Strategic Management
Volume II

The International Library of Critical Writings on Business and Management

1. Cross-Cultural Management (Volumes I and II)
    Gordon Redding and Bruce W. Stening

2. The Management of Innovation (Volumes I and II)
    John Storey

3. Strategic Management (Volumes I and II)
    Julian Birkinshaw

Future titles will include:

Negotiation, Decision Making and Conflict Management
Max H. Bazerman

Human Resource Management
Paul R. Sparrow

International Marketing
Stanley J. Paliwoda and John K. Ryans, Jr.

Organisation Theory
Barbara Czarniawska

Wherever possible, the articles in these volumes have been reproduced as originally published using facsimile reproduction, inclusive of footnotes and pagination to facilitate ease of reference.

For a list of all Edward Elgar published titles visit our site on the World Wide Web at
www.e-elgar.com

Strategic Management
Volume II

Edited by

Julian Birkinshaw

Professor and Chair of Strategic and International Management
London Business School, UK

THE INTERNATIONAL LIBRARY OF CRITICAL WRITINGS ON BUSINESS AND
MANAGEMENT

An Elgar Reference Collection
Cheltenham, UK • Northampton, MA, USA

Published by
Edward Elgar Publishing Limited
Glensanda House
Montpellier Parade
Cheltenham
Glos GL50 1UA
UK

Edward Elgar Publishing, Inc.
136 West Street
Suite 202
Northampton
Massachusetts 01060
USA

A catalogue record for this book is available from the British Library.

ISBN   1 84376 278 1 (2 volume set)

Printed and bound in Great Britain by MPG Books Ltd, Bodmin, Cornwall

Contents

Acknowledgements

The editor and publishers wish to thank the authors and the following publishers who have kindly given permission for the use of copyright material.

Academy of Management and the Copyright Clearance Center, Inc. for articles: Robert A. Burgelman (1983), 'A Model of the Interaction of Strategic Behavior, Corporate Context, and the Concept of Strategy', *Academy of Management Review*, **8** (1), January, 61–70; Elaine Romanelli and Michael L. Tushman (1994), 'Organizational Transformation as Punctuated Equilibrium: An Empirical Test', *Academy of Management Journal*, **37** (5), October, 1141–66.

Administrative Science Quarterly for articles: Michael L. Tushman and Phillip Anderson (1986), 'Technological Discontinuities and Organizational Environments', *Administrative Science Quarterly*, **31** (1), March, 439–65; Rebecca M. Henderson and Kim B. Clark (1990), 'Architectural Innovation: The Reconfiguration of Existing Product Technologies and the Failure of Established Firms', *Administrative Science Quarterly*, **35** (1), Special Issue, March, 9–30; Wesley M. Cohen and Daniel A. Levinthal (1990), 'Absorptive Capacity: A New Perspective on Learning and Innovation', *Administrative Science Quarterly*, **35** (1), March, 128–52.

Blackwell Publishing Ltd for article: Raymond Vernon (1979), 'The Product Cycle Hypothesis in a New International Environment', *Oxford Bulletin of Economics and Statistics*, **41** (4), November, 255–67.

Business History Review for figures: 'Examples of sustaining technological change in componentry and product architecture' and 'Patterns of entry and improvement in disruptive disk drive technologies' included in article: Clayton M. Christensen and Joseph L. Bower (1996), 'Customer Power, Strategic Investment, and the Failure of Leading Firms', *Strategic Management Journal*, **17** (3), 197–218.

California Management Review and the Regents of the University of California for articles: Richard T. Pascale (1984), 'Perspectives on Strategy: The Real Story Behind Honda's Success', *California Management Review*, **XXVI** (3), Spring, 47–72; Michael E. Porter (1986), 'Changing Patterns of International Competition', *California Management Review*, **XXVIII** (2), Winter, 9–40.

Harvard Business School Publishing for articles: Larry E. Greiner (1972), 'Evolution and Revolution as Organizations Grow', *Harvard Business Review*, **50**, July–August, 37–44; W. Chan Kim and Renée Mauborgne (1997), 'Value Innovation: The Strategic Logic of High Growth', *Harvard Business Review*, **75** (1), January–February, 103–12; Gary Hamel (1999), 'Bringing Silicon Valley Inside', *Harvard Business Review*, **77** (5), September–October, 70–84.

Institute for Operations Research and the Management Sciences for articles: James G. March (1991), 'Exploration and Exploitation in Organizational Learning', *Organization Science*, **2** (1), Special Issue, February, 71–87; Bruce Kogut and Udo Zander (1992), 'Knowledge of the Firm, Combinative Capabilities, and the Replication of Technology', *Organization Science*, **3** (3), August, 383–97.

MIT Press Journals and the President and Fellows of Harvard College for article: Raymond Vernon (1966), 'International Investment and International Trade in the Product Cycle', *Quarterly Journal of Economics*, **80** (2), May, 190–207.

Palgrave Macmillan for article: John H. Dunning (1980), 'Toward an Eclectic Theory of International Production: Some Empirical Tests', *Journal of International Business Studies*, **11** (1), Spring–Summer, 9–31.

Tribune Media Services International for articles: James Brian Quinn (1978), 'Strategic Change: "Logical Incrementalism"', *Sloan Management Review*, **20** (1), Fall, 7–21; David J. Teece (1981), 'The Multinational Enterprise: Market Failure and Market Power Considerations', *Sloan Management Review*, **22** (3), Spring, 3–17; Christopher A. Bartlett and Sumantra Ghoshal (1987), 'Managing across Borders: New Strategic Requirements', *Sloan Management Review*, **28** (4), Summer, 7–17; George S. Yip (1989), 'Global Strategy . . . In a World of Nations?', *Sloan Management Review*, **31** (1), Fall, 29–41; Constantinos Markides (1997), 'Strategic Innovation', *Sloan Management Review*, **38** (3), Spring, 9–23.

John Wiley and Sons Ltd for articles: Henry Mintzberg and James A. Waters (1985), 'Of Strategies, Deliberate and Emergent', *Strategic Management Journal*, **6** (3), Jul–Sep, 257–72; C.K. Prahalad and Richard A. Bettis (1986), 'The Dominant Logic: A New Linkage Between Diversity and Performance', *Strategic Management Journal*, **7**, 485–501; Sumantra Ghoshal (1987), 'Global Strategy: An Organizing Framework', *Strategic Management Journal*, **8** (5), September–October, 425–40; Dorothy Leonard-Barton (1992), 'Core Capabilities and Core Rigidities: A Paradox in Managing New Product Development', *Strategic Management Journal*, **13**, Summer, 111–25; Sumantra Ghoshal and Christopher A. Bartlett (1994), 'Linking Organizational Context and Managerial Action: The Dimensions of Quality of Management', *Strategic Management Journal*, **15**, Special Issue, Summer, 91–112; Julian Birkinshaw, Allen Morrison and John Hulland (1995), 'Structural and Competitive Determinants of a Global Integration Strategy', *Strategic Management Journal*, **16** (8), 637–55; Clayton M. Christensen and Joseph L. Bower (1996), 'Customer Power, Strategic Investment, and the Failure of Leading Firms', *Strategic Management Journal*, **17** (3), 197–218; William Ocasio (1997), 'Towards an Attention-based View of the Firm', *Strategic Management Journal*, **18**, Special Issue, Summer, 187–206.

In addition the publishers wish to thank the Library of the University of Warwick and the Library of Indiana University at Bloomington, USA for their assistance in obtaining these articles.

Part I
The Strategy Process

[1]

©Academy of Management Review 1983, Vol. 8, No. 1, 61-70

A Model of the Interaction of Strategic Behavior, Corporate Context, and the Concept of Strategy[1]

ROBERT A. BURGELMAN
Stanford University

Based on a review of previous landmark studies and in the light of findings of recent research on internal corporate venturing, a model of the strategic process in large, complex firms is presented under which the propositions "structure follows strategy" and "strategy follows structure" can both be subsumed. Current corporate strategy induces some strategic behavior but changes in corporate strategy follow other, autonomous, strategic behavior.

The study of the relationships between strategy and structure in large, complex firms remains of central concern to scholars in the fields of strategic management and macro organizational behavior. Previous research has, indeed, produced apparently conflicting propositions regarding the directionality of these relationships. Depending on which body of empirical evidence is used to bolster the argument, "structure follows strategy" and "strategy follows structure" both seem to be valid propositions (Bower & Doz, 1979; Galbraith & Nathanson, 1979; Hall & Saias, 1980). The present paper contributes to the resolution of this apparent contradiction by elucidating further the conditions under which each of these propositions may be valid.

The analysis presented here rests on two critical insights. First, both propositions need to be considered in terms of what they imply about the nature of the strategic *process*. As previous researchers have observed (Bower & Doz, 1979), the strategic process in large, complex firms consists of the strategic activities of managers from different levels in the organization. Second, these strategic activi-

ties are of two kinds. Most strategic activities are *induced* by the firm's current concept of corporate strategy, but also emerging are some *autonomous* strategic activities, that is, activities that fall outside the scope of the current concept of strategy. The consequences of this distinction for the strategic process have not previously been made the subject of systematic analysis.

Autonomous strategic activities have been documented by the students of unrelated diversification through internal corporate venturing (ICV) (Biggadike, 1979; Burgelman, 1980, Fast, 1979). Fast's study of new venture divisions in large, diversified firms, for instance, has provided incidental evidence of the autonomous nature of the strategic activities involved in new venturing. As a participant in one of the firms in Fast's study observed:

> Top management saw a need for ventures and said, "Go ahead and do it." Nobody really managed or directed it. So the whole company began to get into ventures but there was no clear direction or purpose (1979, p. 76).

Biggadike's (1979) large sample study of new entries at the business level of analysis also suggests the autonomous nature of new venture activities. Even though ICV projects required the commitment of substantial amounts of resources over substantial periods of time and changed the scope of the corporate business portfolio when they were successful, there seemed to come little guidance

[1]Support for this paper from New York University's Graduate School of Business Administration and from the Strategic Management Program of Stanford University's Graduate School of Business is gratefully acknowledged. Michael L. Tushman (Columbia University), Eric J. Walton (New York University), L. Jay Bourgeois, David B. Jemison, and Steven C. Wheelwright (all of Stanford University) have made helpful comments on earlier drafts of this manuscript.

from the firms' current corporate strategy for these ICV efforts.

Neither Fast nor Biggadike has attempted to conceptualize the corporate strategic process in which new ventures take shape. Yet both researchers have suggested that the research of Bower (1970) and his students could be useful to conceptualize the corporate strategic processes involved in ICV. Independent of these suggestions, Burgelman's (1980) study of ICV project development in the diversified major firm has found that Bower's model is indeed useful but needs to be extended. This study has provided systematic field data from which the category of autonomous strategic behavior has been induced. It also has provided additional insight in the corporate context processes in which ICV project development is embedded (Burgelman, 1982).

These insights concerning the nature of strategic behavior and corporate context processes provide the basis for reanalyzing the landmark studies from which the two apparently contradictory propositions concerning the relationships between strategy and structure have been derived.

Structure Follows Strategy

The proposition that structure follows strategy became firmly established as a result of Chandler's (1962) study of the historical development of major U.S.-based industrial firms in the period 1919-1959. Subsequent empirical research in the multinational context, and in firms situated in other countries of the Western world, generally has corroborated the structure follows strategy proposition (Galbraith & Nathanson, 1979). Relatively little can be learned about the strategic process underlying Chandler's proposition from these large sample, verification-oriented follow-up studies. The original field study, however, can be reexamined to evaluate the extent to which the original theoretical generalizations were grounded.

Strategy Follows Autonomous Strategic Behavior

Chandler's case materials indicate that major structural adjustments followed the experience of severe management problems *after* strategic initiatives had been undertaken in areas unrelated, or only marginally related, to the traditional lines of business of the firm.

The case data also indicate that these strategic initiatives were not the result of an a priori clearly formulated corporate strategy on the part of top management. Rather, the corporate strategy emerged through a somewhat haphazard process. It was the result of final authorizations by top management of strategic projects that had successfully absorbed the firm's excess resources and promised to do so profitably in the future.

Chandler raised the important question: "Why did the new strategy which called for a change in structure, arise in the first place?" (1962, p. 14). He refers to the major changes in the external environment that had created opportunities for the use of existing excess resources of the firm. At the conclusion of the study, Chandler refers to Penrose's (1968) work and suggests that his data supports her theoretical analysis of the growth of the firm.

Penrose's analysis, however, emphasizes the *internal* impulse toward growth. She observes that the recognition of opportunities takes place in the mind of managers and is often independent of changes in the external environment. In fact, Penrose forebodes the concept of the "enacted environment" (Weick, 1979):

> In the last analysis, the "environment" rejects or confirms the soundness of the judgments about it, but the relevant environment is not an objective fact discoverable before the events (Penrose, 1968, p. 41).

Implicit in the affirmation of the relevance of Penrose's analysis seems to be the recognition that corporate development was not really the result of top management taking a fresh look at the environment, then formulating a strategy, and then establishing the appropriate structural arrangements to implement the strategy. In reality, the structural rearrangements reflected efforts to *consolidate* the results of autonomous strategic behavior. The new strategy reflected the recognition of the importance of these strategic actions. In the final analysis, Chandler's study seems to indicate that changes in corporate strategy followed autonomous strategic behavior.

Heroic View of Top Management

Chandler's case data suggest that multiple layers of management were involved in the strategic initiatives that produced the extensive diversification, and in response to which the new strategy and the new structure eventually emerged. The theoretical generalizations, however, collapse this strategic process into a top management activity. Even though the influence of lower levels in the determination of the content of the strategy is recognized, the major emphasis is on the role of top management. Yet, as the du Pont case materials suggest, top management's influence before the reorganization was very limited, with the real influence over strategic behavior situated at the department head level. It was only after H. Fletcher Brown wrote a penetrating analysis of this situation (Chandler, 1962) that the strategic role of the executive committee (representing the whole corporation) became firmly established.

In spite of a preoccupation with the role of top management in the strategic development of the firms studied, Chandler presents data that question the relative importance of this role, ironically even with respect to the decisions to change the structural arrangements:

> At du Pont, General Motors, and Jersey Standard, the initial awareness of the structural inadequacies caused by the new complexity came from executives close to top management, but who were not themselves in a position to make organizational changes. *In all cases, the president gave no encouragement to the proposers of change* (1962, p. 308, emphasis provided).

And after reflecting on the meaning of the data, Chandler puts forward another key question:

> But if the stockholders and the board became captives of the fulltime administrators, were not the professional entrepreneurs themselves captives of their subordinates? Were not the information and alternatives available to the top determined, possibly quite unconsciously, by junior executives down the line? Must not then the enterprise or the organization as a whole be considered responsible for the basic economic decisions? If this is so, then no individual or team of individuals can be identified as the key decision makers in the private sector of the American economy (1962, p. 313).

Chandler concludes that the case data challenge the view that the role of top management was not predominant. This conclusion, however, is based on the observation that the new structure had facilitated top management's role in strategy formulation and entrepreneurship after it had been put in place. The case data relating to the situation before the reorganization do not support the heroic view of the role of top management. Furthermore, the proposition that the new type of structural arrangement would lead to a greater role for top management in the formulation of corporate strategy

can be verified in the light of the findings of another major line of research in the field of strategic management.

Strategy Follows Structure

The process oriented line of research in strategic management has taken the concepts of the "decision making" (Cohen, March, & Olsen, 1972; Cyert & March, 1963; March & Simon, 1958) and "institutional" (Selznick, 1957) orientations in organization theory, and the "incrementalist" theory in strategy making (Lindblom, 1959) as its points of departure. These theories allow for a bottom-up conception of strategy formulation in which top management's role is not necessarily critical—one in which the concepts of strategy and structure are not clearly delineated from each other (Bower, 1974), nor are operational decisions delineated from strategic decisions (Ansoff, 1965). Basically, this is Chandler's view upside down. Important empirical research has investigated the usefulness of these theoretical orientations for the understanding of the process whereby key decisions are made in complex organizations. It has extended the theory by clarifying the role of top management in these processes (Aharoni, 1966; Allison, 1971; Carter, 1971).

A landmark study concerning the strategic process is Bower's (1970) carefully designed, longitudinal field study of the management of strategic capital investment projects in the "diversified major" firm. Probably the most complex type of divisionalized firm, the latter encompasses an agglomeration of widely diversified but partially related businesses grouped into major divisions whose general managers report to corporate management.

Strategy Making—A Multilayered Process

Bower's study documents the manner in which the strategic capital investment process in such firms is spread over the management hierarchy. Three major subprocesses could be discerned, each of which, in turn, comprised three major phases related to activities of managers at particular levels in the organization.

At the product/market level in a division, proposals are defined in technical/economic terms. This *definition* process is triggered by a perceived discrepancy between strategic business objectives and existent physical plant capacity available to attain these. Projects survive only if they receive impetus from divisional level management. This *impetus* process is highly political, because managers at the divisional level are aware that their career prospects depend, to a large extent, on developing a good "batting average" in supporting strategic projects. Thus managers will evaluate proposals in the light of the reward and measurement systems that determine whether it is in their interest to provide impetus for a particular project. At the corporate level, the major contribution is precisely the manipulation of the *structural context* within which the proposal generation takes shape. Through the manipulation of structural context, top management can influence the type of proposals that will be defined and given impetus.

Whereas definition and impetus are primarily, if not exclusively, bottom-up processes, the design of the structural context is primarily, if again not exclusively, a top-down process. Thus, to the extent that capital investment proposals reflect strategic business planning, it is possible to posit that strategy making is both a bottom-up and top-down multilayered process (Bower, 1974). Because of the effects of structural context on the generation and shaping of strategic projects, it also is possible to posit that strategy follows structure. However, to the extent that the structural context reflects a given concept of corporate strategy, Bower's study actually indicates that corporate strategy induces strategic behavior.

A Less Heroic View of Top Management

Bower's study has provided the basis for further research of the strategic process in various types of organizations and concerning different classes of strategic decisions. These have further elucidated the social and political forces in and around the strategic process (Hofer, 1976).

Recently, Bower and Doz have articulated a major implication of this line of research, which concerns an alternative view of the role of top management in the strategic process:

> Thus, in contrast to strategy formulation as the critical direction-setting general management activity, this new process school of research suggested an alternative, that is, managing the strategic process (1979, p. 158).

Yet, as the authors point out, it is not clear how the management of the corporate phase can be done:

> If structure is to shape strategy, what vision shapes structure and how is that vision to be developed? Who has a say in the process? More research is needed (1979, p. 159).

A Model of the Interaction of Strategic Behavior, Corporate Context, and the Concept of Strategy

Based on the findings of the process study of ICV, and on the insights derived from the preceding review of Chandler's and Bower's studies in the light of these findings, a new model of the strategic process in large, complex firms can be constructed. This new model sheds additional light on the important questions raised by Bower and Doz. It provides a conceptual framework from which the two major, apparently contradictory, propositions in the field of strategic management can be deduced simultaneously. Figure 1 represents this model.

Variation, Enactment, and Strategic Behavior

This model, inductively derived, is isomorphous to the variation-selection-retention model currently emerging as a major conceptual framework for explaining organizational survival, growth, and development (Aldrich, 1979). Its orientation also is in line with current theoretical efforts (White & Hamermesh, 1981) to integrate research done in industrial organization economics, organization theory, and business policy. The model presented here, however, integrates the business and corporate levels of analysis and applies to the class of firms that are large enough and sufficiently resource-rich to be relatively independent of the tight control of external environment selection. Such firms are able to engage in "strategic choice" (Child, 1972) and, as pointed out earlier, their strategic choice process involves substantive inputs from managers from different levels in the organization. Internally generated variation, resulting from the "enactment" (Weick, 1979) of the environment is, at the minimum, a very important source of variation in such firms (Penrose, 1968). Strategic behavior, in the model presented here, refers to such enactments.

The model proposes that two generic categories of strategic behavior can be discerned in such large, complex firms: induced and autonomous. *Induced* strategic behavior uses the categories provided by the current concepts of strategy to identify oppor-

Figure 1
A Model of the Interaction of Strategic Behavior,
Corporate Context, and the Concept of Strategy

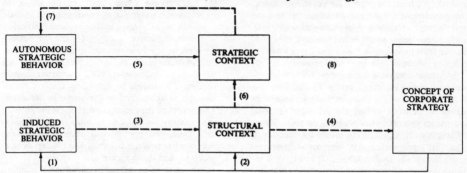

——————— STRONG INFLUENCE
– – – – WEAK INFLUENCE

tunities in the "enactable environment" (Weick, 1979). Being consistent with the existing categories used in the strategic planning system of the firm, such strategic behavior generates little equivocality in the corporate context. Examples of such strategic behavior emerge around, among others, new product development projects for existing businesses, market development projects for existing products, and strategic capital investment projects for existing businesses. Such strategic behavior is shaped by the current structural context. For instance, it can be judged relatively easily in the light of current evaluation and measurement systems. This is the type of strategic behavior documented by Bower (1970). It follows corporate strategy. Hence, the feedback loop (1) in Figure 1 between concept of strategy and induced strategic behavior.

During any given period of time, the bulk of strategic activity in a firm is likely to be of the induced variety. The present model, however, proposes that large, resource-rich firms are likely to possess a reservoir of entrepreneurial potential at operational levels that will express itself in autonomous strategic initiatives. *Autonomous* strategic behavior introduces new categories for the definition of opportunities. Entrepreneurial participants, at the product/market level, conceive new business opportunities, engage in project championing efforts to mobilize corporate resources for these new opportunities, and perform strategic forcing efforts to

create momentum for their further development. Middle level managers attempt to formulate broader strategies for areas of new business activity and try to convince top management to support them. This is the type of strategic behavior encountered in the study of internal corporate venturing (Burgelman, 1980; Roberts, 1980). The strategic initiatives leading up to the corporate managerial problems documented by Chandler (1962) also would seem to fall under this category. Such autonomous strategic initiatives attempt to escape the selective effects of the current structural context, and they make the current concept of corporate strategy problematical. They lead to a redefinition of the corporation's relevant environment and provide the raw material for strategic renewal. They precede changes in corporate strategy.

Corporate Context and Selection

One of the key insights of the study of ICV, reflected in the model presented here, is that the corporate context within which the strategic process takes place encompasses two distinct, selective processes: structural context determination and strategic context determination.

Structural context determination is a broad envelope concept used to denote the various administrative mechanisms that corporate management can manipulate to change the perceived interests of the strategic actors in the organization. In the study of

ICV, it was found to encompass the choices of top management regarding the overall structural configuration, the degree of formalization of positions and relationships, the criteria for project screening, the measures of managerial performance, and the appointment of middle level managers with particular orientations toward entrepreneurial initiative. Bower (1970), of course, had identified earlier the selective nature of this important process.

Structural context determination reflects the efforts of corporate management to fine-tune the selective effects of the administrative arrangements so as to keep (or bring) the strategic proposal generating process in line with the current concept of strategy. This part of the model corresponds to Chandler's propostion that structure follows strategy. Hence, the feedback loop (2) in Figure 1 between concept of strategy and structural context.

Over time, this fine-tuning may make the structural context more elaborate, with more rules applied to the induced strategic behavior. As a result, the range and scope of these strategic behaviors may become narrower while their probability of failure may decrease. One major consequence of the increased selective efficiency of the structural context is that fewer of the selected strategic projects have the potential to force a significant change in the concept of strategy. Standardized, quantitative procedures for project screening, uniform categories of strategic planning unit systems, selection of higher level managers with strong corporate orientation in their decision making, all tend to reduce the variation in the strategic proposals selected by the firm and provide the basis for the proposition that strategy eventually follows structure. Thus, structural context intervenes between induced strategic behavior and the concept of strategy—(3) and (4) in Figure 1. This part of the model corresponds to Bower's findings.

Chandler's proposition focused on the role of top management in bringing structure in line with new strategy. Bower focused on the effects of structure, given strategy. Both studies paid relatively little attention, at least in the conceptualization of the findings, to the role of autonomous strategic behavior in the process through which corporate strategy becomes articulated and changed. The study of ICV has focused on the latter process. This has allowed identification of the process of strategic context determination.

Strategic context determination reflects the efforts of middle level managers to link autonomous strategic behaviors at the product/market level into the corporation's concept of strategy. To do so, the middle level managers must make sense out of these autonomous strategic initiatives and formulate workable, attractive strategies for the corresponding areas of new business development. In addition, they must engage in political activities to convince top management to rationalize, retroactively, these successful initiatives by amending the concept of strategy to accommodate the strategic initiatives. This aspect of the process underlies the proposition that strategy follows autonomous strategic behavior. Thus, strategic context intervenes between autonomous strategic behavior and concept of strategy—(5) and (8) in Figure 1.

The intervening effect of structural context is limited here. In the ICV study, this influence was reflected only in the concerns of the actors to demonstrate large potential size and fast growth rate for the ICV projects. Hence, the dotted arrow (6) from structural context to strategic context in Figure 1.

The degree to which middle management is successful in activating the process of strategic context determination provides guidance for further entrepreneurial initiatives at the operational level. This is represented by the dotted feed-forward loop (7) in Figure 1. It is a feed-forward loop because it guides further strategic initiatives in a particular new area before this area has become incorporated in the concept of strategy of the firm. It is represented as a dotted line because the guidance is relatively tentative and ambiguous.

The Concept of Strategy and Retention

From the perspective of a process study, the concept of strategy of large, complex firms can be viewed as the result of the selective effects of the corporate context on the stream of strategic behaviors at operational levels. The present model proposes that the *concept of corporate strategy* represents the more or less explicit articulation of the firm's theory about its past concrete achievements. This theory defines the identity of the firm at any moment in time. It provides a basis for the maintenance of this identity and for the continuity in strategic activity. It induces further strategic initiative in line with it.

Corporate level managers in large, diversified major firms tend to rise through the ranks, having earned their reputation as head of one or more of the operating divisions. By the time they reach the top management level they have developed a highly reliable frame of reference to evaluate business strategies and resource allocation proposals pertaining to the main lines of business of the corporation. Top managers, basically, are strategies-in-action whose fundamental strategic premises are unlikely to change (Kissinger, 1979). It therefore is not surprising that corporate management focuses on the manipulation of the structural context to keep strategic behavior in line with the current concept of strategy. In the operating system of the firm, this fosters predictability and integration of strategic activity: strategy-making takes on a "planning" mode (Mintzberg, 1973).

To the extent that the current concept of strategy is deeply ingrained in corporate management, its capacity to deal with the substantive issues pertaining to new technological and market developments can be expected to be low. Rather than activating the process of strategic context determination, top management is likely to rely also on the manipulation of the structural context to bring autonomous behavior under control. Ironically, from this analytical perspective, the establishment of a new venture division constitutes a manipulation of the structural context to reduce the variability in the operating divisions rather than the implementation of a strategy of unrelated diversification. Also, from this perspective, Fast's (1979) finding that the position of a new venture division in the corporate context is precarious and Burgelman's (1980) observation of wide oscillations in new venture activity are not surprising. Nor is the finding that the activation of the strategic context requires great conceptual and political skills on the part of middle level managers.

Conclusions and Implications

The widening of the scope of a corporation's business portfolio as a result of successful autonomous strategic activity puts strain on its administrative machinery. Periods of unrelated diversification thus are likely to be followed by periods of consolidation. Chandler's study has documented such cycles during the period 1919-1959, out of which the

divisionalized firm emerged as a new generic type. Once the concept of strategy of the firm has been established through top management's ratification of successful autonomous strategic behavior, structures can be designed and refined to select and shape strategic proposals compatible with this concept of strategy. Bower's study has documented the latter processes. Structural design, however, does not work like a well-calibrated sieve. Autonomous strategic activities continue to escape the selective effects of the structural context by mere chance or because alert actors are able to circumvent, or play to their advantage, the selective mechanisms. In any case, the result can be strategic activity falling outside the established strategy. In a more deterministic sense, structure may motivate or impede strategic activity in unanticipated ways (Greiner, 1972; Mintzberg, 1978).

Structure and strategy thus exist in a reciprocal relationship to each other. Depending on which part of the strategic process is observed, both "structure follows strategy" and "strategy follows structure" can be correct propositions.

The present paper has attempted to provide further insight in the strategic process of large, complex firms by focusing on the interaction between the corporate level process of relating structure to strategy, and the process of strategic behavior at the product/market and middle levels in the firm. The model presented here accommodates the conventional, normative proposition that corporate strategy induces strategic behavior. In addition, and perhaps more fundamentally, the model reflects the new proposition that the more dramatic changes in the corporate strategy of large, complex firms are likely to have been preceded by autonomous strategic initiatives at the operational and middle levels of the organization: strategy follows autonomous strategic behavior. The complete list of propositions embedded in the model presented in this paper are summarized in Table 1. It is hoped that these will stimulate further theoretical and empirical research in the field of strategic management.

The present paper focuses the attention of practitioners of strategic management on the dilemmas that result from the opposing tendencies in large, complex firms toward stability and change. Coherence, continuity, and stability in corporate strategy require the institutionalization of strategic behavior through strategic planning systems. Corporate en-

Table 1
Propositions Concerning the Interaction of Strategic Behavior, Corporate Context, and the Concept of Strategy

(1) The current concept of strategy induces some but usually not all strategic activity in large, diversified firms. Therefore, at any moment in time, the totality of strategic activity of such firms is usually a mixture of induced and autonomous strategic behavior.
(2) The current concept of strategy leads to the establishment of a structural context aimed at keeping strategic behavior at lower levels in line with the concept of corporate strategy. In this sense, structure follows strategy.
(3) Structural context intervenes in the relationship between induced strategic behavior and concept of strategy. It operates as a selection mechanism on the stream of induced strategic behavior. In this sense, strategy follows structure.
(4) Over time, structural context reduces the variation in induced strategic behavior, and may thereby prevent strategic learning on the part of the firm. This is another aspect of the strategy follows structure proposition.
(5) Strategic context intervenes in the relationship between autonomous strategic behavior and concept of strategy. Through the activation of the process of strategic context determination, autonomous strategic behavior can become integrated in the concept of strategy of the firm.
(6) Structural context intervenes only to a limited extent in the relationship between autonomous strategic behavior and concept of strategy.
(7) The activation of the process of strategic context determination has a weak influence on maintaining the volume of autonomous strategic behavior in the firm.
(8) Over time, changes in the concept of strategy are the result of the retroactive rationalization of autonomous strategic behavior. This, in turn, changes the basis for the further inducement of strategic behavior.

trepreneurship and the resulting strategic renewal of large, complex firms, on the other hand, require the interlocking autonomous strategic initiatives of individuals at operational and middle levels, and an experimentation-and-selection approach at the corporate level. Maintaining a pragmatic balance between these fundamentally different requirements presents a major challenge for top management. This is evident, for instance, in the problems of dealing with performance differences between divisions (Hamermesh, 1977) and in the need to provide strategic guidance for different types of strategic business units (SBUs) in the corporate business portfolio. The present paper suggests that such challenges may be met more readily by recognizing the different requirements of different strategic situations existing simultaneously in the organization.

The distinction between autonomous and induced strategic behavior in the model presented in this paper also provides a theoretical foundation for the deduction of the categories in Miles and Snow's (1978) typology. "Analyzers" are firms high on

both induced and autonomous strategic behavior. They attempt to strike the kind of balance discussed in the previous paragraph. "Prospectors" emphasize autonomous strategic behavior. They, however, face the problem of maintaining coherence and continuity in their corporate strategy. "Defenders" emphasize induced strategic behavior based on a very clear concept of corporate strategy. Such firms face the long run danger of a lack of creativity and renewal in their corporate strategy. Finally, "reactors" have neither a clear corporate strategy to induce strategic behavior nor the entrepreneurial capabilities related to autonomous strategic behavior. They find themselves in a dangerously unstable situation.

The model of the strategic process presented here seems also relevant for the emerging theory of organizational learning. The concept of strategy of a corporation and the corresponding structural arrangements impound the learning of the firm over time. The concept of strategy provides a more or less explicit, and more or less shared, frame of reference or "paradigm" (Duncan & Weiss, 1979; Jelinek, 1979) concerning the bases of the firm's past success. Not unlike the sociological notion of a paradigm (Kuhn, 1970; Masterman, 1970), it provides guidance for further strategic action in line with it. At the same time, it crystallizes the attitudinal and social factors that were selected together with the cognitive, substantive factors underlying the past success. As such, it also is likely to prescribe, often implicitly and tacitly, attitudes and managerial styles and an ideology deemed necessary for the prolongation of the firm's success. Autonomous strategic behavior, identified here as the major source of strategic renewal, thus is likely to encounter nonrational obstacles in its efforts to convince top management that changes in corporate strategy are necessary.

Further research may find it useful to explore these less obvious, potentially entropic (Rifkin, 1980) consequences of a concept of corporate strategy for organizational learning. Such research also could shed more light on the factors—external and/or internal to the firm—that influence the balance between induced and autonomous strategic behavior at any given moment in time, and the evolution of this balance over time. In the same line of thought, further research also could investigate the role of acquisition and divestment as compensatory mechanisms—positive and negative, respectively —for the firm's adaptation efforts through autonomous strategic behavior.

Finally, the present paper illustrates an important characteristic of field research. The conceptual frameworks induced from such research seldom exhaust the full content and meaning of the data. Such research allows progress through an iterative process: new conceptual lenses can be brought to bear on old data to generate new insights. Through this process, the old insights can be refined and/or some of their additional implications revealed.

References

Aharoni, Y. *The foreign investment decision process.* Boston, Mass.: Graduate School of Business Administration, Harvard University, 1966.

Aldrich, H. E. *Organizations and environments.* Englewood Cliffs, N. J.: Prentice Hall, 1979.

Allison, G. T. *Essence of decision.* Boston, Mass.: Little Brown, 1971.

Ansoff, H. T. *Corporate strategy.* New York: McGraw-Hill, 1965.

Biggadike, E. R. *Corporate diversification: Entry, strategy, and performance.* Cambridge, Mass.: Harvard University Press, 1979.

Bower, J. L. *Managing the resource allocation process.* Boston, Mass.: Graduate School of Business Administration, Harvard University, 1970.

Bower, J. L. Planning and Control: Bottom-up or top-down. *Journal of General Management,* 1974, 1, 20-31.

Bower, J. L., & Doz, I. Strategy formulation: A social and political view. In D. E. Schendel & C. W. Hofer (Eds.), *Strategic management.* Boston, Mass.: Little Brown, 1979, 152-166.

Burgelman, R. A. *Managing innovating systems: A study of the process of internal corporate venturing.* Unpublished doctoral dissertation, Columbia University, 1980.

Burgelman, R. A. A process model of internal corporate venturing in the diversified major firm. Research paper #636, Graduate School of Business, Stanford University, 1982.

Carter, E. E. The behavioral theory of the firm and top level corporation decisions. *Administrative Science Quarterly,* 1971, 17, 413-428.

Chandler, A. D. *Strategy and structure.* Cambridge, Mass.: M.I.T. Press, 1962.

Child, J. Organization structure, environment, and performance —The role of strategic choice. *Sociology,* 1972, 6, 1-22.

Cohen, M. D., March, J. G., & Olsen, J. P. A garbage can model of organizational choice. *Administrative Science Quarterly,* 1972, 17, 1-25.

Cyert, R. M., & March, J. G. *A behavioral theory of the firm.* Englewood Cliffs, N. J.: Prentice Hall, 1963.

Duncan, R., & Weiss, A. Organizational learning: Implications for organizational design. In B. Shaw (Ed.), *Research in organizational behavior* (Vol. 1). Greenwich, Conn.: JAI Press, 1979, 75-124.

Fast, N. D. *The rise and fall of corporate new venture divisions.* Ann Arbor, Mich.: U.M.I. Research Press, 1979.

Galbraith, J. R., & Nathanson, D. A. The role of organizational structure and process in strategy implementation. In D. E. Schendel & C. W. Hofer (Eds.), *Strategic management.* Boston, Mass.: Little Brown, 1979, 249-284.

Greiner, L. E. Evolution and revolution as organizations grow. *Harvard Business Review,* 1972, 50 (4), 37-46.

Hall, D. J., & Saias, M. A. Strategy follows structure. *Strategic Management Journal,* 1980, 1, 149-163.

Hamermesh, R. G. Responding to divisional profit crises. *Harvard Business Review,* 1977, 55 (2), 124-130.

Hofer, C. W. Research on strategic planning: A survey of past studies and suggestions for future efforts. *Journal of Business and Economics,* 1976, 28 (3), 261-286.

Jelinek, M. *Institutionalizing innovation.* New York: Praeger, 1979.

Kissinger, H. A. *White house years.* Boston, Mass.: Little Brown, 1979.

Kuhn, T. *The structure of scientific revolutions.* Chicago: Ill.: University of Chicago Press, 1970.

Lindblom, C. E. The science of "muddling through." *Public Administration Review,* 1959, 19, 79-88.

March, J. G., & Simon, H. A. *Organizations.* New York: Wiley, 1958.

Masterman, M. The nature of a paradigm. In I. Lakatos & A. Musgrave (Eds.), *Criticism and the growth of knowledge.* Cambridge University Press, 1970, 59-89.

Miles, R. E., & Snow, C. C. *Organizational strategy, structure, and process.* New York: McGraw-Hill, 1978.

Mintzberg, H. Strategy-making in three modes. *California Management Review,* 1973, 16, 44-53.

Mintzberg, H. Patterns of strategy formation. *Management Science,* 1978, 24, 934-948.

Penrose, E. *The theory of the growth of the firm.* Oxford, England: Blackwell, 1968.

Rifkin, J. *Entropy.* New York: The Viking Press, 1980.

Roberts, E. New ventures for corporate growth. *Harvard Business Review,* 1980, 58 (4), 134-142.

Selznick, P. *Leadership in administration.* New York: Row, 1957.

Weick, K. *The social psychology of organizing*. Reading, Mass.: Addison-Wesley, 1979.

White, R. E., & Hamermesh, R. G. Toward a model of business unit performance: An integrative approach. *Academy of Management Review*, 1981, 6, 213-223.

Robert A. Burgelman is Assistant Professor of Management in the Graduate School of Business, Stanford University.

[2]

Sloan Management Review   Fall 1978   7

Strategic Change: "Logical Incrementalism"

James Brian Quinn   Dartmouth College

If you are a devotee of publications like the SMR, you may have come to believe that formal planning, replete with the latest analytical models, provides the ideal means by which corporate strategic goals should be established. Your faith may have been shaken, however, if you read this author's "Strategic Goals: Process and Politics" in the Fall 1977 SMR. This article, the second in what will be a three-part series, goes on to explain how "logical incrementalism" operates in several major corporations. The author further argues that such "muddling," far from being a "necessary evil," may provide the normative model for strategic decision making. *Ed.*

"When I was younger I always conceived of a room where all these [strategic] concepts were worked out for the whole company. Later I didn't find any such room. . . . The strategy [of the company] may not even exist in the mind of one man. I certainly don't know where it is written down. It is simply transmitted in the series of decisions made." Interview quote.

When well-managed major organizations make significant changes in strategy, the approaches they use frequently bear little resemblance to the rational-analytical systems so often touted in the planning literature. The full strategy is rarely written down in any one place. The processes used to arrive at the total strategy are typically fragmented, evolutionary, and largely intuitive. Although one can usually find embedded in these fragments some very refined pieces of formal strategic analysis, the real strategy tends to evolve as internal decisions and external events flow together to create a new, widely shared consensus for action among key members of the top management team. Far from being an abrogation of good management practice, the rationale behind this kind of strategy formulation is so powerful that it perhaps provides the normative model for strategic decision making — rather than the step-by-step "formal systems planning" approach so often espoused.

The Formal Systems Planning Approach
A strong normative literature states what factors *should* be included in a systematically planned strategy[1] and how to analyze and relate these factors step-by-step.[2] The main elements of this "formal planning approach" include: (1) analyzing one's own *internal situation:* strengths, weaknesses, competencies, problems; (2) *projecting* current prod-

uct lines, profits, sales, investment needs into the future; (3) analyzing selected *external environments* and opponents' actions for opportunities and threats; (4) establishing *broad goals* as targets for subordinate groups' plans; (5) *identifying the gap* between expected and desired results; (6) communicating *planning assumptions* to the divisions; (7) requesting *proposed plans* from subordinate groups with more specific target goals, resource needs, and supporting action plans; (8) occasionally asking for *special studies of alternatives, contingencies,* or longer-term opportunities; (9) *reviewing and approving divisional plans* and *summing* these for corporate needs; (10) developing *long-term budgets* presumably related to plans; (11) *implementing* plans; and (12) *monitoring and evaluating* performance (presumably against plans, but usually against budgets).

While this approach is excellent for some purposes, it tends to focus unduly on measurable quantitative factors and to under-emphasize the vital qualitative, organizational, and power-behavioral factors which so often determine strategic success in one situation versus another. In practice, such planning is just one building block in a continuous stream of events that really determine corporate strategy.

The Power-Behavioral Approach
Other investigators have provided important insights on the crucial psychological, power, and behavioral relationships in strategy formulation. Among other things, these have enhanced understanding about: the *multiple goal structures* of organizations,[3] the *politics* of strategic decisions,[4] executive *bargaining* and *negotiation* processes,[5] *satisficing* (as opposed to maximizing) in decision making,[6] the role of *coalitions* in strategic man-

James Brian Quinn is
the William and
Josephine Buchanan
Professor of Manage-
ment at The Amos
Tuck School of Busi-
ness Administration,
Dartmouth College. Dr.
Quinn holds the B.S.
degree in engineering
from Yale University,
the M.B.A. degree from
the Harvard Business
School, and the Ph.D.
degree from Columbia
University. As a re-
nown lecturer and a
special consultant to
the U.S. Congress and
the State Department,
Dr. Quinn has served
on a number of Na-
tional Academy of Sci-
ences panels and is
currently a member on
its Board on Science
and Technology for
International Devel-
opment. Dr. Quinn has
written widely on the
topic of corporate and
national policy ques-
tions.

agement,[7] and the practice of "*muddling*" in
the public sphere.[8] Unfortunately, however,
many power-behavioral studies have been
conducted in settings far removed from the
realities of strategy formulation. Others have
concentrated solely on human dynamics,
power relationships, and organizational processes and ignored the ways in which systematic data analysis shapes and often
dominates crucial aspects of strategic decisions. Finally, few have offered much normative guidance for the strategist.

The Study

Recognizing the contributions and limitations of both approaches, I attempted to
document the dynamics of actual strategic
change processes in some ten major companies as perceived by those most knowl-
edgeably and intimately involved in them.
These companies varied with respect to
products, markets, time horizons, technological complexities, and national versus international dimensions.[9] While the problems of
this kind of research are well recognized,[10]
many precautions were taken in order to in-
sure accuracy.[11]

Summary Findings

Several important findings have begun to
emerge from these investigations.

— Neither the "power-behavioral" nor the
"formal systems planning" paradigm
adequately characterizes the way successful strategic processes operate.

— Effective strategies tend to emerge from a
series of "strategic subsystems," each of
which attacks a specific class of strategic
issue (e.g., acquisitions, divestitures, or
major reorganizations) in a disciplined
way, but which is blended incrementally
and opportunistically into a cohesive pattern that becomes the company's strategy.

— The logic behind each "subsystem" is so
powerful that, to some extent, it may serve

as a normative approach for formulating
these key elements of strategy in large
companies.

— Because of cognitive and process limits,
almost all of these subsystems — and the
formal planning activity itself — must be
managed and linked together by an approach best described as "logical incrementalism."

— Such incrementalism is not "muddling."
It is a purposeful, effective, proactive
management technique for improving and
integrating both the analytical and behavioral aspects of strategy formulation.

This article will document these findings,
suggest the logic behind several important
"subsystems" for strategy formulation, and
outline some of the management and
thought processes executives in large organizations use to synthesize them into effective corporate strategies. Such strategies embrace those patterns of high leverage decisions (on major goals, policies, and action
sequences) which affect the viability and direction of the entire enterprise or determine
its competitive posture for an extended time
period.

Critical Strategic Issues

Although certain "hard data" decisions (e.g.,
on product-market position or resource allocations) tend to dominate the analytical literature,[12] executives identified other "soft"
changes that have at least as much importance in shaping their concern's strategic
posture. Most often cited were changes in
the company's:

1. Overall organizational structure or its
basic management style;

2. Relationships with the government or
other external interest groups;

3. Acquisition, divestiture, or divisional

Sloan Management Review   Fall 1978   9

control practices;

4. International posture and relationships;

5. Innovative capabilities or personnel motivations as affected by growth;

6. Worker and professional relationships reflecting changed social expectations and values;

7. Past or anticipated technological environments.

When executives were asked to "describe the processes through which their company arrived at its new posture" vis-à-vis each of these critical domains, several important points emerged. First, few of these issues lent themselves to quantitative modeling techniques or perhaps even formal financial analyses. Second, successful companies used a different "subsystem" to formulate strategy for each major class of strategic issues, yet these "subsystems" were quite similar among companies even in very different industries. Finally, no single formal analytical process could handle all strategic variables simultaneously on a planned basis. Why?

Precipitating Events

Often external or internal events, over which managements had essentially no control, would precipitate urgent, piecemeal, interim decisions which inexorably shaped the company's future strategic posture. One clearly observes this phenomenon in: the decisions forced on General Motors by the 1973-74 oil crisis,[13] the shift in posture pressed upon Exxon by sudden nationalizations, or the dramatic opportunities allowed for Haloid Corporation[14] and Pilkington Brothers, Ltd.[15] by the unexpected inventions of xerography and float glass.

In these cases, analyses from earlier formal planning cycles did contribute greatly, as long as the general nature of the contingency had been anticipated. They broadened the information base available (as in Exxon's

case), extended the options considered (Haloid-Xerox), created shared values to guide decisions about precipitating events in consistent directions (Pilkington), or built up resource bases, management flexibilities, or active search routines for opportunities whose specific nature could not be defined in advance (General Mills, Pillsbury).[16] But no organization — no matter how brilliant, rational, or imaginative — could possibly foresee the timing, severity, or even the nature of all such precipitating events. Further, when these events did occur there might be neither time, resources, nor information enough to undertake a full formal strategic analysis of all possible options and their consequences. Yet early decisions made under stress conditions often meant new thrusts, precedents, or lost opportunities that were difficult to reverse later.

An Incremental Logic

Recognizing this, top executives usually consciously tried to deal with precipitating events in an incremental fashion. Early commitments were kept broadly formative, tentative, and subject to later review. In some cases neither the company nor the external players could understand the full implications of alternative actions. All parties wanted to test assumptions and have an opportunity to learn from and adapt to the others' responses. Such behavior clearly occurred during the 1973-74 oil crisis; the ensuing interactions improved the quality of decisions for all. It also recurred frequently in other widely different contexts. For example:

◊ Neither the potential producer nor user of a completely new product or process (like xerography or float glass) could fully conceptualize its ramifications without interactive testing. All parties benefited from procedures which purposely delayed decisions and allowed mutual feedback. Some companies, like IBM or Xerox, have formalized this concept into "phase program planning" systems. They make concrete decisions only on individual phases (or stages) of new product developments, establish interactive testing procedures with customers, and postpone final configuration commitments until the latest possible moment.

Similarly, even under pressure, most top executives were extremely sensitive to organizational and power relationships and consciously managed decision processes to improve these dynamics. They often purposely delayed initial decisions, or kept such decisions vague, in order to encourage lower-level participation, to gain more information from specialists, or to build commitment to solutions. Even when a crisis atmosphere tended to shorten time horizons and make decisions more goal oriented than political, perceptive executives consciously tried to keep their options open until they understood how the crisis would affect the power bases and needs of their key constituents. For example:

◇ General Motors's top management only incrementally restructured its various car lines as it understood, step-by-step, the way in which the oil crisis and environmental demands would affect the viability of each existing divisional and dealership structure. In the aggregate these amounted to the greatest shift in balance and positioning among GM's automobile lines since Alfred P. Sloan, and management was deeply concerned about the way its decisions would influence the power and prosperity of various groups.[17]

To improve both the informational content and the process aspects of decisions surrounding precipitating events, logic dictates and practice affirms that they should normally be handled on an incremental basis.

Incrementalism in Strategic Subsystems

One also finds that an incremental logic applies in attacking many of the critical subsystems of corporate strategy. Those subsystems for considering diversification moves,

divestitures, major reorganizations, or government-external relations are typical and will be described here. In each case, conscious incrementalism helps to: (1) cope with both the cognitive and process limits on each major decision, (2) build the logical-analytical framework these decisions require, and (3) create the personal and organizational awareness, understanding, acceptance, and commitment needed to implement the strategies effectively.

The Diversification Subsystem

Strategies for diversification, either through R&D or acquisitions, provide excellent examples. The formal analytical steps needed for successful diversification are well documented.[18] However, the precise directions that R&D may project the company can only be understood step-by-step as scientists uncover new phenomena, make and amplify discoveries, build prototypes, reduce concepts to practice, and interact with users during product introductions. Similarly, only as each acquisition is sequentially identified, investigated, negotiated for, and integrated into the organization can one predict its ultimate impact on the total enterprise.

A step-by-step approach is clearly necessary to guide and assess the strategic fit of each internal or external diversification candidate. Incremental processes are also required to manage the crucial psychological and power shifts that ultimately determine the program's overall direction and consequences. These processes help unify both the analytical and behavioral aspects of diversification decisions. They create the broad conceptual consensus, the risk-taking attitudes, the organizational and resource flexibilities, and the adaptive dynamism that determine both the timing and direction of diversification strategies. Most important among these processes are:

— *Generating a genuine, top-level psychological commitment to diversification.* General Mills, Pillsbury,[19] and Xerox all started their major diversification programs with

Sloan Management Review   Fall 1978   11

broad analytical studies and goal-setting exercises designed both to build top-level consensus around the need to diversify and to establish the general directions for diversification. Without such action, top-level bargaining for resources would have continued to support only more familiar (and hence apparently less risky) old lines, and this could delay or undermine the entire diversification endeavor.

— *Consciously preparing to move opportunistically.* Organizational and fiscal resources must be built up in advance to exploit candidates as they randomly appear. And a "credible activist" for ventures must be developed and backed by someone with commitment power. All successful acquirers created the potential for "profit centered" divisions within their organizational structures, strengthened their financial-controllership capabilities, took action to create low-cost capital access, and maintained the shortest possible communication lines from the "acquisitions activist" to the resource-committing authority. All these actions integrally determined which diversifications actually could be made, the timing of their accession, and the pace they could be absorbed.

— *Building a "comfort factor" for risk taking.* Perceived risk is largely a function of one's knowledge about a field. Hence well-conceived diversification programs should anticipate a trial-and-error period during which top managers reject early proposed fields or opportunities until they have analyzed enough trial candidates to "become comfortable" with an initial selection. Early successes tend to be "sure things" close to the companies' past (real or supposed) expertise. After a few successful diversifications, managements tend to become more confident and accept other candidates — farther from traditional lines — at a faster rate. Again the way this process is handled affects both the direction and pace of the actual program.

— *Developing a new ethos.* If new divisions

are more successful than the old — as they should be — they attract relatively more resources and their political power grows. Their most effective line managers move into corporate positions, and slowly the company's special competency and ethos change. Finally, the concepts and products which once dominated the company's culture may decline in importance or even disappear. Acknowledging these ultimate consequences to the organization at the beginning of a diversification program would clearly be impolitic, even if the manager both desired and could predict the probable new ethos. These factors must be handled adaptively, as opportunities present themselves and as individual leaders and power centers develop.

Each of the above processes interacts with all others (and with the random appearance of diversification candidates) to affect action sequences, elapsed time, and ultimate results in unexpected ways. Complexities are so great that few diversification programs end up as initially envisioned. Consequently, wise managers recognize the limits to systematic analysis in diversification, and use formal planning to build the "comfort levels" executives need for risk taking and to guide the program's early directions and priorities. They then modify these flexibly, step-by-step, as new opportunities, power centers, and developed competencies merge to create new potentials.

The Divestiture Subsystem
Similar practices govern the handling of divestitures. Divisions often drag along in a less-than-desired condition for years before they can be strategically divested. In some cases, ailing divisions might have just enough yield or potential to offer hoped-for viability. In others, they might represent the company's vital core from earlier years, the creations of a powerful person nearing retirement, or the psychological touchstones of the company's past traditions.

Again, in designing divestiture strategies, top executives had to reinforce vaguely felt concerns with detailed data, build up managers' comfort levels about issues, achieve participation in and commitment to decisions, and move opportunistically to make actual changes. In many cases, the precise nature of the decision was not clear at the outset. Executives often made seemingly unrelated personnel shifts or appointments which changed the value set of critical groups, or started a series of staff studies which generated awareness or acceptance of a potential problem. They might then instigate goal assessment, business review, or "planning" programs to provide broader forums for discussion and a wider consensus for action. Even then they might wait for a crisis, a crucial retirement, or an attractive sale opportunity to determine the timing and conditions of divestiture. In some cases, decisions could be direct and analytical. But when divestitures involved the psychological centers of the organization, the process had to be much more oblique and carefully orchestrated. For example:

◇ When General Rawlings became president at General Mills, he had his newly developed Staff (Corporate Analysis) Department make informal presentations to top management on key issues. Later these were expanded to formal Management Operating Reviews (MORs) with all corporate and divisional top managers and controllers present. As problem operations were identified (many "generally known for a long time"), teams of corporate and divisional people were assigned to investigate them in depth. Once needed new data systems were built and studies came into place, they focused increasing attention on some hasty post-World War II acquisitions.

First to go was a highly cyclical — and unprofitable — formula feeds business for which "there was no real heavy philosophical commitment." Then followed some other small divisions and the low-profit electronics business "which the directors didn't feel very comfortable with because it was so different. . . ." At the time, this business was headed by a recently appointed former Finance Department man, "who had no strong attachments to electronics." Only then did the Annual Reports begin to refer to these conscious moves as ones designed "to concentrate on the company's major strengths." And only then, despite earlier concern, frustration, and discontent about its commodity aspects, could the traumatic divestiture of flour milling, the core of the company's traditions, be approached.

Careful incrementalism is essential in most divestitures to disguise intentions yet create the awareness, value changes, needed data, psychological acceptance, and managerial consensus required for such decisions. Early, openly acknowledged, formal plans would clearly be invitations to disaster.

The Major Reorganization Subsystem
It is well recognized that major organizational changes are an integral part of strategy.[20] Sometimes they constitute a strategy themselves, sometimes they precede and/or precipitate a new strategy, and sometimes they help to implement a strategy. However, like many other important strategic decisions, macro-organizational moves are typically handled incrementally and outside of formal planning processes. Their effects on personal or power relationships preclude discussion in the open forums and reports of such processes.

In addition, major organizational changes have timing imperatives (or "process limits") all their own. In making any significant shifts, the executive must think through the new roles, capabilities, and probable individual reactions of the many principals affected. He may have to wait for the promotion or retirement of a valued colleague before consummating any change. He then frequently has to bring in, train, or test new people for substantial periods before he can staff key posts with confidence. During this testing period he may substantially modify his original concept of the reorganization, as he evaluates individuals' potentials, their performance in specific roles, their personal drives, and their relationships with other

Sloan Management Review   Fall 1978   13

team members.

Because this chain of decisions affects the career development, power, affluence, and self-image of so many, the executive tends to keep close counsel in his discussions, negotiates individually with key people, and makes final commitments as late as possible in order to obtain the best matches between people's capabilities, personalities, and aspirations and their new roles. Typically, all these events do not come together at one convenient time, particularly the moment annual plans are due. Instead the executive moves opportunistically, step-by-step, selectively moving people toward a broadly conceived organizational goal, which is constantly modified and rarely articulated in detail until the last pieces fit together.

Major organizational moves may also define entirely new strategies the guiding executive cannot fully foresee. For example:

◇ When Exxon began its regional decentralization on a worldwide basis, the Executive Committee placed a senior officer and board member with a very responsive management style in a vaguely defined "coordinative role" vis-à-vis its powerful and successful European units. Over a period of two years this man sensed problems and experimented with voluntary coordinative possibilities on a pan-European basis. Only later, with greater understanding by both corporate and divisional officers, did Exxon move to a more formal "line" relationship for what became Exxon Europe. Even then the move had to be coordinated step-by-step with similar experimental shifts to regionalized consolidations in other areas of the world. All of these changes together led to an entirely new internal power balance toward regional and non-U.S. concerns and to a more responsive worldwide posture for Exxon.

◇ At General Mills, General Rawlings and his team of outside professional managers actively redefined the company's problems and opportunities in ways the prior management could not have. Once the divesti-

tures noted above were made, the funds released were used for acquisitions, thus automatically increasing the visibility and power of the Controllership-Financial group. Similarly, with fewer large divisions competing for funds, the Consumer-Food groups rapidly increased in their importance. This ultimately led to a choice between these two groups' leaders for the next chairmanship of the company — and hence for control over the corporation's future strategy.

In such situations, executives may be able to predict the broad direction, but not the precise nature, of the ultimate strategy which will result. In some cases, such as Exxon, the rebalance of power and information relationships *becomes* the strategy, or at least its central element. In others, such as General Mills, organizational shifts are primarily means of triggering or implementing new strategic concepts and philosophies. But in all cases, major organizational changes create unexpected new stresses, opportunities, power bases, information centers, and credibility relationships that can affect both previous plans and future strategies in unanticipated ways. Effective reorganization decisions, therefore, allow for testing, flexibility, and feedback. Hence, they should, and usually do, evolve incrementally.

The Government-External Relations Subsystem

Almost all companies cited government and other external activist groups as among the most important forces causing significant changes in their strategic postures during the periods examined. However, when asked "how did your company arrive at its own strategy vis-à-vis these forces?" it became clear that few companies had cohesive strategies (integrated sets of goals, policies, and programs) for government-external relations, other than lobbying for or against specific legislative actions. To the extent that other strategies did exist, they were piecemeal, ad hoc, and had been derived in a very evolutionary manner. Yet there seemed to be very good reasons for such incrementalism. The following are two of the best short explanations of the way these practices develop:

We are a very large company, and we understand that any massive overt action on our part could easily create more public antagonism than support for our viewpoint. It is also hard to say in advance exactly what public response any particular action might create. So we tend to test a number of different approaches on a small scale with only limited or local company identification. If one approach works, we'll test it further and amplify its use. If another bombs, we try to keep it from being used again. Slowly we find a series of advertising, public relations, community relations actions that seem to help. Then along comes another issue and we start all over again. Gradually the successful approaches merge into a pattern of actions that becomes our strategy. We certainly don't have an overall strategy on this, and frankly I don't think we devote enough [organizational and fiscal] resources to it. This may be our most important strategic issue.

I [the president] start conversations with a number of knowledgeable people . . . . I collect articles and talk to people about how things get done in Washington in this particular field. I collect data from any reasonable source. I begin wide-ranging discussions with people inside and outside the corporation. From these a pattern eventually emerges. It's like fitting together a jigsaw puzzle. At first the vague outline of an approach appears like the sail of a ship in a puzzle. Then suddenly the rest of the puzzle becomes quite clear. You wonder why you didn't see it all along. And once it's crystallized, it's not difficult to explain to others.

In this realm, uncontrollable forces dominate. Data are very soft, often can be only subjectively sensed, and may be costly to quantify. The possible responses of individuals and groups to different stimuli are difficult to determine in advance. The number of potential opponents with power is very high, and the diversity in their viewpoints and possible modes of attack is so substantial that it is physically impossible to lay out probabilistic decision diagrams that would have much meaning. Results are unpredictable and error costs extreme. Even the best intended and most rational-seeming strategies can be converted into disasters unless they are thoroughly and interactively tested. For example:

◇ In the 1960s General Motors found that technical discussions of cost vs. benefit tradeoffs were useless against demagogic slogans like "smog kills" or "GM is the worst polluter in the world." It publicly resisted some early attempts to impose pollution standards, stating that they were "beyond the state of the art." Then after successfully completing the costly and risky development of the catalytic converter, GM had its earlier concerns thrown in its face as "foot dragging" or "lying" about technical potentials. As one executive said, "You were damned if you did and damned if you didn't."

Only after prolonged interaction with regulators, legislators, and public interest groups did GM truly understand the needs and pressure potentials of its opponents. Area by area it learned to communicate better with various major interests. Only then could it identify effective *patterns* for dealing with all parties.

For such reasons, companies will probably always have to derive major portions of their government-external relations strategies in an experimental, iterative fashion. But such incrementalism could be much more proactive than it often has been in the past. Favorable public opinion and political action take a long time to mold. There is a body of knowledge about how to influence political action. There are also methods of informal and formal analyses which can help companies anticipate major political movements and adjust their goals or policies in a timely fashion. Once potential approaches are experimentally derived (without destroying needed flexibilities), more cohesive planning can ensure that the resources committed are sufficient to achieve the desired goals, that all important polities are included in plans, and that rigorous and adaptive internal controls maintain those high performance, attitude, service, and image qualities that lend credibility to the strategy. But again, one sees logical incrementalism as the essential thread linking together information gathering, analysis, testing, and the behav-

Sloan Management Review   Fall 1978   15

ioral and power considerations in this strategic subsystem.

Formal Planning in Corporate Strategy

What role do classical formal planning techniques play in strategy formulation? All companies in the sample do have formal planning procedures embedded in their management direction and control systems. These serve certain essential functions. In a process sense, they:

— Provide a discipline forcing managers to take a careful look ahead periodically;
— Require rigorous communications about goals, strategic issues, and resource allocations;
— Stimulate longer-term analyses than would otherwise be made;
— Generate a basis for evaluating and integrating short-term plans;
— Lengthen time horizons and protect long-term investments such as R&D;
— Create a psychological backdrop and an information framework about the future against which managers can calibrate short-term or interim decisions.

In a decision-making sense, they:

— Fine tune annual commitments,
— Formalize cost reduction programs;
— Help implement strategic changes once decided on (for example, coordinating all elements of Exxon's decision to change its corporate name);

Finally, "special studies" had high impact at key junctures for specific decisions.

Formal Plans Also "Increment"

Although individual staff planners were often effective in identifying potential problems and bringing them to top management's attention, the annual planning process itself was rarely (if ever) the initiating source of really new key issues or radical departures into new product/market realms. These almost always came from precipitat-

ing events, special studies, or conceptions implanted through the kinds of "logical incremental" processes described above.

In fact, formal planning practices actually institutionalize incrementalism. There are two reasons for this. *First*, in order to utilize specialized expertise and to obtain executive involvement and commitment, most planning occurs "from the bottom up" in response to broadly defined assumptions or goals, many of which are longstanding or negotiated well in advance. Of necessity, lower-level groups have only a partial view of the corporation's total strategy, and command only a fragment of its resources. Their power bases, identity, expertise, and rewards also usually depend on their existing products or processes. Hence, these products or processes, rather than entirely new departures, should and do receive their primary attention. *Second*, most managements purposely design their plans to be "living" or "ever green." They are intended only as "frameworks" to guide and provide consistency for future decisions made incrementally. To act otherwise would be to deny that further information could have a value. Thus, properly formulated formal plans are also a part of an incremental logic.

Special Studies

Formal planning was most successful in stimulating significant change when it was set up as a "special study" on some important aspect of corporate strategy. For example:

◇ In 1958, when it became apparent that Pilkington's new float glass process would work, the company formed a Directors Flat Glass Committee consisting of all internal directors associated with float glass "to consider the broad issues of flat glass [strategy] in both the present and the future." The Committee did not attempt detailed plans. Instead, it tried to deal in broad concepts, identify alternate routes, and think through the potential consequences of each route some ten years ahead. Of some of the key strategic decisions Sir Alastair later said, "It would be difficult to identify an exact moment when the decision was made. . . . Nevertheless, over a period of time a consensus crystallized with great clarity."

◇ In the late 1960s, after the extraordinary success of the 914 copier, Xerox's Chairman Wilson and President McColough began to worry about the positioning of their total product line. At their request the company's engineers worked with the product planning department to evaluate a series of experimental products (which were then in development) from which top management could choose. These groups developed a series of strategies (from A through Q) concerning these alternative products — where to concentrate and where to deploy lesser resources. Top management chose Strategy Q, which led to the development of the product lines on which the company concentrated in the 1970s. Yet many of the initial targets for product positioning, timing, and price were adjusted as cost and market realities became clearer.

In each case there were also important precursor events, analyses, and political interactions, and each was followed by organizational, power, and behavioral changes. But interestingly, such special strategic studies also represent a "subsystem" of strategy formulation distinct from both annual planning activities and the other subsystems exemplified above. Each of these develops some important aspect of strategy, incrementally blending its conclusions with those of other subsystems, and it would be virtually impossible to force all these together to crystallize a completely articulated corporate strategy at any one instant.

Total Posture Planning
Occasionally, however, managements do attempt very broad assessments of their companies' total posture. Two examples follow:

◇ Shortly after becoming CEO of General Mills, Mr. James McFarland decided that his job was "to take a very good company and move it to greatness," but that it was up to his management group, not himself alone, to decide what a great company was and how to get there. Consequently he took some thirty-five of the company's topmost managers away for a three day management retreat. On the first day, after agreeing to broad financial goals, the group broke up into units of six to eight people. Each unit was to answer the question, "what is a great company?" from the viewpoints of stockholders, employees, suppliers, the public, and society. Each unit reported back at the end of the day, and the whole group tried to reach a consensus through discussion.

On the second day the groups, in the same format, assessed the company's strengths and weaknesses relative to the defined posture of "greatness." The third day focused on how to overcome the company's weaknesses and move it toward a great company. This broad consensus led, over the next several years, to the surveys of fields for acquisition, the building of management's initial "comfort levels" with certain fields, and the acquisition-divestiture strategy that characterized the McFarland era at General Mills.

◇ Xerox Corporation used several such posture analyses between 1965 and 1974. The first of these was the Strategy Q analysis described above. In 1971, Mr. McColough formed another committee of top-line officers to define for the company how it should develop itself around a coalescing theme, "the architecture of information," which had seemed to catch the imagination of the company. This produced a plan defining some eight business areas for the company. This was flexibly implemented through acquisition and internal development.

In 1974, Mr. McColough asked another group, with the full support of internal staffs and external consultants, to help define for the company what its posture should be vis-à-vis many of the great issues of the times (food shortages, energy, ecology, materials supplies, the world's poor, etc.). They were to "discard every taboo written, stated, or believed objective of the company." They were to "write strategies and comment on strategies in a broad frame" and report to the chairman and president on these matters. The committee was to use a full array of all the available formal strategic analysis techniques in arriving at its conclusions. These resulted in a series of discussions with the CEO and president.

Yet even such major endeavors were only portions of a total strategic process. Values which had been built up over decades stimulated or constrained alternatives. Precipitating events, acquisitions, divestitures, external relations, and organizational changes developed important segments of each strategy incrementally. Even the strategies articulated left key elements to be defined as new information became available, polities permitted, or particular opportunities appeared (like Pilkington's Electro-float invention or Xerox's Daconics acquisition). Major product thrusts (like Pilkington's TV tubes or Xerox's computers) proved unsuccessful. Actual strategies therefore evolved as each company overextended, consolidated, made errors, and rebalanced various thrusts over time. And it was both logical and expected that this would be the case.

Logical Incrementalism

All of the above suggest that strategic decisions do not lend themselves to aggregation into a single massive decision matrix where all factors can be treated relatively simultaneously in order to arrive at a holistic optimum. Many have spoken of the "cognitive limits"[21] which prevent this. Of equal importance are the "process limits" — i.e., the timing and sequencing imperatives necessary to create awareness, build comfort levels, develop consensus, select and train people, etc. — which constrain the system, yet ultimately determine the decision itself. Unlike the preparation of a fine banquet, it is virtually impossible for the manager to orchestrate all internal decisions, external environmental events, behavioral and power relationships, technical and informational

needs, and actions of intelligent opponents so that they come together at any precise moment.

Can the Process Be Managed?

Instead, the executive usually deals with the logic of each "subsystem" of strategy formulation largely on its own merits and usually with a different subset of people. He tries to develop or maintain in his own mind a consistent pattern among the decisions made in each subsystem. Knowing his own limitations and the unknowability of the events he faces, he consciously tries to tap the minds and psychic drives of others. He often purposely keeps questions broad and decisions vague in early stages to avoid creating undue rigidities and to stimulate others' creativity. Logic, of course, dictates that he make final commitments *as late as possible* consistent with the information he has.

Consequently, many a successful executive will initially set only broad goals and policies which can accommodate a variety of specific proposals from below, yet give a sense of guidance to the proposers.[22] As they come forward the proposals automatically and beneficially attract the support and identity of their sponsors. Being only proposals, the executive can treat these at less politically charged levels, as specific projects rather than as larger goal or policy precedents. Therefore, he can encourage, discourage, or kill alternatives with considerably less political exposure. As events and opportunities emerge, he can incrementally guide the pattern of escalated or accepted proposals to suit his own purposes without getting prematurely committed to any rigid solution set which unpredictable events might prove wrong or which opponents find sufficiently threatening to coalesce against.

A Strategy Emerges

Successful executives link together and bring order to a series of strategic processes and decisions spanning years. At the beginning of the process it is literally impossible to predict all the events and forces which will shape the future of the company. The best executives can do is to forecast the most likely forces which will impinge on the company's affairs and the ranges of their possible impact. They then attempt to build a resource base and a corporate posture that are so strong in selected areas that the enterprise can survive and prosper despite all but the most devastating events. They consciously select market/technological/product segments which the concern can "dominate" given its resource limits, and place some "side bets"[23] in order to decrease the risk of catastrophic failure or to increase the company's flexibility for future options.

They then proceed incrementally to handle urgent matters, start longer-term sequences whose specific future branches and consequences are perhaps murky, respond to unforeseen events as they occur, build on successes, and brace up or cut losses on failures. They constantly reassess the future, find new congruencies as events unfurl, and blend the organization's skills and resources into new balances of dominance and risk aversion as various forces intersect to suggest better — but never perfect — alignments. The process is dynamic, with neither a real beginning nor end. Pilkington Brothers Ltd. provides an excellent example:[24]

◇ After carefully formulating its broad float glass strategy in 1958, Pilkington Brothers Ltd. quickly developed a technical dominance in flat glass throughout the world. With its patents and established businesses it could control access to selected growth markets in specific countries. Float generated high growth and, after an initial investment period, high cash flows. These gave the company the resources to diversify geographically and into new product lines in order to decrease the risks inherent in the company's one product emphasis in a rapidly weakening British economy. It acquired, formed joint ventures, and expanded in selected product and geographical areas as opportunities became available. Meanwhile, socialism and modern communications combined to break down traditional dependencies among workers, employers, and communities. Growth and diversity required new professional managers and workers, and these executives created a new element in the lengthening gap between workers and owners. All these added to Pilkington's size and complexity.

By 1965, the company had become too complex to manage with its old centralized organization. When a key executive, Mr. Phelps, retired, this opened a chain of promotional possibilities, and after a number of formal and informal studies, the organization was decentralized. The process went too far, however, and the company had to be tightened up through further planning, reorganization, and new controls. Meanwhile, float technology led to entirely new product possibilities, even higher profits, and increased credibility for its successful (non-family) inventor, knighted as Sir Alastair Pilkington. All of these elements reinforced a decision made broadly in the early 1960s to go public near the end of the decade in order to help with the family owners' death duties and to provide a more flexible capital base for the company. In 1970, just before the company was to go public, a strike convinced the owners to ask Lord Pilkington, who was about to retire as chairman, to stay on for three more years before Sir Alastair became chairman. The strike also speeded moves away from Pilkington's paternalistic management style to a more professional one. In the mid-1970s, the company's strategy and posture were still being shaped by the key personalities and decisions of the 1950s.

When the original float strategy was formulated, no one could have forecast or foreseen the interaction of all these events. Any rigid posture would have been doomed. Logic, therefore, dictated the kind of constantly adjusted incrementalism one sees in this vignette. The history of all other companies studied would lead to similar conclusions. Strategy deals with the unknowable, not the uncertain. It involves forces of such great number, strength, and combinatory powers that one cannot predict events in a probabilistic sense. Hence logic dictates that one proceed flexibly and experimentally from broad concepts toward specific commitments, making the latter concrete as late as possible in order to narrow the bands of uncertainty and to benefit from the best available information. This is the process of "logical incrementalism."

Conclusion

"Logical incrementalism" is not "muddling," as most people use that word. It is conscious, purposeful, proactive, good management. Properly managed, it allows the executive to bind together the contributions of rational systematic analyses, political and power theories, and organizational behavior concepts. It helps the executive achieve cohesion and identity with new directions. It allows him to deal with power relationships and individual behavioral needs, and permits him to use the best possible informational and analytical inputs in choosing his major courses of action. This article discusses the rationale behind "logical incrementalism" in strategy formulation. A succeeding article is planned which will treat the management of this process in detail.

Funds for this project were provided by the Associates Program of Amos Tuck School, Dartmouth College, and by the author's chair, the William and Josephine Buchanan Professorship of Management. Sample data include Professor Mariann Jelinek's descriptions of strategic processes at Texas Instruments, Inc. The author gratefully acknowledges her contributions to the early sections of this paper and her insights on the intellectual and behavioral processes which helped interpret the data from this study.

References

1

M. L. Mace, "The President and Corporate Planning," *Harvard Business Review*, January-February 1965, pp. 49–62;

W. D. Guth, "Formulating Organizational Objectives and Strategy: A Systematic Approach," *Journal of Business Policy* (Fall 1971);

K. J. Cohen and R. M. Cyert, "Strategy: Formulation, Implementation, and Monitoring," *Journal of Business* (July 1973): 349–367;

G. J. Skibbins, "Top Management Goal Appraisal," *International Management* (1974);

F. Goronzy and E. Gray, "Factors in Corporate Growth," *Management International Review* (1974): 75–90;

W. E. Rothschild, *Putting It All Together: A Guide to Strategic Thinking* (New York: AMACOM, 1976).

2

J. T. Cannon, *Business Strategy and Policy* (New York: Harcourt, Brace & World, 1968);

G. A. Steiner, *Top Management Planning* (New York: Macmillan Co., 1969);

R. L. Katz, *Management of the Total Enterprise* (Englewood Cliffs, NJ: Prentice-Hall, 1970);

E. K. Warren, *Long-Range Planning: The Executive Viewpoint* (Englewood Cliffs, NJ: Prentice-Hall, 1970);

R. L. Ackoff, *A Concept of Corporate Planning* (New York: Wiley-Interscience, 1970);

H. I. Ansoff, "Managerial Problem Solving," *Journal of Business Policy* (1971): 3–20;

E. C. Miller, *Advanced Techniques for Strategic Planning* (New York: American Management Association, 1971);

R. F. Vancil and P. Lorange, "Strategic Planning in Diversified Companies," *Harvard Business Review*, January-February 1975, pp. 81–90;

R. F. Vancil, "Strategy Formulation in Complex Organizations," *Sloan Management Review*, Winter 1976, pp. 1–18.

3

H. A. Simon, "On the Concept of Organization Goal," *Administrative Science Quarterly* (June 1964): 1–22;

P. Diesing, "Noneconomic Decision-Making," *Organizational Decision Making*, by M. Alexis and C. Z. Wilson (Englewood Cliffs, NJ: Prentice-Hall, 1967), pp. 185–200;

C. Perrow, "The Analysis of Goals in Complex Organizations," *American Sociological Review* (February 1961): 854–866;

P. Georgiou, "The Goal Paradigm and Notes towards a Counter Paradigm," *Administrative Science Quarterly* 18, no. 2 (1973): 291–311.

4

R. M. Cyert, H. A. Simon, and D. B. Trow, "Observation of a Business Decision," *Journal of Business* (October 1956): 237–248;

J. M. Pfiffner, "Administrative Rationality," *Public Administration Review*, 1960, pp. 125–132;

W. J. Gore, *Administrative Decision-Making: A Heuristic Model* (New York: John Wiley & Sons, 1964);

J. L. Bower, "Planning within the Firm," *American Economic Review*, May 1970, pp. 186–194;

A. Zaleznik, "Power and Politics in Organizational Life," *Harvard Business Review*, May-June 1970, pp. 47–58;

R. A. Bauer and K. J. Gergen, eds., *The Study of Policy Formation* (New York: Free Press, 1968);

G. T. Allison, *Essence of Decision: Explaining the Cuban Missile Crisis* (Boston: Little, Brown & Co., 1971);

A. M. Pettigrew, "Information Control as a Power Resource," *Sociology*, May 1972, pp. 187–204.

5

R. M. Cyert and J. G. March, *A Behavioral Theory of the Firm* (Englewood Cliffs, NJ: Prentice-Hall, 1963);

L. R. Sayles, *Managerial Behavior: Administration in Complex Organizations* (New York: McGraw-Hill Book Co., 1964);

Bower (May 1970);

E. E. Carter, "The Behavioral Theory of the Firm and Top-Level Corporate Decisions," *Administrative Science Quarterly* (1971): 413–428;

H. Mintzberg, D. Raisinghani, and A. Théorêt, "The Structure of 'Unstructured' Decision Processes," *Administrative Science Quarterly* 21, no. 2 (June 1976): 246–275;

J. Pfeffer, G. R. Salancik, and H. Leblebici, "The Effect of Uncertainty on the Use of Social Influence in Organizational Decision Making," *Administrative Science Quarterly* 21, no. 2 (June 1976): 227–245;

R. E. Miles and C. C. Snow, *Organizational Strategy: Structure and Process* (New York: McGraw-Hill Book Co., 1978).

6

Simon (June 1964);

Cyert and March (1963).

7

W. H. Riker, *The Theory of Political Coalitions* (New Haven, CT: Yale University Press, 1962);

Cyert and March (1963);

W. D. Guth, "Toward a Social System Theory of Corporate Strategy," *Journal of Business* (July 1976): 374–388.

8

C. E. Lindblom, "The Science of Muddling Through," *Public Administration Review* (Spring 1959);

D. Braybrooke and C. E. Lindblom, *A Strategy of Decision: Policy Evaluation as a Social Process* (New York: Free Press, 1963);

H. E. Wrapp, "Good Managers Don't Make Policy Decisions," *Harvard Business Review*, September-October 1967, pp. 91–99;

J. B. Quinn, "Strategic Goals: Process and Politics,"

Sloan Management Review, Fall 1977, pp. 21–37.

9
Cooperating companies included: General Motors Corp., Chrysler Corp., Volvo (AB), General Mills, Pillsbury Co., Xerox Corp., Texas Instruments, Exxon, Continental Group, and Pilkington Brothers.

10
C. I. Barnard, *The Function of the Executive* (Cambridge, MA: Harvard University Press, 1968); E. H. Bowman, "Epistemology, Corporate Strategy, and Academe," *Sloan Management Review*, Winter 1974, pp. 35–50; Mintzberg, Raisinghani, and Théorèt (June 1976).

11
For each company the author has attempted to create a background of secondary source data; interview at least ten of the executives most intimately associated with the strategic change process; cross-check viewpoints wherever possible; compare internal references with published materials; seek internal documentation if available; draw up a case history describing the process; submit each quotation or paraphrase used to the executive who was its source; clear the entire case for accuracy with an appropriate corporate authority. All quotations in this article have been released by their sources or are derived from secondary sources as noted.

12
For example, H. I. Ansoff, *Corporate Strategy: An Analytic Approach to Business Policy for Growth and Expansion* (New York: McGraw-Hill Book Co., 1965); R. L. Katz, *Cases and Concepts in Corporate Strategy* (Englewood Cliffs, NJ: Prentice-Hall, 1970); S. Schoeffler, R. D. Buzzell, and D. F. Heany, "Impact of Strategic Planning on Profit Performance," *Harvard Business Review*, March-April 1974, pp. 137–145.

13
J. B. Quinn, "General Motors Corporation" (unpublished case, Amos Tuck School, 1978).

14
J. B. Quinn, "Xerox Corporation (A)" (secondary source case, Amos Tuck School, 1978).

15
J. B. Quinn, "Pilkington Brothers" (unpublished case, Amos Tuck School, 1977).

16
J. B. Quinn and M. Jelinek, manuscripts in preparation.

17
Quinn (General Motors case, 1978).

18
These include: (1) clarifying the overall objectives of the corporation, (2) setting forth broad goals for the diversification program within these overall objectives, (3) defining specific criteria which acquisitions or developments should meet, (4) systematically searching out new product or acquisition candidates, (5) setting priorities for pursuing these, (6) evaluating specific candidates in technical, operational, and financial terms, (7) pricing acquisition deals or controlling R&D projects for adequate returns, (8) planning the integration of the new division or line into the enterprise, (9) implementing its integration and following up to see that intended yields are realized; M. L. Mace and G. G. Montgomery, *Management Problems of Corporate Acquisitions*, (Cambridge, MA: Harvard University Press, 1962); J. B. Quinn and J. A. Mueller, "Transferring Research Results to Operations," *Harvard Business Review*, January-February 1963.

19
Quinn and Jelinek, manuscripts in preparation.

20
A. D. Chandler, *Strategy and Structure* (Cambridge, MA: MIT Press, 1962).

21
J. G. March and H. A. Simon, *Organizations* (New York: John Wiley & Sons, 1958).

22
For a more thorough explanation of goal-setting processes, see Quinn (Fall 1977).

23
Ansoff (1965) details the need for internal and external flexibilities.

24
Quinn (Pilkington Brothers case, 1977).

[3]

CALIFORNIA MANAGEMENT REVIEW
Vol. XXVI, No. 3, Spring 1984
Copyright © 1984, The Regents of the University of California

Perspectives on Strategy: The Real Story Behind Honda's Success

Richard T. Pascale

Perspective One: The Honda Effect

At face value, "strategy" is an innocent noun. Webster defines it as the large-scale planning and direction of operations. In the business context, it pertains to a process by which a firm searches and analyzes its environment and resources in order to 1) select opportunities defined in terms of markets to be served and products to serve them, and 2) makes discrete decisions to invest resources in order to achieve identified objectives.[1]

But for a vast and influential population of executives, planners, academics, and consultants, strategy is more than a conventional English noun. It embodies an implicit model of how organizations should be guided and consequently, preconfigures our way of thinking. Strategy formulation 1) is generally assumed to be driven by senior management whom we expect to set strategic direction; 2) has been extensively influenced by empirical models and concepts; and 3) is often associated with a laborious strategic planning process that, in some companies, has produced more paper than insight.

A $500-million-a-year "strategy" industry has emerged in the United States and Europe comprised of management consultants, strategic planning staffs, and business school academics. It caters to the unique emphasis that American and European companies place upon this particular aspect of managing and directing corporations.

Words often derive meaning from their cultural context. *Strategy* is one such word and nowhere is the contrast of meanings more pronounced than between Japan and the United States. The Japanese view the emphasis we place on "strategy" as we might regard their enthusiasm for Kabuki or sumo wrestling. They note our interest not with an intent of acquiring similar ones but for insight into our peculiarities. The Japanese are somewhat distrustful of a single "strategy," for in their view any idea that focuses attention does so at the expense of peripheral vision. They strongly believe that *peripheral vision* is essential to discerning changes in the customer, the technology or competition, and is the key to corporate survival over the long haul. They regard any propensity to be driven by a single-minded strategy as a weakness.

The Japanese have particular discomfort with strategic concepts. While they do not reject ideas such as the experience curve or portfolio theory outright they regard them as a stimulus to perception. They have often ferreted out the "formula" of their concept-driven American competitors and exploited their inflexibility. In musical instruments, for example, (a mature industry facing stagnation as birthrates in the U.S. and Japan declined), Yamaha might have classified its products as "cash cows" and gone on to better things (as its chief U.S. competitor, Baldwin United, had done). Instead, beginning with a negligible share of the U.S. market, Yamaha plowed ahead and destroyed Baldwin's seemingly unchallengeable dominance. YKK's success in zippers against Talon (a Textron division) and Honda's outflanking of Harley-Davidson (a former AMF subsidiary) in the motorcycle field provide parallel illustrations. All three cases involved American conglomerates, wedded to the portfolio concept, that had classified pianos, zippers, and motorcycles as mature businesses to be harvested rather than nourished and defended. Of course, those who developed portfolio theory and other strategic concepts protest that they were never intended to be mindlessly applied in setting strategic direction. But most would also agree that there is a widespread tendency in American corporations to misapply concepts and to otherwise become strategically myopic—ignoring the marketplace, the customer, and the problems of execution. This tendency toward misapplication, being both pervasive and persistent over several decades, is a phenomenon that the literature has largely ignored.[2] There is a need to explicitly identify the factors that influence how we conceptualize strategy—and which foster its misuse.

Honda: The Strategy Model—In 1975, Boston Consulting Group presented the British government its final report: *Strategy Alernatives for the British Motorcycle Industry*. This 120-page document identified two key factors leading to the British demise in the world's motorcycle industry:
- market share loss and profitability declines, and
- scale economy disadvantages in technology, distribution, and manufacturing.

During the period 1959 to 1973, the British share of the U.S. motorcycle industry had dropped from 49 percent to 9 percent. Introducing BCG's recommended strategy (of targeting market segments where sufficient production volumes could be attained to be price competitive) the report states:

> The success of the Japanese manufacturers originated with the growth of their domestic market during the 1950s. As recently as 1960, only 4 percent of Japanese

PERSPECTIVES ON STRATEGY   49

motorcycle production was exported. By this time, however, the Japanese had developed huge production volumes in small motorcycles in their domestic market, and volume-related cost reductions had followed. This resulted in a highly competitive cost position which the Japanese used as a springboard for penetration of world markets with small motorcycles in the early 1960s.[3]

The BCG study was made public by the British government and rapidly disseminated in the United States. It exemplifies the necessary (and I argue, insufficient) strategist's perspective of

- examining competition primarily from an intercompany perspective,
- at a high level of abstraction,
- with heavy reliance on micro-economic concepts (such as the experience curve).

Case writers at Harvard Business School, UCLA, and the University of Virginia quickly condensed the BCG report for classroom use in case discussions. It currently enjoys extensive use in first-term courses in Business Policy.

Of particular note in the BCG study, and in the subsequent Harvard Business School rendition, is the historical treatment of Honda.

The mix of competitors in the U.S. motorcycle market underwent a major shift in the 1960s. Motorcycle registrations increased from 575,000 in 1960 to 1,382,000 in 1965. Prior to 1960 the U.S. market was served mainly by Harley-Davidson of U.S.A., BSA, Triumph and Norton of U.K. and Moto-Guzzi of Italy. Harley was the market leader with total 1959 sales of $16.6 million. After the second world war, motorcycles in the U.S.A. attracted a very limited group of people other than police and army personnel who used motorcycles on the job. While most motorcyclists were no doubt decent people, groups of rowdies who went around on motorcycles and called themselves by such names as "Hell's Angels," "Satan's Slaves" gave motorcycling a bad image. Even leather jackets which were worn by motorcyclists as a protective device acquired an unsavory image. A 1953 movie called "The Wild Ones" starring a 650cc Triumph, a black leather jacket and Marlon Brando gave the rowdy motorcyclists wide media coverage. The stereotype of the motorcyclist was a leather-jacketed, teenage trouble-maker. Honda established an American subsidiary in 1959—American Honda Motor Company. This was in sharp contrast to other foreign producers who relied on distributors. Honda's marketing strategy was described in the 1963 annual report as "With its policy of selling, not primarily to confirmed motorcyclists but rather to members of the general public who had never before given a second thought to a motorcycle . . . . " Honda started its push in the U.S. market with the smallest, lightweight motorcycles. It was superior to the lightweight being sold by Sears, Roebuck in America at that time. It had a three-speed transmission, an automatic clutch, five horsepower (the American cycle only had two and a half), an electric starter and step through frame for female riders. And it was easier to handle. The Honda machines sold for under $250 in retail compared with $1,000-$1,500 for the bigger American or British machines. Even at that early date Honda was probably superior to other competitors in productivity.

By June 1960 Honda's Research and Development effort was staffed with 700 designers/engineers. This might be contrasted with 100 engineers/draftsmen employed by . . . (European and American competitors). In 1962 production per man-year was running at 159 units, (a figure not reached by Harley-Davidson until 1974). Honda's net fixed asset investment was $8170 per employee . . . (more than twice

50   RICHARD T. PASCALE

its European and American competitors). With 1959 sales of $55 million Honda was already the largest motorcycle producer in the world.

Honda followed a policy of developing the market region by region. They started on the West Coast and moved eastward over a period of four-five years. Honda sold 2,500 machines in the U.S. in 1960. In 1961 they lined up 125 distributors and spent $150,000 on regional advertising. Their advertising was directed to the young families, their advertising theme was "You Meet the Nicest People on a Honda." This was a deliberate attempt to dissociate motorcycles from rowdy, Hell's Angels type people.

Honda's success in creating demand for lightweight motorcycles was phenomenal. American Honda's sales went from $500,000 in 1960 to $77 million in 1965. By 1966 the market share data showed the ascendancy of Japanese producers and their success in selling lightweight motorcycles.

U.S.
Market Share
(%)

Honda	63
Yamaha	11
Suzuki	11
Harley-Davidson	4
BSA/Triumph and Others	11

starting from virtually nothing in 1960, the lightweight motorcycles had clearly established their lead.[4]

Quoting from the BCG report:

The Japanese motorcycle industry, and in particular Honda, the market leader, present a [consistent] picture. The basic philosophy of the Japanese manufacturers is that high volumes per model provide the potential for high productivity as a result of using capital intensive and highly automated techniques. Their marketing strategies are therefore directed towards developing these high model volumes, hence the careful attention that we have observed them giving to growth and market share.

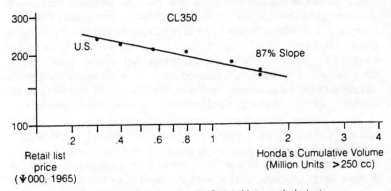

Source: BCG "Strategy Alternatives for the British Motorcycle Industry.

> The overall result of this philosophy over time has been that the Japanese have now developed an entrenched and leading position in terms of technology and production methods . . . . The major factors which appear to account for the Japanese superiority in both these areas are . . . (specialized production systems, balancing engineering and market requirements, and the cost efficiency and reliability of suppliers.[5]

As evidence of Honda's strategy of taking position as low cost producer and exploiting economies of scale, other sources cite Honda's construction in 1959 of a plant to manufacture 30,000 motorcycles per month well ahead of existing demand at the time. (Up until then Honda's most popular models sold 2,000–3,000 units per month.)[6]

The overall picture depicted by the quotes above exemplifies the "strategy model." Honda is portrayed as a firm dedicated to being the low price producer, utilizing its dominant market position in Japan to force entry into the U.S. market, expanding that market by redefining a leisure class ("Nicest People") segment, and exploiting its comparative advantage via aggressive pricing and advertising. Richard Rumelt, writing the teaching note for the UCLA adaptation of the case states: "The fundamental contribution of BCG is not the experience curve per se but the ever-present assumption that differences in cost (or efficiency) are the fundamental components of strategy."[7]

The Organizational Process Perspective—On September 10, 1982, the six Japanese executives responsible for Honda's entry into the U.S. motorcycle market in 1959 assembled in Honda's Tokyo headquarters. They had gathered at my request to describe in fine grain detail the sequence of events that had led to Honda's ultimate position of dominance in the U.S. market.[8] All were in their sixties; three were retired. The story that unfolded, greatly abbreviated below, highlights miscalculation, serendipity, and organizational learning—counterpoints to the streamlined "strategy" version related earlier.

Any account of Honda's successes must grasp at the outset the unusual character of its founder, Sochiro Honda and his partner, Takeo Fujisawa. Honda was an inventive genius with a large ego and mercurial temperament, given to bouts of "philandering" (to use his expression).[9] In the formative stages of his company, Honda is variously reported to have tossed a geisha out a second-story window,[10] climbed inside a septic tank to retrieve a visiting supplier's false teeth (and subsequently placed the teeth in his mouth),[11] appeared inebriated and in costume before a formal presentation to Honda's bankers requesting financing vital to the firm's survival (the loan was denied),[12] hit a worker on the head with a wrench,[13] and stripped naked before his engineers to assemble a motorcycle engine.[14]

Post-war Japan was in desperate need of transportation. Motorcycle manufacturers proliferated, producing clip-on engines that converted bicycles into makeshift "mopeds." Honda was among these but it was not until

52   RICHARD T. PASCALE

he teamed up with Fujisawa in 1949 that the elements of a successful enterprise began to take shape. Fujisawa provided money as well as financial and marketing strengths. In 1950 their first D type motorcycle was introduced. They were, at that juncture, participating in a fragmented industry along with 247 other manufacturers. Other than its sturdy frame, this introductory product was unnoteworthy and did not enjoy great commercial success.[15]

Honda embodied a rare combination of inventive ability and ultimate self-confidence. His motivation was not primarily commerical. Rather, the company served as a vehicle to give expression to his inventive abilities. A successful company would provide a resource base to pursue, in Fujisawa's words, his "grandiose dream." Fujisawa continues, "There was no end to his pursuit of technology."[16]

Fujisawa, in an effort to save the faltering company, pressed Honda to abandon their noisy two-stroke engine and pursue a four-stroke design. The quieter four-stroke engines were appearing on competitive motorcycles, therefore threatening Honda with extinction. Mr. Honda balked. But a year later, Honda stunned Fujisawa with a breakthrough design that doubled the horsepower of competitive four-stroke engines. With this innovation, the firm was off and putting, and by 1951 demand was brisk.[17] There was no organization, however, and the plant was chaotic.[18] Strong demand, however, required early investment in a simplified mass production process. As a result, *primarily* due to design advantages, and secondarily to production methods, Honda became one of the four or five industry leaders by 1954 with 15 percent market share.[19]

For Fujisawa, the engine innovation meant increased sales and easier access to financing. For Mr. Honda, the higher horsepower engine opened the possibility of pursuing one of his central ambitions in life—to race his motorcycle and win. Winning provided the ultimate confirmation of his design abilities. Racing success in Japan came quickly. As a result, in 1959 Honda raised his sights to the international arena and committed the firm to winning at Great Britain's Isle of Man—the "Olympics" of motorcycle racing. Again, Honda's inventive genius was called into play. Shifting most of the firm's resources into this racing effort, Honda embarked on studies of combustion that resulted in a new configuration of the combustion chamber that doubled horsepower and halved weight. Honda leapfrogged past European and American competitors—winning in one class, then another, winning the Isle of Man manufacturer's prize in 1959 and sweeping the first five positions by 1961.[20]

Fujisawa, throughout the fifties, sought to turn Honda's attention from his enthusiasm with racing to the more mundane requirements of running an enterprise. By 1956, as the innovations gained from racing had begun to pay off in vastly more efficient engines, Fujisawa pressed Honda to adapt this technology for a commercial motorcycle.[21] Fujisawa had a particular segment in mind. Most motorcyclists in Japan were male and the machines were used primarily as an alternative form of transportation to trains and buses. There were, however, a vast number of small commercial establishments in Japan that still delivered goods and ran errands on bicycles. Trains and buses were inconvenient for these activities. The purse-strings of these small enterprises were controlled by the Japanese wife—who resisted buying conventional motorcycles because they were expensive, dangerous, and hard to handle. Fujisawa challenged Honda: Can you use what you've learned from racing to come up with an inexpensive, safe-looking motorcycle that can be driven with one hand (to facilitate carrying packages).[22]

In 1958, the Honda 50cc Supercub was introduced—with an automatic clutch, three-speed transmission, automatic starter, and the safe, friendly look of a bicycle (without the stigma of the outmoded mopeds). Owing almost entirely to its high horsepower but *lightweight 50cc engine* (not to production efficiencies), it was affordable. Overnight, the firm was overwhelmed with orders. Engulfed by demand, they sought financing to build a new plant with a 30,000 unit per month capacity. "It wasn't a speculative investment," recalls one executive. "We had the proprietary technology, we had the market, and the demand was enormous."[23] (The plant was completed in mid-1960.) Prior to its opening, demand was met through makeshift, high cost, company-owned assembly and farmed-out assembly through subcontractors.[24] By the end of 1959, Honda had skyrocketed into first place among Japanese motorcycle manufacturers. Of its total sales that year of 285,000 units, 168,000 were Supercubs.[25]

Fujisawa utilized the Supercub to restructure Honda's channels of distribution. For many years, Honda had rankled under the two-tier distribution system that prevailed in the industry. These problems had been exacerbated by the fact that Honda was a late entry and had been carried as secondary line by distributors whose loyalties lay with their older manufacturers. Further weakening Honda's leverage, all manufacturer sales were on a consignment basis.

Deftly, Fujisawa had characterized the Supercub to Honda's distributors as "something much more like a bicycle than a motorcycle." The traditional channels, to their later regret, agreed. Under aimicable terms Fujisawa began selling the Supercub directly to retailers—and primarily through bicycle shops. Since these shops were small and numerous (approximately 12,000 in Japan), sales on consignment were unthinkable. A cash-on-delivery system was installed, giving Honda significantly more leverage over its dealerships than the other motorcycle manufacturers enjoyed.[26]

The stage was now set for exploration of the U.S. market. Mr. Honda's racing conquests in the late fifties had given substance to his convictions about his abilities. While still heavily occupied by the Isle of Man, success fueled his quest for new and different challenges.

To the onlooker from Japan, the American market was vast, untapped,

RICHARD T. PASCALE

and affluent. In addition, Honda had experimented with local Southeast Asian markets in 1957–58 with little success. With little disposable income and poor roads, total Asian exports had reached a meager 1,000 units in 1958.[27] The European market, while larger, was heavily dominated by its own name brand manufacturers, and the popular mopeds dominated the low price, low horsepower end. Spurred in part by ambition and in part by a process of deduction, Fujisawa and Honda focused attention on the United States.

Two Honda executives—the soon-to-be named president of American Honda, Kihachiro Kawashima and his assistant—arrived in the U.S. in late 1958.* Their itenerary: San Francisco, Los Angeles, Dallas, New York, and Columbus. Mr. Kawashima recounts his impressions:

> My first reaction after travelling across the United States was: How could we have been so stupid as to start a war with such a vast and wealthy country! My second reaction was discomfort. I spoke poor English. We dropped in on motorcycle dealers who treated us discourteously and in addition, gave the general impression of being motorcycle enthusiasts who, secondarily, were in business. There were only 3,000 motorcycle dealers in the United States at the time and only 1,000 of them were open five days a week. The remainder were open on nights and weekends. Inventory was poor, manufacturers sold motorcycles to dealers on consignment, the retailers provided consumer financing; after-sales service was poor. It was discouraging.
>
> My other impression was that everyone in the United States drove an automobile—making it doubtful that motorcycles could ever do very well in the market. However, with 450,000 motorcycle registrations in the U.S. and 60,000 motorcycles imported from Europe each year it didn't seem unreasonable to shoot for 10 percent of the import market. I returned to Japan with that report.
>
> In truth, we had no strategy other than the idea of seeing if we could sell something in the United States. It was a new frontier, a new challenge, and it fit the "success against all odds" culture that Mr. Honda had cultivated. I reported my impressions to Fujisawa—including the seat-of-the-pants target of trying, over several years, to attain a 10 percent share of U.S. imports. He didn't probe that target quantitatively. We did not discuss profits or deadlines for breakeven. Fujisawa told me if anyone could succeed, I could and authorized $1 million for the venture.
>
> The next hurdle was to obtain a currency allocation from the Ministry of Finance. They were extraordinarily skeptical. Toyota had launched the Toyopet in the U.S. in 1958 and had failed miserably. "How could Honda succeed?" they asked. Months went by. We put the project on hold. Suddenly, five months after our application, we were given the go-ahead—but at only a fraction of our expected level of commitment. "You can invest $250,000 in the U.S. market," they said, "but only $110,000 in cash." The remainder of our assets had to be in parts and motorcycle inventory.
>
> We moved into frantic activity as the government, hoping we would give up on the idea, continued to hold us to the July 1959 start-up timetable. Our focus, as mentioned earlier, was to compete with the European exports. We knew our products at the time were good but not far superior. Mr. Honda was especially confident of the 250cc and 305cc machines. The shape of the handlebar on these larger machines looked like the eyebrow of Buddha, which he felt was a strong selling point. Thus,

* Mr. Kihachiro Kawashima subsequently became Executive Vice President of Honda Motor Co., Ltd. Japan.

after some discussion and with no compelling criteria for selection, we configured our start-up inventory with 25 percent of each of our four products—the 50cc Supercub and the 125cc, 250cc, and 305cc machines. In dollar value terms, of course, the inventory was heavily weighted toward the larger bikes.

The stringent monetary controls of the Japanese government together with the unfriendly reception we had received during our 1958 visit caused us to start small. We chose Los Angeles where there was a large second and third generation Japanese community, a climate suitable for motorcycle use, and a growing population. We were so strapped for cash that the three of us shared a furnished apartment that rented for $80 per month. Two of us slept on the floor. We obtained a warehouse in a run-down section of the city and waited for the ship to arrive. Not daring to spare our funds for equipment, the three of us stacked the motorcycle crates three high—by hand, swept the floors, and built and maintained the parts bin.

We were entirely in the dark the first year. We were not aware the motorcycle business in the United States occurs during a seasonable April-to-August window— and our timing coincided with the closing of the 1959 season. Our hard-learned experiences with distributorships in Japan convinced us to try to go to the retailers direct. We ran ads in the motorcycle trade magazine for dealers. A few responded. By spring of 1960, we had forty dealers and some of our inventory in their stores— mostly larger bikes. A few of the 250cc and 305cc bikes began to sell. Then disaster struck.

By the first week of April 1960, reports were coming in that our machines were leaking oil and encountering clutch failure. This was our lowest moment. Honda's fragile reputation was being destroyed before it could be established. As it turned out, motorcycles in the United States are driven much farther and much faster than in Japan. We dug deeply into our precious cash reserves to air freight our motorcycles to the Honda testing lab in Japan. Throughout the dark month of April, Pan Am was the only enterprise in the U.S. that was nice to us. Our testing lab worked twenty-four-hour days bench testing the bikes to try to replicate the failure. Within a month, a redesigned head gasket and clutch spring solved the problem. But in the meantime, events had taken a surprising turn.

Throughout our first eight months, following Mr. Honda's and our own instincts, we had not attempted to move the 50cc Supercubs. While they were a smash success in Japan (and manufacturing couldn't keep up with demand there), they seemed wholly unsuitable for the U.S. market where everything was bigger and more luxurious. As a clincher, we had our sights on the import market—and the Europeans, like the American manufacturers, emphasized the larger machines.

We used the Honda 50s ourselves to ride around Los Angeles on errands. They attracted a lot of attention. One day we had a call from a Sears buyer. While persisting in our refusal to sell through an intermediary, we took note of Sears's interest. But we still hesitated to push the 50cc bikes out of fear they might harm our image in a heavily macho market. But when the larger bikes started breaking, we had no choice. We let the 50cc bikes move. And surprisingly, the retailers who wanted to sell them weren't motorcycle dealers, they were sporting goods stores.

The excitement created by the Honda Supercub began to gain momentum. Under restrictions from the Japanese government, we were still on a cash basis. Working with our initial cash and inventory, we sold machines, reinvested in inventory, and sunk the profits into additional inventory and advertising. Our advertising tried to straddle the market. While retailers continued to inform us that our Supercub customers were normal everyday Americans, we hesitated to target toward this segment out of fear of alienating the high margin end of our business—sold through the traditional motorcycle dealers to a more traditional "black leather jacket" customer.[28]

Honda's phenomenal sales and share gains over the ensuing years have been previously reported. History has it that Honda *"redefined"* the U.S. motorcycle industry. In the view of American Honda's start-up team, this was an innovation they backed into—and reluctantly. It was certainly not the strategy they embarked on in 1959. As late as 1963, Honda was still working with its original Los Angeles advertising agency, its ad campaigns straddling all customers so as not to antagonize one market in pursuit of another.

In the spring of 1963, an undergraduate advertising major at UCLA submitted, in fulfillment of a routine course assignment, an ad campaign for Honda. Its theme: You Meet the Nicest People on a Honda. Encouraged by his instructor, the student passed his work on to a friend at Grey Advertising. Grey had been soliciting the Honda account—which with a $5 million a year budget was becoming an attractive potential client. Grey purchased the student's idea—on a tightly kept nondisclosure basis. Grey attempted to sell the idea to Honda.[29]

Interestingly, the Honda management team, which by 1963 had grown to five Japanese executives, was badly split on this advertising decision. The President and Treasurer favored another proposal from another agency. The Director of Sales, however, felt strongly that the Nicest People campaign was the right one—and his commitment eventually held sway. Thus, in 1963, through an inadvertent sequence of events, Honda came to adopt a strategy that directly identified and targeted that large untapped segment of the marketplace that has since become inseparable from the Honda legend.[30]

The Nicest People campaign drove Honda's sales at an even greater rate. By 1964, nearly one out of every two motorcycles sold was a Honda. As a result of the influx of medium income leisure class consumers, banks and other consumer credit companies began to finance motorcycles—shifting away from dealer credit, which had been the traditional purchasing mechanism available. Honda, seizing the opportunity of soaring demand for its products, took a courageous and seemingly risky position. Late in 1964, they announced that thereafter, they would cease to ship on a consignment basis but would require cash on delivery. Honda braced itself for revolt. While nearly every dealer questioned, appealed, or complained, none relinquished his franchise. In one fell swoop, Honda shifted the power relationship from the dealer to the manufacturer. Within three years, this would become the pattern for the industry.[31]

The "Honda Effect"—The preceding account of Honda's inroads in the U.S. motorcycle industry provides more than a second perspective on reality. It focuses our attention on different issues and raises different questions. What factors permitted two men as unlike one another as Honda and Fujisawa to function effectively as a team? What incentives and understandings permitted the Japanese executives at American Honda to respond to the market as it emerged rather than doggedly pursue the 250cc and 305cc strategy that Mr. Honda favored? What decision process permitted the relatively junior sales director to overturn the bosses' preferences and choose the Nicest People campaign? What values or commitment drove Honda to take the enormous risk of alienating its dealers in 1964 in shifting from a consignment to cash? In hindsight, these pivotal events all seem ho-hum common sense. But each day, as organizations live out their lives without the benefit of hindsight, few choose so well and so consistently.

The juxtaposed perspectives reveal what I shall call the "Honda Effect." Western consultants, academics, and executives express a preference for oversimplifications of reality and cognitively linear explanations of events. To be sure, they have always acknowledged that the "human factor" must be taken into account. But extensive reading of strategy cases at business schools, consultants' reports, strategic planning documents as well as the coverage of the popular press, reveals a widespread tendency to overlook the process through which organizations experiment, adapt, and learn. We tend to impute coherence and purposive rationality to events when the opposite may be closer to the truth. How an organization deals with mis-calculation, mistakes, and serendipitous events *outside its field of vision is often crucial to success over time.* It is this realm that requires better understanding and further research if we are to enhance our ability to guide an organization's destiny.

Perspective Two: Shifts in the Nature of Competition

The "microeconomic" and "miscalculation" models focus on different fac-tors and attribute success to different causal events. Both perspectives are valuable; which one is more valuable depends, in part, on the environ-ment in which an organization finds itself. Which view of reality is most appropriate in the environmental context of the eighties?

Two decades ago, American companies were, with rare exception, the flagships of the world's industrial armada. Across a diverse range of prod-ucts and services, one found dominant American companies, each a world leader in its industry, each having carved out a seemingly impregnable strategic enclave. In twenty years, this picture has changed.

Let us consider the extent and nature of this change. Beginning with the Department of Commerce's list of twenty major industries, eliminating those industries heavily regulated (e.g., transportation (railroads and air-lines), utilities, banking); those industries selling primarily to government (e.g., defense and aerospace); and those industries where competition is primarily of a regional rather than a national nature (e.g., construction, food chains). We are left with thirteen industries within which firms compete on a national and often international basis and whose success is primarily self-determined (i.e., not heavily dependent upon geographical advantages or governmental regulation). Identifying the leading firm in each of these

58   RICHARD T. PASCALE

Figure 1. Market Share and Comparative Advantage Trends in Thirteen Key Industries, 1962–1982

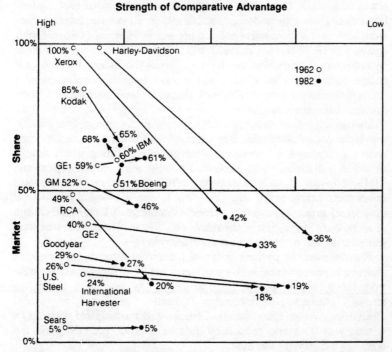

Markets defined as follows: Xerox: plain copiers; Harley-Davidson: motorcycles; Kodak: photographic film; IBM: mainframe computers; GE (General Electric)1: generators; GE2: electrical appliances (refrigerators); GM: passenger cars; Boeing: commercial widebody jet aircraft; RCA: color TVs; Goodyear: OEM tires; U.S. Steel: finished steel; International Harvester: farm tractors; Sears: mass-market retailing.

industries based on *Fortune* 500 rankings, we can trace their movements over the past twenty years—1962 through 1982—in terms of market share positions and gains or losses in comparative advantage. These provide the coordinates for Figure 1.

Individual companies focus on changes *within* their industrial environment. When we aggregate across industries, we observe trends impacting upon all participants. Figure 1 reveals that nine of the leading firms declined both in share and competitive advantage. Two additional companies lost competitive advantage while retaining parity in share. Only Boeing and IBM gained along the market share and competitive advantage dimensions. What factors account for this deterioration in competitive position over the past twenty years?

The early sixties was, above all, a period of industrial expansion. The

Index of Industrial Production registered a 15.6 percent *increase* from 1960 to 1963, compared with a *decrease* of 9.1 from 1979 to 1982.[32] In nearly all sectors, there were increases in primary demand enabling participants to grow without doing so at one another's expense. Interest rates were low (prime rates averaging 4.5 percent in 1961, as compared with an average 18.87 percent in 1981), and investors embraced risks in their determination to capitalize on the optimism of the times. Technological change fuelled continual product and process innovation with the result that productivity increases followed almost effortlessly. Table 1 summarizes these and other factors.

Another ingredient important in securing a firm's competitive position was technological advantage. Bell Laboratories's patents for the first transistors guaranteed a seven-year strategic haven during which time it exploited high margins and recouped its investments. Xerox copiers and IBM's 360 enjoyed much the same competitive respite as did, in one form or another, nearly every other industrial leader. However, patents and proprietary process technology preserve advantage as long as the players of an industrial family honor the rules. This was to change as competition shifted from the domestic to the international arena.

The international pecking order of the sixties (that is, one nation's standing in relation to others), was determined by factors largely separate from the industrial sphere. National status was dependent on military strength, technological leadership (measured by Nobel prizes and megafeats such as space shots), Olympic gold medals, and a country's centrality in the world geopolitical dialogue. NATO, not GNP, was the dominant acronym at the time.

The environment fostered set piece competition. To oversimplify, oligopolistic competitors focused primarily on domestic markets, participants shared implicit rules. These factors fostered competitive stability— abundantly the case in automotive manufacturing and consumer electronics. That is not to say that some industries, such as steel, had not begun to encounter competitive pressures. But relatively speaking, from the postwar period through the mid-sixties, a strategic enclave, once established was defended with comparative ease.

The arts of war have been forever at the mercy of changing armaments; technology changes faster than beliefs. Each leap—from arrow to rifle to infrared seeking missile—renders an era of military knowledge obsolete and imposes a painful reexamination and transition. Military science is the kin of managerial science. The stable industrial world culminating in the sixties was accompanied by a body of managerial beliefs which in the hindsight of the eighties, endowed us with the tactics of Gallipoli in a theater more akin to Vietnam.

The perceived nature of competition in the sixties made strategy the king of management functions. Conceptual rather than operational thinking

60   RICHARD T. PASCALE

Table 1. Dramatic changes over two decades undermine secure market position.

| | Environmental Shifts | |
	From (1960s)	To (1980s)
Growth Rates	• Rapid growth in most industries with room for most serious competitors	• Slowed growth or stagnation; squeezing incremental growth out of competition
Nature of Competition	• Oligopolistic competitors in most industries	• Encroachment of international rivals
	• Primary focus on domestic markets and competitors	• Focus on international competition • Domestic scale economies finance penetration pricing in overseas markets
	• Implicit "rules" shared by domestic competitors foster stability	• New competitors each playing by different rules (e.g., niche vs. scale strategies) force continued innovation, price cutting, quality improvements all resulting in competitive instability
Expressions of Nationalism	• National status dependent on military, technological leadership and level of involvement in international diplomatic dialogue	• The "new mercantilism" • International status and domestic prosperity linked to trade expansionism
	• Internal domestic focus	• Focus on international trade and economic linkages among trading partners
Economic Environment	• Expansionistic, low interest rates	• Stable or contracting economic climate
	• Risk seeking investor climate	• High interest rates • Risk adverse investor climate in most industries
	• Inflation	
Technology	• Rapid technological changes with numerous products early in life cycle	• Slowed technological change in many industries • Maturing products
	• Patents serve to protect technological advantage with secure domestic	• Fierce international competitive surveillance and "reverse engineering" dilute patent protection and rapidly equalize technological advance
IMPLICATIONS:	• Few secure enclaves. • Changing rules. • Intense competition from international rivals.	• Relative stability, security.

prevailed, giving impetus to management consulting firms armed with matrices, experience curves, and other microeconomic paraphernalia. Business schools proliferated as did courses emphasizing the quantitative sciences in an era when success was secured via bold-stroke actions rather than nuance. Qualitative refinements in organizational process and operations management were frosting on the managerial cake. The danger, as our military analogue implies, is that such beliefs, once internalized, tend to persist beyond their time—even when environmental circumstances render them inappropriate.

In the late sixties, research at Harvard Business School exposed an industrial anomaly that has proven a precursor of our times.[33] The major home appliance industry (refrigerators, stoves, dishwashers, washers, and dryers) was revealed to defy the conventional wisdom of market behavior. Dominated by large oligopolistic competitors (Sears, General Electric, Westinghouse) the industry's most profitable participants were its smaller firms (such as Maytag). Whereas other oligopolistic markets fostered stability and protection for their dominant members, in this topsy-turvy industry, the large manufacturers (e.g., G.E.) were squeezed on one hand by continual price pressures from retailers (e.g., Sears) and on the other by the continuing technological innovation of smaller manufacturers (e.g., Tappan and Maytag). The consumer was the prime beneficiary: quality increased, technological innovation blossomed, and prices in real dollars remained steady or declined.

The explanation for this harsh competitive behavior lay in the asymmetry of the participants. Sears, a mass retailer, competed via price leadership; G.E., the manufacturer, competed on quality leadership, innovation parity, and required market share to support its production economies; smaller survivors lived by their technological wits and innovated in order to keep G.E. and Sears at bay. (By achieving sufficient product differentiation, they were able to justify higher margins.)

Enter the 1980s—We have read, ad nauseam, about the industrial climate of this decade, of the iron law of economic stagnation by which one firm's gain is via another's loss. We have read, too, of higher interest rates and more conservative investors. These are no doubt contributing factors. But in addition, slower technological change in many industries has been accompanied by intense competitive surveillance and rapid technological transfer. Particularly across international boundaries, patent protection is mitigated by reverse engineering and outright infringement. As a result, technology is rapidly equalized.

Another powerful, but often underemphasized, factor in these environmental shifts, is the increasing centrality of the "new mercantilism." National status and, indeed, a nation's domestic prosperity are linked directly to trade. Balance of payments, exchange rates, GNP growth, and unemployment are all inextricably intertwined. Heightened national self-interest has placed the spotlight on the success of each country's contestants in key industries. One firm's competitive response is thus linked to a coordinated national response—involving diplomatic exchanges, threats of trade sanctions, central bank behavior, and protective domestic pricing.

In aggregate, the forces depicted have drastically reshaped competitive activity. Most importantly, they have transformed a great many stable and secure domestic markets into battle zones that more closely resemble the major home appliance example cited earlier. International competitors seem more prone to play by different rules. Some invest to achieve scale economies, some for quality leadership, others for price leadership, still others pursue a niche strategy stressing innovation. Under these circumstances, there is no impregnable strategic stance. As in the home appliance example, every participant, in order to survive, behaves in a way that destabilizes his counterparts. Innovators achieve a breakthrough, draw off customers, and start a share swing. To avoid losing share, the most cost efficient producer must follow, rendering his existing product and process technology obsolete. The low price strategy of still another player, content to follow in technology, creates a cost/price squeeze on the rest . . . forcing further innovation and the cycle repeats itself.

Survival for all but the most favored players requires a new competitive response and new organizational capabilities. For those remaining in the upper left-hand corner of Figure 1, defense of the status quo is sufficient. (IBM and Boeing, for example, seem to need to do no more than what they have always done.) For those with high share and weakening competitive advantage, the microeconomic concepts of scale efficiencies are highly applicable. (Insofar as price is *the* key success factor, being larger and reinvesting to sustain low price position assures continued success.) As long as a firm's position remains secure, much of what the old strategy model prescribes still obtains.

But for the vast majority of the firms charted in Figure 1, the shift is down scale, with weakening share position and weakening competitive advantage. For these firms, future success is more dependent on flexibility. In particular, three organizational factors become important:
• operational efficiency
• incremental product improvements, and
• the capacity to sense opportunity and execute an effective response.

For most of the firms in Figure 1, these are the key success factors for the eighties. Older, generalized ways of thinking about strategy must expand to adequately grapple with this new challenge.

Perspective Three: The Case for Multiple Perspectives

The argument developed thus far is as follows: first, traditional biases favor analytical and microeconomic tools shaping corporate strategy. Secondly, strategy alone, even if more broadly defined, is not adequate to achieve the levels of innovation and responsiveness that competition in the eighties demands. This is not to assert that management thinking has been solely limited to formulations of strategy alone. In fact, if we pick up *Business Week, Forbes,* or *Fortune* the odds are high stories about efforts to change or turnaround will focus on not one but three "essentials": a new *strategy,* a *reorganization* to fit the strategy, and a new or rejuvenated *system* to track the factors meriting central attention.

We need a still broader framework. A 1972 study comparing a dozen Japanese subsidiaries in the United States with a dozen American counterparts produced a surprising finding: the Japanese firms had no monopoly on high productivity. In fact, a near-equal mix of Japanese and American firms shared these honors.[34] When the high performing firms (regardless of national ownership) were aggregated, they were found to share much in common. Most notably, they explicitly focused on more than strategy, structure, and systems:

- they paid conscious and concrete attention to management style and had devised ways of transforming style from the intangible realm of personality into a pragmatic instrument of executive direction;
- they did not relegate the hiring and socialization of new employees to a haphazard process governed by personnel departments: instead these firms shared amazing commonality in the step-by-step process through which they welded employees into a productive and committed workforce; and
- they paid attention to the firm's overarching value system, linking its relationship to employees, customer, and society as a whole.

In sum, in addition to 1) strategy, 2) structure, and 3) systems, the high performing firms paid equal attention to 4) style, 5) staff (i.e., their human resources), and 6) shared values. Their use of all *six* of these levers, and their ability to get them all to mesh together, contributed centrally to squeezing more out of their organizations in terms of innovations, responsiveness, and operational efficiency. Let us examine each dimension in sequence.

Perspective #1: Strategy—An earlier section has addressed the shortcomings of the narrowly defined microeconomic strategy model. The Japanese avoid this pitfall by adopting a broader notion of "strategy." In our recent awe of things Japanese, most Americans forget that the original products of the Japanese automotive manufacturers badly mised the mark. Toyota's Toyopet was square, sexless, and mechanically defective. It failed miserably, as did Datsun's first several entries into the U.S. market. More recently, Mazda miscalculated badly with its first rotary engine and nearly went bankrupt. Contrary to myth, the Japanese did not from the onset embark on a strategy to seize the high-quality small car market. They manufactured what they were accustomed to building in Japan and tried to sell it abroad. Their success, as any Japanese automotive executive will

64   RICHARD T. PASCALE

readily agree, did not result from a bold insight by a few big brains at the top. On the contrary, success was achieved by senior managers humble enough not to take their initial strategic positions too seriously. What saved Japan's near-failures was the cumulative impact of "little brains" in the form of salesmen and dealers and production workers, all contributing incrementally to the quality and market position these companies enjoy today. Middle and upper management saw their primary task as guiding and orchestrating this input from below rather than steering the organization from above along a predetermined strategic course.

The Japanese don't use the term "strategy" to describe a crisp business definition or competitive master plan. They think more in terms of "strategic accomodation," or "adaptive persistence," underscoring their belief that corporate direction evolves from an incremental adjustment to unfolding events. Rarely, in their view, does one leader (or a strategic planning group) produce a bold strategy that guides a firm unerringly. Far more frequently, the input is from below. It is this ability of an organization to move information and ideas from the bottom to the top and back again in continuous dialogue that the Japanese value above all things. As this dialogue is pursued, what in hindsight may be "strategy" evolves. In sum, "strategy" is defined as "all the things necessary for the successful functioning of organization as an adaptive mechanism." Skillful use of the other levers help make adaptation possible.

Perspective #2: Organizational Structure—For many American managers, reorgnizing is the ultimate quick fix. Rearrange the boxes; never mind whether you change behavior inside the boxes.

There is no contention here that how one clusters various activities in an organization is unimportant to getting work done. The problem is, as with *any* of the other six factors taken in isolation, organizational structure is necessary but insufficient. The Coca-Cola Company spent the decades of the 1960s and 1970s in a continuous state of reorganization. The field force was decentralized, matrixed, recentralized. Pepsi-Cola steadily gained ground. Not until the eighties, under steadier guidance and with meticulous attention given to support *systems,* field management *style,* recruitment and training of *staff,* and *shared values,* did Coca-Cola begin to recapture its leadership against its major competitor.

Organizational fads, especially in rapid succession of one another, are a strong indicator of naiveté. No survey of American enterprise over the past two decades could fail to notice the succession of structural fads that have come and gone, each promoting itself as the optimum solution. There was functional organization, then the decentralization of the fifties and sixties, followed by the matrix format of the late sixties and seventies— organizational equivalents of a face-lift—and often just as cosmetic. These solutions almost always failed to live up to expectations. The boxes changed but most everything else stayed the same.

One's ability to get things done in corporations seldom depends upon one's job description and formal authority alone. A great part of one's efficacy stems from knowledge, proven track record, reputation and the trust and confidence of others. These factors are especially important at the *interfaces* between one's job and someone else's. No matter how well conceived an organization is structured, these interfaces between functions exist and successful managers build bridges across them with informal relationships. When a reorganization occurs it destroys these relationships. Not surprisingly, organizations then require six to eighteen months for its members to reestablish new interfaces. Frequent reorganizations are very traumatic as they continually disrupt these essential networks before they become fully rooted.

Reorganization is like open heart surgery—sometimes it is necessary. But if a patient can contain a heart ailment through adequate rest, regular exercise, and by not smoking, it is preferable to the risks of the operating table. Organizations would do well to use other mechanisms to get their existing structure to work whenever possible—rather than resorting too quickly to a structural remedy.

The structural "lever" encounters a fatal flaw in that it imposes a two-dimensional way of thinking upon a phenomenon that cannot be captured in two dimensions. The givens of organizations are ambiguity, uncertainty, imperfection, and paradox. Structural remedies, by their unambiguous two-dimensional nature, impose a falsehood—organizational charts:

- suggest a clarity in reporting relationships that, in fact, retain significant elements of interpersonal *ambiguity*;
- announce finite changes that are, in fact, the outcome of an *uncertain* stream of events;
- suggest mechanistic linkages that deny systemic and interpersonal *imperfections*; and
- by the very act of representing *one* organizational solution (rather than another) deny an inherent *paradox*—that paradox being that today's solution to how one organizes, however appropriate, sows the seeds for the next generation of problems.

Structural solutions are simply not fine enough instruments in and of themselves to assure these delicate tradeoffs. To succeed, structure requires reinforcement from the other managerial factors.

Perspective #3: Systems—Systems pertain to such things as forms and computer printouts, to how information flows up, down, and across the hierarchy of an organization. Systems to a large extent prescribe how communication occurs—and as a result, tend to configure how appropriately and quickly an organization can respond. Senior management can revise a strategy by a simple decree. Likewise, a structural reorganization is readily conceived and announced. But systems often remain unchanged.

66   RICHARD T. PASCALE

Stop to consider the forms we fill in, the reports we receive and promulgate, the incentive systems that reward us, and the procedures that guide us and regulate our lives. Systems condition us like mice in a maze; they gobble up an enormous portion of our discretionary energies. They are not chic, they are not pretty, they're not fast in how they work or how they change. (In fact, their maintenance in organizations is regarded as a low-status activity.) But systems insidiously and powerfully influence how people spend their lives at work each day.

"Hard copy" systems focus on things written in ink on paper—procedures that are written down, computer printouts, tables of numbers, forms, and so forth. In addition, all organizations have informal systems, that is, unwritten understandings that employees internalize about "how business gets done around here." Every organization has unwritten habits and routines. Two important ones are systems for conflict resolution and meeting formats. All organizations evolve rules about how one deals with conflict. In some organizations, it is dealt with openly and directly; in others it is handled in a roundabout way. Likewise, most organizations develop acceptable patterns for meetings. Informal rules provide guidelines as to who talks, who listens, whether presentations are formal monologues or informal dialogues, whether presenters use models and data with lots of analysis, whether they focus on the competition, market assumptions, or the bottom line. Informal systems also determine who gets mentored and the legitimate avenues for favoritism. Informal criteria are usually the first to signal fast-track candidates. These largely unseen and unwritten rules account for a great deal.

The Japanese culture pays attention to informal systems. A great many of the most important rules are implicit. There are rituals for bowing and for who has to bow most deeply, for gift giving, and for eating. Japanese life, to a much greater extent than is true in the Western world, is regulated by these unwritten rituals. As a result, survival in Japanese society requires a certain degree of astuteness at perceiving these unwritten rules. This contributes to the ability of Japanese managers to read the unwritten rules of their organization as clearly as most Westerners can read a balance sheet. Not surprisingly, they expect the informal rules to mesh with the formal ones. In most American organizations, we are far less conscious of whether this meshing occurs and, as a result, many of our formal systems are undermined by the informal ones. In summary, fuller and more meticulous attention to both formal and informal systems is a precondition to improved organizational functioning.

Perspective #4: Style—A manager's style breathes life into strategy and systems. Regrettably, most readers equate style with certain personality traits. Once so defined, "style" is relegated to the idiosyncratic and intangible domain of psychology.

A most useful way of thinking about style is to equate it to how a manager allocates time and attention. Henry Mintzberg once researched the managerial span of attention.[36] The average length of time spent on any one thing is nine minutes. Management time is chaotic, fragmented, and filled with interruptions. This is the nature of managerial work. Nonetheless, from that chaos subordinates perceive a pattern, whether intended or not. Subordinates observe how bosses allocate their time, what issues really capture their attention, and from this they interpolate what the boss really cares about.

The three most powerful mechanisms for conveying time and attention messages are within an arm's length of where one sits each day. One of them is the in-basket, another is the telephone, and the third is one's calendar. What goes into the pending tray and yellows with age and what items get turned around immediately? What things get circled, and what comments are written in the margins? Is the "metamessage" of style— cost? quality? budget overruns? new product innovation? The people down the line read these messages with uncanny accuracy.

Consider the telephone. Who gets calls? Who doesn't? What question does the boss ask? What behavior is complimented? What draws criticisms, and what doesn't draw comments at all? What is the cumulative pattern that derives from the way the boss uses the phone?

Lastly the calendar. Who gets in, and who's screened out? When the boss is outside the office, where is he—with the controllers, customers, on the production line?

In aggregate, the calendar, the in-basket, and the telephone tell us a lot about one's style. "Style" defined as symbolic behavior provides every manager with a potent lever of influence and we need not transform our personalities to use it. The effective employment of this managerial lever results from nothing less or more than the self-discipline to allocate our time and attention to *do* what we *say* our priorities are.

Perspective #5: Staff—There is a set of consistent steps that organizations go through to develop a cadre of committed and productive employees. IBM and Procter & Gamble, each in very different ways, do this well. First of all, they target malleable applicants just beginning or very early in their careers. They invest in careful selection. They avoid overselling the candidate and hiding blemishes. They allow the applicant to see rather clearly what the firm is like, permitting applicants to deselect themselves. In addition, of course, the firm plays its part in screening out those who don't fit the mold.

Socialization process begins in the trenches. No employee skips this step. One needs to learn the territory via immersion in the basics of the industry. It's like the infantry: one has to learn to shoot a gun, dig a foxhole, and hit a target.

Next comes coherent, frequently spaced, and predictable rewards. IBM sets quotas that 80 percent of its sales force can reach, then provides

68   RICHARD T. PASCALE

detailed and frequent performance reviews to stretch each candidate beyond to reach his own potential. At IBM, almost everyone on the marketing side has to be able to sell computers and keep the customer happy; one doesn't get promoted otherwise, no matter how good one is at other things. Procter & Gamble establishes a six-rung performance ladder that every successful professional candidate is expected to climb within the first two years. The reward systems are unambiguous and generally unbeatable. This clarity and impartiality, it should be noted, derives from *systems* measures and incentives that are honed for simplicity. At P&G it's: What have you done for market share? What are you doing for profits? At IBM it's: What have you sold? Is the customer satisfied?

Nothing enforces reward systems as powerfully as social leverage. Every high performing firm in the sample had periodic get-togethers in which results were reviewed across one's peer group: The boss would start with one person, ask for his report or result and go around the circle. It creates a powerful incentive. The participant finding himself at the bottom one week is powerfully motivated to avoid that embarrassment the next.

We have noted that socialization is sparked by a shared boot camp experience among a cadre of carefully selected young employees. It is strengthened by the social lever of peer comparisons and group norms and reinforced by reward systems that establish unequivocal standards of performance. Yet a fourth support derives from reinforcing folklore. Every organization has a folklore about watershed events or actions. Odds are high, if we listen carefully, that employees can summarize in one or two pithy sentences the essence of what they interpret the folklore to be. When the moral of the stories are inconsistent with what management is striving to achieve, folklore breeds cynicism and a wait-and-see attitude. Folklore acts as a guiding theory of how the firm really works. As such, it powerfully influences how employees respond to management's initiatives.

Last among the determinants of a coherent and committed staff is the availability of consistent role models. There is no more powerful way for instructing younger members of an organization than role models who present a consistent picture of what a person needs to be like to be a winner. Amazingly, many organizations leave role models to chance. The result is a mixed and confusing picture: one promotion seems related to people skills; another seems to underscore office politics; still another honors a reclusive financial wizard. There is no clear pattern. No training program in existence can instruct more powerfully than consistent role models.

Effective socialization requires consistency and meticulous attention to all the ingredients we have discussed. When managed carefully, it promotes behavioral congruence and cohesiveness. For some, this smacks of an Orwellian nightmare. For others it is ho-hum common sense. Nonetheless, most organizations do it very badly, and our outstanding organizations tend to do it well.

The socialization process described is found in most self-sustaining Japanese, American, and European companies. Its primary dividend is the coherence it provides about "how we do business around here." As such, it greatly enhances the strategic process by facilitating the dialogue up and down the hierarchy. Senior managers who shared the same socialization process and common career experiences as those in the field, can communicate with the field in a kind of shorthand. Remember: organizational responsiveness relies on effective communication with minimum politics and the minimal friction loss resulting from conflicting agendas. A meticulous socialization process directly serves this objective.

Perspective #6: Shared Values[37]—Shared values refer to the overarching value system that ties the purposes of the corporation to the customer, society, and higher order human values. They do not pertain to economic goals such as profit, sales, R.O.I., or market share. For example, IBM's Thomas Watson once stated: "We must be prepared to change all the things we are in order to remain competitive in the environment, but we must never change our three basic beliefs: 1) Respect for the dignity of the individual, 2) Offering the best customer service in the world, and 3) Excellence." In a similar vein, AT&T's value system has for ninety years emphasized 1) "Universal" service, 2) Fairness in handling personnel matters, 3) A belief that work should be held in balance with commitments to one's family and community, and 4) Relationships (i.e., from one manager to another). These four factors are deemed essential in getting things done in a large highly structured company. What makes IBM's or AT&T's value systems so important is that they are not empty slogans. They are deeply internalized. It is hard to talk to an employee of one of these organizations at any length before they surface in one way or another.

What does a strong set of shared values accomplish? It provides a kind of "magnetic north" for an organization which keeps it true to its commitments to employees, the customer, and society. The problem with secular economic values is that their ends often justify inappropriate means: in order to achieve sales or R.O.I. objectives an executive may cut corners on customer service or treat employees in a capricious manner. Having a "magnetic north" helps define the permissible range of behavior in such circumstances. It acts as a kind of "tie breaker," assisting an employee in making a close call, tilting him or her in the direction that the boss would want taken even though the boss isn't there to personally guide the decision.

Employment involves a social contract as well as a contract prescribing the exchange of labor for capital. In many Western organizations, that contract, while never explicit, often assumes little trust by either party in the other. If the only basis for the relation of company and employee is an instrumental one, it should not be surprising that many people in our organizations do what they must do to get their paycheck but little more. Shared values that concern themselves with the development and well-being of employees establish the moral context for this social contract. If such shared values are consistently honored, then employees tend to identify more fully with the company. They see the firm's interest and their own as more congruent and tend to invest themselves more fully in the organization.

Most consultants will confirm that they have been called in to solve a client's problem only to discover in the course of conducting interviews that someone in the client organization already had the solution. But because communication channels were blocked, or, more often, because the individual with the good idea was "turned off" and convinced that the organization wouldn't listen, no initiative was taken. The potential initiator hesitated to invest himself, in the last analysis, because trying is linked to caring, and history had taught him that the firm was not worth caring that much about. We begin to see here the direct connection between shared values and an organization's ability to tap into the "little brains."

Without a doubt, the most significant outcome of the way Japanese organizations manage themselves is that they are better at getting employees to be alert, to look for opportunities to do things better, and to strive by virtue of each small contribution to make the company succeed. It is like building a pyramid or watching a colony of ants: thousands of "little people" doing "little" things, *all with the same basic purpose*, can move mountains.

A recent study of product innovation in the scientific instruments and tool machinery industries indicates that 80 percent of all product innovations are initiated by the customer.[38] The majority of ideas doesn't flow from R&D labs down but from the customer up. To be sure, customers don't do the actual inventing, but their inquiries and complaints plant the seeds for improvements. Given these statistics, it matters a lot whether a company's sales force and others operating out at the tentacles of its field system are vigilant. They need to be open to new ideas *and* willing to initiate within their organization. Here is a key to success of many Japanese companies. We saw this occurring at American Honda. Staying alert and taking entrepreneurial initiative were major tenets of the Honda value system. The Japanese executives at American Honda could count on the fact that if they "erred" in these directions, they were acting as top management would want them to.

To be sure, the case for shared values can be overstated. Self-sustaining firms tend to have a *style* of management that is open to new ideas, ways of handling *staff* that encourage innovation, *systems* that are customer focused and that reward innovation, *skills* at translating ideas into action and so forth. But the ideas don't flow unless the employee *believes* in the corporation and identifies enough with its purposes to "give up" his good ideas. Further, any of us who work in organizations knows how hard they are to move. One has to *really* believe an organization *cares* in order to invest the energy and effort needed to help it change. Such commitment derives from shared values. And if we look at outstanding American firms that have a sustained track record of keeping up with or ahead of competition, we see this to be the case. Hewlett-Packard, Procter & Gamble, 3M, Boeing, Caterpillar are examples. Each has a highly developed value system that causes its employees to identify strongly with the firm. Perhaps the intense loyalty that these firms inspire is just an interesting idiosyncrasy. I believe, on the contrary, that this bond of shared values is fundamental to all of the rest. It is probably the most underpublicized "secret weapon" of great self-sustaining companies.

Conclusion

The intent of the "strategy model" has always been to assess the relationship of a firm with its environment, and identify the key elements of the managerial mix that are relevant to an effective organizational response. Given this charter to view the firm and its environment as an organic whole, our challenge is to develop a more adequate model. The central contention of this paper is that six dimensions are better than one or two or even three. Strategy, structure, and systems are not enough.

A multiple perspective disciplines us against the cognitive and perceptual biases that produce the "Honda Effect." It keeps us honest by drawing us into the interior of organization, forcing us to focus on the fine grain details that drive an effective strategic process. So doing, we learn how each of the S dimensions goes back in history—how the *strategies* that have been attempted, the firm's history of *reorganizations*, the *systems* that have been layered one upon another, the different *styles* of former leaders, and so forth—how each contributes to the legacy of what the firm is today and what stands in the way of moving it forward. Finally, attention to multiple dimensions causes us to grapple with the interdependence of each—that neither strategy nor structure nor any of the factors stands alone. Change efforts that shift only one or two of the factors and leave the remainder alone almost always fail. Only when we move on the multiple fronts across all six factors do we achieve lasting change. This has powerful implications for diagnosis and for practice.

References

1. Joseph L. Bower, *Managing the Resource Allocation Process*, Division of Research, Graduate School of Business Administration, Harvard University, Cambridge, Massachusetts, 1970, pp. 7-8.
2. A recent set of articles have begun to address this problem. See R. H. Hayes and W. J. Abernathy, "Managing Our Way to Economic Decline," *Harvard Business Review* (July/August 1980), p. 67; see also R. H. Hayes, and J. G. Garvin, "Managing As If Tomorrow Mattered," *Harvard Business Review* (May/June 1982), p. 71.
3. Boston Consulting Group, *Strategy Alternatives for the British Motorcycle Industry*, Her Majesty's Stationary Office, London, 30 July 1975, p. XIV.

72   RICHARD T. PASCALE

4. D. Purkayastha, "Note on the Motorcycle Industry—1975," 9–578–210, Harvard Business School, Cambridge, Massachusetts, Rev. 1/81, p. 5, 10, 11, 12.

5. Boston Consulting Group, *Strategy Alternatives*, p. 59; also p. 40.

6. Tetsuo Sakiya, *Honda Motor: The Men, The Management, The Machines* (Tokyo, Japan: Kadonsha International, 1982), p. 119.

7. Richard P. Rumelt, "A Teaching Plan for *Strategy Alternatives for the British Motorcycle Industry*," *Japanese Business: Business Policy*, The Japan Society, New York, NY (1980), p. 2.

8. Anon. *Honda: A Statistical View*, Overseas Public Relations Department of Honda Motor Co., Ltd., Tokyo, Japan (1982), p. 11.

9. Tetsuo Sakiya, "The Story of Honda's Founders," *Asahi Evening News*, June 1–August 29, 1979, Series #19, Series #12; also Series #10, Series #2 and 3.

10. Interviews with Honda executives, Tokyo, Japan, July 1980.

11. Sakiya, *Honda Motor*, p. 69; also Sakiya, "Honda's Founders," Series #4.

12. Sakiya, "Honda's Founders," Series #7 and 8.

13. Sakiya, *Honda Motor*, p. 72.

14. Sakiya, "Honda's Founders," Series #2.

15. Sakiya, *Honda Motor*, pp. 65-69; Sakiya, "Honda's Founders," Series #6.

16. Sakiya, *Honda Motor*, p. 73.

17. Ibid, pp. 71-72.

18. Ibid, p. 71.

19. Data provided by Honda Motor Company, Tokyo, Japan, September 10-12, 1982.

20. Sakiya, "Honda's Founders," Series #11.

21. Ibid, Series #13; also Sakiya, *Honda Motor*, p. 117.

22. Sakiya, "Honda's Founders," Series #11.

23. Richard T. Pascale, Interviews with Honda executives, Tokyo, Japan. September 10, 1982.

24. Ibid.

25. Data provided by Honda Motor Company.

26. Pascale interviews.

27. Ibid.

28. Ibid.

29. Ibid.

30. Ibid.

31. Ibid.

32. The U.S. Federal Reserve Board's "Index of Industrial Production," based on 235 different data series, registered a 15.6% increase (from 66.2 to 76.5) from 1960 to 1963 compared with a 9.1% decrease (from 152.5 to 138.6) from 1979 to 1982.

33. Michael Hunt, "Strategy in the Electric Appliance Industry" (Unpublished Ph.D. dissertation, Harvard Graduate School of Business Administration, Cambridge, Massachusetts, 1971). Also see Michael Hunt, "Teaching Note on the Home Appliance Series," Harvard Graduate School of Business Administration, Cambridge, Massachusetts, 1971.

34. Richard T. Pascale, and A. G. Athos, *The Art of Japanese Management* (New York, NY: Simon & Schuster, 1981).

35. Development of the managerial implications of structure, systems, style, and staff draw heavily on the ideas of Thomas J. Peters. Also see R. H. Waterman, T. J. Peters, and J. R. Phillips, "Structure Is Not Organization," *Business Horizons*, No. 80302 (June 1980).

36. Henry Mintzberg, *The Nature of Managerial Work* (New York, NY: Harper & Row, 1973).

37. Much of this material on shared values is built upon the ideas of Anthony G. Athos. See Pascale and Athos, *The Art of Japanese Management*.

38. Eric von Hippel, "Users as Innovators, *Technology Review* (January 1978) pp. 31-39.

[4]

Strategic Management Journal, Vol. 6, 257–272 (1985)

Of Strategies, Deliberate and Emergent

HENRY MINTZBERG
Faculty of Management, McGill University, Montreal, Quebec,
Canada

JAMES A. WATERS
Faculty of Administrative Studies, York University, Toronto,
Ontario, Canada

Summary

*Deliberate and emergent strategies may be conceived as two ends of
a continuum along which real-world strategies lie. This paper seeks
to develop this notion, and some basic issues related to strategic
choice, by elaborating along this continuum various types of
strategies uncovered in research. These include strategies labelled
planned, entrepreneurial, ideological, umbrella, process,
unconnected, consensus and imposed.*

How do strategies form in organizations? Research into the question is necessarily shaped by the underlying conception of the term. Since strategy has almost inevitably been conceived in terms of what the leaders of an organization 'plan' to do in the future, strategy formation has, not surprisingly, tended to be treated as an analytic process for establishing long-range goals and action plans for an organization; that is, as one of formulation followed by implementation. As important as this emphasis may be, we would argue that it is seriously limited, that the process needs to be viewed from a wider perspective so that the variety of ways in which strategies actually take shape can be considered.

For over 10 years now, we have been researching the process of strategy formation based on the definition of strategy as 'a pattern in a stream of decisions' (Mintzberg, 1972, 1978; Mintzberg and Waters, 1982, 1984; Mintzberg *et al.*, 1986, Mintzberg and McHugh, 1985; Brunet, Mintzberg and Waters, 1986). This definition was developed to 'operationalize' the concept of strategy, namely to provide a tangible basis on which to conduct research into how it forms in organizations. Streams of behaviour could be isolated and strategies identified as patterns or consistencies in such streams. The origins of these strategies could then be investigated, with particular attention paid to exploring the relationship between leadership plans and intentions and what the organizations actually did. Using the label strategy for both of these phenomena—one called *intended*, the other *realized*—encouraged that exploration. (Indeed, by this same logic, and because of practical necessity, we have been drawn into studying strategies as patterns in streams of actions, not decisions, since the latter represent intentions, too. A paper explaining this shift more fully is available from the authors.)

Comparing intended strategy with realized strategy, as shown in Figure 1, has allowed us to distinguish *deliberate* strategies—realized as intended—from *emergent* strategies— patterns or consistencies realized despite, or in the absence of, intentions. These two concepts, and especially their interplay, have become the central themes in our research, which has involved 11 intensive studies (as well as a larger number of smaller ones),

0143-2095/85/030257–16$01.60
©1985 by John Wiley & Sons, Ltd.

Received 28 March 1983
Revised 4 June 1984

258   *Henry Mintzberg and James A. Waters*

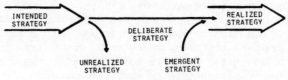

Figure 1. Types of strategies

including a food retailer, a manufacturer of women's undergarments, a magazine, a newspaper, an airline, an automobile firm, a mining company, a university, an architectural firm, a public film agency and a government fighting a foreign war.

This paper sets out to explore the complexity and variety of strategy formation processes by refining and elaborating the concepts of deliberate and emergent strategy. We begin by specifying more precisely what pure deliberate and pure emergent strategies might mean in the context of organization, describing the conditions under which each can be said to exist. What does it mean for an 'organization'—a collection of people joined together to pursue some mission in common—to act deliberately? What does it mean for a strategy to emerge in an organization, not guided by intentions? We then identify various types of strategies that have appeared in our empirical studies, each embodying differing degrees of what might be called deliberateness or emergentness. The paper concludes with a discussion of the implications of this perspective on strategy formation for research and practice.

PURE DELIBERATE AND PURE EMERGENT STRATEGIES

For a strategy to be perfectly deliberate—that is, for the realized strategy (pattern in actions) to form exactly as intended—at least three conditions would seem to have to be satisfied. First, there must have existed precise intentions in the organization, articulated in a relatively concrete level of detail, so that there can be no doubt about what was desired before any actions were taken. Secondly, because organization means collective action, to dispel any possible doubt about whether or not the intentions were organizational, they must have been common to virtually all the actors: either shared as their own or else accepted from leaders, probably in response to some sort of controls. Thirdly, these collective intentions must have been realized exactly as intended, which means that no external force (market, technological, political, etc.) could have interfered with them. The environment, in other words, must have been either perfectly predictable, totally benign, or else under the full control of the organization. These three conditions constitute a tall order, so that we are unlikely to find any perfectly deliberate strategies in organizations. Nevertheless, some strategies do come rather close, in some dimensions if not all.

For a strategy to be perfectly emergent, there must be order—consistency in action over time—in the absence of intention about it. (No consistency means no strategy or at least unrealized strategy—intentions not met.) It is difficult to imagine action in the *total* absence of intention—in some pocket of the organization if not from the leadership itself—such that we would expect the purely emergent strategy to be as rare as the purely deliberate one. But again, our research suggests that some patterns come rather close, as when an environment directly imposes a pattern of action on an organization.

Thus, we would expect to find tendencies in the directions of deliberate and emergent strategies rather than perfect forms of either. In effect, these two form the poles of a continuum along which we would expect real-world strategies to fall. Such strategies would combine various states of the dimensions we have discussed above: leadership intentions would be more or less precise, concrete and explicit, and more or less shared, as would intentions existing elsewhere in the organization; central control over organizational actions would be more or less firm and more or less pervasive; and the environment would be more or less benign, more or less controllable and more or less predictable.

Below we introduce a variety of types of strategies that fall along this continuum, beginning with those closest to the deliberate pole and ending with those most reflective of the characteristics of emergent strategy. We present these types, not as any firm or exhaustive typology (although one may eventually emerge), but simply to explore this continuum of emergentness of strategy and to try to gain some insights into the notions of intention, choice and pattern formation in the collective context we call organization.

THE PLANNED STRATEGY

Planning suggests clear and articulated intentions, backed up by formal controls to ensure their pursuit, in an environment that is acquiescent. In other words, here (and only here) does the classic distinction between 'formulation' and 'implementation' hold up.

In this first type, called *planned strategy*, leaders at the centre of authority formulate their intentions as precisely as possible and then strive for their implementation—their translation into collective action—with a minimum of distortion, 'surprise-free'. To ensure this, the leaders must first articulate their intentions in the form of a plan, to minimize confusion, and then elaborate this plan in as much detail as possible, in the form of budgets, schedules and so on, to pre-empt discretion that might impede its realization. Those outside the planning process may act, but to the extent possible they are not allowed to decide. Programmes that guide their behaviour are built into the plan, and formal controls are instituted to ensure pursuit of the plan and the programmes.

But the plan is of no use if it cannot be applied as formulated in the environment surrounding the organization so the planned strategy is found in an environment that is, if not benign or controllable, then at least rather predictable. Some organizations, as Galbraith (1967) describes the 'new industrial states', are powerful enough to impose their plans on their environments. Others are able to predict their environments with enough accuracy to pursue rather deliberate, planned strategies. We suspect, however, that many planned strategies are found in organizations that simply extrapolate established patterns in environments that they assume will remain stable. In fact, we have argued elsewhere (Mintzberg and Waters, 1982) that strategies appear not to be *conceived* in planning processes so much as elaborated from existing visions or copied from standard industry recipes (see Grinyer and Spender, 1979); planning thus becomes programming, and the planned strategy finds its origins in one of the other types of strategies described below.

Although few strategies can be planned to the degree described above, some do come rather close, particularly in organizations that must commit large quantities of resources to particular missions and so cannot tolerate unstable environments. They may spend years considering their actions, but once they decide to act, they commit themselves firmly. In effect, they deliberate so that their strategies can be rather deliberate. Thus, we studied a

260   *Henry Mintzberg and James A. Waters*

mining company that had to engage in a most detailed form of planning to exploit a new ore body in an extremely remote part of Quebec. Likewise, we found a very strong planning orientation in our study of Air Canada, necessary to co-ordinate the purchase of new, expensive jet aircraft with a relatively fixed route structure. Our study of the United States government's escalation of military activity in Vietnam also revealed a rather planned strategy. Once Lyndon Johnson announced his decision to escalate in 1965, the military planners took over and articulated the intentions in detail (or pulled out existing contingency plans), and pursued the strategy vigorously until 1968 when it became clear that the environment was less controllable than it had seemed (Mintzberg, 1978).

(Note the distinction here between unrealized strategy—that is, intentions not successfully realized—and realized strategy that is unsuccessful in its consequences. The intention to escalate was realized, in fact from Johnson's point of view, *over*-realized; it just did not achieve its objective. In contrast, John F. Kennedy's earlier intention to provide advisers to the Vietnam army was not realized to the extent that those advisers became combatants. It should be noted, however, that the degree of deliberateness is not a measure of the potential success of a strategy. In our research, we have come across rather emergent strategies as well as rather deliberate ones that have been highly successful (see the discussion of the experimental film strategy later in the text for an example of the former) and others of both types that have been dramatic failures.)

THE ENTREPRENEURIAL STRATEGY

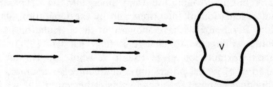

In this second type of strategy, we relax the condition of precise, articulated intentions. Here, one individual in personal control of an organization is able to impose his or her vision of direction on it. Because such strategies are rather common in entrepreneurial firms, tightly controlled by their owners, they can be called *entrepreneurial strategies*.

In this case, the force for pattern or consistency in action is individual vision, the central actor's *concept* of his or her organization's place in its world. This is coupled with an ability to impose that vision on the organization through his or her personal control of its actions (e.g. through giving direct orders to its operating personnel). Of course, the environment must again be co-operative. But entrepreneurial strategies most commonly appear in young and/or small organizations (where personal control is feasible), which are able to find relatively safe niches in their environments. Indeed, the selection of such niches is an integral part of the vision. These strategies can, however, sometimes be found in larger organizations as well, particularly under conditions of crisis where all the actors are willing to follow the direction of a single leader who has vision and will.

Is the entrepreneurial strategy deliberate? Intentions do exist. But they derive from one individual who need not articulate or elaborate them. Indeed, for reasons discussed below, he or she is typically unlikely to want to do so. Thus, the intentions are both more difficult to identify and less specific than those of the planned strategy. Moreover, there is less overt acceptance of these intentions on the part of other actors in the organization. Nevertheless, so long as those actors respond to the personal will of the leader, the strategy would appear to be rather deliberate.

In two important respects, however, that strategy can have emergent characteristics as well. First, as indicated in the previous diagram, vision provides only a general sense of direction. Within it, there is room for adaptation: the details of the vision can emerge *en route*. Secondly, because the leader's vision is personal, it can also be changed completely. To put this another way, since here the formulator is the implementor, step by step, that person can react quickly to feedback on past actions or to new opportunities or threats in the environment. He or she can thus reformulate vision, as shown in the figure below.

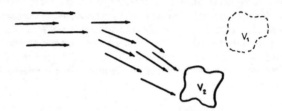

It is this adaptability that distinguishes the entrepreneurial strategy from the planned one. Visions contained in single brains would appear to be more flexible, assuming the individual's willingness to learn,[1] than plans articulated through hierarchies, which are comprised of many brains. Adaptation (and emergentness) of planned strategies are discouraged by the articulation of intentions and by the separation between formulation and implementation. Psychologists have shown that the articulation of a strategy locks it into place, impeding willingness to change it (e.g. Kiesler, 1971). The separation of implementation from formulation gives rise to a whole system of commitments and procedures, in the form of plans, programmes and controls elaborated down a hierarchy. Instead of one individual being able to change his or her mind, the whole system must be redesigned. Thus, despite the claims of flexible planning, the fact is that organizations plan not to be flexible but to realize specific intentions. It is the entrepreneurial strategy that provides flexibility, at the expense of the specificity and articulation of intentions.

Entrepreneurial strategies have appeared in our research, not surprisingly, in two companies that were controlled personally by their aggressive owners—one the food retail chain, the other the manufacturer of women's undergarments. Here, typically, when important aspects of the environment changed, strong new visions emerged rather quickly, followed by long periods of deliberate pursuit of these visions. But as both organizations grew and became more formalized, the visions became the basis for planning (programming), and thereafter decisive changes were less in evidence. This led us to suspect that planned strategies often follow entrepreneurial ones, based on the vision of leaders, sometimes ones who have departed the organization (see Mintzberg and Waters, 1982, 1984).

---

[1] An interesting situation arises when the vision is beyond even the control of the individual himself, so that he or she pursues a pattern of action due to inner, subconscious forces (as, say, when the leader chooses to produce only unconventional products, perhaps because of a phobia about being ordinary). Such 'subconscious' strategies would probably be more difficult to change than those based on more conscious visions.

262   *Henry Mintzberg and James A. Waters*

THE IDEOLOGICAL STRATEGY

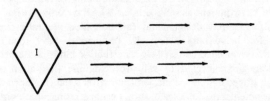

Vision can be collective as well as individual. When the members of an organization share a vision and identify so strongly with it that they pursue it as an ideology, then they are bound to exhibit patterns in their behaviour, so that clear realized strategies can be identified. These may be called *ideological strategies*.

Can an ideological strategy be considered deliberate? Since the ideology is likely to be somewhat overt (e.g. in programmes of indoctrination), and perhaps even articulated (in rough, inspirational form, such as a credo), intentions can usually be identified. The question thus revolves around whether these intentions can be considered organizational and whether they are likely to be realized as intended. In an important sense, these intentions would seem to be most clearly organizational. Whereas the intentions of the planned and entrepreneurial strategies emanate from one centre and are accepted passively by everyone else, those of the ideological strategy are positively embraced by the members of the organization.

As for their realization, because the intentions exist as a rough vision, they can presumably be adapted or changed. But collective vision is far more immutable than individual vision. All who share it must agree to change their 'collective mind'. Moreover, ideology is rooted in the past, in traditions and precedents (often the institutionalization of the vision of a departed, charismatic leader: one person's vision has become everyone's ideology). People, therefore, resist changing it. The object is to interpret 'the word', not to defy it. Finally, the environment is unlikely to impose change: the purpose of ideology, after all, is to change the environment or else to insulate the organization from it. For all these reasons, therefore, ideological strategy would normally be highly deliberate, perhaps more so than any type of strategy except the planned one.

We have not as yet studied any organization dominated by an ideology. But such strategies do seem to occur in certain organizations described in the literature, notably in certain Israeli kibbutzim, 'distinctive colleges', and some charitable institutions (see Clark, 1970, 1972; Sills, 1957; also Mintzberg, 1983: Chapters 11 and 21).

THE UMBRELLA STRATEGY

Now we begin to relax the condition of tight control (whether bureaucratic, personal or ideological) over the mass of actors in the organization and, in some cases, the condition of tight control over the environment as well. Leaders who have only partial control over other actors in an organization may design what can be called *umbrella strategies*. They set general guidelines for behaviour—define the boundaries—and then let other actors manoeuvre within them. In effect, these leaders establish kinds of umbrellas under which organizational actions are expected to fall—for example that all products should be designed for the high-priced end of the market (no matter what those products might be).

When an environment is complex, and perhaps somewhat uncontrollable and unpredictable as well, a variety of actors in the organization must be able to respond to it. In other words, the patterns in organizational actions cannot be set deliberately in one central place, although the boundaries may be established there to constrain them. From the perspective of the leadership (if not, perhaps, the individual actors), therefore, strategies are allowed to emerge, at least within these boundaries. In fact, we can label the umbrella strategy not only deliberate and emergent (intended at the centre in its broad outlines but not in its specific details), but also 'deliberately emergent' (in the sense that the central leadership intentionally creates the conditions under which strategies can emerge).

Like the entrepreneurial strategy, the umbrella one represents a certain vision emanating from the central leadership. But here those who have the vision do not control its realization; instead they must convince others to pursue it. The umbrella at least puts limits on the actions of others and ideally provides a sense of direction as well. Sometimes the umbrella takes the form of a more specific target, as in a NASA that concentrated its efforts during the 1960s on putting a man on the moon. In the light of this specific target, all kinds of strategies emerged, as various technical problems were solved by thousands of different specialists.

The architectural firm in our research provides a good example of umbrella strategy. The partners made it clear what kinds of buildings they wished to design: unique, excellent and highly visible ones that would 'celebrate the spirit of the community'. Under that umbrella, anything went—performing arts centres, office buildings, hotels, etc. The firm occasionally filled in gaps with smaller projects of a more mundane nature, but it never committed itself to a major undertaking that strayed from those central criteria (Mintzberg *et al.*, 1986).[2]

We have so far described the umbrella strategy as one among a number of types that are possible. But, in some sense, virtually all real-world strategies have umbrella characteristics. That is to say, in no organization can the central leadership totally pre-empt the discretion of others (as was assumed in the planned and entrepreneurial strategies) and, by the same token, in none does a central leadership defer totally to others (unless it has ceased to lead). Almost all strategy making behaviour involves, therefore, to some degree at least, a central leadership with some sort of intentions trying to direct, guide, cajole or nudge others with ideas of their own. When the leadership is able to direct, we move towards the realm of the planned or entrepreneurial strategies; when it can hardly nudge, we move toward the realm of the more emergent strategies. But in the broad range between these two can always be found strategies with umbrella characteristics.

In its pursuit of an umbrella strategy—which means, in essence, defining general direction subject to varied interpretation—the central leadership must monitor the behaviour of other actors to assess whether or not the boundaries are being respected. In

---

[2] Of course, to the extent that other architects in the firm embraced these criteria, instead of merely accepting them as the intentions of the central leadership, the strategy could have been labelled ideological.

264   *Henry Mintzberg and James A. Waters*

essence, like us, it searches for patterns in streams of actions. When actors are found to stray outside the boundaries (whether inadvertently or intentionally), the central leadership has three choices: to stop them, ignore them (perhaps for a time, to see what will happen), or adjust to them. In other words, when an arm pokes outside the umbrella, you either pull it in, leave it there (although it might get wet), or move the umbrella over to cover it.

In this last case, the leadership exercises the option of altering its own vision in response to the behaviour of others. Indeed, this would appear to be the place where much effective strategic learning takes place—through leadership response to the initiatives of others. The leadership that is never willing to alter its vision in such a way forgoes important opportunities and tends to lose touch with its environment (although, of course, the one too willing to do so may be unable to sustain any central direction). The umbrella strategy thus requires a light touch, maintaining a subtle balance between proaction and reaction.

THE PROCESS STRATEGY

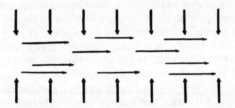

Similar to the umbrella strategy is what can be called the *process strategy*. Again, the leadership functions in an organization in which other actors must have considerable discretion to determine outcomes, because of an environment that is complex and perhaps also unpredictable and uncontrollable. But instead of trying to control strategy content at a general level, through boundaries or targets, the leadership instead needs to exercise influence indirectly. Specifically, it controls the *process* of strategy making while leaving the *content* of strategy to other actors. Again, the resulting behaviour would be deliberate in one respect and emergent in others: the central leadership designs the system that allows others the flexibility to evolve patterns within it.

The leadership may, for example, control the staffing of the organization, thereby determining who gets to make strategy if not what that strategy will be (all the while knowing that control of the former constitutes considerable influence over the latter). Or it may design the structure of the organization to determine the working context of those who get to make strategy. Thus, it was claimed recently that '75 per cent of the (Hewlett Packard) plan is devoted to the new product portfolio generation *process*'.[3]

Divisionalized organizations of a conglomerate nature commonly use process strategies: the central headquarters creates the basic structure, establishes the control systems and appoints the division managers, who are then expected to develop strategies for their own businesses (typically planned ones for reasons outlined by Mintzberg, 1979:384–392); note that techniques such as those introduced by the Boston Consulting Group to manage the

---

[3] Statement by Thomas Peters at the Strategic Management Society Conference 'Exploring the Strategy-making Process', Montreal, 8 October, 1982; emphasis added.

business portfolios of divisionalized companies, by involving headquarters in the business strategies to some extent, bring their strategies back into the realm of umbrella ones.

THE UNCONNECTED STRATEGIES

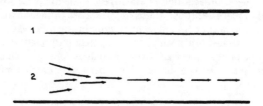

The *unconnected strategy* is perhaps the most straightforward one of all. One part of the organization with considerable discretion—a subunit, sometimes even a single individual—because it is only loosely coupled to the rest, is able to realize its own pattern in its stream of actions. Our clearest example of this appeared in the study of the National Film Board of Canada, a producer of primarily short films, where the central leadership seldom dictated the content of films. From the 1940s to the mid-1960s, the Film Board produced, among many others, a thin but steady stream of experimental films; after that, their number increased significantly. In fact, with one exception, every single film up to 1960 was made by one person, Norman McLaren, the Board's most celebrated film-maker. McLaren, in other words, pursued his own personal strategy—'did his own thing', as the saying goes—for decades, quite independently of the activities of other film-makers.

How deliberate or emergent are these unconnected strategies? Since they come neither from a central leadership nor from intentions in the organization at large, they would seem to be relatively emergent from the perspective of the entire organization. But from the perspective of the unit or individual involved, clearly they can be deliberate or emergent, depending on the prior existence of intentions.

Identifying intentions is a tricky business in any context. Who can be sure that what was articulated was truly intended. Moreover, in the collective context, there is the problem of determining whose intentions really matter, and of dealing with conflicting intentions. These problems may be absent in the context of the individual, but they are replaced by others. For example, the individual pursuing a personal strategy is unlikely to have to articulate his or her intentions before actions are taken, and that can influence the very existence of intentions. Consider the experimental film strategy of Norman McLaren. Was it deliberate? For McLaren himself, it could conceivably have been. That is, he may have developed a general intention to make a stream of experimental films, at least after his initial successes. But why should he have done so? Surely McLaren did not say to himself in 1943: 'I shall make experimental films for the next 30 years'. More likely, he just decided on one film at a time, in effect being deliberate about individual films (although these too may have emerged) but not about the pattern in the sequence of them.

The fact that a Norman McLaren has no need to articulate his intentions (unlike, at least in some cases, a leader in charge of other people) means that no one can ever be sure what he intended (or, more exactly, what he would have claimed he intended). To take another example, used in a previous paper to illustrate the definition of realized strategy (Mintzberg,

1978: 935), Picasso's blue period can be called a personal blue strategy, since there was consistency in his use of colour across a sequence of his paintings. But did Picasso 'decide' to paint blue for a given period of his life, or did he simply feel like using that blue each time he painted during these years?

The fact that neither a McLaren nor a Picasso had to explain their intentions to anyone (McLaren at least not beyond saying enough in his organizational context to get funding for a single film at a time) meant that neither was forced to think them through. This probably allowed those intentions to remain rather vague, to themselves as well as to others around them, and so probably encouraged a degree of emergentness in their behaviours.

The example of Norman McLaren is indicative of the fact that unconnected strategies tend to proliferate in organizations of experts, reflecting the complexity of the environments that they face and the resulting need for considerable control by the experts over their own work, providing freedom not only from administrators but sometimes from their own peers as well. Thus, many hospitals and universities appear to be little more than collections of personal strategies, with hardly any discernible central vision or umbrella, let alone plan, linking them together. Each expert pursues his or her own strategies—method of patient care, subject of research, style of teaching. On the other hand, in organizations that do pursue central, rather deliberate strategies, even planned ones, unconnected strategies can sometimes be found in remote enclaves, either tolerated by the system or lost within it.

As indicated in the previous diagram, unconnected strategies may be deliberate or emergent for the actors involved (although always emergent from the perspective of the organization at large). Also, although they are shown within an umbrella strategy, clearly they can fall outside of these, too. Indeed, some unconnected strategies directly contradict umbrella ones (or even more centrally imposed planned or entrepreneurial ones), in effect developing on a clandestine basis. Allison (1971), for example, describes how President Kennedy's directive to defuse the missile bases in Turkey during the Cuban Missile Crisis was deliberately ignored by the military leaders. We show such clandestine strategies in the figure below as a sequence of arrows breaking out of an umbrella strategy. These arrows signify that even though the strategy is likely to be deliberate from the point of view of its proponents, it cannot be articulated as such: they cannot reveal their intentions. To minimize their risk of exposure, they seek to realize intentions subtly, action by action, as if the strategy was emergent. Of course, that increases the chances that the intentions will get deflected along the way. If they do not, there is still the risk that the leadership will realize what is happening—will recognize the pattern in the stream of actions—and stop the strategy. The leadership can, however, play the game too, waiting to see what happens, knowing it too can learn from clandestine behaviour. If the strategy should prove successful, it can always be accepted and broadened—internalized in the system as a (henceforth) deliberate strategy. Our suspicion is that much strategic adaptation results from unconnected strategies (whether or not clandestine) that succeed and so pervade the organization.

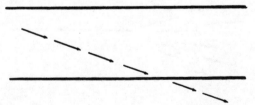

THE CONSENSUS STRATEGY

In no strategy so far discussed have we totally dropped the condition of prior intention. The next type is rather more clearly emergent. Here many different actors naturally converge on the same theme, or pattern, so that it becomes pervasive in the organization, without the need for any central direction or control. We call it the *consensus strategy*. Unlike the ideological strategy, in which a consensus forms around a system of beliefs (thus reflecting intentions widely accepted in the organization), the consensus strategy grows out of the mutual adjustment among different actors, as they learn from each other and from their various responses to the environment and thereby find a common, and probably unexpected, pattern that works for them.

In other words, the convergence is not driven by any intentions of a central management, nor even by prior intentions widely shared among the other actors. It just evolves through the results of a host of individual actions. Of course, certain actors may actively promote the consensus, perhaps even negotiate with their colleagues to attain it (as in the congressional form of government). But the point is that it derives more from collective action than from collective intention.

Our clearest example of a consensus strategy formed so fast that it seemed literally spontaneous. In the early 1950s, the National Film Board of Canada made its first film for television and in a matter of months the organization found itself concentrating two-thirds of its efforts in that medium. Despite heated debate and indications of managerial intentions to the contrary, one film-maker set the precedent by making that first film, and many of the others quickly followed suit. (In fact, the strategy lasted about 4 years and then disappeared just as spontaneously as it began.) Such spontaneity presumably reflects a strong drive for consistency (the Film Board having been groping for a new focus of attention for several years). As soon as the right idea comes along, the consensus crystallizes quickly, much as does a supersaturated solution the moment it is disturbed. We have been speculating on possible uses for the term intuition in a collective context; the spontaneous strategy might be a good example of 'organizational intuition'.

When the convergence is on a general theme rather than a specific activity (such as making films for television), the consensus is likely to develop more gradually: individual actions would take time to be understood and to pervade the organization as precedents. An electronics manufacturer may find itself concentrating on high quality products after it had achieved success with a number of such products, or a university may find itself over the years favouring the sciences over the humanitites as its members came to realize that this is where its real strengths lie.

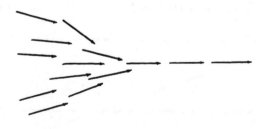

THE IMPOSED STRATEGIES

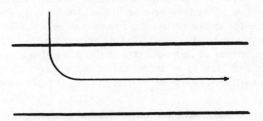

All the strategies so far discussed have derived in part at least from the will (if not the intentions) of actors within the organization. The environment has been considered, if not benign, then at least acquiescent. But strategies can be *imposed* from outside as well; that is, the environment can directly force the organization into a pattern in its stream of actions, regardless of the presence of central controls. The clearest case of this occurs when an external individual or group with a great deal of influence over the organization imposes a strategy on it. We saw this in our study of the state-owned Air Canada, when the minister who created and controlled the airline in its early years forced it to buy and fly a particular type of aircraft. Here the imposed strategy was clearly deliberate, but not by anyone in the organization. However, given its inability to resist, the organization had to resign itself to the pursuit of the strategy, so that it became, in effect, deliberate.

Sometimes the 'environment' rather than people *per se* impose strategies on organizations, simply by severely restricting the options open to them. Air Canada chose to fly jet aeroplanes and later wide-body aeroplanes. But did it? Could any 'world class' airline have decided otherwise? Again the organization has internalized the imperative so that strategic choice becomes a moot point. To draw from another of our studies, did Lyndon Johnson 'choose' to escalate the United States' involvement in Vietnam in 1965? Kennedy's earlier intended strategy of providing advisers for the South Vietnamese became an emergent strategy of engagement in a hot war, imposed by the environment (namely the actions of the Vietcong; of course, to the extent that the military advisers intended to fight, the strategy might be more accurately described as clandestine). The result was that by the time Johnson faced the decision to escalate, the pressures were almost inescapable. So he 'decided', and the strategy became a planned one.

Many planned strategies in fact seem to have this determined quality to them—pursued by organizations resigned to co-operating with external forces. One is reminded here of the king in the Saint-Exupéry (1946) story of *The Little Prince*, who only gave orders that could be executed. He claimed, for example, that he could order the sun to set, but only at a certain time of the day. The point is that when intentions are sufficiently malleable, everything can seem deliberate.

Reality, however, seems to bring organizations closer to a compromise position between determinism and free choice. Environments seldom pre-empt all choice, just as they seldom offer unlimited choice. That is why purely determined strategies are probably as rare as purely planned ones. Alternatively, just as the umbrella strategy may be the most realistic reflection of leadership intention, so too might the partially imposed strategy be the most realistic reflection of environmental influence. As shown in the figure below, the environment bounds what the organization can do, in this illustration determining under what part of the umbrella the organization can feasibly operate. Earlier we described the umbrella strategy of the architectural firm we studied. During one period in its history, it was repeatedly selected to design performing arts centres, even though it was prepared to work on a wide variety of building types. The environment (namely the clients) made its choices for it and so determined its specific strategy for a time, but only within the strategic umbrella acceptable to it. Just as we argued earlier that virtually all real-world strategies have umbrella characteristics, so too do we add here that virtually all have environmental boundaries.

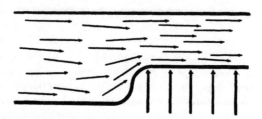

This completes our discussion of various types of strategies. Table 1 summarizes some of their major features.

EMERGING CONCLUSIONS

This paper has been written to open up thinking about strategy formation, to broaden perspectives that may remain framed in the image of it as an *a priori*, analytic process or even as a sharp dichotomy between strategies as either deliberate or emergent. We believe that more research is required on the process of strategy formation to complement the extensive work currently taking place on the content of strategies; indeed, we believe that research on the former can significantly influence the direction taken by research on the latter (and vice versa).

One promising line of research is investigation of the strategy formation process and of the types of strategies realized as a function of the structure and context of organizations. Do the various propositions suggested in this paper, based on our own limited research, in fact hold up in broader samples, for example, that strategies will tend to be more deliberate in tightly coupled, centrally controlled organizations and more emergent in decentralized, loosely coupled ones?

It would also be interesting to know how different types of strategies perform in various contexts and also how these strategies relate to those defined in terms of specific content. Using Porter's (1980) categories, for example, will cost leadership strategies prove more deliberate (specifically, more often planned), differentiation strategies more emergent (perhaps umbrella in nature), or perhaps entrepreneurial? Or using Miles and Snow's (1978) typology, will defenders prove more deliberate in orientation and inclined to use planned strategies, whereas prospectors tend to be more emergent and more prone to rely on umbrella or process, or even unconnected, strategies? It may even be possible that highly deliberate strategy making processes will be found to drive organizations away from

270 *Henry Mintzberg and James A. Waters*

Table 1. Summary description of types of strategies

Strategy	Major features
Planned	Strategies originate in formal plans: precise intentions exist, formulated and articulated by central leadership, backed up by formal controls to ensure surprise-free implementation in benign, controllable or predictable environment; strategies most deliberate
Entrepreneurial	Strategies originate in central vision: intentions exist as personal, unarticulated vision of single leader, and so adaptable to new opportunities; organization under personal control of leader and located in protected niche in environment; strategies relatively deliberate but can emerge
Ideological	Strategies originate in shared beliefs: intentions exist as collective vision of all actors, in inspirational form and relatively immutable, controlled normatively through indoctrination and/or socialization; organization often proactive *vis-à-vis* environment; strategies rather deliberate
Umbrella	Strategies originate in constraints: leadership, in partial control of organizational actions, defines strategic boundaries or targets within which other actors respond to own forces or to complex, perhaps also unpredictable environment; strategies partly deliberate, partly emergent and deliberately emergent
Process	Strategies originate in process: leadership controls process aspects of strategy (hiring, structure, etc.), leaving content aspects to other actors; strategies partly deliberate, partly emergent (and, again, deliberately emergent)
Unconnected	Strategies originate in enclaves: actor(s) loosely coupled to rest of organization produce(s) patterns in own actions in absence of, or in direct contradiction to, central or common intentions; strategies organizationally emergent whether or not deliberate for actor(s)
Consensus	Strategies originate in consensus: through mutual adjustment, actors converge on patterns that become pervasive in absence of central or common intentions; strategies rather emergent
Imposed	Strategies originate in environment: environment dictates patterns in actions either through direct imposition or through implicitly pre-empting or bounding organizational choice; strategies most emergent, although may be internalized by organization and made deliberate

prospecting activities and towards cost leadership strategies whereas emergent ones may encourage the opposite postures.

The interplay of the different types of strategies we have described can be another avenue of inquiry: the nesting of personal strategies within umbrella ones or their departure in clandestine form from centrally imposed umbrellas; the capacity of unconnected strategies to evoke organizational ones of a consensus or even a planned nature as peripheral patterns that succeed pervade the organization; the conversion of entrepreneurial strategies into ideological or planned ones as vision becomes institutionalized one way or another; the possible propensity of imposed strategies to become deliberate as they are internalized within the organization; and so on. An understanding of how these different types of strategies blend into each other and tend to sequence themselves over time in different contexts could reveal a good deal about the strategy formation process.

At a more general level, the whole question of how managers learn from the experiences of their own organizations seems to be fertile ground for research. In our view, the fundamental difference between deliberate and emergent strategy is that whereas the former focuses on direction and control—getting desired things done—the latter opens up this notion of 'strategic learning'. Defining strategy as intended and conceiving it as deliberate, as has traditionally been done, effectively precludes the notion of strategic learning. Once the intentions have been set, attention is riveted on realizing them, not on adapting them.

Messages from the environment tend to get blocked out. Adding the concept of emergent strategy, based on the definition of strategy as realized, opens the process of strategy making up to the notion of learning.

Emergent strategy itself implies learning what works—taking one action at a time in search for that viable pattern or consistency. It is important to remember that emergent strategy means, not chaos, but, in essence, *unintended order*. It is also frequently the means by which deliberate strategies change. As shown in Figure 2, in the feedback loop added to our basic diagram, it is often through the identification of emergent strategies—its patterns never intended—that managers and others in the organization come to change their intentions. This is another way of saying that not a few deliberate strategies are simply emergent ones that have been uncovered and subsequently formalized. Of course, unrealized strategies are also a source of learning, as managers find out which of their intentions do not work, rejected either by their organizations themselves or else by environments that are less than acquiescent.

We wish to emphasize that emergent strategy does not have to mean that management is out of control, only—in some cases at least—that it is open, flexible and responsive, in other words, willing to learn. Such behaviour is especially important when an environment is too unstable or complex to comprehend, or too imposing to defy. Openness to such emergent strategy enables management to act before everything is fully understood—to respond to an evolving reality rather than having to focus on a stable fantasy. For example, distinctive competence cannot always be assessed on paper *a priori*; often, perhaps usually, it has to be discovered empirically, by taking actions that test where strengths and weaknesses really lie. Emergent strategy also enables a management that cannot be close enough to a situation, or to know enough about the varied activities of its organization, to surrender control to those who have the information current and detailed enough to shape realistic strategies. Whereas the more deliberate strategies tend to emphasize central direction and hierarchy, the more emergent ones open the way for collective action and convergent behaviour.

Of course, by the same token, deliberate strategy is hardly dysfunctional either. Managers need to manage too, sometimes to impose intentions on their organizations—to provide a sense of direction. That can be partial, as in the cases of umbrella and process strategies, or it can be rather comprehensive, as in the cases of planned and entrepreneurial strategies. When the necessary information can be brought to a central place and environments can be largely understood and predicted (or at least controlled), then it may be appropriate to suspend strategic learning for a time to pursue intentions with as much determination as possible (see Mintzberg and Waters, 1984).

Our conclusion is that strategy formation walks on two feet, one deliberate, the other emergent. As noted earlier, managing requires a light deft touch—to direct in order to realize intentions while at the same time responding to an unfolding pattern of action. The relative emphasis may shift from time to time but not the requirement to attend to both sides of this phenomenon.

STRATEGIC LEARNING

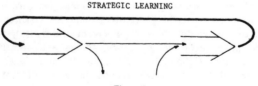

Figure 2

272   *Henry Mintzberg and James A. Waters*

We need to know more about the responding side of this directing/responding dialectic. More specifically, we would like to know more about how managers track the realized strategies of their own organizations. A major component of that elusive concept called 'strategic control' may be in managers doing what we do as researchers: searching for patterns in streams of organizational actions. Pattern recognition is likely to prove a crucial ability of effective managers and crucial to effective organizations may be the facilitation of self-awareness on the part of all its members of the patterns of its own actions and their consequences over time. Strategic choice requires that kind of awareness; a high degree of it is likely to characterize effective managers and effective organizations.

REFERENCES

Allison, G. T. *Essence of Decision: Explaining the Cuban Missile Crisis*, Little, Brown, Boston, 1971.

Brunet, J. P. H. Mintzberg and J. Waters. 'Does planning impede strategic thinking? The strategy of Air Canada 1937-1976,' in Lamb, R (ed.) *Advances in Strategic Management*, Volume 4, Prentice-Hall, Englewood Cliffs, N. J., 1986.

Chandler, A. D. *Strategy and Structure*, MIT Press, Cambridge, 1962.

Clark, B. R. *The Distinctive College*, Aldino, Chicago, 1970.

Clark, B. R. 'The organizational saga in higher education', *Administrative Science Quarterly*, 1972, pp. 178-184.

Galbraith, J. K. *The New Industrial State*, Houghton Mifflin, Boston, 1967.

Grinyer, P. H. and J. C. Spender. *Turnaround: the Fall and Rise of the Newton Chambers Group*, Association Business Press, London, 1979.

Kiesler, C. H. *The Psychology of Commitment: Experiments Linking Behaviour to Belief*, Academic Press, New York, 1971.

Miles, R. and C. Snow. *Organizational Strategy, Structure, and Process*, McGraw-Hill, New York, 1978.

Mintzberg, H. 'Research on strategy-making', *Proceedings of the 32nd Annual Meeting of the Academy of Management*, Minneapolis, 1972.

Mintzberg, H. 'Patterns in strategy formation', *Management Science*, 1978, pp. 934-948.

Mintzberg, H. *The Structuring of Organizations*, Prentice-Hall, Englewood Cliffs, N.J., 1979.

Mintzberg, H. *Power in and Around Organization*, Prentice-Hall, Englewood Cliffs, N.J., 1983.

Mintzberg, H. and A. McHugh. 'Strategy Formation in Adhocracy', *Administrative Science Quarterly*, forthcoming in 1985.

Mintzberg, H., D. Raisinghani and A. Theoret. 'The structure of "unstructured" decision processes', *Administrative Science Quarterly*, 1976, pp. 246-275.

Mintzberg, H. and J. A. Waters. 'Tracking strategy in an entrepreneurial firm', *Academy of Management Journal*, 1982, pp. 465-499.

Mintzberg, H. and J. A. Waters. 'Researching the formation of strategies: the history of Canadian Lady, 1939-1976', in Lamb, R. (ed.) *Competitive Strategic Management*, Prentice-Hall, Englewood Cliffs, N.J., 1984.

Mintzberg, H., S. Otis, J. Shamsie and J. A. Waters. 'Strategy of design: a study of "architects in co-partnership"', Grant, John (ed.) *Strategic Management Frontiers*, JAI Press, Greenwich, CT, 1986.

Porter, M. E. *Competitive Strategy: Techniques for Analyzing Industries and Competitors*, Free Press, New York, 1980.

Saint-Exupery, A. *Le Petit Prince*, English translation by Katherine Woods, Reynal and Hitchcock, New York, 1943.

Sills, D. L. *The Volunteers*, Free Press, New York, 1957.

Strategic Management Journal, Vol. 15, 91–112 (1994)

LINKING ORGANIZATIONAL CONTEXT AND MANAGERIAL ACTION: THE DIMENSIONS OF QUALITY OF MANAGEMENT

SUMANTRA GHOSHAL
The Corporate Renewal Initiative (CORE), INSEAD, Fontainebleau, France

CHRISTOPHER A. BARTLETT
Graduate School of Business Administration, Harvard University, Boston, Massachusetts, U.S.A.

Organizational context is created and renewed through tangible and concrete management actions. The context, in turn, influences the actions of all those within the company. In this article, we elaborate this theme of an interactive development of context and action that, we argue, lies at the core of a company's management process and is a key influencer of its performance. Based on a longitudinal field-study in one company, we identify discipline, stretch, trust and support as the primary dimensions of organizational context and we describe how each of these dimensions can be developed and how these dimensions, in turn, influence the levels of individual initiative, mutual cooperation and collective learning within companies. Shaping the organizational context, we suggest, is the central task of general managers and we propose our model of context as a way to assess an organization's quality of management.

The performance of a firm is influenced by its relative position in the industry and by its stock of relevant, valuable and unique resources. The firm's ability to develop and deploy such resources and to build attractive market positions in its businesses is, in turn, influenced by its organizational capabilities (Rumelt, Schendel, and Teece, 1991). Underlying both the strategic positions and the organizational capabilities are what Porter (1991) describes as 'managerial choices', i.e., the decisions and actions that actors within the firm have taken over time. While neither comprehensive nor nuanced, this crude recapitulation of the last two decades of work in the strategy field points to the next question in the chain of causation: what factors influence these choices and actions of individuals within the firm?

This is the question we address in this paper. Following Barnard, the question can be put another way: why do individuals, in some organizations but not in others, routinely do so much more 'for the good of the organization' (1938: 200) than their personal economic or political rewards would justify? Barnard described such behavior as 'the willingness of individuals to contribute force to the cooperative system' (1938: 83): why do people, in some organizations, contribute this force?

Our answer to this question, based on a rich and longitudinal field study in a company we will refer to as Semco, suggests the primacy of an organization's work ethic in influencing the behaviors and actions of its members. This work ethic is embedded in what has been described in the strategy process literature as the organizational context (Bower, 1970; Burgelman, 1983; Haspeslagh, 1986) and in the organizational theory literature as climate or culture (Tagiuri and Litwin, 1968; Pettigrew, 1979; Ouchi, 1981;

Key words: Organizational context, quality of management, managerial action

CCC 0143–2095/94/090091–22
© 1994 by John Wiley & Sons, Ltd.

92   *S. Ghoshal and C. A. Bartlett*

Deal and Kennedy, 1982; Schneider, 1985; Gordon, 1985; Schein, 1985; Denison, 1990). While we will refer to and build on this prior work in the course of presenting our analysis, the voices in the literature closest to the spirit of our arguments go much further back.

In his analysis of the rise of Western capitalism, Weber had asked the question why people pursued wealth and material gain for its own sake, not because of necessity. While recognizing the influence of a variety of other factors, he had located the main answer to this question in the puritan ethic that sought to achieve salvation through economic activity, thereby transforming the acquisitive motive from personal eccentricity to a moral order (see Furnham, 1990). We suggest in this article that an organization can similarly create and embed in its context a work ethic that would induce rational yet value-oriented actions on the part of its members in furthering the interests of the organization as an end in itself, not just a means to an end. Such a context emerged in Semco. It was created through tangible and concrete management actions. The context, over time, significantly altered the company's strategic processes and the behaviors and actions of its employees. We will describe here the key attributes of such an organizational context and present some propositions, based on our field-study, on the management actions necessary for developing these attributes and on how these attributes, in turn, influence individual and collective action of members. Overall, we will propose a model of the interactive development of context and action in organizations and suggest how these interactions influence organizational effectiveness.

Based on his life-long experience as a practitioner, Barnard had similarly identified the importance of an embedded work-ethic—what he called 'the moral factor' (1938: 261)—as a central requirement for effective organizations. He saw the main role of general managers as creating this moral factor by inspiring peoples' faith: 'faith in common understanding, faith in the probability of success, faith in the ultimate satisfaction of personal motives, faith in the integrity of objective authority, faith in the superiority of common purpose as a personal aim of those who partake in it' (1938: 259). The model of organizational context we present in this article describes the anatomy of such faith: the characteristics of context that inspire it, and the tools available to general managers for developing those characteristics.

Following the causal chain we sketched in the introductory paragraph, this faith is the 'origin of origins' (Porter, 1991)—the ultimate and invisible shaper of organizational performance. If, as suggested by Barnard, inspiring such faith through the creation of an appropriate corporate context is the key task of general managers, then the quality of the organizational context, in terms of its ability to influence individual behavior by the inducement of such faith, is a good measure of what Doz and Prahalad (1988) have referred to as an organization's 'quality of management'.

Two themes have historically been of central concern to strategic management as a field of research and teaching: a focus on the overall performance of the firm, and an interest in the role of general managers in influencing such performance (Rumelt *et al.*, 1991). These two themes had been highly interrelated in the work of those who pioneered the field (Selznick, 1957; Chandler, 1962; Andrews, 1971; Ansoff, 1965). In more recent work, as strategy has evolved to become what Galunic and Eisenhardt (1993) have described as another 'functional imperative', its link with management has eroded. Our analysis here of the first theme of organizational performance also provides a perspective on the second theme of the roles and tasks of management. To this extent, the article also represents an effort to rebuild the bridge that created and legitimized the field.

TALE OF A TURNAROUND: AND OF A MESSY RESEARCH PROCESS

After losing money and market share for 3 years, in 1989, Semco registered an unexpectedly high operating loss of $300 million on sales of $1.8 billion. But for the financial support of the $30 billion diversified group of which it was a part, the company, a manufacturer of electronics-based industrial products, would have been close to bankruptcy. A detailed group-level investigation revealed the situation to be 'hopeless'. In a scale-intensive global industry, Semco was ranked 10th, and its products were positioned in low growth and highly cost competitive market segments. Furthermore, the business was extremely investment intensive with average industry R&D spending of 15 percent of sales, and capital investment of 130 percent of depreciation. To meet such investment needs, the group report concluded that a company needed at least a 6 percent global market share; Semco's share was less than 1 percent.

Internally, the group-level manager responsible for Semco described the environment as 'catastrophic'. Management conflict was rife: the powerful head of the only profitable business unit strongly and openly disagreed with the chief executive's strategy of investing heavily in a new technology; two of the four business unit managers did not even speak to each other; and relations between the line management and the relatively autonomous R&D group was extremely strained. At the operating level, there was what one manager described as 'complete paralysis' made worse by a very political environment.

In March 1989, in response to the company's deteriorating financial and competitive situation but prior to the sudden downturn, Semco's chief executive had been replaced by the head of one of the company's four business units. Unlike his predecessor who had limited company and industry background, the new chief executive had spent his entire three-decade long career at Semco, rising through its technical and marketing ranks. His agreement with the group management had envisaged nursing the business back to break-even point by 1992, and during his first 15 months he had focused his attention on trimming R&D and controlling expenses.

All this changed in May, 1990, when the financial results of 1989 were announced. Stung by adverse reactions from the financial market to the unexpectedly large losses, the newly appointed chief executive of the group demanded more urgent action. Over the next 3 months, Semco managers prepared a plan to reduce personnel by 20 percent, to cut the R&D budget by more than 50 percent, and to close several facilities eliminating the related products from the line.

Our involvement began in October 1990, 3 months after implementation of the plan had begun, when one of the authors was invited to facilitate a meeting of Semco's 50 seniormost managers. The objective was to review the situation and to develop a detailed plan for implementation of the proposed changes. This 3-day meeting evolved into a system of quarterly meetings and triggered a cascade of activities at lower levels as the senior level participants organized preparatory or follow-up meetings with their own subordinates. Between 1990 and 1992 we participated in several such meetings, at different levels of Semco, interviewing managers and collecting relevant data to help structure the agenda and facilitate the discussion process. We also reviewed the ongoing changes with several key actors individually on a regular basis outside the meetings.

Over these 3 years, a plethora of actions was initiated. Despite the recession-plagued industry situation in which both demand and prices of Semco's products declined, financial performance improved steadily from a loss of about $150 million in 1990, to break-even in 1991, and a profit of $200 million on sales of $1.7 billion in 1992. Industry analysts believed that Semco's 1992 profits were structurally sustainable, at least in the medium term. In the middle of 1993, pro-rata profitability continued on the upward slope.

The task of making sense of the detailed data and rich descriptions gathered over almost 3 years of intensive interaction was made manageable only by a multistaged iterative process of data gathering, verification and analysis. In March 1993, at the invitation of group management who wanted to transfer the lessons of the turnaround to other group companies, we returned to Semco to expand on and verify our data. From knowledge gained in our early involvement, we prepared a detailed summary of the key incidents and actions (Figure 1 provides a highly simplified version). Using this as a point of departure, and with the help of a research associate, we interviewed 26 managers at various levels (including 12 we had never met before); we conducted group meetings with office and factory employees; and we collected additional internal documents, detailing the changes. Our objective was to improve the completeness and accuracy of the descriptions, and also to elicit a wide range of opinion and analysis of the events. The observations and findings from this stage of the research process were summarized in the form of a case study which described not only the internal actions and changes within Semco but also incorporated a fairly detailed analysis of the changes in the company's external environment.

94   S. *Ghoshal and C. A. Bartlett*

The data gathering continued into the next phase when the case study was discussed, on two different occasions, with the 100 senior most managers of different group companies. Because the 10-person top management team of Semco was present on each occasion, the discussions of the company's successes and failures, and management's comments and responses, revealed new information which was incorporated in a revised version of the case. It was this detailed record of the changes that became the base document for the analysis reported in this paper.

During this process, we became increasingly aware that while all our interviewees acknowledged the financial impact of the specific actions we had highlighted in our summary (e.g., the 25% employment reduction, the working capital cuts, etc.), they were much more focused on a deeper change in the internal environment, caused in part by these actions but also in part by numerous others that were nowhere as dramatic or as visible. As described by a junior employee in one of Semco's overseas production plants:

What matters most is that the smell of the place has changed. I now enjoy coming to work. It's not one thing, but overall it's become a very different company.

As we pursued this issue of 'the smell of the place', we obtained many descriptions and illustrations of *what* the 'smell' was and *how* it came about. In our subsequent analysis of the data, some patterns began to emerge. First, in response to the 'what' question, a detailed content analysis of the interview notes led us to categorize the various attributes of the new context along one of four dimensions which we finally labeled as (i) discipline, (ii) stretch, (iii) trust, and (iv) support. Then, to summarize 'how' these dimensions of context came about, we identified and sorted the interviewees' descriptions that linked key events and activities into one or more of the four dimensions of context. Some interviewees identified the same activity (e.g., the benchmarking exercise) as influencing more than one dimension of context (e.g., stretch and discipline). In other instances, while some interviewees identified one particular action (such as the introduction of a new cost accounting system) as contributing to the development of one dimension (e.g., discipline), others described the same action as contributing to another dimension (e.g., trust). Table 1 provides a list of the six key events or actions that were associated by a significant number of interviewees with the four different dimensions of context.

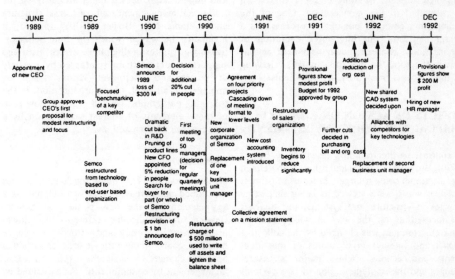

Figure 1.   Key events and actions in the turnaround of Semco: 1989–1992

Table 1.   Effects of actions on dimensions of context: Semco

Key events/actions	No. of interviewees (out of 26) linking the event/action to dimensions of context			
	Discipline	Stretch	Trust	Support
1. Announcement and implementation of drastic cuts, particularly in number of employees	14	3	2	4
2. Focused benchmarking of a key competitor	6	10	4	6
3. Introduction of a new accounting system	11	4	8	5
4. System of quarterly meetings of senior managers	12	9	9	8
5. New formal structure	—	3	4	6
6. Personal style of the CEO	8	6	14	6
Number of employees highlighting the dimension as a key element of the new context of Semco	18	12	16	11

Finally, following Pettigrew's (1992) suggestions, we prepared detailed charts reflecting the sequence of key activities and events, across multiple levels of analysis. The detail and complexity of the data required mapping on multiple charts, each linking a specific set of actions to the different key outcomes. Highly simplified versions of some of these charts will be presented in the next section. One of the findings that emerged out of this process was a clearer sense of the interactive evolution of organizational context and management action. This is the topic we will now pursue, drawing on the concepts framed by the data analysis.

EFFECTS OF ACTION ON CONTEXT: SHAPING THE WORK ENVIRONMENT

In contrast to the founding research by Bower (1970), Burgelman (1983) and others who defined organizational context largely in terms of process variables which were viewed as being shaped by changes in structure and systems, our analysis has focused us on the way in which Semco's work environment was changed by the collective impact and interaction of scores of individual events and actions. While major structural changes and the implementation of new systems were certainly influential, so too were a variety

of much more routine and seemingly minor activities and decisions: the composition of a task force, the handling of a lay off procedure, or the gathering of competitive information, for example.

Our concept of context, therefore, is framed not in familiar process terms such as definition and impetus, nor does it focus primarily on the traditional management tools of formal structure and systems (cf., Bower, 1970). Instead, it highlights the way in which the four behavior-framing attributes of discipline, stretch, trust and support were created and reinforced by a variety of macro and microlevel actions taken by managers at all levels of the organization. In the following paragraphs, we will describe how each of these elements of context was shaped by a convergence of such actions.

Discipline

As shown in Table 1, 18 out of the 26 interviewees mentioned an increased level of discipline as a key element of the new context at Semco. Beyond the predictable reference to timely management reporting and efforts to achieve financial goals, many interviewees described a broader change to what they referred to as 'management by commitments'. As explained by one manager:

96   *S. Ghoshal and C. A. Bartlett*

We now send our samples to customers on time, or at least we try our best. We phone back if we have said we would, and we turn up in meetings on time. If something has been decided in an earlier meeting, we don't reopen the issue. In fact, meeting your commitments has become kind of an ego issue, not just the inventory, cost or revenue targets but, more generally, doing what you promised.

As we put together the interviewees' explanations of why and how discipline became a key element in the context of Semco, it appeared that the actions listed in Table 1, collectively and interactively, led to the development of (i) clear standards and expectations, (ii) a system of open and fast-cycle feedback, and (iii) consistency in the application of sanctions. These three attributes, in turn, contributed to the building of discipline within the company (see Figure 2).

Clear standards

The establishment of clear standards required not only the development of a set of standards but also an acceptance of and commitment to them. While earlier benchmarking exercises, using data provided by external consultants or from public sources, had allowed Semco managers

to develop the first element, it was the quality and detail of the data collected in the 1990 benchmarking (furnished directly by a leading competitor, in the course of an acquisition negotiation) that made it much more credible. The highly disaggregated and fine-grained information prevented debates on authenticity and comparability, while management's realization that the business might be divested led to an emotional commitment to bridging this visible performance gap. The clarity and credibility of this performance gap was further reinforced by the data generated by the new cost accounting system which was fine-grained enough to establish specific responsibilities, expectations and standards at the level of individuals responsible for small, disaggregated units.

This represented a major change in the company's philosophy of accountability. Historically, in Semco, a manager's ability to get activities to be seen as of vital long-term strategic importance was a viable alternative to the unpleasant task of eliminating slack. However, in choosing items for the drastic cuts of 1990, the new CEO had firmly discredited this concept of 'strategic importance' by retrenching activities such as R&D spending that were earlier considered sacrosanct. The fear generated from this

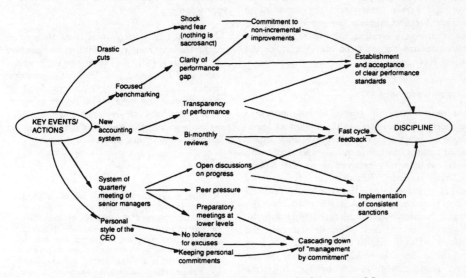

Figure 2.   Emergence of discipline as a key element in the context of Semco

credible threat of retrenchment coupled with the embarrassment caused by unflattering benchmark comparisons played key roles in creating emotional commitment to achieving the new performance standards.

Fast-cycle feedback

Discipline in Semco's management was also developed through activities that increased the frequency and the quality of internal feedback. First, by eliminating certain kinds of information needs, the new accounting system allowed rough weekly figures to be compiled by the following Tuesday, and generated detailed results for any 2-week period within 4 days. The chief executive and the chief financial officer closely monitored these results and personally followed-up on unanticipated outcomes.

While the accounting system improved the frequency of feedback and the demand for explanations, the quarterly management meetings enhanced openness, honesty and candor in the review process. The chief executive's personal style (in his own words, 'calling shit, shit') resulted in these meetings becoming an open review of all aspects of performance. By creating such a process of indirect peer-review, norms were established discrediting overtly political or obfuscating behaviors. By creating similar meetings within their own organizations to prepare for and discuss the outcomes of the senior manager's meeting, most managers helped institutionalize the new norms of candid and honest feedback.

Consistent sanctions

The third commonly perceived contributor to management discipline was the consistent application of sanctions. The chief executive established a norm of dealing quickly and firmly with what was internally referred to as 'satisfactory underperformance'. Replacement of a number of key managers including the chief financial officer and the powerful heads of two of the largest business units built credibility for the slogan of 'no excuses.' This helped ease the difficult decisions that all managers faced as they met the challenge of reducing headcount. At the same time, careful review by the corporate human resource group prevented arbitrariness in

the process, and well publicized reversals of two openly political dismissals helped establish the norm of fairness and consistency.

Past research in the organizational behavior field has identified discipline as an important element of climate (Amsa, 1986). A number of authors have also highlighted the importance of some of the specific mechanisms such as the establishment of standards (Litwin and Stringer, 1968), the holding of regular meetings to provide feedback (Pascale, 1985) and the enforcement of accountability through consistent sanctions (Gordon and DiTomaso, 1992) that helped build discipline as an element of Semco's organizational context. Research in the strategy field, in contrast, has focused on the roles of strategic and operational control as important levers of the corporate influence process (Haspeslagh, 1986; Chakravarthy and Lorange, 1991). But discipline represents the behavioral outcomes, influenced in part by such control mechanisms, rather than the exercise of control, *per se*. Discipline is also reflected in a far broader set of day to day activities than the specific performance outcomes that are the focus of the control processes. It represents a way of life, a norm applicable to all tasks, rather than compliance with a well-defined set of contracts embodied in a company's strategic and operational control tools. To summarize our discussions on discipline in the form of a proposition:

Proposition 1:   Discipline is an attribute of an organization's context that induces its members to voluntarily strive for meeting all expectations generated by their explicit or implicit commitments. Establishment of clear standards of performance and behavior, a system of open, candid and fast-cycle feedback, and consistency in the application of sanctions contribute to the establishment of discipline.

Stretch

Another major change is how we think about targets. In the past, everything was 5 percent. If anyone proposed changes bigger than that, he was immature, he didn't know his business. Now, if you propose a 20 percent cut in inventory, you are a bit embarrassed because someone else is shooting for 25 percent. That too has become a part of life—how far can we go? And that is a fun game!

98   *S. Ghoshal and C. A. Bartlett*

This comment by a Semco factory manager highlights another key change in the company's context. Following Hamel and Prahalad (1993), we call this 'stretch'—an environment in which individuals voluntarily stretch their own standards and expectations. Interviewees saw the 1990 to 1992 actions shaping three attributes that collectively built this environment of stretch: (i) the establishment of shared ambition, (ii) the emergence of a collective identity, and (iii) the development of personal significance in the turnaround task (see Figure 3).

Shared ambition

The same process that led to the establishment of clear standards also helped build a shared ambition among Semco managers. Beyond the emotional commitment to achieving highly stretched goals aimed at bridging the recognized performance gap, by 1992, managers had begun to believe in a future of profitable growth and reputation for excellence in specialized market niches. The visible celebration of some early successes played an important role in converting the desire for survival into a shared ambition for the future.

Another important contributing action was the collective decision in an early quarterly senior managers' meeting to focus the entire organization on four key performance objectives: to reduce the development time for new products (the 'time-to-market' project), to cut the cycle time from order entry to product delivery (the 'make-to-market' project), to shorten customer response time (the 'customer satisfaction' project), and to prune the unwieldy list of 15,000 product offerings (the 'portfolio choice' project). While each of the four broadly constituted project teams established performance standards and monitored improvements, a large number of unit-level teams implemented the specific tasks. By mid 1991, some fairly dramatic performance improvements led to a growing confidence that Semco could match, and in some areas, surpass 'best-in-class' performance levels. By late 1991, transfer of best practices and shared work in the project teams started spreading these successes across the organization, feeding a growing confidence that was validated by improving financial performance, and eventually resulting by late 1992 in a fairly widespread shared ambition for excellence.

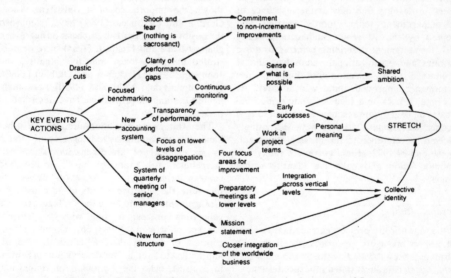

Figure 3.   Emergence of stretch as a key element in the context of Semco

Collective identity

In January 1990, Semco broke away from the holding group's electronics components division, to which it had historically been attached, and became a free standing division by itself. The organizational separation helped Semco's managers develop a greater sense of collective identity. As described by the new chief executive, 'We needed to find our own way to do things together'.

The split from the other businesses also lead to a gradual integration within and across Semco's functional groups. In the past, the sales organizations selling Semco's products in different national markets reported to the overall group country managers and also sold the products of other companies within the old division. After the split, Semco formed its own specialized national sales organizations which were consolidated under a marketing manager in the headquarters of the company. Similar specialization was also achieved in the product development units. Freed from the interdependencies with the other activities, these dedicated units could build stronger links among themselves and the resulting horizontal integration also helped building collective identity.

Finally, although the new chief executive of Semco did not believe in mission statements, he agreed to develop one only at the insistence of his management team. Jointly created and adopted by the 50 senior managers in early 1991, the statement describing Semco's strategic priorities and organizational values had almost no effect in the organization until the company's performance improved about a year later. At that time, it became a focus of some pride, and debates on issues from resource allocation to new product development priority were increasingly resolved by reference to the mission statement. By the end of 1992, it had become a catalyst of common action and collective identity within Semco.

Personal meaning

As the four priority projects cascaded down from the senior managers' quarterly meetings, the broad targets established by the 50 top managers were allocated and translated into specific action. The business unit level meetings broke down the targets for each product group; and the product group level meetings translated them to the level of each factory, development team, and marketing group. As a result, a situation was created in which more and more individuals not only had focused targets but also had a clear picture of how his or her own tasks contributed to the overall performance of the company along one or more of the four priorities. Most of the interviewees believed that this explicit and visible association between ones' own work and the overall priorities of the company created a sense of personal involvement that gave meaning to each individuals' work. This association, in turn, created the motivation for stretch at the individual level.

Evolving from an early emphasis on achievement motivation (Argyris, 1958; McGregor, 1960; Tagiuri and Litwin, 1968), the literature on organizational climate has consistently highlighted the role of stretch, not only as a motivational tool in individual or group-level goal setting tasks (e.g., Latham and Locke, 1979), but also as a broader element of quality in an organization's internal environment that influences the perception of personal impact (Zimmerman and Rappaport, 1988). The three attributes we have identified as contributing to the creation of stretch are consistent with the prior empirical findings in this literature: Denison (1990) has shown the importance of a consistent vision; Gordon and DiTomaso (1992) have established the positive influence of an emphasis on aggressive goals; Allaire and Firsirotu (1984) have demonstrated the need for a collective identity; and Johnston (1976), Hackman and Oldham (1980), and Thomas and Velthouse (1990) have highlighted the impact of what we have described as personal meaning.

The strategy process literature, on the other hand, has underemphasized the role of stretch as an element of an organization's context. Burgelman, for example, has conceptualized context primarily as a selection device 'to fine tune the selective effects of administrative arrangements so as to keep the strategic proposal generating process in line with the current concept of strategy' (1983: 66). Quinn's (1980) concept of logical incrementalism is, indeed, antithetical to stretch. Our observations in Semco, in contrast, echo the arguments of Hamel and Prahalad (1989): while context acts as a selection

100   *S. Ghoshal and C. A. Bartlett*

mechanism, it can also be used to create variation. By developing stretch as a key element of the internal environment, managers can influence the aspiration levels of individuals engaged in all kinds of activities—from ongoing improvement of existing and relatively standardized tasks to the creation of new products and businesses. With stretch, organizational context can be a tool for promoting entrepreneurship, not restraining it. We offer the proposition:

> *Proposition 2: Stretch is an attribute of an organization's context that induces its members to voluntarily strive for more, rather than less, ambitious objectives. Establishment of a shared ambition, the development of a collective identity, and the ability to give personal meaning to the way in which individuals contribute to the overall purpose of the organization contribute to the establishment of stretch.*

Trust

Sixteen of the 26 managers believed that an important change in the environment of Semco was that people had begun to trust one another. This was a sharp departure from the situation in 1989 when managers in one business unit had been discovered advising a customer not to deal with another business unit that was soliciting an order for a very different set of products. In contrast, by 1992, the different business units were collaborating actively—for example, creating a shared CAD/CAM system and jointly developing new products—and growing trust was seen as a key contributor to this spirit of cooperation.

In describing how such trust was developed, the three most important contributing factors identified by the interviewees were: (i) the higher level of perceived fairness and equity in the company's decision processes, (ii) the broader level of involvement in core activities, and (iii) an increase in the overall level of personal competence at all levels of the organization (see Figure 4).

Equity

Interviewees perceived that the first and the most important contributor to the growing sense of fairness in Semco was the process by which the 20 percent reduction of personnel was

implemented. Because of the unprecedented size of the cuts, most expected a politicized decision process based on the political clouts of the unit managers. Instead, decisions were made in collective meetings, based on objective data of benchmarked performance and business priorities, and no changes were made through 'corridor deals'.

The change in the internal structure of Semco also contributed to the development of a sense of fairness. In early 1990, when the new chief executive restructured the business units so they were organized around end user industries rather than around technologies, he increased the level of interdependencies among the units, particularly in the area of technologies and manufacturing. The need for greater coordination led to the creation of new forums which provided a sense of internal equity—both real and perceived—to the dispute resolution process.

Involvement

As described earlier, team work within and across units had increased considerably in Semco. The formation of numerous project-groups between 1990 and 1992 dramatically increased the number of people working on core management issues. Furthermore, the system of cascading quarterly meetings not only served to involve more people in decisions that affected their work, it also broke vertical and horizontal barriers that had previously constrained both participation and information access. For example, regular meetings of the 50 top managers spanned five management grades and all functions and business units—a significant departure from the past practice of specialist meetings involving only those at the same level. Even when decisions ran counter to the interests of individuals, they were exposed to the broader rationale and also had the opportunity of advocating their positions. By enhancing the transparency of outcomes, involvement increased the perception of fairness in the process, thereby improving mutual trust.

Competence

The new chief executive, an engineer and industry expert, believed that a high technology company like Semco had to be managed by specialists, not generalists (like his predecessor). As a result,

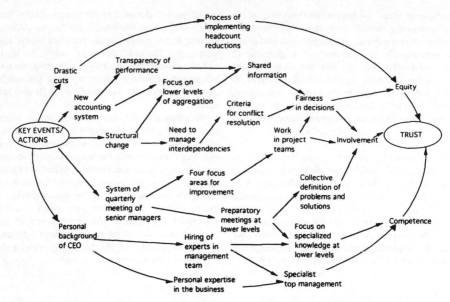

Figure 4.   Emergence of trust as a key element in the context of Semco

the two new business unit managers he appointed had specialized expertise in the industry's technologies and production respectively. In turn, these managers brought in more people with experience in the specialized production process and increased the level of specialization in the company's dedicated sales organization. Overall, by increasing the level of competence, this upgrade in specialist skills also contributed to increasing trust. As described by one manager:

> Trusting someone in the bar is different from trusting someone in the business. Ours is a high-tech outfit. I need someone at the other end who knows what I am talking about. I can spare him a CAD/CAM guy, if he desperately needs one, but I must be sure that he can spare a logistics expert if I need one someday. . . It is easier to build cooperation among people who know the technical aspects of the business.

Given their focus on strategy, structure and systems, neither Bower nor Burgelman explicitly identified trust as a part of an organization's context and implicitly suggested the lack of trust as almost a given in large, complex companies (see, for example, Bower's description of the

highly politicized impetus process). The importance of trust features prominently, however, in the literatures on organizational climate (Campbell, Dunnette, Lawler, and Weick, 1970; Kilmann, 1985) and culture (Deal and Kennedy, 1982; Ouchi, 1981). Existing research has also identified the importance of equity (e.g., Abbey and Dickson, 1983; Alston, 1986; Folger and Konovsky, 1989) and involvement (Johnston, 1976; Denison, 1990; Kim and Mauborgne, 1993) in the building of trust. What we add is the importance of competence as a prerequisite for trust which, though suggested in the early research on climate (McGregor, 1960), has not received adequate attention in more recent work. Instead, following Bandura's (1977) social learning theory, the focus is shifted to the study of competence or, more precisely, self-efficacy as a contributor to the perception of personal empowerment (see Gist and Mitchell, 1992 for a recent review). Particularly for organizations engaged in complex and specialized activities, individual-level competence, we suggest, is almost as important for creating an environment of mutual trust as the process attributes of fairness and participation. Accordingly we propose:

Proposition 3: Trust is an attribute of an organization's context that induces its members to rely on the commitments of each other. Fairness and equity in the organization's decision processes, involvement of individuals in decisions and activities affecting them, and staffing of positions with people who possess and are seen to possess the required capabilities contribute to the establishment of trust.

Support

In identifying support as an element of the context in Semco, the interviewees most often pointed to their increased access to company resources (such as a CAD library) located outside of one's own unit, and the less control-focused and more help-oriented senior management role that was increasing freedom of initiative at lower levels. Collectively, (i) this greater availability of resources together with (ii) increased autonomy and (iii) more help created an environment that supported rather than constrained lower-level initiatives and entrepreneurship (see Figure 5).

Access to resources

Because of conflicts within the top management team and a structure that emphasized the independence of each business unit, cross-unit cooperation had historically been limited in Semco. As a result, for example, each unit had adopted a different IT system, with different CAD/CAM software that prevented access to each others' design libraries.

However, Semco's new market oriented structure required more interdependency, and the changes in personnel increased the number of technically competent individuals with both the interest and the ability to access resources in different parts of the company. A shared CAD system, for example, led to a collective library that all could use. The consolidated sales organization allowed salesmen in one country to use the literature or an order control system developed by another. And the new integrating forums helped a product development team in the U.K. to use the services of an expert in Germany. Such access to resources was seen as a key enabler of decentralized initiative at operational levels.

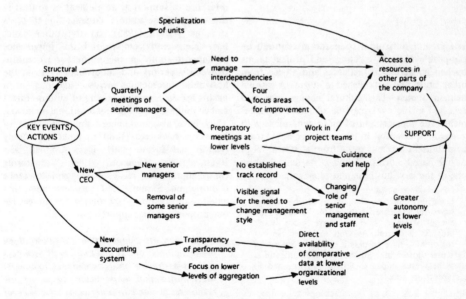

Figure 5.   Emergence of support as a key element in the context of Semco

Autonomy

Most interviewees credited the chief executive's strong commitment to radical decentralization for the growth in front line freedom. Again, key appointments triggered changes throughout the organization. When he found that two of the old-time authoritarian business unit managers were blocking his drive for decentralization, the chief executive replaced them with two technical experts. With limited general management experience, but an inherent preference for decentralization, these two managers played a key role in creating more freedom throughout the units they headed.

The new accounting system also contributed to the decentralization by providing faster, more reliable operating information by product group, in contrast to the earlier system which only provided profitability estimates at the level of the business units. The new system allowed front-line managers to identify problems more quickly, and with a clearer picture of what was going on, senior managers felt less need to interfere with day to day operations. As one manager said, 'The rigor of the new system allowed better control. That, in turn, reduced the need for back seat driving'.

Guidance and help

The greater horizontal cooperation required by the proliferation of meetings and project teams opened up access to resources and advice from other units and established a norm of mutual help in Semco. This cultural change was also reflected in the evolving role of senior management. The replacement of older generalists with younger specialists in the management team contributed to a clear trend from a control focus to one based more on helping. As described by one of the new business unit managers:

I see my role as that of a coach—helper, supporter, teacher. I have to influence the overall strategy, and we have made some progress in specializing units to better use our resources. I have to play a role in coordinating across those units. But beyond that, my job is to help and guide, to provide advice, and to protect my people.

This trend was reinforced by the substantial change in the role of the company's historically powerful central staff groups. With their control over information flows almost destroyed by the large open meeting format, and their power substantially curtailed by budget cuts that shrank their size by over 40 percent, these staff groups could no longer control line managers as they once had. Newly appointed heads of the finance, logistics and human resource functions also brought in a philosophy that the staff must work for the line rather than the other way round. Collectively, these developments led to a new relationship in which the legitimacy and influence of a staff group depended on the extent of support it was recognized as providing to line managers.

Much of the work on organizational context in the strategy field has been carried out in relatively large, divisionalized corporations and from the perspective of the top management. The companies studied by Bower, Burgelman, and Haspeslagh have all represented variations of the fairly hierarchical and bureaucratic M-form structure (Williamson, 1975; Chandler, 1962). In such organizations, at the time these studies were conducted, roles of senior managers tended to focus more on control than on support (Peters, 1992) and, accordingly, there is little reference to support as an element of context in the work of these authors. Organization theorists such as Walton (1985), on the other hand, have consistently emphasized the importance of support—both in the vertical relationships between superiors and subordinates and in the horizontal interactions across functions—as a means for developing a feeling of empowerment and commitment among organizational members. They have also highlighted the importance of access to resources (Kanter, 1988), autonomy (Calori and Sarnin, 1991; Deci, Connell, and Ryan, 1989; Denison, 1990), mentoring (Marcoulides and Heck, 1993) and tolerance (Calori and Sarnin, 1991) as elements that enhance this feature. Accordingly, we summarize our proposition on support:

Proposition 4: Support is an attribute of an organization's context that induces its members to lend assistance and countenance to others. Mechanisms that allow actors to access the resources available to other actors, freedom of initiative at lower levels and personal orientation

104   *S. Ghoshal and C. A. Bartlett*

*of senior functionaries that gives priority to
providing guidance and help over exercising
authority contribute to the establishment of
support.*

EFFECTS OF CONTEXT ON ACTION: INFLUENCING INDIVIDUAL BEHAVIOR

We have argued that management action is
embodied in context, both as its shaper and as
its outcome. In describing the effects of action
on context in the previous section, the careful
charting of observed events and actions and
the detailed content analysis of interviewees'
descriptions provided us with data on which
concepts could be developed. But even in that
analysis we found that such tools could never
provide definitive results or unambiguous
answers.

Yet, as we explored the reciprocal effects of
context on action, the distinction between facts
and interpretation (both the interviewees' and
ours) became even more blurred. For this
analysis, our starting point was the four core
elements of context identified through the pre-

vious process, and our objective was to understand the way in which they interacted as a
gestalt to influence individual behavior. As we
engaged in an intuitive and interpretative process
that led to our conclusions, we found both support
for and some confidence from Weick's (1989)
portrayal of theory building as 'disciplined imagination'. The context model, the charts, and the
interview notes served as sources of both discipline
and imagination, providing the opportunity for
conjecture, while acting collectively as a screening
device against interpretations that did not fit within
a holistic explanation. Through this interaction of
our conceptual model and interpretations, we
identified three behavioral characteristics that
seemed to be central to management activity in
the 'new' Semco that had not been typical of
behavior early in our observations. The three
behavioral elements were distributed and self-
generated initiative, mutual cooperation, and collective learning (see Figure 6).

Distributed initiative

One of the best ways to observe the self-
generated initiative that became a widespread

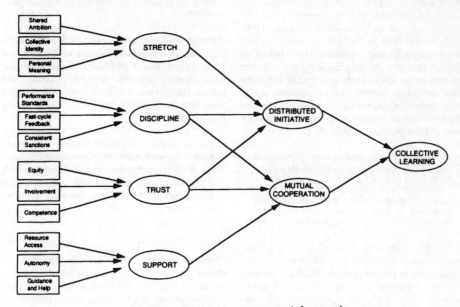

Figure 6. Quality of management: A framework

behavioral norm in Semco by 1992, was to visit the plants that had become a major source of Semco's performance improvement. Beyond implementing the top down initiatives of reductions in headcount and inventory, most of Semco's more than 20 plants had also achieved significant improvements in throughput time, rework, cost, scrap rate and many other operating parameters. Such improvements usually originated from the suggestions and actions of the plants' self-managing production teams. For example, in a small Scottish plant that we studied, throughput time had fallen from 62 days to 24 days through the cumulative effect of worker initiated changes to improve equipment layout, the handling of intermediate products, and the structuring and allocation of tasks. The changes were made despite the fact that many of them led to staffing cuts and over time reduction.

From our own observation and from employee comments, it would appear that such widespread initiative was triggered by the joint effect of stretch, trust and discipline. Initially, the key motivation lay in the desire for survival. The 20 percent headcount reduction had made each employee cognizant of the fact that individual units could be closed and that collectively, the whole business faced potential divestment. The resulting apprehension helped overcome collective indifference and individual shirking. However, as we have described, by early 1992, a desire for achieving excellence had begun to replace the fear of retrenchment as the key motivation for such initiatives. As the following comment of a factory worker indicates, the development of shared ambition was fed by the dissemination of both the competitive benchmark data and the mission statement:

> We see the charts (comparative performance data of key competitors displayed throughout the factory) and we say that's not fair! We can't run behind the Japanese! If we want to get bigger, we must do better than them. We must be the best, as we say (in the mission statement). So, we talk about that in the team, and we try.

A growing level of trust played an equally important role in facilitating such initiatives. The replacement of several poor-performing managers with more capable and experienced individuals restored a feeling of both equity ('managers also lose their jobs') and confidence. Open two-way

information sharing through meetings modeled on General Electric company's 'work-out' process (Tichy and Charan, 1989) strengthened both the reality and the perception of employee involvement. And the replacement of two supervisory layers with a system of self-managed work-teams gave the practical means to exercise their newfound confidence and involvement in work processes.

Finally, discipline was another key requirement in triggering distributed initiative. In particular, continuous measurement and feedback required by the newly adopted total quality process provided the data required by the employees to initiate and maintain such initiatives. As described by the same factory employee we quoted earlier,

> In the past we didn't know how many wafers we put in, how many we got at the end and what time we took. We didn't know how we spent our time. Now we can see, for each team, for each shift—how much we got. That's how we found that we were spending too much time running between the benches. So, instead of one of us looking after two testers, we said let's each look after four and we can have two runners to move the batches. That increased our output 20 percent. We keep making such changes and checking in the charts (showing daily performance data) if things are getting better.

Based on these observations in Semco and on the strength of similar findings in a variety of other organizations (Eisenstadt and Roniger, 1984; Kouzes and Posner, 1987; Bennis and Nanus, 1985; Hamel and Prahalad, 1989; Westley and Mintzberg, 1989), we offer the following proposition:

> *Proposition 5: Organizations that are able to establish stretch, trust and discipline as attributes of their context can motivate and enable distributed and self-generated initiatives that are aligned with the organization's objectives and interests.*

Mutual cooperation

Although conflict and often active opposition to others' initiatives had been widely prevalent in Semco prior to 1989, according to almost everyone we interviewed, the following 3-year period was marked by a highly visible increase in the extent

106   *S. Ghoshal and C. A. Bartlett*

of voluntary cooperation. The collaboration of managers in the German and U.K. units to exploit a new booming market for car phone components is representative of the way in which this cooperative behavior was facilitated by the emerging contextual attributes of trust, discipline and support.

Historically the German unit had focused on producing specialized telephone components, while the U.K. operation had focused on electronic equipment for the automobile industry. As both managers acknowledged, in earlier times both units probably would have mounted parallel and competitive efforts to develop products for a newly emerging market such as car telephone components over which both could claim jurisdiction. As the stiuation developed in 1990–91, however, the two unit managers directly negotiated an agreement whereby the U.K. unit would develop the new product, drawing on its understanding of the automobile market, while the German unit would contribute by allocating two of its engineers with telephone expertise to work full time on the project for 6 months.

According to both unit managers, this cooperative outcome had its roots in the appreciation they had developed for each other's competence in their respective areas, particularly after each had visited the others' plants in the process of working together on a task force. As described by the German manager,

> They had people who knew more about cars than design engineers I know in car companies. While we certainly knew more about telephones, it was obvious that the real trick would like in getting some edge for in-car use, and they were light years ahead of us in being able to do that.

Furthermore, participation in the quarterly meetings had made both managers fully aware of the urgent need for resource conservation. Seeing themselves as among those building the 'new Semco', the cooperative solution was clearly the more consistent with the new rhetoric they had helped fashion. Finally the emerging 'esprit de corps' in Semco convinced the German manager that his contribution would be remembered, reciprocated and rewarded when the opportunity arose.

> Now, there is memory in the system: such actions are openly discussed—so everyone knows. And

> everyone believes it is important to act together; so it is rewarded, at least indirectly. I know John (the U.K. manager) wants to get even, to do something for me in turn, and that's money in the bank.

Together, this mutual recognition of competence, involvement, and sense of equity created a trust that was vital to the cooperation. But trust alone was not enough. One reason most Semco units avoided such cooperative efforts in the past was the time and effort that had to be expended for managing the complex interdependencies joint projects tended to create. With the new norms of discipline, however, the process of developing the new product became considerably more efficient. Clear objectives and schedules were established and conflicts were minimized as units strove to deliver on their commitments. Further, the supportive role of senior managers and the corporate R&D group reduced the time the unit managers had to spend on coordinating the joint efforts.

Cooperation and trust exist in a symbiotic relationship. As we have argued in the preceding section, cooperation produces trust, and as we have illustrated now, trust produces cooperation. This symbiosis is reflected in much of the literature on the causal ordering between these two variables: Dasgupta (1988), Granovetter (1985) and Lewis and Weigert (1985) are among those who have argued for the first relationship, while Boyle and Bonacich (1970) and Williams (1988) have argued for the second. The importance of discipline in building cooperation has been suggested by Zucker (1986) while the need for support has been illustrated by Hargreaves and Dawes (1990). Accordingly, we propose:

Proposition 6: Organizations that are able to establish trust, discipline and support as attributes of their context can motivate and enable voluntary cooperation among actors that are aligned with the organizations' objectives and interests.

Collective learning

> They have broken what used to be considered as an iron-rule: when revenues are below budget, profits must also be below budget. In 1992, because of the recession, their sales were way below plan. But they still made their profit and cash flow numbers.

This comment about Semco's performance by the holding group's CEO emphasized a fundamental change in the company's strategic approach. Historically, management had focused on exploiting economies of scale and accumulating leverageable skills by pursuing high-volume production of standardized products. The pursuit of this strategy based on an industry recipe (Spender, 1989) had led Semco to a high fixed cost infrastructure and, hence, the 'iron rule'. By 1992, however, the company had significantly reduced its break-even point by refocusing on relatively low-volume application-specific products. By converting fixed costs to variable costs, it increased its ability to maintain profits during industry downturns.

Although this change is a good example of double-loop learning (Argyris and Schon, 1978), it emerged not from a formal strategic analysis but as the cumulative effect from a diverse set of actions in different parts of the organization, much in the way described by Mintzberg and McHugh (1985). For example, in spite of strong contrary advice, one particular business unit eliminated a high volume but loss-making activity from its portfolio, then increased profits by reducing its costs to more than offset the loss of revenues. Under pressure for profits, other units began to imitate the same logic. Quite independently, another unit 'sold' its software group to a consulting company to whom they then subcontracted their software development tasks. As the advantages of reduced breakeven levels and improved productivity became clear, others initiated similar actions. Over a 2-year period, the initiation and diffusion of several similar practices cumulated into a new operating logic that gradually gained recognition as 'management by anticipation'. The approach of anticipating contingencies by taking proactive measures to achieve budgeted profits was finally formalized in a revised strategy statement and a new business model.

The process was far from one of random variation, however. Each of the dispersed initiatives was influenced by the same influences of stretch, trust and discipline that triggered the initiatives in the Scottish plant and elsewhere. And the successful diffusion of learning across the units required the same degree of trust, discipline and support we observed in the car phone collaboration. In other words, collective

learning emerged from distributed initiative and mutual cooperation which, in turn, were the products of the four elements of context we have described.

In a recent review of the burgeoning literature on organizational learning, Huber (1991: 92) has lamented that 'in spite of the importance of organizational experiments as learning mechanisms, the literature contains very few studies of experimentation by organizations'. However, his speculations about the antecedent conditions that lead to organizational experiments focus on the attributes of trust, high needs of performance (stretch, in our words) and tolerance for mistakes (which, we believe, requires a combination of trust, discipline and support). Similarly, Duncan and Weiss (1979) have identified the recognition of a performance gap (a source of stretch), trust, and information about the outcomes of actions (fast-cycle feedback) as the key requirements for learning. Accordingly, we offer the proposition:

Proposition 7:   Organizational learning results from a combination of distributed initiative and mutual cooperation which, in turn, require stretch, trust, discipline and support as the antecedent conditions of organizational context.

SUMMARY AND IMPLICATIONS: THE DIMENSIONS OF QUALITY OF MANAGEMENT

How can the management of a company be assessed? For students of management, this is a fundamental question. As described by Lawler (1992), such assessment is routine in practice: stock market evaluations of companies change with the arrival and departure of key executives. Popular magazines rate companies on how well they are managed. Implicit in such evaluation is the assumption that performance is the ultimate management responsibility. Yet, performance is a noisy measure, both unstable and confused for most causal analysis. Any other more direct measure would require a theory of management, for which there is no consensus.

At one end among the contending theories lies what Burgelman (1983) has described as 'the heroic view of top management' and Mintzberg (1990) has caricatured as 'the design school'. Academic scholars have largely rejected this fairly extreme vision of the rational strategy model that implicitly assigned to top management the superhuman role of being the designers of strategy, the architects of structure and the builders of systems. As observed by Eisenhardt and Zbaracki (1992), this model is no longer interesting to strategy researchers even as the 'straw man.' Yet, in the popular press and in the world of practitioners, the model thrives, reinforced by popular autobiographies of charismatic chief executives like Chrysler's Lee Iacocca, ICI's Sir John Harvey Jones and Sony's Akio Morita, and by the larger-than-life portrayal of top management in academic analysis of visibly successful companies like General Electric (Tichy and Sherman, 1993).

At the other extreme lies an equally heroic celebration of the lack of management. Guided by observations of a few cases of poorly managed organizations, organization and management theorists have created, over the last two decades, a growing body of literature that views choices and actions in organizations as severely constrained by ambiguity and uncertainty, on the one hand, and by the opportunism, cognitive limits and political agenda of their members, on the other hand. Given these constraints, decisions emerge either from a process of complex internal bargaining and coalition building (Pettigrew, 1973; Pfeffer, 1992) or pure chance (Cohen, March, and Olsen, 1972) and purposive managerial action, if any, must be hidden behind incremental maneuvering along corridors of indifference in organizational politics (Quinn, 1980). Even after proposing such a 'grass roots model' (Mintzberg and McHugh, 1985), Mintzberg has acknowledged that it 'makes no more sense, since it overstates equally' (1990: 190).

The framework we have put forward in this article is influenced by and expands on the argument that the main influence of general managers lies in their role as shapers of an organization's context. We have suggested that it is the interactions between action and context that lie at the core of a company's management process, and have described the way in which context can be created and renewed by a variety of management actions that develop the characteristics of stretch, trust, discipline and support in the organization's embedded work ethic. We have also shown how these elements of context influence initiative, cooperation and

learning in the day to day behaviors of all those within the organization. While avoiding the false and sterile debate between the advocates of unimpeded voluntarism and unsurmountable determinism, our views reflect what Hamel and Prahalad (1993: 84) have described as an essential paradox of business performance: that 'leadership cannot be planned for, but neither can it happen without a grand and well-considered aspiration.'

As we have shown in this article, we share this middle ground with a number of other authors who have worked on the issues of organizational context, climate and culture. In terms of the specific content of the model, however, we find the most resonance with Barnard's views who had not only emphasized the role of general managers as the builders of organizational context but had also highlighted the importance of stretch and trust—the ingredients for creating a shared purpose in his scheme— as key elements of the work ethic that needs to be embedded in the context for promoting initiative and cooperation. And while he did not explicitly refer to the attributes of discipline and support, the implications of what he called the 'moral factor' are not very different from what the Semco manager described as 'management by commitment.'

Our analysis of the role of general managers can also be related to the increasingly influential resource-based view of strategy. The essential theoretical concept for explaining sustainability of rents in the resource-based view is 'isolating mechanisms' (Rumelt, 1984). As suggested by Barney (1986), Camerer and Vepsalainen (1988), Fiol (1991) and others (see Mahoney and Pandian, 1992 for a detailed review), corporate culture or climate can be perhaps the most inimitable resource and, therefore, the most effective isolating mechanism. Some direct evidence of this hypothesis is provided by Hansen and Wernerfelt (1989) who showed that the attributes of organizational climate explained about twice as much variance in profit rates of firms compared to the combined effect of all the economic factors they considered. Put another way, from the resource-based perspective, shaping the organizational context has a direct and important implication on firm performance and is, therefore, a key task of management.

As we suggested in the introductory section, we believe that the model we have presented provides a starting point for assessing an organization's quality of management. A number of limitations in our research require us to qualify this assertion. Despite excellent precedence (from Barnard to Bower to Burgelman) and well-argued justification (for example, from Mintzberg, 1979), theorizing from a single and, by definition, unique case is inevitably suspect. Our interpretative methodology enhances this suspicion. Yet, the model we have presented is both detailed and testable. Reliable instruments are available for operationalizing most of the variables we have suggested (see, in particular, the work of Denison and Gordon we have referred to). In fact, in his comments on this paper at a Strategic Management Society conference in Michigan, Professor Robert E. Quinn had brought to our attention the recently completed dissertation of Spreitzer (1992) that has operationalized and measured most of the variables in our model. Spreitzer's findings, based on rigorous empirical analysis of large sample data, are also remarkably consistent with our inferences from contextual observations in a single company. Further refinement, modification and elaboration of this model through both conceptual and empirical work, we believe, provides a promising avenue for ultimately developing both a theory and some measures of a firm's quality of management.

At stake in such extension and possible validation of the model is not just the possibility of developing richer normative proposals on how general managers can influence the performance of their companies but also broader issues that are more fundamental to organization theory. Almost since the beginning of formal research on organizations, it has been recognized that the organizing task involves a balancing of two somewhat contradictory objectives (see Reed, 1985). On the one hand, organizational effectiveness depends on the willingness and ability of individuals to take personal initiatives, and on the structure, processes and norms organizations need to facilitate such initiatives. On the other hand, individuals are also subject to certain failures and limitations, so the same structure, processes and norms must also protect the organization from those pathologies of individual behaviors and actions.

Much of the earlier work on organizational theory focused on the first objective, often at the cost of underemphasizing the second. Over the last three decades, however, a set of economic and behavioral theories have come to the fore which focus almost exclusively on the second objective. These theories tend to deny the existence of shared purpose or collective ambition: as stated by Cyert and March, for example, 'individuals have goals, collectivities of people do not' (1963: 26). In this view, goals are presumed to be evoked by problems and by experiences of the past rather than by ambition or from aspirations for the future. Similarly, opportunism rather than trust or self-discipline has become the preferred behavioral assumption (Williamson, 1975). As a result, conflict among disparate subunit goals is seen as pervasive, and incentives and fiat are viewed as the key mechanisms for achieving cooperation. And, while the new analysis has consistently claimed to be inspired by the old (see, for example, Williamson's (1975, 1990) references to Barnard), in reality, the differences in the assumptions about human behavior have led to fundamentally different analyses and conclusions. Although such differences are numerous, nowhere are they more clearly drawn than in the role accorded to incentives in agency theory, transaction cost economics and even in the recent elaboration of the behavioral theory of the firm. These views stand in sharp contrast to those of Barnard who believed that 'it is utterly contrary to the nature of men to be sufficiently induced by material or monetary considerations to contribute enough effort to a cooperative system to enable it to be productively efficient to the degree necessary for persistence over an extended period' (1938: 93).

The underlying assumptions of these dominant theories are just that—assumptions that are either untested or tested only very indirectly. Actual contextual observations within large firms often contradict these assumptions (e.g., Bennis and Nanus, 1985; Ulrich and Wiersema, 1989; Hamel and Prahalad, 1993) but typically these studies are seen as 'practitioner-oriented' and have little impact on the mainstream of theory, much of which was developed in the 1960s and 1970s. As has been widely documented, for most large companies, the environments have changed significantly over the last two decades because of the emergence and strengthening of a set of external forces such as global competition, technological convergence, changing stakeholder demands and shorter product life cycles, and

110   S. Ghoshal and C. A. Bartlett

also because of the availability of a set of more sophisticated management tools and concepts in the form of information systems, quality deployment processes, team organizations and multi-skilled work forces. Collectively, these changes have had some profound impact on the organizational structures and processes of companies and, more specifically, on the roles of individuals and in their relationships with their organizations. As we have shown in an earlier article (Bartlett and Ghoshal, 1993), existing theory is stretched too thin in accommodating these emerging changes not just in organizational forms but in the fundamental assumptions about structure, processes and people that underlie how managers think about the task of organizing. This, we believe, is the principal cause for the widening gap between positive and normative analysis in the fields of strategic management and organizational behavior. Concepts like stretch, trust, discipline or support have little relevance in existing theory. Yet, we believe they are of central importance for the analysis of organizational effectiveness. More and better research to develop a theory of quality of management can perhaps help resolve this contradiction. Our effort here, constrained as it is by limitations of knowledge, skills and data, is a small step in that direction.

ACKNOWLEDGEMENTS

This paper benefitted considerably from ongoing discussions with Heinz Thanheiser who contributed some of the key ideas. Bala Chakravarthy, Mike Brimm, Peter Moran, Robert Quinn, Dan Denison and Yves Doz provided helpful comments. Thanks are also due to Mary Ackenhusen for her help in writing the case on Semco.

REFERENCES

Abbey, A. and J. W. Dickson (1983). 'R&D work climate and innovation in semiconductors', *Academy of Management Journal*, **26**, pp. 362–368.

Allaire, Y. and M. E. Firsirotu (1984). 'Theories of organizational culture, *Organization Studies*, **5**(3), pp. 193–226.

Alston, J. P. (1986). *The American Samurai: Blending American and Japanese Managerial Practices*. de Gruyter, New York.

Amsa, P. (1986). 'Organizational culture and work group behavior: An empirical study', *Journal of Management Studies*, **23**, pp. 347–362.

Ansoff, H. I. (1965). *Corporate Strategy*. McGraw-Hill, New York.

Andrews, K. (1971). *The Concept of Corporate Strategy*. Dow Jones–Irwin, Homewood, IL.

Argyris, C. (1958). 'Some problems in conceptualizing organizational climate: A case study of a bank', *Administrative Science Quarterly*, pp. 501–520.

Argyris, C. and D. Schön (1978). *Organizational Learning*. Addison–Wesley, Reading, MA.

Bandura, A. (1977). 'Self-efficacy: Toward a unifying theory of behavioral change', *Psychological Review*, **84**(2), pp. 191–215.

Barnard, C. I. (1938). *The Functions of the Executive*. Harvard University Press, Cambridge, MA.

Barney, J. B. (1986). 'Organization culture: Can it be a source of sustained competitive advantage?', *Academy of Management Review*, **11**(3), pp. 656–665.

Bartlett, C. A. and S. Ghoshal (1993). 'Beyond the M-form: Toward a managerial theory of the firm', *Strategic Management Journal*, Winter Special Issue, **14**, pp. 23–46.

Bennis, W. and B. Nanus (1985). *The Strategies for Taking Charge*. Harper and Row, New York.

Bower, J. L. (1970). *Managing the Resource Allocation Process*. Harvard University Press, Cambridge, MA.

Boyle, R. and P. Bonacich (1970). 'The development of trust and mistrust in mixed-motive games', *Sociometry*, **23**, pp. 123–139.

Burgelman, R. A. (1983). 'A model of the interaction of strategic behavior, corporate context and the concept of strategy', *Academy of Management Review*, **8**(1), pp. 61–70.

Calori, R. and P. Sarnin (1991). 'Corporate culture and economic performance: A French study', *Organization Studies*, **12**(1), pp. 49–74.

Camerer, C. and A. Vepsalainen (1988). 'The economic efficiency of corporate culture', *Strategic Management Journal*, Summer Special Issue, **9**, pp. 115–126.

Campbell, J. P., M. D. Dunnette, E. E. Lawler and K. E. Weick (1970). *Managerial Behavior, Performance and Effectiveness*. McGraw-Hill, New York.

Chakravarthy, B. S. and P. Lorange (1991). *Managing the Strategy Process*. Prentice-Hall, Englewood Cliffs, NJ.

Chandler, A. D. Jr. (1962). *Strategy and Structure*. MIT Press, Cambridge, MA.

Cohen, M. D., J. G. March and J. P. Olsen (1972). 'A garbage can model of organizational choice', *Administrative Science Quarterly*, **17**, pp. 1–25.

Cyert, R. M. and J. G. March (1963). *A Behavioral Theory of the Firm*. Prentice-Hall, Englewood Cliffs, NJ.

Dasgupta, P. (1988). 'Trust as a commodity'. In D. Gambetta (ed.), *Trust: Making and Breaking Cooperative Relations*. Basil Blackwell, New York, pp. 49–72.

Deal, T. E. and A. A. Kennedy (1982). *Corporate Cultures: The Rites and Rituals of Organizational Life*. Addison–Wesley, Reading, MA.

Deci, E. L., J. P. Connell and R. M. Ryan (1989). 'Self-determination in a work organization', *Journal of Applied Psychology*, **74**, pp. 580–590.

Denison, R. D. (1990). *Corporate Culture and Organizational Effectiveness*. John Wiley, New York.

Doz, Y. and C. K. Prahalad (1988). 'Quality of management: An emerging source of global competitive advantage?'. In N. Hood and J. E. Vahlne (eds.), *Strategies in Global Competition*. Croom Helm, London, pp. 345–369.

Duncan, R. B. and A. Weiss (1979). 'Organizational learning: Implications for organizational design'. In B. Staw (ed.), *Research in Organizational Behavior*. JAI Press, Greenwich, CT, pp. 75–123.

Eisenhardt, K. M. and M. J. Zbaracki (1992). 'Strategic decision making', *Strategic Management Journal*, **13**, pp. 17–37.

Eisenstadt, S. N. and L. Roniger (1984). *Patrons, Clients and Friends: Interpersonal Relations and Structure of Trust in Society*. Cambridge University Press, Cambridge.

Fiol, C. M. (1991). 'Management culture as a competitive resource: An identity-based view of sustainable competitive advantage', *Journal of Management*, **17**, pp. 191–211.

Folger, R. and M. Konovsky (1989). 'Effects of procedural and distributive justice on reactions to pay raise decisions', *Academy of Management Journal*, **32**(1), pp. 115–130.

Furnham, A. (1990). *The Protestant Work Ethic: The Psychology of Work-Related Beliefs and Behaviors*. Routledge, London.

Galunic, D. C. and K. M. Eisenhardt (1993). 'Renewing the strategy–structure–performance paradigm', Department of Industrial Engineering and Engineering Management, Stanford University, Stanford, CA.

Gist, M. and T. N. Mitchell (1992). 'Self-efficacy: A theoretical analysis of its determinants and malleability', *Academy of Management Review*, **17**, pp. 183–211.

Gordon, G. G. (1985). 'The relationship of corporate culture to industry sector and corporate performance'. In R. H. Kilmann, M. J. Saxton, R. Serpa and Associates (eds.), *Gaining Control of the Corporate Culture*. Jossey–Bass, San Francisco, CA, pp. 103–123.

Gordon, G. G. and N. DiTomaso (1992). 'Predicting corporate performance from organizational culture', *Journal of Management Studies*, **29**(6), pp. 783–798.

Granovetter, M. (1985). 'Economic action and social structure: The problem of embeddedness', *American Journal of Sociology*, **91**, pp. 481–510.

Hackman, J. R. and G. R. Oldham (1980). *Work Redesign*. Addison–Wesley, Reading, MA.

Hamel, G. and C. K. Prahalad (1989). 'Strategic intent', *Harvard Business Review*, **67**, pp. 63–76.

Hamel, G. and C. K. Prahalad (1993). 'Strategy as stretch and leverage', *Harvard Business Review*, **71**(2), pp. 75–84.

Hansen, G. S. and B. Wernerfelt (1989). 'Determinants of firm performance: The relative importance of economic and organizational factors', *Strategic Management Journal*, **10**(5), pp. 399–411.

Hargreaves, A. and R. Dawes (1990). 'Paths of professional development: Contrived collegiality, collaborative culture, and the case of peer coaching', *Teaching and Teacher Education*, **6**, pp. 227–241.

Haspeslagh, P. (1986). 'Conceptualising the strategic process in diversified firms: The role and nature of the corporate influence process', INSEAD working paper 86/09.

Huber, G. P. (1991). 'Organizational learning: The contributing processes and literatures', *Organization Science*, **2**(1), pp. 88–115.

Johnston, H. R. (1976). 'A new conceptualization of source of organizational climate', *Administrative Science Quarterly*, **21**, pp. 95–103.

Kanter, R. M. (1988). 'When a thousand flowers bloom: Structural, collective, and social conditions for innovation in organization', *Research in Organizational Behavior*, **10**, pp. 169–211.

Kilmann, R. H. (1985). 'Five steps for closing culture gaps'. In R. H. Kilmann, M. J. Saxton, R. Serpa and Associates (eds.), *Gaining Control of the Corporate Culture*. Jossey–Bass, San Francisco, CA, pp. 351–369.

Kim, W. C. and R. Mauborgne (1993). 'Procedural justice theory and the multinational corporation'. In S. Ghoshal and D. E. Westney (eds.), *Organization Theory and the Multinational Corporation*. St Martin's Press, New York, pp. 237–255.

Kouzes, J. M. and B. Z. Posner (1987). *The Leadership Challenge: How to Get Extraordinary Things Done in Organizations*. Jossey–Bass, San Francisco, CA.

Latham, G. P. and E. A. Locke (1979). 'Goal setting—A motivational technique that works', *Organizational Dynamics*, **8**(2), pp. 68–80.

Lawler, E. E. (1992). *The Ultimate Advantage*. Jossey–Bass, San Francisco, CA.

Lewis, J. D. and A. J. Weigert (1985). 'Social atomism, holism and trust', *The Sociological Quarterly*, **26**, pp. 455–471.

Litwin, G. H. and R. A. Stringer (1968). *Motivation and Organizational Climate*. Harvard Business School: Division of Research, Cambridge, MA.

Mahoney, J. T. and J. R. Pandian (1992). 'The resource-based view within the conversation of strategic management', *Strategic Management Journal*, **3**(5) pp363–392.

Marcoulides, G.A. and R.H. Heck (1993). 'Organizational culture and performance: Proposing and testing a model', *Organization Science*, **4**(2), pp. 209–225.

McGregor, D. M. (1960). *The Human Side of Enterprise*. McGraw–Hill, New York.

Mintzberg, H. (1979). 'An emerging strategy of "direct" research', *Administrative Science Quarterly*, **24**, pp. 582–589.

Mintzberg, H. (1990). 'The Design School: Reconsidering the basic premises of strategic management', *Strategic Management Journal*, **11**(3), pp. 171–195.

112   *S. Ghoshal and C. A. Bartlett*

Mintzberg H. and A. McHugh (1985). 'Strategy formation in an adhocracy', *Administrative Science Quarterly*, **30**, pp. 160–197.

Ouchi, W. G. (1981). *Theory Z*. Addison–Wesley, Reading, MA.

Pascale, R. T. (1985). 'The paradox of "Corporate Culture": Reconciling ourselves to socialization', *California Management Review*, **13**(4), pp. 546–558.

Peters, T. (1992). *Liberation Management*. Alfred A. Knopf, New York.

Pettigrew, A. M. (1973). *Politics of Organisational Decision-Making*. Tavistock, London.

Pettigrew, A. M. (1979). 'On studying organizational cultures', *Administrative Science Quarterly*, **24**, pp. 570–581.

Pettigrew, A. M. (1992). 'The character and significance of strategy research process', *Strategic Management Journal*. Winter Special Issue, **13**, pp. 5–16.

Pfeffer, J. (1992). *Managing With Power: Politics and Influence in Organizations*. Harvard Business School Press, Boston, MA.

Porter M. E. (1991). 'Towards a dynamic theory of strategy', *Strategic Management Journal*, Winter Special Issue, **12**, pp. 95–117.

Quinn, J. B. (1980). *Strategies for Change: Logical Incrementalism*. Richard D. Irwin, Homewood, IL.

Reed, M. (1985). *Redirections in Organizational Analysis*. Tavistock, London.

Rumelt, R. P. (1984). 'Toward a strategic theory of the firm'. In R.Lamb (ed.), *Competitive Strategic Management*, Prentice–Hall, Englewood Cliffs, NJ, pp. 556–570.

Rumelt, R. P., D. Schendel and D. J. Teece (1991). 'Strategic management and economics', *Strategic Management Journal*, Winter Special Issue, **12**, pp. 5–29.

Schein, E. H. (1985). *Organizational Culture and Leadership*. Jossey–Bass, San Francisco, CA.

Schneider, B. (1985). 'Organizational behavior', *Annual Review of Psychology*, **36**, pp. 573–611.

Selznick, P. (1957). *Leadership in Administration*. Harper and Row, New York.

Spender, J. C. (1989). *Industry Recipes: An Enquiry into the Nature and Sources of Managerial Judgement*. Blackwell, Oxford.

Spreitzer, G. M. (1992). 'When organizations dare: The dynamics of individual empowerment in the workplace', unpublished doctoral dissertation, University of Michigan.

Tagiuri, R. and G. H. Litwin (eds.) (1968). *Organizational Climate: Explorations of a Concept*. Harvard Business School: Division of Research, Cambridge, MA.

Thomas, K. W. and B. A. Velthouse (1990). 'Cognitive elements of empowerment: An "Interpretative" model of intrinsic task motivation', *Academy of Management Review*, **15**, pp. 666–681.

Tichy, N. and R. Charan (1989). 'Speed, simplicity, self-confidence: An interview with Jack Welch', *Harvard Business Review*, **67**(5), pp. 112–120.

Tichy, N. M. and S. Sherman (1993). *Control Your Destiny or Someone Else Will*. Doubleday, New York.

Ulrich, D. and M. F. Wiersema (1989). 'Gaining strategic and organizational capability in a turbulent business environment', *Academy of Management Executive*, **3**, pp. 115–122.

Walton, R. (1985). 'From control to commitment in the workplace', *Harvard Business Review*, **63**(2), pp. 77–84.

Weick, K. E. (1989). 'Theory construction as disciplined imagination', *Academy of Management Review*, **14**, pp. 516–531.

Westley, F. and H. Mintzberg (1988). 'Profiles in strategic visions: Leveque and Iacocca'. In J. A. Conger and R. N. Kanungo (eds.), *Charismatic Leadership*. Jossey–Bass, San Francisco, CA, pp. 161–212.

Williams, B. (1988). 'Formal structure and social reality'. In D. Gambetta (ed.), *Trust: Making and Breaking Cooperative Relations*. Basil Blackwell, New York, pp. 3–13.

Williamson, O. E. (1975). *Markets and Hierarchies: Analysis and Antitrust Implications*. Free Press, New York.

Williamson, O. E. (1990). 'Chester Barnard and the incipient science of organization'. In O. E. Williamson (ed.), *Organization Theory from Chester Barnard to the Present and Beyond*. Oxford University Press, New York, pp. 172–206.

Zimmerman, M. A. and J. Rappaport (1988). 'Citizen participation, perceived control, and psychological empowerment', *American Journal of Community Psychology*, **16**, pp. 725–750.

Zucker, L. G. (1986). 'Production of trust: Institutional sources of economic structure, 1840–1920'. In B. M. Staw and L. L. Cummings (eds.), *Research in Organizational Behavior*. JAI Press, Greenwich, CT, pp. 53–111.

Strategic Management Journal, Vol. 18 (Summer Special Issue), 187–206 (1997)

TOWARDS AN ATTENTION-BASED VIEW OF THE FIRM

WILLIAM OCASIO*
J. L. Kellogg Graduate School of Management, Northwestern University, Evanston, Illinois, U.S.A.

The central argument is that firm behavior is the result of how firms channel and distribute the attention of their decision-makers. What decision-makers do depends on what issues and answers they focus their attention on. What issues and answers they focus on depends on the specific situation and on how the firm's rules, resources, and relationships distribute various issues, answers, and decision-makers into specific communications and procedures. The paper develops these theoretical principles into a model of firm behavior and presents its implications for explaining firm behavior and adaptation. © 1997 by John Wiley & Sons, Ltd.

Everyone knows what attention is. It is the taking possession by the mind, in clear and vivid form, of one out of what seem several simultaneously possible objects or trains of thought. Focalization, concentration of consciousness are of its essence. It implies withdrawal from some things in order to deal effectively with others . . .
William James (1890), *The Principles of Psychology*, I: 403–404

Organizations and institutions provide the general stimuli and attention-directors that channelize the behaviors of the members of the group, and that provide the members with the intermediate objectives that stimulate action.
Herbert Simon (1947), *Administrative Behavior*, pp. 100–101

INTRODUCTION

How do firms behave? How do firms determine when, why, and how to respond to or anticipate changes in their environment or internal processes? Why do firms undertake some decisions and moves but not others? Explaining how firms behave is one of the fundamental issues or questions that define the field of strategy, its priorities and concerns, and the contribution it makes to the theory and practice of management (Rumelt, Schendel, and Teece, 1994). In particular, explaining how firms behave allows us to comprehend whether and when firms are able to adapt to changing environments, whether they successfully change their strategies and capabilities, or whether they fail to respond adequately to competition.

Half a century ago, Herbert Simon (1947) introduced a then new perspective on firm behavior, which boldly departed from economists' theories of rational choice and highlighted the limits of human rationality in explaining how firms make decisions. The limited attentional capability of humans—to the range of consequences of their actions, how these consequences would be valued, and the scope of available alternatives—results in their bounded capacity to be rational. For Simon, organizations influence individual decision processes by allocating and distributing the stimuli that channel the attention of administrators in terms of what selected aspects of the situation are to be attended, and what aspects are to be ignored. Firm behavior, for Simon, is both a cognitive and a structural proc-

Key words: attention, cognition, social structure, theory of the firm
* Correspondence to: William Ocasio, Kellogg Graduate School of Management, Northwestern University, Leverone Hall, 2001 Sheridan Road, Evanston, IL 60208, U.S.A.

188   *W. Ocasio*

ess, as decision-making in organizations is the result of both the limited attentional capacity of humans and the structural influences of organizations on an individual's attention.

Fifty years after its initial publication, this paper aims to rediscover the central importance of the structuring of attention in Simon's (1947) early work on administrative behavior, and update it to incorporate our current understanding of social structures, environmental influences, and individual and social cognition. While the concept of attention has a long history and tradition in organization theory, it has not thus far developed into a unified perspective on firm behavior. Different authors have stressed different aspects of attention allocation and structuring, but ignored others. In particular, theories of attention have moved away from Simon's (1947) dual emphasis on structure and cognition to emphasize either how attention is shaped by routines and bounded rationality (March and Simon, 1958; Cyert and March, 1963), or alternatively, how attention is loosely coupled through enactment processes (Weick, 1979) and organized anarchy (Cohen, March, and Olsen, 1972). In the process the effects of the social structure on the channeling and distribution of decision-makers' attention have been greatly deemphasized if not entirely lost.[1] I propose to bring them back in.

The objective of this paper is thus to explicitly link structure and cognition into an attention-based view of the firm. It explicitly links individual information processing and behavior to the organizational structure through the concepts of procedural and communication channels and attention structures. It differs from and extends Simon's (1947) original formulation by providing an explicit treatment of attentional processing as a multilevel process shaped by individuals, organizations, and the environment. While linking

multiple levels, this paper focuses on *organizational attention*, the socially structured pattern of attention by decision-makers within an organization (Ocasio, 1995). The central argument of this open systems perspective (Scott, 1992) is that to explain firm behavior is to explain how firms distribute and regulate the attention of their decision-makers. This idea is based on three interrelated premises:

1. What decision-makers do depends on what issues and answers they focus their attention on (Focus of Attention).
2. What issues and answers decision-makers focus on, and what they do, depends on the particular context or situation they find themselves in (Situated Attention).
3. What particular context or situation decision-makers find themselves in, and how they attend to it, depends on how the firm's rules, resources, and social relationships regulate and control the distribution and allocation of issues, answers, and decision-makers into specific activities, communications, and procedures (Structural Distribution of Attention).

This view provides an alternative explanation for firm behavior both to theories of rational choice, such as game theory and agency theory, and theories that emphasize environmental determinism, such as population ecology. Furthermore, this paper argues that a focus on the structuring of organizational attention to explain firm behavior is of special interest and importance for our understanding of strategic choice (Child, 1972). Corporate strategy, defined by Andrews as the *pattern* of decisions in a company that *determines and reveals* its objectives, purposes, or goals, produces the principal policies and plans for achieving those goals (1971: 13), is understood here as a *pattern of organizational attention*, the distinct focus of time and effort by the firm on a particular set of issues, problems, opportunities, and threats, and on a particular set of skills, routines, programs, projects, and procedures. An attention-based view both shares a strong commonality with and has been influenced by process-based views of strategy formulation and firm behavior (Allison, 1971; Bower, 1970; Burgelman, 1983, 1994), while adding to these an explicit focus on attentional processing.

The next section presents the main outline of

---

[1] In their book-length exposition of the garbage can model of decision-making, March and Olsen (1976) utilize the concept of attention structures as a set of rules that constrain how problems, solutions, and participants get linked in the garbage can. This generalization of the model of organized anarchy provides an independent role for organizational structure in the allocation of attention, and has served as a guide in the preparation of this paper. Their more general model, however, unlike the simple model of organized anarchy, has had limited impact on the organizational or strategic management literature. Furthermore, unlike the arguments found in Simon (1947), or the theory presented here, individual-level attention and information processing are absent from March and Olsen's (1976) formulation.

an attention-based perspective and develops three metatheoretical principles underlying this view of organizations as systems of distributed attention. These principles are put to use in the subsequent section to develop a general process model of how firms behave. While a full theoretical development of the implications of an attention-based view is beyond the scope of this paper, the objective here is to provide a process-based model of how firms behave that integrates our understanding of cognition, organizational structure, and strategy formulation. I draw upon the model to provide a set of implications on how attentional processing helps explain when, why, and how organizations adapt to changes in their environment (Astley and Van de Ven, 1983; Barnett and Carroll, 1995). The last section presents conclusions and reviews the contributions of this paper.

ORGANIZATIONS AS SYSTEMS OF DISTRIBUTED ATTENTION

An attention-based theory views firms as systems of structurally distributed attention in which the cognition and action of individuals are not predictable from the knowledge of individual characteristics but are derived from the specific organizational context and situations that individual decision-makers find themselves in. *Attention* is here defined to encompass the noticing, encoding, interpreting, and focusing of time and effort by organizational decision-makers on both (a) *issues*; the available repertoire of categories for making sense of the environment: problems, opportunities, and threats; and (b) *answers*: the available repertoire of action alternatives: proposals, routines, projects, programs, and procedures.[2] An

important characteristic of this view of the firm as a system of distributed attention is the relationship between individual and organizational-level information processing (Corner, Kinicki, and Keats, 1994). While other perspectives on organizational cognition emphasize either the shared cognitions of organizational members (Schein, 1985; Daft and Weick, 1984), or those of its top management team (Hambrick and Mason, 1984; Eisenhardt, 1990), this attention-based perspective emphasizes the distributed nature of organizational decisions, actions, and cognitions (Simon, 1947; Boland, Tenkaski, and Te'eni, 1994; Hutchins, 1995). While individuals ultimately do the attending, individual attention is situated in the context of the firm's activities and procedures, and these situational contexts, and the decision-makers, issues, and answers they are linked to, are distributed throughout the firm (March and Olsen, 1976). In this section I develop the three interrelated metatheoretical principles or premises, drawn from different levels of analysis, that underlie this perspective on how firms distribute and regulate the attention of its decision-makers:

1. At the level of individual cognition, the principle of focus of attention links attentional processing to individual cognition and behavior.
2. At the level of social cognition, and building on the perspective of Lewinian social psychology (Ross and Nisbett, 1991), the principle of situated attention highlights the importance of the situational context in explaining what decision-makers attend to.
3. At the organizational level, the principle of structural distribution of attention builds on research and theory from organizational decision-making, strategy formulation, and cognitive anthropology to explain how the firm's economic and social structures regulate and channel issues, answers, and decision-makers into the activities, communications, and procedures that constitute the situational context of decision-making.

Principle 1: Focus of attention

The principle of focus of attention indicates, first, that decision-makers will be selective in the issues and answers they attend to at any one time,

---

[2] This definition differs from alternative conceptions that separate attention from encoding and interpretation, with the former as the first of various stages in information processing (e.g., Corner *et al.*, 1994). Cognitive psychologists differ in whether they view attention as occurring only as the first stage of perception followed by encoding, or whether attentional processing is itself shaped by the encoding of information. This paper follows both LaBerge's (1995) model of individual information processing and Simon's (1947) and Weick's (1979) conceptualizations at the organizational level, in which encoding is part of attentional processing. While neither Simon nor Weick discussed encoding directly, their respective concepts of decision premises and enacted environments refer to how organizational decision-makers encode information, and both concepts were considered as central parts of organizational attention.

190   *W. Ocasio*

and second, that what decision-makers do depends on what issues and answers they focus their attention on. At the level of individual cognition, attentional processes focus the energy, effort, and mindfulness of organizational decision-makers on a limited set of elements that enter into consciousness at any given time. Focused attention both facilitates perception and action towards those issues and activities being attended to, and inhibits perception and action towards those that are not (Kahneman, 1973). At the individual level, the heedfulness associated with focused attention is expressed through an elevation of activity in cortical neurons coding for a particular item above the activity in neurons coding for different items when a group of objects or ideas are presented for information processing (LaBerge, 1995). The resulting enhanced mindfulness of individuals generates a selective attention on an object or idea that facilitates perception and action towards the object or idea being considered, and away from others.

The selective focus of attention of decision-makers is ameliorated, at least in part, in the case of routine, or well-learned activities. Shiffrin and Schneider (1977), on the basis of experiments involving visual perception, distinguished between two models of attentional processing: controlled and automatic. Controlled processing is highly demanding of attentional capacity, it is largely under the individual's control, and is strongly dependent on activity load. Automatic processing comes into operation without the active control of individuals, is difficult to alter or suppress, and is dependent on extensive long-term learning. A common example given to distinguish controlled vs. automatic attentional processing is driving: a new driver utilizes controlled processing to maneuver the vehicle and to shift gears, actively mindful of driving; an experienced driver utilizes automatic processing, shifting gears without thinking about it.

The distinction between controlled and automatic attentional processing also helps us to understand the linkage between action and the focus of attention. In the case of automatic processing, action is highly routinized and habitual, as decisions are unreflexively triggered by environmental stimuli that is 'automatically' attended to. In the case of controlled processing, the action of decision-makers is triggered by those issues and answers they are mindful of. But given

their selective focus of attention, decision-makers are limited in the number of issues and answers they can attend to in any particular situation, and only those issues and answers will affect what they do (Simon, 1947).

Principle 2: Situated attention

The principle of situated attention indicates that what decision-makers focus on, and what they do, depends on the particular context they are located in. According to this principle, the focus of attention of individual decision-makers is triggered by characteristics of the situations they confront themselves with, and this situated attention directly shapes individuals' behavior (Ross and Nisbett, 1991). It implies that individual decision-makers will vary their focus of attention depending on the situation, and that consistency (or variance) in attention and behavior is dependent more on consistency (or variance) in the characteristics of the situation rather than characteristics of the individuals.

Cialdini and his collaborators (Cialdini, Reno, and Kallgreen, 1990; Cialdini, Kallgreen, and Reno, 1991) found strong evidence for the principle of situated attention in a series of field experiments. Cialdini and his collaborators discovered that individual decisions to litter or not in public parks and parking garages were dependent on the particular situation they found themselves in: the amount (and placement) of litter, whether other individuals (confederates) littered or not, and their exposure to different written signs on public codes of behavior. They found, not surprisingly, that individuals littered less in litter-free environments than in littered ones. More interestingly, they discovered that littering was even less when either a single piece of litter was found, or when litter was directly lined up along the curb (consistent with litter having been previously swept). The effects of exposure to public codes on littering varied directly with the strength of association between the code of behavior and the antilittering norms.

Cialdini *et al*'s (1990, 1991) experiments indicate that characteristics of the situation trigger the individual's attention to norms of littering, and that this focus of attention directly affects how individuals behave. Cialdini and his collaborators carefully discount other alternative explanations to their experimental results. For example, they found that littering decreased when the confederate littered in an otherwise litter-free environment. This result cannot be explained by direct social influence or modeling of the confederate, but is best explained by positing that the confederate, through his or her violation of the norm, directly focuses the subjects' attention on antilittering norms. The overall pattern of results (Cialdini *et al.*, 1990, 1991) demonstrates how the situation shapes the individuals' focus of attention and how, through this focus of attention, the situation influences individuals' actions.

The principle of situated attention operates at the level of social cognition (Fiske and Taylor, 1991). This principle provides a link between how individuals think and decide in any particular situation, and how the organization and its environment shape the situations that individuals find themselves in. While in the field experiments described above the subjects react to the social environment as manipulated by Cialdini and his collaborators, decision-makers in organizations react to situations as shaped by the organization and its environment. In the case of organizational decision-making and action, the principle of situated attention highlights the effects of the organizational and environmental context in shaping individuals' focus of attention and action.

Principle 3: Structural distribution of attention

This principle indicates that the particular context decision-makers find themselves in, and how they attend to it, depends on how the organization distributes and controls the allocation of issues, answers, and decision-makers within specific firm activities, communications, and procedures. According to this principle, attentional processes of individual and group decision-makers are distributed throughout the multiple functions that take place in organizations, with different foci of attention in each local procedure, communication, or activity. Each local activity within the firm involves a set of procedures and communications, and these procedures and communications focus the attention of decision-makers on a selected set of issues and answers.

The distributed nature of attentional processing and action within the firm is present in Simon's (1947) early formulation of an attention-based perspective. Simon (1947: 220) describes organi-

zational behavior as a complex network of attentional processes. He emphasized the distribution and allocation of decision-making functions and the processes whereby the organization influences the attention of its decision-makers. Organizational actions and decisions are seen as resulting from a composite process whereby, for example, the 'major decisions were made neither by the board nor by any officer, nor formally by any group; they evolved through the interactions of many decisions both of individuals and by committees or boards' (Simon, 1947: 222). For Simon, the firm's economic and social structures create, channel, and distribute the attention of decision-makers into discrete processes, and organizational actions and decisions result from the complex interactions among these discrete attentional processes.

In the strategy literature, Bower's (1970) conceptual and empirical examination of investment decisions in a large U.S. diversified firm illustrates how the distribution of focus among organizational decision-makers affects the content and outcome of the corporate resource allocation process. According to Bower, investment decisions are best understood as an interconnected set of stages in a hierarchical process. At each phase of the process—the initiating, integrating, and corporate levels—managers vary in the definition of the situation and the issues they pay attention to. From an attentional perspective, we can reinterpret Bower's framework as showing how the attentional focus of the firm's decision-makers is distributed throughout the various stages of the resource allocation processes, with each stage containing different procedural and communication channels, and each channel producing different foci of attention.

While the concept of distributed attention is implicit in past research and theory on organizational decision-making and strategy formulation (Simon, 1947; Bower, 1970; March and Olsen, 1976), its development of the linkage between organizational and individual information processing builds on more recent research by cognitive anthropologists (Latour, 1987; Lave, 1988; Hutchins, 1995). This research emphasizes how the division of labor in social organizations requires distributed cognition and information processing in order to coordinate the activities of organizational participants. According to this view, the cognition that takes place within social

192   *W. Ocasio*

organizations is not reducible to the cognitive properties of individuals, but results from the organization of communications and procedures in which social cognition takes place. For example, Hutchins (1995) uses ethnographic methods and cultural analysis to examine how the computations required for ship navigation are distributed among crew members performing different procedures and employing different artifacts and equipment. Human cognition in general, and attentional processing in particular, is not a shared activity of a collective mind, but one that is distributed throughout the various concrete procedures and which reflects both existing technology and the social structure of the organization (Hutchins, 1995).

A MODEL OF SITUATED ATTENTION AND FIRM BEHAVIOR

This section presents an imaginative model of situated attention in firms to explain how firms behave. The model incorporates the three principles of an attention-based view of the firm, described above, into an integrated framework, as shown in Figure 1. The model presents not a full-fledged theory of firm behavior, but a set of constructs and a set of mechanisms relating these constructs, that outline how attentional processing at the individual, social cognitive, and organizational levels interact to shape firm behavior. The constructs and mechanisms here are grounded in exiting cognitive, structural, cultural, and strategy process perspectives on firm behavior. The contribution of the model is to link these con-

structs and mechanisms in a coherent and systematic fashion and to relate them to the central organizing concept of organizational attention.[3] The fundamental components of the model are: (1) the environment of decision; (2) the repertoire of issues and answers; (3) procedural and communicational channels—the firm's situated activities, communications and procedures; (4) the firm's attention structures—its rules of the game, players, structural positions, and resources; (5) decision-makers; and (6) organizational moves. The solid lines in Figure 1 provide a set of mechanisms (1a, 2, 3, 4a, 4b, 4c, 5a, 5b, and 5c) that link the constructs of the model to the three principles of an attention-based view:

1. *Focus of attention*: (5b) Decision-makers focus their attention on a limited set of issues and answers; (5c) the issues and answers they attend to and enact determines what they do.
2. *Situated attention*: The attention of decision-makers is situated in the firm's procedural and communication channels. The situational context of these channels includes: (1a) the environmental stimuli for decision-making; (2) the embodiment of issues and answers in cultural symbols, artifacts, and narratives; and (5a) the interactions among participants in the channel. The context and characteristics of the firm's procedural and communication channels interact to shape the availability and saliency of the repertoire of issues and answers (3).
3. *Structural distribution of attention*; The rules, resources, players, and social positions of the firm generate a distributed focus of attention among decision-makers participating in the firm's procedural and communication channels. The distribution of issues, answers, and decision-makers within the various channels depends on how these attention structures: (4a) generate a set of values that order the importance and relevance of issues and answers; (4b) channel and distribute decision-making into a concrete set of communications and

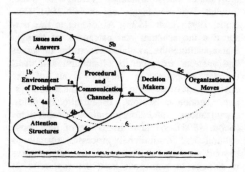

Figure 1. Model of situated attention and firm behavior

[3] The contributions of the model, and the paper more generally, to understanding firm behavior can best be described as a form of architectural innovation (Henderson and Clark, 1990), where existing components (in this case the principles, constructs, and mechanisms presented here), many widely accepted in strategic management and organizational theory, others adapted from cognitive science, sociology, and anthropology, are combined into a new configuration.

procedures; (4c) provide decision-makers with a structured set of interests and identities that shape their understanding of the situation and motivate their actions.

The dotted lines show additional mechanisms, not directly part of the model of firm behavior, of how the firm as a cultural and social system is shaped by the environment of action, (1b) and (1c), and how the environment of decision is shaped by previous organizational moves (6). Note that the numbering of the mechanisms does not reflect temporal order, but the presentation sequence of the constructs of the model. Temporal order is reflected, to a first approximation, by the placement, from left to right, of the origins of the lines representing the various mechanisms.

The firm in this model is an open social system where, through attentional processing and decision-making, the inputs from the environment of decision are transformed by the organization into a set of outputs—the organizational moves. In this model, I represent the elements of the firm's social systems—its culture, structure, processes, and individuals—by the repertoire of issues and answers, the attention structures, the procedural and communication channels, and the decision-makers. In the remainder of this section, I present the constructs of this model and discuss the mechanisms that shape attentional processing and firm behavior.

Environment of decision

The *environment of decision* (Barnard, 1938), represented by the enclosed background in Figure 1, encompasses the multiple material, social, and cultural factors, both internal and external to the firm, that impinge upon any decision activity. The myriad of elements of its external environment include economic and financial markets (competitors, customers, and suppliers), tradable resources (raw materials, labor, and capital), technology, and institutional rules (government laws and regulations, professional norms, industry benchmarks). Note that the diverse elements of the firm itself, including the results of past organizational moves (March and Simon, 1958; Cyert and March, 1963), are an integral part of the firm's environment of decision. In an attention-based view the firm's environment of decisions provides the raw stimuli for the structuring of

organizational practices and decision-making (Barnard, 1938):

> *Mechanism 1a: (Environmental stimuli). In any specific communication or procedural channel, physical, economic, and institutional factors both external and internal to the firm impinge upon the environment of decision and provide a set of stimuli for decision-making.*

While the environment of decision provides the raw inputs into decision-making, this paper follows Weick's (1979) conception of an attention-based view in emphasizing the enactment of the environment in the stimuli that is actually attended to. The environment of decisions is of infinite complexity and firms are bounded in their capacity to attend to all (or even most) environmental stimuli that impinge, directly or indirectly, upon any particular situation. Consequently, decision-makers are selective in those aspects of the environment of decisions that they attend to, as different environmental stimuli are noticed, interpreted, and brought into conscious consideration. Through the enactment of issues and answers, described below, decision-makers selectively restrict their attention to a limited set of stimuli, while ignoring others.

Environmental influences on organizational structures and cognition

With regard to cognitive processes, contemporary cultural and institutional perspectives highlight the treatment of cognitive schemas, symbols, and systems of meaning as external and objective to individual decision-makers (Douglas, 1986; Swidler, 1986; DiMaggio and Powell, 1991; Hutchins, 1995; Scott, 1995). According to this perspective the schemas and categories of thought that constitute the available repertoire of issues and answers are products of cultural and institutional processes at varying levels of the environment of decision, including the world system, economic sectors, organizational fields, organizations, and organizational subsystems (Scott, 1995). While a discussion of how these cultural and institutional processes operate is beyond the scope of this paper, for our purposes it suffices to point out how the repertoire of issues and answers is a product of these cultural and institutional proecsses (Swidler, 1986):

194   W. Ocasio

Mechanism 1b: (Cultural and institutional tool kits). Cultural and institutional processes, at varying levels of the environment, provide decision-makers with a repertoire or 'tool kit' of issues and answers from which to construct actions.

Again, while it is beyond the scope of this paper to discuss how the environment shapes the internal organizational structures—its rules, resources, and social relationships—suffice it to say that these structures are themselves embedded in the economic, social and institutional environment of the firm:

Mechanism 1c: (Environmental embeddedness). The firm's rules, resources, and social relationships are embedded in, and shaped by, the firm's economic, social, and institutional environment.

Issues and answers

Issues and answers are the cultural and cognitive repertoire of schemas available to decision-makers in the firm to make sense of (issues), and to respond to (answers) environmental stimuli. The issues confronted by the firm constitute the cognitive categories of problems, opportunities, and threats that make up the agenda of the firm, which are then available to organizational decision-makers to respond to or to ignore (Dutton and Jackson, 1987; Jackson and Dutton, 1988). Organizational decision-makers possess a cultural repertoire of possible schemas for the problems and opportunities that have been encountered in the past, both by the organization and in its environment. Decision-makers also possess a cultural repertoire of answers or action alternatives that can deal with a wide variety of issues, problems, and opportunities in the firm (March and Simon, 1958). This repertoire of answers is encoded in schemas used by organizational decision-makers to describe and understand the standard operating procedures (Cyert and March, 1963), organizational structures and routines (Nelson and Winter, 1982), and cultural 'tool kit' of plans and programs (Swidler, 1986) available as possible solutions to any problem or opportunity confronted by the firm.

Embodiment of issues and answers

Issues and answers constitute both a set of cognitive schemas and scripts for action and a set

of cultural products embodied in organizational artifacts (Hutchins, 1995; Schein, 1985; Swidler, 1986). As cultural products, issues are reflected in the technology, physical space and arrangements, archives, documents, stories, vocabulary, and narratives that are part of organizational memory (Walsh and Ungson, 1991). Here I would like to highlight how the embodiment of issues and answers in cultural products and artifacts increases their availability (Kahneman and Tversky, 1974) for attentional processing. In particular, the firm's cultural products and artifacts are used in concrete activities, procedures, interactions, and communications of the firm.

Mechanism 2: (Embodiment of issues and answers). Issues and answers are embodied in the cultural products and artifacts used to construct the firm's activities and communications.

Procedural and communication channels

The situated and distributed characteristics of attentional processing emphasize how the firm's organization creates for individual decision-makers a set of situational contexts in which attention and action take place. I have termed these situational contexts procedural and communication channels.[4] *Procedural and communication channels* are the formal and informal *concrete* activities, interactions, and communications set up by the firm to induce organizational decision-makers to action on a selected set of issues. They are termed *concrete* by virtue of their material existence, and specific location in time and space. They include formal and informal meetings, reports (e.g., action memoranda, quarterly and annual reports, customer satisfaction surveys, costs accounts) and administrative protocols (e.g., personnel evaluations, budgetary and capital appropriations requests, requests for proposals). Sutton and Hargadon (1996) examined one particular type of procedural and communication channel used in the product design,

---

[4] The term action channel (Allison, 1971) is equivalent to the concept of procedural and communication channels that I use here. I have settled for the composite term over the simpler one of action channels, first because it is less abstract, and second to connote that both procedures and communications, either independently or jointly, create the situational contexts under which attention takes place.

the brainstorming session, and how it shapes the firm's access to the issues and answers. More generally, Yates (1989) has analyzed the historical use of development of different genres of communications and procedures in large U.S. corporations—including the report, the committee meeting, and the memo—and their role in controlling the flow of information and decision-making.

By focusing the attention of decision-makers, procedural and communication channels are a critical part of the firm's attention allocation and serve as conduits for the processing of issues and answers in the making of organizational moves. The particular form and characteristics of the firm's procedural and communication channels significantly impact when, whether, and how decision-makers focus their attention, and how the attention of various decision-makers interacts within the channel. Stinchcombe (1968) has identified three dimensions—spatial, temporal, and procedural—that shape how these organizational contexts focus the attention of organizational decision-makers. The spatial dimensions regulate the availability of issues and answers and their commonality among decision-makers. The temporal dimensions regulate the amount of time organizational decision-makers have available to respond (i.e., the duration of interaction and communications between decision-makers and the deadlines for response). The procedural dimensions regulate the pattern and duration of attention foci to specific issues and answers available for consideration. Together, these three dimensions shape the availability and saliency (Kahneman and Tversky, 1974) of issues and answers within specific channels.

Take an example—a committee meeting. Its spatial dimensions include the physical location, the seating arrangements, the audiovisual equipment and materials, and the written documents available to committee members. The temporal dimensions include the time it is held, its duration, and its temporal proximity to other meetings and communications both of the same committees and of other groups within the organization. The procedural dimensions include the agenda for the meeting, the formal structure of the committee, if any, voting rules, and the formal and informal norms that guide the duties and responsibilities of committee members. The principle of situated attention suggests that each

of these dimensions affects what decision-makers focus their attention on by increasing the availability and saliency of certain issues and answers, and decreasing others. For instance, whether a committee meeting is held in headquarters location, in a manufacturing plant, or in a restaurant affects the saliency of particular issues and answers; a plant location is likely to make manufacturing and production issues and answers more salient, while off-site locations are often used to invoke the generation of novel issues and answers and to challenge prevailing ones. The duration and the agenda of the meeting affect which issues are considered and how much time and energy are devoted to the generation of answers.

As I discuss in the next subsection, the attention structures of the firm channel specific decisions into specific committee meetings, and regulate the spatial, temporal, and procedural dimensions of any specific meeting. While it is beyond the scope of this paper to develop a theory of how the various spatial, temporal, and procedural dimensions interact to focus the attention of decision-makers, the purpose here is to suggest that they are important factors in determining the availability and saliency of issues and answers for consideration:

Mechanism 3: (Availability and saliency of issues and answers). The spatial, temporal, and procedural dimensions of the firm's communication and procedural channels affect the availability and saliency of issues and answers that decision-makers will attend to.

Attention structures

Attention structures (March and Olsen, 1976) are the social, economic, and cultural structures that govern the allocation of time, effort, and attentional focus of organizational decision-makers in their decision-making activities. Attention structures regulate the valuation and legitimization of issues and answers, the creation and distribution of procedural and communication channels, and the interests and identities that guide decision-makers' actions and interpretations. Four categories of attention regulators will be examined in the conceptual model: rules of the game, players, structural positions, and resources. Together these four sets of factors

explain how firms actively regulate attention to
the internal and external environment of action
and how issues, answers, and decision-makers
are allocated into procedural and communication
channels. These categories of attention structures,
while analytically distinct, do not work independently but interact to organize and allocate the
firm's pattern of attention. Players occupy structural positions and are constrained and enabled
by the organizational rules of the game. They
employ the firm's resources in their attention
processes to collectively direct what, when, and
how organizations enact and respond to the
environment.

The organization's attention structures govern
the allocation and distribution of time, energy,
effort, and attention through three separate
mechanisms. First, the firm's rules, resources, and
social relations structure attention in organizations
by generating a set of values that order the
legitimacy, importance, and relevance of issues
and answers. Second, these attention structures
channel and distribute the decision-making
activity within the firm into a concrete set of
procedures and communications. Third, attention
structures provide the decision-makers with a
structured set of interests and identities. These
interests and identities generate in turn a set of
decision premises and motivations for actions. In
the remainder of the discussion of attention structures I will first describe the four categories of
attention structures and then explicate the three
separate effects, or mechanisms, that comprise
the structural distribution of attention.

Rules of the game

The rules of the game are the formal and informal
principles of action, interaction, and interpretation
that guide and constrain decision-makers in
accomplishing the firm's tasks and in obtaining
social status, credits, and rewards in the process.[5]

---

[5] This concept of rules of the game is closely related to those
of organizational paradigm (Brown, 1978), conceptions of
control (Fligstein, 1990), and institutional logic (Jackall,
1988). I use the term rules of the game rather than institutional
logic to stress not only the cognitive aspects of rules, but
their pragmatic and motivational implications. I use this term
rather than organizational paradigm or conceptions of control
to suggest that the rules of the game may not be fully coherent
and consistent as implied by the concepts of paradigm or
conceptions of control, but are often fragmented and partially contradictory.

These rules constitute a set of assumptions,
norms, values, and incentives—usually implicit—
about how to interpret organizational reality, what
constitutes appropriate behavior, and how to succeed. Organizational games are mixed motive
games of coordination and conflict, of cooperation
and contestation.[6] Organizations are concurrently:
cooperative systems (Barnard, 1938), whose common purpose is the objective of collective action;
shifting political coalitions (Cyert and March,
1963), whose decision-makers have conflicting
interests and goals; and, arenas for contestation,
where participants compete for status, power, and
material rewards (Allison, 1971; Bower, 1970;
White, 1992). The rules of the game provide
both a logic of action and embody a set of
cultural and material values and incentives that
structure and regulate the mixed motives of coordination, bargaining, and contestation that occur
within diverse organizational situations.

The firm's principles for action, interaction,
and interpretation are collective human construc-
tions that reflect the organization's history and
the history of its environment (Selznick, 1957;
Fligstein, 1990). This factor greatly complicates
our understanding and explanations of firm
behavior, as rules must be historically and cul-
turally situated in the social context in which
they were derived and developed. For example,
in the case of competitive strategy and action,
organizational decision-makers develop rules of
competition and anticipate, prepare for, and react
to competitors' actions based on these rules.
These rules of competition define which competitors must be attended to, on what basis competition take place (e.g., price, customer service,
low costs, quality, technological innovation), and
how the firm should prepare for and respond to
competitors' actions. The historical and socially
constructed nature of the rules of competition
held by organizational decision-makers implies
that whether and how a firm attends, anticipates,
and responds to a particularly competitive action
will change as prevailing rules change.

For instance, Microsoft's rapid and vigorous
response to Netscape's entry and early dominance

---

[6] Building on the formal theory of games, Schelling (1960)
distinguished between three forms of games: zero-sum games,
which are governed by pure conflict; coordination (or
cooperation) games, where conflict is to everyone's disadvantage; and mixed motive games, where players must reconcile
their instrumental ambitions with the gains from cooperation.

of Internet platforms is shaped by its rules of competition in the computer industry. According to Microsoft's CEO, Gates (1995), its biggest competitive challenge is to become the first company in the industry to exploit successfully successive shifts in dominant computer technology. This rule, and the example of IBM, and its initial failure to enact accurately the implications of the personal computer, has driven Microsoft to focus many of its strategic efforts and technology development resources to Internet projects.

Players

An important component of the firm's attention regulation are individuals and groups of individuals who are the players in the organizational game. Players affect the firm's attention regulation through the specific skills, beliefs, and values they bring to the firm (March and Olsen, 1976). The most critical players in attention regulation are typically the CEO and the top management group (Hambrick and Mason, 1984; Hambrick, 1994). Other actors and groups of actors both internal and external to the firm may constitute significant players including middle and divisional management, workers and their union representatives, active board members, major customers and suppliers, institutional investors, financial analysts, consultants and, more recently, the business press.

In explaining the influence of players we distinguish the concept of players first from that of decision-makers and second from the structural positions they occupy. Decision-makers are the concrete social actors that participate in the firm's procedural and communication channels. Players are structurally autonomous social actors or groups of actors (Burt, 1982) which, through their social influence, power, and control, influence and regulate the decision and activities of other decision-makers. Not all decision-makers are players, and in a particular situation players who are not decision-makers may influence a particular organizational action or move. For example, the members of the compensation committee of a firm's board of directors who participate in a particular meeting constitute the decision-makers in that particular procedural and communication channel. But not all the participants are players, as some may have little autonomous influence over the committee's actions of decisions. Fur-

thermore, the firm's CEO is typically a player in that meeting, who shapes the attention of decision-makers, through his or her power and social influence over the board (Wade, O'Reilly, and Chandratat, 1990; Westphal and Zajac, 1995). The CEO is not a decision-maker in that specific channel, being neither present in the meeting nor a committee member.

I also distinguish players from the structural positions they occupy (see below). Players have an effect to the extent that they have some discretion over the enactment of the structural position and can bring their own personal set of skills, beliefs, and values to those positions. Players exert control over decision-makers through their individual and structural sources of power. Note that the distinction between players and positions is at the heart of debates over managerial discretion. Here, we argue that managers (and other influential players) have a discretionary role in influencing firm attention and behavior (Hambrick and Finkelstein, 1987).

Players provide an entrepreneurial function in the allocation of attention in organizations. Players may influence the structuring of organizational attention either by affecting the generation and valuation of any of the component issues, answers, or procedural and communication channels, or by regulating the structure of linkages between them. Note that the players' sources of extraorganizational influence are not always beneficial to the firm's performance nor are they a source for change. Players often become committed to prevailing organizational structures and strategies, and their personal interests, values, and orientations may come into conflict with the organization's purpose (Selznick, 1957).

Structural positions

Structural positions are the roles and social identifications that specify (a) the functions and orientations of decision-makers, and (b) their interrelationships with other structural positions internal and external to the firm. Structural positions interact with the rules of the game to provide decision-makers with the interests, values, and identities that regulate how they think and act in organizations. Structural positions and relationships arise from the division of labor both within and between organizations. In large modern business enterprises, specialized structural positions have been developed to attend to the numerous and diverse aspects of the organization's environment. The emergence of structural positions of middle and upper management is associated with an increase in the specialization of function in attending to changes in customers, technologies, competitors, and markets (Chandler, 1962, 1976).

Structural positions provide a source of differentiated attention to different aspects of the organization's environment (Lawrence and Lorsch, 1967) and allow their occupants to focus their time and effort on certain problems and on certain solutions, and to ignore others. Structural positions not only serve to differentiate organizational attention, they also provide structures for their integration. Structural positions shape bargaining, coordination, and contestation within organizations. Structural positions provide for a system of hierarchical authority in organizations that allows conflicts over subunit goals to be resolved and resources to be mobilized.

Resources

Firm *resources* are defined as the set of tangible and intangible assets that allow the firm to perform its activities and to produce its goods and services (Wernerfelt, 1984). Firm resources are embedded in the organization's routines and capabilities (Nelson and Winter, 1982) and provide the organization with the collective skills to perform a wide variety of tasks. In the model, firm resources are the human, physical, technological, and financial capital available to the firm at any moment in time for its objectives.[7] The set of firm resources comprises its distinctive competencies and inimitable assets (Selznick, 1957; Rumelt,1984) which provide a primary source of the firm's competitive advantage, as well as other nondistinctive resources whose yield may be at or below the competitive return.

It is important to distinguish the concept of answers from that of resources in the model and the relationship between them and organizational moves. Answers are the cognitive schemas of

alternatives considered by organizational decision-makers in making decisions and enacting moves. Resources are the tangible and intangible assets utilized in the construction of organizational moves. The repertoire of answers is shaped, but not fully determined, by existing organizational resources. The schemas used by organizational decision-makers to characterize and describe existing resources are part of the repertoire of action alternatives considered. But alternative answers are often considered, such as answers developed by competing firms, that may not be part of the firm's existing resources. Consequently, translating answers selected by organizational decision-makers into organizational moves requires that either existing resources be deployed or that new resources be acquired or developed.

The valuation of issues and answers

A principal mechanism by which attention structures govern and distribute the attentional focus of decision-makers is through the valuation and legitimization of issues and answers. Among the large repertoire of issues and answers available to decision-makers for consideration, decision-makers are more likely to consider and to attend those with greater legitimacy, value, and relevance to the organization. The valuation and rank ordering of the repertoire of issues and answers result from the cultural, social, and economic structures that govern attention in organization.

The rules of the game play a critical role in the allocation of value and legitimacy to the repertoire of issues and answers. These rules embody the organizational identity and purpose (Andrews, 1971; Barnard, 1938; Selznick, 1957; Dutton and Dukerich, 1991) and provide central guiding concepts that legitimate both the issues and problems that firms consider and the appropriateness of the answers and responses to those issues and problems. The rules of the game embody the set of cultural and material values and incentives that structure the coordination, bargaining, and contestation that occur within diverse organizational situations. These values and incentives specify the system of social and economic rewards and recognition obtained by organizational decision-makers in their interactions and links these rewards to specific issues and answers.

---

[7] This definition of resources is more narrow than in some resource-based views of the firm (e.g., Barney, 1991). Note that this paper seeks to explain firm behavior in any specific situation, while resource-based views, to the extent that they directly or indirectly address firm behavior, typically refer to behavior across multiple situations.

This set of incentives regulates the attention of organizational decision-makers so as to recognize and resolve those issues and activities most highly valued by the firm.

While the rules of the game play are central, the allocation of values, legitimacy, and relevance of issues and answers is a joint product of the firm's rules, positions, players and resources. The principle of structural distribution of attention highlights how the values, legitimacy, and relevance of the various issues and answers are not uniform throughout the firm, but are distributed according to the division of labor. The structural positions interact with the rules of the game so that issues and answers are differentially valued throughout the firm. Different values are assigned to different issues and answers according to the structural position held by decision-makers. Players and resources also play a role in the determination of values. Players are involved in selling of issues, answers, and agenda building throughout the various functions of the firm (Dutton, 1988). Answers and solutions embedded in organizational resources are more likely to be highly valued and legitimate than other answers. Attentional and resource constraints bias the firm in the direction of continuing exploitation and development of existing resources and routines, rather than in the development of new ones (March, 1991). Consequently:

Mechanism 4a: (The valuation of issues and answers). The firm's attention structures govern the valuation and legitimization of the repertoire of issues and answers available to decision-makers. These values are not uniform throughout the firm but are differentiated according to the division of labor inherent in the firm's rules, positions, players, and resources.

The channeling of decision-making

The principle of structural distribution of attention suggests that the firm's rules, players, structural positions, and resources allocate the decision-making activities of the firm into a concrete set of procedural and communication channels. Firms establish a wide variety of channels to collect information, measure human, physical, and financial inputs, monitor outcomes, control resource mobilization, and make decisions. Which chan-

nels are created, what specific agendas and procedures are utilized, and where they are located in time and place, are regulated by the firm's rules of coordination and contestation (Simon, 1947), by the division of labor inherent in the firm's resources and structural positions (Henderson and Clark, 1990; Chandler, 1962), and by the power and influence of organizational players (Jackall, 1988). For example, the diverse structural positions of the firm generate a set of quasi-independent channels for the specific decisions including cash management, inventory control, budgeting, investment analysis, marketing, product design, human resource management, performance evaluation, and strategic planning, among others. More generally, these structural positions interact with the rules of the game, the firm resources, and organizational players to regulate the allocation of the diverse decision-making activities throughout the firm:

Mechanism 4b: (The channeling of decision-making). The firm's attention structures channel and distribute the decision-making activities of the firm into a set of procedural and communication channels.

The structuring of interests and identities

A structural perspective on the distribution of attention highlights the role of attention structures in providing the interests and identities that motivate action and that provide decision-makers with the premises for decisions (Simon, 1947). First, the organizational rules of the game provide the normative frames and systems of interests and identities that motivate action and interpret meaning in organizational situations. These interests and identities shape the enactment of issues by specifying how the environment of action is to be interpreted by organizational decision-makers and which elements of the environment are critical to the organizational game. Second, players structure interests and identities through their network of connections with organizational decision-makers (Burt, 1982). Structural perspectives on action highlight the role of players and networks in structuring incentives and influencing perceptions. Third, structural positions provide for a source of variation in the interests and identities of decision-makers. In any situation, decision-makers who hold different structural positions

200   *W. Ocasio*

will have different interests and social identifications (March and Simon, 1958; White,
1992). Finally, the deployment of firm resources
entails a distribution of human capital, with the
interests of decision-makers dependent on the
degree to which their human capital is associated
with the various resources of the firm. Together,
the rules, players, positions, and resources of
the firm structure the interests and identities that
decision-makers face in any situation:

> *Mechanism 4c: (The structuring of interests
> and identities). The firm's attention structures
> provide decision-makers with a structured sys-
> tem of interest and identities to motivate their
> action and to structure their decision premises.*

Decision-makers

Decision-makers are the concrete individuals who
jointly participate, within any specific procedural
and communication channel, in the enactment of
the environment and the social construction of
organizational moves. In an attention-based view
of the firm, decision-makers attend to the environment of action, the inputs of decision-making,
and through their attentional processing selectively construct the mental models that result
in organizational moves, the output of decision-
making. Decision-makers are situated in the firm's
procedural and communication channels, the concrete location in time and space where attentional
processing occurs.

The structuring of participation

The focusing of attention in social organizations
emerges from the social interactions among the
decision-makers who participate in any specific
situation. Organizations are not unitary actors, but
are comprised of multiple decision-makers, with
distinct identities, interests, and social positions
(Cyert and March, 1963). The focusing of attention in organizations is thereby conditional on
whether, when, and how decision-makers participate in the firm's procedural and communication
channels. Participation is in turn conditional on
the time, energy, and effort of decision-makers,
and on the attentional demands on their time
from other channels. Participants bring to any
specific activity or situation knowledge of alternative issues and answers, as well as interests and

identities that shape which issues and answers
become more salient. Who participates in a
decision process shapes which issues and answers
are attended to, and consequently what decision-
makers do (March and Olsen, 1976):

> *Mechanism 5a: (The structuring of
> participation). Decision-making is the product
> of interactions among participants in the firm's
> procedural and action channels. The structur-
> ing of participation is, in turn, conditional on
> the time, energy, interests, and identities of
> organizational decision-makers, and on the
> demands placed on decision-makers by alter-
> native channels.*

The enactment of issues and answers

At the organizational level, the focusing of attention of decision-makers creates a concentration
of their energy and effort on a limited set of
issues and answers. Through the social construction and enactment of issues organizational
decision-makers selectively restrict their attention
to a limited set of stimuli in the complex environment of action, while ignoring others. Decision-
makers are not passive recipients of environmental stimuli, but active creators of the environmental stimuli that they impose upon their actions:
'enactment emphasize[s] that managers construct,
rearrange, single out, and demolish many of the
"objective" features of their surroundings'
(Weick, 1979: 164).

This paper extends Weick's concept of enactment by highlighting how the principles of an
attention-based view interact to shape attentional
processing and the enactment of the environment.
First, decision-makers will be selective in their
focus of attention to issues and answers. Second,
attentional processing is situated in the firm's
procedural and communication channels. This
situational context shapes the enactment of the
environment by increasing the availability and
saliency of certain issues and answers, relative to
others, and by the interaction among participants
in the channel. The structures of attention shape
the enactment of the environment through the
channeling of decision-making activity to specific
channels, through the valuation of issues and
answers, and through the structuring of interests
and identities of decision-makers. These prin-

ciples interact to shape the enactment of issues and answers by decision-makers:

> *Mechanism 5b: (Enactment of issues and answers) Decision-makers will enact the environment of decisions by focusing their attention on a limited number of issues of answers. This attentional focus is shaped both by characteristics of the situation—the availability and saliency of issues and answers (3) and the interactions among participants within the channel (5a)—and by the structural determinants of attention—the values, legitimacy, and relevance accorded to the various issues and answers (4a) and the structured interests and identities of decision-makers.*

This repertoire of available issues and answers is invoked not just in the case of routine situations or standard operating procedures, but is applied to novel situations by seeking analogies and areas of commonality with past situations, activities, and events in the firm (March and Olsen, 1976; Weick, 1979).

Organizational moves

Organizational moves are the output of attentional processing and decision-making which is situated in procedural and communication channels. *Organizational moves are the myriad of actions undertaken by the firm and its decision-makers in response to or in anticipation of changes in its external and internal environment.* Organizational moves include both implicit and explicit decisions made by the organization and its decision-makers, as a result of both controlled and automatic attentional processes. Organizational moves encompass both exchanges of resources and information with the firm's external environment as well as changes in the firm's own resources and attention structures. I use the concept of organizational move instead of the more common concept of organizational decision for several reasons: organizational moves include both the plans for actions implied in an organizational decision and the actions themselves; the concept of moves highlights how they are shaped by the rules of the games, its players, structural positions, and procedural and communication channels; and the term connotes how moves are interdependent and are shaped and affected by the context, order, and timing of other organizational moves. Note, however, that moves may or may not be implemented and lead to strategic change. For example, the adoption of strategic plans by a firm's executive committee is an organization move. Its implementation requires a myriad of subsequent moves by organizational decision-makers.

The selection of organizational moves

The principle of focus of attention implies that the selection of organizational moves depends on the issues and answers that decision-makers attend to. Two interrelated aspects are of particular importance to understanding how the focusing of issues and answers shapes a firm's strategic behavior and the selection of organizational moves. First, the enactment of issues and answers entails both passive attention to the environment and active preparation and focusing of energy and effort. Recent cognitive research has emphasized preparation as one of the principal manifestations of attentional processing (LaBerge, 1995). The preparatory manifestation of attention operates by directing attention to a particular stimulus prior to the time that stimulus occurs and facilitates speed and accuracy of perception and action. Preparatory attention is driven by the importance and relevance of issues and answers and by the interests and identities of decision-makers. Decision-makers will direct their attention to environmental stimuli associated with highly valued issues and answers and which serves to enhance their interests and identities.

Second, decision-makers' enactment of the issues and answers is situated in the firm's procedural and communication channels and may vary across them. For example, the environment may be enacted in terms of long-term competitive opportunities and threats in the firm's strategic plans, and in terms of short-term cash flow considerations in its investment processes. Who participates in procedural and communication channels and the structures that regulate them determine what issues and answers are utilized in specific channels. According to the theory proposed here, firms may not be consistent across channels and situations to the specific aspects of the environment they pay attention to and may vary in the specific moves they undertake. Consequently:

Mechanism 5c: (Selection of organizational moves). Decision-makers will select among alternative organizational moves depending on which issues and answers they attend to. The attention to issues and answers results both from passive response to environmental stimuli and preparatory attention and effort and will vary depending on the procedural and communication channel where decision-making is situated.

Finally, organizational moves, the output of the firm decision-making process, become part of the firm's environment of decision and are an input into the construction of subsequent moves:

Mechanism 6: (Effects on subsequent moves). Organizational moves, once enacted, become part of the firm's environment of decision and are inputs to the construction of subsequent organizational moves.

CHARACTERISTICS OF THE MODEL FOR EXPLAINING FIRM BEHAVIOR AND ADAPTATION

One of the critical issues in strategy to which the model can be applied is whether and how firms adapt to changing environments. In summarizing how an attention-based view of the firm explains organizational adaptation, and more generally how firms behave, the following characteristics are highlighted that differentiate the current theory from alternative explanations of firm adaptation and behavior.

(1) *Small contingencies in the firm's procedural and communication channels may significantly change organizational adaptation and behavior.* An attention-based view of the firm implies that the ability of the firm to adapt successfully to a changing environment is conditional on whether the firm's procedural and communication channels focus the attention of organizational decision-makers on an appropriate set of issues and answers. An attention-based view opens the black box of the firm to highlight the importance of situated attentional processes in selectively focusing decision-makers' attention. Consistent with the principle of situated attention, small differences, or contingencies, in the spatial, temporal, and procedural dimensions of the firm's

procedural and communication channels, and in the spatial and temporal order in which these processes take place, may have significant impacts upon the focus of attention of decision-makers and the subsequent organizational moves.

The importance of contingencies in situated attention in explaining organizational adaptation and behavior is also a central insight of the garbage can model of decision-making (Cohen *et al.*, 1972; March and Olsen, 1976). The role of situational contingencies in the current formulation of an attention-based perspective differs, however, from the garbage can model in two ways. First, as stated earlier, and consistent with Cialdini's research findings (Cialdini *et al.*, 1990, 1991), the contingencies shape decision-making by shaping the focus of attention and cognitive processing of individual decision-makers. Second, the current formulation highlights the importance of rules, norms, and procedural dimensions associated with a firm's procedural and communication channels.

(2) *Inertia, inappropriate change, or successful adaptation may result from situated attentional processes.* An attention-based view of the firm suggests that a firm's ability to adapt to a changing environment is contingent on the firm's enactment of its environment, and on its ability to focus the attention of its decision-makers on the appropriate issues and answers. The determination of inertia and adaptation in an organization remains a central debate in the study of organizations and firm behavior (Astley and Van de Ven, 1983; Barnett and Carroll, 1995). Unlike either theories based on rationality or theories based on environmental determinism, an attention-based view of the firm provides a unified process-based explanation for the conflicting findings of both inertia and successful adaptation in organizations. An attention-based view implies that whether and how firms adapt to a changing environment is not a foregone conclusion but results from specific contingencies arising from the respective firm's procedural and communication channels and attention structures. This is an improvement over the current state of theorizing where different theories are applied to explain different outcomes, but no unified theoretical framework incorporated disparate outcomes.

An attention-based view of the firm extends the explanations of firm adaptation offered by Weick's (1979) perspective on organizational enactment of the environment. Which of multiple enacted environments are selected by the firm to shape organizational response is conditional on the firm's procedural and communication channels and its attention structures. Explaining organizational strategies and action requires an understanding of how the rules of the game, structural positions and arrangements, players, and resources interact to distribute and channel the attention of organizational decision-makers into specific procedural and communication channels, and to draw upon issues and answers in organizational memory. Further research and theoretical development are required to explain how these interactions affect firm adaptation.

(3) *Both structural regularities and cognitive repertoires of issues and answers underlie attentional processes in organizations.* While both structural (Blau, 1994) and cognitive theories (Weick, 1979, 1995) are typically presented as alternative explanations for firm behavior, an attention-based view of the firm highlights how both the social and economic structures of attention and the cultural and cognitive repertoire of issues and answers have independent influences upon the firm's procedural and communication channels and subsequently on the enactment of the environment (Ocasio, 1995). Explanations of how firms adapt to changes in the environment must account for both the effects of social structures and the effects of managerial cognitions and both effects are mediated through the firm's procedural and communication channels.

(4) *Selective focus of attention facilitates firm's strategic actions.* Limited attentional capacity for nonroutine activities by organizational decision-makers implies that alternative issues will compete for his or her selective attention, energy, and effort. This limited capacity for controlled attentional processing underlies the importance of strategic focus. Traditionally, theories of bounded rationality have stressed the inhibitory aspects of selective attention, showing how the limited attentional capability of humans creates a departure from the omniscient rationality of economic theories of choice (Simon, 1947, 1957). But the focalization and concentration of consciousness associated with selective attention create adaptive properties of critical concern to strategic activity, as they facilitate the accuracy, speed, and sustained processing of information in perceptual judgements and actions (LaBerge,

1995: 8–12). The accurate planning and performance of strategic actions and the speed of their execution require that individual and group decision-makers concentrate their energy, effort, and mindfulness on a limited number of issues and tasks. Successful strategic performance thereby requires the sustained focusing of attention and effort associated with controlled attentional processing.

CONCLUSIONS

Fifty years after the introduction of attentional perspectives on administrative behavior (Simon, 1947), this paper brings back an underdeveloped insight into Simon's initial formulation—that to explain firm behavior is to explain how organizations and their structures channel and distribute the attention of their decision-makers. Based on theoretical insights and research findings from cognitive science, social psychology, organizational theory, and strategy process perspectives, this paper presents and develops three theoretical principles that underlie this central insight of an attention-based view of the firm. Existing theories of bounded rationality, enacted environments, and managerial cognition all share the first principle of the theory—that what decision-makers do depends on how they selectively focus their attention on certain characteristics of the organization and its environment, and ignore others. This paper extends these perspectives by adding two additional principles: (1) an emphasis on the situated and variable nature of attentional processes in organizations; and (2) an explicit linkage of managerial cognition to the channeling and distribution of attention by the firm's social, economic, and cultural structures. While a careful reading of *Administrative Behavior* (Simon, 1947: 79–109) reveals that all three principles were present in Simon's initial theory, later theoretical development moved away from these last two premises either towards a theory of satisficing and bounded rationality, or towards loose coupling and enacted environments. This paper rediscovers Simon's insights and updates them to reflect contemporary theoretical developments and research.

This paper builds upon the three theoretical principles of an attention-based view and develops a cross-level, process model of how firms behave—one of the fundamental issues for the field of strategy (Rumelt *et al.*, 1994). This conceptual model does not constitute a fully developed theory of firm behavior, but an initial formulation, based on a set of theoretical constructs and a set of general mechanisms linking those constructs. A central contribution of the model is that it highlights the importance of procedural and communication channels in situating the attention of decision-makers and in contributing to the variations in attentional processing and the enactment of the environment. Another important contribution is that it brings together under the central organizing concept of attentional processing a wide variety of cultural, social, cognitive, and economic mechanisms, at multiple levels of analysis, that shape how firms behave.

The complexity of the model is both a virtue and a weakness. An advantage is its ability, unlike theories of rational choice or theories of environmental determinism, to explain both stability and change in response to changing environmental conditions. Its disadvantage lies in its relatively primitive state of theoretical development, in the generality and high level of abstraction of its mechanisms, and in the large attentional demands it makes on the reader to process and integrate the wide variety of seemingly disparate theories and constructs employed. As the title of this paper suggests, the theoretical development of an attention-based view is still in its preliminary stages. Each of the mechanisms presented in the model is quite general, and allows for significant theoretical elaboration and empirical testing. Given the multiple levels of analysis and concepts employed here, research based on an attentional perspective may rely on multiple methodologies including ethnographies, case studies, historical analysis, field experiments, content analysis, and computer simulations.

An attention-based view helps explain whether and how firms adapt to changing environments. At one level, the theory provides an answer similar to organizational perspectives on the enactment of the environment (Weick, 1979; Ocasio, 1995)—adaptation to the changing environments depends on how firms enact their environment. Failures of adaptation are failures of enactment, failures to successfully attend to the relevant issues and answers. This paper adds to this explanation an emphasis on how the firm's attention structures and its procedural and communication channels are linked to the capacity of the firm to adapt to changing environments. The development and transformation of the modern business enterprise analyzed by Chandler (1962, 1976) and others can be reinterpreted as the development of new forms of attention regulation that increase the firm's adaptability and competitiveness. Chandler focused on what we have called structural arrangements and procedural and communication channels as principal components of what we now know as the modern multibusiness enterprise. Others (e.g., Fligstein, 1990) have emphasized the changing rules of the game (conceptions of control in Fligstein's terms) to explain the corporate transformation. This suggests that an attention-based perspective may help answer another important question of strategy: what is the function of, and the value added, of the headquarters unit in a multibusiness firm (Rumelt, Schendel, and Teece, 1994)? The principal function of the headquarters unit is, in the current model, to regulate and govern organizational attention.

Finally, the paper advances our understanding of firm strategy and behavior by emphasizing how selective attention both facilitates and inhibits perception and action. Previous attentional perspectives in the organization's literature stressed the inhibitory aspects, as selective attention leads to departures from the model of omniscient rationality in economic theories of choice. But the focusing of attention by organizational decision-makers allows for enhanced accuracy, speed, and maintenance of information-processing activities, facilitating perception and action for those activities attended to. Whether attentional processes facilitate or inhibit organizational adaptation and performance is contingent on whether the firm's procedural and communication channels and attention regulators focus and distribute the attention of organizational decision-makers in directions that are congruent with the firm's environmental opportunities and constraints.

While an attention-based view of the firm can bring together multiple dimensions and perspectives into an explanation of firm behavior and strategy, it is not meant to replace the resource-based view of the firm or competitive perspectives on corporate strategy. An attention-based view cannot explain, by itself, the sources of the firm's competitive advantage. Although it may help illustrate sources of firm heterogeneity at any point in time, it cannot explain why firm heterogeneity persists under competitive pressures. I have argued that the channeling and distribution of attention are central to the formulation and implementation of corporate strategy and that attention structures and the deployment of procedural and communication channels can be a major source of the firm's adaptive capabilities. But a full understanding of competitive advantage and firm heterogeneity requires that we integrate an attention-based view of the firm with resource and industry perspectives to develop a dynamic theory of business strategy and value creation.

ACKNOWLEDGEMENTS

I would like to thank Rebecca Henderson, Jim March, Dan Levinthal, Marc Ventresca, Don Lessard, Ranjay Gulati, and the anonymous *SMJ* referees for comments, suggestions, advice, and encouragement.

REFERENCES

Allison, G. T. (1971). *Essence of Decision: Explaining the Cuban Missile Crisis*. Little, Brown, Boston, MA.

Andrews, K. R. (1971). *The Concept of Corporate Strategy*. Dow-Jones, Homewood, IL.

Astley, W. G. and A. H. Van de Ven (1983). 'Central perspectives and debates in organizational theory', *Administrative Science Quarterly*, 28, pp. 245–273.

Barnard, C. I. (1938). *The Functions of the Executive*. Harvard University Press, Cambridge, MA.

Barney, J. B. (1991). 'Firm resources and sustained competitive advantage', *Journal of Management*, 17, pp. 99–120.

Barnett, W. P. and G. Carroll (1995). 'Modeling internal organizational change', *Annual Review of Sociology*, 21, pp. 217–236.

Blau, P. M. (1994). *Structural Contexts of Opportunities*. University of Chicago Press, Chicago, IL.

Boland, R. J., R. V. Tenkaski and D. Te'eni (1994). 'Designing information technology to support distributed cognition', *Organization Science*, 5, pp. 456–475.

Bower, J. L. (1970). *Managing the Resource Allocation Process*. Harvard Business School Press, Boston, MA.

Brown, R. H. (1978). 'Bureaucracy as praxis: Toward a political phenomenology of formal organizations', *Administrative Science Quarterly*, 23, pp. 365–382.

Burgelman, R. (1983). 'A process model of corporate venturing in the diversified major firm', *Administrative Science Quarterly*, 28, pp. 223–244.

Burgelman, R. (1994). 'Fading memories: A process theory of strategic business exit in dynamic environments', *Administrative Science Quarterly*, 39, pp. 24–56.

Burt, R. (1982). *Toward a Structural Theory of Action: Network Models of Social Structure, Perception, and Action*. Academic Press, New York.

Chandler, A. D. (1962). *Strategy and Structure*. MIT Press, Cambridge, MA.

Chandler, A. D. (1976). *The Visible Hand: The Managerial Revolution in American Business*. Harvard University Press, Cambridge, MA.

Child, J. (1972). 'Organizational structure, environment, and performance: The role of strategic choice', *Sociology*, 6, pp. 2–22.

Cialdini, R. B., C. A. Kallgren and R. R. Reno (1991). 'A focus theory of normative conduct', *Advances in Experimental Social Psychology*, 24, pp. 201–234.

Cialdini, R. B., R. R. Reno and C. A. Kallgren (1990). 'A focus theory of normative conduct: Recycling the concept of norms to reduce littering in public places', *Journal of Personality and Social Psychology*, 58, pp. 1015–1026.

Cohen, M. D., J. G. March and J. P. Olsen (1972). 'A garbage can model of organizational choice', *Administrative Science Quarterly*, 17, pp. 1–25.

Corner, P. D., A. J. Kinicki and B. W. Keats (1994). 'Integrating organizational and information processing perspectives on choice', *Organization Science*, 5, pp. 294–308.

Cyert, R. M. and J. G. March (1963). *A Behavioral Theory of the Firm*. Prentice-Hall, Englewood Cliffs, NJ.

Daft, R. L. and K. Weick (1984). 'Toward a model of organizations as interpretation systems', *Academy of Management Review*, 9, pp. 284–295.

DiMaggio, P. D. and W. W. Powell (1991). 'Introduction'. In P. D. DiMaggio and W. W. Powell (eds.), *The New Institutionalism in Organizational Analysis*. University of Chicago Press, Chicago, IL, pp. 1–38.

Douglas, M. (1986). *How Institutions Think*. Syracuse University Press, Syracuse, NY.

Dutton, J. E. (1988). 'Understanding strategic agenda building and its implications for managing change'. In L. R. Pondy, R. Bland and H. Thomas (eds.), *Managing Ambiguity and Change*. Wiley, New York, pp. 127–144.

Dutton, J. E. and J. Dukerich (1991). 'Keeping an eye on the mirror: Image and identity in organizational adaptation', *Academy of Management Journal*, 34(3), pp. 517–554.

Dutton, J. E. and S. E. Jackson (1987). 'Categorizing strategic issues: Links to organizational action', *Academy of Management Review*, 12, pp. 76–90.

Eisenhardt, K. M. (1990). 'Making fast strategic decisions in high-velocity environments', *Academy of Management Journal*, 32, pp. 543–576.

Fiske, S. T. and S. Taylor (1991). *Social Cognition* (2nd ed.). Random House, New York.

Fligstein, N. (1990). *The Transformation of Corporate Control*. Harvard University Press, Cambridge, MA.

Gates, W. P. (1995). *The Road Ahead*. Viking, New York.

Hambrick, D. C. (1994). 'Top management groups: A conceptual integration and reconsideration of the "team" label'. In B. M. Staw and L. L. Cummings (eds.), *Research in Organizational Behavior*, Vol 16. JAI Press, Greenwich, CT, pp. 171–213.

Hambrick, D. C. and S. Finkelstein (1987). 'Managerial discretion: A bridge between polar views on organizations'. In L. L. Cummings and B. M. Staw (eds.), *Research in Organizational Behavior*, Vol. 9. JAI Press, Greenwich, CT, pp. 369–406.

Hambrick, D. C. and P. A. Mason (1984). 'Upper-echelons: The organization as a reflection of its top-managers', *Academy of Management Review*, **9**, pp. 193–206.

Henderson, R. M. and K. B. Clark (1990). 'Architectural innovation: The reconfiguration of existing technologies and the failure of established firms', *Administrative Science Quarterly*, **35**, pp. 9–30.

Hutchins, E. (1995). *Cognition in the Wild*. MIT Press, Cambridge, MA.

Jackall, R. (1988). *Moral Mazes: The World of Corporate Managers*. Oxford University Press, New York.

Jackson, S. E. and J. E. Dutton (1988). 'Discerning threats and opportunities', *Administrative Science Quarterly*, **33**, pp. 370–387.

James, W. (1890). *The Principles of Psychology*. Holt, New York.

Kahneman, D. (1973). *Attention and Effort*. Prentice-Hall, Englewood Cliffs, NJ.

Kahneman, D. and A. Tversky (1974). 'Judgment under uncertainty: Heuristics and biases', *Science*, **185**, pp. 1124–1131.

LaBerge, D. (1995). *Attentional Processing: The Brain's Art of Mindfulness*. Harvard University Press, Cambridge, MA.

Latour, B. (1987). *Science in Action*. Harvard University Press, Cambridge, MA.

Lave, J. (1988). *Cognition in Practice*. Cambridge University Press, Cambridge, UK.

Lawrence, P. R. and J. W. Lorsch (1967). *Organization and Environment: Managing Differentiation and Integration*. Harvard Business School Press, Boston, MA.

March, J. G. (1991). 'Exploration and exploitation in organizational learning', *Organization Science*, **2**, pp. 71–87.

March, J. G. and J. P. Olsen (1976). *Ambiguity and Choice in Organizations*. Universitesforlaget Bergen, Norway.

March, J. G. and H. A. Simon (1958). *Organizations*. Wiley, New York.

Nelson, R. R. and S. G. Winter (1982). *An Evolutionary Theory of Economic Change*. Harvard University Press, Cambridge, MA.

Ocasio, W. (1995). 'The enactment of economic adversity: A reconciliation of theories of failure-induced change and threat rigidity'. In L. L. Cummings and B. M. Staw (eds.), *Research in Organizational Behavior*, Vol. 17. JAI Press, Greenwich, CT, pp. 287–331.

Ross, L. and R. E. Nisbett (1991). *The Person and the Situation: Perspectives of Social Psychology*.

McGraw-Hill, New York.

Rumelt, R. P. (1984). 'Towards a strategic theory of the firm'. In R. B. Lamb (ed.), *Competitive Strategic Management*. Prentice-Hall, Englewood Cliffs, NJ, pp. 556–570.

Rumelt, R. P., D. Schendel and D. J. Teece (1994). *Fundamental Issues in Strategy*. Harvard Business School Press, Boston, MA.

Schein, E. (1985). *Organizational Culture and Leadership*. Jossey-Bass, San Francisco, CA.

Schelling, T. C. (1960). *The Strategy of Conflict*. Oxford University Press, London.

Scott, W. R. (1992). *Organizations: Rational, Natural, and Open Systems* (3rd ed.). Prentice-Hall, Englewood Cliffs, NJ.

Scott, W. R. (1995). *Institutions and Organizations*. Sage, Thousand Oaks, CA.

Selznick, P. (1957). *Leadership in Administration*. Row, Peterson, Evanston, IL.

Shiffrin, R. M. and M. W. Schneider (1977). 'Controlled and automatic human information processing. II. Perceptual learning, automatic attending, and a general theory', *Psychological Review*, **84**, pp. 127–190.

Simon, H. A. (1947). *Administrative Behavior: A Study of Decision-making Processes in Administrative Organizations*. Macmillan, Chicago, IL.

Simon, H. A. (1957). *Models of Man*. Wiley, New York.

Stinchcombe, A. L. (1968). *Constructing Social Theories*. Chicago University Press, Chicago, IL.

Sutton, R. M. and A. Hargadon (1996). 'Brainstorming groups in context: Effectiveness in a product design firm', *Administrative Science Quarterly*, **41**, pp. 685–718.

Swidler, A. (1986). 'Culture in action: Symbols and strategies', *American Sociological Review*, **51**, pp. 273–286.

Walsh, J. P. and G. R. Ungson (1991). 'Organizational memory', *Academy of Management Review*, **16**, pp. 57–91.

Weick, K. M. (1979). *The Social Psychology of Organizing* (2nd edn.). Random House, New York.

Weick, K. M. (1995). *Sensemaking in Organizations*. Sage, Thousand Oaks, CA.

Wade, J. B., C. A. O'Reilly and I. Chandratat (1990). 'Golden parachutes: CEOs and the exercise of social influence', *Administrative Science Quarterly*, **35**, pp. 587–603.

Wernerfelt, B. (1984). 'A resource-based view of the firm', *Strategic Management Journal*, **5**(2), pp. 171–180.

Westphal, J. and E. J. Zajac (1995). 'Who shall govern? CEO/Board power, demographic similarity, and new director selection', *Administrative Science Quarterly*, **40**, pp. 60–83.

White, H. C. (1992). *Identity and Control: A Structural Theory of Social Action*. Princeton University Press, Princeton, NJ.

Yates, J.-A. (1989). *Control through Communication: The Rise of System in American Management*. Johns Hopkins University Press, Baltimore, MD.

Part II
Innovation, Entrepreneurship and Renewal

What separates high-growth companies from the pack is the way managers make sense of how they do business.

Value Innovation:
The Strategic Logic of High Growth

by W. Chan Kim and Renée Mauborgne

After a decade of downsizing and increasingly intense competition, profitable growth is a tremendous challenge many companies face. Why do some companies achieve sustained high growth in both revenues and profits? In a five-year study of high-growth companies and their less successful competitors, we found that the answer lies in the way each group approached strategy. The difference in approach was not a matter of managers choosing one analytical tool or planning model over another. The difference was in the companies' fundamental, implicit assumptions about strategy. The less successful companies took a conventional approach: their strategic thinking was dominated by the idea of staying ahead of the competition. In stark contrast, the high-growth companies paid little attention to matching or beating their rivals. Instead, they sought to make their competitors irrelevant through a strategic logic we call *value innovation*.

Consider Bert Claeys, a Belgian company that operates movie theaters. From the 1960s to the 1980s, the movie theater industry in Belgium was declining steadily. With the spread of videocassette recorders and satellite and cable television, the average Belgian's moviegoing dropped from eight to two times per year. By the 1980s, many cinema operators (COs) were forced to shut down.

The COs that remained found themselves competing head-to-head for a shrinking market. All took similar actions. They turned cinemas into multiplexes with as many as ten screens, broadened their film offerings to attract all customer segments, expanded their food and drink services, and increased showing times.

Those attempts to leverage existing assets became irrelevant in 1988, when Bert Claeys created Kinepolis. Neither an ordinary cinema nor a multiplex, Kinepolis is the world's first megaplex, with 25 screens and 7,600 seats. By offering moviegoers a radically superior experience, Kinepolis won 50% of the market in Brussels in its first year and expanded the market by about 40%. Today many Belgians refer not to a night at the movies but to an evening at Kinepolis.

Consider the differences between Kinepolis and other Belgian movie theaters. The typical Belgian multiplex has small viewing rooms that often have no more than 100 seats, screens that measure 7 meters by 5 meters, and 35-millimeter projection equipment. Viewing rooms at Kinepolis have up to 700 seats, and there is so much legroom that viewers do not have to move when someone passes by.

W. Chan Kim is the Boston Consulting Group Bruce D. Henderson Professor of International Management at INSEAD in Fontainebleau, France. Renée Mauborgne is a senior research fellow in strategy and international management at INSEAD. Their previous HBR article was "Parables of Leadership" (July-August 1992).

DRAWING BY HAROLD LEE MILLER

Researching the Roots of High Growth

Over the last five years, we studied more than 30 companies around the world in approximately 30 industries. We looked at companies with high growth in both revenues and profits and companies with less successful performance records. In an effort to explain the difference in performance between the two groups of companies, we interviewed hundreds of managers, analysts, and researchers. We built strategic, organizational, and performance profiles. We looked for industry or organization patterns. And we compared the two groups of companies along dimensions that are often thought to be related to a company's potential for growth. Did private companies grow more quickly than public ones? What was the impact on companies of the overall growth of their industry? Did entrepreneurial start-ups have an edge over established incumbents? Were companies led by creative, young radicals likely to grow faster than those run by older managers?

We found that none of those factors mattered in a systematic way. High growth was achieved by both small and large organizations by companies in high-tech and low-tech industries, by new entrants and incumbents, by private and public companies, and by companies from various countries.

What did matter—consistently—was the way managers in the two groups of companies thought about strategy. In interviewing the managers, we asked them to describe the strategic moves and the thinking behind them. Thus we came to understand their views on each of the five textbook dimensions of strategy industry assumptions, strategic focus, customers, assets and capabilities, and product and service offerings. We were struck by what emerged from our content analysis of those interviews. The managers of the high-growth companies—irrespective of their industry—all described what we have come to call the logic of value innovation. The managers of the less successful companies all thought along conventional strategic lines.

Intrigued by that finding we went on to test whether the managers of the high-growth companies applied their strategic thinking to business initiatives in the marketplace. We found that they did.

Furthermore in studying the business launches of about 100 companies, we were able to quantify the impact of value innovation on a company's growth in both revenues and profits. Although 86% of the launches were line extensions—that is, incremental improvements—they accounted for 62% of total revenues and only 39% of total profits. The remaining 14% of the launches—the true value innovations—generated 38% of total revenues and a whopping 61% of total profits.

Bert Claeys installed oversized seats with individual armrests and designed a steep slope in the floor to ensure everyone an unobstructed view. At Kinepolis, screens measure up to 29 meters by 10 meters and rest on their own foundations so that sound vibrations are not transmitted from one screen to another. Many viewing rooms have 70-millimeter projection equipment and state-of-the-art sound equipment. And Bert Claeys challenged the industry's conventional wisdom about the importance of prime, city-center real estate by locating Kinepolis off the ring road circling Brussels, 15 minutes from downtown. Patrons park for free in large, well-lit lots. The company was prepared to lose out on foot traffic in order to solve a major problem for the majority of moviegoers in Brussels: the scarcity and high cost of parking.

Bert Claeys can offer this radically superior cinema experience without increasing the price of tickets because the concept of the megaplex results in one of the lowest cost structures in the industry. The average cost to build a seat at Kinepolis is about 70,000 Belgian francs, less than half the industry's average in Brussels. Why? The megaplex's location outside the city is cheaper; its size gives it economies in purchasing, more leverage with film distributors, and better overall margins; and with 25 screens served by a central ticketing and lobby area, Kinepolis achieves economies in personnel and overhead. Furthermore, the company spends very little on advertising because its value innovation generates a lot of word-of-mouth praise.

Within its supposedly unattractive industry, Kinepolis has achieved spectacular growth and profits. Belgian moviegoers now go to the cinema more frequently because of Kinepolis, and people who never went to the movies have been drawn into the market. Instead of battling competitors over targeted segments of the market, Bert Claeys made the competition irrelevant. (See the chart "How Kinepolis Achieves Profitable Growth.")

Why did other Belgian COs fail to seize that opportunity? Like the others, Bert Claeys was an incumbent with sunk investments: a network of cinemas across Belgium. In fact, Kinepolis would have represented a smaller investment for some COs than it did for Bert Claeys. Most COs were thinking—implicitly or explicitly—along these lines: The industry is shrinking, so we should not make major investments – especially in fixed assets. But we can improve our performance by outdoing our competitors on each of the key dimensions of competition. We must have better films, better services, and better marketing.

Bert Claeys followed a different strategic logic. The company set out to make its cinema experience not better than that at competitors' theaters but completely different – and irresistible. The company thought as if it were a new entrant to the market. It sought to reach the mass of moviegoers by focusing on widely shared needs. In order to give most moviegoers a package they would value highly, the company put aside conventional thinking about what a theater is supposed to look like. And the company did all that while reducing its costs. That's the logic behind value innovation.

Conventional Logic Versus Value Innovation

Conventional strategic logic and the logic of value innovation differ along the five basic dimensions of strategy. Those differences determine which questions managers ask, what opportunities they see and pursue, and how they understand risk. (See the table "Two Strategic Logics.")

Industry Assumptions. Many companies take their industry's conditions as given and set strategy accordingly. Value innovators don't. No matter how the rest of the industry is faring, value innovators look for blockbuster ideas and quantum leaps in value. Had Bert Claeys, for example, taken its industry's conditions as given, it would never have created a megaplex. The company would have followed the endgame strategy of milking its business or the zero-sum strategy of competing for share in a shrinking market. Instead, through Kinepolis, the company transcended the industry's conditions.

Strategic Focus. Many companies let competitors set the parameters of their strategic thinking. They compare their strengths and weaknesses with those of their competitors and focus on building advantages. Consider this example. For years, the major U.S. television networks used the same format for news programming. All aired shows in the same time slot and competed on their analysis of events, the professionalism with which they delivered the news, and the popularity of their anchors. In 1980, CNN came on the scene with a focus on creating a quantum leap in value, not on competing with the networks. CNN replaced the networks' format with real-time news from around the world 24 hours a day. CNN not only emerged as the leader in global news broadcasting – and created new de-

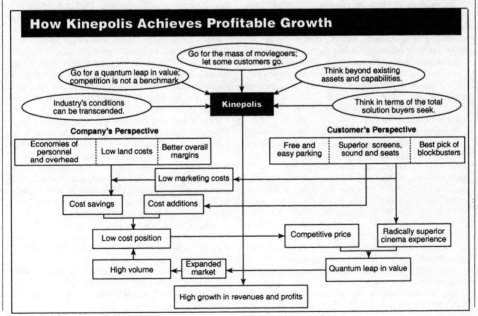

How Kinepolis Achieves Profitable Growth

Two Strategic Logics

The Five Dimensions of Strategy	Conventional Logic	Value Innovation Logic
Industry Assumptions	Industry's conditions are given.	Industry's conditions can be shaped.
Strategic Focus	A company should build competitive advantages. The aim is to beat the competition.	Competition is not the benchmark. A company should pursue a quantum leap in value to dominate the market.
Customers	A company should retain and expand its customer base through further segmentation and customization. It should focus on the differences in what customers value.	A value innovator targets the mass of buyers and willingly lets some existing customers go. It focuses on the key commonalities in what customers value.
Assets and Capabilities	A company should leverage its existing assets and capabilities.	A company must not be constrained by what it already has. It must ask, What would we do if we were starting anew?
Product and Service Offerings	An industry's traditional boundaries determine the products and services a company offers. The goal is to maximize the value of those offerings.	A value innovator thinks in terms of the total solution customers seek, even if that takes the company beyond its industry's traditional offerings.

mand around the world – but also was able to produce 24 hours of real-time news for one-fifth the cost of 1 hour of network news.

Conventional logic leads companies to compete at the margin for incremental share. The logic of value innovation starts with an ambition to dominate the market by offering a tremendous leap in value. Value innovators never say, Here's what competitors are doing; let's do this in response. They monitor competitors but do not use them as benchmarks. Hasso Plattner, vice chairman of SAP, the global leader in business-application software, puts it this way: "I'm not interested in whether we are better than the competition. The real test is, will most buyers still seek out our products even if we don't market them?"

Because value innovators do not focus on competing, they can distinguish the factors that deliver superior value from all the factors the industry competes on. They do not expend their resources to offer certain product and service features just because that is what their rivals are doing. CNN, for example, decided not to compete with the networks in the race to get big-name anchors. Companies that follow the logic of value innovation free up their resources to identify and deliver completely new sources of value. Ironically, value innovators do not set out to build advantages over the competition, but they end up achieving the greatest competitive advantages.

Customers. Many companies seek growth through retaining and expanding their customer

bases. This often leads to finer segmentation and greater customization of offerings to meet specialized needs. Value innovation follows a different logic. Instead of focusing on the differences among customers, value innovators build on the powerful commonalities in the features that customers value. In the words of a senior executive at the French hotelier Accor, "We focus on what unites customers. Customers' differences often prevent you from seeing what's most important." Value innovators believe that most people will put their differences aside if they are offered a considerable increase in value. Those companies shoot for the core of the market, even if it means that they lose some of their customers.

Assets and Capabilities. Many companies view business opportunities through the lens of their existing assets and capabilities. They ask, Given what we have, what is the best we can do? In contrast, value innovators ask, What if we start anew? That is the question the British company Virgin Group put to itself in the late 1980s. The company had a sizable chain of small music stores across the United Kingdom when it came up with the idea of megastores for music and entertainment, which would offer customers a tremendous leap in value. Seeing that its small stores could not be leveraged to seize that opportunity, the company decided to sell off the entire chain. As one of Virgin's executive puts it, "We don't let what we can do today condition our view of what it takes to win tomorrow. We take a clean-slate approach."

This is not to say that value innovators never leverage their existing assets and capabilities. They often do. But, more important, they assess business opportunities without being biased or constrained by where they are at a given moment. For that reason, value innovators not only have more insight into where value for buyers resides – and how it is changing – but also are much more likely to act on that insight.

Product and Service Offerings. Conventional competition takes place within clearly established boundaries defined by the products and services the industry traditionally offers. Value innovators often cross those boundaries. They think in terms of the total solution buyers seek, and they try to overcome the chief compromises their industry forces customers to make – as Bert Claeys did by providing free parking. A senior executive at Compaq Computer describes the approach: "We continually ask where our products and services fit in the total chain of buyers' solutions. We seek to solve buyers' major problems across the entire chain, even if that takes us into a new business. We are not limited by the industry's definition of what we should and should not do."

Creating a New Value Curve

How does the logic of value innovation translate into a company's offerings in the marketplace? Consider the case of Accor. In the mid-1980s, the budget hotel industry in France was suffering from stagnation and overcapacity. Accor's cochairmen, Paul Dubrule and Gérard Pélisson, challenged the company's managers to create a quantum leap in value for customers. The managers were urged to forget everything they knew about the existing rules, practices, and traditions of the industry. They were asked what they would do if Accor were starting fresh.

In 1985, when Accor launched Formule 1, a line of budget hotels, there were two distinct market segments in the budget hotel industry. One segment consisted of no-star and one-star hotels, whose average price per room was between 60 and 90 French francs. Customers came to those hotels just for the low price. The other segment was two-star hotels, with an average price of 200 francs per room. Those more expensive hotels attracted customers by offering a better sleeping environment than the no-star and one-star hotels. People had come to expect that they would get what they paid for: either they would pay more and get a decent night's sleep or they would pay less and put up with poor beds and noise.

Accor's managers began by identifying what customers of all budget hotels – no-star, one-star, and two-star – wanted: a good night's sleep for a low price. Focusing on those widely shared needs, Accor's managers saw the opportunity to overcome the chief compromise that the industry forced customers to make. They asked themselves the following four questions:

☐ Which of the factors that our industry takes for granted should be eliminated?

☐ Which factors should be reduced well below the industry's standard?

☐ Which factors should be raised well above the industry's standard?

☐ Which factors should be created that the industry has never offered?

The first question forces managers to consider whether the factors that companies compete on actually deliver value to consumers. Often those factors are taken for granted, even though they have no value or even detract from value. Sometimes what buyers value changes fundamentally, but companies that are focused on benchmarking one another do not act on – or even perceive – the change. The second question forces managers to determine whether products and services have been overdesigned in the race to match and beat the competition. The third question pushes managers to uncover and eliminate the compromises their industry forces customers to make. The fourth question helps managers break out of the industry's established boundaries to discover entirely new sources of value for consumers.

In answering the questions, Accor came up with a new concept for a hotel, which led to the launch of Formule 1. First, the company eliminated such standard hotel features as costly restaurants and appealing lounges. Accor reckoned that even though it might lose some customers, most people would do without those features.

Accor's managers believed that budget hotels were overserving customers along other dimensions as well. On those, Formule 1 offers less than many no-star hotels do. For example, receptionists are on hand only during peak check-in and check-out hours. At all other times, customers use an automated teller. Rooms at a Formule 1 hotel are small and equipped only with a bed and bare necessities – no stationery, desks, or decorations. Instead of closets and dressers, there are a few shelves and a pole for clothing in one corner of the room. The rooms themselves are modular blocks manufactured in a factory – a method that results in economies of scale in production, high quality control, and good sound insulation.

VALUE INNOVATION

Formule 1 gives Accor considerable cost advantages. The company cut in half the average cost of building a room, and its staff costs dropped from between 25% and 35% of sales – the industry's average – to between 20% and 23%. Those cost savings have allowed Accor to improve the features customers value most to levels beyond those of the average French two-star hotel, but the price is only marginally above that of one-star hotels.

Customers have rewarded Accor for its value innovation. The company has not only captured the mass of French budget-hotel customers but also expanded the market. From truck drivers who previously slept in their vehicles to businesspeople needing a few hours of rest, new customers have been drawn to the budget category. Formule 1 made the competition irrelevant. At last count, Formule 1's market share in France was greater than the sum of the five next-largest players.

The extent of Accor's departure from the conventional logic of its industry can be seen in what we call a *value curve* – a graphic depiction of a company's relative performance across its industry's key success factors. (See the graph "Formule 1's Value Curve.") According to the conventional logic of competition, an industry's value curve follows one basic shape. Rivals try to improve value by offering a little more for a little less, but most don't challenge the shape of the curve.

Like Accor, all the high-performing companies we studied created fundamentally new and superior value curves. They achieved that by a combination of eliminating features, creating features, and reducing and raising others to levels unprecedented in their industries. Take, for example, SAP, a business-application-software company that was started in the early 1970s by five former IBM employees in Walldorf, Germany, and became the worldwide industry leader. Until the 1980s, business-application-software makers focused on subsegmenting the market and customizing their offerings to meet buyers' functional needs, such as production management, logistics, human resources, and payroll.

While most software companies were focusing on improving the performance of particular application products, SAP took aim at the mass of buyers. Instead of competing on customers' differences, SAP sought out important commonalities in what customers value. The company correctly hypothesized that for most customers, the performance advantages of highly customized, individual software modules had been overestimated. Such modules forfeited the efficiency and information advantages of an integrated system, which allows real-time data exchange across a company.

In 1979, SAP launched R/2, a line of real-time, integrated business-application software for mainframe computers. R/2 has no restriction on the platform of the host hardware; buyers can capitalize on the best hardware available and reduce their maintenance costs dramatically. Most important, R/2 leads to huge gains in accuracy and efficiency because a company needs to enter its data only once. And R/2 improves the flow of information. A sales manager, for example, can find out when a product will be delivered and why it is late by cross-referencing the production database. SAP's growth and profits have exceed-

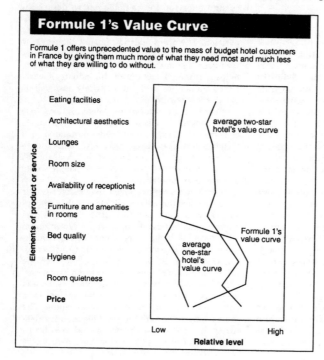

Formule 1's Value Curve

Formule 1 offers unprecedented value to the mass of budget hotel customers in France by giving them much more of what they need most and much less of what they are willing to do without.

Elements of product or service:
Eating facilities
Architectural aesthetics
Lounges
Room size
Availability of receptionist
Furniture and amenities in rooms
Bed quality
Hygiene
Room quietness
Price

average two-star hotel's value curve
Formule 1's value curve
average one-star hotel's value curve

Low   High
Relative level

HARVARD BUSINESS REVIEW   January-February 1997

ed its industry's. In 1992, SAP achieved a new value innovation with R/3, a line of software for the client-server market.

The Trap of Competing, the Necessity of Repeating

What happens once a company has created a new value curve? Sooner or later, the competition tries to imitate it. In many industries, value innovators do not face a credible challenge for many years, but in others, rivals appear more quickly. Eventually, however, a value innovator will find its growth and profits under attack. Too often, in an attempt to defend its hard-earned customer base, the company launches offenses. But the imitators often persist, and the value innovator – despite its best intentions – may end up in a race to beat the competition. Obsessed with hanging on to market share, the company may fall into the trap of conventional strategic logic. If the company doesn't find its way out of the trap, the basic shape of its value curve will begin to look just like those of its rivals.

Consider the following example. When Compaq Computer launched its first personal computer in 1983, most PC buyers were sophisticated corporate users and technology enthusiasts. IBM had defined the industry's value curve. Compaq's first offering – the first IBM-compatible PC – represented a completely new value curve. Compaq's product not only was technologically superb but also was priced roughly 15% below IBM's. Within three years of its start-up, Compaq joined the *Fortune* 500. No other company had ever achieved that status as quickly.

How did IBM respond? It tried to match and beat Compaq's value curve. And Compaq, determined to defend itself, became focused on beating IBM. But while IBM and Compaq were battling over feature enhancements, most buyers were becoming more sensitive to price. User-friendliness was becoming more important to customers than the latest technology. Compaq's focus on competing with IBM led the company to produce a line of PCs that were overengineered and overpriced for most buyers. When IBM walked off the cliff in the late 1980s, Compaq was following close behind.

Could Compaq have foreseen the need to create another value innovation rather than go head-to-head against IBM? If Compaq had monitored the industry's value curves, it would have realized that by the mid to late 1980s, IBM's and other PC makers' value curves were converging with its own. And by the late 1980s, the curves were nearly identical. That should have been the signal to Compaq that it was time for another quantum leap.

Monitoring value curves may also keep a company from pursuing innovation when there is still a huge profit stream to be collected from its current offering. In some rapidly emerging industries, companies must innovate frequently. In many other industries, companies can harvest their successes for a long time: a radically different value curve is difficult for incumbents to imitate, and the volume advantages that come with value innovation make imitation costly. Kinepolis, Formule 1, and CNN, for example, have enjoyed uncontested dominance for a long time. CNN's value innovation was not challenged for almost ten years. Yet we have seen companies pursue novelty for novelty's sake, driven by internal pressures to leverage unique competencies or to apply the latest technology. Value innovation is about offering unprecedented value, not technology or competencies. It is not the same as being first to market.

When a company's value curve is fundamentally different from that of the rest of the industry – and the difference is valued by most customers – managers should resist innovation. Instead, companies should embark on geographic expansion and operational improvements to achieve maximum economies of scale and market coverage. That approach discourages imitation and allows companies to tap the potential of their current value innovation. Bert Claeys, for example, has been rapidly rolling out and improving its Kinepolis concept with Metropolis, a megaplex in Antwerp, and with megaplexes in many countries in Europe and Asia. And Accor has already built more than 300 Formule 1 hotels across Europe, Africa, and Australia. The company is now targeting Asia.

The Three Platforms

The companies we studied that were most successful at repeating value innovation were those that took advantage of all three platforms on which value innovation can take place: product, service, and delivery. The precise meaning of the three platforms varies across industries and companies, but, in general, the product platform is the physical product; the service platform is support such as maintenance, customer service, warranties, and training for distributors and retailers; and the delivery platform includes logistics and the channel used to deliver the product to customers.

Too often, managers trying to create a value innovation focus on the product platform and ignore the other two. Over time, that approach is not likely to yield many opportunities for repeated value innovation. As customers and technologies change, each

How Has Compaq Stayed on Top of the Server Industry?

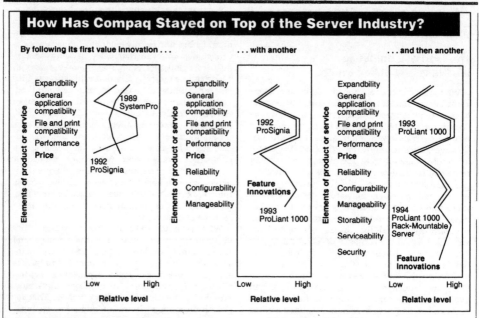

By following its first value innovation . . .   . . . with another   . . . and then another

platform presents new possibilities. Just as good farmers rotate their crops, good value innovators rotate their value platforms. (See the insert "Virgin Atlantic: Flying in the Face of Conventional Logic.")

The story of Compaq's server business, which was part of the company's successful comeback, illustrates how the three platforms can be used alternately over time to create new value curves. (See the graph "How Has Compaq Stayed on Top of the Server Industry?") In late 1989, Compaq introduced its first server, the SystemPro, which was designed to run five network operating systems–SCO UNIX, OS/2, Vines, NetWare, and DOS – and many application programs. Like the SystemPro, most servers could handle many operating systems and application programs. Compaq observed, however, that the majority of customers used only a small fraction of a server's capacity. After identifying the needs that cut across the mass of users, Compaq decided to build a radically simplified server that would be optimized to run NetWare and file and print only. Launched in 1992, the ProSignia was a value innovation on the product platform. The new server gave buyers twice the SystemPro's file-and-print performance at one-third the price. Compaq achieved that value innovation mainly by reducing general application compatibility–a reduction that translated into much lower manufacturing costs.

As competitors tried to imitate the ProSignia and value curves in the industry began to converge, Compaq took another leap, this time from the service platform. Viewing its servers not as stand-alone products but as elements of its customers' total computing needs, Compaq saw that 90% of customers' costs were in servicing networks and only 10% were in the server hardware itself. Yet Compaq, like other companies in the industry, had been focusing on maximizing the price-performance ratio of the server hardware, the least costly element for buyers.

Compaq redeployed its resources to bring out the ProLiant 1000, a server that incorporates two innovative pieces of software. The first, SmartStart, configures server hardware and network information to suit a company's operating system and application programs. It slashes the time it takes a customer to configure a server network and makes installation virtually error-free so that servers perform reliably from day one. The second piece of software, Insight Manager, helps customers manage their server networks by, for example, spotting overheating boards or troubled disk drives before they break down.

By innovating on the service platform, Compaq created a superior value curve and expanded its market. Companies lacking expertise in informa-

VALUE INNOVATION

tion technology had been skeptical of their ability to configure and manage a network server. Smart-Start and Insight Manager helped put those companies at ease. The ProLiant 1000 came out a winner.

As more and more companies acquired servers, Compaq observed that its customers often lacked the space to store the equipment properly. Stuffed into closets or left on the floor with tangled wires, expensive servers were often damaged, were certainly not secure, and were difficult to service.

By focusing on customer value – not on competitors – Compaq saw that it was time for another value innovation on the product platform. The company introduced the ProLiant 1000 Rack-Mountable Server, which allows companies to store servers in a tall, lean cabinet in a central location. The product makes efficient use of space and ensures that machines are protected and are easy to monitor, repair, and enhance. Compaq designed the rack mount to fit both its products and those of other manufacturers, thus attracting even more buyers and discouraging imitation. The company's sales

and profits rose again as its new value curve diverged from the industry's.

Compaq is now looking to the delivery platform for a value innovation that will dramatically reduce the lead time between a customer's order and the arrival of the equipment. Lead times have forced customers to forecast their needs – a difficult task – and have often required them to patch together costly solutions while waiting for their orders to be filled. Now that servers are widely used and the demands placed on them are multiplying rapidly, Compaq believes that shorter lead times will provide a quantum leap in value for customers. The company is currently working on a delivery option that will permit its products to be built to customers' specifications and shipped within 48 hours of the order. That value innovation will allow Compaq to reduce its inventory costs and minimize the accumulation of outdated stock.

By achieving value innovations on all three platforms, Compaq has been able to maintain a gap between its value curve and those of other players.

Virgin Atlantic: Flying in the Face of Conventional Logic

When Virgin Atlantic Airways challenged its industry's conventional logic by eliminating first-class service in 1984, the airline was simply following the logic of value innovation. Most of the industry's profitable revenue came from business class, not first class. And first class was a big cost generator. Virgin spotted an opportunity. The airline decided to channel the cost it would save by cutting first-class service into value innovation for business-class passengers.

First, Virgin introduced large, reclining sleeper seats, raising seat comfort in business class well above the industry's standard. Second, Virgin offered free transportation to and from the airport – initially in chauffeured limousines and later in specially designed motorcycles called LimoBikes – to speed business-class passengers through snarled city traffic.

With those innovations, which were on the product and service platforms, Virgin attracted not only a large share of the industry's business-class customers but also some full-economy-fare and first-class passengers of other airlines. Virgin's value innovation separated the company from the pack for many years, but the competition did not stand still. As the value curves of some other airlines began converging with Virgin's value curve, the company went for another leap in value, this time from the service platform.

Virgin observed that most business-class passengers want to use their time productively before and be-

tween flights and that, after long-haul flights, they want to freshen up and change their wrinkled clothes before going to meetings. The airline designed lounges where passengers can have their clothes pressed, take showers, enjoy massages, and use state-of-the-art office equipment. The service allows busy executives to make good use of their time and go directly to meetings without first stopping at their hotels-a tremendous value for customers that generates high volume for Virgin. The airline has one of the highest sales per employee in the industry, and its costs per passenger mile are among the lowest. The economics of value innovation create a positive and reinforcing cycle.

When Virgin first challenged the industry's assumptions, its ideas were met with a great deal of skepticism. After all, conventional wisdom says that in order to grow, a company must embrace *more*, not fewer, market segments. But Virgin deliberately walked away from the revenue generated by first-class passengers. And it further violated conventional wisdom by conceiving of its business in terms of customer solutions, even if that took the company well beyond an airline's traditional offerings. Virgin has applied the logic of value innovation not just to the airline industry but also to insurance and to music and entertainment retailing. Virgin has always done more than leverage its existing assets and capabilities. The company has been a consistent value innovator.

Despite the pace of competition in its industry, Compaq's repeated value innovations are allowing the company to remain the number one maker of servers worldwide. Since the company's turnaround, overall sales and profits have almost quadrupled.

Driving a Company for High Growth

One of the most striking findings of our research is that despite the profound impact of a company's strategic logic, that logic is often not articulated. And because it goes unstated and unexamined, a company does not necessarily apply a consistent strategic logic across its businesses.

How can senior executives promote value innovation? First, they must identify and articulate the company's prevailing strategic logic. Then they must challenge it. They must stop and think about the industry's assumptions, the company's strategic focus, and the approaches – to customers, assets and capabilities, and product and service offerings – that are taken as given. Having reframed the company's strategic logic around value innovation, senior executives must ask the four questions that translate that thinking into a new value curve: Which of the factors that our industry takes for granted should be eliminated? Which factors should be reduced well below the industry's standard? Which should be raised well above the industry's standard? What factors should be created that the industry has never offered? Asking the full set of questions – rather than singling out one or two – is necessary for profitable growth. Value innovation is the simultaneous pursuit of radically superior value for buyers and lower costs for companies.

For managers of diversified corporations, the logic of value innovation can be used to identify the most promising possibilities for growth across a portfolio of businesses. The value innovators we studied all have been pioneers in their industries, not necessarily in developing new technologies but in pushing the value they offer customers to new frontiers. Extending the pioneer metaphor can provide a useful way of talking about the growth potential of current and future businesses.

A company's *pioneers* are the businesses that offer unprecedented value. They are the most power-

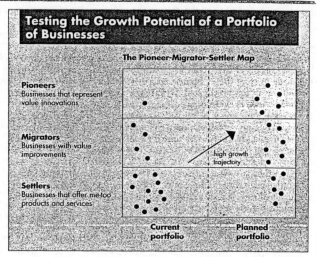

Testing the Growth Potential of a Portfolio of Businesses

The Pioneer-Migrator-Settler Map

Pioneers
Businesses that represent value innovations

Migrators
Businesses with value improvements

Settlers
Businesses that offer me-too products and services

high growth trajectory

Current portfolio   Planned portfolio

ful sources of profitable growth. At the other extreme are *settlers* – businesses with value curves that conform to the basic shape of the industry's. Settlers will not generally contribute much to a company's growth. The potential of *migrators* lies somewhere in between. Such businesses extend the industry's curve by giving customers more for less, but they don't alter its basic shape.

A useful exercise for a management team pursuing growth is to plot the company's current and planned portfolios on a pioneer-migrator-settler map. (See the chart "Testing the Growth Potential of a Portfolio of Businesses.") If both the current portfolio and the planned offerings consist mainly of settlers, the company has a low growth trajectory and needs to push for value innovation. The company may well have fallen into the trap of competing. If current and planned offerings consist of a lot of migrators, reasonable growth can be expected. But the company is not exploiting its potential for growth and risks being marginalized by a value innovator. This exercise is especially valuable for managers who want to see beyond today's performance numbers. Revenue, profitability, market share, and customer satisfaction are all measures of a company's current position. Contrary to what conventional strategic thinking suggests, those measures cannot point the way to the future. The pioneer-migrator-settler map can help a company predict and plan future growth and profit, a task that is especially difficult – and crucial – in a fast-changing economy.   ☐

Reprint 97108   To place an order, call 1-800-545-7685.

[8]

Strategic Innovation

Constantinos Markides

By breaking the rules of the game and thinking of new ways to compete, a company can strategically redefine its business and catch its bigger competitors off guard. The trick is not to play the game better than the competition but to develop and play an altogether different game.

In spring 1902, Jim Penney opened his first dry-goods store in Kemmerer, Wyoming, and began his attack on the big retail chains of the time, including Sears and Woolworth, which date back to 1886 and 1879, respectively. By 1940, J.C. Penney had grown to 1,586 stores and annual sales of $302 million.

• In January 1936, Lever Bros., a subsidiary of Unilever, introduced a new food product in the U.S. market, a vegetable shortening called Spry. The new product went up against Procter & Gamble's established market leader, Crisco, which had been introduced in 1912. Spry's impact was phenomenal: in a single year, it had reached half the market share of Crisco.

• In the early 1960s, Canon, a camera manufacturer, entered the photocopier market — a field totally dominated by Xerox. By the early 1980s, having seen such formidable competitors as IBM and Kodak attack this same market without much success, Canon emerged as the market leader in unit sales. Today, it is a close second to Xerox.

• In 1972, Texas Instruments, a semiconductor chip supplier, entered the calculator business — a field already occupied by Hewlett-Packard, Casio, Commodore, Sanyo, Toshiba, and Rockwell. Within five years, TI was the market leader.

• In 1976, Apple introduced the Apple II in direct competition to IBM, Wang, and Hewlett-Packard in the professional and small business segment and Atari, Commodore, and Tandy in the home segment. Within five years, Apple had become the market leader.

• In 1982, Gannett Company Inc. introduced a new newspaper into a crowded field of 1,700 dailies. By 1993, *USA Today* had become a top-selling newspaper with an estimated 5 million daily readers.

• In 1987, Howard Schultz bought Starbucks Coffee from the original owners. In the next five years, he transformed the company from a chain of 11 stores to some 280 stores in 1993. Sale revenues grew from $1.3 million in 1987 to $163.5 million in 1993.

• In the late 1980s, Yamaha tried to revitalize its declining piano business by developing digital technology so customers could either record live performances by the pianists they'd chosen or buy such recordings on diskettes and play the same composition on their pianos. Sales in Japan have been explosive.

These are certainly nice success stories, but there is more to them than that. The common theme underpinning all these accounts is simple: the companies succeeded dramatically in attacking an established industry leader *without* the help of a radical technological innovation. This feat is not easy. Existing academic evidence shows that attacks on established leaders usually end up in failure — notwithstanding recent well-publicized cases of market leaders, such as IBM and General Motors, losing big to new competitors.[1] A series of studies show that the probability of a first-ranked firm in a particular industry surviving in first place is about 96 percent — almost a certainty.[2] For the second-ranked firm, the probability of survival is

Constantinos Markides is associate professor of strategic and international management, London Business School.

91 percent, and for the third-ranked firm, 80 percent. In fact, most of the turnover that occurs among the top five in an industry is due to mergers rather than to new entrants that outcompete market leaders.

Thus, despite some well-documented cases of dramatic success in competing with an industry leader (e.g., Xerox versus Canon or Caterpillar versus Komatsu), the vast majority of attackers fail quite miserably, while established leaders hang on to their market shares for

> The vast majority of attackers fail quite miserably, while established leaders hang on to their market shares for long periods.

long periods. This is exactly the reason why the success stories I first mentioned are so interesting. Not only have the companies not failed in attacking the established leaders, they have actually succeeded in dramatically increasing their market share and sometimes even emerged as the new industry leader. And they did all this without riding the wave of technological discontinuity. How did they do it?

The Common Element

After studying more than thirty successful attackers, I believe that the simple answer is that they broke the rules of the game in their industry. The common element in all the successful attacks is *strategic innovation*. Significant shifts in market share and fortunes occur not because companies try to play the game better than the competition but because they change the rules of the game.

Consider, for example, the case of Canon. Back in the 1960s, Xerox had a lock on the copier market by following a well-defined, successful strategy. The main elements of Xerox's strategy were: It segmented the market by copier volume and consciously decided to go after the high-speed copier market to tap the corporate reproduction market. This inevitably defined its customers as the big corporations, which by itself determined the distribution method that Xerox adopt-

ed — a direct salesforce. At the same time, Xerox decided to lease rather than sell its machines, a strategic choice that had worked well for the company in its earlier battles with 3M.

This strategy proved to be so successful that several new competitors, such as IBM and Kodak, tried to enter this huge market by adopting the same or similar strategies. Canon, on the other hand, decided to play the game differently. It segmented the market by end user and targeted small and medium-sized businesses, while also producing personal copiers for individuals. Canon also decided to sell its machines outright through a dealer network, and, while Xerox emphasized the speed of its machines, it concentrated on quality and price as its differentiating features. As a result, whereas IBM and Kodak failed to make any significant inroads in the market, Canon emerged as the leader, in unit sales, within twenty years of attacking Xerox.

Another classic example of a company breaking the rules of the game in its industry is Apple Computer. In the mid-1970s, the established leader in the computer business was IBM. The main elements of the successful IBM strategy were to target corporations as customers; to manufacture the heart of the IBM computer, the microprocessor; to write its own software programs; and to sell the computers through a direct salesforce. Apple totally changed these norms: it targeted individuals and small businesses as its customers, purchased its microprocessors from an outside source, and distributed its machines through retail stores across the country. Apple quickly emerged as the new market leader.

There are many other examples of companies that broke the rules. Dell Computer bypassed intermediaries and sold directly to the end consumer. Hanes Corporation created a totally new distribution outlet for women's pantyhose — supermarkets and drugstores. Nucor Steel completely rethought the steel fabricating process and formed minimills. Toyota developed a new inventory and manufacturing philosophy in the car industry. Medco Containment Services provided companies with prescription drugs through the mail rather than through retail drugstores. Perdue differentiated what was widely considered a commodity, chickens. Timex sold cheap watches through drugstores. Southwest Airlines flew point to point rather than using the hub-and-spoke system.

These examples highlight my thesis: without the benefit of a new technological innovation, it is extremely difficult for any firm to successfully attack the established industry leaders or to successfully enter a new market where established players exist. The strategy that seems to improve the probability of success in those situations is the strategy of breaking the rules — strategic innovation.

However, it is *not* enough to proclaim the virtues of breaking the rules and to prompt companies to "just do it." It is easy to argue for innovation and to dissect strategic successes afterward. Over and above deciding *when* it makes sense to break the rules and when it is better to play the existing game (an extremely difficult question in itself), the real question is: How do innovative strategists hit on their strategic masterstrokes? In other words, how do strategists think of new ways of

H ow to break the rules depends on the business that the firm is in as well as the firm's strengths and weaknesses.

competing in a market when everybody else seems to miss them? Is there a systematic way of thinking about the issues that allows a company to come up with ideas that break the rules?

Companies do new or even crazy things, like using a new distribution method in the industry (Hanes), a new selling approach (Bank One), a new manufacturing method (Toyota), or totally bypassing distribution intermediaries (Dell Computer). Their actions, however, are nothing more than the manifestation of innovation.[3] The real question is: "What allowed these companies to think of all these possibilities? What are the sources of their innovation?

Before tackling the issue of how to come up with new strategic ideas, I will make five crucial points:
1. The strategy of breaking the rules is not new. Nor is it something that has suddenly become important because of a more demanding competitive environment. As any military historian would tell us, this old concept is something that military strategists (from Alexander the Great to Hannibal to the South Vietnamese gener-

als in the 1960s) have used to their advantage. Any guerrilla army's tactics — adopted when the odds are stacked against it — are nothing more than breaking the rules. As the company examples suggest, the strategy has been used throughout business history as well.
2. Breaking the rules is *one* way to play the game. All firms should not adopt it, and they should not adopt it all the time. Whether a company should break the rules depends on factors such as the nature of the industry, the nature of the game, the industry payoffs, the firm's competitive position, and so on. Firms have to consider, evaluate, and make decisions on these factors individually.
3. How to break the rules depends on the business that the firm is in as well as the firm's strengths and weaknesses. Whether a company should bypass intermediaries (like Dell) or reposition its product (like Perdue) depends on market realities. The basic criteria for deciding whether to adopt a particular tactic are customer needs or wants and company strengths and weaknesses.
4. The strategy is, by definition, risky. Yet a company can manage the risk, primarily by experimenting in a limited way or limited area before fully adopting the new strategy.
5. Coming up with new ideas does not guarantee success. It's one thing to think of a new idea but another to make it work. The whole organization must be managed appropriately to give the new strategy a chance.

Sources of Strategic Innovation

How can a manager systematically think about breaking the rules? Suppose you are determined to go out and break the rules. How do you do it? How do innovative companies hit on their strategic masterstrokes? As any manager knows, there is nothing more difficult than coming up with really new ideas.

Based on my research, I believe strategic innovation happens like this: As already proposed by Abell, all companies in an industry have to decide three basic issues at the strategic level: *Who* is going to be our customer? *What* products or services should we offer the chosen customer? *How* should we offer these products or services cost efficiently?[4] The answers to the who-what-how questions form the strategy of any company. Some will argue that the answers to these questions *are* the strategy of a company (see Figure 1).

The answers that a company gives to the who-what-how questions are conditioned by what that company thinks its business is. Who you see as your customers depends on what business you believe you are in. If, for example, you think you are in the electricity business, the customers you see will be different from those of the company that believes it is in the energy business. I return to this crucial point later.

Every company makes choices with respect to the who-what-how questions. Thus some companies may choose to focus on specific customer segments and offer specific products or services. Others may choose to be global players offering one or many products or services. Yet others may choose to focus on a specific technology or distribution method and offer specific products or services to one or many customer segments.

> The first requirement for becoming a strategic innovator is to identify gaps before everybody else does.

Once they've made a choice, companies are not stuck with these choices forever. A company can always change its customer orientation or product offering, which may be difficult but not impossible. However, over time, a given industry positioning map becomes filled, i.e., most of the possible customer segments are taken care of; most products and services are offered in one form or another; and most possible distribution or manufacturing methods or technologies are utilized.

Strategic innovation occurs when a company identifies gaps in the industry positioning map, decides to fill them, and the gaps grow to become the new mass market. By gaps, I mean: (1) new, emerging customer segments or existing customer segments that other competitors have neglected; (2) new, emerging customer needs or existing customer needs not served well by other competitors; and (3) new ways of producing, delivering, or distributing existing or new products or services to existing or new customer segments. Gaps appear for a number of reasons, such as changing consumer tastes and preferences, changing technologies, changing gov-

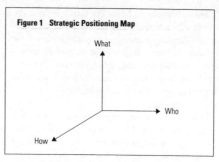

Figure 1   Strategic Positioning Map

ernmental policies, and so on. Gaps can be created by external changes or proactively by the company.

Obviously, the first requirement for becoming a strategic innovator is to identify gaps before everybody else does. However, being the first to identify the right gaps does not guarantee success; a company has to competitively exploit the gap. Based on my research, I believe that companies can identify positioning gaps and thus hit on their strategic masterstrokes in various ways: by accident or luck, by experimenting, through a series of seemingly unrelated steps or actions, or through a proactive thinking process. I now focus on the last option — the thinking approach.

Five Ways to Kick-Start Strategic Innovation

How can a company proactively and systematically think about and develop a new game plan? Five generic approaches of the successful strategic innovators can provide clues:

1. Redefine the business.
2. Redefine the *who*. Who is our customer? A company should think of new customers or new customer segments and develop a game plan that serves them better.
3. Redefine the *what*. What products or services are we offering these customers? A company should think of new customer needs or wants and develop a game plan that better satisfies these needs.
4. Redefine the *how*. Companies should leverage existing core competencies to build new products or a better way of doing business and then find the right customers.
5. Start the thinking process at different points. For example, instead of thinking, "This is our customer, this is what he or she wants, and this is how we can offer it," start by asking: "What are our unique capa-

What Are Mental Models?

A prerequisite to strategic innovation is an honest, fundamental questioning of the mental models or industry recipes that seem to govern the behavior of any individual or organization.[a] A mental model is nothing more than our beliefs about an issue — our family or our business or the world as a whole. Thus, for example, when a person says, "I think everybody should go to church on Sunday," he or she is simply expressing his or her mental model. Other words for the same thing are rules and regulations, habits, managerial frames, assumptions, mind-sets, paradigms, conventional wisdom, industry recipes, customs, institutional memory, and so on.[b]

Research has shown that every human being has a mental model, which develops over time primarily through education and experience. Similarly, organizations develop mental models, manifested in the culture, routines, and unwritten rules of behavior. Thus we hear statements such as, "This is how we do business in this industry," which are the expression of that organization's mental model. Like those of individuals, organizational mental models develop over time through education and experience.

Mental models can be good because they allow us to process information and make decisions quickly. However, very strong mental models can hinder active thinking and the adoption of new ideas because they act as filters that screen incoming information. As a result, if we have very strong mental models, we tend to hear what already supports our existing beliefs and ways of operating, while any new information that does not support what we believe we discard as wrong or not applicable. It is therefore essential that we routinely question our mental models. Questioning does not necessarily mean abandoning. We can question our mental models and decide that nothing's wrong with them. But the questioning should allow us to think actively about assumptions we make about our business and about our behavior in that business.

Usually, human beings and organizations escape their mental models only after a crisis. Many firms discover new ways of competing only when their backs are against the wall. Outsiders who have different mental models from prevailing ones can also be catalysts in prompting an organization to rethink its business. Thus a new CEO, especially one from a totally different industry, can kick-start the strategic innovation process.

Benchmarking can also encourage active questioning of existing mental models and open minds to other possibilities. Or the company can develop an attitude that continually asks why — for example, "Why are we selling our products like this?" When this question is legitimized by, for example, stories of organizations that are profitably selling their products in a different way, the *why* question can produce powerful results. Another tactic is to create a crisis by giving the organization a new objective to aim for — a strategic intent.[c] If people think it is a worthwhile, challenging objective, they will soon realize that it cannot be achieved by doing the same old things better. They'll recognize that they have to think and behave differently to achieve the goal.

There are many tactics that a company can use to escape its mental models.[d] Strategic innovation will not occur unless a company first questions those models.

a. A very good discussion of mental models and how to escape them is found in:
J.C. Spender, *Industry Recipes* (Oxford, England: Basil Blackwell, 1990); and
P. Grinyer and P. McKiernan, "Triggering Major and Sustained Changes in Stagnating Companies," in H. Daems and H. Thomas, eds., *Strategic Groups, Strategic Moves, and Performance* (New York: Elsevier Science, 1994), pp. 173-195.
A very practical discussion is found in:
J.A. Barker, *Paradigms: The Business of Discovering the Future* (New York: HarperCollins, 1992).
b. A recent survey of the academic literature has identified eighty-one words that have been used to describe the same thing. See:
J. Walsh, "Managerial and Organizational Cognition: Notes from a Trip down Memory Lane," *Organization Science*, volume 6, May-June 1995, pp. 280-321.
c. See G. Hamel and C.K. Prahalad, "Strategic Intent," *Harvard Business Review*, volume 67, May-June 1989, pp. 63-76.
d. Other tactics to use to question mental models include: monitor the company's *strategic* health as opposed to its *financial* health, experiment with new ideas, benchmark, ask the "what if" question, monitor maverick competitors and new entrants, talk with noncustomers, bring in outsiders, institutionalize a questioning culture, develop the right incentives, etc.

bilities? What specific needs can we satisfy? Who will be the right customer to approach?

Next I explore each method in turn.

Redefine the Business

Every individual's behavior is conditioned by his or her mental model of the world. Similarly, the behavior of every organization is conditioned by its dominant mental models (see the sidebar). Perhaps a company's most dominant mental model is its perception of what business it is in. The definition that a company gave to its business long ago, either explicitly or implicitly, conditions how that company sees its business, which, in turn, determines how it is going to play the game,

i.e., its strategy. Perhaps the most effective way for a company to start playing the game differently is by questioning the existing definition of its business.

My research suggests that successful strategic innovators all follow very different tactics from those of every other competitor in the industry. Behind these tactics is the thinking process that managers went through and the questions they asked to come up with the tactics. In most cases, the source of strategic innovation is an honest questioning of the answer that managers gave long ago, either explicitly or implicitly, to the question: "What business are we in?"

What business a company believes it is in determines who it sees as its customers, its competitors, its competitive advantage, and so on. It also determines what the company thinks are the success factors in the market and thus ultimately determines how it plays the game. If a company starts playing the game in a totally different way from everyone else, the reason may be that it is playing a different game altogether.

> What business a company believes it is in determines who it sees as its customers, its competitors, its competitive advantage, and so on.

For example, Hal Rosenbluth, president and CEO of Rosenbluth Travel, described how he transformed his company from a $20 million business in 1978 to a $1.3 billion global travel management company by 1990: "Our biggest competitive advantage was to understand that as deregulation changed the rules of travel, we were *no longer in the travel business so much as we were in the information business*" [emphasis added].[5] This fundamental rethinking of its business led Rosenbluth to take a series of actions (such as acquiring computers and airline reservation systems, developing a private reservation data system and relational databases, and so on) that, to an outsider, may have seemed very strange. However, all these actions made perfect sense. If you are in the travel information business, this is what you need to do be successful. Rosenbluth claimed that the company had undergone a similar transformation 100 years before, when his great-grandfather had an insight about the business. He realized that "he wasn't just in travel, selling tickets to people who wanted to cross the Atlantic. He was in family immigration, getting whole clans of people successfully settled in America."

Such redefinition of the business is at the heart of strategic innovation. Many of today's strategic innovators started on their revolutionary journey by first redefining their business. Thus Howard Schultz, president of Starbucks, does not believe he is in the coffee business; instead, he is in the business of creating a consumption experience, of which coffee is a part. A visit to one of his stores is "romance, theatrics, commu-

nity — the totality of the coffee experience."[6] If you think you are in the experience business rather than the coffee business, you will behave very differently from any competitor that thinks it is in the coffee business — not better, just differently.

In another example, Apple Computer's Steve Jobs and Stephen Wozniak did not think they were in the computer business. To them, computers were supposed to be fun. This mind-set led to Macintosh's user-friendliness and to the physical interaction with the computer via a mouse. And Leclerc in France does not see itself as being in the supermarket business, but as a crusader out to change retail distribution in France. Once we understand its conception of who it is, many of its strategic tactics (such as undertaking more than 1,400 legal cases against distributors in France) begin to make sense.

Such redefinition of the business can come only if companies ask: "What business are we really in?" While asking the question does not ensure a new or even better definition, discovering something new will *never* happen if companies never ask the question.

• **How to Define the Business.** There is no right or wrong way to define the business. You can never know beforehand whether a certain definition will be a winner.[7] The important thing is to ask the question, to think of the implications of a possible redefinition, to assess what new tactics to adopt if you were to redefine, to think whether your core competencies will allow you to carry out these tactics efficiently, and so on. Thus, asking the question is only a trigger to thinking actively.

If we look historically at the issue of how to define the business, we can identify three schools of thought. Traditionally, companies defined their business by the *product* they were selling. Thus there were companies in the car business (Ford), the airplane business (Boeing), or the cigarette business (Philip Morris). However, after Levitt's article in the early 1960s, this way of defining the business came under severe attack.[8] Levitt argued that defining the business by product is too narrow and can lead a company astray. He championed the notion that a company should define its business by the *customer function* it is trying to fulfill. Thus "the railroads are in trouble today . . . because they let others take customers away from them because they assumed themselves to be in the railroad business rather than in the transportation business. The reason they defined their industry wrong was because they were railroad-oriented instead of transportation-oriented; they were product-oriented instead of customer-oriented."

This way of looking at the business emphasized the importance of customers and encouraged companies to identify the underlying functionality of their products. By asking what benefits the customer derives from a product, a company can identify its true value-added and define its business. Thus, instead of thinking of your business as the car business, it is better to think of it as the transport or entertainment business or whatever other function your product is fulfilling. A third perspective has emerged that argues that companies must think of their business as a portfolio of *core competencies*.[9] For example, Sony might say it is in the business of selling pocketability, or Apple might say that it is in the business of supplying user-friendliness.

Not one of these three approaches to defining the business is the right one; each has its merits and its limitations. What is a good definition for one company may be bad for another. It all depends on each company's unique capabilities and which definition allows the company to employ its capabilities in the best possible way and thus gain competitive advantage. What usually kick-starts strategic innovation is not the adoption of any one of the three approaches. Rather it is continual switching from one definition to another and continual thinking about the business implications for the company as it switches from one definition to another. The breakthrough usually comes when a company has a dominant way of defining its business, say, customer-driven, and suddenly begins thinking of its business in a different way, say, product-driven.

A company should go through a four-step exercise to define its business:

1. *List all possible definitions of the business* (for example, BMW is in the car business, the prestige car business, the transport business, the ego business, the business of satisfying the transport needs of yuppies, the driving business, the engineering business, the up-market global car business, and so on). Make the list as long as possible.

2. *Evaluate each definition according to a series of criteria.* If we define our business as *x*, who are the customers and what do they need? Who are our competi-

tors? Can we satisfy these customer needs in a unique or better way relative to our competitors? Is our definition of the market attractive (i.e., growing in the future, protected by barriers, and so on)? What will be the key success factors in this business? Can we deliver? How do our competitors behave and what does that imply about how they have defined the business? Does this definition allow us to satisfy our personal objectives for this company? The same questions should be used to evaluate every possible definition. The goal is to identify the definition that gives your company maximum leverage relative to competitors.

3. *Choose one definition.* This is a crucial step. Making a choice implies certain follow-up decisions, for example, that the company will invest in certain products

> **V**ery few companies decide explicitly what business they are in, let alone think about how to redefine the business.

or certain country subsidiaries and not in others. It also implies that certain managers will lose out in the next budget round and others will win. As a result of the serious implications that this decision entails, most companies fail to choose a definition.

4. *Ask these questions* — If our competitor redefined the business, what strategy would it be following? How can we prepare for it?

This is the process that a company should go through to decide how to define its business. Imagine the power of revisiting these questions every year or two — including a follow-up question: Have any changes occurred that make another definition of the business more attractive to our company? This is the source of strategic innovation. Just when everybody else has settled into a certain accepted definition and behaves accordingly, you "discover" a new definition that allows you to start playing the game differently and catch everybody off guard. But, again, to discover a new definition, you must continually explore.

Very few companies decide explicitly what business they are in, let alone think about how to redefine the business. Yet this is the most important element of any strategy. Even the few companies that go through this exercise explicitly either fail to make a specific decision or, having decided what business they are in, fail to revisit the decision, believing that it is cast in concrete, never to be revisited.

Redefine the *Who*

The second source of strategic innovation is a fundamental rethinking of "Who is my customer?" Implicit in this is the notion that the choice of customer is a strategic decision: companies should choose their customers strategically rather than accept as a customer anyone who wants to buy. The criterion for choosing who will be a customer should be an assessment of whether a customer is "good." The trick, therefore, is to identify which customers are good for the company (and keep them or go after them) and which are not (and avoid or get rid of them). A good customer for

> How many companies get rid of existing customers that they have identified as bad customers?

one company may be a bad customer for another, depending not only on the customer's intrinsic characteristics (willing to pay on time, able to pay, profitable) but also on whether the company is able to serve that customer better or more efficiently than its competitors as a result of its unique bundle of assets and capabilities. How many companies think about this question explicitly and proactively? How many have explicit criteria by which they judge every customer? More importantly, how many companies get rid of existing customers that they have identified as bad customers?

In terms of strategic innovation, the purpose of thinking strategically about this question is either to identify new customers or to resegment the existing customer base more creatively and thus form new customer segments. Many companies seem to believe that new customer segments emerge only when new customer *needs* emerge. New customer needs are certainly an important source of new customer segments (and something that I discuss in more length later)

but are not the only one. Often, customer needs remain the same, but customer *priorities* change; for example, customers still need warmth and style in their overcoats, but, compared to thirty years ago, style has risen, for whatever reason, on the list of customer priorities. Thus a company that identifies such changing priorities, not needs, can carve out a specific niche of customers who value style highly.

Similarly, a company can identify a specific customer segment that competitors are not currently serving. The reason this segment is not served is not because companies do not know about the needs of those customers. They may know the needs but have decided that the customer segment is not big enough to go after, or that they cannot serve this segment profitably. If a new company can serve this niche efficiently, it has a new customer segment at its disposal, not because any new customer needs have emerged but because the company has found a more efficient way to fill existing needs.

Another way to identify new customer segments is by more creatively segmenting the existing customer base to put different segments together according to a new logic. Recombination of customer segments may also allow a company to create a new need and grow a particular segment.

My goal is not to make an exhaustive list of all possible ways a company can identify new segments. Rather, I suggest that new customer segments can be developed not only from new customer needs but in various ways. However, a company cannot identify new segments unless it proactively thinks about who its customer really is.

Inevitably, if a company identifies a new customer base, it will start behaving in a way that best satisfies the specific needs of those customers. This behavior will most likely be different from that of established competitors who are serving different customers. Thus the company will be breaking the rules.

Consider, for example, the Canon case: Whereas Xerox leases big photocopiers to corporations through a direct salesforce, Canon sells its personal photocopiers to end users through a dealer network. Thus Canon has adopted a different product, along with different selling and distribution strategies. It is breaking the rules. But how did Canon think of these new rules? Could Canon have started by identifying individuals as a potential customer segment and then asked what these individuals wanted? To Canon, the answer was small personal copiers. It then asked, "How can we get these copiers to them?" Through dealers. Thus the innovative Canon strategy is nothing more than doing exactly what is needed to satisfy the needs of its chosen customer segment.

Many companies that are strategic innovators began this way. They identified a customer segment (usually but not always the low end of the market) or a niche that was not currently served by existing competitors. Then they designed their products and delivery systems to fit the requirements of this customer segment. This source of strategic innovation underpins the success of companies such as Wal-Mart, Canon, Apple, Southwest Airlines, the Body Shop, Texas Instruments (in personal calculators), Lan & Spar Bank, J.C. Penney (in the early 1900s), *USA Today,* Komatsu, Honda (in motorcycles and cars), and so on.

For example, at a time when other airlines were using hub-and-spoke systems, Herb Kelleher, CEO of Southwest Airlines, decided to break the rules: "We wound up with a unique market niche: we are the world's only short-haul, high-frequency, low-fare, point-to-point carrier. . . . We wound up with a market segment that is peculiarly ours, and everything

> For the choice of niche to qualify as strategic innovation, it must grow to eventually become the mass market, and the company's way of playing the game must become the new game in town.

about the airline has been adapted to serving that market segment in the most efficient and economical way possible."[10] Little-known Enterprise Rent-A-Car, America's biggest rental firm, has a strategy that focuses not on the traditional customer segment, people who rent cars at airports, but on people who rent cars not only at airports but wherever they need them. As a result, the company has positioned its 2,400 offices within fifteen minutes of 70 percent of the U.S. population and picks up customers from their homes at no extra cost.[11]

Merely choosing a niche is not strategic innovation. For the choice of niche to qualify as strategic innovation, it must grow to eventually become the mass market, and the company's way of playing the game must become the new game in town. Thus the choice of the *right* niche qualifies as strategic innovation. Therefore, strategic innovators emerge in this manner: At a given time, the mass market is served by a number of competitors. A new company spots a segment or a new niche and goes after it. The existing competitors do not bother because the company is not really taking customers away from them (i.e., they still control the mass market). Given the way the new company plays the game in its little niche, they may not even see it as a competitor. Then, suddenly, the niche grows, and the niche company emerges as the new market leader. All other competitors take notice and search frantically for a response. In the meantime, academics the world over label the new company a maverick competitor that won by breaking the rules. This scenario seems to fit perfectly the success stories of companies like Canon, Apple, Southwest Airlines, Wal-Mart, Dell, Snapple, CNN, MTV, Nucor, and so on.

What eventually led to these companies' success was the choice of a specific market niche that grew phenomenally. But what does it mean when the niche grows to become the new mass market? That what was important to only a few people is now important to almost everybody. For example, concern for the environment grew in the 1980s and along with it the fortunes of the Body Shop. How did this happen? Either the need was already there and a company was lucky or quick enough to climb on the rising wave just in time, or the company helped grow this need so as to exploit it. Thus the important thing is to pick the right niche.[12]

How do strategic innovators pick the right niche? There is really no magic formula. Picking the right niche requires a deep understanding of customer needs and priorities and how they will change. It also requires the courage (most vividly evident in entrepreneurs) to risk pursuing what appears to be a promising customer segment but which may turn out to be a fatal mistake.

Redefine the *What*

The third source of strategic innovation is an honest rethinking of the question: What products or services should we be selling to our customers? Implicit is the notion that the choice of products or services is a strategic decision: companies should decide strategically what to offer their customers. Many companies seem to believe that the choice of customers automatically leads to the choice of products and services to offer. This may be true, but, from a strategic innovation perspective, it also helps to think of the *what* first and then think of *whom* to target. Thus, instead of saying, "These are our customers, so let's think what they want so we can offer

> A company can think ahead and identify new services to offer before the customer even thinks of them.

it to them," it may help to start like this: "These are the products and services that we want to offer, so let's think about who would want to buy them."

Thinking strategically about what to offer the customer should be part of any strategy process. However, for strategic innovation to occur, a company would have to be the first to identify new or changing customer needs, wants, or priorities and therefore be the first to develop new products, services, or better ways to satisfy these needs. For example, at Canon, strategic innovation may have happened in this way: Canon somehow identified (through customer surveys or observation or whatever) that customers did not like waiting in line to use the central photocopier. As a result, Canon came up with the idea of developing personal copiers to serve this need. But, if that were the Canon product, the customer would automatically emerge as the individual to whom Canon would have to sell through dealers. Thus Canon ends up with a strategy that is totally different from Xerox's. How then did Canon identify customers' changing needs or priorities? More importantly, how did Canon go from hearing people say, "I don't like standing in line" to developing the personal copier? In other words, how do strategic innovators identify new customer needs and the products to satisfy those needs?

The first and obvious way to identify new customer needs is, of course, to ask the customer. How-

ever, although absolutely necessary, simply asking the customer or monitoring customer changes in most cases does not lead to strategic innovation, because the customer can only tell you of needs or wants.[13] What must be done to satisfy them requires a creative leap by the company. And this is extremely difficult.

Consider, for example, the case of a German company that manufactures coffee percolators.[14] When it asked customers what they wanted from their percolators, they answered, "Good quality coffee." The problem was that what the company needed to do to achieve this customer need was not immediately obvious. It required a lot of creativity to come up with concrete ideas to satisfy this need. Usually, customer needs or changing customer behaviors are obvious. The real innovation is to go beyond the obvious — to truly understand what is behind what the customer is saying and what products or services the company can develop to satisfy the customer's needs.

Asking customers is only one way to identify new products or services. Equally important is to develop a deep understanding of the customer's business and how the customer is satisfying its own customers' needs. In this way, a company can think ahead and identify new services to offer before the customer even thinks of them. How can you better understand your customers' business? There are several tactics: talk to the customers' customers, talk to their competitors, talk to their suppliers, talk to their employees, understand their value chain, become partners with customers, monitor noncustomers, monitor new entrants, and so on.

To truly understand the customer, a company needs to become customer-oriented, rather than supply-oriented. A company that aspires to be more customer-oriented must, at the very least, change its underlying culture, structure, systems, and incentives to allow its people to achieve this goal. Simply pronouncing the virtues of customer orientation without fundamentally changing the underlying organizational environment will not deliver any results.

Outside benchmarking can be a useful source of new trends and new products. For example, Hanes had its innovative idea to distribute women's pantyhose through supermarkets when, in 1968, the president of Hanes' hosiery division, Robert Elberson, noticed that a West German pantyhose manufacturer had introduced its line to supermarkets in several metropolitan areas in the eastern United States. Similarly, Kresge Co. transformed itself into Kmart in the late 1950s, after its president Harry Cunningham had spent two years studying discount stores, especially Korvette.

Another useful tactic is to experiment continually with new products until you hit on a latent, not obvious need. For example, more than 1,000 new soft drinks appear annually in Japan; only 1 percent survive.[15] A company cannot create a new niche or discover a latent consumer need unless it tries.

Redefine the *How*

Asking customers, thoroughly understanding the customers' business, or becoming a truly customer-oriented company can all be important drivers of strategic innovation. But is that enough? For example, did Sony come up with the Walkman by focusing on the customer? Did Yamaha develop its electronic pianos as a result of deeper customer understanding? Although the answer to both questions may be yes, this line of

W hat Honda learns as it gains experience in managing its dealer network for small cars may help it improve the management of its largely separate network for motorbikes.

questioning points to another possible source of strategic innovation: building on the organization's existing core competencies to create a new product or a new way of doing business that is totally different from the way competitors currently do business.

Consider the following scenario: Canon begins by considering its already-established dealer network that sells cameras to end consumers. In thinking about diversifying into the photocopier business, it therefore recognizes the need to leverage this dealership asset along with its knowledge of marketing to the end consumer. This line of thinking lets Canon identify end consumers as potential customers and so develop the personal copier that it then distributes through dealers.

This plausible scenario suggests that a company can create a new game by leveraging its existing competencies. The classic case, as the Canon example suggests, is to take the knowledge of doing business in one market and utilize it in another market. Thus Canon has developed a deep knowledge of the end consumer as a result of its camera operations and also has an established dealer network. What better solution than to take these two valuable assets and utilize them in the photocopier business by developing personal copiers and targeting the end consumer. To an outsider or to Xerox, this may be breaking the rules, but to Canon, this is simply leveraging its existing strengths.

3M provides another example of the same principle. In 1995, 3M sold nearly $1 billion in microreplication products, ranging from smart adhesives to liquid crystal display film. All these products stem from a single technology, which was first applied in the overhead projector lens thirty years ago. According to the inventor of the first microreplication product, Roger Appeldorn, nobody planned these products: "We didn't sit down and say, 'Microreplication is the next thing to do; let's go do it.' It doesn't work this way. It evolved. It reached a critical mass. And it suddenly proliferated."[16]

Leveraging existing core competencies is certainly one way to create new products or new ways to compete. However, most major breakthroughs occur not so much from amortizing existing competencies but from exploiting them to create and accumulate new strategic assets more quickly and cheaply than competitors. Companies can dynamically exploit existing core competencies in three ways:[17]

1. Share Core Competencies. A company can use a core competence amassed during the building or maintaining of a strategic asset in one small business unit (SBU) to help improve the quality of a strategic asset in another SBU. For example, what Honda learns as it gains experience in managing its dealer network for small cars may help it improve the management of its largely separate network for motorbikes. Similarly, when Canon had successfully established itself in both the camera and photocopier businesses, many of the strategic assets that underpinned the respective SBUs could not be shared directly. The dealer networks and component manufacturing plants were largely specific to each SBU. But, in the course of producing and marketing cameras, the camera division extended this initial asset by a mix of learning by doing and further purchases of assets in the market. As a by-product of this asset accumulation, the camera business also developed a series of competencies such as how to increase the effectiveness of a dealer network, how to develop new products combining optics and electronics, and how to squeeze better productivity from high-volume assembly lines.

Because Canon is in two businesses, cameras and photocopiers, in which the processes of improving dealer effectiveness, speeding up product development, or improving assembly-line productivity are similar, it can improve the quality of the strategic assets in its photocopier business by transferring competencies learned in its camera business and vice versa. This relatedness — similarities in the processes required to improve the effectiveness and efficiency of separate, market-specific stocks of strategic assets in

> # Honda can use the experience of building motorbike distribution to form a new, parallel distribution system for lawn mowers.

two businesses — opens up opportunities for asset improvement advantages that allow a company to play a different game in a different market.

2. Reuse Competencies. A company can use a competence developed during the building of strategic assets in existing businesses to create a *new* strategic asset in a *new* business faster or more cheaply. For example, Honda can use the experience of building motorbike distribution to form a new, parallel distribution system for lawn mowers, which are generally sold through different outlets. Similarly, by operating in the photocopier market and building the asset base required to outcompete rivals, the Canon SBU accumulated its own, additional competencies that the camera SBU had not developed. These included building a marketing organization targeted to business rather than personal buyers and developing and manufacturing a reliable electrostatic printing engine.

When Canon diversified into laser printers, the new

SBU started with an endowment of assets, additional assets acquired in the market, and arrangements to share facilities and core components. But, even more important for its long-term competitiveness, the new laser printer SBU was able to draw on the competencies of its sister businesses in cameras and photocopiers to create new market-specific strategic assets faster and more efficiently than its competitors. This kind of relatedness, in which companies can deploy the competencies amassed by existing SBUs to speed up and to reduce the cost of forming new market-specific strategic assets for a new SBU, is the asset-creation advantage that companies can use to break the rules.

3. Expand Competencies. A company can expand its existing pool of competencies because, as it builds strategic assets in a new business, it learns new skills. For example, in the course of building a new distribution system for lawn mowers, Honda may learn new skills so it can improve its distribution system for motorbikes. Similarly, in creating the assets required to support the design, manufacture, and service of the more sophisticated electronics demanded in the laser printer business, Canon may have developed new competencies to improve its photocopier business. Alternatively, combining the competencies developed in its photocopier and laser printer businesses may have helped it to quickly and cheaply build the strategic assets required to succeed in a fourth market — plain-paper facsimile machines.

Strategic innovation takes place when a company tries to satisfy customer needs based on new strategic assets that are unfamiliar to existing competitors. In the process, the assets of established players become obsolete. Maverick competitors create such new assets by utilizing their core competencies to either develop new assets or bundle existing strategic assets in unique combinations. Successful innovators need therefore to identify and deploy the right core competencies. A better understanding of changing customer needs can lead to a better understanding of which core competencies to emphasize and develop. Similarly, a better understanding of a company's core competencies can lead to better segmentation, choice of customers, and a more productive development of new strategic assets that allow the company to break the rules.

Start the Thinking Process at Different Points
The final source of strategic innovation is the thinking

process for developing new ideas. New ideas emerge more easily if managers can escape their mechanistic way of thinking and look at an issue from different perspectives or angles. The goal, therefore, is to start the thinking process at different points. For example, instead of thinking, "This is our customer, this is what he or she wants, and this is how we can offer it," start by asking, "What are our unique capabilities, what specific needs can we satisfy, and who will be the right customer to approach?"

At the strategic level, a company has to decide the who, the what, and the how: Who are our customers? What do they want? How can we satisfy these wants? The thinking process could, therefore, go through three stages: Start by defining who the selected customers are and then decide on the what and the how. Or start by deciding first what products and services to offer and then decide the who and the how. Or start with the how and then decide the who and the what.

Another useful thinking process is to take the accepted definition of the business as given and then try to think of (1) new customers or new customer segments, (2) new customer needs, or (3) new applications of core competencies. After coming up with a number of ideas, a company can revisit the question, "What is our business?" and, for every possible new definition, repeat the three steps. Again, the objective is to see the business from as many different perspectives as possible so managers can find new ways to play the game.

Conclusion

I began by identifying Canon as a strategic innovator that beat the industry leader, Xerox, by breaking the rules. While there is no question that Canon broke the rules in the copier business, consider the different ways Canon *may* have come up with its innovative strategy:
1. While Xerox plays the game, believing that it is in the photocopier business, Canon begins by seeing itself in the consumer electronics business — perhaps a legacy of its success in the camera business. By thinking of itself as a consumer electronics company, Canon immediately recognizes that the way to play this game is through low price and high quality. It therefore puts all its energy toward developing a reliable copier at an affordable price. When it introduces such a copier, the

first users report how good and cheap this wonderful new machine is, and millions of people suddenly discover that they too need a personal copier at home. The personal copier market explodes, and Canon emerges as the market leader.
2. Based on its experiences in the camera business, Canon starts by identifying individuals as a promising customer segment. Its answer to the question, "What do individuals want?," is small personal copiers. And to, "How can we get these copiers to them?," through dealers. Thus the innovative Canon strategy, when compared to Xerox's strategy, is nothing more than doing exactly what is needed to satisfy the needs of the chosen customer segment.
3. Canon somehow (through customer surveys or observation or whatever) discovers that customers do not like to wait in line for the central photocopier. As a result, Canon comes up with the idea of personal copiers. But if

> Coming up with new ideas is one thing; succeeding in the market is another.

that is the Canon product, the Canon customer automatically emerges as the individual to whom Canon has to sell through dealers. Thus, again, the strategy ends up being totally different from Xerox's.
4. Canon begins by considering its already established dealer network that sells cameras to end consumers. By thinking about diversifying into the photocopier business, it therefore recognizes the need to leverage the dealership asset along with its technology and its knowledge of marketing to the end consumer. This line of thinking lets Canon identify end consumers as the potential customer and develop the personal copier, which it then distributes through dealers.

Each scenario or a combination may have taken place. Perhaps all did. A company can use any one or a combination of the above tactics to strategically innovate.
• **Two Caveats.** It is worth reemphasizing that coming up with new ideas is one thing; succeeding in the market is another. Many readers may rush to identify numerous companies that appear to have strategically innovated in the manner described, only to go bankrupt

in a few years. Osborne Computer is one example. Very much like the founders of Apple Computer, Adam Osborne founded Osborne Computer in 1981 to sell portable personal computers. He went after a new customer niche, one of the sources of strategic innovation. Osborne remarked, "I saw a truck-size hole in the industry, and I plugged it."[18] Osborne Computer grew to $100 million in sales within eighteen months, only to go bankrupt in 1983.

There are many stories of companies that strategically innovated but failed. People Express's failed strategy has similarities to the successful strategy of Southwest Airlines. The demise of the retail chain Next in the United Kingdom contrasts sharply with the success of the Body Shop, even though both companies strategically innovated in the same way, by identifying new customer needs.

Similarly, there are numerous examples of companies that tried to strategically innovate by redefining their business, only to discover that it did not guarantee success: Xerox's attempts to go from the copier business to the office of the future business to the documents business is one case. The failed diversification attempts of the 1960s and 1970s on the shaky ground of a broader business definition should be a warning. Nor is initial success through strategic innovation a guarantee for long-term success — witness the declining fortunes of Apple Computer and Kmart.

All these examples of strategic innovations that failed make the point that any idea, however good, is bound to fail if it is not implemented effectively. Even worse, any idea, however good and however well implemented, will eventually fail if it is not supported by continual innovation. This, however, should not detract from the value of generating new ideas that break the rules. Just because good ideas are only *one* element that determines corporate success and do not guarantee success does not mean that companies should not bother coming up with new ideas.

Finally, I have presented my ideas as if one individual or a group somehow comes up with all these ways to break the rules in a rational manner. This is certainly one way for strategic innovation to take place, but not the only way. A company must also strive to institutionalize innovation by establishing the appropriate culture, structure, incentives, systems, and processes that somehow allow innovation to happen as part of

daily business. How 3M has institutionalized innovation can be a model for other companies that aspire to the same goal. Similarly, a company may want to identify specific obstacles or constraints that prevent it from being entrepreneurial and find ways to remove or bypass them. These are important issues, but not my major concern here. I have been concerned only with the rational approach to strategic innovation. By not discussing institutionalized innovation, I do not suggest that it is unimportant. It is a topic that deserves a separate article. ◆

References

The author thanks Sumantra Ghoshal, Dominic Houlder, Jane Carmichael, Charles Lucier, and Paul Geroski for many useful comments on earlier drafts.

1. There is only one major exception to this generalization: in cases when the attacker utilizes a dramatic technological innovation to attack the leader, seven of ten market leaders lose out. See:
J.M. Utterback, *Mastering the Dynamics of Innovation* (Boston: Harvard Business School Press, 1994).

2. S. Davies, P. Geroski, M. Lund, and A. Vlassopoulos, "The Dynamics of Market Leadership in U.K. Manufacturing Industry, 1979-1986" (London: London Business School, Centre for Business Strategy, working paper 93, 1991); and
P. Geroski and S. Toker, "The Turnover of Market Leaders in U.K. Manufacturing: 1979-1986" (London: London Business School, mimeo, 1993).

3. Whether these new approaches make sense for a particular firm (i.e., whether they will lead to success or failure) depends primarily on the economic merits of these ideas and the company's ability to deliver them competitively. For example, do these new moves allow the company to offer something new to the customer (that he or she wants)? Do they allow the company to offer something better or more efficiently? Are the new offerings something that the customer values? Thus the success of the new ideas will depend on customer needs and on the core competencies of the innovating company.

4. D. Abell, *Defining the Business: The Starting Point of Strategic Planning* (Englewood Cliffs, New Jersey: Prentice-Hall, 1980).

5. H. Rosenbluth, "Tales from a Nonconformist Company," *Harvard Business Review*, volume 69, July-August 1991, p. 32.

6. C. McCoy, "Entrepreneur Smells Aroma of Success in Coffee Bars," *Wall Street Journal*, 8 January 1993, p. B2.

7. The whole purpose of redefining the business is to identify a specific definition that allows you to maximize the impact of your unique capabilities relative to your competitors. Thus what is a good definition for your company may be totally inappropriate for another company; and what is a good definition for your competitor — given its particular strengths — may be totally inappropriate for you. Thus what is a "good" definition is in the eyes of the beholder. However, even if you can find a "good" definition for your company, you just enhance your chances of success, but this does not mean that you are guaranteed success.

8. T. Levitt, "Marketing Myopia," *Harvard Business Review*, volume 38, July-August 1960, pp. 24-47.

9. See, in particular:

G. Hamel and C.K. Prahalad, *Competing for the Future* (Boston: Harvard Business School Press, 1994), p. 83.

10. C.A. Jaffe, "Moving Fast by Standing Still," *Nation's Business*, October 1991, p. 58.

11. "America's Car Rental Business: Driven into the Ground," *The Economist*, 20 January 1996, pp. 76-79.

12. This point is also raised by Gerard Tellis and Peter Golder. Their argument is that "strategic innovators" have a vision of the mass market and actively try to produce quality products at low prices to make them appealing to the mass market. Thus the secret of their success is the fact that they target the mass market and succeed in serving it. Although I agree with the point, my research suggests that the importance of luck, good timing, and external events should not be underestimated as ingredients in the success of the strategic innovators to "pick" the right niche at the right time. See:

G. Tellis and P. Golder, "First to Market, First to Fail? Real Causes of Enduring Market Leadership," *Sloan Management Review*, volume 37, Winter 1996, pp. 65-75.

13. There is a vast literature on the usefulness and the limits of "getting close to the customer." See, in particular:

S. Macdonald, "Too Close for Comfort?: The Strategic Implications of Getting Close to the Customer," *California Management Review*, volume 37, Summer 1995, pp. 8-27; and

I. Simonson, "Get Closer to Your Customers by Understanding How They Make Choices," *California Management Review*, volume 35, Summer 1993, pp. 68-84.

14. K. Ohmae, "Getting Back to Strategy," *Harvard Business Review*, volume 66, November-December 1988, pp. 149-156.

15. "What Makes Yoshio Invent," *The Economist*, 12 January 1991, p. 61.

16. T. Steward, "3M Fights Back" *Fortune*, 5 February 1996, p. 44.

17. For a fuller discussion of this point, see:

C. Markides and P. Williamson, "Related Diversification, Core Competences, and Corporate Performance," *Strategic Management Journal*, volume 15, special issue, 1994, pp. 149-165; and

C. Markides and P. Williamson, "Corporate Diversification and Organizational Structure: A Resource-Based View," *Academy of Management Journal*, volume 39, no. 2, 1996, pp. 340-367.

18. "Osborne: From Brags to Riches," *Business Week*, 22 February 1982, p. 86.

Reprint 3831

[9]

Strategic Management Journal, Vol. 17, 197–218 (1996)

CUSTOMER POWER, STRATEGIC INVESTMENT, AND THE FAILURE OF LEADING FIRMS

CLAYTON M. CHRISTENSEN and JOSEPH L. BOWER
Graduate School of Business Administration, Harvard University, Boston, Massachusetts, U.S.A.

Why might firms be regarded as astutely managed at one point, yet subsequently lose their positions of industry leadership when faced with technological change? We present a model, grounded in a study of the world disk drive industry, that charts the process through which the demands of a firm's customers shape the allocation of resources in technological innovation— a model that links theories of resource dependence and resource allocation. We show that established firms led the industry in developing technologies of every sort—even radical ones— whenever the technologies addressed existing customers' needs. The same firms failed to develop simpler technologies that initially were only useful in emerging markets, because impetus coalesces behind, and resources are allocated to, programs targeting powerful customers. Projects targeted at technologies for which no customers yet exist languish for lack of impetus and resources. Because the rate of technical progress can exceed the performance demanded in a market, technologies which initially can only be used in emerging markets later can invade mainstream ones, carrying entrant firms to victory over established companies.

Students of management have marveled at how hard it is for firms to repeat their success when technology or markets change, for good reason: there are lots of examples. For instance, no leading computer manufacturer has been able to replicate its initial success when subsequent architectural technologies and their corresponding markets emerged. IBM created and continues to dominate the mainframe segment, but it missed by many years the emergence of the minicomputer architecture and market. The minicomputer was developed, and its market applications exploited, by firms such as Digital Equipment and Data General. While very successful in their initial markets, the minicomputer makers largely missed the advent of the desktop computer: a market which was created by entrants such as Apple, Commodore and Tandy, and only later by IBM. The engineering workstation leaders were Apollo

and Sun Microsystems, both entrants to the industry. The pioneers of the portable computing market—Compaq, Zenith, Toshiba and Sharp— were not the leaders in the desktop segment.

And yet even as these firms were missing this sequence of opportunities, they were *very* aggressively and successfully leading their industries in developing and adopting many strategically important and technologically sophisticated technologies. IBM's leadership across generations of multi-chip IC packaging, and Sun Microsystems' embrace of RISC microprocessor technology, are two instances. There are many other examples, discussed below, of firms that aggressively stayed at the forefront of technology development for extended periods, but whose industry leadership was later shaken by shifting technologies and markets.

The failure of leading firms can sometimes be ascribed to managerial myopia or organizational lethargy, or to insufficient resources or expertise. For example, cotton-spinners simply lacked the human, financial and technological resources to

Key words: innovation; resource allocation; strategy change; technological change; failure

CCC 0143–2095/96/030197–22
© 1996 by John Wiley & Sons, Ltd.

Received 20 September 1993
Final revision received 26 May 1995

198   *C.M. Christensen and J.L. Bower*

compete when DuPont brought synthetic fibers into the apparel industry. But in many instances, the firms that missed important innovations suffered none of these problems. They had their competitive antennae up; aggressively invested in new products and technologies; and listened astutely to their customers. Yet they still lost their positions of leadership. This paper examines why and under what circumstances financially strong, customer-sensitive, technologically deep and rationally managed organizations may fail to adopt critical new technologies or enter important markets—failures to innovate which have led to the decline of once-great firms.

Our conclusion is that a primary reason why such firms lose their positions of industry leadership when faced with certain types of technological change has little to do with technology itself—with its degree of newness or difficulty, relative to the skills and experience of the firm. Rather, they fail because they listen too carefully to their customers— and customers place stringent limits on the strategies firms can and cannot pursue.

The term 'technology', as used in this paper, means the processes by which an organization transforms labor, capital, materials, and information into products or services. All firms have technologies. A retailer such as Sears employs a particular 'technology' to procure, present, sell, and deliver products to its customers, while a discount warehouse retailer such as the Price Club employs a different 'technology'. Hence, our concept of technology extends beyond the engineering and manufacturing functions of the firm, encompassing a range of business processes. The term 'innovation' herein refers to a change in technology.

A fundamental premise of this paper is that patterns of resource allocation heavily influence the types of innovations at which leading firms will succeed or fail. In every organization, ideas emerge daily about new ways of doing things— new products, new applications for products, new technical approaches, and new customers—in a manner chronicled by Bower (1970) and Burgelman (1983a, 1983b). Most proposals to innovate require human and financial resources. The patterns of innovation evidenced in a company will therefore mirror to a considerable degree the patterns in how its resources are allocated to, and withheld from, competing proposals to innovate.

We observe that because effective resource allocation is market-driven, the resource allocation procedures in successful organizations provide impetus for innovations known to be demanded by current customers in existing markets. We find that established firms in a wide range of industries have tended to lead in developing and adopting such innovations. Conversely, we find that firms possessing the capacity and capability to innovate may fail when the innovation does *not* address the foreseeable needs of their current customers. When the initial price/performance characteristics of emerging technologies render them competitive only in emerging market segments, and not with current customers, resource allocation mechanisms typically deny resources to such technologies. Our research suggests that the inability of some successful firms to allocate sufficient resources to technologies that initially cannot find application in mainstream markets, but later invade them, lies at the root of the failure of many once-successful firms.

EARLIER VIEWS OF FACTORS INFLUENCING PATTERNS OF RESOURCE ALLOCATION IN THE INNOVATION PROCESS

Our research links two historically independent streams of research, both of which have contributed significantly to our understanding of innovation. The first stream is what Pfeffer and Salancik (1978) call *resource dependence*: an approach which essentially looks *outside* the firm for explanations of the patterns through which firms allocate resources to innovative activities. Scholars in this tradition contend that firms' strategic options are constrained because managerial discretion is largely a myth. In order to ensure the survival of their organizations, managers lack the power to do anything other than to allocate resources to innovative programs that are required of the firm by external customers and investors: the entities that provide the resources the firm needs to survive. Support for this view comes from the work of historians of technological innovation such as Cooper and Schendel (1976) and Foster (1986). The firms they studied generally responded to the emergence of competitively threatening technologies by intensifying their investments to improve the conventional technologies used by their current customers—which provided the resources the firms needed to survive over the short term.

The second stream of ideas, originally taught by Bower (1970) and amplified by Burgelman (1983a, 1983b), describes the resource allocation process internal to the firm. These scholars suggest that most strategic proposals—to add capacity or develop new products or processes—take their fundamental shape at lower levels of hierarchical organizations. Bower observed that the allocation of funding amongst projects is substantially shaped by the extent to which managers at middle levels of the organization decide to support, or lend *impetus*, to some proposals and to withhold it from others. Bower also observed that risk management and career management were closely linked in the resource allocation process. Because the career costs to aspiring managers of having backed an ultimately unsuccessful project can be severe, their tendency was to back those projects where the demand for the product was assured.

Our study links these two streams by showing how the impetus that drives patterns of resource allocation (and hence innovation) within firms does not stem from autonomous decisions of risk-conscious managers. Rather, whether sufficient impetus coalesces behind a proposed innovation is largely determined by the presence or absence of current customers who can capably articulate a need for the innovation in question. There seems to be a powerful linkage from: (1) the expectations and needs of a firm's most powerful customers for product improvements; to (2) the types of innovative proposals which are given or denied impetus within the firm and which therefore are allocated the resources necessary to develop the requisite technological capabilities; to (3) the markets toward which firms will and will not target these innovations; which in turn leads to (4) the firms' ultimate commercial success or failure with the new technology.

A primary conclusion of this paper is that when significant customers demand it, sufficient impetus may develop so that large, bureaucratic firms can embark upon and successfully execute technologically difficult innovations—even those that require very different competencies than they initially possessed.[1] Conversely, we find that

when a proposed innovation addresses the needs of small customers in remote or emerging markets that do not supply a significant share of the resources a firm currently needs for growth and survival, firms will find it difficult to succeed even at innovations that are technologically straightforward. This is because the requisite impetus does not develop, and the proposed innovations are starved of resources.

Our findings build upon the work of earlier scholars who have addressed the question of why leading firms may fail when faced with technological change. Cooper and Schendel (1976) found that new technologies often are initially deployed in new markets, and that these were generally brought into industries by entering firms. They observed that established firms confronted with new technology often intensified investment in traditional technical approaches, and that those that did make initial resource commitments to a new technology rarely maintained adequate resource commitments. Foster (1986) noted that at points when new technologies enter an industry, entrants seem to enjoy an 'attacker's advantage' over incumbent firms. Henderson and Clark (1990) posited that entrant firms enjoyed a particular advantage over incumbents in architectural technology change.

We hope to add additional precision and insight to the work of these pioneering scholars, by stating more precisely the specific sorts of technological innovations that are likely initially to be deployed in new applications, and the sorts that are likely to be used in mainstream markets from the beginning; and to define the types of innovation in which we expect attackers to enjoy an advantage, and the instances in which we expect incumbents to hold the upper hand. By presenting a model of the processes by which resource commitments are made, we hope partially to explain a puzzle posed but not resolved by each of these authors: *why* have incumbent firms generally intensified their commitments to conventional technology, while starving efforts to commercialize new technologies—even while the new technology was gaining ground in the market?

---

[1] Evidence supporting this conclusion is provided below. In making this statement, we contest the conclusions of scholars such as Tushman and Anderson (1986), who have argued that incumbent firms are most threatened by attacking entrants when the innovation in question destroys, or does not build

upon, the competence of the firm. We observe that established firms, though often at great cost, have led their industries in developing critical competence-destroying technologies, when the new technology was needed to meet existing customers' demands.

200   *C.M. Christensen and J.L. Bower*

Finally, by examining why established firms do these things, we hope to provide insights for how managers can more successfully address different types of technological change.

RESEARCH METHODS

Three very different classes of data were used in this study, to establish solid construct validity (Yin, 1989). The first was a data base of the detailed product and performance specifications for every disk drive model announced by every firm participating in the world industry between 1975 and 1990—over 1400 product models in all. These data came from *Disk/Trend Report*, the leading market research publication in the disk drive industry, and from product specification sheets obtained from the manufacturers themselves. The tables and other summary statistics reported in this paper were calculated from this data base, unless otherwise noted. This data set is not a statistical sample, but constitutes a complete census of companies and products for the world industry during the period studied.

The second type of information employed in the study relates to the strategies pursued, and the commercial success and failure, of each of the companies that announced the development of a rigid disk drive between 1976 and 1990. *Disk/Trend* reported each firm's rigid disk drive sales in each of these years, by product category and by market segment. Each monthly issue between 1976 and 1990 of *Electronic Business* magazine, the most prominent trade publication covering the magnetic recording industry, was examined for information about disk drive manufacturers, their strategies and products. We used this information to verify the completeness of the *Disk/Trend* data,[2] and to write a history of the disk drive industry describing the strategies and fortunes of firms in the industry (Christensen, 1993).

The third type of information employed in this study came from over 70 personal, unstructured interviews conducted with executives who are or have been associated with 21 disk drive manufac-

turing companies. Those interviewed included founders; chief executives; vice presidents of sales and marketing, engineering and finance; and engineering, marketing and managerial members of pivotal product development project teams. The firms whose executives were interviewed together account for over 80 percent of the disk drives produced in the world since the industry's inception. Data from these interviews were used to reconstruct, as accurately as possible, the decision-making processes associated with key innovations in each company's history. Wherever possible, accounts of the same decision were obtained from multiple sources, including former employees, to minimize problems with *post hoc* rationalization. Multiple employees were interviewed in 16 of the 21 companies.

The *Disk/Trend* data enabled us to measure the impact that each new component and architectural technology had on disk drive performance. Furthermore, it was possible to identify which firms were the first to develop and adopt each new technology, and to trace the patterns of diffusion of each new technology through the world industry over time, amongst different types of firms. When analysis of the *Disk/Trend* data indicated a particular entrant or established firm had prominently led or lagged behind the industry in a particular innovation, we could determine the impact of that leadership or followership on the subsequent sales and market shares, by product-market segment, for each company.

Analysis of these data essentially enabled us to develop a theory of *what* will happen when different types of technological change occur—whether we would expect entrant and established firms to take leadership in their development. We then used our interview data to write case histories of key decisions in six companies to understand *why* those patterns of leadership and followership in technology development occur. These case studies covered entrant and established firms, over an extended period of time in which each of them made decisions to invest, or delay investing, in a variety of new technologies. These cases were selected in what Yin (1989) calls a multi-case, nested experimental design, so that through pattern-matching across cases, the external validity of the study's conclusions could be established.[3]

---

[2] *Disk/Trend Report* identified 133 firms that participated in the disk drive industry in the period studied. The search of *Electronic Business* magazine yielded information on one additional firm, Peach Tree Technology, that never generated revenues and somehow had escaped detection by the *Disk/Trend* editors.

[3] Table 3 (which refers to Yin, 1989: 35–37) describes this pattern-matching.

We studied the disk drive industry because its history is one of rapid change in technology and market structure. The world rigid disk drive market grew at a 27 percent annual rate to over $13 billion between 1975 and 1990. Of the 17 firms in the OEM industry in 1976, only one was still in operation in 1990. Over 130 firms entered the industry during this period, and more than 100 of them failed. The cost per megabyte (MB) of the average drive in constant 1990 dollars fell from $560 in 1976 to $5 in 1990. The physical size of a 100 MB drive shrank from 5400 to 8 cubic inches over the same period. During this time, six architecturally distinct product generations emerged, and a new company rose to become market leader in four of these six generations. A description of disk drive technology that may be helpful for some readers is provided in Appendix 1.

TYPOLOGIES OF TECHNOLOGICAL CHANGE

Earlier scholars of technology change have argued that incumbent firms may stumble when technological change destroys the value of established technological competencies (Tushman and Anderson, 1986), or when new architectural technologies emerge (Henderson and Clark, 1990). For present purposes, however, we have found it useful to distinguish between those innovations that *sustained* the industry's rate of improvement in product performance (total capacity and recording density were the two most common measures), and those innovations that *disrupted* or redefined that performance trajectory (Dosi, 1982). The following two sections illustrate these concepts by describing prominent examples of trajectory-sustaining and trajectory-disrupting technological changes in the industry's history. The subsequent sections then describe the role these innovations played in the industry's development; the processes through which incumbent and entrant firms responded to these different types of technological change; and the consequent successes and failures these firms experienced.

Sustaining technological changes

In the disk drive industry's history, most of the changes in competent technology, and two of the

six changes in architectural technology, sustained or reinforced established trajectories of product performance improvement. Two examples of such technology change are shown in Figure 1. The left-most graph compares the average recording density of drives that employed conventional particulate oxide disk technology and ferrite head technology, vs. the average density of drives that employed new-technology thin film heads and disks, that were introduced in each of the years between 1976 and 1990. The improvements in the conventional approach are the result of consistent incremental advances such as grinding the ferrite heads to finer, more precise dimensions; and using smaller and more finely dispersed oxide particles on the disk's surface. Note that the improvement in areal density obtainable with ferrite/oxide technology began to level off in the period's later years—suggesting a maturing technology S-curve (Foster, 1986). Note how thin film head and disk technologies emerged to sustain the rate of performance improvement at its historical pace of 35 percent between 1984 and 1990.

The right-most graph in Figure 1 describes a sustaining technological change of a very different character: an innovation in product architecture. In this case, the 14-inch Winchester drive substituted for removable disk packs, which had been the dominant design between 1962 and 1978. Just as in the thin film-for-ferrite/oxide substitution, the impact of Winchester technology was to sustain the historically established rate of performance improvement. Other important innovations, such as embedded servo systems, RLL & PRML recording codes, higher RPM motors and embedded SCSI, SMD, ESDI and AT interfaces, also helped manufacturers sustain the rate of historical performance improvement that their customers had come to expect.[4] Hereafter in this

---

[4] The examples of technology change presented in Figures 1 and 2 in this paper introduce some ambiguity to the unqualified term 'discontinuity', as it has been used by Dosi (1982), Tushman and Anderson (1986), and others. The innovations in head and disk technology described in the left graph of Figure 1 represent *positive discontinuities* in an established technological trajectory, while the development of trajectory-disrupting technologies charted in Figure 2 represent *negative* discontinuities. As will be shown below, established firms seemed quite capable of leading the industry over positive discontinuities. The negative ones were the points at which established firms generally lost their positions of industry leadership.

202   *C.M. Christensen and J.L. Bower*

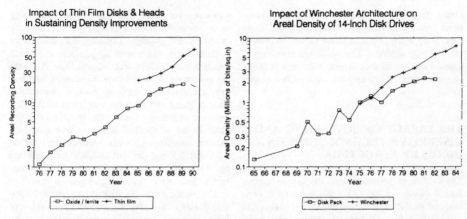

Figure 1. Examples of sustaining technological change in componentry (left) and product architecture (right). Reprinted with permission from *Business History Review*, 1993, **67**, p. 557.

paper, technological changes that have such a sustaining impact on an established trajectory of performance improvement are called *sustaining technologies*.

Disruptive technological changes

Most technological change in the industry's history consisted of sustaining innovations of the sort described above. In contrast, there were just a few trajectory-disrupting changes. The most important of these from a historical viewpoint were the architectural innovations that carried the industry from 14-inch diameter disks to diameters of 8, 5.25 and then 3.5 inches. The ways in which these innovations were disruptive are illustrated in Table 1. Set in 1981, this table compares the attributes of a typical 5.25-inch drive—a new architecture that had been in the market for less than a year at that time—with those of a typical 8-inch drive, which by that time had become the standard drive used by minicomputer manufacturers. Note that along the dimensions of performance which were important to established minicomputer manufacturers—capacity, cost per megabyte, and access time—the 8-inch product was vastly superior. The 5.25-inch architecture did not address the needs of minicomputer manufacturers, as they perceived their needs at that time. On the other hand, the 5.25-inch architecture *did* possess attributes that appealed to the desktop personal computer market segment that

was just emerging in 1980–82. It was small and lightweight—important features for this application. And it was priced at around $2000, which means it could economically be incorporated in desktop machines. Hereafter in this paper, technologies such as this, which disrupt an established trajectory of performance improvement, or redefine what performance means, are called *disruptive technologies*.

In general, sustaining technological changes appealed to established customers in existing, mainstream markets. They provided these customers with more of what they had come to

Table 1. The disruptive impact on performance improvement of the 5.25-inch, vs. the 8-inch architecture

Attribute	8-inch drives	5.25-inch drives
Capacity (megabytes)	**60**	10
Volume (cubic inches)	566	*150*
Weight (pounds)	21	*6*
Access time (ms)	**30**	160
Cost per megabyte	**$50**	$200
Total unit cost	$3000	*$2000*

Key: Attributes valued highly in the minicomputer market in 1981 are presented in **boldface**.
Attributes valued in the emerging desktop computing market in 1981 are shown in *italics*.
Source: Analysis of Disk/Trend Report data; from Christensen (1992a: 90).

expect. In contrast, disruptive technologies rarely could initially be employed in established markets. They tended instead to be valued in remote or emerging markets. This tendency consistently appears not just in disk drives, but across a range of industries (Rosenbloom and Christensen, 1995).

THE IMPACT OF SUSTAINING AND DISRUPTIVE TECHNOLOGIES ON INDUSTRY STRUCTURE

The history of sustaining and disruptive technological change in the disk drive industry is summarized in Figure 2. It begins in 1974, the year after IBM's first Winchester architecture model was introduced to challenge the dominant disk pack architectural design. Almost all drives then were sold to makers of mainframe computers. Note that in 1974 the median-priced mainframe computer was equipped with about 130 MB of hard disk capacity. The typical hard disk storage capacity supplied with the median-priced mainframe increased about 17 percent per year, so that by 1990 the typical mainframe was equipped with 1300 MB of hard disk capacity. This growth in the use of hard disk memory per computer is mapped by the solid line emanating from point A in Figure 2. This trajectory was driven by user learning and software developments in the applications in which mainframes were used (Christensen and Rosenbloom, 1995).

The dashed line originating at point A measures the increase in the average capacity of 14-inch drives over the same period. Note that although the capacity of the average 14-inch drive was equal to the capacity shipped with the typical mainframe in 1974, the rate of increase in capacity provided within the 14-inch architecture exceeded the rate of increase in capacity demanded in the mainframe market—carrying this architecture toward high-end mainframes, scientific computers, and supercomputers. Furthermore, note how the new 14-inch Winchester architecture sustained the capacity trajectory that had been established in the earlier removable disk pack architecture. Appendix 2 describes how these trajectories were calculated.

The solid trajectories emanating from points B, C and D represent the average hard disk capacity *demanded* by computer buyers in each market

segment, over time.[5] The dashed lines emanating from points B, C, and D in Figure 2 measure trends in the average capacity that disk drive manufacturers were able to *provide* with each successive disk drive architecture. Note that with the exception of the 14-inch Winchester architecture, the maximum capacity initially available in each of these architectures was substantially *less* than the capacity required for the typical computer in the established market—these were *disruptive* innovations. As a consequence, the 8, 5.25 and 3.5-inch designs initially were rejected by the leading, established computer manufacturers, and were deployed instead in emerging market applications for disk drives: minicomputers, desktop PCs and portable PCs, respectively. Note, however, that once these disruptive architectures became established in their new markets, the accumulation of hundreds of sustaining innovations pushed each architecture's performance ahead along very steep, and roughly parallel, trajectories.[6]

Note that the trajectory of improvement that the technology was able to *provide* within each architecture was nearly *double* the slope of the increase in capacity *demanded* in each market. As we will see, this disparity between what the technology could provide and what the market demanded seems to have been the primary source of leadership instability in the disk drive industry.

LEADERS IN SUSTAINING AND DISRUPTIVE TECHNOLOGICAL INNOVATIONS

To better understand why leading firms might successfully pioneer in the development and adoption of many new and difficult technologies, and yet lose their positions of industry leadership by failing to implement others, we compared the innovative behavior of *established* firms with that of *entrant* firms, with respect to each of the

---

[5] These trajectories represent the disk capacity *demanded* in each market because in each instance, greater disk capacity could have been supplied to users by the computer manufacturers, had the market demanded additional capacity at the cost for which it could be purchased at the time.
[6] The parallel impact of sustaining innovations across these architectural generations results from the fact that the same sustaining technologies, in the form of componentry, were available simultaneously to manufacturers of each generation of disk drives (Christensen, 1992b).

204   *C.M. Christensen and J.L. Bower*

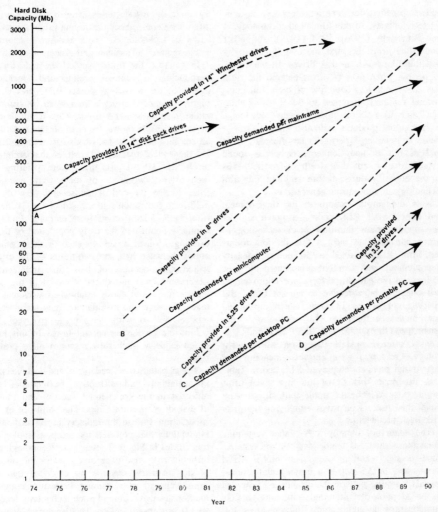

Figure 2. Patterns of entry and improvement in disruptive disk drive technologies. Reprinted with permission from *Business History Review*, 1993, **67**, p. 559.

sustaining and disruptive technological innovations in the history of the disk drive industry. Building upon the approach employed by Henderson and Clark (1990), established firms were defined as firms that had previously manufactured drives which employed an older, established technology, whereas entrant firms were those whose initial product upon entry into the industry employed the new component or architectural technology being analyzed. This approach was used because of this study's longitudinal character, looking at the performance of incumbents and entrants across a sequence of innovations.

In spite of the wide variety in the magnitudes and types of sustaining technological changes in the industry's history, the firms that led in their development and adoption were the industry's leading, established firms. Table 2(a) depicts this leadership pattern for three representative sustaining technologies. In thin-film head technology, it was Burroughs (1976), IBM (1979), and other established firms that first successfully incorporated thin-film heads in disk drives. In the 1981–86 period, when over 60 firms entered the rigid disk drive industry, only five of them (all commercial failures) attempted to do so using thin-film heads as a source of performance advantage in their initial products. All other entrant firms—even aggressively performance-oriented firms such as Maxtor and Conner Peripherals—found it preferable to cut their teeth on ferrite heads in the entry products, before tackling thin-film technology in subsequent generations.

Note the similar pattern in the development and adoption of RLL codes—a much simpler development than thin-film head technology—which consumed at most a few million dollars per firm. RLL enabled a 30 percent density improvement, and therefore represented the type of inexpensive path to performance improvement that ought to be attractive to entrant firms. But in 1985, 11 of the 13 firms which introduced new models employing RLL technology were established firms, meaning that they had previously offered models based on MFM technology. Only two were entrants, meaning that their initial products employed RLL codes. Table 2(a) also notes that six of the first seven firms to introduce Winchester architecture drives were established makers of drives employing the prior disk pack architecture.[7]

The history of literally every other sustaining innovation—such as embedded servo systems, zone-specific recording densities, higher RPM motors and the 2.5-inch Winchester architecture—reveals a similar pattern: the established firms led in the adoption of sustaining technology be it in componentry or architecture. Entrant firms followed. In other words, the failure of leading firms to stay atop the disk drive industry generally was not because they could not keep pace with the industry's movement along the dashed-line technological trajectories mapped in Figure 2. The leading incumbent firms effectively *led* the industry along those trajectories even though many of these were competency-destroying progressions in terms of technologies, skills and manufacturing assets required (Tushman and Anderson, 1986).

In contrast, the firms that led the industry in introducing *disruptive* architectural technologies—in the moves to points B, C and D in Figure 2—tended overwhelmingly to be *entrant*, rather than established firms. This is illustrated in Table 2(b). It shows, for example, that in 1978 an entrant offered the industry's first 8-inch drive. By the end of the second year of that architecture's life (1979), six firms were offering 8-inch drives; two-thirds of them were entrants. Likewise, by the end of the second year of the 5.25-inch generation's life, eight of the 10 firms offering 5.25-inch drives were entrants. Entrants similarly dominated the early population of firms offering 3.5-inch drives. In each of these generations, between half and two-thirds of the established manufacturers of the prior architectural generation *never* introduced a model in the new architecture. And those established drivemakers that did design and manufacture new architecture models did so with an average two-year lag behind the pioneering entrant firms. In this fast-paced industry, such slow response often proved fatal.

These patterns of leadership and followership in sustaining and disruptive technologies are reflected in the commercial success and failure of disk drive manufacturers. The ability of established firms to lead the industry in the sustaining innovations that powered the steep technological trajectories in Figure 2 often were technologically difficult, risky and expensive. Yet in the history of this industry, there is no evidence that the firms that led in sustaining innovations gained market share by virtue of such technology leadership (Christensen, 1992b). This leadership enabled them to maintain their competitiveness only within specific technological trajectories. On the other hand, entrant firms' leadership advantages in disruptive innovations enabled them not only to capture new markets as they emerged, but (because the trajectories of technological progress were steeper than the trajectories of performance demanded) to invade and capture established markets as well.

Hence, all but one of the makers of 14-inch drives were driven from the mainframe computer market by entrant firms that got their start making

---

[7] Note that the statistics shown in Table 2 are not a sample—they represent the entire population of firms in each of the years shown offering models incorporating the technologies in question. For that reason, tests of statistical significance are not relevant in this case.

206   *C.M. Christensen and J.L. Bower*

Table 2.   Trends in technology leadership and followership in sustaining vs. disruptive technologies

(a) Numbers of established and entrant firms introducing models employing selected trajectory-sustaining technologies

		1974	1975	1976	1977	1978	1979	1980	1981	1982	1983	1984	1985	1986	1987	1988
Thin-film	Entrants								1		1	2	1		1	4
heads	Established			1			1	1	3	5	6	8	12	15	17	22
RLL codes	Entrants											1	2	3	6	8
	Established											4	11	20	25	26
Winchester	Entrants				1	4	9									
architecture	Established	1		3	3	7	11									

(b) Numbers of established and entrant firms introducing models based upon disruptive architectural technologies

		1974	1975	1976	1977	1978	1979	1980	1981	1982	1983	1984	1985	1986	1987	1988
8-inch	Entrants					1	4	6	8							
	Established					0	2	5	5							
5.25-inch	Entrants							1	8	8	13					
	Established							1	2	8	11					
3.5-inch	Entrants											1	2	3	4	
	Established											0	1	1	4	

Note: Data are presented in these tables only for those years in which the new technologies were gaining widespread acceptance, to illustrate tendencies in technology leadership and followership. Once the technologies had become broadly accepted, the numbers of firms introducing models using them are no longer reported. Twelve years are covered in the thin-film head category because it took that long for thin film heads to become broadly used in the marketplace. Only 5 years of history are reported for RLL codes because by 1988 the vast majority of established *and* entrant firms had adopted RLL codes. Four years of data are shown for new architectures, because any established firms that had not launched the new architecture within 4 years of its initial appearance in the market had been driven from the industry.

8-inch drives for minicomputers. The 8-inch drive-makers, in turn, were driven from the minicomputer market, and eventually the mainframe market, by firms which led in producing 5.25-inch drives for desktop computers. And the leading makers of 5.25-inch drives were driven from desktop and minicomputer applications by makers of 3.5-inch drives, as mapped in Figure 2.

We began this paper by posing a puzzle: why it was that firms which at one point could be esteemed as aggressive, innovative, customer-sensitive organizations could ignore or attend belatedly to technological innovations with enormous strategic importance. In the context of the preceding analysis of the disk drive industry, this question can be sharpened considerably. The established firms were, in fact, aggressive, innovative, and customer-sensitive in their approaches to sustaining innovations of every sort. But why was it that established firms could not lead their industry in disruptive architectural innovations? For it is only in these innovations that attackers demonstrated an advantage. And unfortunately for the

leading established firms, this advantage enabled attacking entrant firms to topple the incumbent industry leaders each time a disruptive technology emerged.[8]

To understand why disruptive technological change was so consistently vexing to incumbent firms, we personally interviewed managers who played key roles in the industry's leading firms, as incumbents or entrants, when each of these disruptive technologies emerged. Our objective in these interviews was to reconstruct, as accurately and from as many points of view as possible, the forces that influenced these firms' decision-making processes relating to the development and commercialization of disruptive architectural technologies. We found the experiences of the firms, and the forces influencing their decisions, to be

---

[8] We believe this insight—that attacking firms have an advantage in disruptive innovations but not in sustaining ones—clarifies but is not in conflict with Foster's (1986) assertions about the attacker's advantage. The historical examples Foster uses to substantiate his theory generally seem to have been disruptive innovations.

remarkably similar. In each instance, when confronted with disruptive technology change, developing the requisite *technology* was never a problem: prototypes of the new drives often had been developed before management was asked to make a decision. It was in the process of allocating scarce resources amongst competing product and technology development proposals, however, that disruptive projects got stalled. Programs addressing the needs of the firms' most powerful customers almost *always* pre-empted resources from the disruptive technologies, whose markets tended to be small and where customers' needs were poorly defined.

In the following section we have synthesized the data from case studies of the six firms we studied in particular depth, into a *six*-step model that describes the factors that influenced how resources were allocated across competing proposals to develop new sustaining vs. disruptive technology in these firms. The struggle of Seagate Technology, the industry's dominant maker of 5.25-inch drives, to successfully commercialize the disruptive 3.5-inch drive, is recounted here to illustrate each of the steps in the model. Short excerpts from a fuller report of other case histories (Christensen, 1992a) are also presented to illustrate what happened in specific companies at each point in the process. Table 3 describes how the findings from each of the case studies support, or do not support, the principal propositions in the model. In Yin's (1989) terms, the high degree of literal and theoretical replication shown in Table 3, and the extent of 'pattern matching' across case studies where more than one firm encountered the same technological change, lend high degrees of reliability and external validity to the model.[9]

A MODEL OF THE RESOURCE-ALLOCATION PROCESS IN ESTABLISHED FIRMS FACED WITH DISRUPTIVE CHANGE

1. Although entrants were the leaders in *commercializing* disruptive technology, it did not start out that way: the first engineers to develop the disruptive architectures generally did so while employed by a leading established firm, using bootlegged resources. Their work was rarely initiated by senior management. While architecturally innovative, these designs almost always employed off-the-shelf components. For example, engineers at Seagate Technology, the leading 5.25-inch drive maker, were the second in the industry to develop working prototype 3.5-inch models, in 1985. They made over 80 prototype models before the issue of formal project approval was raised with senior management. The same thing happened earlier at Control Data, the dominant 14-inch drivemaker. Its engineers had designed working 8-inch drives internally, nearly 2 years before they appeared in the market.

2. The marketing organization then used its habitual procedure for testing the market appeal of new drives, by showing prototypes to lead customers of the existing product line, asking them to evaluate the new models.[10] Again drawing on the Seagate case, marketers tested the new 3.5-inch drives with IBM and other makers of XT and AT-class desktop personal computers—even though the drives, as shown in Figure 2 above, had significantly less capacity than in the mainstream desktop market demanded.

---

[9] For readers who are unfamiliar with the work of scholars such as Yin (1989) and Campbell and Stanley (1966) on research methodology, a *literal* replication of a model occurs when an outcome happens as the model would predict. A *theoretical* replication of the model occurs when a different outcome happens than what would have been predicted by the model, but where this outcome can be explained by elements in the model. In the instance here, the success of entrants and the failure of established forms at points of disruptive technology change are directly predicted by the model, and would be classed as literal replications. Instances where an established firm succeeded in the face of disruptive technological change because it acted in a way that dealt with the factors in the model that typically precipitated failure, would be classed as *theoretical* replications of the model. Several of these instances occurred in the industry's history, as explained later in this paper.

[10] This is consistent with Burgelman's observation that one of the greatest difficulties encountered by corporate entrepreneurs was finding the right 'beta test sites', where products could be interactively developed and refined with customers. Generally, the entre to the customer was provided by the salesman who sold the firm's established product lines. This helped the firm develop new products for established markets, but did not help it identify new applications for its new technology (Burgelman and Sayles, 1986: 76–80). Professor Rebecca Henderson pointed out to us that this tendency always to take new technologies to mainstream customers reflects a rather narrow *marketing* competence—that although these issues tend to be framed by many scholars as issues of technological competence, a firm's disabilities in finding new markets for new technologies may be its most serious innovative handicap.

208   C.M. Christensen and J.L. Bower

Table 3.   Support of key elements of model found in each of six in-depth case studies

Companies Studied:	Prototypes of disruptive architecture drive developed internally, well before widespread industry adoption (model step 1)	Marketers show early prototypes to lead customers of prior architecture; they reject product; marketing issues pessimistic forecast (model step 2)	Project to commercialize disruptive product is shelved; company aggressively pursues sustaining innovations (model step 3)	New firms are established to commercialize disruptive architecture; they find new markets, where product's attributes are valued (model step 4)	Entrant firms which initially sold product only in new market improve performance faster than initial market requires, enabling them to attack established markets (model step 5)	In response to entrants' attack, established firms belatedly introduce disruptive product. Sales are largely to existing customers, cannibalizing sales of prior architecture products. (model step 6)
Quantum Corp.	L	L	L, T	L, T	L	L, T
Conner Peripherals	L		L	L	L	
Miniscribe		L		L	L	L
Seagate Technology	L	L	L	L	L	L
Micropolis	T	L	L,T	L,T	L	T
Control Data	L	L	L,T	L,T	L	L,T

Note: An 'L' in the matrix indicates that this step was a clear, explicit element in that firm's case history—in Yin's (1989) terms, a 'literal replication'. Where 'T' is shown, the firm avoided the fate described in the model by explicitly recognizing the factors in the model, and dealing with them in the manner described in the final section of this paper. These constitute what Yin calls 'theoretical replications' of the model. Where no 'L' or 'T' is shown, that step was not a clear or prominent part of the firm's encounter with the disruptive technology being studied. Some firms studied confronted only one disruptive architecture. Miniscribe, for example, started making 5.25-inch drives generally in the pattern indicated by our model; and was subsequently driven from the industry. Other firms, such as Quantum and Control Data, confronted a series of disruptive innovations, and dealt with some of them differently than they did with others, as described in the last section of the paper. In such instances, an 'L' and a 'T' are entered in the matrix. As Yin points out, when multiple case studies are used to support a multi-element model, as in this study, each cell in a matrix such as this constitutes an independent 'observation'. Hence, the model is supported in 32 of the 36 observations.

These customers showed little interest in the disruptive drives, because they did not address their need for higher performance within the established architectural framework. As Figure 2 shows, the established customers needed new drives that would take them *along* their existing performance trajectory. As a consequence, the marketing managers were unwilling to support the disruptive technology and offered pessimistic sales forecasts.

Generally, because the disruptive drives were targeted at emerging markets, initial forecasts of sales were small. In addition, because such products were simpler and offered lower performance, forecast profit margins were also lower than established firms had come to require. Financial analysts in established firms, therefore, joined their marketing colleagues in opposing the disruptive programs. As a result, in the ensuing allocation process resources were explicitly withdrawn, and the disruptive projects were slowly starved.

For example, when Seagate's main customer, IBM's PC division, rejected Seagate's 3.5-inch prototypes for insufficient capacity, sales forecasts were cut and senior managers shelved the program—just as 3.5-inch drives

were becoming firmly established in laptops. 'We needed a new model,' recalled a former Seagate manager, 'which could become the next ST412 (a very successful product generating $300 million sales annually in the desktop market that was near the end of its life cycle). Our forecasts for the 3.5-inch drive were under $50 million because the laptop market was just emerging—and the 3.5-inch product just didn't fit the bill.' And earlier, when engineers at Control Data, the leading 14-inch drive maker, developed its initial 8-inch drives, its customers were looking for an average of 300 MB per computer, whereas CDC's earliest 8-inch drives offered less than 60 MB. The 8-inch project was given low priority, and engineers assigned to its development kept getting pulled off to work on problems with 14-inch drives being designed for more important customers. Similar problems plagued the belated launches of Quantum's and Micropolis's 5.25-inch products.

3. In response to the needs of current customers, the marketing managers threw impetus behind alternative *sustaining* projects, such as incorporating better heads or developing new recording codes. These would give their cus-

tomers what they wanted, could be targeted at large markets, and generate the sales and profits required to maintain growth. Although they generally involved greater development expense, such sustaining investments appeared *far* less risky than investments in the disruptive technology, because the customers were there. The rationality of Seagate's decision to shelve the 3.5-inch drive in 1985–86, for example, is stark. Its view downmarket (in terms of Figure 2) was at a $50 million total market forecast for 3.5-inch drives in 1987. What gross margins it could achieve in that market were uncertain, but its manufacturing executives predicted that costs per megabyte in 3.5-inch drives would be much higher than in 5.25-inch products. Seagate's view upmarket was quite different. Volumes in 5.25-inch drives with capacities of 60–100 MB were forecast to be $500 million in size by 1987. And companies serving the 60–100 MB market were earning gross margins of 35–40 percent, whereas Seagate's margins in its high-volume 20 MB drives were between 25 and 30 percent. It simply did not make sense for Seagate to put resources behind the 3.5-inch drive, when competing proposals to move upmarket to develop its ST251 line of drives were also actively being evaluated.

After Seagate executives shelved the 3.5-inch project, it began introducing new 5.25-inch models at a dramatically accelerating rate. In the years 1985, 1986 and 1987, the numbers of new models it introduced each year as a percentage of the total number of its models on the market in the prior year were 57, 78, and 115 percent, respectively. And during the same period, Seagate incorporated complex and sophisticated new component technologies such as thin-film disks, voice coil actuators, RLL codes, and embedded, SCSI interfaces. In each of our other case studies as well, the established firms introduced new models in their established architectures employing an array of new component technologies at an accelerating rate, after the new architectures began to be sold. The clear motivation of the established firms in doing this was to win the competitive wars against each other, rather than to prepare for an attack by entrants from below.

4. New companies, usually including members of the frustrated engineering teams from established firms, were formed to exploit the disruptive product architecture. For example, the founders of the leading 3.5-inch drivemaker, Conner Peripherals, were disaffected employees from Seagate and Miniscribe, the two largest 5.25-inch manufacturers. The founders of 8-inch drive maker Micropolis came from Pertec, a 14-inch manufacturer; and the founders of Shugart and Quantum defected from Memorex.[11] The start-ups were as unsuccessful as their former employers in interesting established computer makers in the disruptive architecture. Consequently, they had to find *new* customers. The applications that emerged in this very uncertain, probing process were the minicomputer, the desktop personal computer, and the laptop (see Figure 2). These are obvious markets for hard drives in retrospect. But at the time, whether these would become significant markets for disk drives was highly uncertain. Micropolis was founded before the market for desk-side minicomputers and word processors, in which its products came to be used, emerged. Seagate was founded 2 years before IBM introduced its PC, when personal computers were simple toys for hobbyists. And Conner Peripherals got its start before Compaq knew the portable computer market had potential. The founders of these firms sold their products without a clear marketing strategy, essentially to whomever would buy them. Out of what was largely a trial-and-error approach to the market, the ultimately dominant applications for their products emerged.

5. Once the start-ups had found an operating base in new markets, they found that by adopting sustaining improvements in new component technologies,[12] they could increase the capacity of their drives at a faster rate than was required by their new market. As shown in Figure 2, they blazed trajectories of 50% annual improvement, fixing their sights on the large, established computer markets immedi-

---

[11] Ultimately, nearly all North American manufacturers of disk drives can trace their founders' genealogy to IBM's San Jose division, which developed and manufactured its magnetic recording products (Christensen, 1993).

[12] In general, these component technologies were developed within the largest of the established firms that dominated the markets above these entrants, in terms of the technology and market trajectories mapped in Figure 2.

210   *C.M. Christensen and J.L. Bower*

ately above them on the performance scale. As noted above, the established firms' views downmarket, and the entrant firms' views upmarket, were asymmetrical. In contrast to the unattractive margins and market size the established firms saw when eyeing the new markets for simpler drives as they were emerging, the entrants tended to view the potential volumes and margins in the upscale, high-performance markets above them as highly attractive. Customers in these established markets eventually embraced the new architectures they had rejected earlier, because once their needs for capacity and speed were met, the new drives' smaller size and architectural simplicity made them cheaper, faster, and more reliable than the older architectures. For example, Seagate, which started in the desktop personal computer market, subsequently invaded and came to dominate the minicomputer, engineering workstation, and mainframe computer markets for disk drives. Seagate, in turn, was driven from the desktop personal computer market for disk drives by Conner and Quantum, the pioneering manufacturers of 3.5-inch drives.

6. When the smaller models began to invade established market segments, the drivemakers that had initially controlled those markets took their prototypes off the shelf (where they had been put in step #3), and defensively introduced them to defend their customer base in their own market.[13] By this time, of course, the new architecture had shed its disruptive character, and had become fully performance-competitive with the larger drives in the established markets. Although some established manufacturers were able to defend their market positions through belated introduction of the new architecture, many found that the entrant firms had developed insurmountable advantages in manufacturing cost and design experience, and they eventually withdrew from the market. For those established manufacturers that did succeed in introducing the new architectures, survival was the only reward. None

of the firms we studied was ever able to win a significant share of the new market whose emergence had been enabled by the new architecture; the new drives simply cannibalized sales of older, larger-architecture products with existing customers. For example, as of 1991 almost none of Seagate's 3.5-inch drives had been sold to portable/laptop manufacturers: its 3.5-inch customers still were desktop computer manufacturers, and many of its 3.5-inch drives continued to be shipped with frames permitting them to be mounted in XT and AT-class computers that had been designed to accommodate 5.25-inch drives. Control Data, the 14-inch leader, never captured even a 1 percent share of the minicomputer market. It introduced its 8-inch drives nearly 3 years after the pioneering start-ups did, and nearly all of its drives were sold to its existing mainframe customers. Miniscribe, Quantum and Micropolis all had the same cannibalistic experience when they belatedly introduced disruptive-technology drives. They failed to capture a significant share of the new market, and at best succeeded in defending a portion of their prior business.

There are curious asymmetries in the *ex post* risks and rewards associated with sustaining and disruptive innovations. Many of the sustaining innovations (such as thin-film heads, thin film disks, and the 14-inch Winchester architecture) were *extremely* expensive and risky from a *technological* point of view. Yet because they addressed well-understood needs of known customers, perceived market risk was low; impetus coalesced; and resources were allocated with only prudent hesitation. Yet, although these innovations clearly helped the innovators retain their customers, there is no evidence from the industry's history that any firm was able to gain observable market share by virtue of such technology leadership.[14]

On the other hand, disruptive innovations were technologically straightforward: several established firms had already developed them by the time formal resource allocation decisions were

---

[13] Note that at this point, because the disruptive innovation invading below had become fully performance-competitive with the established technology, the innovation had essentially acquired the character of a sustaining innovation—it gave customers what they needed.

[14] Christensen (1992b) shows that there was no discernible first-mover advantage associated with trajectory-sustaining innovations, to firms in the disk drive industry. In contrast, there were *very* powerful first-mover advantages to leaders in trajectory-disruptive innovations that fostered the creation of new markets.

made. But these were viewed as extremely risky, because the markets were not 'there'. The most successful of the entrants that accepted the risks of creating new markets for disruptive innovations generated billions in revenues upon foundations of architectural technology that cost at most a few million dollars to put into place.

We argue that although differences in luck, resource endowments, managerial competence, and bureaucratic agility matter, the patterns of technology leadership displayed by established and entrant firms in the disk drive industry accurately reflect differences in the fully informed, rational *ex ante* perceptions of risks and rewards held by managers in the two types of firms. In each of the companies studied, a key task of senior managers was to decide which of the many product and technology development programs continually being proposed to them should receive a formal allocation of resources. The criteria used in these decisions were essentially the total return perceived in each project, adjusted by the perceived riskiness of the project, as these data were presented to them by mid-level managers. Projects targeted at the known needs of big customers in established markets consistently won the rational debates over resource allocation. Sophisticated systems for planning and compensation ensured that this would be the case.[15]

The contrast between the innovative behavior of some *individuals* in the firm, vs. the manner in which the firm's *processes* allocated resources across competing projects, is an important feature of this model.[16] In the cases studied, the pion-

eering engineers in established firms that developed disruptive-architecture drives were innovative not just in technology, but in their view of the market. They intuitively perceived opportunities for a very different disk drive. But organizational processes allocated resources based on rational assessments of data about returns and risks. Information provided by innovating engineers was at best hypothetical: without existing customers, they could only guess at the size of the market, the profitability of products, and required product performance. In contrast, current customers could articulate features, performance, and quantities they would purchase with *much* less ambiguity. Because of these differences in information clarity, firms were led toward particular sorts of innovations—many of which were extremely challenging and risky—and away from others. In the firms studied here, the issue does not seem so much to be innovativeness *per se*, as it is what *type* of innovation the firms' processes could facilitate.

In light of this research, the popular slogan, 'Stay close to your customers' (which is supported by the research of von Hippel, 1988, and others), appears not always to be robust advice. One instead might expect customers to lead their suppliers toward sustaining innovations, and to provide no leadership—or even to explicitly *mis*lead—in instances of disruptive technology change. Henderson (1993) saw similar potential danger for being held captive by customers in her study of photolithographic aligner equipment manufacturers.

We close our discussion of the model with a final note. Neglect of disruptive technologies proved damaging to established drivemakers because the trajectory of performance improvement that the technology *provided* was steeper than the improvement trajectory *demanded* in individual markets (see Figure 2.) The mismatch in these trajectories provided pathways for the firms that entered new markets eventually to become performance-competitive in established markets as well. If the trajectories were parallel, we would expect disruptive technologies to be deployed in new markets and to stay there; each successive market would constitute a relatively stable niche market out of which technologies and firms would not migrate.

---

[15] It is interesting that 20 years after Bower's (1970) study of resource allocation, we see in leading-edge systems for planning and compensation the same bias against risk taking. Morris and Ferguson's description of how IBM allowed Microsoft to gain control of PC operating system standards is centered on the role of mainframe producers in IBM's resource allocation process. In a 1990 interview with one of the authors, one of the most successful innovators in IBM history recounted how time and again he was forced to battle the controlling influence of middle-management's commitment to serve commercial mainframe customers.

[16] We are indebted to Professor Robert Burgelman for his comments on this issue. He has also noted, given the sequence of events we observed—where engineers inside the established firms began pursuing the disruptive product opportunity before the start-up entrants did—that timing matters a lot. It may be that when individuals in the established firms were pressing their ideas internally, they were too far ahead of the market. In the year or two that it took them to leave their employers, create new firms, and create new products, the nascent markets may have become more ready to accept the new drives.

212   *C.M. Christensen and J.L. Bower*

THE LINKAGE BETWEEN MODELS OF RESOURCE DEPENDENCE AND RESOURCE ALLOCATION

We mentioned at the outset that a contribution of this paper is that it establishes a linkage between the school of thought known as *resource dependence* (Pfeffer and Salancik, 1978) and the models of the resource allocation process proposed by Bower (1970) and Burgelman (1983a, 1983b). Our findings support many of the conclusions of the resource dependence theorists, who contend that a firm's scope for strategic change is strongly bounded by the interests of external entities (customers, in this study) who provide the resources the firm needs to survive. We show that the mechanism through which customers wield this power is the process in which impetus coalesces behind investments in sustaining technologies, directing resources to innovations that address current customers' needs.

But although our findings lend support to the theory of resource dependence, they decidedly do not support a contention that managers are powerless to change the strategies of their companies in directions that are inconsistent with the needs of their customers as resource providers (Pfeffer and Salancik, 1978: 263–265).[17] The evidence from this study is that managers can, in fact, change strategy—but that they can successfully do so only if their actions are consistent with, rather than in counteraction to, the principle of resource dependence. In the disk drive industry's history, three established firms achieved a measure of commercial success in disruptive technologies. Two did so by spinning out organizations that were completely independent, in terms of customer relationships, from the mainstream groups. The third launched the disruptive tech-

nology with extreme managerial effort, from within the mainstream organization. This paper closes by summarizing these case histories and their implications for theory.

Distinct organizational units for small drives at Control Data

Control Data (CDC) was the dominant manufacturer of 14-inch disk pack and Winchester drives sold into the OEM market between 1975 and 1982: its market share fluctuated between 55 and 62 per cent. When the 8-inch architecture emerged in the late 1970s, CDC missed it by 3 years. It never captured more than 3–4 percent of the 8-inch market, and those 8-inch drives that it did sell, were sold almost exclusively to its established customer base of mainframe computer manufacturers. The reason given by those interviewed in this study was that engineers and marketers kept getting pulled off the 8-inch program to resolve problems in the launch of next-generation 14-inch products for CDC's mainstream customers.

CDC also launched its first 5.25-inch model 2 years after Seagate's pioneering product appeared in 1980. This time, however, CDC located its 5.25-inch effort in Oklahoma City—according to one manager, 'not to escape CDC's Minneapolis engineering culture, but to isolate the (5.25-inch product) group from the company's mainstream customers. We needed an organization that could get excited about a $50,000 order. In Minneapolis (which derived nearly $1 billion from the sale of 14-inch drives in the mainframe market) you needed a million-dollar order just to turn anyone's head.' Although it was late and never reascended to its position of dominance, CDC's foray into 5.25-inch drives was profitable, and at times it commanded a 20 percent share of higher-capacity 5.25-inch drives.

Having learned from its experience in Oklahoma City, when CDC decided to attack the 3.5-inch market it set up yet another organization in Simi Valley, California. This group shipped its first products in mid-1988, about 18 months behind Conner Peripherals, and enjoyed modest commercial success. The creation of these standalone organizations was CDC's way of handling the 'strategic forcing' and 'strategic context determination' challenges described by Burgelman (1983b, 1984).

---

[17] In Chapter 10 of Pfeffer and Salancik's (1978) book, for example, they assert that the manager's most valuable role is symbolic, and they cite a hypothetical example. When external forces induce hard times in a company, managers can usefully be fired—not because bringing in a new manager will make any difference to the performance of the organization, but because of the symbolic content of that action. It creates the *feeling* in the organization that something is being done to address this problem, even though it will have no effect. The evidence from these case studies does not support this assertion about the ability of managers to change the course of their organizations. *As long as managers act in a manner consistent with the forces of resource dependence*, it appears that they can, indeed, wield significant power.

Quantum Corporation and the 3.5-inch Hardcard

Quantum Corporation, a leading maker of 8-inch drives sold in the minicomputer market, introduced its first 5.25-inch product 3 years after those drives had first appeared in the market. As the 5.25-inch pioneers began to invade the minicomputer market from below, for all of the reasons described above, Quantum launched a 5.25-inch product and was temporarily successful in defending some of its existing customers by selling its 5.25-inch drive to them. But it never sold a single drive into the desktop PC market, and its overall sales began to sag. In 1984 a group of Quantum engineers saw a market for a thin 3.5-inch drive plugged into an expansion slot in IBM XT- and AT-class desktop computers—drives that would be sold to end-users, rather than OEM computer manufacturers. Quantum financed and retained 80 percent ownership of this spin-off venture, called Plus Development Corporation, and set the company up in different facilities. Plus was extremely successful. As sales of Quantum's line of 8-inch drives began to evaporate in the mid-1980s, they were offset by Plus's growing 'Hardcard' revenues. By 1987, sales of 8 and 5.25-inch products had largely evaporated. Quantum purchased the 20 percent of Plus it did not own; essentially closed down the old corporation, and installed Plus's executives in Quantum's most senior positions. They then reconfigured Plus's 3.5-inch products to appeal to desktop computer makers such as Apple, just as the capacity vector for 3.5-inch drives was invading the desktop, as shown in Figure 2. By 1994 the new Quantum had become the largest unit-volume producer of disk drives in the world. Quantum's spin-out of the Hardcard effort and its subsequent strategic reorientation appears to be an example of the processes of strategy change described in Burgelman (1991).

Micropolis: Transition through managerial force

Managers at Micropolis Corporation, also an 8-inch drivemaker, employed a very different approach in which senior management initiated a disruptive program within the mainstream organization that made 8-inch drives. As early

as 1982, Micropolis' founder and CEO, Stuart Mabon, intuitively saw the trends mapped in Figure 2 and decided the firm needed to become primarily a maker of 5.25-inch drives. While initially hoping to keep adequate resources focused on the 8-inch line that Micropolis could straddle both markets,[18] he assigned the company's premier engineers to the 5.25-inch program. Mabon recalls that it took '100% of his time and energy for 18 months' to keep adequate resources focused on the 5.25-inch program, because the organization's own mechanisms allocated resources to where the customers were: 8-inch drives. By 1984 Micropolis had failed to keep pace with competition in the minicomputer market for disk drives, and withdrew its remaining 8-inch models. With Herculean effort, however, it did succeed in its 5.25-inch programs. Figure 3 shows why this was necessary: in the transition, Micropolis assumed a position on a very different technological trajectory (Dosi, 1982). In the process it had to walk away from every one of its major customers, and replace the lost revenues with sales of the new product line to an entirely different group of desktop computer makers. Mabon remembers the experience as the most exhausting of his life. Micropolis aborted a 1989 attempt to launch its first 3.5-inch drive, and as of 1992 the company still had not introduced a 3.5-inch product.

Table 4 arrays the experiences of the six companies we studied in depth, as they addressed disruptive technologies from within their mainstream organization, and through independent organizations. Companies are classed as having been successful in this table if their market share in the new market enabled by the disruptive disk drive technology was at least 25% of its percentage share in the prior, established market in which it was dominant. Hence, Control Data, whose share of the 14-inch mainframe computer disk drive market often exceeded 60 percent, was classed as a

---

[18] The failure of Micropolis to maintain simultaneous competitive commitments to its established technology while adequately nurturing the 5.25-inch technology is consistent with the technological histories recounted in Utterback (1994). Utterback found historically that firms that attempted to develop radically new technology almost always tried simultaneously to maintain their commitments to the old; and that they almost always failed.

214   *C.M. Christensen and J.L. Bower*

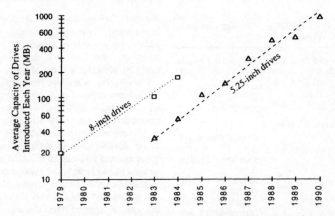

Figure 3. The disruptive impact of 5.25-inch drives on the market position of Micropolis Corp.

failure in its attempt to sell 8-inch drives, because its share of minicomputer disk drives never exceeded 3 percent. Its share of 5.25-inch drives sold to the desktop workstation market, however, reached 20 percent, and it was therefore classed as a success in that effort. An organization was defined as being independent from the mainstream if it was geographically separated; was held accountable for full profit and loss; and included within it all of the functional units of a typical company: sales and marketing, manufacturing, finance, human resources, engineering, and so on.

In addition to the six firms studied in depth, Table 4 lists other firms, shown in *italic type*, whose histories were researched through public sources and a more limited number of personal interviews. The 'L' and 'T' shown next to each company in the table, as in Table 3, denotes whether that firm's experience lends literal or theoretical support (Yin, 1989) to the proposition that managers can effect a strategy change despite resource dependence, by creating independent organizations that depend exclusively upon resources in the targeted market. Micropolis' transition from 8 to 5.25-inch drives is classed as a theoretical replication, because of the enormous managerial effort that was required to counteract the force of resource dependence in that transition.[19] Note that in

every instance except Micropolis' 5.25-inch entry, firms that *fought* the forces of resource dependence by attempting to commercialize disruptive technology from within their mainstream organizations failed, as measured by *Disk/Trend* data. And the firms that *accounted for* the forces of resource dependence by spinning out independent organizations succeeded.

Note in Table 4 that there do not seem to be strong firm or managerial effects, compared to the organizational effect. Control Data, Quantum, and Micropolis encountered multiple disruptive technologies; and *the same general managers sat atop these organizations across each of these transitions*. What seems to have distinguished these firms' successful from failed attempts to commercialize these disruptive technologies was not the talent of the managers *per se*, but whether the managers created organizationally distinct units to accomplish the task—where the forces of resource dependence could work in their favor, rather than against them. The successful cases cited here are the only ones in the industry's history in which a leading incumbent stayed atop its market when faced with disruptive technological change—and as a result, the number of data points in the top half of the matrix is limited. But these

---

[19] The success or failure of these other firms at each point of disruptive technology change was unambiguously determinable from *Disk/Trend Report* data. Similarly, whether these

firms managed the launch of disruptive technology products from within their mainstream organization, or through an organizationally separate unit, was a matter of public record and general industry knowledge. Hence, there were no subjective judgments involved in constructing Table 4.

Table 4. The success and failure of companies addressing disruptive technologies through mainstream vs. independent organizations

Succeeded	Control Data 5.25-inch (L) Control Data 3.5-inch (L) Quantum 3.5-inch (L) *Maxtor 3.5-inch (L)*	Micropolis 5.25-inch (T)
Failed		Control Data 8-inch (L) Quantum 5.25-inch (L) Miniscribe 3.5-inch (L) Seagate 3.5-inch (L) Micropolis 3.5-inch (L) *Memorex 8-inch (L)* *Memorex 5.25-inch (L)* *Priam 5.25-inch (L)* *Century Data 8-inch (L)* *Ampex 8-inch (L)* *Ampex 5.25-inch (L)*
	Commercialized from within an independent organization.	Commercialized from within the mainstream organization.

findings do suggest that, while the forces of resource dependence act as strong constraints on managerial discretion, managers can in fact manipulate those constraints effectively in order to achieve strategic change.

CONCLUSIONS

This study highlights an important issue for managers and scholars who strive to understand the reasons why strong, capably managed firms stumble when faced with particular types of technological change. While many scholars see the issue primarily as an issue of *technological competence*, we assert that at a deeper level it may an issue of *investment*. We have observed that when competence was lacking, but impetus from customers to develop that competence was sufficiently strong, established firms successfully led their industries in developing the competencies required for sustaining technological change. Importantly, because sustaining technologies address the interests of established firms' existing customers, we saw that technological change could be achieved without strategy change.

Conversely, when technological competence existed, but impetus from customers was lacking, we saw consistently that firms were unable to commercialize what they already could do. This is because disruptive technologies initially tend to be saleable only in different markets whose economic and financial characteristics render them unattractive to established firms. Addressing these technologies therefore requires a change in strategy in order to attack a very different market. In the end, it appears that although the stumbles of these established firms are *associated* with technological change, the key issue appears to be firms' disabilities in changing strategy, not technology.

Our model is not presented as the path every firm follows when faced with disruptive technology. We believe, however, that it may contribute several insights for scholars interested in the factors that affect strategic change in firms. First, it notes that the allocation of resources to some product development and commercialization programs, and the denial of resources to others, is a key event or decision in the implementation of strategy. The model highlights the process by which impetus and consequent resources may be denied to technological opportunities that do not contribute to the needs of prominent customers. These findings suggest a causal relationship might exist between resource allocation processes, as modeled by Bower (1970) and Burgelman (1983a, 1983b), and the phenomenon of resource dependence (Pfeffer and Salancik, 1978). Our findings suggest that despite the powerful forces of resource dependence, however, managers can, in fact, wield considerable power, and wield it effectively, in changing the strategic course of their firms in directions other than those in which its resource providers are pulling it. By understanding the processes that link customer needs, impetus, and resource allocation, managers can align efforts to commercialize disruptive technology (which entails a change in strategy) with the forces of resource dependence. This involves managing disruptive technology in a manner that is out of the organizational and strategic context of mainstream organizations—where of necessity,

216   *C.M. Christensen and J.L. Bower*

incentives and resource allocation processes are designed to nourish sustaining innovations that address current customers' needs. In this way, the model and these case studies illustrate the mechanisms through which autonomous and induced strategic behavior (Burgelman, 1983a) can affect, or fail to affect, a company's course.

Much additional research must be done. Efforts to explore the external validity and usefulness of the model through studies of sustaining and disruptive technological change in other industries has begun (Rosenbloom and Christensen, 1995), but much more is required. In addition, we hope that future researchers can develop clearer models for managerial action and strategic change in the face of disruptive technology change that are consistent with the principles of resource dependence and the processes of resource allocation.

ACKNOWLEDGEMENTS

We gratefully acknowledge the financial support of the Harvard Business School Division of Research in conducting the research for this paper, and thank the editors of *Disk/Trend Report* for sharing their industry data with us. We are indebted to Professors Robert Burgelman of Stanford University, Rebecca Henderson of the Massachusetts Institute of Technology, David Garvin and several of our other colleagues at the Harvard Business School, as well as the anonymous referees, for invaluable suggestions for improving earlier versions of this paper. Any remaining deficiencies are our sole responsibility.

REFERENCES

Bower, J. (1970). *Managing the Resource Allocation Process*. Irwin, Homewood, IL.
Burgelman, R. (1983a). 'A model of the interaction of strategic behavior, corporate context, and the concept of strategy', *Academy of Management Review*, 3(1), pp. 61–69.
Burgelman, R. (1983b). 'A process model of internal corporate venturing in the diversified major firm', *Administrative Science Quarterly*, 28, pp. 223–244.
Burgelman, R. (1984). 'Designs for corporate entrepreneurship in established firms', *California Management Review*, 26, Spring, pp. 154–166.
Burgelman, R. (1991). 'Intraorganizational ecology of strategy-making and organizational adaptation: Theory and field research', *Organization Science*, 2, pp. 239–262.
Burgelman, R. and L. Sayles (1986). *Inside Corporate Innovation*. Free Press, New York.
Campbell, D. T. and J. C. Stanley (1966). *Experimental and Quasi-Experimental Designs for Research*. Houghton Mifflin, Boston, MA.
Christensen, C. M. (1992a). 'The Innovator's challenge: Understanding the influence of market demand on processes of technology development in the rigid disk drive industry'. Unpublished DBA dissertation. Graduate School of Business Administration, Harvard University.
Christensen, C. M. (1992b). 'Exploring the limits of the technology S-curve', *Production and Operations Management*, 1, pp. 334–366.
Christensen, C. M. (1993). 'The rigid disk drive industry: A history of commercial and technological turbulence', *Business History Review*, 67, pp. 531–588.
Christensen, C. M. and R. S. Rosenbloom (1995). 'Explaining the attacker's advantage: Technological paradigms, organizational dynamics, and the value network', *Research Policy*, 24, pp. 233–257.
Cooper, A. and D. Schendel (February 1976). 'Strategic responses to technological threats', *Business Horizons*, 19, pp. 61–69.
Data Sources: The Comprehensive Guide to the Information Processing Industry (annual). Ziff-Davis Publishing, New York.
Disk/Trend Report (annual). Disk/Trend, Inc., Mountain View, CA.
Dosi, G. (1982). 'Technological paradigms and technological trajectories', *Research Policy*, 11, pp. 147–162.
Foster, R. J. (1986). *Innovation: The Attacker's Advantage*. Summit Books, New York.
Henderson, R. M. (1993). 'Keeping too close to your customers', working paper, Sloan School of Management, Massachusetts Institute of Technology.
Henderson, R. M. and K. B. Clark (1990). 'Architectural innovation: The reconfiguration of existing systems and the failure of established firms', *Administrative Science Quarterly*, 35, pp. 9–30.
Pfeffer, J. and G. R. Salancik (1978). *The External Control of Organizations: A Resource Dependence Perspective*. Harper & Row, New York.
Rosenbloom, R. S. and C. M. Christensen (1995). 'Technological discontinuities, organizational capabilities, and strategic commitments', *Industrial and Corporate Change*, 4, pp. 655–685.
Tushman, M. L. and P. Anderson (1986). 'Technological discontinuities and organizational environments', *Administrative Science Quarterly*, 31, pp. 439–465.
Utterback, J. (1994). *Mastering the Dynamics of Innovation*. Harvard Business School Press, Boston, MA.
von Hippel, E. (1988). *The Sources of Innovation*. Oxford University Press, New York.
Yin, R. K. (1989). *Case Study Research: Design and Methods*. Sage, Newbury Park, CA.

APPENDIX 1: A BRIEF PRIMER ON HOW DISK DRIVES WORK

Rigid disk drives are comprised of one or more rotating disks—polished aluminum platters coated with magnetic material—mounted on a central spindle. Data are recorded and read on concentric tracks on the surfaces of these disks. Read/write heads—one each for the top and bottom surfaces of each disk on the spindle—are aerodynamically designed to fly a few millionths of an inch over the surface of the disk. They generally rest on the disk's surface when the drive is at rest; 'take off' as the drive begins to spin; and 'land' again when the disks stop. The heads are positioned over the proper track on the disk by an actuator motor, which moves the heads across the tracks in a fashion similar to the arm on a phonograph. The head is essentially a tiny electromagnet which, when current flows in one direction, orients the polarity of the magnetic domain on the disk's surface immediately beneath it. When the direction of current through the electromagnet reverses, its polarity changes. This induces an opposite switch of the polarity of the adjacent domain on the disk's surface as the disk spins beneath the head. In this manner, data are written in binary code on the disk. To read data, changes in magnetic field on the disk as it spins beneath the head are used to induce changes in the direction of current—essentially the reverse process of writing. Disk drives also include electronic circuitry enabling computers to control and communicate with the drive.

As in other magnetic recording products, *areal recording density* (measured in megabits per square inch of disk surface area, or mbpsi) was the pervasive measure of product performance in the disk drive industry. Historically, areal density in the industry has increased at a steady 35 percent annual rate. A drive's total capacity is the product of the available square inches on the top and bottom surfaces of the disks mounted on the spindle of the drive, multiplied by its areal recording density. Historically, the capacity of drives in a given product architecture has increased at about 50 percent annually. The difference between the 35 percent increase in areal density and the 50 percent increase in total capacity has come from mechanical engineering innovations, which enable manufacturers to squeeze additional disks and heads into a given size of drive.

APPENDIX 2: CALCULATION OF THE TRAJECTORIES MAPPED IN FIGURE 2

The trajectories mapped in Figure 2 were calculated as follows. Data on the capacity provided with computers in the mainframe, minicomputer, desktop personal computer, and portable computer classes were obtained from *Data Sources*, an annual publication that lists the technical specifications of all computer models available from each computer manufacturer. Where particular models were available with different features and configurations, the manufacturer provided *Data Sources* with a 'typical' system configuration, with defined RAM capacity, performance specifications of peripheral equipment (including disk drives), list price, and year of introduction. In instances where a given computer model was offered for sale over a sequence of years, the hard disk capacity provided in the typical configuration generally increased. *Data Sources* divides computers into mainframe, mini/midrange, desktop personal, portable and laptop, and notebook computers. For each class of computers, all models available for sale in each year were ranked by price, and the hard disk capacity provided with the median-priced model was identified, for each year. The best-fit line through the resultant time series for each class of computer is plotted as the solid lines in Figure 2. These single solid lines are drawn in Figure 2 for expository simplification, to indicate the trend in typical machines. In reality, of course, there is a wide band around these lines. The leading and trailing edges of performance—the highest and lowest capacities offered with the most and least expensive computers— were substantially higher and lower, respectively, than the typical values mapped in Figure 2.

The dotted lines in Figure 2 represent the best-fit line through the unweighted average capacity of all disk drives introduced for sale in each given architecture, for each year. These data were taken from *Disk/Trend Report*. Again, for expository simplification, only this average line is shown. There was a wide band of capacities introduced for sale in each year, so that the highest-capacity drive introduced in each year was substantially above the average shown. Stated in another way, a distinction must be made between the full range of products available for

218   *C.M. Christensen and J.L. Bower*

purchase, and those in typical systems of use. The upper and lower bands around the median and average trajectories in Figure 2 are generally parallel to the lines shown.

Because higher-capacity drives were available than the capacities offered with the median-priced systems, we state in the text that the solid-line trajectories in Figure 2 represent the capacities 'demanded' in each market. In other words, the capacity per machine was not constrained by technological availability. Rather, it represents a *choice* for hard disk capacity, made by computer users, given the prevailing cost.

[10]

70

ARTWORK BY JANET DREW

In Silicon Valley, exciting new business ideas rapidly attract capital and talent away from less worthy ventures. But in big companies, ideas, capital, and talent are stagnant – prisoners of traditional bureaucratic ways of allocating resources. To capture the Valley's entrepreneurial magic, your company needs to move from resource allocation to resource attraction.

BRINGING SILICON VALLEY INSIDE

BY GARY HAMEL

I T'S A FACT. In most industries, newcomers are creating much of the new wealth. Cisco, Amazon.com, Starbucks, Charles Schwab, America Online, the Gap, MCI WorldCom, Dell, Southwest Airlines, SAP – these companies didn't even exist a generation ago, yet by May 1999 their combined market capitalization had grown to nearly $800 billion. And they are hardly unique. In industry after industry, unorthodox start-ups are challenging complacent incumbents.

Stewardship versus entrepreneurship: that's the fundamental distinction between the mediocre mass and the revolutionary wealth creators. Stewards polish grandma's silver – they buff up the assets and capabilities they inherited from entrepreneurs long retired or long dead. Devoid of passion and imagination, they spend their time trying to unlock wealth by hammering down costs, outsourcing inefficient processes, buying back shares, selling off bad businesses, and spinning out good ones. But in the new economy, investors don't want stewards. They want entrepreneurial heroes – innovators who are obsessed with creating *new* wealth. Stewards conserve. Entrepreneurs create.

If you want your company to join the pantheon of wealth-creating superstars, you have to shift the balance of effort from stewardship to entrepreneurship in your organization. There's nothing wrong with stewardship – someone has to safeguard all those brands, skills, assets, and customers that underpin today's success. But in a world where strategy life cycles are increasingly measured in months, not decades, even the most skilled stewardship won't enable you to capture tomorrow's riches. It may not even enable you to survive.

Face it: Out there in some garage, an entrepreneur is forging a bullet with your company's name on it. Once that bullet leaves the barrel, you won't be able to dodge it. You've got one option: you have to shoot first. You have to out-innovate the innovators, out-entrepreneur the entrepreneurs. Sound impossible for a decades-old incumbent? It is. Unless you're willing to challenge just about every assumption you have about how to drive innovation and wealth creation in your company.

Your classroom is Silicon Valley – a sliver of real estate about 30 miles long and ten miles wide, nestled up against the Santa Cruz mountains. Here you'll find towering eucalyptus trees, verdant hills, a crisp Pacific breeze, and what may be the most perfect climate on earth. But in these bucolic surroundings lurks a raw and restless spirit.

Face it: out there in some garage, an entrepreneur is forging a bullet with your company's name on it. You have only one option: you have to shoot first.

The Valley is the distilled essence of entrepreneurial energy. Its ethos is simple: If it's not new, it's not cool; if it's not cool, it's not worth doing. If you don't own shares, you're getting screwed. If you've been in the same job for more than two years, your career is over. If you haven't been through an IPO, you're a virgin. This is where a $2 million house is a teardown. This is where a Porsche is just one more compact car and sushi's just another fast food. Never has so much wealth been created in so little time by so few people. If the Valley's residents pause to think about it for even a nanosecond, they know they're as blessed as those who lived in Italy during the Renaissance. Like the Florentines and Venetians, they're building a new age – an age of virtual presence, of globally inter-

Gary Hamel is the Thomas S. Murphy Distinguished Research Fellow at Harvard Business School, a visiting professor of strategy and international management at the London Business School, and chairman of Strategos, a consulting firm based in Menlo Park, California. His last article for HBR, "Strategy as Revolution" (July–August 1996), won the McKinsey Prize. Hamel's forthcoming book, Leading the Revolution, *will be published by the Harvard Business School Press.*

To discuss this article, join HBR's authors and readers in the HBR Forum at www.hbr.org/forum.

connected communities, of frictionless commerce, of instantly accessible knowledge and stunningly seductive media.

If your company is going to grab more than its fair share of new wealth, it has to learn how to bring the energy and ethos of the Valley inside. The choice is simple, really. You can sit back and wait for the Valley or some other hotbed of innovation to spawn the revolutionary company that buries your business model. Or you can bring the Valley inside and capture the vast economic benefits that flow from unfettered imagination and unbridled ambition.

Big Stakes

What's the payoff to bringing Silicon Valley inside? Well, let's do a bit of arithmetic. Silicon Valley has about 2 million people. Let's say 50% of them are at work in the private sector – the rest are kids, retirees, government employees, and the like. Of that million, let's say half are of the caliber you'd find in your company – people who haven't spent their entire careers working at 7-Eleven or Jiffy Lube. Let's call those 500,000 people the Silicon Valley gene pool. In 1998, that gene pool produced 41 IPOs, which by January 1999 had a combined market cap of $27 billion. If you divide $27 billion by 500,000, you get $54,000. That's $54,000 in new wealth creation per capita – in a single year.

Multiply $54,000 by the number of employees in your organization. Did your company create that much new wealth last year out of your employee gene pool? Let's see. At the end of 1998, General Motors had 594,000 employees. That's $32 billion in potential new wealth – if only GM could engender the passion and imagination of Silicon Valley. Kmart had 278,000 employees – that's $15 billion in potential new wealth. 3M had 73,000 employees – that's $4 billion.

Okay, so maybe it's unreasonable to aspire to match the heady performance of Silicon Valley. Maybe you can create new wealth at only half the pace or a quarter of the pace. But ask yourself this: Would the potential payoff of bringing Silicon Valley inside be any less than what you're getting with supply chain management or enterprise resource planning or some other stewardship program? If not, doesn't it deserve at least the same effort?

Many corporate leaders envy the success of Silicon Valley's entrepreneurs, but few have thought about how they might bring the Valley inside – how they might ignite the entrepreneurial passions of their own people. They assume the Valley is filled with brilliant visionaries while their own organizations are filled with witless drones. This assumption is, of course, self-fulfilling. Where employees are called on to do no more than service the existing business model, you will indeed find a company filled with witless drones.

Those who populate Silicon Valley don't have brains the size of basketballs. They don't live in some special energy field. What sets the Valley apart is not its people or its climate but its way of doing business. In the Valley, ideas, capital, and talent are allowed to circulate freely. They meld into whatever combinations are most likely to generate innovation and wealth. There are none of the numbing bureaucratic controls that paralyze creativity in traditional businesses. If you want to free the entrepreneurial spirit inside your company, you're going to have to figure out how to set up and sustain dynamic internal markets for ideas, capital, and talent. Sound implausible? There are companies that are already doing it.

Silicon Valley in Royal Dutch/Shell

Royal Dutch/Shell, the Anglo-Dutch oil giant headquartered more than 6,000 miles from Silicon Valley, is seldom mistaken for a lithe and nimble upstart. With $138 billion in revenues and 102,000 employees, it's the epitome of a lumbering industrial behemoth – the last place you'd expect to find entrepreneurial zeal. Within its balkanized organization, which one employee has compared to a maze of 100-foot-high brick walls, access to capital is tightly controlled, investment hurdles are daunting, and radical ideas move slowly, if at all. Shell's globe-trotting managers are famously disciplined, diligent, and methodical; they don't come across as wild-eyed dreamers. Indeed, employees with an entrepreneurial urge would probably prefer skinny-dipping in the North Sea to confronting Shell's conservative bureaucracy.

But a band of renegades, led by Tim Warren, the director of research and technical services in Shell's largest division, Exploration and Production, has been intent on changing all that. Warren and his team have been working hard to free up the flow of ideas, capital, and talent – to make E&P an innovation-friendly zone. Their initial success suggests that it is possible to imbue a global giant with the kind of damn-the-conventions ethos that permeates Silicon Valley. Here's their story.

By late 1996, it had become apparent to Warren and some of his colleagues that E&P was unlikely to meet its earnings targets without radical innovations. In recent years, his team had been under considerable pressure to align its R&D spending with the immediate needs of Shell's national operating units. Long-term projects had been reined in and short-term priorities given more weight. Warren understood the rationale for those moves, but he wondered whether the existing R&D process could be counted on to help Shell invent entirely new businesses and dramatically different business models. He sensed that a wealth of imagination was bottled up in Shell's employees – imagination that might help the company find its way into new, high-growth opportunities.

Looking to stir up some new thinking, he had already encouraged his people to devote up to 10% of their time to "nonlinear" ideas. The results were less than he'd hoped for. His frustration was the genesis for an entirely new approach to innovation, one that was both simple and slightly deviant.

He gave a small panel of freethinking employees the authority to allocate $20 million to rule-breaking, game-changing ideas submitted by their peers. Anyone could submit ideas, and the panel would decide which deserved funding. Proposals would be accepted not just from within E&P but from anywhere across Shell. In this way, unconventional ideas wouldn't have to run the usual approval gauntlet or justify their existence in terms of existing programs and priorities.

The GameChanger process, as it came to be known, went live in November 1996. At first, the availability of venture funding failed to yield an avalanche of new ideas. Though bright and creative, employees long accustomed to working on well-defined technical problems found it difficult to think revolutionary thoughts. Hoping to kick-start the process, the GameChanger panel enlisted the help of a team of consultants from Strategos who designed a three-day "Innovation Lab" to help employees develop rule-busting ideas and to dole out a half million dollars of seed money. Seventy-two enthusiastic would-be entrepreneurs showed up for the initial lab, a much larger group than the panel had anticipated. Many were individuals no one would have suspected of harboring an entrepreneurial impulse.

If you want to free the entrepreneurial spirit inside your company, you're going to have to set up and sustain dynamic internal markets for ideas, capital, and talent. Sound implausible? There are companies that are already doing it.

In the Innovation Lab, the budding revolutionaries were encouraged to learn from radical innovations drawn from outside the energy business. They were taught how to identify and challenge industry conventions, how to anticipate and exploit discontinuities of all kinds, and how to leverage Shell's

Big companies are not markets, they're hierarchies. The guys at the top decide where the money goes. You wanna try something new, something out of bounds, something that challenges the status quo? Good luck.

competencies and assets in novel ways. Groups of eight attendees were then seated at round tables in front of networked laptop computers and encouraged to put their new thinking skills to work. Slowly at first, then in a rush, new ideas began to flow through the network. Some ideas attracted a flurry of support from the group; others remained orphans. By the end of the second day, a portfolio of 240 ideas had been generated. Some were for entirely new businesses, and many more were for new approaches within existing businesses.

The attendees then agreed on a set of screening criteria to determine which of the ideas deserved a portion of the seed money. Twelve ideas were nominated for funding, and a volunteer army of supporters coalesced around each one. Invigorated by their participation in the Innovation Lab, the teams vowed to move quickly to turn their GameChanger ideas into concrete business plans. A second Innovation Lab was held a month later with a new tranche of nascent entrepreneurs, and it produced a similar outpouring of fresh thinking.

Realizing that GameChanger had to be more than a brainstorming exercise, Shell put mechanisms in place to ensure that the ideas were turned into

actions. At the conclusion of the Innovation Labs, internal transfer payments were made to cover the time of the employees serving on the idea development teams. A five-day "Action Lab," again designed with Strategos, was held to teach the teams to create credible venture plans. In the Action Lab, team members were taught how to scope out the boundaries of an opportunity space, identify potential partnerships, enumerate genuine sources of competitive advantage, and identify the broad financial implications. Next, they were coached in developing 100-day action plans: low-cost, low-risk ways of testing the ideas. Finally, each team presented its story to a "venture board" consisting of the GameChanger panel, a sampling of senior managers, and representatives from Shell Technology Ventures – a unit that funds projects that don't fall under the purview of Shell's operating units.

Since the completion of the labs, the Game-Changer panel has been working hard to institutionalize the internal entrepreneurial process. It meets weekly to discuss new submissions – 320 have come in so far, many through Shell's intranet – and its members serve as coaches and advocates for prospective innovators. An employee with a

Shell's various growth initiatives. Others are carried forward as R&D projects, and still others are written off as interesting but unsuccessful experiments.

Several of the GameChanger ventures have themselves grown into major corporate initiatives. Indeed, of the company's five largest growth initiatives in early 1999, four had their genesis in the GameChanger process. One team was granted a charter to work with people throughout Shell to explore an entirely new business focused on renewable geothermal energy sources. GameChanger has also had a significant impact on Tim Warren's own division. Fully 30% of E&P's 1999 R&D budget is focused on ventures that have emerged from the process.

Yet the GameChanger program is still fragile. The 1998 slump in oil prices threw Shell into a frenzy of cost cutting. Whether GameChanger will survive in its current form remains to be seen. But it has demonstrated unequivocally that entrepreneurial passion lurks everywhere – even deep in the canyons of a 92-year-old oil company.

From Resource Allocation to Resource Attraction

Shell is just one of a number of companies, ranging from Monsanto to Virgin to GE Capital, that have internalized the principles of Silicon Valley. To gain a fuller understanding of those principles, we need to head back to the Valley. Let's pop in for breakfast at Buck's – a popular diner in Woodside that attracts cyber-CEOs, venture capitalists, and an unending stream of entrepreneurs on the make. In the parking lot you'll find some of the world's most exotic cars, and maybe a horse or two tied up at a well-used hitching rail. Inside you'll find a restaurant that can be charitably described as eclectic (imagine an explosion in the props department at Paramount Pictures). Now look around. These people are having *fun*. These people know they're creating the new economy. There's a buzz that goes beyond caffeine. No whining Dilberts here. Everyone should have this much fun. Everyone should have the chance to build something that will make a difference. Everyone should have the chance to create new wealth. So why doesn't it happen?

It doesn't happen because few executives can distinguish between Silicon Valley as a place and Silicon Valley as a way of doing business. Silicon Valley's not just an incestuous little cluster of universities, venture capitalists, and eager entrepreneurs perched on a peninsula. At its core are three interconnected markets: a market for ideas, a market for capital, and a market for talent. It is at the

promising idea is invited to give a ten-minute pitch to the panel, followed by a 15-minute Q&A session. If the members agree that the idea has real potential, the employee is invited to a second round of discussions with a broader group of company experts whose knowledge or support may be important to the success of the proposed venture. Before rejecting an idea, the panel looks carefully at what Shell would stand to lose if the opportunity turned out to be all its sponsors claimed. Ideas that get a green light often receive funding – on average, $100,000, but sometimes as much as $600,000 – within eight or ten days. Those that don't pass muster enter a database accessible to anyone who would like to compare a new idea with earlier submissions.

Some months later, each accepted project goes through a proof-of-concept review in which the team has to show that its plan is indeed workable and deserves further funding. This review typically marks the end of the formal GameChanger process, although the panel will often help successful ventures find a permanent home inside Shell. About a quarter of the efforts that get funded ultimately come to reside in an operating unit or in one of intersection of unbounded imagination, opportunity-seeking cash, and energetic freethinking people that wealth gets created. Ideas, capital, and talent whirl through Silicon Valley in a frenetic entrepreneurial dance. In most large companies, by contrast, ideas, capital, and talent are indolent. They don't move unless someone orders them to move. Where Silicon Valley is a vibrant market, the average big company is a smothering bureaucracy.

In fact, the last bastion of Soviet-style central planning can be found in *Fortune* 500 companies – it's called resource allocation. Big companies are not markets, they're hierarchies. The guys at the top decide where the money goes. Unconventional ideas are forced to make a tortuous climb up the corporate pyramid. If an idea manages to survive the gauntlet of skeptical vice presidents, senior vice presidents, and executive vice presidents, some distant CEO or chairman finally decides whether or not to invest. You wanna try something new, something out of bounds, something that challenges the status quo? Good luck. It's no wonder so many Silicon Valley entrepreneurs are corporate exiles. After all, the Valley is nothing more than a refugee camp for frustrated entrepreneurs who couldn't get a hearing elsewhere. (See the sidebar "How Sun Nearly Torched Its Future.")

Silicon Valley is based not on resource *allocation* but on resource *attraction* – a crucial distinction. If an idea has merit, it will attract resources in the form of venture capital and talent. If it doesn't, it won't. There's no CEO of Silicon Valley. There's no giant brain making global allocation decisions. And there's also no reason resource attraction can't be made to work inside a General Motors, an AT&T, or a Procter & Gamble. Everyone doesn't have to work within 50 miles of one another for free markets to function. As we saw at Shell, there are other ways to link passion, imagination, cash, and competence in the service of new business ideas.

Resource allocation is well suited to investments in existing businesses. After all, the guys at the top built the business, and they're well placed to make judgments about investments aimed at perpetuating existing business models. But management veterans are not usually the best ones to judge the merits of investing in entirely new business models or making radical changes to existing models. In these cases, their experience is irrelevant at best. A senior officer at Monsanto put it bluntly: "You can't trust the judgment of a senior vice president to get resources behind the best new ideas."

It's not that top-down resource allocation, and the painstaking financial analysis that underlies it,

has no place in companies. It does. But it can't be the only game in town. If the goal is to create new wealth, something much more spontaneous and less circumscribed is required – something much more like resource attraction. Shell's GameChanger process is totally unsuited to the problem of evaluating the investment case for a new multibillion-dollar offshore oil platform. But, conversely, Shell's comprehensive financial modeling is of no help in deciding whether to make an initial investment in some nontraditional energy venture.

Resource allocation is about managing the downside. Resource attraction is about creating the upside. Who can say which is more important? It's vitally important to manage the downside risk of big investments in the core business. It's equally important to unleash the ideas and passion that will create new businesses or transform the core. For this

How Sun Nearly Torched Its Future

Resource allocation is just as likely to hobble creativity in large and vibrant Silicon Valley companies as it is in boring, old, industrial-age companies. Sun Microsystems is a Valley legend. In the early 1980s, its four founders created the high-end workstation business. Sun's early workstations sold for as much as $40,000. When one of the company's founders, Andy Bechtolsheim, suggested building a $10,000 workstation using a radical new chip technology, he ran headfirst into a wall of internal skepticism. The reason was simple: Sun's process for allocating product development resources heavily favored incremental improvements to existing products. Frustrated, Bechtolsheim left the company and used his own money to build a prototype. When they finally saw the elegant new computer, Sun's top managers quickly invited Bechtolsheim back into the fold. Within three months the new workstation, named the SPARCstation, was out-selling every other product in the Sun line.

Not every entrepreneur is as single-minded as Andy Bechtolsheim, and most lack the resources to fund their dreams. If your company insists on trying to frog-march every new idea through a resource allocation process built for incrementalism, it will leave millions of dollars of potential wealth on the table for future-focused start-ups.

reason every company must become an amalgam of disciplined resource allocation *and* impromptu resource attraction. Hierarchies and markets must coexist.

Hierarchy – you understand that. But what about markets for ideas, capital, and talent. Just how do they work?

The Market for Ideas

An average-sized venture-capital firm in Silicon Valley gets as many as 5,000 unsolicited business plans a year. How many unsolicited business plans does the average senior vice president of a big company get? Five? Ten? Zero? There's not much chance of catching the next wave when your corner of the ocean is as placid as a bathtub.

In Silicon Valley everyone understands that innovation is the only way to create new wealth – both corporately and individually. New-economy billionaires like Jerry Yang, cofounder of Yahoo!, and Pierre Omidyar, chairman and founder of eBay, didn't get rich by wringing the last ounce of efficiency out of dying business models. Everyone in the Valley knows this. The proposition that innovation creates new wealth is so obvious as to be totally unremarkable. But employees in most large companies live in a world where operational efficiency is everything. Reengineering. Workout. Six sigma. Supply chain optimization. Enterprise resource planning. Whatever the name, the goal is the same – get better at what you're already doing. Their spirits crushed by a decade-long efficiency death march, few employees are able to even imagine another route to wealth creation.

If you doubt it, ask yourself how many people in your company believe, *really* believe, that rule-busting innovation is more likely to create shareholder wealth than, say, a flawless SAP implementation. Every successful company was built on radical innovations. But are those innovations still celebrated in your company, or are they relegated to dusty pages in some corporate archive?

And how many people in your company believe that radical innovation is the fastest route to *personal* wealth creation? Two years ago, the CEO of one of America's large information technology companies approached me with a simple question: "What will it take for my company to capture a bigger chunk of Internet-related opportunities?"

"For starters," I replied, "a willingness to create a slew of 30-year-old millionaires."

The CEO furrowed his brow and said, "I can't see us doing that." Not surprisingly, his company has missed the Internet bonanza.

All too often, the risk-reward trade-off for internal entrepreneurs is long on risk and short on reward. Why should employees risk a bruising battle with the defenders of the status quo when the potential payoff is so meager? Unless the champions of the new believe there is a chance for substantial personal wealth creation, the marketplace for ideas will be as barren as the shelves of a Soviet supermarket. It's ironic that companies pay CEOs millions upon millions to unlock shareholder wealth but seem incapable of funneling six- and seven-figure rewards to people who can actually create new wealth. The currency in Silicon Valley is equity. There are many, many companies where every employee is a shareholder and where success has made millionaires out of all those who took a risk and joined the company before it was a sure thing.

It used to be that the difference between working for a large company and working in a start-up was job security. You wouldn't get rich working in a big firm but, short of malfeasance, your job was secure. That bargain was shattered by the endless waves of restructuring that swept through corporate America in the 1990s. In 1998, there were more than 600,000 layoffs in large U.S. companies. That was a record. Recent years have also seen a record number of start-ups. These trends are not unrelated. If job security inside Giganticorp is as precarious as it is in a start-up, why not go for the start-up and the chance for a big personal payoff? Until senior executives spend as much energy fostering innovation as they do efficiency, and until individuals believe they have the opportunity for substantial wealth creation, the marketplace for ideas will remain closed.

Silicon Valley is based not on resource allocation but on resource attraction – a crucial distinction. If an idea has merit, it will attract both money and talent immediately.

There's a second reason large companies fail to spur much true innovation. Inside their walls, the marketplace for ideas is a monopsony – there's only one buyer. There's only one place to pitch a new idea – up the chain of command – and all it takes is one *nyet* to kill that idea. In the Valley, there's no one person who can say no to a new idea. Power is diffuse, and there are many sources of capital. It's rare to find a successful start-up whose initial business plan wasn't rejected by several venture capitalists before finding a sponsor. In an analogous way, Shell's GameChanger process invites protagonists to present their business plans to a wide cross section of senior executives. The hope is that if one says no, another will say yes.

The third reason why the market for ideas is much more vibrant in Silicon Valley is that there's no prejudice about who is or is not capable of inventing a new business model. The hierarchy of imagination counts for far more than the hierarchy of experience. As Steve Jobs puts it, "Silicon Valley is a meritocracy. It doesn't matter how old you are. It doesn't matter what you wear. What matters is how smart you are." In the Valley, no one assumes that the next great thing will come from a senior vice president running the last great thing.

There's an implicit belief in most large companies that strategy is the province of senior management. Not so long ago, a disaffected employee in one of America's largest companies caught up with me at a conference where I was speaking. In his hands was the company's glossy new performance-assessment manual, which had recently been distributed to all employees. He drew my attention to the fact that only "senior executives" were to be accountable for "creating strategy." The performance criteria for "managers" and "associates" said not a word about strategy. Vibrating with indignation, he accused his employer of being uniquely stupid in having excused 99% of its employees from any responsibility for strategic thinking. Surely, no other company would be so backward as to assume that only top executives could create strategy. Yes, I assured him, he had a right to be indignant. But no, his company was far from unique. What he faced was no different from what mavericks face in big companies everywhere.

Think about the corporate pyramid and ask yourself three questions. First, where in the pyramid will you find the least genetic diversity in terms of how people think about the business? Second, where in the organization will you find people who have most of their emotional equity invested in the past? And third, where will you find people who have, for the most part, already "made it"? The answer to all three questions is, "at the top." What's the chance, then, that a truly revolutionary idea will emerge from the ranks of top management? Jeff Bezos, the founder of Amazon.com, wasn't some big muckety-muck at Barnes & Noble or Borders. Wayne Huizenga, the founder of Blockbuster and AutoNation, got his start in the garbage business. And Anita Roddick, founder of the Body Shop, had no prior experience in the cosmetics industry.

Every day of the week, venture capitalists get pitched new ideas by kids who haven't reached their 30th birthday. When was the last time you saw a 20-something pitch a radical new business idea in your company with any kind of success? If it's not happening, your company has already relinquished most of its wealth-creating potential. [See the sidebar "Virgin's Amazing Business-Making Machine."]

The explosive growth of GE Capital has come in large part from its ability to bring Silicon Valley inside. Like venture capitalists, executives running GE Capital's 28 businesses devote much of their time to hunting down opportunities outside current business boundaries. In the 1998 planning round, someone suggested that every business put together a team of lower- to midlevel managers, all of them under 30, and give them the task of finding opportunities that their "stodgy old managers" had missed. The young teams came back with a bunch of novel ideas, including several focused on how GE

Virgin's Amazing Business-Making Machine

While most large companies have to work had to stoke the fires of entrepreneurship, they burn with a ferocious intensity at the Virgin Group. Described by one senior executive as a "branded venture-capital company," Virgin would never be mistaken for a hidebound incumbent. But as a £3 billion company that has created nearly 200 new businesses, it stands as clear evidence that ideas, capital, and talent can flow as freely in big, far-flung organizations as the can among the start-ups of Silicon Valley.

Virgin's eclectic business mix includes entertainment megastores, cinemas, a funky fun-to-fly airline, an all-in-one consumer-banking arm, a hip radio station, and a passenger-train service. (At one time the company even hawked condoms, though in that case they wisely avoided using the Virgin brand.) Unlike other business visionaries, Virgin's chairman, Richard Branson, doesn't limit his vision to one particular industry, he has a vision about what it takes to spawn entirely new business models. He hasn't invented a new business so much as he's invented a business-making machine.

Business ideas can come from anywhere in Virgin. As the company has grown, Branson has remained accessible to employees who have novel proposals. There was a time when every employee had Branson's phone number, and he would receive two or three calls a day from workers wanting to try something new. Today he gets around 50 letters a day from employees. And the annual "house party" he hosts for employees, which has grown into a week-long 35,000-person extravaganza, is another occasion to buttonhole the chairman.

Capital could leverage the Internet. New wealth is created by new ideas. New ideas tend to come from new voices. Are you listening to those voices in your organization?

The Market for Capital

Over the last decade it would have been great to be a shareholder in Silicon Valley Inc., a holding company encompassing all the high-tech start-ups in the Valley. Look at the numbers. Of the 63 companies that received venture funding in the fourth quarter of 1993, 26 had gone public by the end of 1998. An investor who bought into each of those

companies at the offer price would have achieved a return of 1,700% by the end of last year. The internal rate of return of the average venture capital firm is estimated to be about 40% – hardly shabby – and the best do substantially better than that.

Venture capitalists are not financially stupid people, but they sure don't think like CFOs. While both may be in the business of funding projects, the market for capital in Silicon Valley isn't anything like the market for capital in large companies. The first difference is access. How easy is it for someone seven levels down in a large company to get a few hundred thousand dollars to try out a new idea? Whether the sum is half a million or $50 million,

In one telling incident, a woman who believed the company's airline should offer passengers onboard massages camped on Branson's doorstep until she was allowed to give him a neck and shoulder rub. Now, an in-flight massage is a valued perk in Virgin Atlantic's Upper Class. On another occasion, a soon-to-be-married flight attendant came up with the idea of offering an integrated bridal-planning service – everything from wedding apparel to catering to limousines to honeymoon reservations. She became the first CEO of Virgin Bride. And Virgin's burgeoning Internet business was started by an employee who was working in another company within Virgin's Media Group.

Branson and his deputies have worked hard to instill a "speak up" culture at Virgin. There is no gleaming corporate headquarters, just a large and slightly tatty house in London's Holland Park, where meetings are often held in a small conservatory overlooking an equally small garden. There are no trappings of executive privilege to intimidate employees. There are no job descriptions because they're believed to limit what people can do. In the company's pancake-flat organization, senior executives work shoulder-to-shoulder with first-line employees. It's probably safe to say that the level of discourse between top executives and "ordinary" employees is unprecedented in an organization of Virgin's size. One example: the managing director of the company's financial services arm, Virgin Direct, regularly books eight seats at a local restaurant. Anyone with a new idea can apply for a spot.

In addition to all the informal conversations, Virgin has instituted formal mechanisms to ensure that good ideas come to light and receive adequate attention and funding. Its business development function, once led by a former venture capitalist, canvasses managers from across the company for ideas and pulls together ad hoc

teams to evaluate the most promising ones. Virgin Management, the nearest thing Virgin has to a head office, is a small team of creative people who help launch new businesses and work to inculcate them with the company's values. The role of business development and Virgin Management is not all that different from the role a venture capital board would play in bringing a new business into existence. Indeed, Will Whitehorn, one of Branson's key aides, describes the chairman as an investment "angel" of the type who gives first-stage funding to Silicon Valley start-ups.

Virgin's approval process for new business ventures doesn't look much like the traditional corporate planning process. The investment screen essentially consists of four questions: What is the potential for restructuring the market and bringing new benefits to consumers? Is the opportunity radical enough to justify the Virgin brand? (Me-too strategies are anathema.) Will the opportunity benefit from the skills and expertise Virgin has accumulated in its other businesses? Is there a way to keep the investment risk within acceptable boundaries? As Gordon McCallum, the current director of Virgin's business development function, puts it, "The ultimate business case is not a financial one, but one that is based upon deep customer needs and an understanding of how to meet them in a new way. The numbers will take care of themselves if we get things right for our customers."

Virgin's model for business creation is as unique as it is productive. In how many companies does every employee know they're in the business of creating new businesses? In how many companies does everyone deeply believe that to succeed they have to shatter the rules? In how many companies does everyone know they have the opportunity to be heard at the highest levels? Outside Silicon Valley, you won't find many.

the investment hurdles usually appear insurmountable to someone far removed from top management.

Most companies have a system of graduated approval limits, where senior executives have the authority to make bigger financial commitments than lower-level managers do. Yet whatever the level and dollar amount involved, the aversion to risk is the same. What is a trivial risk for the company as a whole may be a substantial risk for a small unit and for the career of a young manager. An eager entrepreneur wanting to risk a few hundred grand has to make the same airtight business case as a divisional vice president who's going to risk tens of millions of dollars. But does it really make sense to set the same hurdles for a small investment in a new experiment as for a large and irreversible investment in an existing business? Why should it be so difficult for someone with an unconventional idea to get the funding needed to build a prototype, design a little market trial, or merely flesh out a business case –particularly when the sum involved is peanuts?

Imagine that every innovator in Silicon Valley had to go to Bill Gates for funding. Pretty soon everyone in the Valley would be working to extend the Windows franchise. Goodbye to Netscape. Goodbye to Java. Goodbye to PalmPilot.

In most companies, there's an assumption that anything nonincremental is high risk and anything incremental is low risk. But in a fast-changing world, the reverse is often true. Venture capitalists are risk takers, but they're not *big* risk takers. Motorola investing in Iridium, AT&T buying into the cable TV industry, Monsanto spending billions on seed companies, Sony betting a billion on a new video game chip – these are big risks. VCs look for opportunities that don't need a lot of cash to get started. The initial investment in Hotmail was $300,000; the company was sold to Microsoft for something north of $400 million. Silicon Valley runs on nifty new ideas, not zillions of greenbacks. VCs work hard to enforce a culture of frugality in the companies they back. And because they are intimately involved in those companies – helping to appoint the management team, sitting on the board, plotting strategy with the owners – they are well positioned to know when to double their bets and when to cut and run. Compared with VCs, the average CFO is a spendthrift.

Roughly two-thirds of Silicon Valley start-ups receive their initial funding from "angels" – wealthy individuals who pool their investments to fund new companies. The average angel puts in around $50,000, and the average first-round investment for a start-up is $500,000. That's a rounding error in the average annual report. Yet how easy would it be for an ardent entrepreneur in your company to find ten angels willing to invest $50,000 each?

Creative new business ideas seldom make it through traditional financial screens. If estimates of market size and market growth seem the tiniest bit fuzzy, the proposal gets canned. If key business assumptions seem a bit shaky, no funds are forthcoming. If financial projections can't be supported with reams of analysis, top management takes a pass. Typical is the logic a senior car-company exec gave me for his firm's initial reluctance to invest in minivans: "There was no segment there, so how could we invest? We couldn't make a business case." By the time the company amassed enough evidence to assure itself that the minivan opportunity was real, it was a million units behind Chrysler, the minivan pioneer.

The market for capital works very differently in Silicon Valley. Talk to Steve Jurvetson, who funded Hotmail and is one of the Valley's hottest young VCs. Ask him how he evaluates a potential business idea, and this is what he'll tell you:

The first thing I ask is, Who will care? What kind of difference will this make? Basically, How high is up? I want to fund things that have just about unlimited upside. The second thing I ask is, How will this snowball? How will you scale this thing? What's the mechanism that drives increasing returns? Can it spread like a virus? Finally, I want to know how committed the person is. I never invest in someone who says they're *going* to do something; I invest in people who say they're *already* doing something and just want the funding to drive it forward. Passion counts for more than experience.

A VC has a very different notion of what constitutes a business plan than the typical CFO. Again, listen to Jurvetson:

The business plan is not a contract in the way a budget is. It's a story. It's a story about an opportunity, about the migration path and how you're going to create and capture value.

I never use Excel at work. I never run the numbers or build financial models. I know the forecast is a delusional view of reality. I basically ignore this. Typically, there are no IRR forecasts or EVA calculations. But I spend a lot of time thinking about how big the thing could be.

The point is this: in most companies the goal of capital budgeting is to make sure the firm never ever makes a bet-the-business investment that fails to deliver an acceptable return. But in attempting to guarantee that there's never an unexpected downside, the typical capital-budgeting process places an absolute ceiling on the upside. Dollars lost are highly visible (everyone knows whose projects have lost money), but dollars foregone are totally invisible.

Venture capitalists start with a very different set of expectations about success and failure. Out of 5,000 ideas, a five-partner VC firm may invest in ten, which it views as a portfolio of options. Out of that ten, five will be total write-offs, three will be modest successes, one will double the initial investment, and one will return the investment 50- to 100-fold. The goal is to make sure you have a big winner, not to make sure there are no losers.

In most large companies, someone with a vision of a radical new business model has to go to the defenders of the old business model to get funding. All too often the guy running the old thing has veto power over the new thing. To understand the problem this creates, imagine that every innovator in Silicon Valley had to go to Bill Gates for funding. Pretty soon everyone in the Valley would be working to extend the Windows franchise. Goodbye to Netscape. Goodbye to the Network Computer. Goodbye to Java and Jini. Goodbye to PalmPilot. And goodbye to anything else that might challenge Microsoft's current business model.

A VC doesn't ask how one venture plays off against the success of another venture. There's no search for synergy. Nobody asks, Is this new venture consistent with our strategy? Now, synergy is good, and consistency is a virtue. But in a world where the life span of the average business model is longer than a butterfly's but shorter than a dog's, one needs the chance to regularly consider a few opportunities that are *inconsistent* with the current strategy. One of those opportunities might just turn out to be a whole lot more attractive than what you're already working on. But how will you ever know unless you're willing to create a market for capital that puts a bit of cash behind the unorthodox? (See the sidebar "Spin-Ups, Not Spin-Outs.")

> *In attempting to guarantee that there's never an unexpected downside, the typical capital-budgeting process places an absolute ceiling on the upside.*

New ideas get squashed when they threaten to cannibalize the sales of existing businesses – businesses protected by powerful constituents. Yet every company is told that it must cannibalize its own business before competitors do. Solving the cannibalization problem isn't difficult. You simply have to make sure that individuals seeking funding for nontraditional opportunities don't have to go cup in hand to the guardians of the past. That's what Shell did. In the GameChanger process, Shell created a market for capital that is entirely separate from the traditional capital-budgeting process, a process dominated by the investment needs of yesterday's businesses. Rather than wait for the annual budgeting cycle to roll around, innovators can go to the GameChanger panel at any time and present their business case. And they are guaranteed an almost immediate response. So yes, it is possible to create an innovation-friendly market for capital inside a big company.

Spin-Ups, Not Spin-Outs

The goal of bringing Silicon Valley inside is not only to create new businesses but also to reinvent existing business models. Too often companies think of internal entrepreneurship as focused solely on new business – ones that typically lie far outside the company's core. Once such businesses start to gain momentum, they're often spun out into separate companies with their own equity structures and stock market listings. But spin-outs do little to transform the base business. Xerox's Palo Alto Research Center has spun off a number of successful entrepreneurial companies while Xerox's core business has languished with less than double-digit growth.

Spin-ups are often more valuable than spin-outs. An idea that has the power to radically improve the economics of an existing business shouldn't languish in some backwater. Instead it should be spun up into a corporatewide initiative. A company that succeeds in bringing Silicon Valley inside should expect to create, as Shell has done, dozens of game-changing experiments inside existing businesses – a new pricing strategy here, an unconventional distribution model over there, a fresh approach to merchandising somewhere else. The experiments should be small and tightly bounded. But if they show promise, they can be spun up into major business-transforming programs.

The Market for Talent

Imagine what would happen if 20% of your best people up and left in a single year. It happens all the time in Silicon Valley. Valley workers change companies with less angst than most people change jobs within companies. Sure, they jump for money, but more than that they jump at the chance to work on the next great thing. Companies pursuing killer opportunities attract the best talent. As one venture capitalist bluntly puts it: "'A' people work on 'A' opportunities."

Every Silicon Valley CEO knows that if you don't give your people truly exhilarating work – and a dramatic upside – they'll start turning in their badges.

Isn't it amazing that while every company has at least some kind of process for capital allocation, almost no company has a process for talent allocation.

In recent years, companies like Apple and Silicon Graphics hemorrhaged talent, while up-and-comers like Cisco and Yahoo! have been magnets for the cerebrally gifted. Scott Cook, the chairman of Intuit, understands the hard reality of the talent market: "I wake up every morning knowing that if my people don't sense a compelling vision and a big upside, they'll simply leave." Not to worry. Intuit's restless innovators are busy turning the company into a dominant financial services player on the Internet.

The talent merry-go-round spins fast enough in Silicon Valley to make the average HR manager nauseous. In the old economy, employees are often viewed as something akin to indentured servants. Divisional vice presidents think they own their key people. And if those people work in South Bend, St. Louis, Des Moines, Nashville, or a hundred other cities that don't have the kind of superheated economy that exists in Silicon Valley, they may not find it so easy to jump ship. But that's no reason to chain ambitious and creative employees to the deck of a slowly sinking strategy.

Isn't it amazing that while every company has at least some kind of process for capital allocation, almost no company has a process for talent allocation – much less an open market for talent? Capital budgeting may be sclerotic and filled with nostalgia for old businesses, but at least there's a process for addressing the question of how much capital each business deserves every year. And there are measures like EVA that let one judge whether or not a particular business is using its capital wisely. Yet there's no knowing whether a company's very best people are lined up behind its biggest new opportunities or slowly suffocating in moribund businesses. You can look at retention rates, but that's only part of the story. People often quit emotionally long before they quit physically. Novelty, meaning, and impact are the oxygen that gives life to the entrepreneurial spirit. Denied that oxygen, even the most talented folks are soon brain dead.

As difficult as it is for a prospective entrepreneur to get seed capital in a large company, it's even harder to grab a few of the very best engineering or marketing folks. There's an enormous sense of entitlement among divisional vice presidents and business heads. "Hey, we make all the money, we ought to have the best people," they'll say. But the marginal value a talented employee adds to a business running on autopilot is often a fraction of the value that individual could add to a venture not yet out of the proverbial garage.

Disney understands this. The company has excelled at moving its very best talent into new and nontraditional business areas. Whether it's producing Broadway shows, starting a cruise line, or opening the company's first live-animal theme park, Disney's most capable "cast members" vie for the chance to work on the new and the unique. Helping to break new ground is regarded as a career coup. For their part, Disney's senior executives have worked to soften the kind of narrowly parochial profit-center thinking that so often scuppers the movement of people out of existing businesses and into new ones.

Shell, too, has been working hard to lower the barriers to employee mobility. The company has recently moved to what it terms an "open resourcing" model for talent. Jobs are listed on Shell's intranet, and with a two-month notice, employees can go and work on anything that interests them. There are no barriers hindering people from going to work on whatever fires their imagination. Monsanto has adopted a similar approach. One of the architects of Monsanto's metamorphosis from chemical giant to biotech pioneer puts it this way:

Because we don't have a lot of structure, people will flow toward where success and innovation are taking place. We have a free-market system where people can move, so you have an outflow of people in areas where not much progress is being made. Before, the HR function ran processes like management development and performance evaluation. Now it also facilitates this movement of people.

At Monsanto, everyone across the company can point to the few critical projects that are redefining the company and opening up new vistas. What about your company? Could your most creative people point to ten unconventional ventures within your organization aimed at reinventing the company and its industry? And how easy would it be for those people to nominate themselves onto those teams?

Sure, many companies post internal job openings. But a market for talent is more than that. Employees have to believe that the best way to win big is to be part of building something new. That means providing additional incentives for employees who are willing to take a risk on something out of the ordinary. It means celebrating every courageous employee who abandons the security of a legacy business for an untested opportunity. It's not enough to remove the barriers to migration – one must positively provide incentives for employees to abandon the familiar for the unconventional.

Mobility fuels commitment. When employees are truly attracted to the projects and teams they work on, commitment is a foregone conclusion. And while they may not stay committed forever, particularly if a business model is running out of gas, people who've voted with their feet, and their lives, aren't likely to join the ranks of disaffected Dilberts.

Many companies are already paying a price for having failed to create internal markets for talent. People who have the passion and the aptitude to create new wealth are abandoning the old economy for the new. When AT&T vice presidents start leaving for the left coast, something's up. Even America's best MBA grads – kids who've been groomed for corporate life – have been forsaking the old guard for the vanguard. Today, 20% of Harvard MBAs join companies with fewer than 100 people, and 20% of Stanford MBAs join companies with fewer than 50. Yeah, some still want to go into consulting and devote their lives to making the world safe for vice presidents, but more and more want to go kick incumbent butt. Confident in their talents and ambitious as hell, they're going to companies where the market for talent is brutally efficient. They're going to companies where there are no constraints on their contribution, where there are no apprenticeships to serve, no senior partners to carry, and no corporate posteriors to kiss. If you fail to create a vibrant and vital market for talent in your company, you're never even going to have the chance to hire these people, and your leaky tap of talent will become a torrent.

The bottom line is this: if you have highly creative and ambitious people who feel trapped in moribund businesses, they *are* going to leave. The only question is whether they leave to join some other company or whether they leave to join a GameChanger kind of team in your company. Or, to put it more simply, are they going to create wealth for themselves and somebody else or are they going to create wealth for themselves and your shareholders? Creating an internal market for talent won't happen until you have the courage to blow up the entitlement mentality that so often imprisons both talent and capital. And it won't hap-

pen until you come to believe, truly, that there's more wealth to be had by setting ambitious and capable employees free than by holding them hostage in businesses that have already reached their sell-by date.

The Innovation Frontier

We are at the dawn of a new industrial order. We are leaving behind a world in which scale, efficiency, and replication were everything. We are taking our first tentative steps into a world where imagination, experimentation, and agility are, if not everything, at least the essential catalysts for wealth creation. Resource allocation worked fine for the old world, but companies need something more, and quite different, if they are to capture their fair share of wealth in the new world. In concept and in reality, resource attraction is well tuned to the new world of self-organization, spontaneity, and speed.

Opportunities are fleeting in this new world. By the time some cautious vice president decides to pull the trigger, some hot, young entrepreneur is already a billionaire. So you'd best not wait any longer to start building your own internal markets for ideas, capital, and talent. Shell, Virgin, GE Capital, and Monsanto are setting the pace, but you shouldn't expect to distill a neat little guide from their experience. If there were a best-practice manual, you'd be even further behind the curve than you already are. Instead, recognize that resource attraction is not something as simple as a new process – this isn't knowledge management or data mining. It's a fundamentally new approach to the challenge of creating wealth.

If you have highly creative and ambitious people who feel trapped in moribund businesses, they are going to leave.

Silicon Valley companies are challenging the industrial aristocracy in fields as diverse as auto retailing, insurance, bookselling, and broadcast media. But the real competition between the old economy and the new economy is occurring not between individual companies but between remarkably different regimes. Just as communism and capitalism were competing economic regimes, resource allocation and resource attraction are competing innovation regimes. Resource allocation works fine where innovation is largely incremental to the existing business model (think Cherry Coke versus regular Coke). But where the goal is the invention of novel business models (music downloaded off the Web versus CDs bought at Tower Records), or the radical redesign of existing business models (Dell's build-to-order direct-selling approach), resource allocation is wholly inadequate. The shift to a postindustrial economy, accelerating by the minute, is perhaps the greatest economic sea change in history. Any company that hopes to profit from this transition must first ask itself whether its innovation regime is up to the challenge.

There is a persistent yet unfounded belief that big companies must always lose to nimble start-ups, that no incumbent can ever match the entrepreneurial fervor of Silicon Valley or its analogues around the globe. I heartily disagree. In fact, when it comes to innovation, large companies have their own advantages that in many ways offsets those of Silicon Valley. Large companies have resources. They have a ready source of capital – if they can learn how to supplement risk-averse resource allocation with opportunity-focused resource attraction. They often have brands and distribution assets that can give a new venture a quick start. Mighty Microsoft would still be a minnow if it hadn't found a way to tap into IBM's brand and distribution strengths. In theory, it should be easier for large companies to re-

deploy talent into new areas than it is for start-ups to induce prospective employees to endure the hassles of changing companies. And where a venture capitalist will often lose a hot idea to a rival source of funds, large companies should at least enjoy preferential access to the ideas that emerge from their own employees.

Silicon Valley exists not because large companies are incapable of innovation but because they have been unwilling to abandon the tightly knit safety net of resource allocation. A disciplined, top-down approach to allocating money and talent gives top management a sense of control. But in a world where the risk of being rendered irrelevant by an impertinent interloper is ever present, such control is illusory. Yes, you can do your best to ensure that you never put a dollar of capital or a great employee into anything that doesn't come wrapped in an ironclad business case. But in the process, you'll surrender the future and its wealth to more intrepid souls. ▽

Reprint 99504   To order reprints, see the last page of this issue.

"I'll tell you Jennings, we're nothing but pawns in this company."

[11]

Absorptive Capacity: A
New Perspective on
Learning and Innovation

Wesley M. Cohen
Carnegie Mellon University
Daniel A. Levinthal
University of Pennsylvania

In this paper, we argue that the ability of a firm to recognize the value of new, external information, assimilate it, and apply it to commercial ends is critical to its innovative capabilities. We label this capability a firm's absorptive capacity and suggest that it is largely a function of the firm's level of prior related knowledge. The discussion focuses first on the cognitive basis for an individual's absorptive capacity including, in particular, prior related knowledge and diversity of background. We then characterize the factors that influence absorptive capacity at the organizational level, how an organization's absorptive capacity differs from that of its individual members, and the role of diversity of expertise within an organization. We argue that the development of absorptive capacity, and, in turn, innovative performance are history- or path-dependent and argue how lack of investment in an area of expertise early on may foreclose the future development of a technical capability in that area. We formulate a model of firm investment in research and development (R&D), in which R&D contributes to a firm's absorptive capacity, and test predictions relating a firm's investment in R&D to the knowledge underlying technical change within an industry. Discussion focuses on the implications of absorptive capacity for the analysis of other related innovative activities, including basic research, the adoption and diffusion of innovations, and decisions to participate in cooperative R&D ventures.[•]

INTRODUCTION

Outside sources of knowledge are often critical to the innovation process, whatever the organizational level at which the innovating unit is defined. While the example of Japan illustrates the point saliently at the national level (e.g., Westney and Sakakibara, 1986; Mansfield, 1988; Rosenberg and Steinmueller, 1988), it is also true of entire industries, as pointed out by Brock (1975) in the case of computers and by Peck (1962) in the case of aluminum. At the organizational level, March and Simon (1958: 188) suggested most innovations result from borrowing rather than invention. This observation is supported by extensive research on the sources of innovation (e.g., Mueller, 1962; Hamberg, 1963; Myers and Marquis, 1969; Johnston and Gibbons, 1975; von Hippel, 1988). Finally, the importance to innovative performance of information originating from other internal units in the firm, outside the formal innovating unit (i.e., the R&D lab), such as marketing and manufacturing, is well understood (e.g., Mansfield, 1968).

[•]

We appreciate the comments of Kathleen Carley, Robyn Dawes, Mark Fichman, Tom Finholt, Sara Kiesler, Richard Nelson, Linda Pike, and three anonymous referees. The representations and conclusions presented herein are those of the authors. They have not been adopted in whole or in part by the Federal Trade Commission, its Bureau of Economics, or any other entity within the commission. The FTC's Disclosure Avoidance Officer has certified that the data included in this paper do not identify individual company line-of-business data.

The ability to exploit external knowledge is thus a critical component of innovative capabilities. We argue that the ability to evaluate and utilize outside knowledge is largely a function of the level of prior related knowledge. At the most elemental level, this prior knowledge includes basic skills or even a shared language but may also include knowledge of the most recent scientific or technological developments in a given field. Thus, prior related knowledge confers an ability to recognize the value of new information, assimilate it, and apply it to commercial ends. These abilities collectively constitute what we call a firm's "absorptive capacity."

Absorptive Capacity

At the level of the firm—the innovating unit that is the focus here—absorptive capacity is generated in a variety of ways. Research shows that firms that conduct their own R&D are better able to use externally available information (e.g., Tilton, 1971; Allen, 1977; Mowery, 1983). This implies that absorptive capacity may be created as a byproduct of a firm's R&D investment. Other work suggests that absorptive capacity may also be developed as a byproduct of a firm's manufacturing operations. Abernathy (1978) and Rosenberg (1982) have noted that through direct involvement in manufacturing, a firm is better able to recognize and exploit new information relevant to a particular product market. Production experience provides the firm with the background necessary both to recognize the value of and implement methods to reorganize or automate particular manufacturing processes. Firms also invest in absorptive capacity directly, as when they send personnel for advanced technical training. The concept of absorptive capacity can best be developed through an examination of the cognitive structures that underlie learning.

Cognitive Structures

The premise of the notion of absorptive capacity is that the organization needs prior related knowledge to assimilate and use new knowledge. Studies in the area of cognitive and behavioral sciences at the individual level both justify and enrich this observation. Research on memory development suggests that accumulated prior knowledge increases both the ability to put new knowledge into memory, what we would refer to as the acquisition of knowledge, and the ability to recall and use it. With respect to the acquisition of knowledge, Bower and Hilgard (1981: 424) suggested that memory development is self-reinforcing in that the more objects, patterns and concepts that are stored in memory, the more readily is new information about these constructs acquired and the more facile is the individual in using them in new settings.

Some psychologists suggest that prior knowledge enhances learning because memory—or the storage of knowledge—is developed by associative learning in which events are recorded into memory by establishing linkages with pre-existing concepts. Thus, Bower and Hilgard (1981) suggested that the breadth of categories into which prior knowledge is organized, the differentiation of those categories, and the linkages across them permit individuals to make sense of and, in turn, acquire new knowledge. In the context of learning a language, Lindsay and Norman (1977: 517) suggested the problem in learning words is not a result of lack of exposure to them but that "to understand complex phrases, much more is needed than exposure to the words: a large body of knowledge must first be accumulated. After all, a word is simply a label for a set of structures within the memory system, so the structures must exist before the word can be considered learned." Lindsay and Norman further suggested that knowledge may be nominally acquired but not well utilized subsequently because the individual did not already possess the appropriate contextual knowledge necessary to make the new knowledge fully intelligible.

The notion that prior knowledge facilitates the learning of new related knowledge can be extended to include the case in which the knowledge in question may itself be a set of learning skills. There may be a transfer of learning skills across bodies of knowledge that are organized and expressed in similar ways. As a consequence, experience or performance on one learning task may influence and improve performance on some subsequent learning task (Ellis, 1965). This progressive improvement in the performance of learning tasks is a form of knowledge transfer that has been referred to as "learning to learn" (Ellis, 1965; Estes, 1970). Estes (1970: 16), however, suggested that the term "learning to learn" is a misnomer in that prior experience with a learning task does not necessarily improve performance because an individual knows how to learn (i.e., form new associations) better, but that an individual may simply have accumulated more prior knowledge so that he or she needs to learn less to attain a given level of performance. Notwithstanding what it is about prior learning experience that may affect subsequent performance, both explanations of the relationship between early learning and subsequent performance emphasize the importance of prior knowledge for learning.

The effect of prior learning experience on subsequent learning tasks can be observed in a variety of tasks. For instance, Ellis (1965: 4) suggested that "students who have thoroughly mastered the principles of algebra find it easier to grasp advanced work in mathematics such as calculus." Further illustration is provided by Anderson, Farrell, and Sauers (1984), who compared students learning LISP as a first programming language with students learning LISP after having learned Pascal. The Pascal students learned LISP much more effectively, in part because they better appreciated the semantics of various programming concepts.

The literature also suggests that problem-solving skills develop similarly. In this case, problem-solving methods and heuristics typically constitute the prior knowledge that permits individuals to acquire related problem-solving capabilities. In their work on the development of computer programming skills, Pirolli and Anderson (1985) found that almost all students developed new programs by analogy-to-example programs and that their success was determined by how well they understood why these examples worked.

We argue that problem solving and learning capabilities are so similar that there is little reason to differentiate their modes of development, although exactly what is learned may differ: learning capabilities involve the development of the capacity to assimilate existing knowledge, while problem-solving skills represent a capacity to create new knowledge. Supporting the point that there is little difference between the two, Bradshaw, Langley, and Simon (1983) and Simon (1985) suggested that the sort of necessary preconditions for successful learning that we have identified do not differ from the preconditions required for problem solving and, in turn, for the creative process. Moreover, they argued that the processes themselves do not differ much. The prior possession of relevant knowledge and skill is what gives rise to creativity, permitting the sorts of associations and linkages that may have never been considered before. Likewise, Ellis (1965: 35) suggested that Harlow's (1959) findings on the development of learning sets provide a possible explanation for the behavioral

Absorptive Capacity

phenomenon of "insight" that typically refers to the rapid solution of a problem. Thus, the psychology literature suggests
that creative capacity and what we call absorptive capacity
are quite similar.

To develop an effective absorptive capacity, whether it be for
general knowledge or problem-solving or learning skills, it is
insufficient merely to expose an individual briefly to the relevant prior knowledge. Intensity of effort is critical. With regard
to storing knowledge in memory, Lindsay and Norman (1977:
355) noted that the more deeply the material is processed—
the more effort used, the more processing makes use of associations between the items to be learned and knowledge
already in the memory—the better will be the later retrieval
of the item. Similarly, learning-set theory (Harlow, 1949, 1959)
implies that important aspects of learning how to solve
problems are built up over many practice trials on related
problems. Indeed, Harlow (1959) suggested that if practice
with a particular type of problem is discontinued before it is
reliably learned, then little transfer will occur to the next
series of problems. Therefore, he concluded that considerable
time and effort should be spent on early problems before
moving on to more complex problems.

Two related ideas are implicit in the notion that the ability to
assimilate information is a function of the richness of the pre-
existing knowledge structure: learning is cumulative, and
learning performance is greatest when the object of learning
is related to what is already known. As a result, learning is
more difficult in novel domains, and, more generally, an individual's expertise—what he or she knows well—will change
only incrementally. The above discussion also suggests that
diversity of knowledge plays an important role. In a setting in
which there is uncertainty about the knowledge domains
from which potentially useful information may emerge, a diverse background provides a more robust basis for learning
because it increases the prospect that incoming information
will relate to what is already known. In addition to strengthening assimilative powers, knowledge diversity also facilitates
the innovative process by enabling the individual to make
novel associations and linkages.

From Individual to Organizational Absorptive Capacity

An organization's absorptive capacity will depend on the absorptive capacities of its individual members. To this extent,
the development of an organization's absorptive capacity will
build on prior investment in the development of its constituent, individual absorptive capacities, and, like individuals' absorptive capacities, organizational absorptive capacity will
tend to develop cumulatively. A firm's absorptive capacity is
not, however, simply the sum of the absorptive capacities of
its employees, and it is therefore useful to consider what
aspects of absorptive capacity are distinctly organizational.
Absorptive capacity refers not only to the acquisition or assimilation of information by an organization but also to the organization's ability to exploit it. Therefore, an organization's
absorptive capacity does not simply depend on the organization's direct interface with the external environment. It also
depends on transfers of knowledge across and within subunits that may be quite. removed from the original point of

entry. Thus, to understand the sources of a firm's absorptive capacity, we focus on the structure of communication between the external environment and the organization, as well as among the subunits of the organization, and also on the character and distribution of expertise within the organization.

Communication systems may rely on specialized actors to transfer information from the environment or may involve less structured patterns. The problem of designing communication structures cannot be disentangled from the distribution of expertise in the organization. The firm's absorptive capacity depends on the individuals who stand at the interface of either the firm and the external environment or at the interface between subunits within the firm. That interface function may be diffused across individuals or be quite centralized. When the expertise of most individuals within the organization differs considerably from that of external actors who can provide useful information, some members of the group are likely to assume relatively centralized "gatekeeping" or "boundary-spanning" roles (Allen, 1977; Tushman, 1977). For technical information that is difficult for internal staff to assimilate, a gatekeeper both monitors the environment and translates the technical information into a form understandable to the research group. In contrast, if external information is closely related to ongoing activity, then external information is readily assimilated and gatekeepers or boundary-spanners are not so necessary for translating information. Even in this setting, however, gatekeepers may emerge to the extent that such role specialization relieves others from having to monitor the environment.

A difficulty may emerge under conditions of rapid and uncertain technical change, however, when this interface function is centralized. When information flows are somewhat random and it is not clear where in the firm or subunit a piece of outside knowledge is best applied, a centralized gatekeeper may not provide an effective link to the environment. Under such circumstances, it is best for the organization to expose a fairly broad range of prospective "receptors" to the environment. Such an organization would exhibit the organic structure of Burns and Stalker (1961: 6), which is more adaptable "when problems and requirements for action arise which cannot be broken down and distributed among specialist roles within a clearly defined hierarchy."

Even when a gatekeeper is important, his or her individual absorptive capacity does not constitute the absorptive capacity of his or her unit within the firm. The ease or difficulty of the internal communication process and, in turn, the level of organizational absorptive capacity are not only a function of the gatekeeper's capabilities but also of the expertise of those individuals to whom the gatekeeper is transmitting the information. Therefore, relying on a small set of technological gatekeepers may not be sufficient; the group as a whole must have some level of relevant background knowledge, and when knowledge structures are highly differentiated, the requisite level of background may be rather high.

The background knowledge required by the group as a whole for effective communication with the gatekeeper highlights the more general point that shared knowledge and expertise

Absorptive Capacity

is essential for communication. At the most basic level, the relevant knowledge that permits effective communication both within and across subunits consists of shared language and symbols (Dearborn and Simon, 1958; Katz and Kahn, 1966; Allen and Cohen, 1969; Tushman, 1978; Zenger and Lawrence, 1989). With regard to the absorptive capacity of the firm as a whole, there may, however, be a trade-off in the efficiency of internal communication against the ability of the subunit to assimilate and exploit information originating from other subunits or the environment. This can be seen as a trade-off between inward-looking versus outward-looking absorptive capacities. While both of these components are necessary for effective organizational learning, excessive dominance by one or the other will be dysfunctional. If all actors in the organization share the same specialized language, they will be effective in communicating with one another, but they may not be able to tap into diverse external knowledge sources. In the limit, an internal language, coding scheme, or, more generally, any particular body of expertise could become sufficiently overlapping and specialized that it impedes the incorporation of outside knowledge and results in the pathology of the not-invented-here (NIH) syndrome. This may explain Katz and Allen's (1982) findings that the level of external communication and communication with other project groups declines with project-group tenure.

This trade-off between outward- and inward-looking components of absorptive capacity focuses our attention on how the relationship between knowledge sharing and knowledge diversity across individuals affects the development of organizational absorptive capacity. While some overlap of knowledge across individuals is necessary for internal communication, there are benefits to diversity of knowledge structures across individuals that parallel the benefits to diversity of knowledge within individuals. As Simon (1985) pointed out, diverse knowledge structures coexisting in the same mind elicit the sort of learning and problem solving that yields innovation. Assuming a sufficient level of knowledge overlap to ensure effective communication, interactions across individuals who each possess diverse and different knowledge structures will augment the organization's capacity for making novel linkages and associations—innovating—beyond what any one individual can achieve. Utterback (1971), summarizing research on task performance and innovation, noted that diversity in the work setting "stimulates the generation of new ideas." Thus, as with Nelson and Winter's (1982) view of organizational capabilities, an organization's absorptive capacity is not resident in any single individual but depends on the links across a mosaic of individual capabilities.

Beyond diverse knowledge structures, the sort of knowledge that individuals should possess to enhance organizational absorptive capacity is also important. Critical knowledge does not simply include substantive, technical knowledge; it also includes awareness of where useful complementary expertise resides within and outside the organization. This sort of knowledge can be knowledge of who knows what, who can help with what problem, or who can exploit new information. With regard to external relationships, von Hippel (1988) has shown the importance for innovation of close relationships with both buyers and suppliers. To the extent that an organization develops a broad and active network of internal and external relationships, individuals' awareness of others' capabilities and knowledge will be strengthened. As a result, individual absorptive capacities are leveraged all the more, and the organization's absorptive capacity is strengthened.

The observation that the ideal knowledge structure for an organizational subunit should reflect only partially overlapping knowledge complemented by nonoverlapping diverse knowledge suggests an organizational trade-off between diversity and commonality of knowledge across individuals. While common knowledge improves communication, commonality should not be carried so far that diversity across individuals is substantially diminished. Likewise, division of labor promoting gains from specialization should not be pushed so far that communication is undermined. The difficulties posed by excessive specialization suggest some liabilities of pursuing production efficiencies via learning by doing under conditions of rapid technical change in which absorptive capacity is important. In learning by doing, the firm becomes more practiced and hence more capable at activities in which it is already engaged. Learning by doing does not contribute to the diversity that is critical to learning about or creating something that is relatively new. Moreover, the notion of "remembering by doing" (Nelson and Winter, 1982) suggests that the focus on one class of activity entailed by learning by doing may effectively diminish the diversity of background that an individual or organization may have at one time possessed and, consequently, undercut organizational absorptive capacity and innovative performance.

It has become generally accepted that complementary functions within the organization ought to be tightly intermeshed, recognizing that some amount of redundancy in expertise may be desirable to create what can be called cross-function absorptive capacities. Cross-function interfaces that affect organizational absorptive capacity and innovative performance include, for example, the relationships between corporate and divisional R&D labs or, more generally, the relationships among the R&D, design, manufacturing, and marketing functions (e.g., Mansfield, 1968: 86–88). Close linkages between design and manufacturing are often credited for the relative success of Japanese firms in moving products rapidly from the design stage through development and manufacturing (Westney and Sakakibara, 1986). Clark and Fujimoto (1987) argued that overlapping product development cycles facilitate communication and coordination across organizational subunits. They found that the speed of product development is strongly influenced by the links between problem-solving cycles and that successful linking requires "direct personal contacts across functions, liaison roles at each unit, cross-functional task forces, cross-functional project teams, and a system of 'product manager as integrator' " (Clark and Fujimoto, 1987: 24). In contrast, a process in which one unit simply hands off the design to another unit is likely to suffer greater difficulties.

Some management practices also appear to reflect the belief that an excessive degree of overlap in functions may reduce

Absorptive Capacity

the firm's absorptive capacity and that diversity of backgrounds is useful. The Japanese practice of rotating their R&D personnel through marketing and manufacturing operations, for example, while creating knowledge overlap, also enhances the diversity of background of their personnel. Often involving the assignment of technical personnel to other functions for several years, this practice also suggests that some intensity of experience in each of the complementary knowledge domains is necessary to put an effective absorptive capacity in place; breadth of knowledge cannot be superficial to be effective.

The discussion thus far has focused on internal mechanisms that influence the organization's absorptive capacity. A question remains as to whether absorptive capacity needs to be internally developed or to what extent a firm may simply buy it via, for example, hiring new personnel, contracting for consulting services, or even through corporate acquisitions. We suggest that the effectiveness of such options is somewhat limited when the absorptive capacity in question is to be integrated with the firm's other activities. A critical component of the requisite absorptive capacity for certain types of information, such as those associated with product and process innovation, is often firm-specific and therefore cannot be bought and quickly integrated into the firm. This is reflected in Lee and Allen's (1982) findings that considerable time lags are associated with the integration of new technical staff, particularly those concerned with process and product development. To integrate certain classes of complex and sophisticated technological knowledge successfully into the firm's activities, the firm requires an existing internal staff of technologists and scientists who are both competent in their fields and are familiar with the firm's idiosyncratic needs, organizational procedures, routines, complementary capabilities, and extramural relationships. As implied by the discussion above, such diversity of knowledge structures must coexist to some degree in the same minds. Moreover, as Nelson and Winter's (1982) analysis suggests, much of the detailed knowledge of organizational routines and objectives that permit a firm and its R&D labs to function is tacit. As a consequence, such critical complementary knowledge is acquired only through experience within the firm. Illustrating our general argument, Vyssotsky (1977), justifying the placement of Bell Labs within AT&T, argued: "For research and development to yield effective results for Bell System, it has to be done by . . . creative people who understand as much as they possibly can about the technical state of the art, and about Bell System and what System's problems are. The R&D people must be free to think up new approaches, and they must also be closely coupled to the problems and challenges where innovation is needed. This combination, if one is lucky, will result in insights which help the Bell System. That's why we have Bell Labs in Bell System, instead of having all our R&D done by outside organizations."

Path Dependence and Absorptive Capacity

Our discussion of the character of absorptive capacity and its role in assimilating and exploiting knowledge suggests a simple generalization that applies at both the individual and organizational levels: prior knowledge permits the assimilation and exploitation of new knowledge. Some portion of that prior knowledge should be very closely related to the new knowledge to facilitate assimilation, and some fraction of that knowledge must be fairly diverse, although still related, to permit effective, creative utilization of the new knowledge. This simple notion that prior knowledge underlies absorptive capacity has important implications for the development of absorptive capacity over time and, in turn, the innovative performance of organizations. The basic role of prior knowledge suggests two features of absorptive capacity that will affect innovative performance in an evolving, uncertain environment (Cohen and Levinthal, 1989b). Accumulating absorptive capacity in one period will permit its more efficient accumulation in the next. By having already developed some absorptive capacity in a particular area, a firm may more readily accumulate what additional knowledge it needs in the subsequent periods in order to exploit any critical external knowledge that may become available. Second, the possession of related expertise will permit the firm to better understand and therefore evaluate the import of intermediate technological advances that provide signals as to the eventual merit of a new technological development. Thus, in an uncertain environment, absorptive capacity affects expectation formation, permitting the firm to predict more accurately the nature and commercial potential of technological advances. These revised expectations, in turn, condition the incentive to invest in absorptive capacity subsequently. These two features of absorptive capacity—cumulativeness and its effect on expectation formation—imply that its development is domain-specific and is path- or history-dependent.

The cumulativeness of absorptive capacity and its effect on expectation formation suggest an extreme case of path dependence in which once a firm ceases investing in its absorptive capacity in a quickly moving field, it may never assimilate and exploit new information in that field, regardless of the value of that information. There are two reasons for the emergence of this condition, which we term "lockout" (Cohen and Levinthal, 1989b). First, if the firm does not develop its absorptive capacity in some initial period, then its beliefs about the technological opportunities present in a given field will tend not to change over time because the firm may not be aware of the significance of signals that would otherwise revise its expectations. As a result, the firm does not invest in absorptive capacity and, when new opportunities subsequently emerge, the firm may not appreciate them. Compounding this effect, to the extent that prior knowledge facilitates the subsequent development of absorptive capacity, the lack of early investment in absorptive capacity makes it more costly to develop a given level of it in a subsequent period. Consequently, a low initial investment in absorptive capacity diminishes the attractiveness of investing in subsequent periods even if the firm becomes aware of technological opportunities.[1] This possibility of firms being "locked-out" of subsequent technological developments has recently become a matter of concern with respect to industrial policy. For instance, Reich (1987: 64) declaims Monsanto's exit from "float-zone" silicon manufacturing because he believes that the decision may be an irreversible exit from a technology, in that ". . . each new generation of technology

[1]
A similar result emerges from models of adaptive learning. Levitt and March (1988: 322) noted that "a competency trap can occur when favorable performance with an inferior procedure leads an organization to accumulate more experience with it, thus keeping experience with a superior procedure inadequate to make it rewarding to use."

Absorptive Capacity

builds on that which came before, once off the technological escalator it's difficult to get back on.''

Thus, the cumulative quality of absorptive capacity and its role in conditioning the updating of expectations are forces that tend to confine firms to operating in a particular technological domain. If firms do not invest in developing absorptive capacity in a particular area of expertise early on, it may not be in their interest to develop that capacity subsequently, even after major advances in the field. Thus, the pattern of inertia that Nelson and Winter (1982) highlighted as a central feature of firm behavior may emerge as an implication of rational behavior in a model in which absorptive capacity is cumulative and contributes to expectation formation. The not-invented-here syndrome, in which firms resist accepting innovative ideas from the environment, may also at times reflect what we call lockout. Such ideas may be too distant from the firm's existing knowledge base—its absorptive capacity—to be either appreciated or accessed. In this particular setting, NIH may be pathological behavior only in retrospect. The firm need not have acted irrationally in the development of the capabilities that yields the NIH syndrome as its apparent outcome.

A form of self-reinforcing behavior similar to lockout may also result from the influence of absorptive capacity on organizations' goals or aspiration levels. This argument builds on the behavioral view of organizational innovation that has been molded in large part by the work of March and Simon (1958). In March and Simon's framework, innovative activity is instigated due to a failure to reach some aspiration level. Departing from their model, we suggest that a firm's aspiration level in a technologically progressive environment is not simply determined by past performance or the performance of reference organizations. It also depends on the firm's absorptive capacity. The greater the organization's expertise and associated absorptive capacity, the more sensitive it is likely to be to emerging technological opportunities and the more likely its aspiration level will be defined in terms of the opportunities present in the technical environment rather than strictly in terms of performance measures. Thus, organizations with higher levels of absorptive capacity will tend to be more proactive, exploiting opportunities present in the environment, independent of current performance. Alternatively, organizations that have a modest absorptive capacity will tend to be reactive, searching for new alternatives in response to failure on some performance criterion that is not defined in terms of technical change per se (e.g., profitability, market share, etc.).

A systematic and enduring neglect of technical opportunities may result from the effect of absorptive capacity on the organization's aspiration level when innovative activity (e.g., R&D) contributes to absorptive capacity, which is often the case in technologically progressive environments. The reason is that the firm's aspiration level then depends on the very innovative activity that is triggered by a failure to meet the aspiration level itself. If the firm engages in little innovative activity, and is therefore relatively insensitive to the opportunities in the external environment, it will have a low aspiration level with regard to the exploitation of new technology, which in turn implies that it will continue to devote little effort to innovation. This creates a self-reinforcing cycle. Likewise, if an organization has a high aspiration level, influenced by externally generated technical opportunities, it will conduct more innovative activity and thereby increase its awareness of outside opportunities. Consequently, its aspiration level will remain high. This argument implies that reactive and proactive modes of firm behavior should remain rather stable over time. Thus, some organizations (like Hewlett-Packard and Sony) have the requisite technical knowledge to respond proactively to the opportunities present in the environment. These firms do not wait for failure on some performance dimension but aggressively seek out new opportunities to exploit and develop their technological capabilities.[2]

The concept of dynamically self-reinforcing behavior that may lead to the neglect of new technological developments provides some insight into the difficulties firms face when the technological basis of an industry changes—what Schumpeter (1942) called "the process of creative destruction." For instance, the change from electromechanical devices to electronic ones in the calculator industry resulted in the exit of a number of firms and a radical change in the market structure (Majumdar, 1982). This is an example of what Tushman and Anderson (1986) termed competence-destroying technical change. A firm without a prior technological base in a particular field may not be able to acquire one readily if absorptive capacity is cumulative. In addition, a firm may be blind to new developments in fields in which it is not investing if its updating capability is low. Accordingly, our argument implies that firms may not realize that they should be developing their absorptive capacity due to an irony associated with its valuation: the firm needs to have some absorptive capacity already to value it appropriately.

Absorptive Capacity and R&D Investment

The prior discussion does not address the question of whether we can empirically evaluate the importance of absorptive capacity for innovation. There is a key insight that permits empirical tests of the implications of absorptive capacity for innovative activity. Since technical change within an industry—typically incremental in character (Rosenberg and Steinmueller, 1988)—is often closely related to a firm's ongoing R&D activity, a firm's ability to exploit external knowledge is often generated as a byproduct of its R&D. We may therefore consider a firm's R&D as satisfying two functions: we assume that R&D not only generates new knowledge but also contributes to the firm's absorptive capacity.[3] If absorptive capacity is important, and R&D contributes to it, then whatever conditions the firm's incentives to learn (i.e., to build absorptive capacity) should also influence R&D spending. We may therefore consider the responsiveness of R&D activity to learning incentives as an indication of the empirical importance of absorptive capacity. The empirical challenge then is to understand the impact of the characteristics of the learning environment on R&D spending.

We construct a simple static model of firm R&D intensity, which is defined as R&D divided by sales. Normalization of R&D by firm sales controls for the effect of firm size, which

2

This argument that such reactive and proactive behavior may coexist in an industry over the long run assumes that there is slack in the selection environment and that technologically progressive behavior is not essential to survival. One can, alternatively, identify a number of industries, such as semiconductors, in which it appears that only firms that aggressively exploit technical opportunities survive.

3

We refer readers interested in the details of the theoretical and subsequent empirical analysis and results to Cohen and Levinthal (1989a), from which the following discussion is drawn.

Absorptive Capacity

affects the return per unit of R&D effort. This model is developed in the broader context of what applied economists have come to believe to be the three classes of industry-level determinants of R&D intensity: demand, appropriability, and technological opportunity conditions (Cohen and Levin, 1989). Demand is often characterized by the level of sales and the price elasticity of demand. The latter indicates the degree to which a firm's revenue will increase due to a reduction in price. For example, in the case of a process innovation that reduces the cost of production and, in turn, the product price, the price elasticity of demand reflects the associated change in total revenue that influences the economic return to innovative effort. Appropriability conditions refer to the degree to which firms capture the profits associated with their innovative activity and are often considered to reflect the degree to which valuable knowledge spills out into the public domain. The emphasis here is on valuable knowledge, because if a competitor's knowledge spills out but the competitor has already exploited a first-mover advantage in the marketplace, this knowledge is no longer valuable to the firm and does not constitute a spillover by our definition. The level of spillovers, in turn, depends on the strength of patents within an industry, the efficacy of secrecy, and/or first-mover advantages. Technological opportunity represents how costly it is for the firm to achieve some normalized unit of technical advance in a given industry. As typically conceived, there are two dimensions of technological opportunity (Cohen and Levin, 1989). The first, incorporated in our model, refers simply to the quantity of extraindustry technological knowledge, such as that originating from government or university labs, that effectively complements and therefore leverages the firm's own knowledge output. The second dimension of technological opportunity is the degree to which a unit of new knowledge improves the technological performance of the firm's manufacturing processes or products and, in turn, the firm's profits. For example, given the vitality of the underlying science and technology, an advance in knowledge promises to yield much larger product-performance payoffs in the semiconductor industry than in steel.[4]

The basic model of how absorptive capacity affects the determination of R&D expenditures is represented diagramatically in Figure 1. We postulate that learning incentives will have a direct effect on R&D spending. We also suggest that where the effect of other determinants, such as technological opportunity and appropriability, depend on the firm's or rivals' assimilation of knowledge, absorptive capacity—and therefore learning incentives—will mediate those effects. Finally, we suggest that the effect of appropriability conditions (i.e., spillovers) will be conditioned by competitor interdependence. In this context, we define interdependence as the extent to which a rival's technical advances diminish the firm's profits.

There are two factors that will affect a firm's incentives to learn, and, therefore, its incentives to invest in absorptive capacity via its R&D expenditures. First, there is the quantity of knowledge to be assimilated and exploited: the more there is, the greater the incentive. Second, there is the difficulty (or, conversely, the ease) of learning. Some types of information are more difficult to assimilate and use than others. We inter-

[4]
This second dimension is incorporated in the model developed in Cohen and Levinthal (1989a). We do not incorporate this second dimension in the present model because all the qualitative theoretical and empirical results associated with this second dimension of technological opportunity are the same as those associated with the first considered here.

Figure 1. Model of absorptive capacity and R&D incentives.

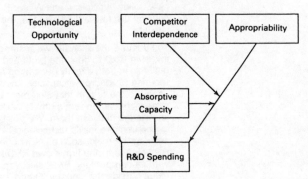

pret this to mean that per unit of knowledge, the cost of its absorption may vary depending on the characteristics of that knowledge. As learning is more difficult, more prior knowledge has to have been accumulated via R&D for effective learning to occur. As a result, this is a more costly learning environment. In such a setting, R&D is more important to building absorptive capacity and the more R&D effort the firm will need to have expended to achieve some level of absorptive capacity. Thus, for a given level of a firm's own R&D, the level of absorptive capacity is diminished in environments in which it is more difficult to learn. In addition, we are suggesting that a more difficult learning environment increases the marginal effect of R&D on absorptive capacity. In contrast, in environments in which learning is less demanding, a firm's own R&D has little impact on its absorptive capacity. In the extreme case in which external knowledge can be assimilated without any specialized expertise, a firm's own R&D would have no effect on its absorptive capacity.

We have argued that the ease of learning is in turn determined by the characteristics of the underlying scientific and technological knowledge. Although it is difficult to specify a priori all the relevant characteristics of knowledge affecting the ease of learning, they would include the complexity of the knowledge to be assimilated and the degree to which the outside knowledge is targeted to the needs and concerns of the firm. When outside knowledge is less targeted to the firm's particular needs and concerns, a firm's own R&D becomes more important in permitting it to recognize the value of the knowledge, assimilate, and exploit it. Sources that produce less targeted knowledge would include university labs involved in basic research, while more targeted knowledge may be generated by contract research labs, or input suppliers. In addition, the degree to which a field is cumulative, or the field's pace of advance, should also affect how critical R&D is to the development of absorptive capacity. The more that findings in a field build on prior findings, the more necessary is an understanding of prior research to the assimilation of subsequent findings. The pace of advance of a field affects the importance of R&D to developing absorptive capacity because the faster the pace of knowledge generation, the larger

Absorptive Capacity

the staff required to keep abreast of new developments. Finally, following Nelson and Winter (1982), the less explicit and codified the relevant knowledge, the more difficult it is to assimilate.

To structure the analysis, we assumed that firms purposefully invest in R&D to generate profit and take into account R&D's dual role in both directly generating new knowledge and contributing to absorptive capacity. Knowledge is assumed to be useful to the firm in that increments to a firm's own knowledge increase the firm's profits while increments to rivals' knowledge diminish them. We posit a simple model of the generation of a firm's technological knowledge that takes into account the major sources of technological knowledge utilized by a firm: the firm's own R&D knowledge that originates with its competitors' R&D, spillovers, and that which originates outside the industry. Figure 2 provides a stylized representation of this model in which, first, the firm generates new knowledge directly through its own R&D, and second, extramural knowledge, drawn from competitors as well as extraindustry sources such as government and university labs, also contribute to the firm's knowledge. A central feature of the model is that the firm's absorptive capacity determines the extent to which this extramural knowledge is utilized, and this absorptive capacity itself depends on the firm's own R&D. Because of this mediating function, absorptive capacity influences the effects of appropriability and technological opportunity conditions on R&D spending. Thus, the effects of appropriability and technological opportunity are not independent of R&D itself.

Figure 2. Model of sources of a firm's technical knowledge.

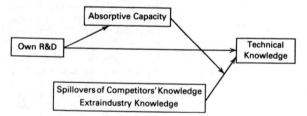

A key assumption in the model is that exploitation of competitors' research findings is realized through the interaction of the firm's absorptive capacity with competitors' spillovers. This interaction signifies that a firm is unable to assimilate externally available knowledge passively. Rather, to utilize the accessible R&D output of its competitors, the firm invests in its absorptive capacity by conducting R&D. Figure 2 also illustrates that, like its assimilation of competitors' R&D output, a firm's assimilation of extraindustry knowledge—the dimension of technological opportunity considered here—is constrained by its absorptive capacity. According to our model, therefore, the factors that affect learning incentives (i.e., the ease of learning and the quantity of available knowledge) influence the effects of appropriability and technological opportunity conditions on R&D.

Direct effect of ease of learning. As shown formally in Cohen and Levinthal (1989a), this model implies that as the ease of learning diminishes, learning becomes more dependent on a firm's own R&D, and R&D spending increases because of two effects. First, the marginal impact of R&D on absorptive capacity is greater in more difficult learning environments. As the learning environment becomes more difficult, however, there is a second, more subtle effect. Since, ceteris paribus, a more difficult learning environment lowers firms' absorptive capacities, R&D activity becomes more of a private good in the sense that competitors are now less able to tap into the firm's R&D findings that spill out.

Technological opportunity. We predict that an increase in technological opportunity—the amount of available relevant external technical knowledge—will elicit more R&D in more difficult learning environments. Greater technological opportunity signifies greater amounts of external information, which increase the firm's incentive to build absorptive capacity, and a more challenging learning environment increases the level of R&D necessary to build absorptive capacity.

Appropriability. We predict that spillovers will provide, in part, a positive incentive to conduct R&D due to the interaction of spillovers with an endogenous absorptive capacity. Traditionally, spillovers have been considered only a deterrent to R&D activity (e.g., Nelson, 1959; Arrow, 1962; Spence, 1984). In the standard view, a firm's incentive to invest in R&D is diminished to the extent that any findings from such activities are exploited by competitors and thereby diminish the innovator's own profits. In our framework, however, this negative appropriability incentive associated with spillovers is counterbalanced by a positive absorptive-capacity-building incentive. The more of its competitors' spillovers there are out there, the more incentive the firm has to invest in its own R&D, which permits it to exploit those spillovers.

We have shown elsewhere (Cohen and Levinthal, 1989a) that when this absorption incentive is large, as when learning is difficult, spillovers may actually encourage R&D. The relative magnitude of the absorption incentive is greater when firms within an industry are less interdependent in the sense that rivals' technical advances have less of an effect on the firm's own profits. With less interdependence, the degree to which rivals gain from the firm's R&D spillovers at the firm's expense diminishes relative to the benefit of being able to exploit the rivals' spillovers. Either a more competitive market structure or a higher price elasticity of demand for the firm's product can diminish interdependence in an industry.

METHODS

Data and Measures

To test the predictions of our framework for R&D activity, we used cross-sectional survey data on technological opportunity and appropriability conditions in the American manufacturing sector collected from R&D lab managers by Levin et al. (1983, 1987), and the Federal Trade Commission's Line of Business Program data on business unit sales, transfers, and R&D expenditures. The dependent variable, R&D intensity, was de-

Absorptive Capacity

fined as company-financed business-unit research and
development expenditures, expressed as a percentage of
business unit sales and transfers over the period 1975
through 1977. The data on interindustry differences in technological opportunity and appropriability are industry (line of
business) mean scores computed as an average over all respondents within a given industry. The sample consists of
1,719 business units representing 318 firms in 151 lines of
business.

The data pose two estimation issues. First, some 24 percent
of the firms performed no R&D in at least one year. If the independent variables reflect both the probability of conducting
R&D, as well as the amount of R&D spending, then a Tobit
analysis would be appropriate. Alternatively, a firm may require some initial level of absorptive capacity before it is influenced by the characteristics of the learning environment. In
this case, the variables reflecting the ease of learning only affect the amount of R&D conducted by firms engaging in
R&D activity and not the probability of engaging in R&D activity. In light of the uncertainty over the appropriate estimation technique, we explored the robustness of the results by
analyzing a Tobit and an OLS (or GLS) specification. The
second estimation issue is the presence of heteroscedasticity. We found the assumption of homoscedasticity to be violated, with the logarithm of the error variance being a linear
function of the exogenous variables and the number of respondents to Levin et al.'s (1983, 1987) survey. Unless otherwise noted, the results we report in this section reflect
robust effects that hold across three different estimation
methods, including ordinary least squares (OLS), generalized
least squares (GLS) in which we adjust for heteroscedasticity,
and Tobit, which was used when we included the observations for which R&D expenditures were zero.

We tested our predictions in the context of an empirical
model of business unit R&D intensity in which technological
opportunity, appropriability, and demand conditions are considered as the principal industry-level determinants of firms'
R&D spending. While data constraints do not permit observation of the direct effect of the ease of learning or its determinants on firms' R&D spending, we were able to examine
how these variables condition the influence on R&D of technological opportunity and appropriability conditions.

Technological opportunity was assessed with variables measuring the "relevance" or "importance" for technological
progress in each line of business of what are considered to
be two critical sources of technological opportunity—the
science base of the industry and extraindustry sources of
knowledge (Cohen and Levin, 1989). These measures are
drawn from Levin et al.'s survey, in which R&D managers indicated on a 7-point Likert scale the relevance of eleven basic
and applied fields of science and the importance of external
sources of knowledge to technological progress in a line of
business. The basic fields of science include biology, chemistry, mathematics, and physics, and the applied fields of
science include agricultural science, applied math/operations
research, computer science, geology, materials science,
medical science, and metallurgy.[5] The five extraindustry

5
Although geology was classed as a basic science by Levin et al., we classed it as an applied science because of its inductive methodology and intensive use by firms in the extractive sector.

sources of knowledge considered here included equipment suppliers (EQUIPTECH), materials suppliers (MATERIAL-TECH), downstream users of the industry's products (USER-TECH), government laboratories and agencies (GOVTECH), and universities (UNIVTECH). We interpreted the measures of the relevance or importance of each field or knowledge source to index the relative quantity of knowledge generated by that field or source that is potentially useful. We then distinguished across the eleven scientific fields and the five extraindustry knowledge source variables on the basis of the ease of learning associated with each. We suggested above that one important determinant of the ease of learning is the degree to which outside knowledge is targeted to a firm's needs and concerns. One can readily distinguish among both the eleven fields and the five extraindustry knowledge sources on that basis. The knowledge associated with the basic sciences is typically less targeted than that associated with the applied sciences. We also distinguished among the extraindustry knowledge sources on the same basis. A priori, we ranked university labs, government labs, materials suppliers, and equipment suppliers as providing increasingly more targeted knowledge to firms. We did not rank the relative effect of knowledge originating from users because, as suggested by von Hippel (1978), users will often provide a product idea to potential suppliers, but the informativeness of the "solution concept" is quite variable. Therefore, the targeted quality of the information is variable as well.

To represent intraindustry spillovers of R&D, we employed measures from Levin et al.'s survey of the effectiveness of six mechanisms used by firms to capture and protect the competitive advantages of new processes and new products: patents to prevent duplication, patents to secure royalty income, secrecy, lead time, moving quickly down the learning curve, and complementary sales and service efforts. We employed the maximum value of the effectiveness scores attained by these mechanisms as our measure of appropriability or spillovers, and label this variable APPROPRIABILITY; a high level of APPROPRIABILITY reflects a low level of spillovers.

In our theory, we predicted an interaction effect by which, as the ease of learning diminishes, or firms become less interdependent, the effect of spillovers on R&D spending should become more positive (or less negative). In the absence of any direct measure of the ease of learning, we distinguished categorically between those industries in which basic science was more relevant to technical progress than the relatively more targeted applied sciences and assumed that learning was generally less difficult in industries that fell into the latter category. Thus, we created a dummy variable, DUMBAS, that equals one when the average value of the relevance scores associated with the basic fields exceeds that associated with the applied fields and that equals zero otherwise. We specified the dummy variable, DUMAPP, analogously. To capture the interdependence of firms, we employed measures of industries' competitiveness as represented by each industry's four-firm concentration ratio (C4) and industry-level estimates of the price elasticity of demand (PELAS).

To further control for industry demand conditions, we used industry estimates developed by Levin (1981) of price elas-

Absorptive Capacity

ticity (PELAS) and income elasticity (INCELAS) and a demand time-shift parameter (DGROWTH). Finally, we included another control variable that may also reflect technological opportunity, industry maturity. We used a somewhat crude measure of industry maturity, NEWPLANT, that measures the percentage of an industry's property, plant, and equipment installed within the preceding five years.

RESULTS

Technological opportunity. Our theory suggests that when the targeted quality of knowledge is less (i.e., learning is more difficult), an increase in the relevance (i.e., quantity) of knowledge should have a more positive effect on R&D intensity. Therefore, the coefficient estimates of the variables measuring the relevance of the four basic scientific fields should exceed those of the variables measuring the relevance of the seven applied scientific fields. Confirming the prediction, Table 1 indicates that the estimated coefficients for the applied sciences are, with the exception of computer science, lower than that for the basic sciences. The similarity of the estimate of the effect of the relevance of computer science, an applied science, to those of some of the basic sciences suggests that the assumption may not be correct that only one determinant of the ease of learning, the targeted quality of the field, varies systematically across the fields of applied and basic science. Another determinant of the ease of learning postulated above is a field's pace of advance, where faster pace should require more R&D to permit assimilation, and the pace of advance in computer science has been relatively rapid over the past two decades.

To further test the prediction that the coefficient values of the less targeted, basic science field variables would exceed those of the applied fields, we estimated a specification, otherwise identical to the first, in which we constrained the coefficients of the basic sciences to be the same and the coefficients of the applied sciences to be the same. This shows the effect on R&D spending as the overall technological opportunity associated with basic science and applied science, respectively, change. The constrained coefficient estimates of the effect of the technological opportunity associated with the basic and applied sciences are significantly different (at the $p < .01$ level) across all estimation methods, with the former equal to .189 and the latter equal to $-.080$ in the GLS estimation. Therefore, relative to the effect of an increase in the technological opportunity associated with applied science, an increase in that associated with basic science elicits more R&D.

Our predicted ranking of the coefficient magnitudes associated with the extraindustry sources of knowledge, reflecting increasingly targeted knowledge from these sources, is largely confirmed. The coefficient estimate for the importance of knowledge originating from universities exceeds that for government labs, which, in turn, is greater than that for materials suppliers, which exceeds that for equipment suppliers. The difference between coefficient values is statistically significant in the case of government sources versus materials suppliers for both the OLS and Tobit results ($p < .01$) and in the case of materials suppliers versus equipment suppliers in

Table 1

Analysis of R&D Intensity*

	Regression Coefficient		
Variable	OLS (N = 1302)	GLS (N = 1302)	Tobit (N = 1719)
Intercept	−5.184**	−2.355*	−4.086**
	(1.522)	(1.037)	(1.461)
APPROPRIABILITY × C4	.213	.342**	.368**
	(.128)	(.103)	(.130)
APPROPRIABILITY × PELAS	−.192	−.200*	−.176
	(.106)	(.091)	(.103)
APPROPRIABILITY × DUMAPP	.448*	.248	.211
	(.202)	(.143)	(.194)
APPROPRIABILITY × DUMBAS	.302	.174	.094
	(.208)	(.144)	(.206)
USERTECH	.470**	.397**	.612**
	(.104)	(.069)	(.107)
UNIVTECH	.374**	.318**	.395**
	(.131)	(.091)	(.147)
GOVTECH	.221*	.069	.137
	(.106)	(.079)	(.107)
MATERIALTECH	−.258**	−.074	−.303**
	(.098)	(.070)	(.100)
EQUIPTECH	−.401**	−.484**	−.574**
	(.111)	(.077)	(.117)
Biology	.314**	.185**	.276*
	(.102)	(.071)	(.114)
Chemistry	.289**	.081	.191*
	(.084)	(.062)	(.088)
Math	.184	.151	.123
	(.131)	(.097)	(.143)
Physics	.373**	.323**	.310*
	(.117)	(.091)	(.128)
Agricultural Science	−.441**	−.273**	−.308**
	(.088)	(.064)	(.099)
Applied Math/Operations Research	−.237	−.117	−.366*
	(.148)	(.102)	(.152)
Computer Science	.294*	.116	.433**
	(.124)	(.090)	(.122)
Geology	−.363**	−.240**	−.365**
	(.084)	(.061)	(.097)
Materials Science	−.110	−.150	.116
	(.125)	(.095)	(.118)
Medical Science	−.179	−.133	−.133
	(.093)	(.070)	(.103)
Metallurgy	−.315**	−.195**	−.393**
	(.077)	(.053)	(.089)
NEWPLANT	.057**	.049**	.045**
	(.008)	(.006)	(.007)
PELAS	.936	1.082*	.892
	(.611)	(.527)	(.573)
INCELAS	1.077**	.587**	1.112**
	(.170)	(.131)	(.188)
DGROWTH	.068	−.074	.004
	(.090)	(.053)	(.105)
R^2	.287		

* $p < .05$; ** $p < .01$.
* Reproduced from Cohen and Levinthal (1989a: 590–591, 569–596). Standard errors are in parentheses.

the GLS results ($p < .01$). While we had no prediction regarding the coefficient value for USERTECH, the consistently high value of the coefficient estimate may reflect some element of demand conditions. Consistent with this, we have observed the variable USERTECH to be significantly correlated with measures of the importance of product differentiation (cf. Cohen and Levinthal, 1989a).

Absorptive Capacity

Appropriability. The results largely support the prediction that the ease of learning conditions the effect of knowledge spillovers. The effect on R&D intensity of increasing appropriability (i.e., diminishing spillovers) was significantly greater ($p < .05$) in those industries in which the applied sciences are more relevant to innovation than the basic sciences. This result suggests that the positive absorption incentive associated with spillovers is greater in industries in which the difficulty of learning is greater. Second, there is a significant positive effect ($p < .01$) of the interaction between market concentration and the appropriability level. As market concentration increases (indexing a diminution in competitiveness), the positive effect of a given appropriability level on R&D intensity increases, as predicted. Likewise, the effect of the interaction of the price elasticity of demand and the level of appropriability is negative (but only significant at $p < .05$ in the GLS estimate), providing additional support for the proposition that the positive effect of spillovers will increase in industries in which firms are less interdependent. The results suggest that the learning environment affects the impact of spillovers on R&D spending and that the importance of the positive absorptive-capacity-building incentive relative to that of the negative appropriability incentive is conditioned by the degree of competitor interdependence.

While we have shown that the learning environment modifies the effect of appropriability conditions, the question remains whether spillovers may, on balance, actually encourage R&D in some industries. To explore this possibility, we examined the effect of spillovers in the four two-digit SIC code level industries for which our sample contains enough lines of business to permit separate industry regressions. These include SICs 20 (food processing), 28 (chemicals), 35 (machinery), and 36 (electrical equipment). Due to the reduction in the degrees of freedom for industry-level variables, we simplified the estimating equation to consider only the direct effect of APPROPRIABILITY, and the science field variables were summarized as the maximum relevance scores attained by the basic and applied fields, respectively. In SICs 28 and 36, the effect of the APPROPRIABILITY variable was negative and significant at conventional levels, implying that R&D intensity rises with spillovers. In the Tobit results, the sign was also positive for SICs 28 and 36, but the coefficient estimates were not quite significant at the .05 confidence level. Thus, in SICs 28 (chemicals) and 36 (electrical equipment), R&D intensity rose with spillovers when we controlled for other industry-level variables conventionally thought to drive R&D spending, including technological opportunity and demand conditions. Although the analyses showing a positive effect of spillovers in these two industry groups do not represent a direct test of our model, the results suggest, particularly when considered with the interaction results, that the positive absorption incentive associated with spillovers may be sufficiently strong in some cases to more than offset the negative appropriability incentive.

IMPLICATIONS FOR INNOVATIVE ACTIVITY

Drawing on our prior work (Cohen and Levinthal, 1987, 1989a), we offer some implications of absorptive capacity for the analysis of other innovative activities, including basic research, the adoption and diffusion of innovations, and decisions to participate in cooperative R&D ventures, that follow from the preceding analyses.

The observation that R&D creates a capacity to assimilate and exploit new knowledge provides a ready explanation of why some firms may invest in basic research even when the preponderance of findings spill out into the public domain. Specifically, firms may conduct basic research less for particular results than to be able to provide themselves with the general background knowledge that would permit them to exploit rapidly useful scientific and technological knowledge through their own innovations or to be able to respond quickly—become a fast second—when competitors come up with a major advance (see also Rosenberg, 1990). In terms of our discussion of the cognitive and organizational aspects of absorptive capacity, we may think of basic research as broadening the firm's knowledge base to create critical overlap with new knowledge and providing it with the deeper understanding that is useful for exploiting new technical developments that build on rapidly advancing science and technology.

This perspective on the role of basic research offers a rather different view of the determinants of basic research than that which has dominated thinking in this area for the thirty years since Nelson's (1959) seminal article. Nelson hypothesized that more diversified firms will invest more heavily in basic research because, assuming imperfect markets for information, they will be better able to exploit its wide-ranging and unpredictable results. Nelson thus saw product-market diversification as one of the key determinants of basic research.[6] Emphasizing the role of basic research in firm learning, our perspective redirects attention from what happens to the knowledge outputs from the innovation process to the nature of the knowledge inputs themselves. Considering that absorptive capacity tends to be specific to a field or knowledge domain means that the type of knowledge that the firm believes it may have to exploit will affect the sort of research the firm conducts. From this vantage point, we would conjecture that as a firm's technological progress becomes more closely tied to advances in basic science (as has been the case in pharmaceuticals), a firm will increase its basic research, whatever its degree of product-market diversification. We also suggest, with reference to all firm research, not just basic research, that as the fields underlying technical advance within an industry become more diverse, we may expect firms to increase their R&D as they develop absorptive capacities in each of the relevant fields. For example, as automobile manufacturing comes to draw more heavily on newer fields such as microelectronics and ceramics, we expect that manufacturers will expand their basic and applied research efforts to better evaluate and exploit new findings in these areas.

The findings on the role of absorptive capacity and the ways in which it may be developed also have implications for the analysis of the adoption and diffusion of innovations. Our perspective implies that the ease of learning, and thus technology adoption, is affected by the degree to which an innovation is related to the pre-existing knowledge base of

6
Markets for information often fail because they inherently represent a situation of information asymmetry in which the less informed party cannot properly value the information he or she wishes to purchase, and the more informed party, acting self-interestedly, attempts to exploit that inability (Williamson, 1975).

Absorptive Capacity

prospective users. For example, personal computers diffused more rapidly at the outset among consumers and firms who had prior experience on mainframes or minicomputers. Likewise, software engineering practices seem to be adopted more readily by programmers with previous Pascal rather than Fortran experience because the structure of Pascal more closely reflects some of the underlying principles of software engineering (Smith et al., 1989). Our argument also suggests that an innovation that is fully incorporated in capital equipment will diffuse more rapidly than more disembodied innovations that require some complementary expertise on the part of potential users. This is one of the anticipated benefits of making computers more "user friendly."

The importance of absorptive capacity also helps explain some recent findings regarding firms' cooperative research ventures. First, Link (1987) has observed that cooperative research ventures are actually found more typically in industries that employ more mature technologies rather than in industries in which technology is moving ahead quickly—as seems to be suggested by the popular press. Second, it has been observed that cooperative ventures that have been initiated to pursue basic research, as well as more applied research objectives, have been subject over the years to increasing pressure to focus on more short-term research objectives (Mowery and Rosenberg, 1989). The simple notion that it is important to consider the costs of assimilating and exploiting knowledge from such ventures provides at least a partial explanation for these phenomena. Many cooperative ventures are initiated in areas in which the cost to access the output of the venture is low, or they often gravitate toward such areas over time. Conversely, those who are attempting to encourage cooperative research ventures in quickly advancing fields should recognize that the direct participation in the venture should represent only a portion of the resources that it will take to benefit from the venture. Participating firms also must be prepared to invest internally in the absorptive capacity that will permit effective exploitation of the venture's knowledge output.

CONCLUSION

Our empirical analysis of R&D investment suggested that firms are in fact sensitive to the characteristics of the learning environment in which they operate. Thus, absorptive capacity appears to be part of a firm's decision calculus in allocating resources for innovative activity. Despite these findings, because absorptive capacity is intangible and its benefits are indirect, one can have little confidence that the appropriate level, to say nothing of the optimal level, of investment in absorptive capacity is reached. Thus, while we have proposed a model to explain R&D investment, in which R&D both generates innovation and facilitates learning, the development of this model may ultimately be as valuable for the prescriptive analysis of organizational policies as its application may be as a positive model of firm behavior.

An important question from a prescriptive perspective is When is a firm most likely to underinvest in absorptive capacity to its own long-run detriment? Absorptive capacity is more likely to be developed and maintained as a byproduct of routine activity when the knowledge domain that the firm wishes to exploit is closely related to its current knowledge base. When, however, a firm wishes to acquire and use knowledge that is unrelated to its ongoing activity, then the firm must dedicate effort exclusively to creating absorptive capacity (i.e., absorptive capacity is not a byproduct). In this case, absorptive capacity may not even occur to the firm as an investment alternative. Even if it does, due to the intangible nature of absorptive capacity, a firm may be reluctant to sacrifice current output as well as gains from specialization to permit its technical personnel to acquire the requisite breadth of knowledge that would permit absorption of knowledge from new domains. Thus, while the current discussion addresses key features of organizational structure that determine a firm's absorptive capacity and provides evidence that investment is responsive to the need to develop this capability, more research is necessary to understand the decision processes that determine organizations' investments in absorptive capacity.

REFERENCES

Abernathy, William J.
1978 The Productivity Dilemma. Baltimore: Johns Hopkins University Press.

Allen, Thomas J.
1977 Managing the Flow of Technology. Cambridge, MA: MIT Press.

Allen, Thomas J., and Stephen D. Cohen
1969 "Information flows in R&D labs." Administrative Science Quarterly, 20: 12–19.

Anderson, John R., Robert Farrell, and Ron Sauers
1984 "Learning to program in LISP." Cognitive Science, 8: 87–129.

Arrow, Kenneth J.
1962 "Economic welfare and the allocation of resources for invention." In R. R. Nelson (ed.), The Rate and Direction of Inventive Activity: 609–625. Princeton, NJ: Princeton University Press.

Bower, Gordon H., and Ernest R. Hilgard
1981 Theories of Learning. Englewood Cliffs, NJ: Prentice-Hall.

Bradshaw, Gary F., Patrick W. Langley, and Herbert A. Simon
1983 "Studying scientific discovery by computer simulation." Science, 222: 971–975.

Brock, Gerald W.
1975 The U.S. Computer Industry. Cambridge, MA: Ballinger.

Burns, Tom, and George M. Stalker
1961 The Management of Innovation. London: Tavistock.

Clark, Kim B., and Takahiro Fujimoto
1987 "Overlapping problem solving in product development." Technical Report, Harvard Business School.

Cohen, Wesley M., and Richard C. Levin
1989 "Empirical studies of innovation and market structure." In R. C. Schmalensee and R. Willig (eds.), Handbook of Industrial Organization: 1059–1107. Amsterdam: Elsevier.

Cohen, Wesley M., and Daniel A. Levinthal
1987 "Participation in cooperative research ventures and the cost of learning." Technical Report, Dept. of Social and Decision Sciences, Carnegie Mellon University.
1989a "Innovation and learning: The two faces of R&D." Economic Journal, 99: 569–596.
1989b "Fortune favors the prepared firm." Technical Report, Dept. of Social and Decision Sciences, Carnegie Mellon University

Dearborn, R., and Herbert A. Simon
1958 "Selective perception in executives." Sociometry, 21: 140–144.

Ellis, Henry Carlton
1965 The Transfer of Learning. New York: MacMillan.

Estes, William Kaye
1970 Learning Theory and Mental Development. New York: Academic Press.

Hamberg, Daniel
1963 "Invention in the industrial research laboratory." Journal of Political Economy, 71: 95–115.

Harlow, H. F.
1949 "The formation of learning sets." Psychological Review, 56: 51–65.
1959 "Learning set and error factor theory." In S. Koch (ed.), Psychology: A Study of Science, 2: 492–537. New York: McGraw-Hill.

Johnston, R., and M. Gibbons
1975 "Characteristics of information usage in technological innovation." IEEE Transactions on Engineering Management, 27–34, EM-22.

Katz, Daniel, and Robert L. Kahn
1966 The Social Psychology of Organizations. New York: Wiley.

Katz, Ralph
1982 "The effects of group longevity on project communication and performance." Administrative Science Quarterly, 27: 81–104.

Katz, Ralph, and Thomas J. Allen
1982 "Investigating the not invented here (NIH) syndrome: A look at the performance, tenure, and communication patterns of 50 R&D project groups." R&D Management, 12: 7–12.

Lee, Denis M. S., and Thomas J. Allen
1982 "Integrating new technical staff: Implications for acquiring new technology." Management Science, 28: 1405–1420.

Absorptive Capacity

Levin, Richard C.
1981 "Toward an empirical model of Schumpeterian competition." Technical Report, Dept. of Economics, Yale University.

Levin, Richard C., Alvin K. Klevorick, Richard R. Nelson, and Sidney G. Winter
1983 "Questionnaire on industrial research and development." Dept. of Economics, Yale University.
1987 "Appropriating the returns from industrial R&D." Brookings Papers on Economic Activity, 783–820.

Levitt, Barbara, and James G. March
1988 "Organizational learning." Annual Review of Sociology, 14: 319–340.

Lindsay, Peter H., and Donald A. Norman
1977 Human Information Processing. Orlando, FL: Academic Press.

Link, Albert N.
1987 "Cooperative research activity in U.S. Manufacturing." Technical Report, University of North Carolina, Greensboro, Final report submitted to the National Science Foundation under grant PRA 85-212664.

Majumdar, Bodiul Alam
1982 Innovations, Product Developments and Technology Transfers: An Empirical Study of Dynamic Competitive Advantage, The Case of Electronic Calculators. Lanham, MD: University Press of America.

Mansfield, Edwin
1968 Economics of Technological Change. New York: Norton.
1988 "The speed and cost of industrial innovation in Japan and the United States: External vs. internal technology." Management Science, 34(10): 1157–1168.

March, James G., and Herbert A. Simon
1958 Organizations. New York: Wiley.

Mowery, David C.
1983 "The relationship between intrafirm and contractual forms of industrial research in American manufacturing, 1900–1940." Explorations in Economic History, 20: 351–374.

Mowery, David C., and Nathan Rosenberg
1989 Technology and the Pursuit of Economic Growth. New York: Cambridge University Press.

Mueller, Willard F.
1962 "The origins of the basic inventions underlying DuPont's major product and process innovations, 1920 to 1950." In R. R. Nelson (ed.), The Rate and Direction of Inventive Activity: 323–358. Princeton: Princeton University Press.

Myers, Sumner, and Donald C. Marquis
1969 "Successful industrial innovations." Washington, DC: National Science Foundation, NSF 69-17.

Nelson, Richard R.
1959 "The simple economics of basic research." Journal of Political Economy, 67: 297–306.

Nelson, Richard R., and Sidney Winter
1982 An Evolutionary Theory of Economic Change. Cambridge, MA: Harvard University Press.

Peck, Merton J.
1962 "Inventions in the postwar American aluminum industry." In R. R. Nelson (ed.), The Rate and Direction of Inventive Activity: 279–298. Princeton: Princeton University Press.

Pirolli, Peter L., and John R. Anderson
1985 "The role of learning from example in the acquisition of recursive programming skill." Canadian Journal of Psychology, 39: 240–272.

Reich, Robert B.
1987 "The rise of techno-nationalism." Atlantic, May: 63–69.

Rosenberg, Nathan
1982 Inside the Black Box: Technology and Economics. New York: Cambridge University Press.
1990 "Why do firms do basic research (with their own money)?" Research Policy (in press).

Rosenberg, Nathan, and W. Edward Steinmueller
1988 "Why are Americans such poor imitators?" American Economic Review, 78(2): 229–234.

Schumpeter, Joseph A.
1942 Capitalism, Socialism and Democracy. New York: Harper and Row.

Simon, Herbert A.
1985 "What we know about the creative process." In R. L. Kuhn (ed.), Frontiers in Creative and Innovative Management: 3–20. Cambridge, MA: Ballinger.

Smith, Gordon, Wesley M. Cohen, William Hefley, and Daniel A. Levinthal
1989 "Understanding the adoption of Ada: A field study report." Technical Report, Software Engineering Institute, Carnegie Mellon University.

Spence, A. Michael
1984 "Cost reduction, competition, and industry performance." Econometrica, 52: 101–122.

Tilton, John E.
1971 International Diffusion of Technology: The Case of Semiconductors. Washington, DC: Brookings Institution.

Tushman, Michael L.
1977 "Special boundary roles in the innovation process." Administrative Science Quarterly, 22: 587–605.
1978 "Technical communication in R&D laboratories: The impact of project work characteristics." Administrative Science Quarterly, 21: 624–644.

Tushman, Michael L., and Philip Anderson
1986 "Technological discontinuities and organizational environments." Administrative Science Quarterly, 31: 439–465.

Utterback, James M.
1971 "The process of technological innovation within the firm." Academy of Management Journal, 12: 75–88.

von Hippel, Eric
1978 "Successful industrial products from customer ideas." Journal of Marketing, 42: 39–49.
1988 The Sources of Innovation. New York: Oxford University Press.

Vyssotsky, V. A.
1977 "The innovation process at Bell Labs." Technical Report, Bell Laboratories.

Westney, D. Eleanor, and Kiyonori
Sakakibara
1986 "The role of Japan-based R&D
     in global technology strategy."
     In M. Hurowitch (ed.), Tech-
     nology in the Modern Corpora-
     tion: 217–232, London:
     Pergamon.

Williamson, Oliver E.
1975 Markets and Hierarchies:
     Analysis and Antitrust Implica-
     tions. New York: Free Press.

Zenger, Todd R., and Barbara S.
Lawrence
1989 "Organizational demography:
     The differential effects of age
     and tenure distributions on
     technical communication."
     Academy of Management
     Journal, 32: 353–376.

[12]

Strategic Management Journal, Vol. 13, 111–125 (1992)

CORE CAPABILITIES AND CORE RIGIDITIES: A PARADOX IN MANAGING NEW PRODUCT DEVELOPMENT

DOROTHY LEONARD-BARTON
Graduate School of Business Administration, Harvard University, Boston, Massachusetts, U.S.A.

This paper examines the nature of the core capabilities of a firm, focusing in particular on their interaction with new product and process development projects. Two new concepts about core capabilities are explored here. First, while core capabilities are traditionally treated as clusters of distinct technical systems, skills, and managerial systems, these dimensions of capabilities are deeply rooted in values, which constitute an often overlooked but critical fourth dimension. Second, traditional core capabilities have a down side that inhibits innovation, here called core rigidities. Managers of new product and process development projects thus face a paradox: how to take advantage of core capabilities without being hampered by their dysfunctional flip side. Such projects play an important role in emerging strategies by highlighting the need for change and leading the way. Twenty case studies of new product and process development projects in five firms provide illustrative data.

INTRODUCTION

Debate about the nature and strategic importance of firms' distinctive capabilities has been heightened by the recent assertion that Japanese firms understand, nurture and exploit their core competencies better than their U.S.-based competitors (Prahalad and Hamel, 1990). This paper explores the interaction of such capabilities with a critical strategic activity: the development of new products and processes. In responding to environmental and market changes, development projects become the focal point for tension between innovation and the *status quo*—microcosms of the paradoxical organizational struggle to maintain, yet renew or replace core capabilities.

In this paper, I first examine the history of core capabilities, briefly review relevant

Key words: Core capabilities, innovation, new product development

0143–2095/92/060125–15$12.50

literature, and describe a field-based study providing illustrative data. The paper then turns to a deeper description of the nature of core capabilities and detailed evidence about their symbiotic relationship with development projects. However, evidence from the field suggests the need to enhance emerging theory by examining the way that capabilities inhibit as well as enable development, and these arguments are next presented. The paper concludes with a discussion of the project/capabilities interaction as a paradox faced by project managers, observed management tactics, and the potential of product/process development projects to stimulate change.

THE HISTORY OF CORE CAPABILITIES

Capabilities are considered *core* if they differentiate a company strategically. The concept is not new. Various authors have called them distinctive

112   *D. Leonard-Barton*

competences (Snow and Hrebiniak, 1980; Hitt and Ireland, 1985), core or organizational competencies (Prahalad and Hamel, 1990; Hayes, Wheelwright and Clark, 1988), firm-specific competence (Pavitt, 1991), resource deployments (Hofer and Schendel, 1978), and invisible assets (Itami, with Roehl, 1987). Their strategic significance has been discussed for decades, stimulated by such research as Rumelt's (1974) discovery that of nine diversification strategies, the two that were built on an existing skill or resource base in the firm were associated with the highest performance. Mitchell's (1989) observation that industry-specific capabilities increased the likelihood a firm could exploit a new technology within that industry, has confirmed the early work. Therefore some authors suggest that effective competition is based less on strategic leaps than on incremental innovation that exploits carefully developed capabilities (Hayes, 1985; Quinn, 1980).

On the other hand, institutionalized capabilities may lead to 'incumbent inertia' (Lieberman and Montgomery, 1988) in the face of environmental changes. Technological discontinuities can enhance or destroy existing competencies within an industry (Tushman and Anderson, 1986). Such shifts in the external environment resonate within the organization, so that even 'seemingly minor' innovations can undermine the usefulness of deeply embedded knowledge (Henderson and Clark, 1990). In fact, all innovation necessarily requires some degree of 'creative destruction' (Schumpeter, 1942).

Thus at any given point in a corporation's history, core capabilities are evolving, and corporate survival depends upon successfully managing that evolution. New product and process development projects are obvious, visible arenas for conflict between the need for innovation and retention of important capabilities. Managers of such projects face a paradox: core capabilities *simultaneously* enhance and inhibit development.[1] Development projects reveal friction between technology strategy and current corporate practices; they also spearhead potential new strategic directions (Burgelman, 1991). However, most studies of industrial innovation focus on the new

product project as a self-contained unit of analysis, and address such issues as project staffing or structure (Souder, 1987; Leonard-Barton, 1988a; Clark and Fujimoto, 1991. Chapter 9).[2] Therefore there is little research-based knowledge on managing the interface between the project and the organization, and the interaction between development and capabilities in particular. Observing core capabilities through the lens of the project places under a magnifying glass one aspect of the 'part-whole' problem of innovation management, which Van de Ven singles out as '[p]erhaps the most significant structural problem in managing complex organizations today. . . ' (1986:598).

Recent field research on 20 new product and process development projects provided an opportunity to explore and conceptually model the relationship between development practices and a firm's core capabilities. As described in the Appendix, four extensive case studies in each of five companies (Ford, Chaparral Steel, Hewlett Packard, and two anonymous companies, Electronics and Chemicals) were conducted by joint teams of academics and practitioners.[3] (Table 1). Before describing the interactions observed in the field, I first define core capabilities.

Dimensions of core capabilities

Writers often assume that descriptors of core capabilities such as 'unique,' 'distinctive,' 'difficult to imitate,' or 'superior to competition' render the term self-explanatory, especially if reference is also made to 'resource deployment' or 'skills.' A few authors include activities such as 'collective learning' and explain how competence is and is not cultivated (Prahalad and Hamel, 1990).Teece, Pisano and Shuen provide one of the clearest definitions: 'a set of differentiated skills, complementary assets, and routines that provide the basis for a firm's competitive capacities and sustainable advantage in a particular business' (1990: 28).

---

[1] According to Quinn and Cameron, '(t)he key characteristic in paradox is the simultaneous presence of contradictory, even mutually exclusive elements' (1988:2.)

[2] Exceptions are historical cases about a developing technical innovation in an industry (see for example, Rosenbloom and Cusumano, 1987.)

[3] Other members of the data-collection team on which I served are: Kent Bowen, Douglas Braithwaite, William Hanson, Gil Preuss and Michael Titelbaum. They contributed to the development of the ideas presented herein through discussion and reactions to early drafts of this paper.

Table 1. Description of projects studied

Company	Product/process description
Ford Motor Company	**FX15** Compressor for automobile air conditioning systems **EN53** New full-sized car built on carryover platform **MN12** All new car platform including a novel supercharged engine **FN9** Luxury automobile built on carryover platform with major suspension system modifications
Chaparral Steel	**Horizontal Caster** New caster used to produce higher grades steel **Pulpit Controls** Furnace control mechanism upgrade from analog to digital **Microtuff 10** New special bar quality alloy steel **Arc Saw** Electric arc saw for squaring ends of steel beams
Hewlett-Packard Company	**Deskjet** Low cost personal computer and office printer using new technology **Hornet** Low cost spectrum analyzer **HP 150** Terminal/PC linked to high-end computer **Logic Analyzer** Digital logic analyzer
Chemicals	Special use camera Large format printer for converting digital input to continuous images New polymer used in film 21st century 'factory of the future'
Electronics	New RISC/UNIX workstation Local area network linking multiple computer networks Software architecture for desktop publishing High-density storage disk drive

In this article, I adopt a knowledge-based view of the firm and define a core capability as the knowledge set that distinguishes and provides a competitive advantage. There are four dimensions to this knowledge set. Its content is embodied in (1) employee *knowledge and skills* and embedded in (2) *technical systems*. The processes of knowledge creation and control are guided by (3) *managerial systems*. The fourth dimension is (4) the *values and norms* associated with the various types of embodied and embedded knowledge and with the processes of knowledge creation and control. In managerial literature, this fourth dimension is usually separated from the others or ignored.[4] However, understanding it is crucial to managing both new product/process development and core capabilities.

The first dimension, knowledge and skills embodied in people, is the one most often associated with core capabilities (Teece *et al.*, 1990) and the one most obviously relevant to new product development. This knowledge/skills dimension encompasses both firm-specific techniques and scientific understanding. The second, knowledge embedded in technical systems, results from years of accumulating, codifying and structuring the tacit knowledge in peoples' heads. Such physical production or information systems represent compilations of knowledge, usually derived from multiple individual sources; therefore the whole technical system is greater than the sum of its parts. This knowledge constitutes both information (e.g. a data base of product tests conducted over decades) and procedures (e.g. proprietary design rules.) The third dimension, managerial systems, represents formal and informal ways of creating knowledge (e.g. through

---

[4] Barney (1986) is a partial exception in that it poses organizational culture as a competitive advantage.

114   *D. Leonard-Barton*

sabbaticals, apprenticeship programs or networks with partners) and of controlling knowledge (e.g. incentive systems and reporting structures).

Infused through these three dimensions is the fourth: the value assigned within the company to the content and structure of knowledge (e.g. chemical engineering vs. marketing expertise; 'open-systems' software vs. proprietary systems), means of collecting knowledge (e.g. formal degrees v. experience) and controlling knowledge (e.g. individual empowerment vs. management hierarchies). Even physical systems embody values. For instance, organizations that have a strong tradition of individual vs. centralized control over information prefer an architecture (software and hardware) that allows much autonomy at each network node. Such 'debatable, overt, espoused values' (Schein, 1984: 4) are one 'manifestation' of the corporate culture (Schein, 1986: 7).[5]

Core capabilities are 'institutionalized' (Zucker, 1977). That is, they are part of the organization's taken-for-granted reality, which is an accretion of decisions made over time and events in corporate history (Kimberly, 1987; Tucker, Singh and Meinhard, 1990; Pettigrew, 1979). The technology embodied in technical systems and skills usually traces its roots back to the firm's first products. Managerial systems evolve over time in response to employees' evolving interpretation of their organizational roles (Giddens, 1984) and to the need to reward particular actions. Values bear the 'imprint' of company founders and early leaders (Kimberly, 1987). All four dimensions of core capabilities reflect accumulated behaviors and beliefs based on early corporate successes. One advantage of core capabilities lies in this unique heritage, which is not easily imitated by would-be competitors.

Thus a core capability is an interrelated, interdependent knowledge system. See Figure 1. The four dimensions may be represented in very different proportions in various capabilities. For instance, the information and procedures embedded in technical systems such as computer programs are relatively more important to credit card companies than to engineering consulting firms, since these latter firms likely rely more on

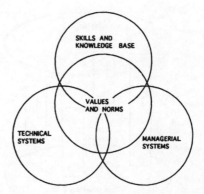

Figure 1. The four dimensions of a core capability.

the knowledge base embodied in individual employees (the skills dimension).[6]

Interaction of development projects and core capabilities: Managing the paradox

The interaction between development projects and capabilities lasts over a period of months or years and differs according to how completely aligned are the values, skills, managerial and technical systems required by the project with those currently prevalent in the firm. (See Figure 2). Companies in the study described above identified a selected, highly traditional and strongly held capability and then one project at each extreme of alignment: highly congruent vs. not at all (Table 2). Degree of congruence does not necessarily reflect project size, or technical or market novelty. Chaparral's horizontal caster and Ford's new luxury car, for instance, were neither incremental enhancements nor small undertakings. Nor did incongruent projects necessarily involve 'radical' innovations, by market or technological measures. Electronic's new workstation used readily available, 'state-of-the-shelf' components. Rather, unaligned projects

---

[5] Schein distinguishes between these surface values and 'preconscious' and 'invisible' 'basic assumptions' about the nature of reality (1984: 4).

[6] Each core capability draws upon only *some* of a company's skill and knowledge base, systems and values. Not only do some skills, systems and norms lie outside the domain of a particular core capability, but some may lie outside *all* core capabilities, as neither unique nor distinctly advantageous. For instance, although every company has personnel and pay systems, they may not constitute an important dimension of any core capability.

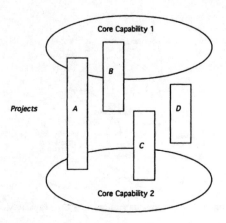

Figure 2.   Possible alignments of new product and process development projects with current core capabilities at a point in time.

were nontraditional for the organization along several dimensions of the selected core capability.

For instance, Chemicals' project developing a new polymer used in film drew heavily on traditional values, skills and systems. In this company, film designers represent the top five

percent of all engineers. All projects associated with film are high status, and highly proprietary technical systems have evolved to produce it. In contrast, the printer project was nontraditional. The key technical systems, for instance, were hardware rather than chemical or polymer and required mechanical engineering and software skills. Similarly, whereas the spectrum analyzer project at Hewlett Packard built on traditional capabilities in designing measurement equipment, the 150 terminal as a personal computer departed from conventional strengths. The 150 was originally conceived as a terminal for the HP3000, an industrial computer already on the market and as a terminal, was closely aligned with traditional capabilities. The attempt to transform the 150 into a personal computer was not very successful because different technical and marketing capabilities were required. Moreover, the greater system complexity represented by a stand-alone computer (e.g. the need for disk drives) required very untraditional cross-divisional cooperation.

Similar observations could be made about the other projects featured in Table 2. Chaparral's horizontal caster pushed the traditional science of molds to new heights, whereas the arc saw required capabilities that turned out to be

Table 2.   Relationship of selected projects with a very traditional core capability in each company studied

Company name	Traditional core capability	Degree of alignment	
		Very high	Very low
Ford Motor Co.	Total Vehicle Architecture	luxury car built on carryover platform (FN9)	compressor for air conditioner system (FX15)
Chaparral Steel	Science of Casting Molds	horizontal caster	electric arc saw
Hewlett Packard	Measurement Technology	low cost spectrum analyzer	150 terminal/ personal computer
Chemicals	Silver Halide Technology	new polymer for film	factory of the future
Electronics	Networking	local area network link	stand-alone workstation

116   *D. Leonard-Barton*

unavailable. The local area networks project at Electronics grew directly out of networking expertise, whereas the new RISC/UNIX workstation challenged dominant and proprietary software/hardware architecture. At Ford, the three car projects derived to varying degrees from traditional strengths—especially the new luxury car. However, the air-conditioner compressor had never been built in-house before. Since all new product development departs somewhat from current capabilities, project misalignment is a matter of degree. However, as discussed later, it is also a matter of kind. That is, the type as well as the number of capability dimensions challenged by a new project determines the intensity of the interaction and the project's potential to stimulate change.

THE UP SIDE: CAPABILITIES ENHANCE DEVELOPMENT

In all projects studied, deep stores of knowledge embodied in people and embedded in technical systems were accessed; all projects were aided by managerial systems that created and controlled knowledge flows, and by prevalent values and norms. That is, whether the projects were aligned or not with the prominent core capability identified by the company, *some* dimensions of that capability favored the project. However, the closer the alignment of project and core knowledge set, the stronger the enabling influence.

In order to understand the dynamic interaction of project with capabilities, it is helpful to tease apart the dimensions of capabilities and put each dimension separately under the microscope. However, we must remember that these dimensions are interrelated; each is supported by the other three. Values in particular permeate the other dimensions of a core capability.

Skills/knowledge dimension

Excellence in the dominant discipline

One of the most necessary elements in a core capability is excellence in the technical and professional skills and knowledge base underlying major products. The professional elite in these companies earn their status by demonstrating remarkable skills. They expect to 'achieve the

impossible'—and it is often asked of them. Thus managers of development projects that draw upon core capabilities have rich resources. In numerous cases, seemingly intractable technical problems were solved through engineering excellence. For instance, although engineers working on the thin film media project at Electronics had little or no prior experience with this particular form of storage technology, (because the company had always used ferrite-based media) they were able to *invent* their way out of difficulties. Before this project was over, the geographically dispersed team had invented new media, new heads to read the data off the thin film media, as well as the software and hardware to run a customized assembly and test line for the new storage device.

Pervasive technical literacy

Besides attracting a cadre of superbly qualified people to work in the dominant discipline, time-honored core capabilities create a reservoir of complementary skills and interests outside the projects, composed of technically skilled people who help shape new products with skilled criticism. In the Electronics Software Applications project, the developers enlisted employees through computer networks to field test emerging products. After trying out the software sent them electronically, employees submitted all reactions to a computerized 'Notes' file. This internal field testing thus took advantage of both willing, technically able employees and also a computer system set up for easy world-wide networking. Similarly, Electronics Workstation developers recruited an internal 'wrecking crew' to evaluate their new product. Employees who found the most 'bugs' in the prototype workstations were rewarded by getting to keep them. At Chemicals, developers tested the special purpose camera by loading down an engineer going on a weekend trip with film, so that he could try out various features for them. In these companies, internal testing is so commonplace that it is taken for granted as a logical step in new product/process creation. However, it represents a significant advantage over competitors trying to enter the same market without access to such technically sophisticated personnel. Internal 'field testers' not only typify users but can translate their reactions into technical enhancements; such swift feedback helps development teams hit market windows.

The technical systems dimension

Just as pervasive technical literacy among employees can constitute a corporate resource, so do the systems, procedures and tools that are artifacts left behind by talented individuals, embodying many of their skills in a readily accessible form. Project members tap into this embedded knowledge, which can provide an advantage over competitors in timing, accuracy or amount of available detail. At Ford Motor Company, the capability to model reliability testing derives in part from proprietary software tools that simulate extremely complex interactions. In the full-sized car project, models simulating noise in the car body allowed engineers to identify nonobvious root causes, some originating from interaction among physically separated components. For instance, a noise apparently located in the floor panel could be traced instead to the acoustical interaction of sound waves reverberating between roof and floor. Such simulations cut development time as well as costs. They both build on and enhance the engineers' skills.

The management systems dimension

Managerial systems constitute part of a core capability when they incorporate unusual blends of skills, and/or foster beneficial behaviors not observed in competitive firms. Incentive systems encouraging innovative activities are critical components of some core capabilities, as are unusual educational systems. In Chaparral Steel, all employees are shareholders. This rewards system interacts with development projects in that employees feel that every project is an effort to improve a process they own. 'I feel like this company partly belongs to me,' explains a millwright. Consequently, even operators and maintenance personnel are tenacious innovation champions. The furnace controls upgrade (incorporating a switch from analog to digital) was initiated by a maintenance person, who persevered against opposition from his nominal superiors. Chaparral Steel also has a unique apprenticeship program for the entire production staff, involving both classroom education and on-the-job training. Classes are taught by mill foremen on a rotating basis. The combination of mill-specific information and general education (including such unusual offerings as interpersonal

skills for furnace operators) would be difficult to imitate, if only because of the diversity of abilities required of these foremen. They know what to teach from having experienced problems on the floor, and they must live on the factory floor with what they have taught. This managerial system, tightly integrating technical theory and practice, is reflected in every development project undertaken in the company (Leonard-Barton, 1991).

Values dimension

The values assigned to knowledge creation and content, constantly reinforced by corporate leaders and embedded in management practices, affect all the development projects in a line of business. Two subdimensions of values are especially critical: the degree to which project members are empowered and the status assigned various disciplines on the project team.

Empowerment of project members

Empowerment is the belief in the potential of every individual to contribute meaningfully to the task at hand and the relinquishment by organizational authority figures to that individual of responsibility for that contribution. In HP, 'Electronics,' and Chaparral, the assumption is that empowered employees will create multiple potential futures for the corporation and these options will be selected and exercised as needed. The future of the corporation thus rests on the ability of such individuals to create new businesses by championing new products and processes. Since strategy in these companies is 'pattern in action' or 'emergent' rather than 'deliberate' (Mintzberg, 1990), empowerment is an especially important element of their core capabilities, and project members initiating new capabilities were exhilarated by the challenges they had created. The Hewlett Packard printer and the Electronics storage teams actually felt that they had turned the course of their mammoth corporate ship a critical degree or two.

High status for the dominant discipline

A business generally recognized for certain core capabilities attracts, holds, and motivates talented people who value the knowledge base underlying that capability and join up for the challenges,

118   *D. Leonard-Barton*

the camaraderie with competent peers, the status associated with the skills of the dominant discipline or function. Each company displays a cultural bias towards the technical base in which the corporation has its historical roots. For Chemicals, that base is chemistry and chemical engineering; for Hewlett Packard and Electronics, it is electronics/computer engineering and operating systems software. A history of high status for the dominant discipline enables the corporation and the projects to attract the very top talent. Top chemical engineers can aspire to become the professional elites constituting the five percent of engineers who design premier film products at Chemicals. At Hewlett Packard and Electronics, design engineers are the professional elite.

A natural outgrowth of the prominence of a particular knowledge base is its influence over the development process. In many firms, a reinforcing cycle of values and managerial systems lends power and authority to the design engineer. That is, design engineers have high status because the new products that are directly evaluated by the market originate in design engineering; in contrast, the expertise of manufacturing engineers is expended on projects less directly tied to the bottom line and more difficult to evaluate. The established, well-paid career path for product designers attracts top engineering talent, who tend to perform well. The success (or failure) of new products is attributed almost entirely to these strong performers, whose high visibility and status constantly reinforce the dominance of their discipline.

As the above discussion suggests, projects derive enormous support from core capabilities. In fact, such capabilities continually spawn new products and processes because so much creative power is focused on identifying new opportunities to apply the accumulated knowledge base. However, these same capabilities can also prove dysfunctional for product and process development.

THE DOWN SIDE: CORE RIGIDITIES INHIBIT DEVELOPMENT

Even in projects that eventually succeed, problems often surface as product launch approaches. In response to gaps between product specifi-

cations and market information, or problems in manufacture, project managers face unpalatable choices. They can cycle back to prior phases in the design process (Leonard-Barton, 1988a), revisiting previous decisions higher up the design hierarchy (Clark, 1985), but almost certainly at the cost of schedule slippage. Or they may ship an inadequate product. Some such problems are idiosyncratic to the particular project, unlikely to occur again in the same form and hence not easily predicted. Others, however, occur repeatedly in multiple projects. These recurring shortfalls in the process are often traceable to the gap between current environmental requirements and a corporation's core capabilities. Values, skills, managerial systems, and technical systems that served the company well in the past and may still be wholly appropriate for some projects or parts of projects, are experienced by others as core rigidities—inappropriate sets of knowledge. Core rigidities are the flip side of core capabilities. They are not neutral; these deeply embedded knowledge sets actively create problems. While core rigidities are more problematic for projects that are deliberately designed to create new, nontraditional capabilities, rigidities can affect all projects—even those that are reasonably congruent with current core capabilities.

Skills and knowledge dimension

Less strength in nondominant disciplines

Any corporation's resources are limited. Emphasizing one discipline heavily naturally makes the company somewhat less attractive for top people in a nondominant one. A skilled marketing person knows that she will represent a minority discipline in an engineering-driven firm. Similarly, engineers graduating from top U.S. schools generally regard manufacturing in fabrication industries less attractive than engineering design, (see Hayes *et al.*, 1988) not only because of noncompetitive salaries, but because of a lower level of expertise among potential colleagues.

In each of the nonaligned and hence more difficult projects (Table 2), specific nontraditional types of knowledge were missing. Chaparral Steel's electric arc saw project required understanding electromagnetic fields for a variety of alloys—a very different knowledge set than the usual metallurgical expertise required in casting.

The Hewlett Packard 150 project suffered from a lack of knowledge about personal computer design and manufacture. The company has a long history of successful instrument development based on 'next-bench' design, meaning the engineering designers based their decisions on the needs and skills of their colleagues on the bench next to them. However, such engineers are not representative of personal computer users. Therefore traditional sources of information and design feedback were not applicable for the 150 project. Similarly, the new workstation project of Electronics met with less than optimal market acceptance because the traditional focus on producing a 'hot box,' i.e. excellent hardware, resulted in correspondingly less attention to developing software applications. The knowledge relevant to traditional hardware development flows through well-worn channels, but much less knowledge exists about creating application software. Therefore, the first few working proto-types of the UNIX/RISC workstation were shipped to customers rather than to third-party software developers. While this practice had worked well to stimulate interest in the company's well-established lines of hardware, for which much software is available, it was less appropriate for the new hardware, which could not be used and evaluated without software.

Technical systems dimension

Physical systems can embody rigidities also, since the skills and processes captured in software or hardware become easily outdated. New product designers do not always know how many such systems they are affecting. For example, in the RISC/UNIX workstation project at Electronics, the new software base posed an extreme challenge to manufacturing because hundreds of diagnostic and test systems in the factory were based on the corporate proprietary software. The impact of this incompatibility had been underestimated, given the very tight 8 month product delivery targets.

Management systems dimension

Management systems can grow just as intractable as physical ones—perhaps more so, because one cannot just plug in a new career path when a new project requires strong leadership in a hithertofore underutilized role. Highly skilled people are understandably reluctant to apply their abilities to project tasks that are undervalued, lest that negative assessment of the importance of the task contaminate perceptions of their personal abilities. In several companies, the project manager's role is not a strong one—partly because there is no associated career path. The road to the top lies through individual technical contribution. Thus a hardware engineer in one project considered his contribution as an engineering manager to be much more important than his simultaneous role as project manager, which he said was 'not my real job.' His perception of the relative unimportance of project leadership not only weakened the power of the role in that specific project but reinforced the view held by some that problem-solving in project management requires less intelligence than technical problem-solving.

Values dimension

Core rigidities hampered innovation in the development projects especially along the values dimension. Of course, certain generic types of corporate cultures encourage innovation more than others (Burns and Stalker, 1961; Chakravarthy, 1982). While not disagreeing with that observation, the point here is a different one: the very same values, norms and attitudes that support a core capability and thus enable development can also constrain it.

Empowerment as entitlement

A potential down side to empowerment observed is that individuals construe their empowerment as a psychological contract with the corporation, and yet the boundaries of their responsibility and freedom are not always clear. Because they undertake heroic tasks for the corporation, they expect rewards, recognition and freedom to act. When the contract goes sour, either because they exceed the boundaries of personal freedom that the corporation can tolerate, or their project is technically successful but fails in other ways, or their ideas are rejected, or their self-sacrifice results in too little recognition, they experience the contract as abrogated and often leave the company—sometimes with a deep sense of betrayal.

Engineers in projects that fall towards the 'incongruity' end of the spectrum speak of 'betting

120   *D. Leonard-Barton*

their [corporate identification] badges,' on the outcome, and of having 'their backs to the cliff' as ways of expressing their sense of personal risk. One engineering project manager describes 'going into the tunnel,' meaning the development period, from which the team emerges only when the job is done. 'You either do it or you don't. . . You don't have any other life.' Such intrapreneurs seem to enjoy the stress—as long as their psychological contract with the company remains intact. In this case the manager believed her contract included enormous freedom from corporate interference with her management style. When corporate management imposed certain restrictions, she perceived her contract as abrogated, and left the company just 2 months before product launch, depriving the project of continuity in the vision she had articulated for an entire stream of products.

Empowerment as a value and practice greatly aids in projects, therefore, until it conflicts with the greater corporate good. Because development requires enormous initiative and yet great discipline in fulfilling corporate missions, the management challenge is to channel empowered individual energy towards corporate aims—without destroying creativity or losing good people.

Lower status for non-dominant disciplines

When new product development requires developing or drawing upon technical skills traditionally less well respected in the company, history can have an inhibiting effect. Even if multiple subcultures exist, with differing levels of maturity, the older and historically more important ones, as noted above, tend to be more prestigious. For instance, at Chemicals, the culture values the chemical engineers and related scientists as somehow 'more advanced' than mechanical engineers and manufacturing engineers. Therefore, projects involving polymers or film are perceived as more prestigious than equipment projects. The other companies displayed similar, very clear perceptions about what disciplines and what kinds of projects are high status. The lower status of nondominant disciplines was manifested in pervasive but subtle negatively reinforcing cycles that constrained their potential for contributions to new product development and therefore limited the cross-functional integration so necessary to innovation

(Pavitt, 1991). Four of these unacknowledged but critical manifestations are: who travels to whom, self-fulfilling expectations, unequal credibility and wrong language.[7]

One seemingly minor yet important indication of status affecting product/process development is that lower status individuals usually travel to the physical location of the higher. Manufacturing engineers were far more likely to go to the engineering design sites than vice versa, whether for one-day visits, or temporary or permanent postings. Not only does such one-way travel reinforce manufacturing's lower status, but it slows critical learning by design engineers, reinforcing their isolation from the factory floor. The exception to the rule, when design engineers traveled to the manufacturing site, aided cross-functional coordination by fostering more effective personal relationships. Such trips also educated the design engineers about some of the rationale behind design for manufacture (Whitney, 1988). A design engineer in one project returned to alter designs after seeing 'what [manufacturing] is up against' when he visited the factory floor.

Expectations about the status of people and roles can be dangerously self-fulfilling. As dozens of controlled experiments manipulating unconscious interpersonal expectations have demonstrated, biases can have a 'pygmalion effect': person A's expectations about the behavior of person B affect B's actual performance—for better or worse (Rosenthal and Rubin, 1978). In the engineering-driven companies studied, the expectation that marketing could not aid product definition was ensured fulfillment by expectations of low quality input, which undermined marketers' confidence. In the Electronics Local Area Network project, the marketing people discovered early on that users would want certain very important features in the LAN. However, they lacked the experience to evaluate that information and self-confidence to push for inclusion of the features. Not until that same information was gathered directly from customers by two experienced consulting engineers who presented it strongly was it acted upon. Precious time was lost as the schedule was slipped

---

[7] Such cycles, or 'vicious circles' as psychiatry has labeled them, resemble the examples of self-fulfilling prophecies cited by Weick (1979: 159–164).

four months to incorporate the 'new' customer information. Similarly, in the Hewlett Packard printer project, marketing personnel conducted studies in shopping malls to discover potential customers' reactions to prototypes. When marketing reported need for 21 important changes, the product designers enacted only five. In the next mall studies, the design engineers went along. Hearing from the future customers' own lips the same information rejected before, the product developers returned to the bench and made the other 16 changes. The point is certainly not that marketing always has better information than engineering. Rather history has conferred higher expectations and greater credibility upon the dominant function, whereas other disciplines start at a disadvantage in the development process.

Even if nondominant disciplines are granted a hearing in team meetings, their input may be discounted if not presented in the language favored by the dominant function. Customer service representatives in the Electronics LAN project were unable to convince engineering to design the computer boards for field repair as opposed to replacing the whole system in the field with a new box and conducting repairs back at the service center, because they were unable to present their argument in cost-based figures. Engineering assumed that an argument not presented as compelling financial data was useless.

Thus, nondominant roles and disciplines on the development team are kept in their place through a self-reinforcing cycle of norms, attitudes and skill sets. In an engineering-dominated company, the cycle for marketing and manufacturing is: low status on the development team, reinforced by the appointment of either young, less experienced members or else one experienced person, whose time is splintered across far too many teams. Since little money is invested in these roles, little contribution is expected from the people holding them. Such individuals act without confidence, and so do not influence product design much—thus reinforcing their low status on the team.

THE INTERACTION OF PRODUCT/PROCESS DEVELOPMENT PROJECTS WITH CORE RIGIDITIES

The severity of the paradox faced by project managers because of the dual nature of core capabilities depends upon both (1) the number and (2) the types of dimensions comprising a core rigidity. The more dimensions represented, the greater the misalignment potentially experienced between project and capability. For example, the Arc Saw project at Chaparral Steel was misaligned with the core metallurgical capability mostly along two dimensions: technical systems (not originally designed to accommodate an arc saw), and more importantly, the skills and knowledge-base dimension. In contrast, the Factory-of-the-Future project at Chemicals challenged all four dimensions of the traditional core capability. Not only were current proprietary technical systems inadequate, but existing managerial systems did not provide any way to develop the cross-functional skills needed. Moreover, the values placed on potential knowledge creation and control varied wildly among the several sponsoring groups, rendering a common vision unattainable.

The four dimensions vary in ease of change. From technical to managerial systems, skills and then values, the dimensions are increasingly less tangible, less visible and less explicitly codified. The technical systems dimension is relatively easy to alter for many reasons, among them the probability that such systems are local to particular departments. Managerial systems usually have greater organizational scope (Leonard-Barton, 1988b), i.e. reach across more subunits than technical systems, requiring acceptance by more people. The skills and knowledge content dimension is even less amenable to change because skills are built over time and many remain tacit, i.e. uncodified and in employees' heads (see von Hippel, 1990). However, the value embodied in a core capability is the dimension least susceptible to change; values are most closely bound to culture, and culture is hard to alter in the short term (Zucker, 1977), if it can be changed at all (Barney, 1986).

Effects of the paradox on projects

Over time, some core capabilities are replaced because their dysfunctional side has begun to inhibit too many projects. However, that substitution or renewal will not occur within the lifetime of a single project. Therefore, project managers cannot wait for time to resolve the paradox they face (Quinn and Cameron, 1988).

In the projects observed in this study, managers handled the paradox in one of four ways: (1) abandonment; (2) recidivism, i.e. return to core capabilities; (3) reorientation; and (4) isolation. The arc saw and factory-of-the-future projects were abandoned, as the managers found no way to resolve the problems. The HP150 personal computer exemplifies recidivism. The end product was strongly derivative of traditional HP capabilities in that it resembled a terminal and was more successful as one than as a personal computer. The special-use camera project was reoriented. Started in the film division, the stronghold of the firm's most traditional core capability, the project languished. Relocated to the equipment division, where the traditional corporate capability was less strongly ensconced, and other capabilities were valued, the project was well accepted. The tactic of isolation, employed in several projects to varying degrees, has often been invoked in the case of new ventures (Burgelman, 1983). Both the workstation project at Electronics and the HP Deskjet project were separated physically and psychologically from the rest of the corporation, the former without upper management's blessing. These project managers encouraged their teams by promoting the group as hardy pioneers fighting corporate rigidities.

Effects of the paradox on core capabilities

Although capabilities are not usually dramatically altered by a single project, projects do pave the way for organizational change by highlighting core rigidities and introducing new capabilities. Of the companies studied, Chaparral Steel made the most consistent use of development projects as agents of renewal and organization-wide learning. Through activities such as benchmarking against best-in-the-world capabilities, Chaparral managers use projects as occasions for challenging current knowledge and for modeling alternative new capabilities. For instance, personnel from vice presidents to operators spent months in Japan learning about horizontal casting and in the case of the new specialty alloy, the company convened its own academic conference in order to push the bounds of current capabilities.

In other companies, negative cycles reinforcing the lower status of manufacturing or marketing were broken—to the benefit of both project and corporation. In the workstation project at

Electronics, the manufacturing engineers on the project team eventually demonstrated so much knowledge that design engineers who had barely listened to 20 percent of their comments at the start of the project, gave a fair hearing to 80 percent, thereby allowing manufacturing to influence design. In the deskjet printer project at Hewlett Packard, managers recognized that inequality between design and manufacturing always created unnecessary delays. The Vancouver division thus sought to raise the status of manufacturing engineering skills by creating a manufacturing engineering group within R&D and then, once it was well established, moving it to manufacturing. A rotation plan between manufacturing and R&D was developed to help neutralize the traditional status differences; engineers who left research to work in manufacturing or vice versa were guaranteed a 'return ticket.' These changes interrupted the negative reinforcing cycle, signalling a change in status for manufacturing and attracting better talent to the position. This same project introduced HP to wholly unfamiliar market research techniques such as getting customer reactions to prototypes in shopping malls.

As these examples indicate, even within their 1–8-year lifetime, the projects studied served as small departures from tradition in organizations providing a 'foundation in experience' to inspire eventual large changes (Kanter, 1983). Such changes can be *precipitated* by the introduction of new capabilities along any of the four dimensions. However, for a capability to become *core*, all four dimensions must be addressed. A core capability is an interconnected set of knowledge collections—a tightly coupled system. This concept is akin to Pfeffer's definition of a paradigm, which he cautions is not just a view of the world but 'embodies procedures for inquiring about the world and categories into which these observations are collected. Thus', he warns, 'paradigms have within them an internal consistency that makes evolutionary change or adaptation nearly impossible' (1982: 228). While he is thinking of the whole organization, the caution might apply as well to core capabilities. Thus, new technical systems provide no inimitable advantage if not accompanied by new skills. New skills atrophy or flee the corporation if the technical systems are inadequate, and/or if the managerial systems such as training are incompatible. New values will not take root if associated behaviors are not rewarded. Therefore, when the development process encounters rigidities, projects can be managed consciously as the 'generative' actions characteristic of learning organizations (Senge, 1990) only if the multidimensional nature of core capabilities is fully appreciated.

CONCLUSION

This paper proposes a new focus of inquiry about technological innovation, enlarging the boundaries of 'middle range' project management theory to include interactions with development of capabilities, and hence with strategy. Because core capabilities are a collection of knowledge sets, they are distributed and are being constantly enhanced from multiple sources. However, at the same time that they enable innovation, they hinder it. Therefore in their interaction with the development process, they cannot be managed as a single good (or bad) entity.[x] They are not easy to change because they include a pervasive dimension of values, and as Weick (1979: 151) points out, 'managers unwittingly collude' to avoid actions that challenge accepted modes of behavior.

Yet technology-based organizations have no choice but to challenge their current paradigms. The swift-moving environment in which they function makes it critical that the 'old fit be consciously disturbed. . . ' (Chakravarthy, 1982: 42). Itami points out that 'The time to search out and develop a new core resource is when the current core is working well,' (1987: 54)—a point that is echoed by Foster (1982). Development projects provide opportunities for creating the 'requisite variety' for innovation (Van de Ven, 1986: 600; Kanter, 1986). As micro-level social systems, they create conflict with the macro system and hence a managerial paradox. Quinn and Cameron argue that recognizing and managing paradox is a powerful lever for change: 'Having multiple frameworks available. . . is probably the single most powerful attribute of self-renewing. . . organizations' (1988: 302).

---

[x] This observation is akin to Gidden's argument that structure is 'always both constraining and enabling' (1984: 25).

Thus project managers who constructively 'discredit' (Weick, 1979) the systems, skills or values traditionally revered by companies may cause a complete redefinition of core capabilities or initiate new ones. They can consciously manage projects for continuous organizational renewal. As numerous authors have noted, (Clark and Fujimoto, 1991; Hayes *et al.*, 1988; Pavitt, 1991) the need for this kind of emphasis on organizational learning over immediate output alone is a critical element of competition.

ACKNOWLEDGEMENTS

The author is grateful to colleagues Kim Clark, Richard Hackman and Steven Wheelwright as well as members of the research team and two anonymous reviewers for comments on earlier drafts of this paper, to the Division of Research at Harvard Business School for financial support, and to the companies that served as research sites.

A full report on the research on which this paper is based will be available in Kent Bowen, Kim Clark, Chuck Holloway and Steven Wheelwright, *Vision and Capability: High Performance Product Development in the 1990s*, Oxford University Press, New York.

REFERENCES

Barney, J. B. 'Organizational culture: Can it be a source of sustained competitive advantage?, *Academy of Management Review*, **11**(3), 1986, pp. 656–665.

Burgelman, R. 'A process model of internal corporate venturing in the diversified major firms', *Administrative Science Quarterly*, **28**, 1983, pp. 223–244.

Burgelman, R. 'Intraorganizational ecology of strategy making and organizational adaptation: Theory and field research', *Organization Science* **2**(3), 1991, pp. 239–262.

Burns, T. and G. M. Stalker. *The Management of Innovation*, Tavistock, London, 1961.

Chakravarthy, B. S. 'Adaptation: A promising metaphor for strategic management', *Academy of Management Review*, **7**(1), 1982, pp. 35–44.

Clark, K. 'The interaction of design hierarchies and market concepts in technological evolution' *Research Policy*, **14**, 1985, pp. 235–251.

Clark, K. and T. Fujimoto. *Product Development Performance*, Harvard Business School Press, Boston, MA, 1991.

124   D. Leonard-Barton

Foster, R. 'A call for vision in managing technology,' *Business Week*, May 24, 1982, pp. 24–33.

Giddens, A. *The Constitution of Society: Outline of the Theory of Structuration*. Polity Press, Cambridge, UK, 1984.

Hayes, R. H. 'Strategic planning—forward in reverse?', *Harvard Business Review*, November–December 1985, pp. 111–119 (Reprint # 85607).

Hayes, R. H., S. C. Wheelwright and K. B. Clark. *Dynamic Manufacturing: Creating the Learning Organization*, Free Press, New York, 1988.

Henderson, R. and K. B. Clark. 'Architectural innovation: The reconfiguration of existing product technologies and the failure of established firms', *Administrative Science Quarterly*, **35**, 1990, pp. 9–30.

Hitt, M. and R. D. Ireland. 'Corporate distinctive competence, strategy, industry and performance', *Strategic Management Journal*, **6**, 1985, pp. 273–293.

Hofer, C. W. and D. Schendel. *Strategy Formulation: Analytical Concepts*. West Publishing, St. Paul, MN, 1978.

Huber, G. and D. J. Power. 'Retrospective reports of strategic-level managers: Guidelines for increasing their accuracy', *Strategic Management Journal*, **6**(2), 1985, pp. 171–180.

Itami, H. with T. Roehl. *Mobilizing Invisible Assets*, Harvard University Press, Cambridge, MA, 1987.

Kanter, R. M. *The Change Masters*. Simon and Schuster, New York, 1983.

Kanter, R. M. 'When a thousand flowers bloom: Structural, collective and social conditions for innovation in organizations', Harvard Business School Working Paper #87–018, 1986.

Kimberly, J. R. 'The study of organization: Toward a biographical perspective'. In J. W. Lorsch (ed.), *Handbook of Organizational Behavior*, Prentice-Hall, Englewood Cliffs, NJ, 1987, pp. 223–237.

Leonard-Barton, D. 'Implementation as mutual adaptation of technology and organization', *Research Policy*, **17**, 1988a, pp. 251–267.

Leonard-Barton, D. 'Implementation characteristics in organizational innovations', *Communication Research*, **15**(5), October 1988b, pp. 603–631.

Leonard-Barton, D. 'The factory as a learning laboratory', Harvard Business School Working Paper # 92–023, 1991.

Lieberman, M. and D. B. Montgomery. 'First-mover advantages', *Strategic Management Journal*, **9**, Summer 1988, pp. 41–58.

Mintzberg, H. 'Strategy formation: Schools of thought'. In J. W. Fredrickson (ed.), *Perspectives on Strategic Management*, Harper & Row, New York, 1990.

Mitchell, W. 'Whether and when? Probability and timing of incumbents' entry into emerging industrial subfields', *Administrative Science Quarterly*, **34**, 1989, pp. 208–230.

Pavitt, K. 'Key characteristics of the large innovating firm', *British Journal of Management*, **2**, 1991, pp. 41–50.

Pettigrew, A. 'On studying organizational cultures', *Administrative Science Quarterly*, **24**, 1979,

pp. 570–581.

Pfeffer, J. *Organizations and Organization Theory*, Ballinger Publishing, Cambridge, MA, 1982.

Prahalad, C K. and G. Hamel. 'The core competence of the corporation', *Harvard Business Review*, **68**(3), 1990, pp. 79–91, (Reprint # 90311).

Quinn, J. B. *Strategies for Change: Logical Incrementalism*, Richard D. Irwin, Homewood, IL, 1980.

Quinn, R. and K. Cameron. 'Organizational paradox and transformation'. In R. Quinn and K. Cameron (eds), *Paradox and Transformation*, Cambridge, MA, Ballinger Publishing, 1988.

Rosenbloom, R. and M. Cusumano. 'Technological pioneering and competitive advantage: The birth of the VCR industry', *California Management Review*, **29**(4), 1987, pp. 51–76.

Rosenthal, R. and D. Rubin. 'Interpersonal expectancy effects: The first 345 studies', *The Behavioral and Brain Sciences*, **3**, 1978, pp. 377–415.

Rumelt, R. P. *Strategy, Structure and Economic Performance*, Harvard Business School Classics, Harvard Business School Press, Boston, MA, 1974 and 1986.

Schein, E. 'Coming to a new awareness of organizational culture', *Sloan Management Review*, Winter, 1984, pp. 3–16.

Schein, E. *Organizational Culture and Leadership*, Jossey-Bass, San Francisco, CA, 1986.

Schumpeter, J. *Capitalism, Socialism, and Democracy*, Harper, New York, 1942.

Senge, P.'The leader's new work: Building a learning organization', *Sloan Management Review*, **32**(1), 1990, pp. 7–23, (Reprint # 3211).

Snow, C. C. and L. G. Hrebiniak. 'Strategy, distinctive competence, and organizational performance', *Administrative Science Quarterly*, **25**, 1980, pp. 317–335.

Souder, W. E. *Managing New Product Innovations*, Lexington Books, Lexington, MA, 1987.

Teece, D. J., G. Pisano and A. Shuen. 'Firm capabilities, resources and the concept of strategy', Consortium on Competitiveness and Cooperation Working Paper # 90–9, University of California at Berkeley, Center for Research in Management, Berkeley, CA, 1990.

Tucker, D., J. Singh and A. Meinhard. 'Founding characteristics, imprinting and organizational change'. In J.V. Singh (ed.), *Organizational Evolution: New Directions*, Sage Publications, Newbury Park, CA, 1990.

Tushman, M. L. and P. Anderson. 'Technological discontinuities and organizational environments', *Administrative Science Quarterly*, **31**, 1986, pp. 439–465.

Van de Ven, A. 'Central problems in management of innovations', *Management Science*, **32**(5), 1986, pp. 590–607.

von Hippel, E. 'The impact of 'Sticky Data' on innovation and problem-solving', Sloan Management School, Working Paper # 3147-90-BPS, 1990.

Weick, K. E. 'Theory construction as disciplined imagination', *Academy of Management Review*,

14(4), 1989, pp. 516–531.
Weick, K. E. *The Social Psychology of Organizing*,
    Random House, New York, 1979.
Whitney, D. 'Manufacturing by design', *Harvard*

Business Review, **66**(4), 1988, pp. 83–91.
Zucker, L. G. 'The role of institutionalization in
    cultural persistence', *American Sociological Review*,
    42, 1977, pp. 726–743.

APPENDIX: METHODOLOGY

Structure of research teams

Four universities (Harvard, M.I.T., Standford
and Purdue) participated in the 'Manufacturing
Visions' project. Each research team was composed of at least one engineering and one
management professor plus one or two designated
company employees. The research was organized
into a matrix, with each research team having
primary responsibility for one company and also
one or more specific research 'themes' across
sites and companies. Some themes were identified
in the research protocol; others (such as the
capabilities/project interaction) emerged from
initial data analysis. In data collection and
analysis, the internal company and outside
researchers served as important checks on each
other—the company insiders on the generalizability of company observations from four cases
and the academics on the generalizability of
findings across companies.

Data-gathering

Using a common research protocol, the teams
developed case histories by interviewing development team members, including representatives
from all functional groups who had taken active
part and project staff members. These in-person
interviews, conducted at multiple sites across the
U.S., each lasted 1–3 hours. Interviewers toured
the manufacturing plants and design laboratories
and conducted follow-up interview sessions as
necessary to ensure comparable information
across all cases. The data-gathering procedures
thus adhered to those advocated by Huber
and Power (1985) to increase reliability of
retrospective accounts (e.g. interviews conducted

in tandem, motivated informants selected from
different organizational levels, all responses
probed extensively). In addition, the interviewers'
disparate backgrounds guarded against the dominance of one research bias, and much archival
evidence was collected. I personally interviewed
in 3 of the 5 companies.

Data analysis

Notes compiled by each team were exchanged
across a computer network and joint sessions
were held every several months to discuss
and analyze data. Company-specific and theme-
specific reports were circulated, first among team
members and then among all research teams to
check on accuracy. Team members 'tested' the
data against their own notes and observations
and reacted by refuting, confirming or refining
it. There were four within-team iterations and
an additional three iterations with the larger
research group. Thus observations were subjected
to numerous sets of 'thought trials' (Weick,
1989).

Each team also presented interim reports to
the host companies. These presentations offered
the opportunity to check data for accuracy, obtain
reactions to preliminary conclusions, fill in missing
data and determine that observations drawn from
a limited number of projects were in fact
representative of common practice in the company. The examples of traditional core capabilities
presented in Table 2 were provided by the
companies as consensus judgments, usually
involving others besides the company team
members. While the 20 projects vary in the
degree of success attributed to them by the
companies, only two were clear failures. The
others all succeeded in some ways (e.g. met a
demanding schedule) but fell short in others (e.g.
held market leadership for only a brief period).

[13]

Technological Discontinuities and Organizational Environments

Michael L. Tushman
Columbia University
Philip Anderson
Cornell University

This paper focuses on patterns of technological change and on the impact of technological breakthroughs on environmental conditions. Using data from the minicomputer, cement, and airline industries from their births through 1980, we demonstrate that technology evolves through periods of incremental change punctuated by technological breakthroughs that either enhance or destroy the competence of firms in an industry. These breakthroughs, or technological discontinuities, significantly increase both environmental uncertainty and munificence. The study shows that while competence-destroying discontinuities are initiated by new firms and are associated with increased environmental turbulence, competence-enhancing discontinuities are initiated by existing firms and are associated with decreased environmental turbulence. These effects decrease over successive discontinuities. Those firms that initiate major technological changes grow more rapidly than other firms.•

Since Barnard's (1938) and Selznick's (1949) seminal work, one of the richest streams of research in organizational theory has centered on organization-environment relations (see Starbuck, 1983, for a review). Recent work on organizational life cycles (Miller and Friesen, 1984; Tushman and Romanelli, 1985), organizational adaptation (Aldrich and Auster, 1986), population dynamics (Freeman, 1982), executive succession (Carroll, 1984), and strategy (e.g., Harrigan, 1983) hinges on environment-organization linkages. Environments pose constraints and opportunities for organizational action (Hrebiniak and Joyce, 1985).

If organizational outcomes are critically influenced by the context within which they occur, then better understanding of organizational dynamics requires that we more fully understand determinants of environmental change. While there has been substantial research on environmental conditions and organizational relations (see review in Downey and Ireland, 1979), relatively little research has examined how competitive environments change over time. While it is agreed that environmental conditions are shaped by competitive, legal, political, and technological factors (e.g., Starbuck, 1983; Romanelli and Tushman, 1986), and the interplay between them (Horwitch, 1982; Noble, 1984), there is little data on how these factors change over time or how they affect environmental conditions.

This paper focuses on technology as a central force in shaping environmental conditions. As technological factors shape appropriate organizational forms (McKelvey, 1982), fundamental technological change affects the rise and fall of populations within organizational communities (Astley, 1985). Basic technological innovation affects not only a given population, but also those populations within technologically interdependent communities. For example, major changes in semiconductor technology affected semiconductor firms as well as computer and automotive firms. Technology is, then, an important source of environmental variation and hence a critical factor affecting population dynamics.

This paper specifically investigates patterns of technological change and their impact on environmental conditions. Building on a considerable body of research on technological change, we argue and empirically demonstrate that patterned changes

•
This research was generously supported by funds from the Strategy Research Center at Columbia University, the Center for Entrepreneurial Studies at New York University, and the Center for Innovation Management Studies at Lehigh University. We would like to thank Graham Astley, Ellen Auster, Robert Drazin, Kathryn Harrigan, and anonymous *ASQ* reviewers for their helpful comments.

Technological Discontinuities

in technology dramatically affect environmental conditions.
There exist measurable patterns of technological change that
generate consistent patterns of environmental change over
time across three diverse industries. While technology is but
one force driving the course of environmental evolution, it is a
key building block to better understand how environments and
ultimately organizations evolve over time.

TECHNOLOGY AND TECHNOLOGICAL DISCONTINUITIES

Technology can be defined as those tools, devices, and knowledge that mediate between inputs and outputs (process technology) and/or that create new products or services (product
technology) (Rosenberg, 1972). Technological change has an
unequivocal impact on economic growth (Solow, 1957; Klein,
1984) and on the development of industries (Lawrence and
Dyer, 1983). The impact of technology and technological
change on environmental conditions is, however, less clear.

For over thirty years, technology and workflows have been central topics in organizational theory (e.g., Gerwin, 1981). Most
studies of technology in organizational theory, however, have
been either cross sectional in design (e.g., Woodward, 1965),
have taken place in technologically stable settings (e.g., public
and not-for-profit settings), or simply have treated technology
as a constant (Astley, 1985). Since technology has been taken
as a given, there has been a conspicuous lack of clarity concerning how and why technologies change and how technological change affects environmental and/or organizational
evolution. An exception is the work of Brittain and Freeman
(1980).

There is a substantial literature on technological evolution and
change (e.g., Mensch, 1979; Sahal, 1981; Dutton and Thomas,
1985). Some suggest that technological change is inherently a
chance or spontaneous event driven by technological genius,
as did Taton (1958) in his discussion of penicillin and radioac-
tivity, and Schumpeter (1961). Others, like Gilfillan (1935), who
described the multiple independent discoveries of sail for
ships, suggest that technological change is a function of historical necessity; still others view technological progress as a
function of economic demand and growth (Schmookler, 1966;
Merton, 1968). An analysis of many different technologies over
years of evolution strongly indicates that none of these perspectives alone captures the complexity of technological
change. Technology seems to evolve in response to the interplay of history, individuals, and market demand. Technological
change is a function of both variety and chance as well as structure and patterns (Morison, 1966; Sahal, 1981).

Case studies across a range of industries indicate that technological progress constitutes an evolutionary system punctuated by discontinuous change. Major product breakthroughs
(e.g., jets or xerography) or process technological breakthroughs (e.g., float glass) are relatively rare and tend to be
driven by individual genius (e.g., C. Carlson and xerography; A.
Pilkington and float glass). These relatively rare discontinuities
trigger a period of technological ferment. As a new product
class opens (or following substitution of one product or process
for a previous one), the rate of product variation is substantial
as alternative product forms compete for dominance. An exam-

ple is the competition between electric, wood, and internal combustion engines in automobiles or the competition between incompatible videocassette or microcomputer technologies. This technological experimentation and competition persists within a product class until a dominant design emerges as a synthesis of a number of proven concepts (Utterback and Abernathy, 1975; Abernathy, 1978).

A dominant design reflects the emergence of product-class standards and ends the period of technological ferment. Alternative designs are largely crowded out of the product class, and technological development focuses on elaborating a widely accepted product or process; the dominant design becomes a guidepost for further product or process change (Sahal, 1981; Abernathy and Clark, 1985). Dominant designs and associated shifts in product or process change have been found across industries. The Model T, the DC-3, the Fordson tractor, the Smith Model 5 typewriter and the PDP-11 minicomputer were dominant designs that dramatically shaped the evolution of their respective product classes.

Once a dominant design emerges, technological progress is driven by numerous incremental, improvement innovations (Myers and Marquis, 1969; Dutton and Thomas, 1985). For example, while the basic technology underlying xerography has not changed since Carlson's Model 914, the cumulative effect of numerous incremental changes on this dominant design has dramatically improved the speed, quality, and cost per unit of reprographic products (Dessauer, 1975). A similar effect was documented by Yin and Dutton (1986), who described the enormous performance benefits of incremental process improvement in oil refining.

Incremental technological progress, unlike the initial breakthrough, occurs through the interaction of many organizations stimulated by the prospect of economic returns. This is evident in Hollander's (1965) discussion of rayon, Tilton's (1971) study of semiconductors, and Rosenbloom and Abernathy's (1982) study of VCR technology. These incremental technological improvements enhance and extend the underlying technology and thus reinforce an established technical order.

Technological change is a bit-by-bit, cumulative process until it is punctuated by a major advance. Such discontinuities offer sharp price-performance improvements over existing technologies. Major technological innovations represent technical advance so significant that no increase in scale, efficiency, or design can make older technologies competitive with the new technology (Mensch, 1979; Sahal, 1981). Product discontinuities are reflected in the emergence of new product classes (e.g., airlines, automobiles, plain-paper copiers), in product substitution (e.g., transistors vs. vacuum tubes; diesel vs. steam locomotives), or in fundamental product improvements (e.g., jets vs. turbojets; LSI vs. VSLI semiconductor technology). Process discontinuities are reflected either in process substitution (e.g., mechanical ice making vs. natural ice harvesting; thermal vs. catalytic cracking in crude oil refining; artificial vs. natural gems) or in process innovations that result in radical improvements in industry-specific dimensions of merit (e.g., Dundee kiln in cement; Lubbers machinery in glass).

Technological Discontinuities

These major technological shifts can be classified as *competence-destroying* or *competence-enhancing* (see also Abernathy and Clark, 1985), because they either destroy or enhance the competence of existing firms in an industry. The former require new skills, abilities, and knowledge in both the development and production of the product. The hallmark of competence-destroying discontinuities is that mastery of the new technology fundamentally alters the set of relevant competences within a product class. For example, the knowledge and skills required to make glass using the float-glass method are quite different from those required to master other glass-making technologies. Diesel locomotives required new skills and knowledge that steam-engine manufacturers did not typically possess. Similarly, automatically controlled machine tools required wholesale changes in engineering, mechanical, and data-processing skills. These new technical and engineering requirements were well beyond and qualitatively different from those skills necessary to manufacture conventional paper-punched machine tools (Noble, 1984).

A competence-destroying product discontinuity either creates a new product class (e.g., xerography or automobiles) or substitutes for an existing product (e.g., diesel vs. steam locomotive; transistors vs. vacuum tubes). Competence-destroying process discontinuities represent a new way of making a given product. For example, the float-glass process in glass manufacture substituted for continuous grinding and polishing; mechanical ice making substituted for natural ice harvesting; planar processes substituted for the single-wafer process in semiconductors. In each case, the product remained essentially unchanged while the process by which it was made was fundamentally altered. Competence-destroying process breakthroughs may involve combining previously discrete steps into a more continuous flow (e.g., float glass) or may involve a completely different process (e.g., man-made gems).

Competence-destroying discontinuities are so fundamentally different from previously dominant technologies that the skills and knowledge base required to operate the core technology shift. Such major changes in skills, distinctive competence, and production processes are associated with major changes in the distribution of power and control within firms and industries (Chandler, 1977; Barley, 1986). For example, the ascendance of automatically controlled machine tooling increased the power of industrial engineers within the machine-tool industry (Noble, 1984), while the diffusion of high-volume production processes led to the rise of professional managers within more formally structured organizations (Chandler, 1977).

Competence-enhancing discontinuities are order-of-magnitude improvements in price/performance that build on existing know-how within a product class. Such innovations substitute for older technologies, yet do not render obsolete skills required to master the old technologies. Competence-enhancing product discontinuities represent an order-of-magnitude improvement over prior products yet build on existing know-how. For example, IBM's 360 series was a major improvement in price, performance, and features over prior models yet was developed through the synthesis of familiar technologies (Pugh, 1984). Similarly, the introduction of fan jets or of the screw propeller dramatically improved the speed of jets and ocean-going steamships, and aircraft producers and boatyards were able to take advantage of existing knowledge and skills and rapidly absorb these complementary technologies (Davies, 1972; Headrick, 1981).

Competence-enhancing process discontinuities are process innovations that result in an order-of-magnitude increase in the efficiency of producing a given product. For example, the Edison kiln was a major process innovation in cement manufacture that permitted enormous increases in production capacity yet built on existing skills in the cement industry (Lesley, 1924). Similarly, major process advances in semiconductor integration, strip steel, and glass production eliminated barriers to future growth in their product classes. These advances built on existing knowledge and skills and provided the core for subsequent incremental improvements (Dutton and Thomas, 1985).

Table 1 gives a typology of technological changes with examples of competence-destroying and competence-enhancing product and process technologies.

Table 1

A Typology of Product and Process Technological Changes

	Technological Changes	
Competence-Destroying		Competence-Enhancing
Product		
New Product Class:		*Major Product Improvements:*
Airlines (1924)		Jet ⟶ turbofan
Cement (1872)		LSI ⟶ VSLI semiconductors
Plain-paper copying (1959)		Mechanical ⟶ electric typewriters
		Continuous aim cannons
		Nonreturnable ⟶ returnable bottles
		Thin-walled iron cylinder block engine
Product Substitution:		
Vacuum tubes ⟶ transistors		
Steam ⟶ diesel locomotives		*Incremental Product Changes*
Piston ⟶ jet engines		
Records ⟶ compact disks		*Dominant Designs:**
Punched paper ⟶ automatic control machine tooling		PDP-11, VHS technology
Discrete ⟶ integrated circuits		IBM 360, DC-3
Open ⟶ closed steel auto bodies		Numerical control machine tools
Process		
Process Substitution:		*Major Process Improvements:*
Natural ⟶ mechanical ice		Edison kiln
Natural ⟶ industrial gems		Resistive metal deposition (semiconductors)
Open hearth ⟶ basic oxygen furnace		Gob feeder (glass containers)
Individual wafer ⟶ planar process		Catalytic cracking ⟶ catalytic reforming
Continuous grinding ⟶ float glass		
Thermal cracking ⟶ catalytic cracking		*Incremental Process Improvements:*
Vertical ⟶ rotary kiln		Learning by doing; numerous process improvements
Blown ⟶ drawn window glass		

*Some dominant designs are incremental improvements (e.g., PDP-11), while others are major improvements (e.g., DC-3, IBM 360).

Both technological discontinuities and dominant designs are only known in retrospect — technological superiority is no guarantee of success. The dominance of a substitute product (e.g., Wankel engines, supersonic jets, or bubble memory), sub-

Technological Discontinuities

stitute process (e.g., continuous casting), or a dominant design (e.g., VHS vs. beta videocasette systems) is a function of technological, market, legal, and social factors that cannot be fully known in advance. For example, the choice by vacuum tube makers such as RCA, GE, and Philco to concentrate on a dominant design for electron tubes in the early transistor days turned out, in retrospect, to have been an error (Tilton, 1971). Similarly, choices of standard record speeds, widths of railroad track, automatically controlled machine tool technologies or automated office equipment standards are often less a function of technical merit than of market or political power (Noble, 1984).

A number of product-class case studies indicate that technology progresses in stages through relatively long periods of incremental, competence-enhancing change elaborating a particular dominant design. These periods of increasing consolidation and learning-by-doing may be punctuated by competence-destroying technological discontinuities (i.e., product or process substitution) or by further competence-enhancing technological advance (e.g., revitalizing a given product or process with complementary technologies). Technological discontinuities trigger a period of technological ferment culminating in a dominant design and, in turn, leading to the next period of incremental, competence-enhancing, technological change. Thus, we hypothesize:

Hypothesis 1: Technological change within a product class will be characterized by long periods of incremental change punctuated by discontinuities.

Hypothesis 1a: Technological discontinuities are either competence enhancing (build on existing skills and know-how) or competence destroying (require fundamentally new skills and competences).

Competence-destroying and competence-enhancing discontinuities dramatically alter previously attainable price/performance relationships within a product class. Both create technological uncertainty as firms struggle to master an untested and incompletely understood product or process. Existing firms within an industry are in the best position to initiate and exploit new possibilities opened up by a discontinuity if it builds on competence they already possess. Competence-enhancing discontinuities tend to consolidate industry leadership; the rich are likely to get richer.

Competence-destroying discontinuities, in contrast, disrupt industry structure (Mensch, 1979). Skills that brought product-class leaders to preeminence are rendered largely obsolete; new firms founded to exploit the new technology will gain market share at the expense of organizations that, bound by traditions, sunk costs, and internal political constraints, remain committed to outmoded technology (Tilton, 1971; Hannan and Freeman, 1977). We thus hypothesize:

Hypothesis 2: The locus of innovation will differ for competence-destroying and competence-enhancing technological changes. Competence-destroying discontinuities will be initiated by new entrants, while competence-enhancing discontinuities will be initiated by existing firms.

TECHNOLOGICAL DISCONTINUITIES AND ORGANIZATIONAL ENVIRONMENTS

To determine the extent to which technological discontinuities affect environmental conditions, we build on Dess and Beard's (1984) review of environmental dimensions and examine two critical characteristics of organizational environments: uncertainty and munificence. Uncertainty refers to the extent to which future states of the environment can be anticipated or accurately predicted (Pfeffer and Salancik, 1978). Munificence refers to the extent to which an environment can support growth. Environments with greater munificence impose fewer constraints on organizations than those environments with resource constraints.

Both competence-enhancing and competence-destroying technological discontinuities generate uncertainty as firms struggle to master an incompletely understood product or process. Technological breakthroughs trigger a period of technological ferment as new technologies are tried, established price-performance ratios are upset, and new markets open. During these periods of technological upheaval, it becomes substantially more difficult to forecast demand and prices. Technological discontinuities, then, will be associated with increases in environmental uncertainty:

Hypothesis 3: Competitive uncertainty will be higher after a technological discontinuity than before the discontinuity.

Technological discontinuities drive sharp decreases in price-performance or input-output ratios. These factors, in turn, fuel demand in a product class. The role of technological progress in stimulating demand is well documented (e.g., Solow, 1957; Mensch, 1979). As both competence-enhancing and competence-destroying discontinuities reflect major price-performance improvements, both will be associated with increased demand and environmental munificence:

Hypothesis 4: Environmental munificence will be higher after a technological discontinuity than before the discontinuity.

Environments can also be described in terms of different competitive conditions (Scherer, 1980). Important dimensions of competitive conditions include entry-exit patterns and degree of order within a product class. Orderliness within a product class can be assessed by interfirm sales variability. Those environments with substantial net entry and substantial interfirm sales variability will be very different competitive arenas than those environments in which exits dominate and there is minimal interfirm sales variability.

Competence-destroying technological discontinuities have quite different effects on competitive conditions than competence-enhancing discontinuities. Competence-enhancing advances permit existing firms to exploit their competence and expertise and thereby gain competitive advantage over smaller or newer firms. Competence-enhancing discontinuities consolidate leadership in a product class; the rich get richer as liabilities of newness plague new entrants. These order-creating breakthroughs increase barriers to entry and minimum scale requirements. These processes will be reflected in relatively fewer entries relative to exits and a decrease in interfirm sales variability — those remaining firms will

Technological Discontinuities

share more equally in product-class sales growth.

Competence-destroying discontinuities break the existing order. Barriers to entry are lowered; new firms enter previously impenetrable markets by exploiting the new technology (Astley, 1985; Abernathy and Clark, 1985). These discontinuities favor new entrants at the expense of entrenched defenders. New entrants take advantage of fundamentally different skills and expertise and gain sales at the expense of formerly dominant firms burdened with the legacy (i.e., skills, abilities, and expertise) of prior technologies and ways of operating (Astley, 1985; Tushman and Romanelli, 1985). Competence-destroying discontinuities will be associated with increased entry-to-exit ratios and an increase in interfirm sales variability:

Hypothesis 5: Competence-enhancing discontinuities will be associated with decreased entry-to-exit ratios and decreased interfirm sales variability. These patterns will be reversed for competence-destroying discontinuities.

If competence-destroying discontinuities do not emerge to alter a product class, successive competence-enhancing discontinuities will result in increased environmental orderliness and consolidation. Each competence-enhancing breakthrough builds on prior advances and further raises barriers to entry and minimum scale requirements. As product classes mature, the underlying resource base becomes ever more limited by physical and resource constraints. Successive competence-enhancing discontinuities will have smaller impacts on uncertainty and munificence as successive advances further exploit a limited technology and market-resource base:

Hypothesis 6: Successive competence-enhancing discontinuities will be associated with smaller increases in uncertainty and munificence.

Environmental changes induced by a technological discontinuity present a unique opportunity or threat for individual organizations (Tushman and Romanelli, 1985). Technological discontinuities alter the competitive environment and reward those innovative firms that are first to recognize and exploit technological opportunities. The superiority of a new technology presents organizations with a stark choice: adapt or face decline. Those firms that are among the first to adopt the new product or process proceed down the learning curve ahead of those that follow. The benefits of volume and experience provide early movers with a competitive edge not easily erased (Porter, 1985; MacMillan and McCaffrey, 1984). Therefore, we hypothesize:

Hypothesis 7: Those organizations that initiate major technological innovations will have higher growth rates than other firms in the product class.

RESEARCH DESIGN AND MEASURES

Three product classes were selected for study: domestic scheduled passenger airline transport, Portland cement manufacture, and minicomputer manufacture (excluding firms that merely add peripherals and/or software to another firm's minicomputer and resell the system). These three product classes represent assembled products, nonassembled products, and services; this product-class diversity increases the generalizability of our results. These industries were also selected because most participants historically had been undiversified, so environmental conditions outside the industry had little effect on these firms. Data on each product class was gathered from the year of the niche's inception (1872 for cement, 1924 for airlines, and 1956 for minicomputers) through 1980.

The three populations studied included all U.S. firms that produced cement, flew airplane passengers, or produced minicomputers. These industries were chosen partly because archival sources exist permitting a complete census of population members over time. Two outstanding books (Lesley, 1924; Davies, 1972) chronicle the history of the cement and airline industries and include meticulously researched profiles of early entrants into those product classes. In the airline industry, the Civil Aeronautics Board (CAB) lists of entries and exits after 1938 are definitive, due to licensing requirements. In cement, the very high degree of agreement among two trade journals and two industry directories from 1900 on suggests substantially all firms that ever produced cement are included. Similarly, in minicomputers, the very high degree of agreement among trade journals, an exhaustive annual industry directory in *Computers and Automation*, and International Data Corporation (IDC) product listings indicates that virtually all firms that ever produced a minicomputer are included. All sources included very small firms that survived only briefly; any firms that might have been overlooked in this study have never received published mention in three industries thoroughly covered by numerous archival sources.

Technological change. A thorough review of books and trade publications permitted the identification of price-performance changes and key technological events within the three product classes. Technological change was measured by examining key performance parameters for all new kilns, airplanes, or minicomputers introduced in each year of the industry's existence. For cement and airlines, percentage improvement in the state of the art was calculated by dividing the seat-mile-per-year or barrel-per-day capacity of the most capable plane or largest kiln in existence in a given year by the same capacity figure for the most capable plane or largest kiln in existence the previous year. This review of new equipment also permitted the identification of initiators and early adopters of significant innovations. Technological discontinuities were relatively easy to identify because a few innovations so markedly advanced the state of the art that they clearly stand out from less dramatic improvements.

The key performance parameter in cement production is kiln capacity in barrels of cement per day. For every new kiln, this capacity is reported by the manufacturer and is widely published in trade journals and industry directories. For airlines, the key economic factor is the number of passenger-seat-miles per year a plane can fly, calculated by multiplying the number of seats normally in an aircraft model by the number of miles per year it can fly at normal operating speeds for the average number of flight hours per year it proved able to log. These figures are reported in Davies (1972) for all aircraft models flown by U.S. airliners. In minicomputers, a key performance parameter is the amount of time required for the central processing unit to complete one cycle; this is the primary determinant of computer speed and throughput capability. Both *Computers and Automation*, a leading trade journal and industry directory, and

Technological Discontinuities

the International Data Corporation (IDC), a leading computer-industry research firm, report cycle time for all minicomputers.

Uncertainty. Uncertainty is typically measured as a function of variance measures (Dess and Beard, 1984). Because environmental uncertainty refers to the extent to which future states of the environment cannot be predicted accurately, we measured uncertainty in terms of forecasting error — the ability of industry analysts to predict industry outcomes. Published forecasts for every SIC code are collected and indexed in *Predicasts Forecasts*. For each of the three niches, published one-year demand growth forecasts were collected and compared to actual historical results. Forecast error is defined as

$$\frac{(\mid \text{Forecast demand growth} - \text{Actual demand growth} \mid \times 100)}{(\text{Actual demand growth})}$$

To measure environmental uncertainty, the mean forecast error for the five-year period before each technological discontinuity was compared to the mean forecast error for the five-year period following the discontinuity. The choice of five-year periods is arbitrary. Major technological changes do not have an overnight impact; it takes several years for their effect on uncertainty and munificence to appear. Yet in the longer run, extraneous events create demand fluctuations whose noise can drown out the patterns generated by major technological advances. Since the industries selected included discontinuities seven and ten years apart, five years was selected as the maximum practicable period of observation that would not create serious overlap problems between the era following one discontinuity and the era preceding another.

Munificence. Munificence was measured in terms of demand, the basic resource available to niche participants. Annual sales growth in units was obtained from the CAB and Bureau of Mines for the airline and cement niches, respectively. Minicomputer sales data were obtained from the International Data Corporation and from *Computers and Automation*. Since sales figures grow as a result of both inflation and growth in the economy as a whole, these factors were eliminated by dividing demand figures by an index of real GNP growth. Mean demand growth was calculated for five-year periods before and after each technological discontinuity.

Two possible objections may be raised to comparing the means of five-year periods preceding and following a discontinuity. First, if there is a strong upward trend in the time series, then for practically any year chosen, demand in the five succeeding years will be significantly higher than demand in the five preceding years. If this is so, there is nothing special about the eras surrounding a technological discontinuity. On the other hand, it may be that the findings are very sensitive to the exact year chosen to mark the discontinuity. If results are significant comparing, for example, 1960–1964 with 1965–1969, but not significant if the comparison is between 1959–1963 and 1964–1968, or between 1961–1965 and 1966–1970, then the finding is not robust.

Accordingly, the difference-of-means test was performed for every possible combination of two adjacent five-year periods for each industry. In each industry, it was found that eras of significant before and after demand shift are rare. Sixteen of 96 possible comparisons were significant at the .05 level in the cement industry (17 percent), 17 of 45 possible comparisons of airline demand (38 percent), and 2 of 7 possible comparisons of minicomputer demand (28 percent). This suggests that technological discontinuities are not the only events that seem to be associated with sharp increases in demand. However, neither do such shifts occur frequently or at random. In each case, a difference of one year either way in identifying the discontinuity would have made no difference; the demand shift is not particularly sensitive to the specific year chosen as the discontinuity.

Table 2

Summary of Variables, Measures, and Data Sources

Variable	Industry	Measure	Data Source	N	Range	Mean	SD
Technological change	Cement	% improvement in barrel/ day production capacity of largest kiln.	Published specifications of new kilns in *Rock Products.*	90	0–320%		
	Airlines	% improvement in seat-miles per year capacity of most capable plane flown.	Davies (1972).	54	0–248%		
	Minicomputers	Central processor unit speed.	Published specifications in *Computers and Automation.*	24	.2–9000		
Locus of innovation	Cement	Proportion of new firms among earliest to adopt an innovation.	Reports on new kilns in *Rock Products* and trade directories.	4	.1–1.0		
	Airlines		Davies (1972), CAB annual studies of airplane purchases.	4	0–.9		
	Minicomputers		Published specifications in *Computers and Automation.*	3	0–.5		
Uncertainty	Cement	Mean percentage error of one-year demand growth forecasts	*Predicasts Forecasts.*	28	5.2–266.9	52.0	61.6
	Airlines			88	.1–381.4	59.2	58.4
	Minicomputers			36	3.5–811	138.1	167.1
Munificence	Cement	Annual cement consumption (tons).	U.S. Bureau of Mines.	101	8–85513	30296	27103
	Airlines	Annual passenger-seat-miles (mil.).	Civil Aeronautics Board.	52	1–156.6	34.6	46.1
	Minicomputers	Annual minicomputer sales (000 units)	International Data Corporation.	16	1–168	47.3	49.6
Entries	Cement	Number of firms producing for first time (mean, range and SD are entries per year, N is number of entries).	*Cement Industry Trade Directory; Rock Products.*	281	0–24	2.8	4.2
	Airlines		Davies (1972); CAB annual reports.	147	1–33	11.3	9.8
	Minicomputers		*Computers and Automation;* International Data Corporation.	173	3–30	10.8	7.3
Exits	Cement	Number of firms acquired or no longer producing (mean, SD and range are exits per year, N is number of exits).	*Cement Industry Trade Directory; Rock Products.*	218	0–23	2.2	3.9
	Airlines		Davies (1972); CAB annual reports.	126	1–28	9.7	8.2
	Minicomputers		*Computers and Automation;* International Data Corporation.	82	0–14	5.1	4.2
Interfirm sales variance	Airlines	Unweighted variance in five-year sales growth percentage among all firms in the industry.	Same as munificence measure.	4	2.0–13.4	5.5	4.6
	Minicomputers		Same as munificence measure.	4	2.6–21.3	11.2	8.6
Firm growth rate	Airlines	Firm sales at end of five-year era divided by sales at beginning of five-year era.	CAB annual reports.	46	−269–346	61.4	79.9
	Minicomputers		International Data Corporation.	67	−96–11900	635.6	1561.6

Technological Discontinuities

At a few comparatively rare periods in the history of an industry, then, one can locate a demand breakpoint, an era of two or three years during which average demand for the five years following any of these critical years significantly exceeds the average demand in the five years preceding the chosen year. Some of these critical eras are not associated with technological discontinuities. Without exception, every technological discontinuity is associated with such a demand shift.

Entry and exit. Entry and exit data were gathered from industry directories and books chronicling the histories of each product class. An entry was recorded in the year when a firm first began cement production, an airline flew its first passenger-mile, or a firm produced its first minicomputer. An exit was recorded when a firm ceased producing cement, flying passengers, or producing at least one minicomputer. Bankruptcy was recorded as an exit only if production ceased. An exit was recorded whenever a firm was acquired; an entry was recorded only if the acquiring firm did not already produce cement, fly passengers, or produce minicomputers. An entrant was classified as new if the company sold no products prior to its entry into the industry or as an existing firm if it sold at least one product before entering the industry. Entry and exit statistics are not calculated for the airline industry from 1938 through 1979, because entries were forbidden by the CAB, and exits depended more on regulatory action than on market forces. Table 2 provides measures, data sources, and summary data for each variable.

Early adopters. To test hypothesis 7, that those firms initiating technological discontinuities would have higher growth rates than other firms in the product class, we examined the growth rates of the first four adopters. Data were available for airlines after 1955 and for minicomputers. The number of early adopters chosen was arbitrary. Four were selected to provide a group large enough for a mean to be meaningful, yet small enough to argue reasonably that the firms considered were quicker to adopt the innovation than the rest of the industry.

RESULTS

Hypothesis 1 suggested that technological evolution would be characterized by periods of incremental change punctuated by either competence-destroying or competence-enhancing discontinuities. Hypothesis 2 argued that competence-destroying advances would be initiated by new entrants, while competence-enhancing advances would be initiated by existing firms. Table 3 summarizes the key technological discontinuities for each niche, while Figures 1a–1c provide more detailed data on key performance dimensions over time.

The cement, airline, and minicomputer niches opened in 1872, 1924, and 1956, respectively. After the three niche openings, there were six competence-enhancing technological discontinuities and two competence-destroying discontinuities (see Table 3). Each discontinuity had a marked effect on a key measure of cost or performance, far greater than the impact of other, more incremental technological events.[1]

Figure 1a documents the three significant technological changes that have punctuated the history of the Portland cement industry. Portland cement, invented in Europe, was first

1
Other industries may not exhibit such marked differences and eventually a coefficient of technological progress could be developed to help distinguish incremental from discontinuous change; one approach might be to pool annual percentage improvements and select those more than two standard deviations above the mean.

Table 3

Significant Technological Discontinuities

Industry	Year	Event	Importance	Type of discontinuity	Locus of Innovation New firms	Locus of Innovation Existing firms	Probability
Cement	1872	First production of Portland cement in the United States.	Discovery of proper raw materials and importation of knowledge opens new industry.	Niche opening	10 of 10	1 of 10	
	1896	Patent for process burning powdered coal as fuel.	Permits economical use of efficient rotary kilns.	Competence-destroying	4 of 5	1 of 5	.333
	1909	Edison patents long kiln (150 ft.).	Higher output with less cost.	Competence-enhancing	1 of 6	5 of 6	.001*
	1966	Dundee Cement installs huge kiln, far larger than any previous.	Use of process control permits operation of very efficient kilns.	Competence-enhancing	1 of 8	7 of 8	.000*
Airlines	1924	First airline.	Mail contracts make transport feasible.	Niche opening	9 of 10	1 of 10	
	1936	DC3 airplane.	First large and fast enough to carry passengers economically.	Competence-enhancing	0 of 4	4 of 4	.005*
	1959	First jet airplane in commercial use.	Speed changes economics of flying.	Competence-enhancing	0 of 4	4 of 4	.005*
	1969	Widebody jets debut.	Much greater capacity and efficiency.	Competence-enhancing	0 of 4	4 of 4	.005*
Minicomputer manufacture	1956	Burroughs E-101.	First computer under $50,000.	Niche opening	1 of 8	7 of 8	
	1965	Digital Equipment Corp. PDP-8.	First integrated-circuit minicomputer.	Competence-destroying	3 of 6	3 of 6	.019*
	1971	Data General Supernova SC.	Semiconductor memory much faster than core.	Competence-enhancing	0 of 7	7 of 7	.533

*$p < .01$.
Note: Fisher's exact test compares the pool of firms that are among the first to enter the niche with the pool of firms that introduce or are among the first to adopt a major technological innovation. The null hypothesis is that the proportion of new firms is the same in each sample; probability is the probability of obtaining the observed proportions if the null hypothesis is correct.

made in this country about 1872, but early attempts to compete with established European brands were largely failures. Two events effectively established the domestic industry. The development of the rotary kiln made the manufacture of large volumes of cement with little labor practicable, and the invention in 1896 of a method for creating a continuous flame fed by powdered coal meant that a high-quality, uniform cement could be made without expensive hand-stoking.

During the following decade, rotary kilns 60 feet in length were standard. In 1909, Thomas Edison patented a technique for making kilns over 150 feet in length, enormously increasing the production capacity of a kiln, and the industry rapidly adopted the new "long kiln." Subsequent progress, though, was gradual; kiln capacity increased greatly over a period of decades, but in a series of incremental advances. In 1960, the industry began experimenting with computerized control of kilns. The introduction of computers permitted the construction of huge kilns, much larger than any that had preceded them. The experimental models of the early 1960s culminated in the enormous Dundee kiln in 1967; previously kilns of such capacity could not have been used because their huge size and weight made them impossible to regulate.

Technological Discontinuities

The revolution that brought powdered coal and rotary kilns to
the industry was competence-destroying, rendering almost
completely obsolete the know-how required to operate wood-
fired vertical kilns. A totally new set of competences was required to make cement, and most vertical kiln operators went
out of business. The Edison and Dundee kilns were
competence-enhancing innovations; each markedly extended
the capability of coal-fired rotary kiln technology. A large investment in new kilns and process-control equipment was required, but existing cement-making techniques were not made
obsolete, and the leading firms in the industry proved most able
to make the necessary capital expenditures.

Figure 1a. Barrels-per-day production capacity of the largest U.S. cement kiln, 1890–1980.

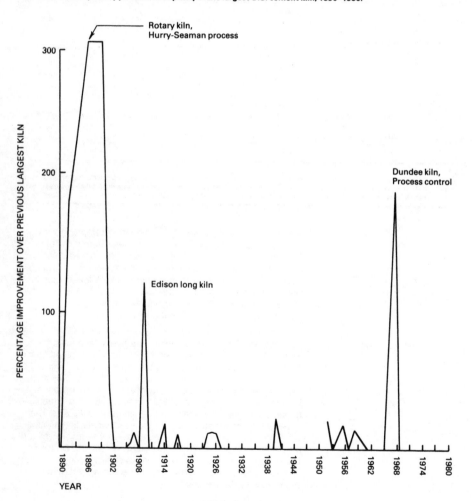

New developments in aircraft construction have been the major technological breakthroughs that have affected the economics of the airline industry, as illustrated in Figure 1b. Numerous flimsy, slow aircraft were flown until the early 1930s, when a flurry of development produced the Boeing 247, Douglas DC-2, and Douglas DC-3 in a span of three years, each a significant improvement on its immediate predecessor. The DC-3, which incorporated some 25 major improvements in aircraft design (Davies, 1972), superseded all other models to become so dominant that by the outbreak of World War II, 80 percent of U.S. airliners in service were DC-3s. Further aircraft improvements were incremental until 1959, when the debut of jet aircraft, with their considerably greater speed and size, again changed the economics of the airline industry. The final breakthrough event was the introduction in 1969 of the Boeing 747, beginning an era dominated by widebody jets.

All three of these major advances were competence enhancing from the perspective of the air carriers (though not from the perspective of aircraft manufacturers). Each advance generated significant economies of scale; airlines could carry many more passengers with each plane than was possible before. Though new skills were required to fly and maintain the new machines, airlines were able to build on their existing competences and take advantage of increased scale economies permitted with new aircraft.

In contrast to cement and airlines, in the minicomputer industry established firms built the first inexpensive computers (usually as an extension of their accounting machine lines). These early minicomputers were based on vacuum tubes and/or transistor technology. The first transistor minicomputer was far faster than its vacuum-tube predecessors, but transistor architecture was replaced by integrated circuitry within two years and thus never diffused widely. Sales were meager until integrated-

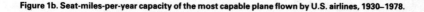

Figure 1b. Seat-miles-per-year capacity of the most capable plane flown by U.S. airlines, 1930–1978.

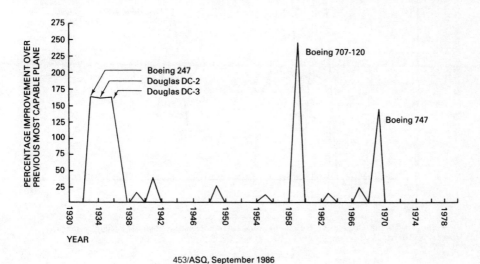

Technological Discontinuities

circuit minicomputers were introduced by a combination of new and older firms. Figure 1c depicts the enormous impact of transistors, immediately followed by integrated circuitry, on computer performance. Integrated circuitry increased minicomputer speed more than 100 times between 1963 and 1965, while size and assembly complexity also decreased substantially. Integrated circuits permitted the construction of compact machines at a greatly reduced cost by eliminating most of the wiring associated with transistors. Integrated-circuit technology was competence-destroying, since expertise in designing, programming, and assembling transistor-based computers was not especially transferable to the design and manufacture of integrated-circuit machines (Fishman, 1981).

The introduction of semiconductor memory in 1971 caused another abrupt performance improvement (see Figure 1c) but did not challenge the fundamental competence of existing minicomputer firms; most companies were able to offer customers versions of their existing models equipped with either magnetic core or semiconductor memory. The effect of semiconductor memory was to increase order in the product class as existing firms were able easily to incorporate this innovation into their existing expertise. For memory manufacturers, however, semiconductor memory was a competence-destroying discontinuity.

Figure 1c. Central-processor-unit cycle time of the fastest minicomputer in production, 1956–1980.

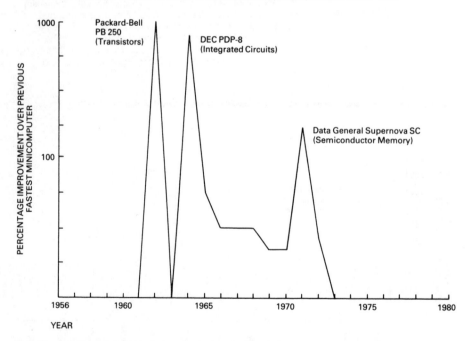

Note: The vertical scale is logarithmic, because the impact of transistors and integrated circuitry on processor speed was so great.

These patterns of incremental technological progress punctuated by discontinuities strongly support hypothesis 1. As suggested in hypothesis 2, the locus of technological innovation for competence-enhancing breakthroughs significantly differs from that of competence-destroying discontinuities. The first cement and airline firms were overwhelmingly new start-ups, not existing companies entering a new industry (Table 3). No product classes existed in 1872 or 1924 whose competences were transferable to cement manufacture or flying airplanes. In contrast, early minicomputers were made by existing accounting machine and electronics manufacturers, who found their existing know-how was readily transferable to the first small, crude computers. New industries can be started either by new organizations or by established ones from other industries; a key variable seems to be whether analogous product classes with transferable competences exist when a new product class emerges.

Patterns in the locus of innovation for discontinuities subsequent to product-class openings are remarkably consistent. The two competence-destroying discontinuities were largely pioneered by new firms (i.e., 7 of 11), while the six competence-enhancing discontinuities were almost exclusively introduced by established industry members (i.e., 35 of 37 firms were existing firms; Fisher's exact test; $p = .0002$). Across these three industries, competence-destroying breakthroughs are significantly more likely to be initiated by new firms, while competence-enhancing breakthroughs are significantly more likely to be initiated by existing firms. Similarly, within each industry, Fisher's exact tests indicate that the proportion of new firms that initiate competence-destroying discontinuities is significantly greater than the proportion of new firms initiating competence-enhancing discontinuities (see last column in Table 3).

Hypothesis 3 suggested that environmental uncertainty would be significantly higher after a technological discontinuity than before it. Since the forecasts we used to test this hypothesis are not available before 1950, only four of the eight technological discontinuities could be tested. In three of the four cases examined, mean forecast error after the discontinuity was significantly higher ($p < .05$) than before the discontinuity (see

Table 4

Forecast Error over Time*

Industry	Era	Mean forecast error	$t(1)$	D.f.	$t(2)$	D.f.
Airlines	1955–1959	16.15%	1.78•	18		
	1960–1964	77.81%				
Airlines	1965–1969	18.52%	4.35••	66	1.91•	54
	1970–1974	49.13%				
Cement	1963–1967	38.31%	1.85•	26		
	1968–1972	80.26%				
Minicomputers	1967–1971	146.31%	−.14	34		
	1972–1976	136.12%				

•$p < .05$; ••$p < .01$.
*$t(1)$ compares mean forecast error of the first period to the mean forecast error of the second period; $t(2)$ compares 1960–1964 with 1970–1974.

Technological Discontinuities

Table 4). Except for the period following the introduction of semiconductor memory in minicomputers, the ability of experienced industry observers to predict demand one year in advance was significantly poorer following technological disruption than before.[2] In the semiconductor case, forecast errors were very high both before and after the discontinuity.

Hypothesis 4 suggested that environmental munificence would be higher after a technological discontinuity than before it. The results in Table 5 strongly support the hypothesis. In every case, demand growth following the discontinuity was significantly higher than it was immediately prior to the discontinuity. Further, these demand data indicate the enormous impact of initial discontinuities on product-class demand. Initial discontinuities were associated with, on average, a 529-percent increase in product-class demand. Subsequent discontinuities spark smaller (though still relatively large) increases in demand (226 percent, on average). Technological discontinuities were, then, associated with significantly higher demand after each discontinuity; this effect, though significant in each case, was smaller over successive discontinuities (except for minicomputers, where demand increased substantially after both technological discontinuities).

Table 5

Demand before and after Technological Discontinuity

Industry	Era	Mean annual demand	t^*
Cement	1892–1896	168	–3.16**
	1897–1901	1249	
	1905–1909	9271	–6.35**
	1910–1914	15612	
	1963–1967	63348	–2.16*
	1968–1972	77122	
Airlines	1932–1936	2326	–3.01**
	1937–1941	8019	
	1955–1959	244625	–3.68**
	1960–1964	355678	
	1965–1969	742838	–4.42**
	1970–1974	1165943	
Minicomputers	1960–1964	435	–1.96*
	1965–1969	2181	
	1967–1971	7274	–4.60*
	1972–1976	47149	

$*p < .05$; $**p < .01$.
$*$ t-statistic compares mean demand of first period with mean demand of second period. In each case, there are 8 degrees of freedom.

2
Since data on published forecasts, annual growth in demand, and entry and exit data are available for the three populations, sampling error is not an issue; one could simply report the differences between populations. However, the critical question here is whether consistent differences between pre- and post-discontinuity environments can be discerned. The significance tests show that the probability is small that chance processes could have produced the reported differences between pre- and post-discontinuity eras (Blalock, 1979: 241).

Hypothesis 5 argued that competence-enhancing discontinuities would be associated with decreased entry-to-exit ratios and decreased interfirm sales variability. Opposite effects were hypothesized for competence-destroying discontinuities. Entry-to-exit ratios were calculated for five years before and after each discontinuity (except for the 1938–1979 period in airlines). Results in Table 6 are partially supportive of hypothesis 5. The ratio of entries to exits was higher in each of the five years before a competence-enhancing discontinuity than during the five subsequent years. None of the differences is statistically significant, though pre-discontinuity entry-to-exit ratios range from 1.15 to over 7 times greater than post-discontinuity entry-to-exit ratios. Entry-to-exit ratios prevailing before a discontinuity are markedly shifted in favor of exits following competence-enhancing discontinuities.

It was expected that entry-to-exit ratios would rise following the two competence-destroying discontinuities; the opposite was observed. Entry-to-exit ratios were quite high following these competence-destroying innovations but were smaller than the extremely large entry-to-exit ratios prevailing just before the discontinuity. Many firms entered and few departed the cement and minicomputer niches in the 1892–1896 and 1960–1964 periods, respectively. Both of these eras were themselves periods of technological ferment in emerging product classes – rotary kilns began to replace vertical kilns in the early 1890s, and transistors began to replace vacuum tubes in the early 1960s. It may be that the rush of new firms to enter emerging product classes confounds the effects of competence-destroying discontinuities.

Table 6

Entry-to-Exit Ratio before and after Discontinuity

Industry	Era	Entry-to-exit ratio*	Discontinuity type
Cement	1872–1896	3.25	Niche opening
	1892–1896	46.00	Competence-destroying
	1897–1901	12.00	
	1905–1909	1.489	Competence-enhancing
	1910–1914	.814	
	1963–1967	1.250	Competence-enhancing
	1968–1972	.160	
Airlines	1913–1930	1.730	Niche opening
	1930–1934	.820	Competence-enhancing†
	1935–1939	.714	
Minicomputers	1956–1960	Not finite‡	Niche opening
	1960–1964	5.500	Competence-destroying
	1965–1969	2.917	
	1967–1971	4.933	Competence-enhancing
	1972–1976	2.708	

*The difference between the pre-discontinuity entry-to-exit ratios and the corresponding post-discontinuity entry-to-exit ratios, while consistent, do not reach statistical significance, due to the large variance between individual years.
†Airline data for subsequent periods were not reported, because entry and exit were regulated.
‡Six entries, no exits.

Entry-to-exit patterns are consistent across these three divergent industries. Entries dominate exits early on, reflecting the rush of new entrants. After competence-enhancing discontinuities in cement and airlines, exits dominate entries, reflecting industry consolidation. In minicomputers, while entry-to-exit ratios decrease over time, entries dominate exits throughout this 20-year period.

Hypothesis 5 also suggested that competence-enhancing discontinuities would decrease interfirm sales variability as those remaining firms adopt industry standards in both products and processes. Small firms drop out of the industry, entry barriers

Technological Discontinuities

are raised, and firms exploiting similar existing competences experience relatively similar outcomes. Following competence-destroying discontinuities, though, we expected marked variability in sales growth as firms compete with each other on fundamentally different bases; some firms' sales grow explosively while others experience dramatic sales decline.

The results in Table 7 for airlines and minicomputers support this prediction. In minicomputers, integrated circuits triggered explosive growth in the product class and increased interfirm sales variability. Following the other three competence-enhancing discontinuities, though, interfirm sales variability decreased significantly; niche occupants experienced similar results as they built on their existing competences to exploit demand growth.

Table 7

Interfirm Sales Variability before and after Discontinuity

Industry	Era	Discontinuity type	Interfirm variance	F^*	D.f.
Airlines	1955–1959	Competence-enhancing	79.24	2.726•	12,12
	1960–1964		29.07		
	1965–1969	Competence-enhancing	103.63	4.096••	11,11
	1970–1974		25.30		
Minicomputers	1960–1964	Competence-destroying	5599.32	−17.480••	8,11
	1965–1969		97873.25		
	1967–1971	Competence-enhancing	86.26	9.960••	9,35
	1972–1976		8.65		

•$p < .05$; ••$p < .01$.
*The F-statistic compares the ratio of interfirm sales variance before the discontinuity to interfirm sales variance after the discontinuity.

Hypothesis 6 suggested that successive competence-enhancing discontinuities would be associated with relatively smaller effects on uncertainty and munificence. Because forecast data are not available before 1950, this hypothesis could only be partially tested in the case of uncertainty. As predicted, the mean forecast error in airlines for the 1960–1964 period is higher than that for the 1970–1974 period ($t = 1.91$; $p < .05$; see Table 4). Hypothesis 6 receives stronger support with respect to munificence. In cement and airlines, mean growth rates in demand are smaller for each successive competence-enhancing discontinuity. These differences are significant for two of the three comparisons (see Table 8). These data suggest that as technology matures, successive competence-enhancing discontinuities increase both uncertainty and munificence, but not as much as those discontinuities that preceded them in establishing the product class. These data, as well as those entry-to-exit data in Table 6, suggest that successive competence-enhancing advances result in increased product-class maturity, reflected in decreased uncertainty, decreased demand growth-rates, and increased product-class consolidation.

Hypothesis 7 argued that those firms initiating technological discontinuities would have higher growth rates than other firms in the product class. Table 9 compares five-year growth rates for the four early adopters to all other firms before and after

Table 8

Demand Patterns Following Successive Competence-Enhancing Discontinuities

Industry	Era	Mean growth*	*t*(1)	D.f.
Cement	1910–1914	48.3%	12.03••	8
	1968–1972	8.4%		
Airlines	1937–1941	161.5%		
	1960–1964	33.4%	30.79••	8
	1970–1974	32.3%	.75	8

••*p* < .01.
*Mean growth is the average annual *percentage* gain in sales for the industry (in contrast to Table 5, which measures demand in units). The *t*-statistic compares consecutive post-discontinuity periods; e.g., a comparison of mean percentage growth for 1910–1914 with mean percentage growth for 1968–1972 yields a *t*-statistic of 12.03, failing to support the null hypothesis that there is no difference in percentage growth rates between successive post-discontinuity eras.

technological discontinuities. As hypothesized in each of the four comparisons, early adopters experienced more growth than other firms. Early adopters had significantly higher five-year growth rates than other firms in the airline industry. For jets, early adopters had growth rates similar to others before the discontinuity, while for widebody jets, the early adopters had higher sales growth before and after the discontinuity (see Table 9). In minicomputers, early adopters had annual percentage growth rates that were 105 percentage points higher, on average, than other firms. Technological discontinuities are, then, sources of opportunities (or threats) for firms. While dominant technologies cannot be known in advance, those firms that recognize and quickly adopt a technological breakthrough grow more rapidly than others.

Table 9

Relative Sales Growth of First Four Adopters of a Major Innovation

Industry	Innovation*	Era	Mean sales growth first 4 adopters	Growth all others	*t*†	D.f.
Airlines	Jet aircraft	1955–1959	38.1%	22.2%	1.268	10
		1960–1964	44.3%	12.3%	2.121••	10
	Widebody jets	1965–1969	101.1%	19.2%	2.487•	9
		1970–1974	16.1%	1.0%	2.642•	9
Minicomputer	Integrated circuits	1960–1964	Not available (new firms)			
		1965–1969	339.2%	179.6%	.44	10
	Semiconductor memory	1967–1971	Not available (new firms)			
		1972–1976	238.0%	188.4%	.14	34

•*p* < .05; ••*p* < .06.
*The first four adopters in each case are: *Jet aircraft:* American, TWA, United, Eastern; *Widebody jet:* American, TWA, Continental, United; *Integrated circuits:* Digital Equipment, Computer Control Co., Scientific Data Systems, Systems Engineering Laboratories; *Semiconductors:* Data General, Digital Computer Controls, Interdata, Microdata.
†The *t*-test compares the mean annual percentage growth rates of the four firms who first introduced or adopted each innovation with the mean annual percentage growth rates of all other firms in the industry. Two periods do not yield interpretable statistics because annual growth for new firms cannot be calculated when the base year contains zero sales.

DISCUSSION

The purpose of this paper has been to explore technological evolution and to investigate its impact on environmental conditions. A better understanding of technological evolution may in-

Technological Discontinuities

crease our understanding of a range of phenomena at the population (e.g., structural evolution, population dynamics, strategic groups) as well as the organizational levels of analysis (e.g., organizational adaptation, executive succession patterns, executive demographics, and political dynamics) (Astley, 1985; Tushman and Romanelli, 1985).

Longitudinal data across three diverse industries indicate that technology evolves through relatively long periods of incremental change punctuated by relatively rare innovations that radically improve the state of the art. Such discontinuities occurred only eight times in the 190 total years observed across three industries. Yet in each product class, these technological shifts stand out clearly and significantly altered competitive environments.

The effect of major technological change on the two fundamental dimensions of uncertainty and munificence is unambiguous. Environmental conditions following a discontinuity are sharply different from those that prevailed before the technical breakthrough: the advance makes available new resources to fuel growth within the niche and renders observers far less able to predict the extent of future resource availability. Major technical change opens new worlds for a product class but requires niche occupants to deal with a considerable amount of ambiguity and uncertainty as they struggle to comprehend and master both the new technology and the new competitive environment.

It is also clear that technological discontinuities are not all alike. Competence-enhancing discontinuities significantly advance the state of the art yet build on, or permit the transfer of, existing know-how and knowledge. Competence-destroying discontinuities, on the other hand, significantly advance the technological frontier, but with a knowledge, skill, and competence base that is inconsistent with prior know-how. While competence-enhancing discontinuities build on existing experience, competence-destroying discontinuities require fundamentally new skills and technological competence.

The locus of innovation and the environmental consequences of competence-destroying versus competence-enhancing discontinuities are quite different. Competence-enhancing breakthroughs are overwhelmingly initiated by existing, successful firms. Competence-enhancing discontinuities result in greater product-class consolidation, reflected in relatively smaller entry-to-exit ratios and decreased interfirm sales variability. As competence-enhancing discontinuities build on existing know-how, it appears that the rich get richer, while new firms face liabilities of newness (Stinchcombe, 1965). Product-class conditions become ever more consolidated over successive order-creating discontinuities.

Competence-destroying discontinuities are more rare than competence-enhancing technological advances. Competence-destroying breakthroughs are watershed events in the life of a product class; they open up new branches in the course of industrial evolution (Astley, 1985). These discontinuities are initiated by new firms and open up the product class to waves of new entrants unconstrained by prior technologies and organizational inertia. While liabilities of newness plague new firms confronting competence-enhancing breakthroughs, liabilities of age and tradition constrain existing, successful firms in the face of competence-destroying discontinuities. Although the data were limited, competence-destroying discontinuities seem to break the grip of established firms in a product class. Interfirm sales variability jumped after integrated circuits were introduced in minicomputers, as new firms and established firms pursued different strategies, with markedly different results. Similarly in cement, new firms initiated rotary kilns and went on to dominate the industry.

These patterns are seen most vividly in minicomputer manufacture. The first inexpensive computers were built by established office-equipment firms (e.g., Monroe), electronics firms (e.g., Packard-Bell), and computer firms (e.g., Burroughs). This new product class continued unchanged until the advent of integrated circuits. Without exception, established firms floundered in the face of a technology based on active components. Integrated circuits rendered obsolete much of the engineering knowledge embodied in the first minicomputers. Office-equipment and the existing computer firms were unable to produce a successful model embodying semiconductor technology. Only the few firms explicitly founded to make minicomputers (e.g., DEC) were able to make the transition. By 1965, almost every firm that produced early minicomputers had exited the product class.

Technological discontinuities, whether competence-destroying or competence-enhancing, appear to afford a rare opportunity for competitive advantage for firms willing to risk early adoption. In all four cases, early adopters of major innovations had greater five-year growth rates than the rest of the product class. While these data are not unequivocal, firms that recognize and seize opportunities presented by major advances gain first-mover advantages. Those firms that do not adopt the innovation early or, worse, increase investment in obsolete technology, risk failing, because product-class conditions change so dramatically after the discontinuity.

Technological advance seems to be an important determinant of market as well as intraorganizational power. Competence-enhancing discontinuities are order creating in that they build on existing product-class know-how. These breakthroughs increase the market power of existing firms as barriers to entry are raised and dependence on buyers and suppliers decreases in the face of larger and more dominant producers. Competence-destroying technological advances, on the other hand, destroy order in a product class. These discontinuities create fundamental technological uncertainty as incompatible technologies compete for dominance. New firms, unconstrained by prior competence and history, take advantage of technological opportunities and the lethargy of organizations burdened with the consequences of prior success. Given the enormous impact of technological advance on product-class order, future research could explore the politics of technological change as interest groups attempt to shape technological progress to suit their own competences (e.g., Noble, 1984).

Within the firm, technological discontinuities affect the distribution of power and, in turn, decision-making processes. Those who control technological advances (whether competence destroying or enhancing) will gain power at others' expense (e.g.,

Technological Discontinuities

Morison, 1966; Pettigrew, 1973). Because technological dominance is rarely known in advance, the control of technological
assumptions and the locus of technological decisions will be an
important arena for intraorganizational political processes.
Shaping technological advance may be a critical organizational
issue, since technology affects both intra- and interorganizational bases of power.

Because technology affects organizational adaptation, organizations may be able to use investment in R&D and technological innovation to shape environmental conditions in their favor.
While technological dominance cannot be predicted at the outset (e.g., Wankel engines, bubble memory), organizations that
create technological variation, or are able to adopt technological
change quickly, maximize their probability of being able to
move with a changing technological frontier. Organizations that
do not contribute to or keep up with multiple technological
bases may lose their ability to be aware of and deal with technological evolution (Dutton and Thomas, 1985).

The patterns of technological change are similar across these
three diverse industries. It appears that new product classes
are associated with a wave of new entrants, relatively few
exits, and substantial technological experimentation.
Competence-destroying discontinuities occurred early in both
cement and minicomputer manufacture. After competence-
destroying breakthroughs, successive competence-enhancing
discontinuities resulted in an ever more consolidated and mature product class. While we have no data, subsequent
competence-destroying discontinuities may, in turn, break up a
mature product class and restart the product class's evolutionary clock (e.g., microcomputers vs. minicomputers or compact
disks vs. records).

Competence-destroying discontinuities initiate a period of
technological ferment, as alternative technologies compete for
dominance. This period of technological competition lasts until
a dominant design emerges as a synthesis of prior technological experimentation (e.g., Dundee kiln, DC-3, PDP-11). Dominant designs reflect a consolidation of industry standards.
These designs crowd out alternative designs and become
guideposts for incremental product as well as major process
change (Utterback and Abernathy, 1975). Thus, quite apart
from major technological advance, the establishment of a dominant design may also be an important lever in shaping environmental conditions and organizational fate.

CONCLUSION

While these data indicate that technological discontinuities exist and that these discontinuities have important effects on environmental conditions, the data are not conclusive. Though the
data are consistent across three diverse industries, the number
of cases is relatively small, and some of the tests were limited
by data availability. Future research needs to focus more
closely on patterns of technological change. If technology is an
important determinant of competitive conditions, we need to
know more about differences between competence-
destroying and competence-enhancing technological advances, what distinguishes between incremental improvements and dramatic advances, what are dominant designs and

how they occur, and what are the impacts of competence-destroying advances in mature product classes.

Both product and process innovation are important. While the data here are only suggestive, it may be that different kinds of innovation are relatively more important in different product classes. For nonassembled products (e.g., cement, glass, oil), major process innovations may be relatively more important than product innovations. For assembled products (e.g., mini-computers, VCRs, scientific instruments), major product improvements or substitutions may be relatively more important than process innovations. Future research might explore the differential importance of major product and process innovations by different product-class type.

The effects of nontechnological discontinuities must also be examined to understand more fully how competitive environments change. Technological change does not occur in a vacuum. If frequently sparks a response from the legal, political, or social environments. For example, bioengineering, automatic control machinery, nuclear power, and supersonic transportation each has been directly affected by a complex set of interactions among technological and political, social, and legal considerations (e.g., Horwitch, 1982; Astley and Fombrun, 1983; Noble, 1984). Further, periods of incremental technological change and standardization may become turbulent for nontechnological reasons (e.g., airline deregulation or the outlawing of basing-point pricing in cement). More complete analyses of the technology-environment linkages must also take into account the linkages between technological change and these other important social, political, and legal forces.

Technological change clearly affects organizational environments. Beyond exploring more deeply the nature of technological change, future research could also explore the linkage between technological evolution and population phenomena, such as structural evolution, mortality rates, or strategic groups, as well as organizational issues, such as adaptation, succession, and political processes. These results suggest that technology is not a static environmental resource. Rather, technology advances through the competition between alternative technologies promoted by rivalrous organizations. At the organization level, technological action, such as investment in R&D and internal venturing, may be a powerful lever in directly shaping environmental conditions and, in turn, organizational adaptation.

REFERENCES

Abernathy, William
1978 The Productivity Dilemma. Baltimore, MD: Johns Hopkins University Press.

Abernathy, William, and Kim B. Clark
1985 "Innovation: Mapping the winds of creative destruction." Research Policy, 14: 3–22.

Aldrich, Howard, and Ellen R. Auster
1986 "Even dwarfs started small: Liabilities of age and size and their strategic implications." In L. L. Cummings and Barry M. Staw (eds.), Research in Organizational Behavior, 8: 165–198. Greenwich, CT: JAI Press.

Astley, W. Graham
1985 "The two ecologies: Population and community perspectives on organizational evolution." Administrative Science Quarterly, 30: 224–241.

Astley, W. Graham, and Charles Fombrun
1983 "Technological innovation and industrial structure: The case of telecommunications." In Robert Lamb (ed.), Advances in Strategic Management, 1: 205–229. Greenwich, CT: JAI Press.

Barley, Stephen R.
1986 "Technology as an occasion for structuring: Evidence from observations of CT scanners and the social order of radiology departments." Administrative Science Quarterly, 31: 78–108.

Technological Discontinuities

Barnard, Chester
1938 The Functions of the Executive. Cambridge, MA: Harvard University Press.

Blalock, Hubert
1979 Social Statistics, rev. 2d ed. New York: McGraw-Hill.

Brittain, Jack, and John Freeman
1980 "Organizational proliferation and density-dependent selection." In John R. Kimberly and Robert Miles (eds.), The Organizational Life Cycle: 291–338. San Francisco: Jossey-Bass.

Carroll, Glenn R.
1984 "Dynamics of publisher succession in newspaper organizations." Administrative Science Quarterly, 29: 93–113.

Chandler, Alfred D., Jr.
1977 The Visible Hand: The Managerial Revolution in American Business. Cambridge, MA: Belknap Press.

Davies, R. E. G.
1972 Airlines of the United States Since 1914. London: Putnam.

Dess, Gregory G., and Donald W. Beard
1984 "Dimensions of organizational task environments." Administrative Science Quarterly, 29: 52–73.

Dessauer, John H.
1975 My Years with Xerox. New York: Manor Books.

Downey, H. Kirk, and R. Duane Ireland
1979 "Quantitative versus qualitative: Environmental assessment in organizational studies." Administrative Science Quarterly, 24: 630–637.

Dutton, John, and Annie Thomas
1985 "Relating technological change and learning by doing." In Richard D. Rosenbloom (ed.), Research on Technological Innovation, Management, and Policy, 2: 187–224. Greenwich, CT: JAI Press.

Fishman, Katherine
1981 The Computer Establishment. New York: Harper & Row.

Freeman, John
1982 "Organizational life cycles and natural selection processes." In Barry M. Staw and L. L. Cummings (eds.), Research in Organizational Behavior, 4: 1–32. Greenwich, CT: JAI Press.

Gerwin, Donald
1981 "Relationships between structure and technology." In Paul Nystrom and William Starbuck (eds.), Handbook of Organizational Design, 2: 3–31. New York: Oxford University Press.

Gilfillan, S. Colum
1935 Inventing the Ship. Chicago: Follett.

Hannan, Michael, and John Freeman
1977 "The population ecology of organizations." American Journal of Sociology, 82: 929–964.

Harrigan, Kathryn
1983 Strategies for Vertical Integration. Lexington, MA: D. C. Heath, Lexington Books.

Headrick, Daniel
1981 The Tools of Empire. Oxford: Oxford University Press.

Hollander, Samuel
1965 The Sources of Increased Efficiency. Cambridge, MA: MIT Press.

Horwitch, Mel
1982 Clipped Wings: A Study of the Supersonic Transport. Cambridge, MA: MIT Press.

Hrebiniak, Lawrence G., and William F. Joyce
1985 "Organizational adaptation: Strategic choice and environmental determinism." Administrative Science Quarterly, 30: 336–349.

Klein, Burton
1984 Wages and Business Cycles: A Dynamic Theory. New York: Pergamon Press.

Lawrence, Paul, and Davis Dyer
1983 Renewing American Industry. New York: Free Press.

Lesley, Robert
1924 A History of the United States Portland Cement Industry. Chicago: Portland Cement Association.

MacMillan, Ian, and M. L. McCaffrey
1984 "Strategy for financial services: Cashing in on competitive inertia." Journal of Business Strategy, 4: 58–73.

McKelvey, Bill
1982 Organizational Systematics — Taxonomy, Evolution, Classification. Berkeley, CA: University of California Press.

Mensch, Gerhard
1979 Stalemate in Technology: Innovations Overcome the Depression. Cambridge, MA: Ballinger.

Merton, Robert
1968 Social Theory and Social Structure. New York: Free Press.

Miller, Danny, and Peter Friesen
1984 Organizations: A Quantum View. Englewood Cliffs, NJ: Prentice-Hall.

Morison, Elting E.
1966 Men, Machines, and Modern Times. Cambridge, MA: MIT Press.

Myers, Sumner, and Donald G. Marquis
1969 Successful Industrial Innovations. Washington, DC: National Science Foundation.

Noble, David
1984 Forces of Production: A Social History of Industrial Automation. New York: Knopf.

Pettigrew, Andrew
1973 Politics of Organizational Decision-Making. London: Tavistock.

Pfeffer, Jeffrey, and Gerald Salancik
1978 The External Control of Organizations. New York: Harper & Row.

Porter, Michael
1985 Competitive Advantage: Creating and Sustaining Superior Performance. New York: Free Press.

Pugh, Emerson W.
1984 Memories That Shaped an Industry: Decisions Leading to the IBM System 360. Cambridge, MA: MIT Press.

Romanelli, Elaine, and Michael L. Tushman
1986 "Inertia, environments and strategic choice: A quasi-experimental design for comparative-longitudinal research." Management Science, 32: 608–621.

Rosenberg, Nathan
1972 Technology and American Economic Growth. Armonk, NY: M.E. Sharpe.

Rosenbloom, Robert, and William Abernathy
1982 "The climate for innovation in industry: The role of management attitudes and practices in consumer electronics." Research Policy, 11: 209–225.

Sahal, Devendra
1981 Patterns of Technological Innovation. Reading, MA: Addison-Wesley.

Scherer, Frederick
1980 Industrial Market Structure and Economic Performance. Boston: Houghton Mifflin.

Schmookler, Jacob
1966 Invention and Economic Growth. Cambridge, MA: Harvard University Press.

Schumpeter, Josef
1961 History of Economic Analysis. New York: Oxford University Press.

Selznick, Philip
1949 TVA and the Grass Roots: A Study of Politics and Organization. Berkeley, CA: University of California Press.

Solow, Robert M.
1957 "Technical change and the aggregate production function." Review of Economics and Statistics, 39: 312–320.

Starbuck, William
1983 "Organizations and their environments." In Marvin D. Dunnette (ed.), Handbook of Organizational and Industrial Psychology: 1069–1123. New York: Wiley.

Stinchcombe, Arthur
1965 "Social structure and organization." In James G. March (ed.), Handbook of Organizations: 142–193. Chicago: Rand McNally.

Taton, René
1958 Reason and Chance in Scientific Discovery. New York: Philosophical Library.

Tilton, John W.
1971 International Diffusion of Technology: The Case of Semiconductors. Washington, DC: Brookings Institution.

Tushman, Michael, and Elaine Romanelli
1985 "Organizational evolution: A metamorphosis model of convergence and reorientation." In L. L. Cummings and Barry M. Staw (eds.), Research in Organizational Behavior, 7: 171–222. Greenwich, CT: JAI Press.

Utterback, James, and William Abernathy
1975 "A dynamic model of process and product innovation." Omega, 33: 639–656.

Woodward, Joan
1965 Industrial Organization: Theory and Practice. Oxford: Oxford University Press.

Yin, Zun-Sheng, and John M. Dutton
1986 "Systems learning and technological change: The evolution of 20th century U.S. domestic petroleum-refining processes." Working paper, New York University Graduate School of Business Administration.

[14]

Architectural Innovation: The Reconfiguration of Existing Product Technologies and the Failure of Established Firms

Rebecca M. Henderson
Massachusetts Institute of Technology
Kim B. Clark
Harvard University

This paper demonstrates that the traditional categorization of innovation as either incremental or radical is incomplete and potentially misleading and does not account for the sometimes disastrous effects on industry incumbents of seemingly minor improvements in technological products. We examine such innovations more closely and, distinguishing between the components of a product and the ways they are integrated into the system that is the product "architecture," define them as innovations that change the architecture of a product without changing its components. We show that architectural innovations destroy the usefulness of the architectural knowledge of established firms, and that since architectural knowledge tends to become embedded in the structure and information-processing procedures of established organizations, this destruction is difficult for firms to recognize and hard to correct. Architectural innovation therefore presents established organizations with subtle challenges that may have significant competitive implications. We illustrate the concept's explanatory force through an empirical study of the semiconductor photolithographic alignment equipment industry, which has experienced a number of architectural innovations.•

The distinction between refining and improving an existing design and introducing a new concept that departs in a significant way from past practice is one of the central notions in the existing literature on technical innovation (Mansfield, 1968; Moch and Morse, 1977; Freeman, 1982). Incremental innovation introduces relatively minor changes to the existing product, exploits the potential of the established design, and often reinforces the dominance of established firms (Nelson and Winter, 1982; Ettlie, Bridges, and O'Keefe, 1984; Dewar and Dutton, 1986; Tushman and Anderson, 1986). Although it draws from no dramatically new science, it often calls for considerable skill and ingenuity and, over time, has very significant economic consequences (Hollander, 1965). Radical innovation, in contrast, is based on a different set of engineering and scientific principles and often opens up whole new markets and potential applications (Dess and Beard, 1984; Ettlie, Bridges, and O'Keefe, 1984; Dewar and Dutton, 1986). Radical innovation often creates great difficulties for established firms (Cooper and Schendel, 1976; Daft, 1982; Rothwell, 1986; Tushman and Anderson, 1986) and can be the basis for the successful entry of new firms or even the redefinition of an industry.

Radical and incremental innovations have such different competitive consequences because they require quite different organizational capabilities. Organizational capabilities are difficult to create and costly to adjust (Nelson and Winter, 1982; Hannan and Freeman, 1984). Incremental innovation reinforces the capabilities of established organizations, while radical innovation forces them to ask a new set of questions, to draw on new technical and commercial skills, and to employ new problem-solving approaches (Burns and Stalker, 1966; Hage, 1980; Ettlie, Bridges, and O'Keefe, 1984; Tushman and Anderson, 1986).

© 1990 by Cornell University.
0001-8392/90/3501-0009/$1.00.

•

This research was supported by the Division of Research, Harvard Business School. Their support is gratefully acknowledged. We would like to thank Dataquest and VLSI Research Inc for generous permission to use their published data, the staffs at Canon, GCA, Nikon, Perkin Elmer and Ultratech, and all those individuals involved with photolithographic alignment technology who gave so generously of their time. We would also like to thank the editors of this journal and three anonymous reviewers who gave us many helpful comments. Any errors or omissions remain entirely our responsibility.

The distinction between radical and incremental innovation has produced important insights, but it is fundamentally incomplete. There is growing evidence that there are numerous technical innovations that involve apparently modest changes to the existing technology but that have quite dramatic competitive consequences (Clark, 1987). The case of Xerox and small copiers and the case of RCA and the American radio receiver market are two examples.

Xerox, the pioneer of plain-paper copiers, was confronted in the mid-1970s with competitors offering copiers that were much smaller and more reliable than the traditional product. The new products required little new scientific or engineering knowledge, but despite the fact that Xerox had invented the core technologies and had enormous experience in the industry, it took the company almost eight years of missteps and false starts to introduce a competitive product into the market. In that time Xerox lost half of its market share and suffered serious financial problems (Clark, 1987).

In the mid-1950s engineers at RCA's corporate research and development center developed a prototype of a portable, transistorized radio receiver. The new product used technology in which RCA was accomplished (transistors, radio circuits, speakers, tuning devices), but RCA saw little reason to pursue such an apparently inferior technology. In contrast, Sony, a small, relatively new company, used the small transistorized radio to gain entry into the U.S. market. Even after Sony's success was apparent, RCA remained a follower in the market as Sony introduced successive models with improved sound quality and FM capability. The irony of the situation was not lost on the R&D engineers: for many years Sony's radios were produced with technology licensed from RCA, yet RCA had great difficulty matching Sony's product in the marketplace (Clark, 1987).

Existing models that rely on the simple distinction between radical and incremental innovation provide little insight into the reasons why such apparently minor or straightforward innovations should have such consequences. In this paper, we develop and apply a model that grew out of research in the automotive, machine tool, and ceramics industries that helps to explain how minor innovations can have great competitive consequences.

CONCEPTUAL FRAMEWORK

Component and Architectural Knowledge

In this paper, we focus on the problem of product development, taking as the unit of analysis a manufactured product sold to an end user and designed, engineered, and manufactured by a single product-development organization. We define innovations that change the way in which the components of a product are linked together, while leaving the core design concepts (and thus the basic knowledge underlying the components) untouched, as "architectural" innovation.[1] This is the kind of innovation that confronted Xerox and RCA. It destroys the usefulness of a firm's architectural knowledge but preserves the usefulness of its knowledge about the product's components.

1
In earlier drafts of this paper we referred to this type of innovation as "generational." We are indebted to Professor Michael Tushman for his suggestion of the term architectural.

Architectural Innovation

This distinction between the product as a whole—the system—and the product in its parts—the components—has a long history in the design literature (Marples, 1961; Alexander, 1964). For example, a room fan's major components include the blade, the motor that drives it, the blade guard, the control system, and the mechanical housing. The overall architecture of the product lays out how the components will work together. Taken together, a fan's architecture and its components create a system for moving air in a room.

A component is defined here as a physically distinct portion of the product that embodies a core design concept (Clark, 1985) and performs a well-defined function. In the fan, a particular motor is a component of the design that delivers power to turn the fan. There are several design concepts one could use to deliver power. The choice of one of them—the decision to use an electric motor, for example, establishes a core concept of the design. The actual component—the electric motor—is then a physical implementation of this design concept.

The distinction between the product as a system and the product as a set of components underscores the idea that successful product development requires two types of knowledge. First, it requires component knowledge, or knowledge about each of the core design concepts and the way in which they are implemented in a particular component. Second, it requires architectural knowledge or knowledge about the ways in which the components are integrated and linked together into a coherent whole. The distinction between architectural and component knowledge, or between the components themselves and the links between them, is a source of insight into the ways in which innovations differ from each other.

Types of Technological Change

The notion that there are different kinds of innovation, with different competitive effects, has been an important theme in the literature on technological innovation since Schumpeter (1942). Following Schumpeter's emphasis on creative destruction, the literature has characterized different kinds of innovations in terms of their impact on the established capabilities of the firm. This idea is used in Figure 1, which classifies innovations along two dimensions. The horizontal dimension captures an innovation's impact on components, while the vertical captures its impact on the linkages between components.[2] There are, of course, other ways to characterize different kinds of innovation. But given the focus here on innovation and the development of new products, the framework outlined in Figure 1 is useful because it focuses on the impact of an innovation on the usefulness of the existing architectural and component knowledge of the firm.

Framed in this way, radical and incremental innovation are extreme points along both dimensions. Radical innovation establishes a new dominant design and, hence, a new set of core design concepts embodied in components that are linked together in a new architecture. Incremental innovation refines and extends an established design. Improvement occurs in individual components, but the underlying core design concepts, and the links between them, remain the same.

2
We are indebted to one of the anonymous *ASQ* reviewers for the suggestion that we use this matrix.

Figure 1. A framework for defining innovation.

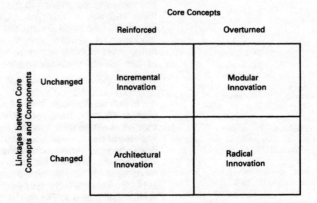

Figure 1 shows two further types of innovation: innovation that changes only the core design concepts of a technology and innovation that changes only the relationships between them. The former is a modular innovation, such as the replacement of analog with digital telephones. To the degree that one can simply replace an analog dialing device with a digital one, it is an innovation that changes a core design concept without changing the product's architecture. Our concern, however, is with the last type of innovation shown in the matrix: innovation that changes a product's architecture but leaves the components, and the core design concepts that they embody, unchanged.

The essence of an architectural innovation is the reconfiguration of an established system to link together existing components in a new way. This does not mean that the components themselves are untouched by architectural innovation. Architectural innovation is often triggered by a change in a component—perhaps size or some other subsidiary parameter of its design—that creates new interactions and new linkages with other components in the established product. The important point is that the core design concept behind each component—and the associated scientific and engineering knowledge—remain the same.

We can illustrate the application of this framework with the example of the room air fan. If the established technology is that of large, electrically powered fans, mounted in the ceiling, with the motor hidden from view and insulated to dampen the noise, improvements in blade design or in the power of the motor would be incremental innovations. A move to central air conditioning would be a radical innovation. New components associated with compressors, refrigerants, and their associated controls would add whole new technical disciplines and new interrelationships. For the maker of large, ceiling-mounted room fans, however, the introduction of a portable fan would be an architectural innovation. While the primary components would be largely the same (e.g., blade, motor, control system), the architecture of the product would be quite different. There would be significant changes in the

Architectural Innovation

interactions between components. The smaller size and the
co-location of the motor and the blade in the room would
focus attention on new types of interaction between the
motor size, the blade dimensions, and the amount of air that
the fan could circulate, while shrinking the size of the apparatus would probably introduce new interactions between the
performance of the blade and the weight of the housing.

The distinctions between radical, incremental, and architectural innovations are matters of degree. The intention here is
not to defend the boundaries of a particular definition, particularly since there are several other dimensions on which it
may be useful to define radical and incremental innovation.
The use of the term architectural innovation is designed to
draw attention to innovations that use many existing core design concepts in a new architecture and that therefore have a
more significant impact on the relationships between components than on the technologies of the components themselves. The matrix in Figure 1 is designed to suggest that a
given innovation may be less radical or more architectural, not
to suggest that the world can be neatly divided into four
quadrants.

These distinctions are important because they give us insight
into why established firms often have a surprising degree of
difficulty in adapting to architectural innovation. Incremental
innovation tends to reinforce the competitive positions of established firms, since it builds on their core competencies
(Abernathy and Clark, 1985) or is "competence enhancing"
(Tushman and Anderson, 1986). In the terms of the framework developed here, it builds on the existing architectural
and component knowledge of an organization. In contrast,
radical innovation creates unmistakable challenges for established firms, since it destroys the usefulness of their existing
capabilities. In our terms, it destroys the usefulness of both
architectural and component knowledge (Cooper and
Schendel, 1976; Daft, 1982; Tushman and Anderson, 1986).

Architectural innovation presents established firms with a
more subtle challenge. Much of what the firm knows is
useful and needs to be applied in the new product, but some
of what it knows is not only not useful but may actually
handicap the firm. Recognizing what is useful and what is not,
and acquiring and applying new knowledge when necessary,
may be quite difficult for an established firm because of the
way knowledge—particularly architectural knowledge—is organized and managed.

The Evolution of Component and Architectural Knowledge

Two concepts are important to understanding the ways in
which component and architectural knowledge are managed
inside an organization. The first is that of a dominant design.
Work by Abernathy and Utterback (1978), Rosenberg (1982),
Clark (1985), and Sahal (1986) and evidence from studies of
several industries show that product technologies do not
emerge fully developed at the outset of their commercial lives
(Mansfield, 1977). Technical evolution is usually characterized
by periods of great experimentation followed by the acceptance of a dominant design. The second concept is that organizations build knowledge and capability around the recurrent
tasks that they perform (Cyert and March, 1963; Nelson and

Winter, 1982). Thus one cannot understand the development of an organization's innovative capability or of its knowledge without understanding the way in which they are shaped by the organization's experience with an evolving technology.

The emergence of a new technology is usually a period of considerable confusion. There is little agreement about what the major subsystems of the product should be or how they should be put together. There is a great deal of experimentation (Burns and Stalker, 1966; Clark, 1985). For example, in the early days of the automobile industry, cars were built with gasoline, electric, or steam engines, with steering wheels or tillers, and with wooden or metal bodies (Abernathy, 1978).

These periods of experimentation are brought to an end by the emergence of a dominant design (Abernathy and Utterback, 1978; Sahal, 1986). A dominant design is characterized both by a set of core design concepts that correspond to the major functions performed by the product (Marples, 1961; Alexander, 1964; Clark, 1985) and that are embodied in components and by a product architecture that defines the ways in which these components are integrated (Clark, 1985; Sahal, 1986). It is equivalent to the general acceptance of a particular product architecture and is characteristic of technical evolution in a very wide range of industries (Clark, 1985). A dominant design often emerges in response to the opportunity to obtain economies of scale or to take advantage of externalities (David, 1985; Arthur, 1988). For example, the dominant design for the car encompassed not only the fact that it used a gasoline engine to provide motive force but also that it was connected to the wheels through a transmission and a drive train and was mounted on a frame rather than on the axles. A dominant design incorporates a range of basic choices about the design that are not revisited in every subsequent design. Once the dominant automobile design had been accepted, engineers did not reevaluate the decision to use a gasoline engine each time they developed a new design. Once any dominant design is established, the initial set of components is refined and elaborated, and progress takes the shape of improvements in the components within the framework of a stable architecture.

This evolutionary process has profound implications for the types of knowledge that an organization developing a new product requires, since an organization's knowledge and its information-processing capabilities are shaped by the nature of the tasks and the competitive environment that it faces (Lawrence and Lorsch, 1967; Galbraith, 1973).[3]

In the early stages of a technology's history, before the emergence of a dominant design, organizations competing to design successful products experiment with many different technologies. Since success in the market turns on the synthesis of unfamiliar technologies in creative new designs, organizations must actively develop both knowledge about alternate components and knowledge of how these components can be integrated. With the emergence of a dominant design, which signals the general acceptance of a single architecture, firms cease to invest in learning about alternative configurations of the established set of components. New component knowledge becomes more valuable to a firm than

[3] For simplicity, we will assume here that organizations can be assumed to act as boundedly rational entities, in the tradition of Arrow (1974) and Nelson and Winter (1982).

Architectural Innovation

new architectural knowledge because competition between designs revolves around refinements in particular components. Successful organizations therefore switch their limited attention from learning a little about many different possible designs to learning a great deal about the dominant design. Once gasoline-powered cars had emerged as the technology of choice, competitive pressures in the industry strongly encouraged organizations to learn more about gasoline-fired engines. Pursuing refinements in steam- or electric-powered cars became much less attractive. The focus of active problem solving becomes the elaboration and refinement of knowledge about existing components within a framework of stable architectural knowledge (Dosi, 1982; Clark, 1985).

Since in an industry characterized by a dominant design, architectural knowledge is stable, it tends to become embedded in the practices and procedures of the organization. Several authors have noted the importance of various institutional devices like frameworks and routines in completing recurring tasks in an organization (Galbraith, 1973; Nelson and Winter, 1982; Daft and Weick, 1984). The focus in this paper, however, is on the role of communication channels, information filters, and problem-solving strategies in managing architectural knowledge.

Channels, filters, and strategies. An organization's communication channels, both those that are implicit in its formal organization (A reports to B) and those that are informal ("I always call Fred because he knows about X"), develop around those interactions within the organization that are critical to its task (Galbraith, 1973; Arrow, 1974). These are also the interactions that are critical to effective design. They are the relationships around which the organization builds architectural knowledge. Thus an organization's communication channels will come to embody its architectural knowledge of the linkages between components that are critical to effective design. For example, as a dominant design for room fans emerges, an effective organization in the industry will organize itself around its conception of the product's primary components, since these are the key subtasks of the organization's design problem (Mintzberg, 1979; von Hippel, 1990). The organization may create a fan-blade group, a motor group, and so on. The communication channels that are created between these groups will reflect the organization's knowledge of the critical interactions between them. The fact that those working on the motor and the fan blade report to the same supervisor and meet weekly is an embodiment of the organization's architectural knowledge about the relationship between the motor and the fan blade.

The information filters of an organization also embody its architectural knowledge. An organization is constantly barraged with information. As the task that it faces stabilizes and becomes less ambiguous, the organization develops filters that allow it to identify immediately what is most crucial in its information stream (Arrow, 1974; Daft and Weick, 1984). The emergence of a dominant design and its gradual elaboration molds the organization's filters so that they come to embody parts of its knowledge of the key relationships between the components of the technology. For instance, the relationships between the designers of motors and controllers for a room fan are likely to change over time as they are able to express the nature of the critical interaction between the motor and the controller in an increasingly precise way that allows them to ignore irrelevant information. The controller designers may discover that they need to know a great deal about the torque and power of the motor but almost nothing about the materials from which it is made. They will create information filters that reflect this knowledge.

As a product evolves, information filters and communication channels develop and help engineers to work efficiently, but the evolution of the product also means that engineers face recurring kinds of problems. Over time, engineers acquire a store of knowledge about solutions to the specific kinds of problems that have arisen in previous projects. When confronted with such a problem, the engineer does not reexamine all possible alternatives but, rather, focuses first on those that he or she has found to be helpful in solving previous problems. In effect, an organization's problem-solving strategies summarize what it has learned about fruitful ways to solve problems in its immediate environment (March and Simon, 1958; Lyles and Mitroff, 1980; Nelson and Winter, 1982). Designers may use strategies of this sort in solving problems within components, but problem-solving strategies also reflect architectural knowledge, since they are likely to express part of an organization's knowledge about the component linkages that are crucial to the solution of routine problems. An organization designing fans might learn over time that the most effective way to design a quieter fan is to focus on the interactions between the motor and the housing.

The strategies designers use, their channels for communication, and their information filters emerge in an organization to help it cope with complexity. They are efficient precisely because they do not have to be actively created each time a need for them arises. Further, as they become familiar and effective, using them becomes natural. Like riding a bicycle, using a strategy, working in a channel, or employing a filter does not require detailed analysis and conscious, deliberate execution. Thus the operation of channels, filters, and strategies may become implicit in the organization.

Since architectural knowledge is stable once a dominant design has been accepted, it can be encoded in these forms and thus becomes implicit. Organizations that are actively engaged in incremental innovation, which occurs within the context of stable architectural knowledge, are thus likely to manage much of their architectural knowledge implicitly by embedding it in their communication channels, information filters, and problem-solving strategies. Component knowledge, in contrast, is more likely to be managed explicitly because it is a constant source of incremental innovation.

Problems Created by Architectural Innovation

Differences in the way in which architectural and component knowledge are managed within an experienced organization give us insight into why architectural innovation often creates problems for established firms. These problems have two sources. First, established organizations require significant time (and resources) to identify a particular innovation as architectural, since architectural innovation can often initially be

Architectural Innovation

accommodated within old frameworks. Radical innovation tends to be obviously radical—the need for new modes of learning and new skills becomes quickly apparent. But information that might warn the organization that a particular innovation is architectural may be screened out by the information filters and communication channels that embody old architectural knowledge. Since radical innovation changes the core design concepts of the product, it is immediately obvious that knowledge about how the old components interact with each other is obsolete. The introduction of new linkages, however, is much harder to spot. Since the core concepts of the design remain untouched, the organization may mistakenly believe that it understands the new technology. In the case of the fan company, the motor and the fan-blade designers will continue to talk to each other. The fact that they may be talking about the wrong things may only become apparent after there are significant failures or unexpected problems with the design.

The development of the jet aircraft industry provides an example of the impact of unexpected architectural innovation. The jet engine initially appeared to have important but straightforward implications for airframe technology. Established firms in the industry understood that they would need to develop jet engine expertise but failed to understand the ways in which its introduction would change the interactions between the engine and the rest of the plane in complex and subtle ways (Miller and Sawyers, 1968; Gardiner, 1986). This failure was one of the factors that led to Boeing's rise to leadership in the industry.

This effect is analogous to the tendency of individuals to continue to rely on beliefs about the world that a rational evaluation of new information should lead them to discard (Kahneman, Slovic, and Tversky, 1982). Researchers have commented extensively on the ways in which organizations facing threats may continue to rely on their old frameworks —or in our terms on their old architectural knowledge—and hence misunderstand the nature of a threat. They shoehorn the bad news, or the unexpected new information, back into the patterns with which they are familiar (Lyles and Mitroff, 1980; Dutton and Jackson, 1987; Jackson and Dutton, 1988).

Once an organization has recognized the nature of an architectural innovation, it faces a second major source of problems: the need to build and to apply new architectural knowledge effectively. Simply recognizing that a new technology is architectural in character does not give an established organization the architectural knowledge that it needs. It must first switch to a new mode of learning and then invest time and resources in learning about the new architecture (Louis and Sutton, 1989). It is handicapped in its attempts to do this, both by the difficulty all organizations experience in switching from one mode of learning to another and by the fact that it must build new architectural knowledge in a context in which some of its old architectural knowledge may be relevant.

An established organization setting out to build new architectural knowledge must change its orientation from one of refinement within a stable architecture to one of active search for new solutions within a constantly changing context. As long as the dominant design remains stable, an organization can segment and specialize its knowledge and rely on standard operating procedures to design and develop products. Architectural innovation, in contrast, places a premium on exploration in design and the assimilation of new knowledge. Many organizations encounter difficulties in their attempts to make this type of transition (Argyris and Schön, 1978; Weick, 1979; Hedberg, 1981; Louis and Sutton, 1989). New entrants, with smaller commitments to older ways of learning about the environment and organizing their knowledge, often find it easier to build the organizational flexibility that abandoning old architectural knowledge and building new requires.

Once an organization has succeeded in reorientating itself, the building of new architectural knowledge still takes time and resources. This learning may be quite subtle and difficult. New entrants to the industry must also build the architectural knowledge necessary to exploit an architectural innovation, but since they have no existing assets, they can optimize their organization and information-processing structures to exploit the potential of a new design. Established firms are faced with an awkward problem. Because their architectural knowledge is embedded in channels, filters, and strategies, the discovery process and the process of creating new information (and rooting out the old) usually takes time. The organization may be tempted to modify the channels, filters, and strategies that already exist rather than to incur the significant fixed costs and considerable organizational friction required to build new sets from scratch (Arrow, 1974). But it may be difficult to identify precisely which filters, channels, and problem-solving strategies need to be modified, and the attempt to build a new product with old (albeit modified) organizational tools can create significant problems.

The problems created by an architectural innovation are evident in the introduction of high-strength-low-alloy (HSLA) steel in automobile bodies in the 1970s. The new materials allowed body panels to be thinner and lighter but opened up a whole new set of interactions that were not contained in existing channels and strategies. One automaker's body-engineering group, using traditional methods, designed an HSLA hood for the engine compartment. The hoods, however, resonated and oscillated with engine vibrations during testing. On further investigation, it became apparent that the traditional methods for designing hoods worked just fine with traditional materials, although no one knew quite why. The knowledge embedded in established problem-solving strategies and communication channels was sufficient to achieve effective designs with established materials, but the new material created new interactions and required the engineers to build new knowledge about them.

Architectural innovation may thus have very significant competitive implications. Established organizations may invest heavily in the new innovation, interpreting it as an incremental extension of the existing technology or underestimating its impact on their embedded architectural knowledge. But new entrants to the industry may exploit its potential much more effectively, since they are not handicapped by a legacy of embedded and partially irrelevant architectural knowledge.

Architectural Innovation

We explore the validity of our framework through a brief summary of the competitive and technical history of the semiconductor photolithographic alignment equipment industry. Photolithographic aligners are sophisticated pieces of capital equipment used in the manufacture of integrated circuits. Their performance has improved dramatically over the last twenty-five years, and although the core technologies have changed only marginally since the technique was first invented, the industry has been characterized by great turbulence. Changes in market leadership have been frequent, the entry of new firms has occurred throughout the industry's history, and incumbents have often suffered sharp declines in market share following the introduction of equipment incorporating seemingly minor innovation. We believe that these events are explained by the intrusion of architectural innovation into the industry, and we use three episodes in the industry's history—particularly Canon's introduction of the proximity aligner and Kasper's response to it—to illustrate this idea in detail.

INNOVATION IN PHOTOLITHOGRAPHIC ALIGNMENT EQUIPMENT

Data

The data were collected during a two-year, field-based study of the photolithographic alignment equipment industry. The study was initially designed to serve as an exploration of the validity of the concept of architectural innovation, a concept originally developed by one of the authors during the course of his experience with the automobile and ceramics industry (Clark, 1987).

The core of the data is a panel data set consisting of research and development costs and sales revenue by product for every product development project conducted between 1962, when work on the first commercial product began, and 1986. This data is supplemented by a detailed managerial and technical history of each project. The data were collected through research in both primary and secondary sources. The secondary sources, including trade journals, scientific journals, and consulting reports, were used to identify the companies that had been active in the industry and the products that they had introduced and to build up a preliminary picture of the industry's technical history.

Data were then collected about each product-development project by contacting directly at least one of the members of the product-development team and requesting an interview. Interviews were conducted over a fourteen-month period, from March 1987 to May 1988. During the course of the research, over a hundred people were interviewed. As far as possible, the interviewees included the senior design engineer for each project and a senior marketing executive from each firm. Other industry observers and participants, including chief executives, university scientists, skilled design engineers, and service managers were also interviewed. Interview data were supplemented whenever possible through the use of internal firm records. The majority of the interviews were semistructured and lasted about two hours. Respondents were asked to describe the technical, commercial, and managerial history of the product-development projects with which they were familiar and to discuss the technical and commercial success of the products that grew out of them.

In order to validate the data that were collected during this process, a brief history of product development for each equipment vendor was circulated to all the individuals who had been interviewed and to others who knew a firm's history well, and the accuracy of this account was discussed over the telephone in supplementary interviews. The same validation procedure was followed in the construction of the technical history of the industry. A technical history was constructed using interview data, published product literature, and the scientific press. This history was circulated to key individuals who had a detailed knowledge of the technical history of the industry, who corrected it as appropriate.

We chose to study the semiconductor photolithographic alignment equipment industry for two reasons. The first is that it is very different from the industries in which our framework was first formulated, since it is characterized by much smaller firms and a much faster rate of technological innovation. The second is that it provides several examples of the impact of architectural innovation on the competitive position of established firms. Photolithographic equipment has been shaken by four waves of architectural innovation, each of which resulted in a new entrant capturing the leadership of the industry. In order to ground the discussion of architectural innovation we provide a brief description of photolithographic technology.

The Technology

Photolithographic aligners are used to manufacture solid-state semiconductor devices. The production of semiconductors requires the transfer of small, intricate patterns to the surface of a wafer of semiconductor material such as silicon, and this process of transfer is known as lithography. The surface of the wafer is coated with a light-sensitive chemical, or "resist." The pattern that is to be transferred to the wafer surface is drawn onto a mask and the mask is used to block light as it falls onto the resist, so that only those portions of the resist defined by the mask are exposed to light. The light chemically transforms the resist so that it can be stripped away. The resulting pattern is then used as the basis for either the deposition of material onto the wafer surface or for the etching of the existing material on the surface of the wafer. The process may be repeated as many as twenty times during the manufacture of a semiconductor device, and each layer must be located precisely with respect to the previous layer (Watts and Einspruch, 1987). Figure 2 gives a very simplified representation of this complex process.

A photolithographic aligner is used to position the mask relative to the wafer, to hold the two in place during exposure, and to expose the resist. Figure 3 shows a schematic diagram of a contact aligner, the first generation of alignment equipment developed. Improvement in alignment technology has meant improvement in minimum feature size, the size of the smallest pattern that can be produced on the wafer surface, yield, the percentage of wafers successfully processed, and

Architectural Innovation

Figure 2. Schematic representation of the lithographic process.

STEPS
1. Expose Resist

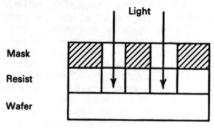

2. Develop Resist

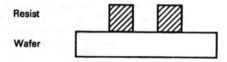

3. Deposit Material

4. Remove Remaining Resist

throughput, the number of wafers the aligner can handle in a given time.

Contact aligners were the first photolithographic aligners to be used commercially. They use the mask's shadow to transfer the mask pattern to the wafer surface. The mask and the wafer are held in contact with each other, and light shining through the gaps in the mask falls onto the wafer surface. Contact aligners are simple and quick to use, but the need to bring the mask and the wafer into direct contact can damage the mask or contaminate the wafer. The first proximity aligner was introduced in 1973 to solve these problems.

Figure 3. Schematic diagram of a contact aligner.

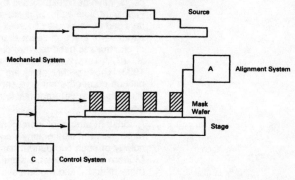

In a proximity aligner the mask is held a small distance away from (in proximity to) the wafer surface, as shown in the simplified drawing in Figure 4. The separation of the mask and the wafer means that they are less likely to be damaged during exposure, but since the mask and wafer are separated from each other, light coming through the mask spreads out before it reaches the resist, and the mask's shadow is less well defined than it is in the case of a contact aligner. As a result, users switching to proximity aligners traded off some minimum feature size capability for increased yield.

The basic set of core design concepts that underlie optical photolithography—the use of a visible light source to transmit the image of the mask to the wafer, a lens or other device to focus the image of the mask on the wafer, an alignment system that uses visible light, and a mechanical system that holds the mask and the wafer in place—have remained unchanged since the technology was first developed, although aligner performance has improved dramatically. The minimum-feature-size capability of the first aligners was about fifteen to twenty microns. Modern aligners are sometimes specified to have minimum feature sizes of less than half a micron.

Figure 4. Schematic diagram of a proximity aligner.

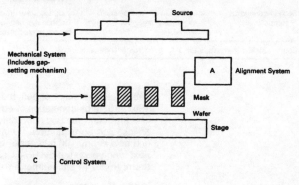

Architectural Innovation

Radical alternatives, making use of quite different core concepts, have been explored in the laboratory but have yet to be widely introduced into full-scale production. Aligners using x-rays and ion beams as sources have been developed, as have direct-write electron beam aligners, in which a focused beam of electrons is used to write directly on the wafer (Chang et al., 1977; Brown, Venkatesan, and Wagner, 1981; Burggraaf, 1983). These technologies are clearly radical. They rely not only on quite different core concepts for the source, but they also use quite different mask, alignment, and lens technologies.

A constant stream of incremental innovation has been critical to optical photolithography's continuing success. The technology of each component has been significantly improved. Modern light sources are significantly more powerful and more uniform, and modern alignment systems are much more accurate. In addition, the technology has seen four waves of architectural innovation: the move from contact to proximity alignment, from proximity to scanning projection alignment, and from scanners to first- and then second-generation "steppers." Table 1 summarizes the changes in the technology introduced by each generation. In each case the core technologies of optical lithography remained largely untouched, and much of the technical knowledge gained in building a previous generation could be transferred to the next. Yet, in each case, the industry leader was unable to make the transition.

Table 1

A Summary of Architectural Innovation in Photolithographic Alignment Technology

Equipment	Major Changes	
	Technology	Critical relationships between components
Proximity aligner	Mask and wafer separated during exposure.	Accuracy and stability of gap is a function of links between gap-setting mechanism and other components.
Scanning projection	Image of mask projected onto wafer by scanning reflective optics.	Interactions beween lens and other components is critical to successful performance.
First-generation stepper	Image of mask projected through refractive lens. Image "stepped" across wafer.	Relationship between lens field size and source energy becomes significant determinant of throughput. Depth of focus characteristics—driven by relationship between source wavelength and lens numerical aperture—become critical. Interactions between stage and alignment system are critical.
Second-generation stepper	Introduction of "site-by-site" alignment, larger 5× lenses.	Throughput now driven by calibration and stepper stability. Relationship between lens and mechanical system becomes crucial means of controlling distortion.

Source: Field interviews, internal firm records (Henderson, 1988).

Table 2 shows share of deflated cumulative sales, 1962–1986, by generation of equipment for the leading firms. The first commercially successful aligner was introduced by Kulicke and Soffa in 1965. They were extremely successful and held nearly 100 percent of the (very small) market for the next nine years, but by 1974 Cobilt and Kasper had replaced them. In 1974 Perkin-Elmer entered the market with the

Table 2

Share of Deflated Cumulative Sales (%) 1962–1986, by Generation, for the Leading Optical Photolithographic Alignment Equipment Manufacturers*

Firm	Contact	Proximity	Alignment Equipment Scanners	Step and repeat (1)	Step and repeat (2)
Cobilt	44		<1		
Kasper	17	8		7	
Canon		67	21	9	
Perkin-Elmer			78	10	<1
GCA				55	12
Nikon					70
Total	61	75	99+	81	82+

* This measure is distorted by the fact that all of these products are still being sold. For second-generation step and repeat aligners this problem is particularly severe, since in 1986 this equipment was still in the early stages of its life cycle. Source: Internal firm records, Dataquest, VLSI Research Inc.

scanning projection aligner and rapidly became the largest firm in the industry. GCA, in turn, replaced Perkin-Elmer through its introduction of the stepper, only to be supplanted by Nikon, which introduced the second-generation stepper.

In nearly every case, the established firm invested heavily in the next generation of equipment, only to meet with very little success. Our analysis of the industry's history suggests that a reliance on architectural knowledge derived from experience with the previous generation blinded the incumbent firms to critical aspects of the new technology. They thus underestimated its potential or built equipment that was markedly inferior to the equipment introduced by entrants.

The Kasper Saga

The case of Kasper Instruments and its response to Canon's introduction of the proximity printer illustrates some of the problems encountered by established firms. Kasper Instruments was founded in 1968 and by 1973 was a small but profitable firm supplying approximately half of the market for contact aligners. In 1973 Kasper introduced the first contact aligner to be equipped with proximity capability. Although nearly half of all the aligners that the firm sold from 1974 onward had this capability, Kasper aligners were only rarely used in proximity mode, and sales declined steadily until the company left the industry in 1981. The widespread use of proximity aligners only occurred with the introduction and general adoption of Canon's proximity aligner in the late 1970s.

The introduction of the proximity aligner is clearly not a radical advance. The conceptual change involved was minor, and most proximity aligners can also be used as contact aligners. However, in a proximity aligner, a quite different set of relationships between components is critical to successful performance. The introduction of the proximity aligner was thus an architectural innovation. In particular, in a proximity aligner, the relationships between the gap-setting mechanism and the other components of the aligner are significantly different.

Architectural Innovation

In both contact and proximity aligners, the mask and the wafer surface must be parallel to each other during exposure if the quality of the final image on the wafer is to be adequate. This is relatively straightforward in a contact aligner, since the mask and the wafer are in direct contact with each other during exposure. The gap-setting mechanism is used only to separate the mask and the wafer during alignment. Its stability and accuracy have very little impact on the aligner's performance. In a proximity aligner, however, the accuracy and precision of the gap-setting mechanism are critical to the aligner's performance. The gap between the mask and the wafer must be precise and consistent across the mask and wafer surfaces if the aligner is to perform well. Thus, the gap-setting mechanism must locate the mask at exactly the right point above the wafer by dead reckoning and must then ensure that the mask is held exactly parallel to the wafer. Since the accuracy and stability of the mechanism is as much a function of the way in which it is integrated with the other components as it is of its own design, the relationships between the gap-setting mechanism and the other components of the aligner must change if the aligner is to perform well. Thus, the successful design of a proximity aligner requires both the acquisition of some new component knowledge— how to build a more accurate and more stable gap-setting mechanism—and the acquisition of new architectural knowledge.

Kasper's failure to understand the challenge posed by the proximity aligner is especially puzzling given its established position in the market and its depth of experience in photolithography. There were several highly skilled and imaginative designers at Kasper during the early 1970s. The group designed a steady stream of contact aligners, each incorporating significant incremental improvements. From 1968 to 1973, the minimum-feature-size capability of its contact aligners improved from fifteen to five microns.

But Kasper's very success in designing contact aligners was a major contributor to its inability to design a proximity aligner that could perform as successfully as Canon's. Canon's aligner was superficially very similar to Kasper's. It incorporated the same components and performed the same functions, but it performed them much more effectively because it incorporated a much more sophisticated understanding of the technical interrelationships that are fundamental to successful proximity alignment. Kasper failed to develop the particular component knowledge that would have enabled it to match Canon's design. More importantly, the architectural knowledge that Kasper had developed through its experience with the contact aligner had the effect of focusing its attention away from the new problems whose solution was critical to the design of a successful proximity aligner.

Kasper conceived of the proximity aligner as a modified contact aligner. Like the incremental improvements to the contact aligner before it, design of the proximity aligner was managed as a routine extension to the product line. The gap-setting mechanism that was used in the contact aligner to align the mask and wafer with each other was slightly modified, and the new aligner was offered on the market. As a result, Kasper's proximity aligner did not perform well. The gap-setting mechanism was not sufficiently accurate or stable to ensure adequate performance, and the aligner was rarely used in its proximity mode. Kasper's failure to understand the obsolescence of its architectural knowledge is demonstrated graphically by two incidents.

The first is the firm's interpretation of early complaints about the accuracy of its gap-setting mechanism. In proximity alignment, misalignment of the mask and the wafer can be caused both by inaccuracies or instability in the gap-setting mechanism and by distortions introduced during processing. Kasper attributed many of the problems that users of its proximity equipment were experiencing to processing error, since it believed that processing error had been the primary source of problems with its contact aligner. The firm "knew" that its gap-setting mechanism was entirely adequate, and, as a result, devoted very little time to improving its performance. In retrospect, this may seem like a wanton misuse of information, but it represented no more than a continued reliance on an information filter that had served the firm well historically.

The second illustration is provided by Kasper's response to Canon's initial introduction of a proximity aligner. The Canon aligner was evaluated by a team at Kasper and pronounced to be a copy of a Kasper machine. Kasper evaluated it against the criteria that it used for evaluating its own aligners—criteria that had been developed during its experience with contact aligners. The technical features that made Canon's aligner a significant advance, particularly the redesigned gap mechanism, were not observed because they were not considered important. The Canon aligner was pronounced to be "merely a copy" of the Kasper aligner.

Kasper's subsequent commercial failure was triggered by several factors. The company had problems designing an automatic alignment system of sufficient accuracy and in managing a high-volume manufacturing facility. It also suffered through several rapid changes of top management during the late 1970s. But the obsolescence of architectural knowledge brought about by the introduction of architectural innovation was a critical factor in its decline.

Kasper's failure stemmed primarily from failures of recognition: the knowledge that it had developed through its experience with the contact aligner made it difficult for the company to understand the ways in which Canon's proximity aligner was superior to its own. Similar problems with recognition show up in all four episodes of architectural innovation in the industry's history. The case of Perkin-Elmer and stepper technology is a case in point. By the late 1970s Perkin-Elmer had achieved market leadership with its scanning projection aligners, but the company failed to maintain that leadership when stepper technology came to dominate the industry in the early 1980s. When evaluating the two technologies, Perkin-Elmer engineers accurately forecast the progress of individual components in the two systems but failed to see how new interactions in component development—including better resist systems and improvements in lens design—would give stepper technology a decisive advantage.

Architectural Innovation

GCA, the company that took leadership from Perkin-Elmer, was itself supplanted by Nikon, which introduced a second-generation stepper. Part of the problem for GCA was recognition, but much of its failure to master the new stepper technology lay in problems in implementation. Echoing Kasper, GCA first pronounced the Nikon stepper a "copy" of the GCA design. Even after GCA had fully recognized the threat posed by the second-generation stepper, its historical experience handicapped the company in its attempts to develop a competitive machine. GCA's engineers were organized by component, and cross-department communication channels were all structured around the architecture of the first-generation system. While GCA engineers were able to push the limits of the component technology, they had great difficulty understanding what Nikon had done to achieve its superior performance.

Nikon had changed aspects of the design—particularly the ways in which the optical system was integrated with the rest of the aligner—of which GCA's engineers had only limited understanding. Moreover, because these changes dealt with component interactions, there were few engineers responsible for developing this understanding. As a result, GCA's second-generation machines did not deliver the kind of performance that the market demanded. Like Kasper and Perkin-Elmer before them, GCA's sales languished and they lost market leadership. In all three cases, other factors also played a role in the firm's dramatic loss of market share, but a failure to respond effectively to architectural innovation was of critical importance.

DISCUSSION AND CONCLUSIONS

We have assumed that organizations are boundedly rational and, hence, that their knowledge and information-processing structure come to mirror the internal structure of the product they are designing. This is clearly an approximation. It would be interesting to explore the ways in which the formulation of architectural and component knowledge are affected by factors such as the firm's history and culture. Similarly, we have assumed that architectural knowledge embedded in routines and channels becomes inert and hard to change. Future research designed to investigate information filters, problem-solving strategies and communication channels in more detail could explore the extent to which this can be avoided.

The ideas developed here could also be linked to those of authors such as Abernathy and Clark (1985), who have drawn a distinction between innovation that challenges the technical capabilities of an organization and innovation that challenges the organization's knowledge of the market and of customer needs. Research could also examine the extent to which these insights are applicable to problems of process innovation and process development.

The empirical side of this paper could also be developed. While the idea of architectural innovation provides intriguing insights into the evolution of semiconductor photolithographic alignment equipment, further research could explore the extent to which it is a useful tool for understanding the impact of innovation in other industries.

The concept of architectural innovation and the related concepts of component and architectural knowledge have a number of important implications. These ideas not only give us a richer characterization of different types of innovation, but they open up new areas in understanding the connections between innovation and organizational capability. The paper suggests, for example, that we need to deepen our understanding of the traditional distinction between innovation that enhances and innovation that destroys competence within the firm, since the essence of architectural innovation is that it both enhances and destroys competence, often in subtle ways.

An architectural innovation's effect depends in a direct way on the nature of organizational learning. This paper not only underscores the role of organizational learning in innovation but suggests a new perspective on the problem. Given the evolutionary character of development and the prevalence of dominant designs, there appears to be a tendency for active learning among engineers to focus on improvements in performance within a stable product architecture. In this context, learning means learning about components and the core concepts that underlie them. Given the way knowledge tends to be organized within the firm, learning about changes in the architecture of the product is unlikely to occur naturally. Learning about changes in architecture—about new interactions across components (and often across functional boundaries)—may therefore require explicit management and attention. But it may also be that learning about new architectures requires a different kind of organization and people with different skills. An organization that is structured to learn quickly and effectively about new component technology may be ineffective in learning about changes in product architecture. What drives effective learning about new architectures and how learning about components may be related to it are issues worth much further research.

These ideas also provide an intriguing perspective from which to understand the current fashion for cross-functional teams and more open organizational environments. These mechanisms may be responses to a perception of the danger of allowing architectural knowledge to become embedded within tacit or informal linkages.

To the degree that other tasks performed by organizations can also be described as a series of interlinked components within a relatively stable framework, the idea of architectural innovation yields insights into problems that reach beyond product development and design. To the degree that manufacturing, marketing, and finance rely on communication channels, information filters, and problem-solving strategies to integrate their work together, architectural innovation at the firm level may also be a significant issue.

Finally, an understanding of architectural innovation would be useful to discussions of the effect of technology on competitive strategy. Since architectural innovation has the potential to offer firms the opportunity to gain significant advantage over well-entrenched, dominant firms, we might expect less-

Architectural Innovation

entrenched competitor firms to search actively for opportunities to introduce changes in product architecture in an industry. The evidence developed here and in other studies suggests that architectural innovation is quite prevalent. As an interpretive lens, architectural innovation may therefore prove quite useful in understanding technically based rivalry in a variety of industries.

REFERENCES

Abernathy, William J.
1978 The Productivity Dilemma: Roadblock to Innovation in the Automobile Industry. Baltimore: Johns Hopkins University Press.

Abernathy, William J., and Kim Clark
1985 "Innovation: Mapping the winds of creative destruction." Research Policy, 14: 3–22.

Abernathy, William J., and James Utterback
1978 "Patterns of industrial innovation." Technology Review, June–July: 40–47.

Alexander, Christopher
1964 Notes on the Synthesis of Form. Cambridge, MA: Harvard University Press.

Argyris, Chris, and Donald Schön
1978 Organizational Learning. Reading, MA: Addison-Wesley.

Arrow, Kenneth
1974 The Limits of Organization. New York: Norton.

Arthur, Brian
1988 "Competing technologies: An overview." In Giovanni Dosi et al. (eds.), Technical Change and Economic Theory: 590–607. New York: Columbia University Press.

Brown, William L., T. Venkatesan, and A. Wagner
1981 "Ion beam lithography." Solid State Technology, August: 60–67.

Burggraaf, Pieter
1983 "X-Ray lithography: Optical's heir." Semiconductor International, September: 60–67.

Burns, Tom, and George Stalker
1966 The Management of Innovation. London: Tavistock.

Chang, T. H. P., M. Hatzakis, A. D. Wilson, and A. N. Broers
1977 "Electron-beam lithography draws a finer line." Electronics, May: 89–98.

Clark, Kim B.
1985 "The interaction of design hierarchies and market concepts in technological evolution." Research Policy, 14: 235–251.
1987 "Managing technology in international competition: The case of product development in response to foreign entry." In Michael Spence and Heather Hazard (eds.), International Competitiveness: 27–74. Cambridge, MA: Ballinger.

Cooper, Arnold C., and Dan Schendel
1976 "Strategic response to technological threats." Business Horizons, 19: 61–69.

Cyert, Richard M., and James G. March
1963 A Behavioral Theory of the Firm. Englewood Cliffs, NJ: Prentice-Hall.

Daft, Richard L.
1982 "Bureaucratic versus nonbureaucratic structure and the process of innovation and change." In Samuel B. Bacharach (ed.), Research in the Sociology of Organizations, 1:129–166. Greenwich, CT: JAI Press.

Daft, Richard L., and Karl E. Weick
1984 "Towards a model of organizations as interpretation systems." Academy of Management Review, 9: 284–295.

David, Paul A.
1985 "Clio and the economics of QWERTY." American Economic Review, 75: 332–337.

Dess, Gregory G., and Donald Beard
1984 "Dimensions of organizational task environments." Administrative Science Quarterly, 29: 52–73.

Dewar, Robert D., and Jane E. Dutton
1986 "The adoption of radical and incremental innovations: An empirical analysis." Management Science, 32: 1422–1433.

Dosi, Giovanni
1982 "Technological paradigms and technological trajectories: A suggested interpretation of the determinants and directions of technical change." Research Policy, 11: 147–162.

Dutton, Jane E., and Susan E. Jackson
1987 "Categorizing strategic issues: Links to organizational action." Academy of Management Review, 12: 76–90.

Ettlie, John E., William P. Bridges, and Robert D. O'Keefe
1984 "Organizational strategy and structural differences for radical vs. incremental innovation." Management Science, 30: 682–695.

Freeman, Christopher
1982 The Economics of Industrial Innovation, 2d ed. Cambridge, MA: MIT Press.

Galbraith, Jay
1973 Designing Complex Organizations. Reading, MA: Addison-Wesley.

Gardiner, J. P.
1986 "Design trajectories for airplanes and automobiles during the past fifty years." In Christopher Freeman (ed.), Design, Innovation and Long Cycles in Economic Development: 121–141. London: Francis Pinter.

Hage, Jerald
1980 Theories of Organization. New York: Wiley Interscience.

Hannan, Michael T., and John Freeman
1984 "Structural inertia and organizational change." American Sociological Review, 49: 149–164.

Hedberg, Bo L. T.
1981 "How organizations learn and unlearn." In P. C. Nystrom and W. H. Starbuck (eds.), Handbook of Organizational Design, 1: 3–27. New York: Oxford University Press.

Henderson, Rebecca M.
1988 "The failure of established firms in the face of technical change: A study of photolithographic alignment equipment." Unpublished Ph.D. dissertation, Harvard University.

Hollander, Samuel
1965 The Sources of Increased Efficiency: A Study of Du Pont Rayon Plants. Cambridge, MA: MIT Press.

Jackson, Susan E., and Jane E. Dutton
1988 "Discerning threats and opportunities." Administrative Science Quarterly, 33: 370–387.

Kahneman, David, Paul Slovic, and Amos Tversky
1982 Judgement under Uncertainty: Heuristics and Biases. Cambridge: Cambridge University Press.

Lawrence, Paul R., and Jay W. Lorsch
1967 Organization and Environment: Managing Differentiation and Integration. Homewood, IL: Irwin.

Louis, Meryl R., and Robert I. Sutton
1989 "Switching cognitive gears: From habits of mind to active thinking." Working Paper, School of Industrial Engineering, Stanford University.

Lyles, Majorie A., and Ian I. Mitroff
1980 "Organizational problem formulation: An empirical study." Administrative Science Quarterly, 25: 102–119.

Mansfield, Edwin
1968 Industrial Research and Technical Innovation. New York: Norton.
1977 The Production and Application of New Industrial Technology. New York: Norton.

March, James G., and Herbert A. Simon
1958 Organizations. New York: Wiley.

Marples, David L.
1961 "The decisions of engineering design." IEEE Transactions on Engineering Management, EM.8 (June): 55–71.

Miller, Ronald, and David Sawyers
1968 The Technical Development of Modern Aviation. New York: Praeger.

Mintzberg, Henry
1979 The Structuring of Organizations. Englewood Cliffs, NJ: Prentice-Hall.

Moch, Michael, and Edward V. Morse
1977 "Size, centralization and organizational adoption of innovations." American Sociological Review, 42: 716–725.

Nelson, Richard, and Sidney Winter
1982 An Evolutionary Theory of Economic Change. Cambridge, MA: Harvard University Press.

Rosenberg, Nathan
1982 Inside the Black Box: Technology and Economics. Cambridge: Cambridge University Press.

Rothwell, Roy
1986 "The role of small firms in the emergence of new technologies." In Christopher Freeman (ed.), Design, Innovation and Long Cycles in Economic Development: 231–248. London: Francis Pinter.

Sahal, Devendra
1986 "Technological guideposts and innovation avenues." Research Policy, 14: 61–82.

Schumpeter, Joseph A.
1942 Capitalism, Socialism and Democracy. Cambridge, MA: Harvard University Press.

Tushman, Michael L., and Philip Anderson
1986 "Technological discontinuities and organizational environments." Administrative Science Quarterly, 31: 439–465.

von Hippel, Eric
1990 "Task partitioning: An innovation process variable." Research Policy (in press).

Watts, Roderick K., and Norman G. Einspruch (eds.)
1987 Lithography for VLSI, VLSI Electronics—Microstructure Science. New York: Academic Press.

Weick, Karl E.
1979 "Cognitive processes in organizations." In B. M. Staw and L. L. Cummings (eds.), Research in Organizational Behavior, 1: 41–47. Greenwich, CT: JAI Press.

[15]

ORGANIZATION SCIENCE
Vol. 2, No. 1, February 1991
Printed in U.S.A.

EXPLORATION AND EXPLOITATION IN ORGANIZATIONAL LEARNING*

JAMES G. MARCH

*Graduate School of Business, Stanford University,
Stanford, California 94305*

This paper considers the relation between the exploration of new possibilities and the exploitation of old certainties in organizational learning. It examines some complications in allocating resources between the two, particularly those introduced by the distribution of costs and benefits across time and space, and the effects of ecological interaction. Two general situations involving the development and use of knowledge in organizations are modeled. The first is the case of mutual learning between members of an organization and an organizational code. The second is the case of learning and competitive advantage in competition for primacy. The paper develops an argument that adaptive processes, by refining exploitation more rapidly than exploration, are likely to become effective in the short run but self-destructive in the long run. The possibility that certain common organizational practices ameliorate that tendency is assessed.
(ORGANIZATIONAL LEARNING: RISK TAKING; KNOWLEDGE AND COMPETITIVE ADVANTAGE)

A central concern of studies of adaptive processes is the relation between the exploration of new possibilities and the exploitation of old certainties (Schumpeter 1934; Holland 1975; Kuran 1988). Exploration includes things captured by terms such as search, variation, risk taking, experimentation, play, flexibility, discovery, innovation. Exploitation includes such things as refinement, choice, production, efficiency, selection, implementation, execution. Adaptive systems that engage in exploration to the exclusion of exploitation are likely to find that they suffer the costs of experimentation without gaining many of its benefits. They exhibit too many undeveloped new ideas and too little distinctive competence. Conversely, systems that engage in exploitation to the exclusion of exploration are likely to find themselves trapped in suboptimal stable equilibria. As a result, maintaining an appropriate balance between exploration and exploitation is a primary factor in system survival and prosperity.

This paper considers some aspects of such problems in the context of organizations. Both exploration and exploitation are essential for organizations, but they compete for scarce resources. As a result, organizations make explicit and implicit choices between the two. The explicit choices are found in calculated decisions about alternative investments and competitive strategies. The implicit choices are buried in many features of organizational forms and customs, for example, in organizational procedures for accumulating and reducing slack, in search rules and practices, in the ways in which targets are set and changed, and in incentive systems. Understanding the choices and improving the balance between exploration and exploitation are complicated by the fact that returns from the two options vary not only with respect to their expected values, but also with respect to their variability, their timing, and their distribution within and beyond the organization. Processes for allocating resources between them, therefore, embody intertemporal, interinstitutional, and interpersonal comparisons, as well as risk preferences. The difficulties involved in making

*Accepted by Lee S. Sproull and Michael D. Cohen; received August 18, 1989.

71

72   JAMES G. MARCH

such comparisons lead to complications in specifying appropriate trade-offs, and in achieving them.

1. The Exploration / Exploitation Trade-Off

Exploration and Exploitation in Theories of Organizational Action

In rational models of choice, the balance between exploration and exploitation is discussed classically in terms of a theory of rational search (Radner and Rothschild 1975; Hey 1982). It is assumed that there are several alternative investment opportunities, each characterized by a probability distribution over returns that is initially unknown. Information about the distribution is accumulated over time, but choices must be made between gaining new information about alternatives and thus improving future returns (which suggests allocating part of the investment to searching among uncertain alternatives), and using the information currently available to improve present returns (which suggests concentrating the investment on the apparently best alternative). The problem is complicated by the possibilities that new investment alternatives may appear, that probability distributions may not be stable, or that they may depend on the choices made by others.

In theories of limited rationality, discussions of the choice between exploration and exploitation emphasize the role of targets or aspiration levels in regulating allocations to search (Cyert and March 1963). The usual assumption is that search is inhibited if the most preferred alternative is above (but in the neighborhood of) the target. On the other hand, search is stimulated if the most preferred known alternative is below the target. Such ideas are found both in theories of satisficing (Simon 1955) and in prospect theory (Kahneman and Tversky 1979). They have led to attempts to specify conditions under which target-oriented search rules are optimal (Day 1967). Because of the role of targets, discussions of search in the limited rationality tradition emphasize the significance of the adaptive character of aspirations themselves (March 1988).

In studies of organizational learning, the problem of balancing exploration and exploitation is exhibited in distinctions made between refinement of an existing technology and invention of a new one (Winter 1971; Levinthal and March 1981). It is clear that exploration of new alternatives reduces the speed with which skills at existing ones are improved. It is also clear that improvements in competence at existing procedures make experimentation with others less attractive (Levitt and March 1988). Finding an appropriate balance is made particularly difficult by the fact that the same issues occur at levels of a nested system—at the individual level, the organizational level, and the social system level.

In evolutionary models of organizational forms and technologies, discussions of the choice between exploration and exploitation are framed in terms of balancing the twin processes of variation and selection (Ashby 1960; Hannan and Freeman 1987). Effective selection among forms, routines, or practices is essential to survival, but so also is the generation of new alternative practices, particularly in a changing environment. Because of the links among environmental turbulence, organizational diversity, and competitive advantage, the evolutionary dominance of an organizational practice is sensitive to the relation between the rate of exploratory variation reflected by the practice and the rate of change in the environment. In this spirit, for example, it has been argued that the persistence of garbage-can decision processes in organizations is related to the diversity advantage they provide in a world of relatively unstable environments, when paired with the selective efficiency of conventional rationality (Cohen 1986).

The Vulnerability of Exploration

Compared to returns from exploitation, returns from exploration are systematically less certain, more remote in time, and organizationally more distant from the locus of action and adaption. What is good in the long run is not always good in the short run. What is good at a particular historical moment is not always good at another time. What is good for one part of an organization is not always good for another part. What is good for an organization is not always good for a larger social system of which it is a part. As organizations learn from experience how to divide resources between exploitation and exploration, this distribution of consequences across time and space affects the lessons learned. The certainty, speed, proximity, and clarity of feedback ties exploitation to its consequences more quickly and more precisely than is the case with exploration. The story is told in many forms. Basic research has less certain outcomes, longer time horizons, and more diffuse effects than does product development. The search for new ideas, markets, or relations has less certain outcomes, longer time horizons, and more diffuse effects than does further development of existing ones.

Because of these differences, adaptive processes characteristically improve exploitation more rapidly than exploration. These advantages for exploitation cumulate. Each increase in competence at an activity increases the likelihood of rewards for engaging in that activity, thereby further increasing the competence and the likelihood (Argyris and Schön 1978; David 1985). The effects extend, through network externalities, to others with whom the learning organization interacts (Katz and Shapiro 1986; David and Bunn 1988). Reason inhibits foolishness; learning and imitation inhibit experimentation. This is not an accident but is a consequence of the temporal and spatial proximity of the effects of exploitation, as well as their precision and interconnectedness.

Since performance is a joint function of potential return from an activity and present competence of an organization at it, organizations exhibit increasing returns to experience (Arthur 1984). Positive local feedback produces strong path dependence (David 1990) and can lead to suboptimal equilibria. It is quite possible for competence in an inferior activity to become great enough to exclude superior activities with which an organization has little experience (Herriott, Levinthal, and March 1985). Since long-run intelligence depends on sustaining a reasonable level of exploration, these tendencies to increase exploitation and reduce exploration make adaptive processes potentially self-destructive.

The Social Context of Organizational Learning

The trade-off between exploration and exploitation exhibits some special features in the social context of organizations. The next two sections of the present paper describe two simple models of adaptation, use them to elaborate the relation between exploitation and exploration, and explore some implications of the relation for the accumulation and utilization of knowledge in organizations. The models identify some reasons why organizations may want to control learning and suggest some procedures by which they do so.

Two distinctive features of the social context are considered. The first is the mutual learning of an organization and the individuals in it. Organizations store knowledge in their procedures, norms, rules, and forms. They accumulate such knowledge over time, learning from their members. At the same time, individuals in an organization are socialized to organizational beliefs. Such mutual learning has implications for understanding and managing the trade-off between exploration and exploitation in organizations. The second feature of organizational learning considered here is

74   JAMES G. MARCH

the context of competition for primacy. Organizations often compete with each
other under conditions in which relative position matters. The mixed contribution of
knowledge to competitive advantage in cases involving competition for primacy
creates difficulties for defining and arranging an appropriate balance between exploration and exploitation in an organizational setting.

2. Mutual Learning in the Development of Knowledge

Organizational knowledge and faiths are diffused to individuals through various
forms of instruction, indoctrination, and exemplification. An organization socializes
recruits to the languages, beliefs, and practices that comprise the organizational code
(Whyte 1957; Van Maanen 1973). Simultaneously, the organizational code is adapting
to individual beliefs. This form of mutual learning has consequences both for the
individuals involved and for an organization as a whole. In particular, the trade-off
between exploration and exploitation in mutual learning involves conflicts between
short-run and long-run concerns and between gains to individual knowledge and
gains to collective knowledge.

A Model of Mutual Learning

Consider a simple model of the development and diffusion of organizational
knowledge. There are four key features to the model:

(1) There is an external reality that is independent of beliefs about it. Reality is
described as having m dimensions, each of which has a value of 1 or -1. The
(independent) probability that any one dimension will have a value of 1 is 0.5.

(2) At each time period, beliefs about reality are held by each of n individuals in an
organization and by an organizational code of received truth. For each of the m
dimensions of reality, each belief has a value of 1, 0, or -1. This value may change
over time.

(3) Individuals modify their beliefs continuously as a consequence of socialization
into the organization and education into its code of beliefs. Specifically, if the code is
0 on a particular dimension, individual belief is not affected. In each period in which
the code differs on any particular dimension from the belief of an individual,
individual belief changes to that of the code with probability, p_1. Thus, p_1 is a
parameter reflecting the effectiveness of socialization, i.e., learning *from* the code.
Changes on the several dimensions are assumed to be independent of each other.

(4) At the same time, the organizational code adapts to the beliefs of those
individuals whose beliefs correspond with reality on more dimensions than does the
code. The probability that the beliefs of the code will be adjusted to conform to the
dominant belief within the superior group on any particular dimension depends on
the level of agreement among individuals in the superior group and on p_2.[1] Thus, p_2
is a parameter reflecting the effectiveness of learning *by* the code. Changes on the
several dimensions are assumed to be independent of each other.

Within this system, initial conditions include: a reality m-tuple (m dimensions,
each of which has a value of 1 or -1, with independent equal probability); an
organizational code m-tuple (m dimensions, each of which is initially 0); and n

---

[1]More precisely, if the code is the same as the majority view among those individuals whose overall
knowledge score is superior to that of the code, the code remains unchanged. If the code differs from the
majority view on a particular dimension at the start of a time period, the probability that it will be
unchanged at the end of period is $(1 - p_2)^k$, where k ($k > 0$) is the number of individuals (within the
superior group) who differ from the code on this dimension minus the number who do not. This
formulation makes the effective rate of code learning dependent on k, which probably depends on n. In
the present simulations, n is not varied.

individual m-tuples (m dimensions, with values equal 1, 0, or -1, with equal probabilities).

Thus, the process begins with an organizational code characterized by neutral beliefs on all dimensions and a set of individuals with varying beliefs that exhibit, on average, no knowledge. Over time, the organizational code affects the beliefs of individuals, even while it is being affected by those beliefs. The beliefs of individuals do not affect the beliefs of other individuals directly but only through affecting the code. The effects of reality are also indirect. Neither the individuals nor the organizations experience reality. Improvement in knowledge comes by the code mimicking the beliefs (including the false beliefs) of superior individuals and by individuals mimicking the code (including its false beliefs).

Basic Properties of the Model in a Closed System

Consider such a model of mutual learning first within a closed system having fixed organizational membership and a stable reality. Since realizations of the process are subject to stochastic variability, repeated simulations using the same initial conditions and parameters are used to estimate the distribution of outcomes. In all of the results reported here, the number of dimensions of reality (m) is set at 30, the number of individuals (n) is set at 50, and the number of repeated simulations is 80. The quantitative levels of the results and the magnitude of the stochastic fluctuations reported depend on these specifications, but the qualitative results are insensitive to values of m and n.

Since reality is specified, the state of knowledge at any particular time period can be assessed in two ways. First, the proportion of reality that is correctly represented in the organizational code can be calculated for any period. This is the knowledge level of the code for that period. Second, the proportion of reality that is correctly represented in individual beliefs (on average) can be calculated for any period. This is the average knowledge level of the individuals for that period.

Within this closed system, the model yields time paths of organizational and individual beliefs, thus knowledge levels, that depend stochastically on the initial conditions and the parameters affecting learning. The basic features of these histories can be summarized simply: Each of the adjustments in beliefs serves to eliminate differences between the individuals and the code. Consequently, the beliefs of individuals and the code converge over time. As individuals in the organization become more knowledgeable, they also become more homogeneous with respect to knowledge. An equilibrium is reached at which all individuals and the code share the same (not necessarily accurate) belief with respect to each dimension. The equilibrium is stable.

Effects of learning rates. Higher rates of learning lead, on average, to achieving equilibrium earlier. The equilibrium level of knowledge attained by an organization also depends interactively on the two learning parameters. Figure 1 shows the results when we assume that p_1 is the same for all individuals. Slower socialization (lower p_1) leads to greater knowledge at equilibrium than does faster socialization, particularly when the code learns rapidly (high p_2). When socialization is slow, more rapid learning by the code leads to greater knowledge at equilibrium; but when socialization is rapid, greater equilibrium knowledge is achieved through slower learning by the code. By far the highest equilibrium knowledge occurs when the code learns rapidly from individuals whose socialization to the code is slow.

The results pictured in Figure 1 confirm the observation that rapid learning is not always desirable (Herriott, Levinthal and March 1985; Lounamaa and March 1987).

76JAMES G. MARCH

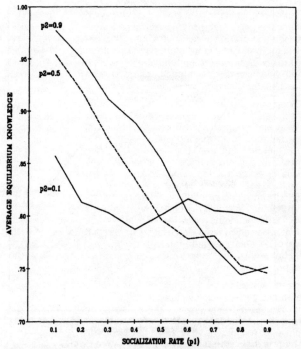

FIGURE 1.Effect of Learning Rates (p_1, p_2) on Equilibrium Knowledge.
$M = 30$; $N = 50$; 80 Iterations.

In previous work, it was shown that slower learning allows for greater exploration of possible alternatives and greater balance in the development of specialized competences. In the present model, a different version of the same general phenomenon is observed. The gains to individuals from adapting rapidly to the code (which is consistently closer to reality than the average individual) are offset by second-order losses stemming from the fact that the code can learn only from individuals who deviate from it. Slow learning on the part of individuals maintains diversity longer, thereby providing the exploration that allows the knowledge found in the organizational code to improve.

Effects of learning rate heterogeneity. The fact that fast individual learning from the code tends to have a favorable first-order effect on individual knowledge but an adverse effect on improvement in organizational knowledge and thereby on long-term individual improvement suggests that there might be some advantage to having a mix of fast and slow learners in an organization. Suppose the population of individuals in an organization is divided into two groups, one consisting of individuals who learn rapidly from the code ($p_1 = 0.9$) and the other consisting of individuals who learn slowly ($p_1 = 0.1$).

If an organization is partitioned into two groups in this way, the mutual learning process achieves an equilibrium in which all individuals and the code share the same beliefs. As would be expected from the results above with respect to homogeneous

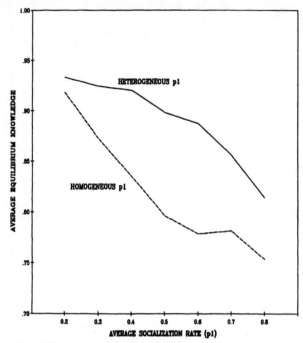

FIGURE 2.   Effect of Heterogeneous Socialization Rates ($p_1 = 0.1, 0.9$) on Equilibrium Knowledge. $M = 30; N = 50; p_2 = 0.5;$ 80 Iterations.

socialization rates, larger fractions of fast learners result in the process reaching equilibrium faster and in lower levels of knowledge at equilibrium than do smaller fractions of fast learners. However, as Figure 2 shows, for any average rate of learning from the code, it is better from the point of view of equilibrium knowledge to have that average reflect a mix of fast and slow learners rather than a homogeneous population. For equivalent average values of the socialization learning parameter (p_1), the heterogeneous population consistently produces higher equilibrium knowledge.

On the way to equilibrium, the knowledge gains from variability are disproportionately due to contributions by slow learners, but they are disproportionately realized (in their own knowledge) by fast learners. Figure 3 shows the effects on period-20 knowledge of varying the fraction of the population of individuals who are fast learners ($p_1 = 0.9$) rather than slow learners ($p_1 = 0.1$). Prior to reaching equilibrium, individuals with a high value for p_1 gain from being in an organization in which there are individuals having a low value for p_1, but the converse is not true.

These results indicate that the fraction of slow learners in an organization is a significant factor in organizational learning. In the model, that fraction is treated as a parameter. Disparities in the returns to the two groups and their interdependence make optimizing with respect to the fraction of slow learners problematic if the rates of individual learning are subject to individual control. Since there are no obvious individual incentives for learning slowly in a population in which others are learning rapidly, it may be difficult to arrive at a fraction of slow learners that is optimal from the point of view of the code if learning rates are voluntarily chosen by individuals.

78   JAMES G. MARCH

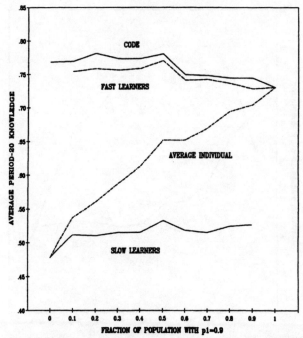

FIGURE 3.   Effect of Heterogeneous Socialization Rates (p_1 = 0.1, 0.9) on Period-20 Knowledge.
M = 30; N = 50; p_1 = 0.1, 0.9; p_2 = 0.5; 80 Iterations.

Basic Properties of the Model in a More Open System

These results can be extended by examining some alternative routes to selective slow learning in a somewhat more open system. Specifically, the role of turnover in the organization and turbulence in the environment are considered. In the case of turnover, organizational membership is treated as changing. In the case of turbulence, environmental reality is treated as changing.

Effects of personnel turnover. In the previous section, it was shown that variability is sustained by low values of p_1. Slow learners stay deviant long enough for the code to learn from them. An alternative way of producing variability in an organization is to introduce personnel turnover. Suppose that each time period each individual has a probability, p_3, of leaving the organization and being replaced by a new individual with a set of naive beliefs described by an m-tuple, having values equal to 1, 0, or -1, with equal probabilities. As might be expected, there is a consistent negative first-order effect of turnover on average individual knowledge. Since there is a positive relation between length of service in the organization and individual knowledge, the greater the turnover, the shorter the average length of service and the lower the average individual knowledge at any point. This effect is strong.

The effect of turnover on the organizational code is more complicated and reflects a trade-off between learning rate and turnover rate. Figure 4 shows the period-20 results for two different values of the socialization rate (p_1). If p_1 is relatively low, period-20 code knowledge declines with increasing turnover. The combination of slow

EXPLORATION & EXPLOITATION IN ORGANIZATIONAL LEARNING   79

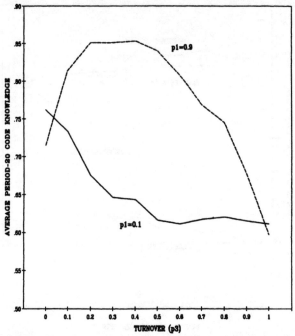

FIGURE 4.   Effect of Turnover (p_3) and Socialization Rate (p_1) on Period-20 Code Knowledge.
$M = 30$; $N = 50$; $p_2 = 0.5$; 80 Iterations.

learning and rapid turnover leads to inadequate exploitation. However, if p_1 is
relatively high, moderate amounts of turnover improve the organizational code.
Rapid socialization of individuals into the procedures and beliefs of an organization
tends to reduce exploration. A modest level of turnover, by introducing less socialized
people, increases exploration, and thereby improves aggregate knowledge. The level
of knowledge reflected by the organizational code is increased, as is the average
individual knowledge of those individuals who have been in the organization for some
time. Note that this effect does not come from the superior knowledge of the average
new recruit. Recruits are, on average, less knowledgeable than the individuals they
replace. The gains come from their diversity.

Turnover, like heterogeneity in learning rates, produces a distribution problem.
Contributions to improving the code (and subsequently individual knowledge) come
from the occasional newcomers who deviate from the code in a favorable way.
Old-timers, on average, know more, but what they know is redundant with knowledge
already reflected in the code. They are less likely to contribute new knowledge on the
margin. Novices know less on average, but what they know is less redundant with the
code and occasionally better, thus more likely to contribute to improving the code.

Effects of environmental turbulence. Since learning processes involve lags in adjustment to changes, the contribution of learning to knowledge depends on the amount
of turbulence in the environment. Suppose that the value of any given dimension of
reality shifts (from 1 to −1 or −1 to 1) in a given time period with probability p_4.

80   JAMES G. MARCH

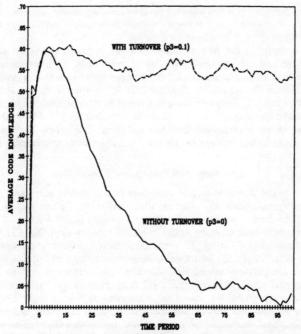

FIGURE 5.   Effect of Turbulence (p_4) on Code Knowledge over Time with and Without Turnover (p_3).
$M = 30$; $N = 50$; $p_1 = 0.5$; $p_2 = 0.5$; $p_4 = 0.02$; 80 Iterations.

This captures in an elementary way the idea that understanding the world may be complicated by turbulence in the world. Exogenous environmental change makes adaptation essential, but it also makes learning from experience difficult (Weick 1979). In the model, the level of knowledge achieved in a particular (relatively early) time period decreases with increasing turbulence.

In addition, mutual learning has a dramatic long-run degenerate property under conditions of exogenous turbulence. As the beliefs of individuals and the code converge, the possibilities for improvement in either decline. Once a knowledge equilibrium is achieved, it is sustained indefinitely. The beliefs reflected in the code and those held by all individuals remain identical and unchanging, regardless of changes in reality. Even before equilibrium is achieved, the capabilities for change fall below the rate of change in the environment. As a result, after an initial period of increasing accuracy, the knowledge of the code and individuals is systematically degraded through changes in reality. Ultimately, the accuracy of belief reaches chance (i.e., where a random change in reality is as likely to increase accuracy of beliefs as it is to decrease it). The process becomes a random walk.

The degeneracy is avoided if there is turnover. Figure 5 plots the average level of code knowledge over time under conditions of turbulence ($p_4 = 0.02$). Two cases of learning are plotted, one without turnover ($p_3 = 0$), the other with moderate turnover ($p_3 = 0.1$). Where there is turbulence without turnover, code knowledge first rises to a moderate level, and then declines to 0, from which it subsequently wanders randomly. With turnover, the degeneracy is avoided and a moderate level of code knowledge is sustained in the face of environmental change. The positive effects of moderate turnover depend, of course, on the rules for selecting new recruits. In the present case, recruitment is not affected by the code. Replacing departing individuals with recruits closer to the current organizational code would significantly reduce the efficiency of turnover as a source of exploration.

Turnover is useful in the face of turbulence, but it produces a disparity between code knowledge and the average knowledge of individuals in the organization. As a result, the match between turnover rate and level of turbulence that is desirable from the point of view of the organization's knowledge is not necessarily desirable from the point of view of the knowledge of every individual in it, or individuals on average. In particular, where there is turbulence, there is considerable individual advantage to having tenure in an organization that has turnover. This seems likely to produce pressures by individuals to secure tenure for themselves while restricting it for others.

3. Knowledge and Ecologies of Competition

The model in the previous section examines one aspect of the social context of adaptation in organizations, the ways in which individual beliefs and an organizational code draw from each other over time. A second major feature of the social context of organizational learning is the competitive ecology within which learning occurs and knowledge is used. External competitive processes pit organizations against each other in pursuit of scarce environmental resources and opportunities. Examples are competition among business firms for customers and governmental subsidies. Internal competitive processes pit individuals in the organization against each other in competition for scarce organizational resources and opportunities. Examples are competition among managers for internal resources and hierarchical promotion. In these ecologies of competition, the competitive consequences of learning by one organization depend on learning by other organizations. In this section, these links among learning, performance, and position in an ecology of competition are discussed by considering some ways in which competitive advantage is affected by the accumulation of knowledge.

Competition and the Importance of Relative Performance

Suppose that an organization's realized performance on a particular occasion is a draw from a probability distribution that can be characterized in terms of some measure of average value (x) and some measure of variability (v). Knowledge, and the learning process that produces it, can be described in terms of their effects on these two measures. A change in an organization's performance distribution that increases average performance (i.e., makes $x' > x$) will often be beneficial to an organization, but such a result is not assured when relative position within a group of competing organizations is important. Where returns to one competitor are not strictly determined by that competitor's own performance but depend on the relative standings of the competitors, returns to changes in knowledge depend not only on the magnitude of the changes in the expected value but also on changes in variability and on the number of competitors.

To illustrate the phenomenon, consider the case of competition for primacy between a reference organization and N other organizations, each having normal performance distributions with mean $= x$ and variance $= v$. The chance of the reference organization having the best performance within a group of identical competitors is $1/(N + 1)$. We compare this situation to one in which the reference organization has a normal performance distribution with mean $= x'$ and variance $= v'$. We evaluate the probability, P^*, that the (x', v') organization will outperform all of the N (x, v) organizations. A performance distribution with a mean of x' and a variance of v' provides a competitive advantage in a competition for primacy if P^* is

82   JAMES G. MARCH

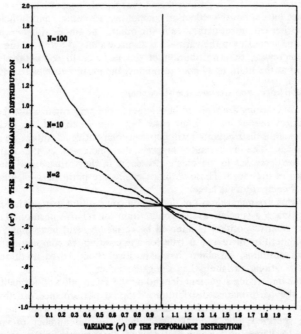

FIGURE 6.   Competitive Equality Lines ($P^* = 1/(N + 1)$) for One ($x'v'$) Organization Competing with N (0, 1) Organizations (Normal Performance Distributions).

greater than $1/(N + 1)$. It results in a competitive disadvantage if P^* is less than $1/(N + 1)$.

If an organization faces only one competitor ($N = 1$), it is easy to see that any advantage in mean performance on the part of the reference organization makes P^* greater than $1/(N + 1) = 0.5$, regardless of the variance. Thus, in bilateral competition involving normal performance distributions, learning that increases the mean always pays off, and changes in the variance—whether positive or negative—have no effect.

The situation changes as N increases. Figure 6 shows the competitive success (failure) of an organization having a normal performance distribution with a mean $= x'$ and a variance $= v'$, when that organization is faced with N identical and independent competitors whose performance distributions are normal with mean $= 0$ and variance $= 1$. Each point in the space in Figure 6 represents a different possible normal performance distribution (x', v'). Each line in the figure is associated with a particular N and connects the (x', v') pairs for which $p^* = 1/(N + 1)$.[2] The area to the right and above a line includes (x', v') combinations for which P^* is greater than $1/(N + 1)$, thus that yield a competitive advantage relative to (0, 1). The area to the left and below a line includes (x', v') combinations for which P^* is less than $1/(N + 1)$, thus that yield a competitive disadvantage relative to (0, 1).

---

[2] The lines are constructed by estimating, for each value of v' from 0 to 2 in steps of 0.05, the value of x' for which $p^* = 1/(N + 1)$. Each estimate is based on 5000 simulations. Since if $x' = 0$ and $v' = 1$, $P^* = 1/(N + 1)$ for any N, each of the lines is constrained to pass through the (0, 1) point.

The pattern is clear. If N is greater than 1 (but finite), increases in either the mean or the variance have a positive effect on competitive advantage, and sufficiently large increases in either can offset decreases in the other. The trade-off between increases in the mean and increases in the variance is strongly affected by N. As the number of competitors increases, the contribution of the variance to competitive advantage increases until at the limit, as N goes to infinity, the mean becomes irrelevant.

Learning, Knowledge, and Competitive Advantage

The effects of learning are realized in changes in the performance distribution. The analysis indicates that if learning increases both the mean and the variance of a normal performance distribution, it will improve competitive advantage in a competition for primacy. The model also suggests that increases in the variance may compensate for decreases in the mean; decreases in the variance may nullify gains from increases in the mean. These variance effects are particularly significant when the number of competitors is large.

The underlying argument does not depend on competition being only for primacy. Such competition is a special case of competition for relative position. The general principle that relative position is affected by variability, and increasingly so as the number of competitors increases, is true for any position. In competition to achieve relatively high positions, variability has a positive effect. In competition to avoid relatively low positions, variability has a negative effect.

Nor does the underlying argument depend on the assumption of normality or other symmetry in the performance distributions. Normal performance distributions are special cases in which the tails of the distribution are specified when the mean and variance are specified. For general distributions, as the number of competitors increases, the likelihood of finishing first depends increasingly on the right-hand tail of the performance distribution, and the likelihood of finishing last depends increasingly on the left-hand tail (David 1981). If learning has different effects on the two tails of the distribution, the right-hand tail effect will be such more important in competition for primacy among many competitors. The left-hand tail will be much more important in competition to avoid finishing last.

Some learning processes increase both average performance and variability. A standard example would be the short-run consequences from adoption of a new technology. If a new technology is so clearly superior as to overcome the disadvantages of unfamiliarity with it, it will offer a higher expected value than the old technology. At the same time, the limited experience with the new technology (relative to experience with the old) will lead to an increased variance. A similar result might be expected with the introduction of a new body of knowledge or new elements of cultural diversity to an organization, for example, through the introduction of individuals with untypical skills, attitudes, ethnicity, or gender.

Learning processes do not necessarily lead to increases in both average performance and variation, however. Increased knowledge seems often to reduce the variability of performance rather than to increase it. Knowledge makes performance more reliable. As work is standardized, as techniques are learned, variability, both in the time required to accomplish tasks and in the quality of task performance, is reduced. Insofar as that increase is reliability comes from a reduction in the left-hand tail, the likelihood of finishing last in a competition among many is reduced without changing the likelihood of finishing first. However, if knowledge has the effect of reducing the right-hand tail of the distribution, it may easily decrease the chance of being best among several competitors even though it also increases average performance. The question is whether you can do exceptionally well, as opposed to better than average, without leaving the confines of conventional action. The answer is complicated, for it depends on a more careful specification of the kind of knowledge involved and its precise effects on the right-hand tail of the distribution. But knowledge that simultaneously increases average performance and its reliability is not a guarantee of competitive advantage.

Consider, for example, the case of modern information and decision technology based on computers. In cases where time is particularly important, information technology has a major effect on the mean, less on the variance. Some problems in environmental scanning for surprises, changes, or opportunities probably fall into such a category. Under such conditions, appropriate use of information technology seems likely to improve competitive position. On the other hand, in many situations the main effect of information technology is to make outcomes more reliable. For example, additional data, or more detailed analyses, seem likely to increase reliability in decisions more rapidly than they will increase their average returns. In such cases, the effects on the tails are likely to dominate the effects on the mean. The net effect of the improved technology on the chance of avoiding being the worst competitor will be positive, but the effect on the chance of finishing at the head of the pack may well be negative.

Similarly, multiple, independent projects may have an advantage over a single, coordinated effort. The average result from independent projects is likely to be lower than that realized from a coordinated one, but their right-hand side variability can compensate for the reduced mean in a competition for primacy. The argument can be extended more generally to the effects of close collaboration or cooperative information exchange. Organizations that develop effective instruments of coordination and communication probably can be expected to do better (on average) than those that are more loosely coupled, and they also probably can be expected to become more reliable, less likely to deviate significantly from the mean of their performance distributions. The price of reliability, however, is a smaller chance of primacy among competitors.

Competition for Relative Position and Strategic Action

The arguments above assume that the several individual performances of competitors are independent draws from a distribution of possible performances, and that the distribution cannot be arbitrarily chosen by the competitors. Such a perspective is incomplete. It is possible to see both the mean and the reliability of a performance distribution (at least partially) as choices made strategically. In the long run, they represent the result of organizational choices between investments in learning and in consumption of the fruits of current capabilities, thus the central focus of this paper. In the short run, the choice of mean can be seen as a choice of effort or attention. By varying effort, an organization selects a performance mean between an entitlement (zero-effort) and a capability (maximum-effort) level. Similarly, in the short run, variations in the reliability of performance can be seen as choices of knowledge or risk that can be set willfully within the range of available alternatives.

These choices, insofar as they are made rationally, will not, in general, be independent of competition. If relative position matters, as the number of competitors increases, strategies for increasing the mean through increased effort or greater knowledge become less attractive relative to strategies for increasing variability. In the more general situation, suppose organizations face competition from numerous competitors who vary in their average capabilities but who can choose their variances. If payoffs and preferences are such that finishing near the top matters a great deal, those organizations with performance distributions characterized by comparatively low means will (if they can) be willing to sacrifice average performance in order to augment the right-hand tails of their performance distributions. In this way, they improve their chances of winning, thus force their more talented competitors to do likewise, and thereby convert the competition into a right-hand tail "race" in which average performance (due to ability and effort) becomes irrelevant. These dynamics comprise powerful countervailing forces to the tendency for experience to eliminate exploration and are a reminder that the learning dominance of exploitation is, under some circumstances, constrained not only by slow learning and turnover but also by reason.

4. Little Models and Old Wisdom

Learning, analysis, imitation, regeneration, and technological change are major components of any effort to improve organizational performance and strengthen competitive advantage. Each involves adaptation and a delicate trade-off between exploration and exploitation. The present argument has been that these trade-offs are affected by their contexts of distributed costs and benefits and ecological interaction. The essence of exploitation is the refinement and extension of existing competences, technologies, and paradigms. Its returns are positive, proximate, and predictable. The essence of exploration is experimentation with new alternatives. Its returns are uncertain, distant, and often negative. Thus, the distance in time and space between the locus of learning and the locus for the realization of returns is generally greater in the case of exploration than in the case of exploitation, as is the uncertainty.

Such features of the context of adaptation lead to a tendency to substitute exploitation of known alternatives for the exploration of unknown ones, to increase the reliability of performance rather more than its mean. This property of adaptive processes is potentially self-destructive. As we have seen, it degrades organizational learning in a mutual learning situation. Mutual learning leads to convergence between organizational and individual beliefs. The convergence is generally useful both for individuals and for an organization. However, a major threat to the effectiveness of such learning is the possibility that individuals will adjust to an organizational code before the code can learn from them. Relatively slow socialization of new organizational members and moderate turnover sustain variability in individual beliefs, thereby improving organizational and average individual knowledge in the long run.

An emphasis on exploitation also compromises competitive position where finishing near the top is important. Knowledge-based increases in average performance can be insufficient to overcome the adverse effects produced by reductions in variability. The ambiguous usefulness of learning in a competitive race is not simply an artifact of representing knowledge in terms of the mean and variance of a normal distribution. The key factor is the effect of knowledge on the right-hand tail of the performance distribution. Thus, in the end, the effects stem from the relation between knowledge and discovery. Michael Polanyi, commenting on one of his contributions to physics, observed (Polanyi 1963, p. 1013) that "I would never have conceived my theory, let alone have made a great effort to verify it, if I had been more familiar with major developments in physics that were taking place. Moreover, my initial ignorance of the powerful, false objections that were raised against my ideas protected those ideas from being nipped in the bud."

These observations do not overturn the renaissance. Knowledge, learning, and education remain as profoundly important instruments of human well-being. At best, the models presented here suggest some of the considerations involved in thinking about choices between exploration and exploitation and in sustaining exploration in the face of adaptive processes that tend to inhibit it. The complexity of the distribution of costs and returns across time and groups makes an explicit determination of optimality a nontrivial exercise. But it may be instructive to reconfirm some elements

86 JAMES G. MARCH

of folk wisdom asserting that the returns to fast learning are not all positive, that rapid socialization may hurt the socializers even as it helps the socialized, that the development of knowledge may depend on maintaining an influx of the naive and ignorant, and that competitive victory does not reliably go to the properly educated.

Acknowledgments

This research has been supported by the Spencer Foundation and the Graduate School of Business, Stanford University. The author is grateful for the assistance of Michael Pich and Suzanne Stout and for the comments of Michael Cohen, Julie Elworth, Thomas Finholt, J. Michael Harrison, J. Richard Harrison, David Matheson, Martin Schulz, Sim Sitkin and Lee Sproull.

References

ARGYRIS, C. AND D. SCHÖN (1978), *Organizational Learning*. Reading, MA: Addison-Wesley.

ARTHUR, W. B. (1984), "Competing Technologies and Economic Prediction," *IIASA Options*, 2, 10–13.

ASHBY, W. R. (1960), *Design for a Brain*. (2nd ed.). New York: Wiley.

COHEN, M. D. (1986), "Artificial Intelligence and the Dynamic Performance of Organizational Designs," in J. G. March and R. Weissinger-Baylon (Eds.), *Ambiguity and Command: Organizational Perspectives on Military Decision Making*. Boston, MA: Ballinger, 53–71.

CYERT, R. M. AND J. G. MARCH (1963), *A Behavioral Theory of the Firm*. Englewood Cliffs, NJ: Prentice Hall.

DAVID, H. A. (1981), *Order Statistics*. (2nd ed.). New York: John Wiley.

DAVID, P. A. (1985), "Clio and the Economics of QWERTY," *American Economic Review*, 75, 332–337.

——— (1990), "The Hero and the Herd in Technological History: Reflections on Thomas Edison and 'The Battle of the Systems'," in P. Higgonet and H. Rosovsky (Eds.), *Economic Development Past and Present: Opportunities and Constraints*. Cambridge, MA: Harvard University Press.

——— AND J. A. BUNN (1988), "The Economics of Gateway Technologies and Network Evolution," *Information Economics and Policy*, 3, 165–202.

DAY, R. H. (1967), "Profits, Learning, and the Convergence of Satisficing to Marginalism," *Quarterly Journal of Economics*, 81, 302–311.

HANNAN, M. T. AND J. FREEMAN (1987), "The Ecology of Organizational Foundings: American Labor Unions, 1836-1985," *American Journal of Sociology*, 92, 910–943.

HERRIOTT, S. R., D. A. LEVINTHAL AND J. G. MARCH (1985), "Learning from Experience in Organizations," *American Economic Review*, 75, 298–302.

HEY, J. D. (1982), "Search for Rules for Search," *Journal of Economic Behavior and Organization*, 3, 65–81.

HOLLAND, J. H. (1975), *Adaptation in Natural and Artificial Systems*. Ann Arbor, MI: University of Michigan Press.

KAHNEMAN, D. AND A. TVERSKY (1979), "Prospect Theory: An Analysis of Decision under Risk," *Econometrica*, 47, 263–291.

KATZ, M. L. AND C. SHAPIRO (1986), "Technology Adoption in the Presence of Network Externalities," *Journal of Political Economy*, 94, 822–841.

KURAN, T. (1988), "The Tenacious Past: Theories of Personal and Collective Conservatism," *Journal of Economic Behavior and Organization*, 10, 143–171.

LEVINTHAL, D. A. AND J. G. MARCH (1981), "A Model of Adaptive Organizational Search," *Journal of Economic Behavior and Organization*, 2, 307–333.

LEVITT, B. AND J. G. MARCH (1988), "Organizational Learning," *Annual Review of Sociology*, 14, 319–340.

LOUNAMAA, P. H. AND J. G. MARCH (1987), "Adaptive Coordination of a Learning Team," *Management Science*, 33, 107–123.

MARCH, J. G. (1988), "Variable Risk Preferences and Adaptive Aspirations," *Journal of Economic Behavior and Organization*, 9, 5–24.

POLANYI, M. (1963). "The Potential Theory of Adsorption: Authority in Science Has Its Uses and Its Dangers," *Science*, 141, 1010–1013.

RADNER, R. AND M. ROTHSCHILD (1975), "On the Allocation of Effort," *Journal of Economic Theory*, 10, 358–376.

SCHUMPETER, J. A. (1934), *The Theory of Economic Development*. Cambridge. MA: Harvard University Press.

SIMON, H. A. (1955), "A Behavioral Model of Rational Choice," *Quarterly Journal of Economics*, 69, 99–118.

Strategic Management II

VAN MAANEN, J. (1973), "Observations on the Making of Policemen," *Human Organization*, 32, 407–418.
WEICK, K. E. (1979), *The Social Psychology of Organizing.* (2nd ed.). Reading, MA: Addison-Wesley.
WHYTE, W. H., JR. (1957), *The Organization Man*. Garden City, NY: Doubleday.
WINTER, S. G. (1971), "Satisficing, Selection, and the Innovating Remnant," *Quarterly Journal of Economics*, 85, 237–261,

[16]

© Academy of Management Journal
1994, Vol. 37, No. 5, 1141–1166.

ORGANIZATIONAL TRANSFORMATION AS PUNCTUATED EQUILIBRIUM: AN EMPIRICAL TEST

ELAINE ROMANELLI
Georgetown University
MICHAEL L. TUSHMAN
Columbia University

The punctuated equilibrium model of organizational transformation has emerged as a prominent theoretical framework for explaining fundamental changes in patterns of organizational activity. To date, however, few aspects of the model have been tested formally. We tested three basic arguments of the model using data on U.S. minicomputer producers. Supportive results showed that (1) a large majority of organizational transformations were accomplished via rapid and discontinuous change over most or all domains of organizational activity, (2) small changes in strategies, structures, and power distributions did not accumulate to produce fundamental transformations, and (3) major environmental changes and chief executive officer succession influenced transformations.

The punctuated equilibrium model of organizational transformation (e.g., Gersick, 1991; Miller & Friesen, 1980a, 1984; Tushman & Romanelli, 1985) has recently emerged as a prominent theoretical framework for characterizing and investigating fundamental organizational change. As described by its proponents, punctuated equilibrium theory depicts organizations as evolving through relatively long periods of stability (equilibrium periods) in their basic patterns of activity that are punctuated by relatively short bursts of fundamental change (revolutionary periods). Revolutionary periods substantively disrupt established activity patterns and install the basis for new equilibrium periods. Gersick (1991) described the largely independent emergence of punctuated equilibrium models over a number of social and physical science disciplines, including biology (e.g., Gould, 1989), sociology (Kuhn, 1970), and psychology (Levinson, 1986), and at several levels of analysis in organizational theory, such as groups (Gersick,

---

We are grateful to Howard Aldrich, Sarah Freeman, Connie Gersick, Christopher Gresov, Heather Haveman, Katherine Lyman, Kaye Schoonhoven, and the reviewers of the *Academy of Management Journal* for comments and suggestions on earlier drafts. The research was supported by the Center for Strategic Management, Columbia University, and a grant from the National Science Foundation.

1988, 1989) and organizations (Miller & Friesen, 1980a, 1984; Tushman & Romanelli, 1985).

Despite the growing prominence and pervasiveness of punctuated equilibrium theory, little research has explored the empirical validity of the model's basic arguments. A few case histories have supported the idea that fundamental transformations occur according to patterns predicted by the model. For example, Tushman, Newman, and Romanelli (1986) examined the life histories of four organizations, AT&T, General Radio, Citibank, and Prime Computers, and described a progression of equilibrium periods during which organizational systems, structures, and strategies were consistently reinforced toward increasing coherence with the organizations' basic missions. The equilibrium periods were punctuated by very brief periods of intense and pervasive change, culminating in the formulation of new missions and the initiation of new equilibrium periods. Bartunek (1984) described repeated failures of a religious order to accomplish fundamental transformation until both the structure and the interpretive schemes of the organization were rapidly and dramatically revised.

Other studies have explored some of the correlates and consequences of revolutionary transformation. For example, Lant and Mezias (1992) linked the punctuated equilibrium model to processes of organizational learning that accounted for tensions between the forces for stability and change that generate revolutionary transformations. Miller and Friesen (1982, 1984) showed that organizations that radically and quickly altered their formal structures, decision-making routines, and information-processing devices performed better over their lives than organizations that changed gradually or incrementally. Similarly, Virany, Tushman, and Romanelli (1992) showed that organizations that accomplished transformations discontinuously and in response to basic changes in their environments performed better over their lives than organizations that were either never transformed or were transformed excessively without the clear stimulus of environmental change.

Although case histories have supported the descriptive validity of the punctuated equilibrium theory, and though tests of the antecedents and consequences of fundamental transformation have offered important insights into its processes and practical outcomes, no study has tested the model directly. At its heart, punctuated equilibrium is a theoretical explanation for how organizations will typically accomplish fundamental transformation. Critical empirical questions regarding the frequency with which organizations undergo fundamental transformations according to patterns predicted by the punctuated equilibrium model remain unanswered. In this study, we sought to fill that empirical gap.

THEORY AND HYPOTHESES

Punctuated equilibrium models first and foremost enable predictions about patterns of fundamental organizational transformation. Proponents of the general theory argue that the common state of organizational activity is one of stability or equilibrium. Organizations establish an initial pattern of activity (Boeker, 1988; Eisenhardt & Schoonhoven, 1990; Selznick, 1949; Stinchcombe, 1965), based on the environmental conditions prevailing and the managerial decisions made during their time of founding. Then, as a result of inertia (Hannan & Freeman, 1984) and institutionalization (Meyer & Rowan, 1977; Scott, 1987; Zucker, 1988), organizations develop coherent systems of shared understandings that support continuation of the established patterns. According to the punctuated equilibrium model, radical and discontinuous change of all or most organizational activities is necessary to break the grip of strong inertia. Thus, the first and principal hypothesis of the punctuated equilibrium model is that the pattern of fundamental organizational transformation is one of radical, brief, and pervasive change.

> Hypothesis 1: Organizational transformations will most frequently occur in short, discontinuous bursts of change involving most or all key domains of organizational activity.

As Gersick (1991) discussed, punctuated equilibrium theorists typically contrast their prediction of discontinuous and pervasive transformation with a view of nonrevolutionary, or gradual, incremental transformation. For example, Miller and Friesen, following Cyert and March (1963), characterized the nonrevolutionary view as depicting "individual subunits of organizations dealing incrementally and disjointedly with one problem and one goal at a time while emphasizing short-run reaction to short-run feedback" (1984: 222). Nonrevolutionary views of organizational transformation thus emphasize the relative independence of organizational subunits as managers seek to adapt to changes in their local internal and external environments. Over time, as subunits repeatedly alter their goals and relationships to local environments, the organization as a whole becomes transformed. Nonrevolutionary views suggest that fundamental organizational transformations can be observed by comparing organizational activity patterns over distant points in time, though no specific transforming event may be identifiable. Miller and Friesen associated the gradual transformation perspective with familiar arguments from policy theorists (e.g., Lindblom, 1959; Hedberg, Nystrom, & Starbuck, 1976; Quinn, 1980) about the potential efficacy of incremental change but noted that such arguments merely assume the prevalence of incremental change processes.

Punctuated equilibrium theorists, by contrast, stress the interdependence of organizational subunits. Following Khandwalla (1973) and Mintzberg (1979), Miller and Friesen argued that organizations "must be constructed so as to ensure a complementary alignment among structural variables" (1982: 870). Similarly, building on arguments from population ecology (e.g., Hannan & Freeman, 1984) and institutional theory (e.g., Tolbert & Zucker, 1983; Zucker, 1988), we concluded in an earlier work that organizations develop "webs of interdependent relationships with buyers, suppliers, and financial backers ... and patterns of culture, norms, and ideology" (Tushman & Romanelli, 1985: 177) that legally and normatively constrain organizations to an ongoing commitment to established activities and relationships. Finally, Gersick described "organizational deep structure" (1991: 14) as a system of interrelated organizational parts that is maintained by mutual dependencies among the parts and with competitive, regulatory, and technological systems outside the organization that reinforce the legitimacy of managerial choices that produced the parts.

According to this view, the result of interdependence is not cascading adaptation over related organizational subunits, but rather resistance to change as subunit managers seek to maintain a complex network of commitments and relationships. Resistance to change is critical to punctuated equilibrium theory in that it establishes the key condition that supports revolutionary transformation as the principal means by which organizations can accomplish transformation. Resistance to change prevents small changes in organizational subunits from taking hold or substantially influencing activities in related subunits. Thus,

> Hypothesis 2: Small changes in individual domains of organizational activity will not accumulate incrementally to yield a fundamental transformation.

Finally, punctuated equilibrium theorists have addressed the question of how organizational transformation can be stimulated. Especially since the theory posits strong inertia as the common state of organizational affairs, consideration of how such inertia can be broken or disrupted is critical. Severe crisis in the performance of an organization, major changes in its environment, and succession of its chief executive officer have been posited as forces potentially strong enough to overcome inertia and to stimulate fundamental organizational transformation.

Numerous studies have explored the influence of organizational performance on fundamental transformation. For example, Oster (1982) and Boeker (1989) showed that organizations tend to persist in established activity patterns when performance is good or improving. Harrigan (1980) and D'Aveni (1989) showed that organizations tend to alter their activities principally when performance is poor or declining. Although declines in organizational performance may challenge the legitimacy of established courses of action, several authors (e.g., Hambrick & D'Aveni, 1988; Staw, Sandelands, & Dutton, 1981) have noted that incumbent management teams may tend to minimize the importance of performance declines or seek to explain them optimistically in terms of a need for greater commitment of resources. We have thus previously argued (Tushman & Romanelli, 1985) that only large or long-sustained declines in performance are likely to trigger fundamental organizational transformations.

> Hypothesis 3: *Major declines in the short-term perfor-*
> *mance of an organization or sustained declines over sev-*
> *eral years will substantially increase the likelihood of*
> *revolutionary transformation.*

Much attention has been paid to the influence of major environmental change on the likelihood of organizational transformation. Indeed, the literature on the effects of changes in the demand for an organization's product (e.g., Delacroix & Swaminathan, 1991; Miles & Cameron, 1982), technological innovation (e.g., Abernathy & Utterback, 1978), changes in environmental uncertainty, complexity, and turbulence (Keats & Hitt, 1988; Meyer, 1982; Meyer, Brooks, & Goes, 1990; Miner, Amburgey, & Stearns, 1990), and changes in institutional conditions (Mezias, 1990; Oliver, 1991; Tolbert & Zucker, 1983) is one of the richest in organization theory. Although most of these studies have not distinguished among degrees or types of organizational transformation, all have generally predicted a positive relationship between changes in environmental conditions and organizational change. Studies by Meyer and his colleagues (Meyer, 1982; Meyer et al., 1990) have directly explored the influence on revolutionary change of "environmental jolts," discontinuous changes that dramatically alter the competitive and operating conditions of an environment. Through longitudinal analysis of the hospital industry, these researchers concluded that environmental jolts do tend to provoke crises in organizations that facilitate revolutionary transformation.

> Hypothesis 4: *Major changes in environmental conditions*
> *will significantly increase the likelihood of revolutionary*
> *transformation.*

Finally, chief executive officer (CEO) succession, even in the absence of performance declines or major environmental change, should increase the likelihood of organizational transformation (Tushman & Romanelli, 1985). Fundamental organizational transformation requires not only a vision of the type of transformation that will promote organizational interests but also an opportunity for instigating transformations. New chief executive officers, especially those who come from outside organizations (Helmich & Brown, 1972), stand uncommitted to the strategies and policies established by their predecessors. Moreover, their information and experience may lead them to have different understandings of effective or appropriate organizational actions than their predecessors had (Dearborn & Simon, 1985). Finally, new CEOs often begin work in an atmosphere of expectancy about change. The periods closely following their installation provide the best opportunity for signaling that new regimes are in place (Gabarro, 1987).

> Hypothesis 5: *Installation of a new chief executive officer*
> *will significantly increase the likelihood of revolutionary*
> *transformation.*

1146   *Academy of Management Journal*   October

METHODS

Data and Setting

This study examined the life histories of 25 minicomputer producers that were founded in the United States over a three-year period, 1967 through 1969. The firms studied represent 54.4 percent of the 46 minicomputer producers that were founded during this period, which covers the peak of founding activities in the minicomputer segment of the computer industry. The group of firms was selected to maximize organizational similarities on dimensions of organizational age and the environmental characteristics that the organizations faced both during founding and later in their lives. We considered such similarity to be critical for ruling out alternative explanations for patterns in organizational transformation that might be observed. All 46 companies were founded as single-product manufacturers of minicomputers with initial market and distribution targets restricted to the United States. We chose the 25 companies on the basis of the availability of data regarding their products, markets, strategies, structures, and the composition of their executive teams over their lives. Since all 25 companies were publicly traded early in their lives, substantial information about their activities was available from public documents. Detailed, longitudinal data about organizations' activities were critical to ensuring that we would discover all transformations, whether revolutionary or nonrevolutionary.

These sampling procedures may have limited the generalizability of our findings to firms founded during the high-growth period of technology-based industries and acquiring early public funding. For this study, however, we were principally concerned that enough data be available on a large enough number of firms competing over time in the same general environment to ensure the discovery of fundamental transformations, whether revolutionary or nonrevolutionary. Threats to generalizability are considered in the discussion section of this article.

Domains of Organizational Activity

Investigation of organizational transformation as a discontinuous event involving most or all domains of organizational activity requires measuring organizational characteristics over several different domains. As McKelvey (1982) and Freeman (1982) noted, domains should also be selected on the basis of their importance to organizational survival and centrality to an organization's core competencies (Prahalad & Hamel, 1990). We take it as axiomatic that organizations are changing in some ways virtually every day. The study of organizational transformation as a process or outcome that is distinct from routine replacements of personnel, normal improvements of equipment and control processes, and regular changes in customer composition requires that we explore domains in which substantial change can systematically alter the overall pattern of organizational activity.

In our earlier work on organizational transformation (Tushman & Romanelli, 1985), we identified five domains of organizational activity—

organizational culture, strategy, structure, power distributions, and control systems—that met the criteria of being important to organizational survival and central to organizational activities. In developing these domains we drew on Zald's (1970) matrix of organizational activities, framed by internal and external orientations and by social and economic objectives. These domains are highly similar to other characterizations of core organizational activities that have appeared in the literature. For example, Hannan and Freeman (1984) defined organizational forms in terms of stated goals, forms of authority, core technology, and marketing strategy, including both product characteristics and types of markets targeted. Mintzberg (1979) described five basic parts of organizations: the strategic apex, the technostructure, the middle line, the support staff, and the operating core. Thus, as these domains appear generally in the literature as characteristic of organizations' fundamental activity patterns, we think they are appropriate for studying organizational transformation.

The study of organizational transformation also demands that measures of organizational activities be taken frequently over organizations' lives. We collected data on organizational cultures, strategies, structures, power distributions, and control systems for all years of the organizations' lives from a variety of sources, including 10-K forms required by the Securities and Exchange Commission, annual reports, prospectuses, and industry and business press reports. Detailed information about strategies, structures, and power distributions was available for all organizations in the study group throughout their lives. However, the organizations reported information about cultures and control systems infrequently and inconsistently. Thus, we dropped the culture and control system domains of activity from further analysis.

Because some of our information about organizational strategies, structures, and power distributions came from stories reported in the industry and business press and other information came from descriptions and interpretations of events described in company documents, some of the information was more objective than the rest. Accordingly, we used different methods to characterize activities occurring over the organizations' lives and to identify important changes. In the following sections, we discuss the qualitative and objective methods used for identifying substantial change in the strategies, structures, and power distributions of the organizations. Examination of the similarity of findings derived by these two methods provides a basis for ensuring the validity of measures of change by either method.

Qualitative Measures of Changes in Activity Domains

A rich base of "stories" about organizational activities was available from business press articles, 10-K forms, annual reports, and prospectuses. Two independent coding teams developed company histories from these sources. One coding team (four individuals) mined documents prepared by the firms themselves. The other coding team (two individuals) considered information from business press articles and other noncompany publications. We divided the information sources in this way because we were concerned about biases in information, particularly from firm-generated documents.

Each coder was instructed to organize materials in chronological order and to write objective, year-by-year event histories of the firms. For this portion of the coding, we did not specify any precise meanings of strategy, structure, or power distribution. Coders were simply told to record, as fully and objectively as possible, everything that happened to or that was discussed by the firms. For a few of the firms, coders exchanged documents and wrote independent histories. No differences in the event histories were observed, either between coders or between different document sources.

Only when the objective histories were completed was any attempt made to organize and interpret the information. Three individuals, who were coders of only some of the objective histories, reviewed the event histories and noted all changes in strategies, structures, and power distributions that appeared to represent substantial changes in organizational activities. For this phase of the research, we employed specific definitions.

Strategy changes. Changes in strategy were coded whenever companies introduced or abandoned either major new lines of minicomputers or non-minicomputer product lines such as software systems, peripherals, mainframes, or microcomputers. A strategy change was also coded if a company entered or abandoned an important market segment, shifting, for instance, from original equipment manufacturers as principal customers to end users. For example, Data General began marketing minicomputers directly to end users in 1972, an activity that substantially deviated from its prior and publicly stated emphasis on sales to original equipment manufacturers. Rolm Corporation initiated a major product reorientation in 1976 when it began marketing computerized telephone switching equipment in addition to its traditional "ruggedized" minicomputers for severe environments. We considered movements into or out of major product lines and changes in principal customer targets to be important strategic changes on the basis of companies' own discussions of such movements as representing substantial shifts in market targets and activities.

Structure changes. Changes in structure were coded whenever business press articles or company documents reported a general reorganization of a firm, from, for instance, a functional to a divisional structure, or major changes in centralization or decentralization. For example, Datapoint decentralized its sales and research operations in 1976 by establishing a network of sales offices and research laboratories throughout the United States. In 1974, Computer Automation abandoned its traditional, engineering-dominated functional structure in favor of a product divisional structure supporting its diversifying product line.

Power distribution changes. Changes in power distributions were coded whenever an organization experienced a high turnover of senior executives or when additions to an executive team reflected a shift in the functional orientation of a firm—for instance, from emphasis on research and development to emphasis on sales and marketing. For example, when Microdata began manufacturing, as opposed to licensing, its minicomputer designs in 1970, a number of new executives were installed to handle not only the production function but also the new requirement for marketing expertise. Additions to the executive team were accompanied by exits of other executives whose expertise had addressed R&D almost exclusively. The new executives publicly discussed these changes as indicative of a major new strategic orientation.

It should be noted that we did not code CEO successions as indicators of major shifts in power distributions. This decision was made for two reasons. First, as numerous succession studies (e.g., Carlson, 1962; Helmich & Brown, 1972; Gabarro, 1987) have shown, CEO succession often precedes changes in the composition of the executive team as well as the balance of power over various functional and divisional domains of activity. Hypothesis 5 in this research explicitly predicts that CEO succession can be an important triggering event for organizational transformation. Second, as Mintzberg and Waters (1982) described, major changes in power distributions can occur even in the absence of a CEO change. Thus, we considered that shifts in power distributions should be counted toward organizational transformations only when an executive team, minus the CEO, and its collective expertise were substantially altered.

For any year in which a substantial change on any of these dimensions was observed, a 1 was coded in the appropriate category for the particular year; otherwise, a 0 was coded. Coders agreed on the majority (87%) of classifications. Disagreements were usually resolved in favor of coding a change since no objective criterion existed for determining substantialness. Changes and nonchanges in the strategy, structure, and power distribution domains were coded for all years of the organizations' lives except for their first years of existence and the last years of acquired or failed firms. No substantial change or transformation can reasonably occur during the first year of an organization's life. And significant changes during the last year of a failed or acquired firm's existence probably reflect closing out operations or transferring assets more than they reflect substantial change in activities.

On the basis of these data, a total of 149 substantial changes were identified out of a possible 669 over all 25 organizations. We calculated the total number of possible changes by multiplying the number of years of a firm's life (minus the first and last years) by three, the number of core activity domains being considered. Over all companies, the average number of substantial changes per year was .223 (s.d. = .416). The minimum number of substantial changes exhibited by a firm was 0; the maximum was 17.

Objective Measures of Changes in Activity Domains

Qualitative measures of organizational changes yield a rich picture of organizational histories, but we were concerned that all significant changes might not have been observed for all companies. Some companies (e.g., Microdata, Viatron) were written about often and at length in the business press; other companies were mentioned only infrequently or very briefly. It was possible the qualitative data indicated that some firms exhibited few or no changes on the different dimensions of organizational activity simply because less information was available. Thus, we developed objective measurements of the firms' strategies, structures, and power distributions from information consistently available for all companies and used these measurements separately to identify substantial changes.

Strategy changes. Four measures of substantial change in organizational strategy were defined. First, consistent with the qualitative measures, strategy change was coded whenever a company entered or exited a non-minicomputer product line, such as peripherals or microcomputers. Major product line listings for all companies were reported annually in the *Computer Directory and Buyers' Guide*. For the years 1957 through 1981, entries and exits were coded (0 = no entry or exit, 1 = entry or exit) for the year in which a line first appeared or disappeared from the lists. Second, substantial change was coded whenever a company shifted its basic market orientation from original equipment manufacturers (OEMs) to end users, or vice versa. Companies formally reported categories of customer segments, which included OEMs as a separate category, to describe the range of their customer markets. Shifts into or out of an OEM customer segment were coded (0 = no shift, 1 = shift) for the year in which the original equipment manufacturer category was either first indicated or was eliminated.

Although these measures capture the basic product and market orientations of the minicomputer producers, they do not indicate variation in the organizations' strategies for designing and marketing minicomputers themselves. Thus, following procedures described in Romanelli (1989), we also coded changes in the market breadth and market aggressiveness of the organizations' minicomputer strategies. Market breadth was measured as the number of distinct applications segments in which a company competed. The companies competed in six segments—scientific and engineering laboratories, industrial automation and process control, communications, distributed data processing, small business, and severe environments—over the period of the study. Market aggressiveness was measured as the number of distinct product lines offered, independent of the number of markets addressed. Minicomputer product lines were differentiated on the basis of fundamental system architecture as indicated in documents prepared by International Data Corporation. No significant correlation was found between measures of market aggressiveness and breadth; minicomputer producers varied widely in their tendencies to offer many different product lines to a single market segment or to offer a single product line to many segments. Change in market breadth was coded as the number of markets entered plus the number of markets exited over the total remaining number of markets in which a company operated. Change in market aggressiveness was coded as the number of product lines added plus the number of lines eliminated over the remaining number of product lines offered. For both variables, we considered additions and deletions to be representative of change since both clearly necessitate substantial reallocations of resources.

Structure changes. Changes in organizational structure were measured using titles of senior executives as basic indicators. Titles were classified as general management where no specific functional or divisional responsibilities were indicated (for instance, president, treasurer, comptroller); as functional where no product- or geographic-specific responsibilities were attached (e.g., vice president of research and development, sales manager); and as divisional if a product or geographical division was indicated (e.g., vice president, Western United States, or vice president, airlines reservations systems). We used two measures of organizational structure based on yearly data on ratios of executive titles: (1) the number of general management titles relative to the total number of executives and (2) the number of functional titles relative to the number of functional and divisional titles. These measures reflect the extent to which organizations organized on a functional or a divisional basis and, given some emphasis on one or the other type, the extent to which functional or divisional concerns were dominant. Changes in organizational structure were measured as the absolute value of percentage increases or decreases in the executive title ratios.

Power distribution changes. Changes in power distributions were coded in three ways. First, turnover in a company's executive team was measured as the number of new executives plus the number of executives eliminated over the total number of executives remaining. We considered both additions and deletions to an executive team to represent change since remaining executives will be aware of, and presumably respond to, both the presence of new members and the absence of old. Second, to assess the relative power of research and development concerns over marketing and sales concerns, or vice versa, we calculated percentage changes in the ratio between research expenditures and the total of research expenditures and marketing and sales expenditures. Finally, we calculated changes in the ratio between the number of research executive titles and the total number of titles in research plus titles in marketing and sales. Minicomputer organizations, like companies in many other technology-based industries, struggle routinely with the relative sways that R&D and marketing and sales should hold over strategic decisions. Thus, shifts in the proportion of expenditures and executive titles over these domains seemed to offer good measures of shifts in organizational power distributions.

Table 1 presents descriptive statistics for all the strategy, structure, and power distribution variables that were measured objectively. As described above, some of the measures used to identify substantial change were categorical, such as entry into or exit from a non-minicomputer product line. For these measures, substantial change was coded whenever the indicated event occurred. Other measures, however, such as minicomputer product line change and executive team turnover, are continuous, and no objective criterion could be established to determine how substantial a change was. To

1152 *Academy of Management Journal* October

TABLE 1
Descriptive Statistics and Pearson Correlations, Objective Measures[a]

Variables	Means	s.d.	1	2	3	4	5	6	7	8
Measures of strategic change										
1. Entries/exits: Non-minicomputer products	.18	.39								
2. OEM–end user shifts[b]	.06	.23	.15							
3. Percent change in market aggressiveness	.15	.27	.15	.04						
4. Percent change in market breadth	.08	.24	.21	.22	.33					
Measures of structure change										
5. Percent change in general management titles	.19	.23	.05	−.01	.09	−.03				
6. Percent change in functional titles	.12	.26	.15	−.03	.02	−.05	.03			
Measures of change in power distributions										
7. Executive team turnover	.33	.44	.10	.04	.03	.11	.07	.01		
8. Percent change in R&D expenditures	.18	.25	−.04	−.05	−.01	−.06	−.01	−.07	−.03	
9. Percent change in R&D titles	.19	.33	.09	.08	.04	.01	.28	−.01	−.11	.15

[a] Ns vary between 156 and 225 according to data availability—some companies, for example, did not always separate R&D and other expenditures.
[b] OEM is "original equipment manufacturer."

obtain a first estimate of substantial change, we simply classified all year-to-year changes at four levels of percentage change (30, 40, 50, and 60 percent). Results regarding the number of substantial changes over the three activity domains and patterns in organizational transformation, which rely on these data, will be presented for all criterion levels. This approach supports analysis of the sensitivity of our findings to different assumptions about substantial change. Table 2 shows the number of substantial changes identified by both qualitative and objective methods, the latter at each of the four change-criterion levels.

Table 2 also shows the mean number of substantial changes observed over all activity domains for each of the measurement types. Not surprisingly, the mean number of changes per year was highest for changes measured objectively at the 30 percent criterion level. Even at this level, however, change in any domain occurred relatively rarely, at the rate of .390 changes per year. As discussed above, theoretical interest in the topic of organizational transformation hinges conceptually on a distinction between routine and revolutionary organizational changes. This finding suggests that our measures captured relatively major changes in the strategies, structures, and power distributions of the organizations.

We noted earlier that one advantage of using both qualitative and objective measures is the opportunity that is gained for assessing their agreement. Since the two procedures were almost completely independent in terms of the coders and kinds of data used, substantial agreement between qualitative and objective measures would indicate that important organizational changes were being measured reliably. To assess the degree of agreement between qualitative and objective measures, we simply counted the number of times that the measures agreed for each year of a company's existence. Agreements were counted separately for each of the four criterion levels and then calculated as proportions of the total number of possible agreements for each company. We then averaged these proportions over all the companies studied to arrive at the average proportion of agreements shown in Table 3.

As Table 3 shows, agreement between qualitative and objective measures was quite high for all four criterion levels, ranging from an average proportion of .808 (s.d. = .119) at the 30 percent criterion level to .872 (s.d. = .103) at the 60 percent criterion level. Apparently, the qualitative and objective measures of substantial change in domain activities largely captured the same information. Thus, we were confident that our procedures for measuring organizational transformations were based on reliable indicators of substantial change in domain activities.

Identifying Organizational Transformations

Fundamental organizational transformations were coded as occurring whenever substantial changes were observed in the strategy, structure, and power distribution domains of organizational activity. No restriction was imposed for the length of time over which substantial changes had to be observed over all three domains. For example, if a company exhibited a significant change in strategy during year 3 of its existence, a structure change in year 9, and a power distribution change in year 12, we counted the firm as having completed a transformation in its 12th year. Whenever a

TABLE 2
Frequencies of Substantive Change by Domain and Type of Measure

Variables	Qualitative Measures	Objective Criterion Levels			
		60%	50%	40%	30%
Strategy changes	61	57	74	75	90
Structure changes	35	17	37	39	61
Power distribution changes	53	53	69	86	110
Total number of changes	149	127	180	200	261
Mean number of changes annually	.223	.190	.269	.299	.390
Standard deviation	.416	.392	.444	.458	.488

TABLE 3
Average Proportion of Agreement Between Qualitative and Objective Measures

Agreement	Objective Criterion Levels			
	60%	50%	40%	30%
Mean	.872	.869	.868	.808
Standard deviation	.10	.10	.10	.12

transformation was identified in this manner, we restarted the count of substantial changes.

A revolutionary transformation was coded as occurring whenever changes in all three strategy, structure, and power distributions occurred within any two-year time period. A more stringent criterion for classifying transformations would require that changes occur in all three domains in a single year. The majority of the revolutionary transformations observed, defined by either qualitative or objective measures, in fact did occur within single years. However, because some of the data were presented for corporate fiscal years and some for calendar years, the two-year criterion seemed best.

Nonrevolutionary transformations were identified in two ways. First, following the procedures described above, we coded a nonrevolutionary transformation as having occurred whenever there were substantial changes over a period longer than two years. This measure permitted direct examination of the frequency of revolutionary and nonrevolutionary transformations in which the components of change were entirely comparable except in the timing of their occurrence. We also wished to examine, however, whether nonrevolutionary transformations might be observed through the accumulation over time of even very small changes in the activity domains. Thus, we also coded a nonrevolutionary transformation whenever changes in each of the three activity domains accumulated to 30 percent through addition of multiple small annual changes and when all three domains exhibited this level of change. For this approach, the count of small annual changes was halted whenever a one-year change of at least 30 percent was encountered.

Counting toward accumulation was begun again immediately after the occurrence of a large annual change.

Measures of Extrasystemic Pressures for Transformation

We coded three measures of extrasystemic pressure to investigate the possibility that organizational transformations typically occur when organizations are facing crises resulting from declines in performance or major changes in environmental conditions, or when a CEO succession has recently occurred.

Performance crisis. Organizational performance was measured as the percentage change in a firm's market share over successive annual periods. Crisis was coded whenever the market share percentage change was − .42 or lower, a level representing the lowest 10th percentile of market share changes over all firms for all years. The data were coded as a dummy variable (0 = crisis, 1 = no crisis). Market share data were available for all firms for all years of their lives from information compiled in the *EDP Industry Report*, published by International Data Corporation. This publication supplies monthly information on the number and prices of all minicomputer models marketed by all producers. We calculated market share by contrasting each firm's minicomputer sales with the total number of minicomputers sold by all competitors. Although market share does not directly specify profitability, it does indicate the relative strengths and ongoing viability of organizations' competitive positions. Thus, we considered a substantial decline in market share to constitute an organizational crisis.

Major environmental changes. Major changes in environmental conditions were coded as dummy variables (1 = major change, 0 = no major change) to test the effect of environmental change on the likelihood of organizational transformation. Three major shifts, occurring during 1971, 1976, and 1980, seemed severe enough to pose a crisis for competing organizations. Previous research (Romanelli & Tushman, 1986; Tushman & Anderson, 1986) contains detailed discussions of the major environmental changes that occurred in the minicomputer industry during those years. Thus, we only briefly characterize the periods here. The year 1971 presented the first serious challenge to minicomputer producers since the industry's inception in 1957. Previous steep increases in the rate of organizational foundings, rapid changes in basic minicomputer technology, and steep declines in competitive concentration gave way to a stable technological design, a dramatic decline in the organizational birth rate, and a stabilization of competitive concentration. Perhaps most important, venture capital dried up and public markets for funds tightened severely. We have described (Romanelli & Tushman, 1986) 1971 as the first period of shakeout and consolidation experienced in this industry. The year 1976 showed a sharp increase in both the failure rates of minicomputer producers and four- and eight-firm concentration ratios. This was the first year in which sales of desktop computers made a dent in overall computer sales. Traditional minicomputer markets were also beginning to be squeezed by the introduction of superminis, 32-bit minicomputers; the previous standard had been the 16-bit minicomputer. Demand for minicomputers continued to increase throughout the mid-1970s, but the rate of increase began to slow substantially in 1976. Finally, 1980 exhibited the first absolute decline ever in the sales of minicomputers. Only one new firm was founded in 1980. Four-firm concentration ratios increased to almost 75 percent of minicomputer sales. Industry analysts and executives alike began to hail the end of the traditional minicomputer market.

CEO succession. Succession of a CEO was coded as a dummy variable (1 = a year in which a CEO was replaced, 0 = otherwise) to test the effect of succession on the likelihood of organizational transformation.

RESULTS

Hypothesis 1 predicts that organizational transformations most frequently follow the patterns described in the punctuated equilibrium model, occurring as short, discontinuous bursts of change over most or all domains of organizational activity. Table 4 shows the number of transformations identified and classified as revolutionary and nonrevolutionary according to the methods described above. As shown, whether measured qualitatively or objectively and calculated at any level of percentage change, revolutionary transformations outnumbered nonrevolutionary transformations by at least six to one. Hypothesis 1 is clearly supported. Organizational transformations occurred most frequently according to the patterns described by the punctuated equilibrium model.

Although these results were striking in the overwhelming preponderance of revolutionary transformations over nonrevolutionary transformations, a question remains as to whether our observation of revolutionary transformations was simply a function of chance. Chance observation would be especially likely to occur for organizations with high base rates of sub-

TABLE 4
Frequencies and Average Durations of Transformations

Variables	Qualitative Measures	Objective Criterion Levels			
		60%	50%	40%	30%
Frequencies					
Revolutionary transformations	23	10	26	29	40
Nonrevolutionary transformations	3	2	4	6	7
Total	26	12	30	35	47
Average durations					
Revolutionary transformations					
Means	1.17	1.30	1.39	1.38	1.28
s.d.	.38	.48	.50	.49	.45
Nonrevolutionary transformations					
Means	4.67	3.00	3.25	3.33	3.29
s.d.	2.08	1.00	.50	.58	.49

stantial change over the three activity domains. The firms studied were heterogeneous with respect to base rates of change. A more direct test of Hypothesis 1 would involve examination of the frequency of revolutionary transformations for each organization relative to its particular base rate of substantial change. The arguments of punctuated equilibrium theory would be more strongly supported if revolutionary transformations were observed even where base rates of change were low.

To explore this possibility, we calculated expected numbers of revolutionary transformations by computing, for each company, the expected number of substantial changes over any two-year period for each of the three activity domains. We then computed the intersection of these expected values for each company to obtain an expected number of revolutionary transformations for each company. For example, Digital Computer Controls, which was founded in 1969 and acquired and disbanded by Data General in 1977, exhibited two substantial changes in strategy, one substantial change in structure, and four substantial changes in power distributions using the 50 percent change criterion. This computation yielded an expected value of substantial change per year of .33, .17, and .67 for each of the three domains. Multiplying these figures together yields an expected number of .037 revolutionary transformations per year for Digital Computer Controls, which translates to an expectation of .222 revolutionary transformations over the life of the company. We observed 1 revolutionary transformation over the life of the company. We followed this procedure for each company studied, calculating observed rates of revolutionary transformation using both qualitative and objective data, entering the latter at each of the four levels of percentage change. Chi-square tests for independence between observed and expected frequencies showed that, for both the qualitative and objective measures, the observed frequencies of revolutionary transformation significantly outnumbered the expected rates even when organizations' individual base rates of substantial change were taken into account. For example, the observed frequency of revolutionary transformations at the 50 percent change criterion level was significantly greater than the expected frequency ($\chi^2 = 178.64_{15}$, $p < .01$). Chi-square values were of similar magnitude and significance for all qualitative and objective measures of substantial change.

Hypothesis 1 is thus directly supported. Regardless of differences in the base rates of substantial change over the three activity domains, the organizations tended to accomplish fundamental organizational transformations according to patterns predicted by the punctuated equilibrium model.

Hypothesis 2 predicts that small changes in individual domains of organizational activity will not accumulate incrementally to yield a fundamental transformation. To explore this hypothesis, we arrayed all objective measures of change for each of the three domains over all years of all organizations' lives. We then summed annual percentage changes for each variable over successive years. Incremental accumulation of small changes toward large differences—30 percent or greater—would disconfirm one of the main arguments of punctuated equilibrium. The striking result of these analyses was that in not one single case did accumulated changes total more than 18 percent before a one-year increase of at least 30 percent occurred. Apparently, small organizational changes do not accumulate to produce nonrevolutionary transformations. These findings provide additional evidence that fundamental organizational transformations tend to occur in short, discontinuous bursts.

Finally, punctuated equilibrium theories contain predictions about when organizations will be likely to undergo revolutionary transformations. Hypotheses 3 through 5 predict that revolutionary transformations will typically occur in the presence of some external stimulus for change. Specifically, we hypothesized that major declines in an organization's performance, major changes in its environmental conditions, and succession of its chief executive officer would increase the likelihood of fundamental, revolutionary transformation. We tested these hypotheses using "logit" regression analysis, which Yamaguchi (1991) noted as an appropriate procedure to use when time-dependent processes, such as organizational age, are not specified theoretically. Table 5 shows results of these analyses.

As Table 5 shows, major changes in environmental conditions and succession of a CEO significantly and positively influence revolutionary transformations. Thus findings support Hypotheses 4 and 5. Hypothesis 3, however, which predicts a negative relationship between performance crisis and the occurrence of revolutionary transformation, was not supported. The coefficient was insignificant. We examined whether lags in the performance change variable might improve the results, but the coefficient was again insignificant (results are not shown).

DISCUSSION

We began this research with the simple idea that research was needed to verify the basic arguments of the punctuated equilibrium model before reliable insights about the antecedents and consequences of revolutionary transformation could be established. Results of this study demonstrate that

TABLE 5
Results of Regression Analyses: Effects of External Pressures on Revolutionary Transformation

Variables	Means	s.d.	b	s.e.
Constant			$-2.427**$	.505
Performance crisis	.785	.412	-0.593	.495
Major environmental change	.238	.427	$1.513**$	.466
CEO succession	.112	.316	$1.684**$	.544
χ^2			21.853^a	
df			3	
pseudo R^2			.140	

[a] $\alpha \leq .001$
** $p < .01$

revolutionary transformation, as predicted by the punctuated equilibrium model, is a principal means by which organizations fundamentally alter their systems, strategies, and structures. The organizations studied overwhelmingly accomplished fundamental transformations within two-year periods. The few transformations that occurred over a period longer than 2 years averaged between 3 and 4.67 years, depending on whether we were looking at qualitative or objective measures. No evidence was found to support an argument that very small changes accumulated over longer periods to accomplish fundamental transformation. This result supports a key argument of punctuated equilibrium theory regarding the likely inability of organizations to instigate or conclude a fundamental transformation via incremental or gradual changes in organizational characteristics. Finally, the results support hypotheses regarding the ability of extrasystemic pressure to initiate fundamental transformation. Revolutionary transformations were shown to be positively and significantly influenced by major changes in environmental conditions and successions of chief executive officers.

Although these results provide good support for the arguments of the punctuated equilibrium model, we do not suggest that debate about either the descriptive validity or prescriptive consequences of revolutionary transformation can or should be laid to rest. Questions about the processes and outcomes of fundamental organizational transformation remain important, both theoretically and practically. We close this study by offering a few thoughts about directions for future research that should both improve the quality of debate about the modes of fundamental transformation (revolutionary versus nonrevolutionary) and extend investigation of the punctuated equilibrium model.

Replications and Extensions of the Research

Several aspects of this research merit future investigation using different samples of organizations and data that are different in certain respects. First, results of this study must be considered limited in their generalizability in that the activities of the minicomputer producers were examined during a period of high turbulence in technology and competition. We chose this setting precisely because such conditions should generate a high number of fundamental transformations. This density of incident was crucial to testing the null hypothesis that revolutionary transformations do not occur more frequently than nonrevolutionary transformations. It is possible, however, that the high degree of environmental turbulence in this industry actually led to faster and more dramatic transformations. Future studies should explore whether organizations competing in more stable environments exhibit similar patterns of fundamental transformation.

Second, the punctuated equilibrium argument that resistance to change, or deep structure, is the mechanism that accounts for the rarity of nonrevolutionary transformations needs to be tested more directly. Because we used archival data, we were only able to show here that small changes in individual activity domains tended not to accumulate toward fundamental transformation. This finding is consistent with a resistance-to-change argument, but it does not directly demonstrate the mechanism. Future research will need to examine finer-grained data on the attempts at change that subunits try and on the responses, whether adaptation or rejection, of related subunits.

A related issue concerns our procedure for classifying nonrevolutionary transformations. As was described, we simply coded a nonrevolutionary transformation as occurring whenever substantial changes in all three activity domains occurred over a period of longer than two years. This procedure raises the possibility, when the period of nonrevolutionary transformation is very long, that the substantial changes observed over the three domains were unrelated. Archival data unfortunately make investigating such a possibility difficult. Our purpose for this research, however, was to explore whether organizational transformations fit the pattern predicted in the punctuated equilibrium model. Possible relationships among changes are not directly germane to this research question. Future research should certainly explore patterns of influence among substantial changes over different domains for both revolutionary and nonrevolutionary transformations.

Finally, findings did not support our hypothesis regarding the influence of performance declines on revolutionary transformations. Perhaps the measure of performance used in this study, change in market share, is inappropriate as a signal of performance declines. As noted, market share for any one organization is directly affected by the activities of other organizations. Organizations can experience an inverse relationship between profitability and market share, especially in a high-growth market. Our experience with this data set suggests that this is not the case, however; organizations that did not increase or at least maintain steady levels of market share failed earlier and more frequently than other organizations (Romanelli, 1989). Nevertheless, future studies should explore the impact of changes in profitability directly.

Future Directions

In its strong finding that revolutionary transformation was the principal means by which these organizations fundamentally altered their activity patterns, this research also sets the stage for the examination of related questions regarding the consequences and temporal patterns of revolutionary transformations. Even as research proceeds to verify our findings, it is important to the development of the punctuated equilibrium paradigm (Gersick, 1991) to elaborate and test the full implications of the model.

Performance consequences. Researchers have examined whether revolutionary transformation improves the performance of organizations more than nonrevolutionary transformation. Studies by Miller and Friesen (1984) and by Virany and colleagues (1992) have showed that organizations that have accomplished revolutionary transformation outperformed organizations pursuing more gradual, incremental approaches to transformation.

These results suggest that, when transformation occurs, revolutionary change confers a performance benefit.

In earlier work, however (Tushman & Romanelli, 1985), we have argued that revolutionary transformation nonetheless constitutes a dangerous endeavor for organizations, increasing their risk of short-term failure. Revolutionary transformation fundamentally disrupts established activities and understandings, and nothing guarantees that the resulting configuration of activities will be better than the previous configuration. Hambrick and D'Aveni (1988) described a dangerous "downward spiral" of decline that is characterized by increasingly frequent and more radical changes as an organization seeks to reestablish some basic alignment with environmental conditions. Miner and colleagues (1990) also found support for the dangers of transformation in their study of Finnish newspapers from 1771 to 1963; transformations significantly increased the probability of failure for all these organizations.

A few studies have examined organizational and environmental conditions that tend to increase the likelihood of successful revolutionary transformation. Miner and colleagues also found that newspaper organizations that were protected by interorganizational linkages showed a significantly lower probability of failure following transformation than organizations without such protection. Haveman (1992) argued that the timing of fundamental transformations and the relationship of changes to established routines and competencies also influenced post-transformation performance and survival chances. In her study of California savings and loan institutions, Haveman showed that transformations accomplished in close temporal proximity with major environmental changes improved both the short-term financial performance of the organizations and their long-term survival likelihood. Among these organizations, financial performance was also improved when changes were related in some fashion to previous organizational competencies. In an interesting reinforcement of this finding, Virany and colleagues (1992) found that although the majority of the transformations they observed occurred immediately following the succession of a CEO, organizations that accomplished revolutionary transformations without change in CEO performed better over the long term than organizations that coupled transformation with CEO succession.

Post-transformation performance was not examined here, but it is interesting to consider how findings from studies of the consequences of transformation compare with our results about the triggers of transformation. Our findings showed that an organization is significantly more likely to undergo a revolutionary transformation when environmental conditions are changing dramatically and its CEO has been replaced. Apparently, the occurrence of transformation when environments are changing improves an organization's performance and survival likelihood. New CEOs, however, although they demonstrate a clear tendency to radically alter their organizations following the assumption of power, might do better to avoid or delay transformation. Virany and colleagues argued that new CEOs, especially outsiders, may not understand established competencies and important interorganizational relationships well enough to determine successful post-transformation activity patterns.

Paths of revolutionary transformation. Punctuated equilibrium theorists have also begun to consider questions about longer-term relationships among activity patterns over equilibrium periods. If organizations are most effectively transformed when links to prior equilibrium periods are maintained, a real chance is gained for examining the paths or directions of transformational development. Rather than merely theorizing about organizational life cycles, researchers can begin to consider whether organizations develop according to regular, and thus ultimately predictable, sequences of equilibrium periods, or follow their own idiosyncratic paths.

Miller and Friesen (1980b, 1984) have argued in favor of the first view, suggesting that organizational configurations cluster over a few basic types. Each type, they stated, presents basic constraints on the transformation that will likely occur. In contrast, we have suggested (Tushman & Romanelli, 1985) that there may be great variety in the temporal patterns of configuration over organizations' lives. Given the radical nature of revolutionary transformation, organizations, even very similar organizations facing similar changes in their environments, may emphasize different competencies as links over successive transformational periods. Prior activity patterns probably constrain subsequent patterns to some extent; the nature and direction of change, however, is left open in our model.

It would be premature at this stage of investigation to draw conclusions about the degree of constraint that may characterize longitudinal patterns in organizational transformation. Punctuated equilibrium theory, however, as it specifies periods of stable organizational activity, presents a clear basis for conducting research on this question. Periods could be investigated across organizations, with researchers looking for similarities in pattern and temporal sequencing. More generally, we might explore, within organizations, whether characteristics of earlier periods systematically influence the degrees or directions of future change. The punctuated equilibrium model thus establishes a basis for exploring path dependencies in long-term patterns of organizational transformation.

CONCLUSIONS

This article has addressed the question of whether organizations are typically transformed via the discontinuous change processes predicted in the punctuated equilibrium model. Our findings strongly support the conclusion that revolutionary transformation is the most common mode of fundamental transformation. Researchers may thus proceed with further investigation of the processes and outcomes of revolutionary transformation with greater assurance that organizations do frequently alter their systems, strategies, and structures through short, discontinuous bursts of change over most or all domains of organizational activity.

At the same time, we suggest that this study should serve as the starting point for more systematic debate among proponents of revolutionary and nonrevolutionary theories of fundamental organizational transformation. Competing theories of fundamental transformation appear to embody systematically different assumptions about organizational capacities for change at the subunit level and about the degree of interconnectedness among subunits. These issues address the most basic understandings about organizations. At the same time as researchers explore the performance consequences of alternative modes of transformation, they should continue to examine both the frequencies of revolutionary and nonrevolutionary transformations and the underlying organizational systems and conditions that may give rise to the different modes.

REFERENCES

Abernathy, W. J., & Utterback, J. 1978. Patterns of industrial innovation. *Technology Review*, 80(7): 41–47.

Bartunek, J. M. 1984. Changing interpretive schemes and organizational restructuring: The example of a religious order. *Administrative Science Quarterly*, 29: 355–372.

Boeker, W. P. 1988. Organizational origins: Entrepreneurial and environmental imprinting at the time of founding. In G. R. Carroll (Ed.), *Ecological models of organization:* 33–55. Cambridge, MA: Ballinger.

Boeker, W. P. 1989. Strategic change: The effects of founding and history. *Academy of Management Journal*, 32: 489–515.

Carlson, R. O. 1962. *Executive succession and organizational change.* Chicago: University of Chicago, Midwest Administration Center.

Computer Directory and Buyers' Guide. 1957–1981. Newtonville, MA: Berkeley Enterprises.

Cyert, R., & March, J. 1963. *A behavioral theory of the firm.* Englewood Cliffs, NJ: Prentice-Hall.

D'Aveni, R. A. 1989. The aftermath of organizational decline: A longitudinal study of the strategic and managerial characteristics of declining firms. *Academy of Management Journal*, 32: 577–605.

Dearborn, D. C., & Simon, H. A. 1958. Selective perception: A note on the departmental identification of executives. *Sociometry*, 21: 140–144.

Delacroix, J., & Swaminathan, A. 1991. Cosmetic, speculative, and adaptive organizational change in the wine industry: A longitudinal study. *Administrative Science Quarterly*, 36: 631–661.

EDP industry report. 1964–81. Framingham, MA: International Data Corporation.

Eisenhardt, K. M., & Schoonhoven, C. B. 1990. Organizational growth: Linking founding team, strategy, environment, and growth among U.S. semiconductor ventures. *Administrative Science Quarterly*, 35: 504–529.

Freeman, J. 1982. Organizational life cycles and natural selection processes. In B. M. Staw & L. L. Cummings (Eds.), *Research in organizational behavior*, vol. 4: 1–32. Greenwich, CT: JAI Press.

Gabarro, J. 1987. *The dynamics of taking charge.* Boston: Harvard University Press.

Gersick, C. J. G. 1988. Time and transition in work teams: Toward a new model of group development. *Academy of Management Journal*, 31: 9–41.

Gersick, C. J. G. 1989. Marking time: Predictable transitions in task groups. *Academy of Management Journal*, 32: 274–309.

Gersick, C. J. G. 1991. Revolutionary change theories: A multilevel exploration of the punctuated equilibrium paradigm. *Academy of Management Review*, 16: 10–36.

Gould, S. J. 1989. Punctuated equilibrium theory in fact and theory. *Journal of Social Biological Structures*, 12: 117–136.

Hambrick, D. C., & D'Aveni, R. A. 1988. Large corporate failures as downward spirals. *Administrative Science Quarterly*, 33: 1–23.

Hannan, M. T., & Freeman, J. 1984. Structural inertia and organizational change. *American Sociological Review*, 49: 149–164.

Harrigan, K. R. 1980. *Strategies for declining businesses.* Lexington, MA: Heath.

Haveman, H. A. 1992. Between a rock and a hard place: Organizational change and performance under conditions of fundamental environmental transformation. *Administrative Science Quarterly*, 37: 48–75.

Hedberg, B., Nystrom, P., & Starbuck, W. 1976. Camping on seesaws: Prescriptions for a self-designing organization. *Administrative Science Quarterly*, 21: 41–65.

Helmich, D. L., & Brown, W. B. 1972. Successor type and organizational change in the corporate enterprise. *Administrative Science Quarterly*, 17: 371–381.

Keats, B. W., & Hitt, M. A. 1988. A causal model of linkages among environmental dimensions, macro organizational characteristics, and performance. *Academy of Management Journal*, 31: 570–598.

Khandwalla, P. 1973. Environment and its impact on the organization. *Academy of Management Journal*, 16: 481–495.

Kuhn, T. S. 1970. *The structure of scientific revolutions.* Chicago: University of Chicago Press.

Lant, T. K., & Mezias, S. J. 1992. An organizational learning model of convergence and reorientation. *Organization Science*, 3: 47–71.

Levinson, D. J. 1986. A conception of adult development. *American Psychologist*, 41: 3–13.

Lindblom, C. E. 1959. The science of muddling through. *Public Administration Review*, 19: 79–88.

McKelvey, B. 1982. *Organizational systematics: Taxonomy, evolution, classification.* Berkeley: University of California Press.

Meyer, A. D. 1982. Adapting to environmental jolts. *Administrative Science Quarterly*, 27: 515–537.

Meyer, A. D., Brooks, G. R., & Goes, J. B. 1990. Environmental jolts and industry revolutions: Organizational responses to discontinuous change. *Strategic Management Journal*, 11: 93–110.

Meyer, J. W., & Rowan, B. 1977. Institutionalized organizations: Formal structures as myth and ceremony. *American Journal of Sociology*, 83: 340–363.

Mezias, S. 1990. An institutional model of organizational practice: Financial reporting at the Fortune 200. *Administrative Science Quarterly*, 35: 431–457.

Miles, R. H., & Cameron, K. S. 1982. *Coffin nails and corporate strategies.* Englewood Cliffs, NJ: Prentice-Hall.

Miller, D., & Friesen, P. H. 1980a. Momentum and revolution in organizational adaptation. *Academy of Management Journal*, 23: 591–614.

Miller, D., & Friesen, P. H. 1980b. Archetypes of organizational transition. *Administrative Science Quarterly*, 25: 268–299.

Miller, D., & Friesen, P. H. 1982. Structural change and performance: Quantum vs. piecemeal-incremental approaches. *Academy of Management Journal*, 25: 867–892.

Miller, D., & Friesen, P. H. 1984. *Organizations: A quantum view.* Englewood Cliffs, NJ: Prentice-Hall.

Miner, A. S., Amburgey, T. L., & Stearns, T. M. 1990. Interorganizational linkages and population dynamics: Buffering and transformational shields. *Administrative Science Quarterly*, 35: 689–713.

Mintzberg, H. 1979. *The structure of organizations.* Englewood Cliffs, NJ: Prentice-Hall.

Mintzberg, H., & Waters, J. A. 1982. Tracking strategy in an entrepreneurial firm. *Academy of Management Journal*, 25: 465–499.

Oliver, C. 1991. Strategic responses to institutional processes. *Academy of Management Review*, 16: 145–179.

Oster, S. M. 1982. Intraindustry structure and the ease of strategic change. *Review of Economics and Statistics*, 20: 376–384.

Prahalad, C. K., & Hamel, G. 1990. The core competence of corporations. *Harvard Business Review*, 90(3): 79–91.

Quinn, J. B. 1980. *Strategies for change: Logical incrementalism.* Homewood, IL: Irwin.

Romanelli, E. 1989. Environments and strategies of organizational start-ups: Effects on early survival. *Administrative Science Quarterly*, 34: 369–387.

Romanelli, E., & Tushman, M. L. 1986. Inertia, environments, and strategic choice: A quasi-experimental design for comparative-longitudinal research. *Management Science*, 32: 608–621.

Scott, W. R. 1987. The adolescence of institutional theory. *Administrative Science Quarterly*, 32: 493–511.

Selznick, P. 1949. *TVA and the grass roots.* Berkeley: University of California Press.

Staw, B. M., Sandelands, L. E., & Dutton, J. E. 1981. Threat-rigidity effects in organizational behavior: A multilevel analysis. *Administrative Science Quarterly*, 26: 501–524.

Stinchcombe, A. L. 1965. Social structure and organizations. In J. G. March (Ed.), *Handbook of organizations:* 142–193. Chicago: Rand-McNally.

Tolbert, P., & Zucker, L. G. 1983. Institutional sources of change in the formal structure of organizations: The diffusion of civil service reform, 1880–1935. *Administrative Science Quarterly*, 28: 22–39.

Tushman, M. L., & Anderson, A. 1986. Technological discontinuities and organizational environments. *Administrative Science Quarterly*, 31: 439–465.

Tushman, M. L., Newman, W. H., & Romanelli, E. 1986. Convergence and upheaval: Managing the unsteady pace of organizational evolution. *California Management Review*, 29(1): 1–16.

Tushman, M. L., & Romanelli, E. 1985. Organizational evolution: A metamorphosis model of convergence and reorientation. In L. L. Cummings & B. M. Staw (Eds.), *Research in organizational behavior,* vol. 7: 171–222. Greenwich, CT: JAI Press.

Yamaguchi, K. 1991. *Event history analysis.* Newbury Park, CA: Sage.

Virany, B., Tushman, M. L., & Romanelli, E. 1992. Executive succession and organization outcomes in turbulent environments: An organization learning approach. *Organization Science*, 3: 72–91.

Zald, M. N. 1970. Political economy: A framework for comparative analysis. In M. N. Zald (Ed.), *Power in organizations:* 221–261. Nashville: Vanderbilt University Press.

Zucker, L. G. 1988. Where do institutional patterns come from? Organizations as actors in social systems. In L. G. Zucker (Ed.), *Institutional patterns and organizations:* 23–52. Cambridge, MA: Ballinger.

Elaine Romanelli is an associate professor in management and strategy at the School of Business, Georgetown University. Her current research interests include longitudinal studies of the contexts, processes, and consequences of organizational foundings in the motion picture and biotechnology industries. She received her Ph.D. degree from the Graduate School of Business, Columbia University.

Michael L. Tushman is the Phillip Hettleman Professor of Management at the Graduate School of Business, Columbia University. He received his Ph.D. degree from the Sloan School of Management, Massachusetts Institute of Technology. His current research interests include the relationship between technological change, executive teams, and organizational evolution.

[17]

Strategic Management Journal, Vol. 7, 485–501 (1986)

The Dominant Logic: a New Linkage Between Diversity and Performance

C. K. PRAHALAD
Graduate School of Business, The University of Michigan, Ann Arbor, Michigan, U.S.A.

RICHARD A. BETTIS
Edwin L. Cox School of Business, Southern Methodist University, Dallas, Texas, U.S.A.

Summary
Current research offers alternative explanations to the 'linkage' between the pattern of diversification and performance. At least four streams of research can be identified. None of these can be considered to be a reliable, predictive theory of successful diversification. They are, at best, partial explanations. The purpose of this paper is to propose an additional 'linkage', conceptual at this stage, that might help our understanding of the crucial connection between diversity and performance. The conceptual argument is intended as a 'supplement' to the current lines of research, rather than as an alternative explanation.

For the past 35 years product-market diversification of large firms has continued at a rapid pace. Today, over two-thirds of the firms in the U.S.A. *Fortune* 500 are highly diversified and similar patterns of diversification exist in Western Europe and Japan (Rumelt, 1974; Pavan, 1972; Thanheiser, 1972; Pooley, 1972; Channon, 1973; Suzuki, 1980). As a consequence, interest in the relationship between corporate diversification and financial performance has grown among practitioners, academics, and public policy-makers.

Accompanying this interest has been a spate of research on the patterns of diversification and the determinants of performance in diversified firms by the academic community. Concurrently, consulting firms have been actively promoting a variety of approaches for managing diversified firms. The results of these efforts have been mixed at best. There is, as yet, no overall theory that links diversification with performance and the linkage, if any, remains elusive.

The purpose of this paper is to propose a crucial linkage, which has largely been ignored in the literature on the relationship between diversification and performance; and to show how this approach can add significantly to our managerial understanding of performance in the diversified firm.

This linkage is referred to as the 'dominant general management logic' (or dominant logic) and consists of the mental maps developed through experience in the core business and sometimes applied inappropriately in other businesses.

A BRIEF REVIEW OF RESEARCH ON DIVERSITY AND PERFORMANCE

The purpose of this section is to review briefly the major academic research streams and consulting framework relevant to the relationships between diversity and performance.

0143-2095/86/060485-17$08.50
© 1986 by John Wiley & Sons, Ltd.

Received 8 November 1983
Revised 5 April 1985

486   *C. K. Prahalad and R. A. Bettis*

These represent alternative approaches to research in this area. While significant literature exists in support of each of the streams of research outlined below, we will only reference and discuss the seminal works in each area.

The strategy of diversification

Pioneering work by Chandler (1962) and Ansoff (1965) established the motivations for diversification and the general nature of the diversified firm. Wrigley (1970) refined and extended Chandler's study by investigating the various options open to a diversifying firm. Building on the work of Chandler, Wrigley, and others, Rumelt (1974, 1977) investigated the relationships among diversification strategy, organizational structure, and economic performance. Rumelt used four major and nine minor categories to characterize the diversification strategy of firms. The major categories were single business, dominant business, related business and unrelated business. These categories provide a spectrum of diversification strategies—from firms that remained essentially undiversified to firms that diversified significantly into unrelated areas. Using statistical methods, Rumelt was able to relate diversification strategy to performance. The related diversification strategies— related–constrained and related–linked (e.g. General Foods and General Electric) were found to outperform the other diversification strategies on the average (relatedness was defined in terms of products, markets and technology). The related–constrained was found to be the highest performing on the average. (In related–constrained firms most component businesses are related to each other, whereas in related–linked firms only one-to-one relationships are required.) By contrast, the unrelated conglomerate strategy was found to be one of the lowest performing on the average.

Recently Nathanson and Cassano (1982) conducted a statistical study of diversity and performance using a sample of 206 firms over the years 1973–78. They developed a two-dimensional typology (market diversity and product diversity) for capturing diversification strategy that refines Rumelt's categories. They found that returns (on the average) declined as product diversity increased, while returns remained relatively steady as market diversity increased. However, they also found that size plays an important moderating role on the relationships. For both the market and product diversity, smaller firms did well relative to larger firms in categories marked by no diversification and in categories of extremely high diversification. Larger firms did significantly better than smaller firms in the in-between categories—those characterized by intermediate levels of diversification.

In both these studies linking diversification and performance (Rumelt and Nathanson/Cassano) the key point to note is that *choosing the generic strategy of diversification (how much and what kind of relatedness)* is the key to achieving performance.

Economic characteristics of individual businesses

Porter (1980), among others, established that the characteristics of the various industries in which a firm participates, and the position of the firm's businesses in these industries, impacts overall firm performance.

Two studies have in fact empirically validated these influences for diversified firms. The widely discussed PIMS program of the Marketing Science Institute (see Schoeffler, Buzzell and Heany, 1974, for an introduction) has shown that variables such as market share and relative product quality directly influence the profitability of constituent businesses in large diversified firms. More recently, Montgomery (1979) has examined the performance differences in diversified firms using the market structure variables of industrial organization economics. Montgomery found that diversified firms with higher levels of performance tended to have well-positioned businesses in industries with 'favorable' market structures.

In summary, for both studies (PIMS and Montgomery) *the structure of the industries in which the firm competes and the competitive position of the firm's businesses within these industries are the key determinants of performance.*

Portfolio concepts

What are here called 'portfolio concepts' go by various names such as portfolio grids, SBU concepts, and SBU matrices. Although there are numerous slight variations among the approaches used by various consultant groups and firms, they all rely on a matrix or grid with two axes. The matrix classifies businesses by product-market attractiveness, or some variant of it, along one axis and by competitive position or some variant of it along the other axis. Typically these matrices are divided into either four or nine boxes. (For a thorough discussion see Hofer and Schendel, 1978.) The position (box) that each business occupies represents its strategic position and determines the role that the business should play in the corporate portfolio. This role involves varying degrees of cash generation or cash usage. Studies by Bettis (1979), and Haspeslagh (1982) suggest that managers use these concepts to varying degrees—as a tool or as dogma—in managing a diversified portfolio of businesses.

For each variant of the portfolio concept the key points are: (1) *the strategic position of each business determines its cash flow characteristics; and (2) it is the 'balance' of these cash flow characteristics of the collection of businesses that determines the overall performance of the diversified firm.*

Et cetera

In addition to the streams of research discussed above, a number of studies focusing on performance in large firms, by researchers concerned with organizational theory and human motivation, have appeared recently. Representative of this line of research are Peters and Waterman (1982), Deal and Kennedy (1982), Pascale and Athos (1981), and Ouchi (1981). While these studies do not consider the problems of managing diversity explicitly, they often do make some implicit recommendations on the issue, but the nature of the recommendations varies widely. (For example, Peters and Waterman suggest that 'excellent firms' confine their operations to businesses they know or 'they stick to the knitting'.)

The three streams of research lead to somewhat different conclusions. To summarize, the linkage between diversity and performance would appear to be a function of:

1. the generic diversification strategy (how much and what kind of relatedness), or
2. the profit potential of the industries in which the individual businesses are positioned and the actual competitive position of the businesses in each industry, or
3. the cash flow characteristics of the various businesses and the internal cash flow balance for the total firm.

Undoubtedly all three perspectives *provide partial answers* to the question. Just how partial these answers are becomes more obvious when you consider that Rumelt (1974) was only able to explain less than 20 percent of the variance in performance, while Montogomery could only explain about 38 percent of the variance in performance. These results suggest that further conceptual development could enhance our understanding of diversity and performance.

The importance of 'quality of management'

Bettis, Hall and Prahalad (1978) have argued that, if we move away from the traditional research preoccupation with central tendencies, but focus on outliers—the very high and very poor performers—we may learn more about the elusive linkage between diversity and performance. By studying just 12 firms, six of which were high performers and six low performers, across the three generic categories of dominant, related, and unrelated diversifiers (with a sample of four firms each, two in high- and two in low-performance categories), they concluded that the quality of management was as critical in explaining performance as any other factor. (It should be noted that their definition of quality was somewhat ambiguous.) The study was not based on the large sample (and it could not be by design, as their concern was with outliers), and the conclusions were tentative. (In a much larger study, Bettis and Mahajan (forthcoming) were able to show that the high-performance attributes usually attributed to related diversification were *not* recognized in the overwhelming majority of related diversifiers.) The real departure in the academic perspective on diversity and performance indicated by the study was the concern with very good and very poor performances in the same generic diversification category—or a desire to study outliers—and the inclusion of concept of the '*quality of management*' as a major variable linking diversity and performance.

Top management in a diversified firm: a distinct skill?

Two in-depth clinical studies suggest that the skills that constitute the 'quality of management' in a single-business firm are distinct from a diversified firm; and that as firms diversify, top managers have to acquire those skills. Rajan Das (1981) studied one firm's attempt to diversify out of the core business (tobacco) and how it had to learn the process of general management in the new businesses into which it ventured. The conclusion was that it was not the quality of the business—its competitive structure—or the pattern of diversification *per se* that determined early failures and successes later, but the evolution of the top management and its ability to acquire new skills and recognize that its approach to managing a diversifed firm must be different from the way it had managed the single-business firm. The study by Miles (1982) of tobacco companies in the U.S. and their attempts to diversify away from tobacco, also leads to a similar conclusion. The firms *had to learn as much about general management in the diversified firm, as a distinct process and skill*, as about the characteristics of the new businesses. Both these studies indicate that the work of top management in diversified firms is a distinct skill and can contribute to the success or failure of any one of the businesses within the firm or the firm as a whole.

The management of a diversified firm

Studies of the work of top management and the process by which they manage a diversified firm are not numerous. Bower (1972a) demonstrated that top managers influence the strategic choices made by unit-level managers by orchestrating the organizational context— the formal structure and systems. In other words, the tools of top management were administrative in character. He labeled the term 'metamanagement' (Bower, 1972b) to describe the job of top managers in diversified firms. Hamermesh (1977) outlined the process by which top managers intervene in a divisional profit crisis. Prahalad and Doz (1981) outlined, in detail, how top managers can use administrative tools to shift the strategic direction of a business. This line of research established both the broad scope of the work of top management, but more importantly how that influences the strategic choices made by lower-level managers at the business-unit level, thereby impacting on the overall performance. There exists a logical, though only partially empirically, verified link between the quality of management—or the quality of the processes by which top managers influence the business-level managers in their work—and the performance of the firm.

The two questions that we posed ourselves based on the literature were:

1. If top managers in single-business firms had to learn the process of managing a diversified portfolio, *should top managers in diversified firms go through a similar learning process when they add new businesses*? Is the task of top management in the diversified firm dependent on, or at least partially *influenced by, the underlying strategic characteristics* of the businesses?
2. If the tools available to top managers in diversified firms to influence the strategic direction of businesses are essentially administrative as regards the organizational context, does it follow that the substance of businesses is irrelevant? In other words, can the same conceptual organizational context management capabilities suffice if the mix of businesses changes?

THE ELUSIVE LINKAGE

It is important before proceeding to differentiate at least two distinct levels of general management in a diversified firm—that at the SBU or business level and the corporate management team. Often, in diversified firms, there tends to be an intermediate level of general management, called group or sector executives, between business level and corporate management. Our focus will be on the *corporate management team*, and its relationships with business- and group-level managers, as it pertains to managing the totality of the firm.

Given this focus on corporate management the conceptual framework linking diversity and performance, proposed in this paper, is based on the following premises:

1. Top management of a (diversified) firm should not be viewed 'as a faceless abstraction', but as a 'collection of key individuals' (i.e. a dominant coalition) who have significant influence on the way the firm is managed. This collection of individuals, to a large extent, influence the style and process of management, and as a result the key resource allocation choices (Donaldson and Lorsch, 1983).

Few organizational events are approached by these managers (or any managers as being totally unique and requiring systematic study. Instead, they are processed through pre-existing knowledge systems. Known as schemas (see Norman, 1976, for a discussion of schemas), these systems represent beliefs, theories and propositions that have developed over time based on the manager's personal experiences. At a broader unit of analysis, Huff (1982) implied the possibility that organizations' actions can be characterized as schemas. An organizational schema is primarily a product of managers' interpretations of experiences while operating within certain firms and industries.

Schemas permit managers to categorize an event, assess its consequences, and consider appropriate actions (including doing nothing), and to do so rapidly and often efficiently. Without schemas a manager, and ultimately the organizations with which he/she is associated, would become paralyzed by the need to analyze 'scientifically' an enormous number of ambiguous and uncertain situations. In other words, managers must be able to scan environments selectively so that timely decisions can be made (Hambrick, 1982). The selection of environmental elements to be scanned is likely affected by a manager's schema.

Unfortunately, schemas are not infallible guides to the organization and its environments. In fact, some are relatively inaccurate representations of the world, particularly as conditions change. Furthermore, events often are not labeled accurately, and sometimes are processed through inaccurate and/or incomplete knowledge structures.

For the purposes of this research it is important to understand what managers' schemas actually represent. Kiesler and Sproul (1982) offer the following concise description:

> Managers operate on mental representations of the world and those representaions
> are likely to be of historical environments rather than of current ones (p. 557).

(Furthermore, as Weick (1979) discusses, it is the schema concept that provides the vehicle for his concept of the social construction (or enactment) of a firm's environment.)

For the present purposes the schema concept is introduced as a general mental structure that can store a shared dominant general management logic. (The specific nature and content of this 'logic' is discussed below.)

2.   The strategic characteristics of businesses in a diversified firm, determined by the underlying competitive structure, technologies, and customers of specific businesses, vary. The differences in strategic characteristics of the businesses in the portfolio of the firm, a measure of *strategic variety*, impact the ability of a top management group to manage. This premise implies that complexity of the top management process *is a function of the strategic variety, not just the number of distinct businesses* or *the size of those businesses*. For example, the management of a very large, primarily one-industry firm (e.g. General Motors), or the management of a diversified firm in strategically similar businesses (e.g. Procter & Gamble), is a lot simpler than managing a diversified firm in strategically dissimilar industries (e.g. General Electric).

3.   Strategically similar business can be managed using a single *dominant general management logic*. A dominant general management logic is defined as the way in which managers conceptualize the business and make critical resource allocation decisions—be it in technologies, product development, distribution, advertising, or in human resource management. These tasks are performed by managing the infrastructure of administrative tools like choice of key individuals, processes of planning, budgeting, control, compensation, career management and organization structure. If the businesses in a diversified firm are strategically similar, one dominant general management logic would suffice. However, diversified firms with strategic variety, impose the need for multiple dominant logics.

The dominant logic is stored via schemas and hence can be thought of as a structure. However, some of what is stored is process knowledge (e.g. what kind of process should be used in a particular kind of resource alleviation decision or how new technologies should be evaluated). Hence, more broadly the dominant logic can be considered as both a knowledge structure and a set of elicited management processes. (The actual content of this knowledge structure and how this context is established is discussed below.)

4.   The ability of a top management group (a group of key individuals), to manage a diversified firm is limited by the dominant general management logic(s) that they are used to. In other words, the repertoire of tools that top managers use to identify, define, and make strategic decisions, and their view of the world (mind sets), is determined by their experiences. Typically, the dominant top management logic in a diversified firm tends to be

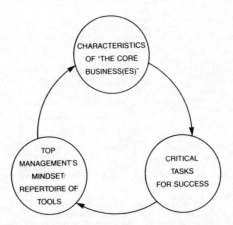

Figure 1.   Dominant general management logic evolves due to . . .

influenced by the largest business or the 'core business' which was the historical basis for the firm's growth (e.g. semiconductors at Texas Instruments, public switching and telephones at GTE). The characteristics of the core business, often the source of top managers in diversified firms, tend to cause managers to define problems in certain ways and develop familiarity with, and facility in the use of, those administrative tools that are particularly useful in accomplishing the critical tasks of the core business (Figure 1).

The sources of dominant logic
Dominant logic, as we have defined it here, is a mind set or a world view or conceptualization of the business and the administrative tools to accomplish goals and make decisions in that business. It is stored as a shared cognitive map (or set of schemas) among the dominant coalition. It is expressed as a learned, problem-solving behavior. As such, in order to understand the difficulties faced by a top management group in changing the dominant logic, we need to first examine the research streams that deal with the development of cognitive maps and the associated problem-solving behavior. We identified four streams of research—operant conditioning, paradigms, cognitive biases, and artificial intelligence—to highlight the process by which a dominant logic evolves (i.e. how the cognitive map originates and changes) and the difficulties in changing it or adding new logics to one's repertoire. The relationships of these four streams to problem-solving behavior are shown in Figure 2.

Operant conditioning
Skinner (1953), in his seminal work on operant conditioning, argued that behavior was a function of its consequences. Behavior could be understood by considering the contingencies that were administered by the environment in response to certain behaviors. Behavior that was *reinforced* was emitted more frequently in the future. By contrast, behavior that was ignored or punished (negative reinforcement) was likely to diminish over time. A dominant logic can be seen as resulting from the reinforcement that results from doing the 'right things' with respect to a set of businesses. In other words, when top managers effectively perform the tasks that are critical for success in the core business they are positively reinforced by economic success. This reinforcement results in their focusing

492   *C. K. Prahalad and R. A. Bettis*

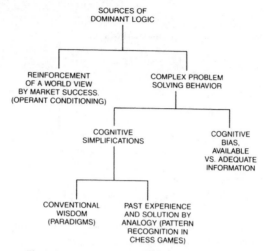

Figure 2.   Conceptual foundations of dominant logic

effort on the behaviors that led to success. Hence they develop a particular mind set and repertoire of tools and preferred processes. This in turn determines the approaches that they are likely to use in resource allocation, control over operations, and the approach to intervention in a crisis. If the firm acquires or develops a business for which the critical tasks for success are substantially different from those in the core business, because of operant conditioning the behaviors of top managers and the approaches they use to manage the new business are likely to remain those that were appropriate for the core business even though they may be inappropriate in the new business. In other words it is difficult for a top management group to be effective in managing a new business by learning and using a new dominant logic in a short time. The problems faced by American Can (e.g. Pickwick International), and Exxon (e.g. office systems), in managing acquisitions of businesses totally different from their core businesses, in the early stages, are an illustration of the power of operant conditioning on the dominant logics used by top management.

The power of paradigms

The concept of dominant logic also derives direct support from Kuhn's (1970) work on scientific paradigms and Allison's (1971) work on the importance of alternate paradigms in the context of analyzing government actions during the Cuban missile crisis.

   Kuhn, a historian of science, argued that a particular science at any point in time can be characterized by a set of 'shared beliefs' or 'conventional wisdom' about the world that constitutes what he called the 'dominant paradigm'. What Kuhn calls 'normal science' is carried out efficiently under this set of shared beliefs. In a sense, Kuhn's 'paradigm' is simply a way of *defining and managing the world and a basis for action in that world*. Kuhn points out how difficult it is to shift dominant paradigms, and illustrates this with several examples such as the shift from the Ptolemaic view of the universe (earth-centered) to the Copernican view of the universe (sun-centered) in astronomy. The analogy from science to a business firm is simple and direct. The dominant paradigm and the dominant logic are conceptually similar but employed in different fields.

Allison used paradigmatic analysis to show how the adoption of a particular paradigm powerfully affects our evaluation of events. He characterized a paradigm as 'a systematic statement of the basic assumptions, concepts and propositions employed by a school of analysis'. Different paradigms resulted in dramatically different analyses of his chosen example: the Cuban missile crisis. The parallel between Allison's use of the word paradigm and our use of dominant logic is obvious.

The pattern-recognition process

As part of the development of 'intelligent' computer programs there have been numerous efforts to develop chess-playing programs (see Newell and Simon, 1972, for a review). Inevitably such research has required intense studies of how chess experts make decisions in a chess game. In particular, the decision-making and problem-solving process used by grandmasters and masters has been compared to that of lesser players (de Groot, 1965). These studies have shown that the better players could remember more 'patterns' of previous games than the lesser players. Simon (1979) estimated that class A players could remember about 1300 familiar patterns while masters or grandmasters remember about 50,000. This 'vocabulary' of previous games lets players make effective decisions by comparison with earlier games. In other words, chess players decide on the basis of experience or 'what worked before', not on the basis of some best strategy or optimizing procedure. Now consider a situation where the design of the gameboard or rules of chess are changed. The stored 'vocabulary' of games is no longer as useful in this new game. Similarly, when the economic gameboard or rules are changed either by structural changes in existing businesses or by a diversification move, the vocabulary of economic moves stored through experience in the core business may no longer be as useful. In other words, solutions based on 'past experience' or solution by 'analogy' may be inappropriate.

Cognitive biases

A final area from which research results are suggestive of the concept of a dominant top management logic is cognitive psychology. The psychology of cognitive biases is the study of how people in making decisions sometimes make systematic (and often severe) errors (see Tversky and Kahneman, 1974, for an introduction and survey). When dealing with uncertain and complex tasks people often rely on a limited number of heuristic principles which greatly simplify the decision process. In general these heuristics are useful, but on some occasions they can result in significant errors.

For present purposes the most interesting of these heuristic principles is what is called the availability heuristic (see Tversky and Kahneman, 1973, for a thorough discussion). Basically, the availability heuristic leads people to make decisions by using information that can easily be brought to mind (i.e. information that is 'available'). This often leads to severe and systematic errors. This field of research also suggests that decision-makers do not necessarily use analytical approaches to evaluate the information content of available data or search for 'adequate information' (Nisbett and Ross, 1980). For example, Tversky and Kahneman (1974) point out that one may assess the risk of heart attack among middle-aged people by recalling such occurrences among one's acquaintances even if it can be shown that it is an inappropriate basis for drawing such a conclusion. Obviously, for top managers, knowledge of the core business and the business they are most familiar with will be a significant source of available information. They tend to apply it to other businesses where it may or may not be appropriate (Das, 1981). Research on cognitive processes suggests that the mind set and repertoire of tools that constitute the dominant logic are likely to be

494   *C. K. Prahalad and R. A. Bettis*

inappropriately applied by managers confronted with a 'different' business, and that there is significant 'learning' that precedes change in those biases. The difficulty of operating in diverse businesses which require multiple dominant logics is obvious.

STRATEGIC VARIETY AND THE DOMINANT LOGIC

The premises outlined above help us develop a framework for assessing the linkage between diversity and performance. Essentially they relate strategic variety amongst businesses in the firm, and changes in it, with the appropriateness of the dominant general management logic(s) that top managers in that firm use. We will examine in the rest of the paper the problems that diversified firms face in relating strategic variety and the dominant general management logic(s).

Strategic variety

Strategic variety in a diversified firm depends on the characteristics of the mix of business the firm is engaged in. During the past decade top managers have tended to reduce the strategic variety (not necessarily the number of district businesses) in the portfolio of the firm. This is accomplished, often, by divesting businesses that do not 'fit'—those that increase strategic variety. Many of the businesses divested are profitable (e.g. Sperry's sale of Vickers to concentrate on information technology, ITT's sale of its bakery division). Divesting businesses to get more 'focus' to the portfolio results from an implicit recognition that the demands on top management of strategic variety can be significant. Not all diversified firms have been proactive in reducing strategic variety. Some have been forced to divest businesses, after years of poor profit performance and an inability on their part to turn around the 'sick businesses'.

An alternative to the approach outlined above—reducing strategic variety by restricting the mix of businesses in the firm to those whose strategic characteristics are similar—is followed by firms like General Electric, Textron, or 3M. Typically, businesses with similar strategic characteristics tend to be grouped together, into 'sectors' for management purposes. As a result there is little strategic variety within a sector, but across sectors there can be significant differences. This approach reduces the strategic variety that top managers have to deal with by creating an intermediate level of general management. These group- or sector-level executives tend to manage the strategic direction of specific businesses within the sector. Conceptually, this arrangement explicitly recognizes the need to contain strategic variety for effective management. However, in practice, the role of sector executives and their relationship both with business-level managers and the top management of the firm can get unclear if top management of the firm attempts to directly influence the conduct of any one business or a group of businesses.

Changing strategic variety

So far we have considered how firms can contain strategic variety in a diversified firm, at a given point in time. But over time, even with an unchanging mix of businesses, the strategic variety can change. For example, the strategic characteristics of businesses can change due to changes in the structure of industries. The toy industry was changed, in a relatively short period of time, by the availability of inexpensive microprocessors. The combination of telecommunication and computers and deregulation is changing the financial services industry. Globalization has changed the nature of competition in several industries such as TV, hi-fi, autos, steel, machine tools, etc. As a result, even firms which do not ostensibly change the mix of businesses will have to cope with increasing strategic variety, as the underlying structural characteristics of businesses change. Top managers, as a result, must possess the ability to revise the dominant logic they used to manage those businesses. The inability of top managers both to identify changing structural characteristics of businesses and accept the need for change in dominant logic(s), may provide at least a partial explanation for the difficulties traditional businesses like steel, machine tools, and autos have faced during the past 5 years in the U.S.

An addition of a new business, either through internal development or acquisition, can also change the strategic variety within the firm. If the new business is distinctly different (e.g. General Motors' acquisition of EDS, or General Electric's acquisition of Utah International) the strategic variety it adds is easily recognized.

In such acquisitions, top managers also recognize that hasty attempts to impose the dominant logic of the firm on the acquired business may be dysfunctional. Often the acquired firm is 'left alone', at least for a time.

When a new business is created through internal development it is harder to recognize the different structural characteristics of that business compared to those in the current mix of businesses; more so if the new business is technologically not dissimilar to existing businesses. For example, the experience of the calculator, digital watch, and personal computer businesses at Texas Instruments illustrates the point. The dominant logic which worked so well for TI in the semiconductor business, when applied to the new business, led to failure. A dramatic contrast is the early recognition at IBM that the personal computer business was structurally quite distinct. This recognition resulted in the creation of an independent business unit for managing that business. It was not subject to the dominant logic of the mainframe business. As the PC business evolves, and as it takes on the characteristics of the mainframe business, at least in some applications and with some customer segments, IBM may reimpose the dominant logic of mainframes on that business.

To summarize, strategic variety in a diversified firm can change due to

1. changes in the structural characteristics of the existing mix of businesses, or
2. changes in the mix of businesses caused by acquisitions or internal development.

In either case, top managers must explicitly examine the implications of changes in strategic variety. In other words, *major structural changes in an industry* have the same effect on the strategic variety of a firm as acquiring a new business.

The task of top management is to constantly re-examine its portfolio to ascertain if there are perceptible changes in the strategic variety as well as explicitly to assess the impact of new businesses on dominant logic(s) in the firm. The task of top management under various combinations of 'sources of strategic variety' and 'top management orientation' give us six possible combinations, as shown in Table 1. In a firm with a single dominant logic, if the nature of the core business changes significantly, then top managers will have to revise the dominant logic (A). If a new business is added, and is strategically similar (B), no change in dominant logic is needed. If, however, the new business is dissimilar, top managers have to create the capacity within the firm to cope with multiple dominant logics (C). In a firm operating with multiple dominant logics, if the nature of a significant business changes, then top managers may have to revise the dominant logic applied to that business or regroup it under a different 'sector' or 'group' (D). If the new business is strategically similar to one

496   *C. K. Prahalad and R. A. Bettis*

Table 1.   Nature of top management tasks in diversified firms

Top management orientation	Sources of strategic variety		
	Significant structural changes in core business	Addition of a new business	
		Similar to existing businesses	Dissimilar from existing businesses
Single dominant logic	(A) Revise the dominant logic	(B) No change required	(C) Create the capacity for Multiple dominant logic(s)
Multiple dominant logic(s)	(D) Revise the dominant logic applied to that business or regroup it under another sector	(E) Assign business to appropriate 'sector'	(F) Add to the variety of dominant logic(s)

of the 'groups' or 'sectors' within the firm, then top managers may assign it to the appropriate sector (E). If the new business is dissimilar to the existing businesses, then top managers have to add variety to the dominant logics within the firm (F).

CONCLUSIONS

The concept of dominant general management logic and the role of top managers in understanding and managing the logic(s), are important aspects to be considered in the research on diversity and performance. There are several implications of including these concepts in the study of diversity and performance. We will list some:

Limits to diversity
We have argued that the 'real diversity' in a managerial sense in a firm does not arise from the variety in technologies or markets or by the number of district businesses *per se*, but from the strategic variety among businesses requiring a variety in the dominant logics used by top management. Further, the variety of dominant logics that a top management can handle depends on the composition of the team, and their experiences, as well as their attitude toward learning. These factors suggest that we ought to recognize that the limit to the diversity of businesses within a firm is determined by the strategic variety, and that the strategic variety that a firm can cope with is dependent on the composition of a top management team.

Undoubtedly, organization structure can help cope with increased strategic variety. One basic aspect of decentralization is to make decisions at the level where the proper expertise is available. In other words, the cognitive map is more likely to fit the strategic imperatives of the business. However, all decision-making cannot be decentralized. For example, resource allocation decisions *among* a firm's portfolio of businesses must be made. Furthermore, plans, strategies and budgets must be reviewed at the corporate level and managerial performance must be assessed. Hence organizational structure, although useful, is limited. It can attenuate the *intensity* of strategic variety that corporate-level management must deal with, but it cannot substitute for the need to handle strategic variety at the corporate level.

An alternative or supplementary approach is to reduce the strategic variety in the businesses of the firm—what has come to be known as 'focus' in the portfolio. An interesting variant on this is to impose a single strategic approach on each business. For example as Porter *et al.* (1983) discuss, Emerson Electric has a uniform goal across businesses of being the low-cost producer in each of its markets. Such an approach reduces strategic variety but may impose an inappropriate logic on a particular business. Interestingly, Emerson usually seeks to divest businesses that cannot meet this goal.

Ultimately many firms exceed the limits of organizational structure in attenuating the intensity of strategic variety and/or cannot reduce or limit strategic variety adequately. These firms face the reality of having to deal intensively with strategic variety at the corporate level and the necessity of developing multiple dominant logics if performance is to be sustained.

The bottom line is that each top management team at a given point in time has an inbuilt limit to the extent of diversity it can manage. Organizational structure and focus in the portfolio can help extend this limit but they cannot eliminate it.

Diversity and performance: the hidden costs

A high level of performance in a diversified firm requires the ability to 'respond fast' to competitor moves, as well as 'respond appropriately'. One of the implications of our thesis, so far, is that top managers are less likely to 'respond appropriately' to situations where the dominant logic is different, as well as not respond quickly enough, as they may be unable to interpret the meaning of information regarding unfamiliar businesses. The 'hidden costs' associated with diversifying into nonfamiliar businesses are shown schematically in Figure 3. These 'hidden costs' are not explicitly recognized when the overall business climate is very favorable. Problems surface when the newly acquired businesses (which are strategically dissimilar) encounter competitive problems or are faced with a profit crisis. Top managers find themselves unable to respond to the crisis under those circumstances (Hamermesh, 1977).

Changing or adding dominant logics

The process of adding dominant logics is, given the previous discussion, obviously an important aspect in the management of diversified firms. Also, as the argument so far suggests, the process of changing dominant logics is important to any firm that encounters rapid change in the structure of the industries in which it competes. These issues revolve around the ability of the firm or its dominant coalition to learn. Fortunately, there is a small but growing literature on organizational learning (see Hedberg, 1981, for an introduction and survey). This literature suggests ways in which organizations can change or add dominant logics.

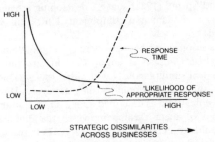

Figure 3.   The diversity and performance

498   *C. K. Prahalad and R. A. Bettis*

First, let us consider the situation involved in changing the dominant logic of a (single-logic) firm. The explicit assumption here is that the structure of the core industry the firm competes in is or has changed significantly.

In general it appears (see March and Simon, 1958; Downs, 1967; Terreberrey, 1968; Cyert and March, 1963; Starbuck, 1976; Hedberg, 1973; Hedberg, Nystrom and Starbuck, 1976) that changes in the ways organizations solve significant new problems (i.e. change dominant logics) are triggered by substantial problems or crises. Hedberg (1981) also suggests that opportunities or changes in key executives may also trigger learning, but here the evidence is small by comparison. (Key executive changes are often made in response to crises.) It would appear that in the overwhelming number of instances a crisis is needed to precipitate change (e.g. 'Why fix it if it is not broke?') Not only must there be a crisis but as Nystrom, Hedberg and Starbuck (1976), propose and illustrate, the initial response to the crisis is likely to be inappropriate. In other words the initial response is likely to draw on the now inappropriate but still current dominant logic. This, of course, provokes a deepening of the crisis and a search for other solutions. In other words survival is likely to become dependent on finding a new logic.

Given that the opportunity for learning has been elicited by a crisis (or other event) the organizational learning literature (e.g. Hedberg, 1981) suggests that unlearning must occur to make way for new mental maps. Unlearning is simply the process by which firms eliminate old logics and behaviors and make room for new ones. Interestingly, the more successful organizations have been, the more difficult unlearning becomes (Argyris and Schon, 1978; Starbuck and Hedberg, 1977).

Given that these two preconditions, a precipitating crisis and a start of unlearning, have occurred, the stage is set for the kind of learning that can result in a new dominant logic. However, as Michael (1973) and Hedberg (1981) have observed, little is known about how organizations' cognitive structures are changed. Hence, the discussion *here must be largely speculative*. Hedberg (1981) makes four general suggestions: (1) making organizations more experimental; (2) regulating organizations' sensitivity to environmental changes to an optimal level (neither too low nor too high); (3) redesigning organizations' inner and outer environments; and (4) achieving a dynamic balance between stabilizing and destabilizing influences. Beyond these general areas the current authors suggest: (1) structuring the top management team to include individuals with significantly different experience bases; (2) encouraging top managers to enrich their experience bases through sabbaticals and educational experiences; (3) rehearsing as a management team for a broad range of future industry scenarios; (4) separating economic evaluation from manager evaluation so that executives can be rewarded for experimenting even when projects fail; and (5) legitimizing dissent. Furthermore, in an interesting article about managerial responses to changing environments, Kiesler and Sproul (1982) suggest developing schemas that incorporate the expectation of change as a fundamental component. Unfortunately, again the 'how to' remains largely undefined.

The discussion in this section so far has considered changing dominant logics, not adding new ones. Adding new logics implies retaining the old one and not unlearning it, but developing the ability to deal simultaneously with other logics. This generally falls beyond what has been studied in the organizational learning literature. Diversification is often not triggered by a crisis, and unlearning as described above is not desirable. It appears that what must occur is some kind of meta-learning in which the dominant coalition learns to simultaneously conceptualize different type businesses. Perhaps some sort of meta-logic evolves that specifies the necessity of, and rules for, picking between partially contradictory mental maps. Further research here is obviously needed.

The meaning of 'relatedness'
The concept of related or conglomerate diversification was typically based on an analysis of the technological and market characteristics. The view presented here suggests that we may have to develop a concept of relatedness based on the 'strategic similarities' of businesses and the cognitive composition of the top management team. In other words relatedness may be as much a cognitive concept as it is an economic and technical concept.

Future research
The concept of a dominant logic presents opportunities to deepen our understanding of the management of diversification and the relationships between diversity and performance. A first necessary step is to move beyond the purely conceptual stage to measurement of the construct, or in other words, to being able to specify just what a particular dominant logic actually is. The authors have had experience in trying to construct the dominant logic of a firm by in-depth interviewing of the top management team, and believe that useful results and insights can be achieved. However, such an approach, though useful as a consulting framework, lacks the rigor necessary to establishing general results. Furthermore, quantification is complicated by the cognitive nature of the dominant logic.

Decision-makers' descriptions of their own policies are often inaccurate (Hoffman, 1960; Slovic, 1969; Balke, Hammond and Meyer, 1973). Similarly, stated policies and intentions often vary from what is actually used. Argyris and Schon (1974) describe this as the difference between 'espoused theories' and 'theories in use' that actually govern behavior. These researchers suggest that a person's theory in use cannot be obtained simply by asking for it. Creative questionnaires and analysis procedures, however, can be developed that elicit the true nature of the dominant logic. For example, the policy-capturing methodology (Slovic and Lichtenstein, 1971; Slovic, Fischoff and Lichtenstein, 1977) would seem to be a powerful approach to measuring a firm's dominant logic.

Another approach to establishing a firm's dominant logic could be through the use of historical analysis. As previous arguments have discussed, the dominant logic is developed as a result of the experiences of the key executives. Hence, delving into the industry and firm experience of these key individuals would seem to be a fruitful approach, especially when coupled with in-depth interviews of the individuals and their immediate subordinates.

A second important area for future research is the previously mentioned process of learning to use multiple dominant logics. The organizational learning literature deals primarily with changing cognitive maps. It does not deal with the process of learning to use multiple, partially contradictory maps. Some firms have obviously been able to solve this problem. Logitudinal clinical investigation is necessary to determine how.

REFERENCES

Allison, Graham J. *Essence of Decision: Explaining the Cuban Missile Crisis*. Little, Brown, Boston, MA, 1971.
Ansoff, H. Igor. *Corporate Strategy*. McGraw-Hill, New York, 1965.
Argyris, C. and D. A. Schon. *Theory in Practice: Increasing Professional Effectiveness*. Jossey-Bass, San Francisco, CA, 1974.
Argyris, C. and D. Schon. *Organizational Learning*. Addison-Wesley, Reading, MA, 1978.
Balke, W. M., K. R. Hammond and G. D. Meyer. 'An alternative approach to labor-management negotiations', *Administrative Science Quarterly*, **18**, 1973, pp. 311–327.
Bettis, R. A. 'Strategic portfolio management in the multibusiness firm: implementing the portfolio concept'. Unpublished doctoral dissertation, University of Michigan, 1979.

500   *C. K. Prahalad and R. A. Bettis*

Bettis, R. and V. Mahajan. 'Risk/return performance of diversified firms', *Management Science,* forthcoming.

Bettis, R. A., W. K. Hall and C. K. Prahalad. 'Diversity and performance in the multibusiness firm', *National Proceedings of the American Institute for Decision Sciences,* 1978, pp. 210-212.

Bower, J. L. *Managing the Resource Allocation Process,* Irwin, Homewood, IL, 1972a.

Bower, J. L. 'Metamanagement: a technology and a philosophy'. Paper presented at the Winter meeting of AAAS, 20 November 1972b.

Chandler, Alfred D. *Strategy and Structure.* MIT Press, Cambridge, MA, 1962.

Channon, Derek. *The Strategy and Structure of British Enterprise,* Graduate School of Business Administration, Harvard University, Boston, 1973.

Cyert, R. and J. March. *A Behavioral Theory of the Firm.* Prentice Hall, Englewood Cliffs, NJ, 1963.

Das, Rajan. *Managing Diversification: The General Management Perspective.* Macmillan India, New Delhi, 1981.

Deal, Terrence E. and Allan A. Kennedy. *Corporate Cultures.* Addison-Wesley, Reading, MA, 1982.

de Groot, A. D. *Thought and Choice in Chess.* Mouton, The Hague, 1965.

Donaldson, G. and Jay Lorsch. *Decision Making at the Top.* Basic Books, New York, 1983.

Downs, A. *Inside Bureaucracy.* Little, Brown, Boston, MA, 1967.

Hambrick, D. C. 'Environmental scanning and organizational strategy', *Strategic Management Journal,* **3,** 1982, pp. 159-174.

Hamermesh, R. G. 'Responding to the divisional profit crisis'. Unpublished doctoral dissertation, Harvard Business School, 1977.

Haspeslagh, P. 'Portfolio planning: uses and limits', *Harvard Business Review,* January–February 1982, pp. 58-73.

Hedberg, B. 'Organizational stagnation and choice of strategy'. Working paper, International Institute of Management, Berlin, 1973.

Hedberg, B. 'How organizations learn and unlearn'. In Nystron, P. and W. Starbuck (eds), *Handbook of Organizational Design.* Oxford University Press, Oxford, 1981.

Hedberg, B., P. Nystrom and W. Starbuck. 'Camping on seesaws: prescriptions for a self-designing organization', *Administrative Science Quarterly,* **21,** 1976, pp. 41-65.

Hofer, Charles W. and Dan Schendel. *Strategy Formulation: Analytical Concepts.* West, St Paul, MN, 1978.

Hoffman, P. 'The paramorphic representation of clinical judgment', *Psychological Bulletin,* **47,** 1960, pp. 116-131.

Huff, A. S. 'Industry influence on strategy reformulation', *Strategic Management Journal,* **3,** 1982, pp. 119-131.

Kiesler, S. and L. Sproul. 'Managerial response to changing environments: perspectives and problem sensing from social cognition', *Administrative Science Quarterly,* **37,** 1982, pp. 548-570.

Kuhn, Thomas S. *The Structure of Scientific Revolutions,* 2nd edn. University of Chicago Press, Chicago, IL, 1970.

March, J. and H. Simon. *Organizations.* Wiley, New York, 1958.

Michael, Donald N. *On Learning to Plan and Planning to Learn.* Jossey-Bass, San Francisco, CA, 1973.

Miles, R. H. *Coffin Nails and Corporate Strategies.* Prentice Hall, Englewood Cliffs, NJ, 1982.

Montgomery, Cynthia. 'Diversification, market structure and firm performance: an extension of Rumelt's model', Ph.D. dissertation, Purdue University, 1979.

Nathanson, Daniel and James Cassano. 'Organization, diversity, and performance', *Wharton Magazine,* Summer 1982, pp. 19-26.

Newell, A. and Herbert Simon. *Human Problem Solving.* Prentice-Hall, Englewood Cliffs, NJ, 1972.

Nisbett, R. and L. Ross. *Human Inference: Strategies and Shortcomings of Social Judgement.* Prentice-Hall, Englewood Cliffs, NJ, 1980.

Norman, D. *Memory and Attention,* 2nd edn. Wiley, New York, 1976.

Nystrom, P., B. Hedberg and W. Starbuck. 'Interacting processes as organizational designs'. In Kilman, R., L. Pondy and D. Slevin (eds) *The Management of Organization Design.* Elsevier, New York, 1976.

Ouchi, William G. *Theory Z.* Addison-Wesley, Reading, MA, 1981.

Pascale, Richard J. and Anthony G. Athos. *The Art of Japanese Management*. Simon and Schuster, New York, 1981.

Pavan, R. J. 'Strategy and structure of Italian enterprise'. Unpublished doctoral dissertation, Harvard Business School, 1972.

Peters, Thomas J. and Robert H. Waterman, Jr. *In Search of Excellence*. Harper and Row, New York, 1982.

Pooley, G. 'Strategy and structure of French enterprise'. Unpublished doctoral dissertation, Harvard Business School, 1972.

Porter, M. *Competitive Strategy*. The Free Press, New York, 1980.

Porter, M., D. Collis, J. DeBelina, J. Elsasser, J. Hornthal and R. Shearer. 'The chain saw industry in 1974'. In Porter, M. (ed.) *Cases in Competitive Strategy*. The Free Press, New York, 1983.

Prahalad, C. K. and Y. Doz. 'An approach to strategic control in MNCs', *Sloan Management Review*, Summer 1981, pp. 5-13.

Rumelt, Richard P. *Strategy, Structure, and Economic Performance*. Division of Research, Graduate School of Business Administration, Harvard University, 1974.

Rumelt, Richard P. 'Diversity and profitability'. Paper MGL-51, Managerial Studies Center, Graduate School of Management, University of California, Los Angeles, 1977.

Schoeffler, Sidney, Robert D. Buzzell and Donald F. Heany. 'Impact of strategic planning on profit performance', *Harvard Business Review*, March-April 1974, pp. 137-145.

Simon, Herbert A. 'Information processing models of cognition', *Annual Review of Psychology*, **30**, 1979, pp. 363-396.

Skinner, B. F. *Science and Human Behavior*. Macmillan, New York, 1953.

Slovic, P. 'Analyzing the expert judge: a descriptive study of stockbroker's decision processes', *Journal of Applied Psychology*, **53**, 1969, pp. 255-263.

Slovic, P. and S. Lichtenstein. 'Comparison of Bayesian and regression approaches to the study of information processing in judgment', *Organizational Behavior and Human Performance*, **6**, 1971, pp. 649-744.

Slovic, P., B. Fischoff and S. Lichtenstein. 'Behavioral decision theory'. In Rosenzweig, R. and L. W. Porter (eds), *Annual Review of Psychology*. Annual Review, Palo Alto, CA, 1977, pp. 1-39.

Starbuck, W. 'Organizations and their environments'. In Dunnette, M. (ed.) *Handbook of Industrial and Organizational Psychology*. Rand McNally, Chicago, IL, 1976.

Starbuck, W. and B. Hedberg. 'Saving an organization from a stagnating environment'. In Thorelli, H. (ed.) *Strategy + Structure = Performance*. Indiana University Press, Bloomington, IN, 1977.

Suzuki, Y. 'The strategy and structure of top 100 Japanese industrial enterprises 1950-1970', *Strategic Management Journal*, **3**, 1980, pp. 265-291.

Terreberry, S. 'The evolution of organizational environments', *Administrative Science Quarterly*, **12**, 1968, pp. 590-613.

Thanheiser, H. 'Strategy and structure of German enterprise'. Unpublished doctoral dissertation, Harvard Business School, 1972.

Tversky, Amos and Daniel Kahneman. 'Availability: a heuristic for judging frequency and probability', *Cognitive Psychology*, **4**, 1973, pp. 207-232.

Tversky, Amos and Daniel Kahneman. 'Judgment under uncertainty: heuristics and biases', *Science*, **185**, 1974, pp. 1124-1131.

Weick, K. *The Social Psychology of Organizing*, 2nd edn. Addison-Wesley, Reading, MA, 1979.

Wrigley, Leonard. 'Divisional autonomy and diversification'. DBA dissertation, Harvard University, 1970.

[18]

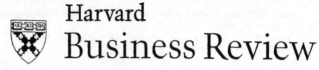

Harvard
Business Review
July-August 1972

Larry E. Greiner

Evolution and revolution as organizations grow

*A company's past has clues for management
that are critical to future success*

Foreword

This author maintains that growing organizations move through five distinguishable phases of development, each of which contains a relatively calm period of growth that ends with a management crisis. He argues, moreover, that since each phase is strongly influenced by the previous one, a management with a sense of its own organization's history can anticipate and prepare for the next developmental crisis. This article provides a prescription for appropriate management action in each of the five phases, and it shows how companies can turn organizational crises into opportunities for future growth.

Mr. Greiner is Associate Professor of Organizational Behavior at the Harvard Business School and is the author of several previous HBR articles on organization development.

A small research company chooses too complicated and formalized an organization structure for its young age and limited size. It flounders in rigidity and bureaucracy for several years and is finally acquired by a larger company.

Key executives of a retail store chain hold on to an organization structure long after it has served its purpose, because their power is derived from this structure. The company eventually goes into bankruptcy.

A large bank disciplines a "rebellious" manager who is blamed for current control problems, when the underlying cause is centralized pro-

Author's note: This article is part of a continuing project on organization development with my colleague, Professor Louis B. Barnes, and sponsored by the Division of Research, Harvard Business School.

Harvard Business Review: July-August 1972

cedures that are holding back expansion into new markets. Many younger managers subsequently leave the bank, competition moves in, and profits are still declining.

The problems of these companies, like those of many others, are rooted more in past decisions than in present events or outside market dynamics. Historical forces do indeed shape the future growth of organizations. Yet management, in its haste to grow, often overlooks such critical developmental questions as: Where has our organization been? Where is it now? And what do the answers to these questions mean for where we are going? Instead, its gaze is fixed outward toward the environment and the future—as if more precise market projections will provide a new organizational identity.

Companies fail to see that many clues to their future success lie within their own organizations and their evolving states of development. Moreover, the inability of management to understand its organization development problems can result in a company becoming "frozen" in its present stage of evolution or, ultimately, in failure, regardless of market opportunities.

My position in this article is that the future of an organization may be less determined by outside forces than it is by the organization's history. In stressing the force of history on an organization, I have drawn from the legacies of European psychologists (their thesis being that individual behavior is determined primarily by previous events and experiences, not by what lies ahead). Extending this analogy of individual development to the problems of organization development, I shall discuss a series of developmental phases through which growing companies tend to pass. But, first, let me provide two definitions:

1. The term *evolution* is used to describe pro-

longed periods of growth where no major upheaval occurs in organization practices.

2. The term *revolution* is used to describe those periods of substantial turmoil in organization life.

As a company progresses through developmental phases, each evolutionary period creates its own revolution. For instance, centralized practices eventually lead to demands for decentralization. Moreover, the nature of management's solution to each revolutionary period determines whether a company will move forward into its next stage of evolutionary growth. As I shall show later, there are at least five phases of organization development, each characterized by both an evolution and a revolution.

Key forces in development

During the past few years a small amount of research knowledge about the phases of organization development has been building. Some of this research is very quantitative, such as time-series analyses that reveal patterns of economic performance over time.[1] The majority of studies, however, are case-oriented and use company records and interviews to reconstruct a rich picture of corporate development.[2] Yet both types of research tend to be heavily empirical without attempting more generalized statements about the overall process of development.

A notable exception is the historical work of Alfred D. Chandler, Jr., in his book *Strategy and Structure*.[3] This study depicts four very broad and general phases in the lives of four large U.S. companies. It proposes that outside market opportunities determine a company's strategy, which in turn determines the company's organization structure. This thesis has a valid ring for the four companies examined by Chandler, largely because they developed in a time of explosive markets and technological advances. But more recent evidence suggests that organization structure may be less malleable than Chandler assumed; in fact, structure can play a critical role in influencing corporate strategy. It is this reverse emphasis on how organization structure affects future growth which is highlighted in the model presented in this article.

From an analysis of recent studies,[4] five key dimensions emerge as essential for building a model of organization development:

1. Age of the organization.

1. See, for example, William H. Starbuck, "Organizational Metamorphosis," in *Promising Research Directions*, edited by R.W. Millman and M.P. Hottenstein (Tempe, Arizona, Academy of Management, 1968), p. 113.

2. See, for example, the *Grangesberg* case series, prepared by C. Roland Christensen and Bruce R. Scott, Case Clearing House; Harvard Business School.

3. *Strategy and Structure: Chapters in the History of the American Industrial Enterprise* (Cambridge, Massachusetts, The M.I.T. Press, 1962).

4. I have drawn on many sources for evidence: (a) numerous cases collected at the Harvard Business School; (b) *Organization Growth and Development*, edited by William H. Starbuck (Middlesex, England, Penguin Books, Ltd., 1971), where several studies are cited; and (c) articles published in journals, such as Lawrence E. Fouraker and John M. Stopford, "Organization Structure and the Multinational Strategy," *Administrative Science Quarterly*, Vol. 13, No. 1, 1968, p. 47; and Malcolm S. Salter, "Management Appraisal and Reward Systems," *Journal of Business Policy*, Vol. 1, No. 4, 1971.

2. Size of the organization.
3. Stages of evolution.
4. Stages of revolution.
5. Growth rate of the industry.

I shall describe each of these elements separately, but first note their combined effect as illustrated in *Exhibit I*. Note especially how each dimension influences the other over time; when all five elements begin to interact, a more complete and dynamic picture of organizational growth emerges.

After describing these dimensions and their interconnections, I shall discuss each evolutionary/revolutionary phase of development and show (a) how each stage of evolution breeds its own revolution, and (b) how management solu-

tions to each revolution determine the next stage of evolution.

Age of the organization

The most obvious and essential dimension for any model of development is the life span of an organization (represented as the horizontal axis in *Exhibit I*). All historical studies gather data from various points in time and then make comparisons. From these observations, it is evident that the same organization practices are not maintained throughout a long time span. This makes a most basic point: management problems and principles are rooted in time. The concept of decentralization, for example, can have meaning for describing corporate practices

Exhibit I. Model of organization development

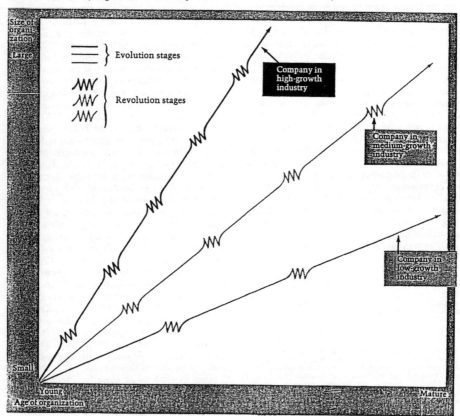

Harvard Business Review: July-August 1972

at one time period but loses its descriptive power at another.

The passage of time also contributes to the institutionalization of managerial attitudes. As a result, employee behavior becomes not only more predictable but also more difficult to change when attitudes are outdated.

Size of the organization

This dimension is depicted as the vertical axis in *Exhibit I.* A company's problems and solutions tend to change markedly as the number of employees and sales volume increase. Thus, time is not the only determinant of structure; in fact, organizations that do not grow in size can retain many of the same management issues and practices over lengthy periods. In addition to increased size, however, problems of coordination and communication magnify, new functions emerge, levels in the management hierarchy multiply, and jobs become more interrelated.

Stages of evolution

As both age and size increase, another phenomenon becomes evident: the prolonged growth that I have termed the evolutionary period. Most growing organizations do not expand for two years and then retreat for one year; rather, those that survive a crisis usually enjoy four to eight years of continuous growth without a major economic setback or severe internal disruption. The term evolution seems appropriate for describing these quieter periods because only modest adjustments appear necessary for maintaining growth under the same overall pattern of management.

Stages of revolution

Smooth evolution is not inevitable; it cannot be assumed that organization growth is linear. *Fortune's* "500" list, for example, has had significant turnover during the last 50 years. Thus we find evidence from numerous case histories which reveals periods of substantial turbulence spaced between smoother periods of evolution.

I have termed these turbulent times the periods of revolution because they typically exhibit a serious upheaval of management practices. Traditional management practices, which were appropriate for a smaller size and earlier time, are brought under scrutiny by frustrated top

managers and disillusioned lower-level managers. During such periods of crisis, a number of companies fail—those unable to abandon past practices and effect major organization changes are likely either to fold or to level off in their growth rates.

The critical task for management in each revolutionary period is to find a new set of organization practices that will become the basis for managing the next period of evolutionary growth. Interestingly enough, these new practices eventually sow their own seeds of decay and lead to another period of revolution. Companies therefore experience the irony of seeing a major solution in one time period become a major problem at a latter date.

Growth rate of the industry

The speed at which an organization experiences phases of evolution and revolution is closely related to the market environment of its industry. For example, a company in a rapidly expanding market will have to add employees rapidly; hence, the need for new organization structures to accommodate large staff increases is accelerated. While evolutionary periods tend to be relatively short in fast-growing industries, much longer evolutionary periods occur in mature or slowly growing industries.

Evolution can also be prolonged, and revolutions delayed, when profits come easily. For instance, companies that make grievous errors in a rewarding industry can still look good on their profit and loss statements; thus they can avoid a change in management practices for a longer period. The aerospace industry in its infancy is an example. Yet revolutionary periods still occur, as one did in aerospace when profit opportunities began to dry up. Revolutions seem to be much more severe and difficult to resolve when the market environment is poor.

Phases of growth

With the foregoing framework in mind, let us now examine in depth the five specific phases of evolution and revolution. As shown in *Exhibit II,* each evolutionary period is characterized by the dominant *management style* used to achieve growth, while each revolutionary period is characterized by the dominant *management problem* that must be solved before growth can continue. The patterns presented in *Exhibit II* seem to be

Exhibit II. The five phases of growth

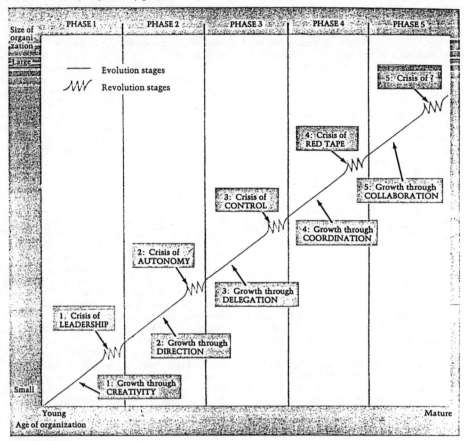

typical for companies in industries with moderate growth over a long time period; companies in faster growing industries tend to experience all five phases more rapidly, while those in slower growing industries encounter only two or three phases over many years.

It is important to note that *each phase is both an effect of the previous phase and a cause for the next phase.* For example, the evolutionary management style in Phase 3 of the exhibit is "delegation," which grows out of, and becomes the solution to, demands for greater "autonomy" in the preceding Phase 2 revolution. The style of delegation used in Phase 3, however, eventually provokes a major revolutionary crisis that

is characterized by attempts to regain control over the diversity created through increased delegation.

The principal implication of each phase is that management actions are narrowly prescribed if growth is to occur. For example, a company experiencing an autonomy crisis in Phase 2 cannot return to directive management for a solution— it must adopt a new style of delegation in order to move ahead.

Phase 1: Creativity ...

In the birth stage of an organization, the emphasis is on creating both a product and a mar-

Harvard Business Review: July-August 1972

ket. Here are the characteristics of the period of creative evolution:

O The company's founders are usually technically or entrepreneurially oriented, and they disdain management activities; their physical and mental energies are absorbed entirely in making and selling a new product.

O Communication among employees is frequent and informal.

O Long hours of work are rewarded by modest salaries and the promise of ownership benefits.

O Control of activities comes from immediate marketplace feedback; the management acts as the customers react.

... e) the leadership crisis: All of the foregoing individualistic and creative activities are essential for the company to get off the ground. But therein lies the problem. As the company grows, larger production runs require knowledge about the efficiencies of manufacturing. Increased numbers of employees cannot be managed exclusively through informal communication; new employees are not motivated by an intense dedication to the product or organization. Additional capital must be secured, and new accounting procedures are needed for financial control.

Thus the founders find themselves burdened with unwanted management responsibilities. So they long for the "good old days," still trying to act as they did in the past. And conflicts between the harried leaders grow more intense.

At this point a crisis of leadership occurs, which is the onset of the first revolution. Who is to lead the company out of confusion and solve the managerial problems confronting it? Quite obviously, a strong manager is needed who has the necessary knowledge and skill to introduce new business techniques. But this is easier said than done. The founders often hate to step aside even though they are probably temperamentally unsuited to be managers. So here is the first critical developmental choice— to locate and install a strong business manager who is acceptable to the founders and who can pull the organization together.

Phase 2: Direction ...

Those companies that survive the first phase by installing a capable business manager usually embark on a period of sustained growth under able and directive leadership. Here are the characteristics of this evolutionary period:

O A functional organization structure is in-troduced to separate manufacturing from marketing activities, and job assignments become more specialized.

O Accounting systems for inventory and purchasing are introduced.

O Incentives, budgets, and work standards are adopted.

O Communication becomes more formal and impersonal as a hierarchy of titles and positions builds.

O The new manager and his key supervisors take most of the responsibility for instituting direction, while lower-level supervisors are treated more as functional specialists than as autonomous decision-making managers.

... e) the autonomy crisis: Although the new directive techniques channel employee energy more efficiently into growth, they eventually become inappropriate for controlling a larger, more diverse and complex organization. Lower-level employees find themselves restricted by a cumbersome and centralized hierarchy. They have come to possess more direct knowledge about markets and machinery than do the leaders at the top; consequently, they feel torn between following procedures and taking initiative on their own.

Thus the second revolution is imminent as a crisis develops from demands for greater autonomy on the part of lower-level managers. The solution adopted by most companies is to move toward greater delegation. Yet it is difficult for top managers who were previously successful at being directive to give up responsibility. Moreover, lower-level managers are not accustomed to making decisions for themselves. As a result, numerous companies flounder during this revolutionary period, adhering to centralized methods while lower-level employees grow more disenchanted and leave the organization.

Phase 3: Delegation ...

The next era of growth evolves from the successful application of a decentralized organization structure. It exhibits these characteristics:

O Much greater responsibility is given to the managers of plants and market territories.

O Profit centers and bonuses are used to stimulate motivation.

O The top executives at headquarters restrain themselves to managing by exception, based on periodic reports from the field.

O Management often concentrates on making

new acquisitions which can be lined up beside other decentralized units.

O Communication from the top is infrequent, usually by correspondence, telephone, or brief visits to field locations.

The delegation stage proves useful for gaining expansion through heightened motivation at lower levels. Decentralized managers with greater authority and incentive are able to penetrate larger markets, respond faster to customers, and develop new products.

... & the control crisis: A serious problem eventually evolves, however, as top executives sense that they are losing control over a highly diversified field operation. Autonomous field managers prefer to run their own shows without coordinating plans, money, technology, and manpower with the rest of the organization. Freedom breeds a parochial attitude.

Hence, the Phase 3 revolution is under way when top management seeks to regain control over the total company. Some top managements attempt a return to centralized management, which usually fails because of the vast scope of operations. Those companies that move ahead find a new solution in the use of special coordination techniques.

Phase 4: Coordination...

During this phase, the evolutionary period is characterized by the use of formal systems for achieving greater coordination and by top executives taking responsibility for the initiation and administration of these new systems. For example:

O Decentralized units are merged into product groups.

O Formal planning procedures are established and intensively reviewed.

O Numerous staff personnel are hired and located at headquarters to initiate company-wide programs of control and review for line managers.

O Capital expenditures are carefully weighed and parceled out across the organization.

O Each product group is treated as an investment center where return on invested capital is an important criterion used in allocating funds.

O Certain technical functions, such as data processing, are centralized at headquarters, while daily operating decisions remain decentralized.

O Stock options and companywide profit shar-

ing are used to encourage identity with the firm as a whole.

All of these new coordination systems prove useful for achieving growth through more efficient allocation of a company's limited resources. They prompt field managers to look beyond the needs of their local units. While these managers still have much decision-making responsibility, they learn to justify their actions more carefully to a "watchdog" audience at headquarters.

... & the red-tape crisis: But a lack of confidence gradually builds between line and staff, and between headquarters and the field. The proliferation of systems and programs begins to exceed its utility; a red-tape crisis is created. Line managers, for example, increasingly resent heavy staff direction from those who are not familiar with local conditions. Staff people, on the other hand, complain about uncooperative and uninformed line managers. Together both groups criticize the bureaucratic paper system that has evolved. Procedures take precedence over problem solving, and innovation is dampened. In short, the organization has become too large and complex to be managed through formal programs and rigid systems. The Phase 4 revolution is under way.

Phase 5: Collaboration...

The last observable phase in previous studies emphasizes strong interpersonal collaboration in an attempt to overcome the red-tape crisis. Where Phase 4 was managed more through formal systems and procedures, Phase 5 emphasizes greater spontaneity in management action through teams and the skillful confrontation of interpersonal differences. Social control and self-discipline take over from formal control. This transition is especially difficult for those experts who created the old systems as well as for those line managers who relied on formal methods for answers.

The Phase 5 evolution, then, builds around a more flexible and behavioral approach to management. Here are its characteristics:

O The focus is on solving problems quickly through team action.

O Teams are combined across functions for task-group activity.

O Headquarters staff experts are reduced in number, reassigned, and combined in interdis-

Harvard Business Review: July-August 1972

ciplinary teams to consult with, not to direct, field units.

O A matrix-type structure is frequently used to assemble the right teams for the appropriate problems.

O Previous formal systems are simplified and combined into single multipurpose systems.

O Conferences of key managers are held frequently to focus on major problem issues.

O Educational programs are utilized to train managers in behavioral skills for achieving better teamwork and conflict resolution.

O Real-time information systems are integrated into daily decision making.

O Economic rewards are geared more to team performance than to individual achievement.

O Experiments in new practices are encouraged throughout the organization.

. . . & the ? crisis: What will be the revolution in response to this stage of evolution? Many large U.S. companies are now in the Phase 5 evolutionary stage, so the answers are critical. While there is little clear evidence, I imagine the revolution will center around the "psychological saturation" of employees who grow emotionally and physically exhausted by the intensity of teamwork and the heavy pressure for innovative solutions.

My hunch is that the Phase 5 revolution will be solved through new structures and programs that allow employees to periodically rest, reflect, and revitalize themselves. We may even see companies with dual organization structures: a "habit" structure for getting the daily work done, and a "reflective" structure for stimulating perspective and personal enrichment. Employees could then move back and forth between the two structures as their energies are dissipated and refueled.

One European organization has implemented just such a structure. Five reflective groups have been established outside the regular structure for the purpose of continuously evaluating five task activities basic to the organization. They report directly to the managing director, although their reports are made public throughout the organization. Membership in each group includes all levels and functions, and employees are rotated through these groups on a six-month basis.

Other concrete examples now in practice include providing sabbaticals for employees, moving managers in and out of "hot spot" jobs, establishing a four-day workweek, assuring job security, building physical facilities for relaxation *during* the working day, making jobs more interchangeable, creating an extra team on the assembly line so that one team is always off for reeducation, and switching to longer vacations and more flexible working hours.

The Chinese practice of requiring executives to spend time periodically on lower-level jobs may also be worth a nonideological evaluation. For too long U.S. management has assumed that career progress should be equated with an upward path toward title, salary, and power. Could it be that some vice presidents of marketing might just long for, and even benefit from, temporary duty in the field sales organization?

Implications of history

Let me now summarize some important implications for practicing managers. First, the main features of this discussion are depicted in *Exhibit III*, which shows the specific management actions that characterize each growth phase. These actions are also the solutions which ended each preceding revolutionary period.

In one sense, I hope that many readers will react to my model by calling it obvious and natural for depicting the growth of an organization. To me this type of reaction is a useful test of the model's validity.

But at a more reflective level I imagine some of these reactions are more hindsight than foresight. Those experienced managers who have been through a developmental sequence can empathize with it now, but how did they react when in the middle of a stage of evolution or revolution? They can probably recall the limits of their own developmental understanding at that time. Perhaps they resisted desirable changes or were even swept emotionally into a revolution without being able to propose constructive solutions. So let me offer some explicit guidelines for managers of growing organizations to keep in mind.

Know where you are in the developmental sequence.

Every organization and its component parts are at different stages of development. The task of top management is to be aware of these stages; otherwise, it may not recognize when the time for change has come, or it may act to impose the wrong solution.

[19]

ORGANIZATION SCIENCE
Vol. 3, No. 3, August 1992
Printed in U.S.A.

KNOWLEDGE OF THE FIRM, COMBINATIVE CAPABILITIES, AND THE REPLICATION OF TECHNOLOGY*

BRUCE KOGUT AND UDO ZANDER

*The Wharton School, University of Pennsylvania, Philadelphia,
Pennsylvania* 19104
*Institute of International Business, Stockholm School of Economics,
Stockholm, Sweden*

How should we understand why firms exist? A prevailing view has been that they serve to keep in check the transaction costs arising from the self-interested motivations of individuals. We develop in this article the argument that what firms do better than markets is the sharing and transfer of the knowledge of individuals and groups within an organization. This knowledge consists of information (e.g., who knows what) and of know-how (e.g., how to organize a research team). What is central to our argument is that knowledge is held by individuals, but is also expressed in regularities by which members cooperate in a social community (i.e., group, organization, or network). If knowledge is only held at the individual level, then firms could change simply by employee turnover. Because we know that hiring new workers is not equivalent to changing the skills of a firm, an analysis of what firms can do must understand knowledge as embedded in the organizing principles by which people cooperate within organizations.

Based on this discussion, a paradox is identified: efforts by a firm to grow by the replication of its technology enhances the potential for imitation. By considering how firms can deter imitation by innovation, we develop a more dynamic view of how firms create new knowledge. We build up this dynamic perspective by suggesting that firms learn new skills by recombining their current capabilities. Because new ways of cooperating cannot be easily acquired, growth occurs by building on the social relationships that currently exist in a firm. What a firm has done before tends to predict what it can do in the future. In this sense, the cumulative knowledge of the firm provides options to expand in new but uncertain markets in the future.

We discuss at length the example of the make/buy decision and propose several testable hypotheses regarding the boundaries of the firm, without appealing to the notion of "opportunism."
(ORGANIZATIONAL KNOWLEDGE; TECHNOLOGY TRANSFER; IMITATION; CAPABILITIES; LEARNING)

A fundamental puzzle, as first stated by Michael Polanyi (1966), is that individuals appear to know more than they can explain. That knowledge can be tacit has broad implications for understanding the difficulty of imitating and diffusing individual skills, a problem lying at the heart of artificial intelligence to the competitive analysis of firms. Though the idea of tacit knowledge has been widely evoked but rarely defined—as if the lack of definition is itself evidence of the concept, it represents a dramatically different vantage point by which to analyze the capabilities and boundaries of firms.

This article seeks to lay out an organizational foundation to a theory of the firm. To rephrase Polanyi's puzzle of tacit knowledge, organizations know more than what their contracts can say. The analysis of what organizations are should be grounded in the understanding of what they know how to do.

*Accepted by Arie Y. Lewin; received September 1988. This paper has been with the authors for three revisions.

383

It is curious that the considerable attention given to how organizations learn has obscured the implication that organizations "know" something. In fact, the knowledge of the firm, as opposed to learning, is relatively observable; operating rules, manufacturing technologies, and customer data banks are tangible representations of this knowledge. But the danger of this simple characterization is that everything that describes a firm becomes an aspect of its knowledge. While this is definitionally true, the theoretical challenge is to understand the knowledge base of a firm as leading to a set of capabilities that enhance the chances for growth and survival.

In our view, the central competitive dimension of what firms know how to do is to create and transfer knowledge efficiently within an organizational context. The following article seeks to describe these capabilities by analyzing the contention put forth by Winter (1987) that technology transfer and imitation are blades of the same scissor. The commonality is that technology is often costly to replicate, whether the replication is desired by the firm or occurs by imitation and unwanted diffusion. Though the terminology may differ, the underlying phenomena impacting the costs of technology transfer and imitation share similarities, regardless whether the replication occurs within the firm, by contract, or among competitors.

That similar factors may determine both the costs of imitation and technology transfer presents an interesting dilemma to the firm. In the efforts to speed the replication of current and new knowledge, there arises a fundamental paradox that the codification and simplification of knowledge also induces the likelihood of imitation. Technology transfer is a desired strategy in the replication and growth of the firm (whether in size or profits); imitation is a principal constraint.

Our view differs radically from that of the firm as a bundle of contracts that serves to allocate efficiently property rights. In contrast to the contract approach to understanding organizations, the assumption of the selfish motives of individuals resulting in shirking or dishonesty is not a necessary premise in our argument. Rather, we suggest that organizations are social communities in which individual and social expertise is transformed into economically useful products and services by the application of a set of higher-order organizing principles. Firms exist because they provide a social community of voluntaristic action structured by organizing principles that are not reduceable to individuals.

We categorize organizational knowledge into information and know-how based, a distinction that corresponds closely to that used in artificial intelligence of declarative and procedural knowledge. To move beyond a simple classification, these types of knowledge are argued to carry competitive implications through their facility to be easily replicated within an organization but difficult to imitate by other firms. Following the suggestions of Rogers (1983) and Winter (1987), the characteristics of both types of knowledge are analyzed along the dimensions of codifiability and complexity. By examining first personal expertise and then social knowledge, the capabilities of the firm in general are argued to rest in the organizing principles by which relationships among individuals, within and between groups, and among organizations are structured.

But organizations serve as more than mechanisms by which social knowledge is transferred, but also by which new knowledge, or learning, is created. The theoretical problem is that if the knowledge of the firm is argued to be competitively consequential, learning cannot be characterized as independent of the current capabilities. To explore this dynamic aspect, we introduce the concept of a **combinative capability** to synthesize and apply current and acquired knowledge. This concept is, then, explored in the context of a competitive environment. By this discussion, we ground such concepts as localized learning to path dependence by developing a micro-behavioral foundation of social knowledge, while also stipulating the effects of the degree of environmental selection on the evolution of this knowledge.

KNOWLEDGE OF THE FIRM   385

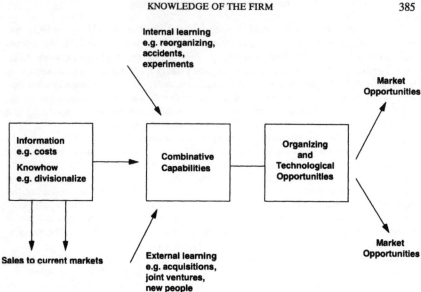

FIGURE 1.   Growth of Knowledge of the Firm.

To ground the abstraction of the argument in an example, we reexamine the empirical findings on the make-buy decision of firms. The importance of the ability to generate new knowledge suggests a different view on the "boundaries" of the firm, that is, what a firm makes and what it buys. Firms invest in those assets that correspond to a combination of current capabilities and expectations regarding future opportunities. Or, in other words, the knowledge of a firm can be considered as owning a portfolio of options, or platforms, on future developments.[1]

Figure 1 provides a roadmap to our argument. We begin by analyzing the knowledge of the firm by distinguishing between information regarding prices and the know-how, say, to divisionalize. This static portrait is the basis by which we explore how knowledge may be recombined through internal and external learning. An important limitation to the capability of developing new skills is the opportunity (or potential) in the organizing principles and technologies for further exploitation. Eventually, there are decreasing returns to a given technology or method of organizing, and there, consequently, results in an incentive to build new, but related skills. These investments in new ways of doing things, we suggest, serve as platforms on future and uncertain market opportunities.

It is important to underline the presumption that the knowledge of the firm must be understood as socially constructed, or, more simply stated, as resting in the organizing of human resources. The issue of the organizing principles underlying the creation, replication, and imitation of technology opens a window on understanding the capabilities of the firm as a set of "inert" resources that are difficult to imitate and redeploy.[2] It is the persistence in the organizing of social relationships in which knowledge is embedded that is the focus of inquiry developed in this article.

---

[1]This notion of a platform is investigated in Kogut (1991) and Kogut and Kim (1991).
[2]See Lippman and Rumelt (1982), Wernerfelt (1984), Rumelt (1984), Barney (1986), and Kogut (1987), as well as the publications that appeared while this article was under review by Dierickx and Cool (1989) and Prahalad and Hamel (1990).

Information and Know-How

There have been many suggestions as to how the knowledge of the firm might be categorized. Nelson (1982), for example, separates techno from logy, the former belonging to a firm, the latter to the public arena. A more common distinction is between research and development, or that between process and product.

For our purposes, we distinguish between two categories of knowledge as information and know-how.[3] By information, we mean knowledge which can be transmitted without loss of integrity once the syntactical rules required for deciphering it are known. Information includes facts, axiomatic propositions, and symbols. Nelson's idea of logy is, in fact, a recognition that within scientific communities, there exists a social agreement regarding the factual evidence by which to communicate the reliability of scientific findings. Similarly, public firms are required to report data to shareholders in a common format so as to facilitate analysis and appraisal. For the objective of public dissemination, information is standardized and released in order to be understood at minimal cost to those with the requisite training.

Of course, information is often proprietary. Firms maintain, as a rule, two sets of accounting data, one for external use, the other to aid managerial decisions and evaluation. Data can also be of competitive value. An obvious example is the value of information to traders of financial securities, but a more prosaic example is the data acquired by grocery stores on consumer expenditures.

Know-how is a frequently used, but rarely defined term. Von Hippel offers the definition that "know-how is the accumulated practical skill or expertise that allows one to do something smoothly and efficiently" (von Hippel 1988). The pivotal word in this definition is "accumulated," which implies that know-how must be learned and acquired.

Knowledge as information implies knowing **what** something means. Know-how is, as the compound words state, a description of knowing **how** to do something. In economics, this distinction is, implicitly, preserved in the often made distinction between exchange and production economies, where the former consists of only traders responding to prices, and the latter to how inputs are transformed into outputs. To use a current example, the problems of the adoption economy in Eastern Europe consist not only of just finding the right prices, but also learning how to organize a market and a firm efficiently.

Though this distinction between information and know-how appears to be a fundamental element in the analysis of organizational knowledge, most efforts in this direction have tended, following March and Simon (1958) and Cyert and March (1963), to investigate the notion of routines in the context of organizational learning. Yet, this vantage point for the investigation of firm knowledge is ill-chosen. Learning has little significance in the absence of a theory of organizational knowledge.

A routine is in itself an insightful but incomplete characterization of knowledge. Because of the broad coverage of the term routine, an appeal is often made to the analogy of a blueprint, an analogy favored by a number of authors.[4] But a blueprint favors much more a description of information than know-how. Knowing how to do something is much like a recipe; there is no substantive content in any of the steps, except for their capacity to produce a desired end.[5] The information is contained in

---

[3]Steve Kimbrough has pointed out in conversation that the terms are similar to Bertrand Russell's distinction between know-that and know-how.

[4]See Nelson and Winter (1982); Hannan and Freeman (1977); March and Simon (1958).

[5]In light of the wide appeal genetics has for organizational analogies, it is of interest to refer to Dawkin's (1987) discussion of genes as recipes (and the phenotype as a blueprint). See also Simon (1962).

the original listing of ingredients, but the know-how is only imperfectly represented in the description.

It is revealing that this distinction between information and know-how as blueprints and recipes is similar to that made between declarative and procedural knowledge used in computer science. Declarative knowledge consists of a statement that provides a state description, such as the information that inventory is equal to a 100 books. Procedural knowledge consists of statements that describe a process, such as a method by which inventory is minimized. This distinction is robust to other phenomena than software, even to a furniture set where the inventory of parts is first described and then the recipe of assembly laid out.

Know-how, like procedural knowledge, is a description of what defines current practice inside a firm. These practices may consist of how to organize factories, set transfer prices, or establish divisional and functional lines of authority and accountability. The knowledge displayed in an organizational chart, as in any blueprint, is limited to providing information on personnel and formal authority. The know-how is the understanding of how to organize a firm along these formal (and informal) lines. It is in the regularity of the structuring of work and of the interactions of employees conforming to explicit or implicit recipes that one finds the content of the firm's know-how.

The Inertness of Knowledge

Firms differ in their information and know-how and these differences, when they are economically interesting, have persisting effects on relative performance. Thus, a central characteristic to be explained is the persisting difference in capabilities, that is, the difficulty in their transfer and imitation. The persistence of differentials in firm performance lies in the joint problem of the difficulty of transferring and imitating knowledge.

There is a need, therefore, to go beyond the classification of information and know-how and consider why knowledge is not easily transmitted and replicated. The transferability and imitability of a firm's knowledge, whether it is in the form of information or know-how, are influenced by several characteristics (Kogut and Zander 1990). Rogers (1983) and Winter (1987) have proposed that knowledge can be analyzed along a number of dimensions.

Consider the two dimensions of codifiability and complexity. Codifiability refers to the ability of the firm to structure knowledge into a set of identifiable rules and relationships that can be easily communicated. Coded knowledge is alienable from the individual who wrote the code. Not all kinds of knowledge are amenable to codification. Drafting a recipe for the manufacturing of a musical instrument is unlikely to capture the requisite skills of a craftsperson.

Nor is this limitation only applicable to know-how. It is not always possible to identify the relevant information which operates as the data to an actor or set of actions. There may be no 'theory' (in the sense used above) by which to identify the relevant information, such as drawing the blueprint. This argument bears similarities to the artificial intelligence debate on the obstacles to formalizing noncodified "background knowledge" to scientific theories (Dreyfus and Dreyfus 1988). Codifiability is a question of the degree that there exists an implied theory by which to identify and symbolically represent knowledge. A theory may be as lacking for information as for know-how.[6]

---

[6]Contrary to Dreyfus' and Dreyfus' doubts, the organization behaviorists, Argyris and Schoen (1978, p. 11), believe it possible to derive the "theory-in-use" from "directly observable data of behavior... to ground... construction of the models of action theories which guide interpersonal behavior."

	Individual	Group	Organization	Network
Information	-facts	-who knows what	-profits -accounting data -formal & informal structure	-prices -whom to contact -who has what
Know-how	-skill of how to communicate -problem solving	-recipes of organizing such as Taylorist methods or craft production	-higher-order organizing principles of how to coordinate groups and transfer knowledge	-how to cooperate -how to sell and buy

FIGURE 2.

Though codifiability is a central characteristic, it does not capture other aspects of knowledge. Knowledge can vary in complexity. There are many ways to define complexity. From a computer science perspective, it can be defined as the number of operations (or CPU time) required to solve a task. Indeed, Simon's notion of nearly decomposable systems is closely related. An ordered system reduces the cost and necessity of complex communication patterns. Drawing upon information theory, Pringle (1951) draws the distinction between order and complexity, defining the latter as the number of parameters to define a system. Within any given ordering (or what we call a code), complexity can be accommodated, but at a cost.

These dimensions are not independent. Codifiability and complexity are related, though not identical. To return to Pringle's definition, it is obvious that the number of parameters required to define, say, a production system is dependent upon the choice of mathematical approaches or programming languages. For a particular code, the costs of transferring a technology will vary with its complexity. A change of code changes the degree of complexity.

Transformation of Personal to Social Knowledge

The final element in our characterization of the static properties of organizational knowledge is the distinction between the knowledge of an individual and that of the organization. Any discussion of firm knowledge confronts, ultimately, the problem of unit of analysis. We leave to the side the important task of specifying a more explicit integration of individual and organizational knowledge (such as via a shared culture, mechanisms of socialization, or an assumption of affiliative needs), but turn rather to laying out a description of the problem by distinguishing between personal, group, organizational, and network knowledge. The following discussion is summarized in Figure 2.[7]

Nelson and Winter (1982) have provided an important contribution by separating skills from routines. Individuals can be skilled in certain activities, such as driving a car or playing tennis. These skills may indeed be difficult to pass on. Variations in human intelligence alone may render difficult the transfer of technology, especially if intelligence is decomposed into aptitudes for solving differentiated tasks.

---

[7]As a way of summarizing our argument, this figure was suggested to us by Gunnar Hedlund. See also Hedlund and Nonaka (1991).

It is, in fact, the problem of communicating personal skills that underlies Polanyi's (1966) well-known idea of tacit knowledge, an idea similar to the dimensions of noncodifiable and complex knowledge. As noted earlier, to Polanyi, the central puzzle is the following: why do individuals know more than they can express. An interpretation of his argument is that tacit knowledge consists of search rules, or heuristics, that identify the problem and the elements consisting of the solution (Polanyi 1966, pp. 23–24). The act of solving a problem rests on a sense of how the phenomena function; the formal expression of the solution is unlikely to capture fully this procedural knowledge, or even the data and information (or clues, as Polanyi describes it) leading to the solution. Thus, even in the arena of problem identification and solving, the know-how of heuristic search precedes the formal knowledge of the solution.[8]

The teaching of know-how and information requires frequently interaction within small groups, often through the development of a unique language or code. Part of the knowledge of a group is simply knowing the information who knows what. But it also consists of how activities are to be organized, e.g., by Taylorist principles.

It is the sharing of a common stock of knowledge, both technical and organizational, that facilitates the transfer of knowledge within groups. This view is widely held across a disparate literature. Arrow (1974) views one of the advantages of the organization as its ability to economize in communication through a common code. Piore (1985, p. xxv) likens the theory of internal labor markets to a "conception of production knowledge as being like a language" common to a particular group of workers. By shared coding schemes, personal knowledge can be transmitted effectively within close-knit groups (Katz and Kahn 1966). Personal knowledge can be transmitted because a set of values are learned, permitting a shared language by which to communicate (Berger and Luckman 1967). It is this language which provides a normative sanction of how activities are to be organized or what information is to be collected and evaluated.

But whereas the accumulation of small group interactions facilitate the creation of shared coding schemes within functions, a fundamental problem arises in the shifting of technologies from research groups to manufacturing and marketing (Dougherty forthcoming). At this point, the identification with a professional orientation conflicts with the need to integrate within the organization. The problems of different professional languages are attenuated when technology transfer is horizontal, that is, within the same function, as when a second plant identical to the first is built. To facilitate this communication, certain individuals play pivotal roles as boundary spanners, both within the firm as well as between firms (Allen and Cohen 1969; Tushman 1977).

The vertical transfer of technology, as when a product is moved from development to production, poses additional problems insofar that the shared codes of functional groups differ. Leonard-Barton's (1988) finding that technology transfer success is dependent upon the mutual adaptation between the two parties highlights the critical transformation of personal and group knowledge in the process of codification. To facilitate this transfer, a set of higher-order organizing principles act as mechanisms by which to codify technologies into a language accessible to a wider circle of individuals. These principles establish how the innovation is transferred to other groups, the responsibility of engineers to respond to complaints, and the allocation of incentives to establish authority over decisions. These organizing principles, which we

---

[8] In the philosophy of the science, this distinction corresponds to the difference between the logic of discovery and the logic of demonstration. See also Dreyfus and Dreyfus (1988) for a discussion in relation to artificial intelligence.

call higher-order as they facilitate the integration of the entire organization, are also supported by data regarding profitability, costs, or task responsibility (as represented in an organizational chart).

In this sense, a firm's functional knowledge is nested within a higher-order set of recipes that act as organizing principles. Complex organizations exist as communities within which varieties of functional expertise can be communicated and combined by a common language and organizing principles. To the extent that close integration within a supplier or buyer network is required, long-term relationships embed future transactions within a learned and shared code. In fact, the trading of know-how among firms often requires the establishment of long-term relationships (von Hippel 1988). In this wider perspective, a firm's knowledge consists also of the information of other actors in the network, as well as the procedures by which resources are gained and transactions and cooperation are conducted.

The Paradox of Replication

There is an important implication for the growth of the firm in the transformation of technical knowledge into a code understood by a wide set of users. An individual is a resource severely restrained by physical and mental limitations. Unless able to train large numbers of individuals **or** to transform skills into organizing principles, the craft shop is forever simply a shop. The speed of replication of knowledge determines the rate of growth; control over its diffusion deters competitive erosion of the market position.

For a firm to grow, it must develop organizing principles and a widely-held and shared code by which to orchestrate large numbers of people and, potentially, varied functions. Whereas the advantages of reducing the costs of intra- or inter-firm technology transfer encourage codification of knowledge, such codification runs the risk of encouraging imitation. It is in this paradox that the firm faces a fundamental dilemma.

The problems of the growth of the firm are directly related to the issues of technology transfer and imitation. Once organizing principles replace individual skills of the entrepreneur, they serve as organizational instructions for future growth. Technology transfer is, from this perspective, the replication of existing activities. The goal of the firm is to reduce the costs of this transfer while preserving the quality and value of the technology.

Because personal and small group knowledge is expensive to re-create, firms may desire to codify and simplify such knowledge as to be accessible to the wider organization, as well as to external users. It is an interesting point, with far-reaching implications, that such a translation rarely occurs without a transformation in the nature of the knowledge. Computer software packages not only reduce the complexity of the knowledge required to use a computer's hardware; knowing how to use software is, in fact, substantively different from knowing how the computer works.

The reason why software has been successful is that it is codified so as to demand a lower fixed cost on the part of the general user. The user is required to understand the function of the program without knowledge of the substantive technology. (A function is an attribute to the product; substantive technology is the knowledge by which the product is created or produced.) The cost of this transformation is that the user's choices are restricted to the expressed functions. The specificity of a software language cannot expand the capabilities of the hardware; rather, it can only reduce the costs of its accessibility. It is, in fact, the possibility to separate the expertise to generate the technology and the ability to use it that permits the nesting of a firm's knowledge, as described above. But it is also this separation, as discussed below, that facilitates the ease of imitation. Being taught the functional skills of how to do something is different than being taught how to create it. We turn to these static and dynamic considerations below.

Combinative Capabilities

The issue of being able to use and being able to create software reflects a distinction commonly made in the literature on technology transfer regarding know-how and know-why.[9] It is, in fact, this distinction between exploiting and developing capabilities that lies at the foundation of Rosenberg's (1976) observation that "reliance on borrowed technology (by developing countries) perpetuates a posture of dependency and passivity." For example, activities involved in a manufacturing production process can be codified and imitated without requiring the knowledge of how the machinery functions. A Japanese factory shop might, conceivably, be organized by rules for inventory management and these rules might be transferred to American operations. Yet, the knowledge that leads to the development of such practices is unlikely to be transferred as easily. Being taught the functional skills of how to do something is different than being taught how to create it.

To return to the development of software as a problem in codifying knowledge, Papert (1979, p. 77) notes the paradox that some languages are simple to learn but become complex in application. He writes:

> But what do we mean by 'simpler' and what do we mean by 'learn the language'? Indeed, the (user)...would learn its vocabulary very quickly, but they would spend the rest of their time struggling with its constraints. They would have to search for devious ways to encode even mildly complex ideas into this small vocabulary. Thus it is well-known that the programming language BASIC...is quickly learned, but its programs quickly become labyrinths.

Papert's objection raises two important points. Some codes may be qualitatively better than others. They might facilitate certain technologies or practices better; the language of chemical pharmaceuticals may be inadequate for the development and transfer of biotechnologies. Even for the same technology, some firms may have evolved codes that differ in their efficacy.

The observation that some languages are more "easily learned" suggests, superficially, a contradiction in the argument. Basic is "simpler" but becomes quickly complex. But in what sense is it simpler other than through its familiarity to what the user already knows and through its design to address specific applications familiar to the user? Then why does it become a "labyrinth"? The implicit suggestion is that Basic does not provide an efficient capability to address a change in the required application.

Let us migrate the argument from the individual to the organizational level by sorting out the two issues of familiarity to the user and, as discussed later, of the capability to create new applications to address changes in the environment, such as changes in market demand. Creating new knowledge does not occur in abstraction from current abilities. Rather, new learning, such as innovations, are products of a firm's **combinative capabilities** to generate new applications from existing knowledge. By combinative capabilities, we mean the intersection of the capability of the firm to exploit its knowledge and the unexplored potential of the technology, or what Scherer (1965) originally called the degree of "technological opportunity."

---

[9] In the interest of avoiding a proliferation of terms, we would add the caveat that since formal science is characterized by recipes through which causal relationships are identified, this distinction may be simply a restatement of the question, identified in footnote 8, whether the methods of scientific discovery can be codified.

In the technological literature, the determinants of "opportunity" are often regarded as physical in character; the speed of electrons is inferior to that of light. But
since physical laws are eternally given, the critical question would then seem to be the
social laws of their discovery and innovative application. Schumpeter (1968) argued
that, in general, innovations are new combinations of existing knowledge and incremental learning.[10] He writes:

> To produce other things, or the same things by a different method, means to combine these
> materials and forces differently... Development in our sense is then defined by the carrying out of
> new combinations (Schumpeter 1934, pp. 65–66).

As widely recognized, firms learn in areas closely related to their existing practice.
As the firm moves away from its knowledge base, its probability of success converges
to that for a start-up operation (as implicit in Lippman and Rumelt 1982). The
abstract explanation for this claim is that the growth of knowledge is experiential,
that is, it is the product of localized search as guided by a stable set of heuristics, or,
in our terminology, know-how and information (Cyert and March 1963, Nelson and
Winter 1982). It is this local search that generates a condition commonly called "path
dependence," that is, the tendency for what a firm is currently doing to persist in the
future.

It should be clear that individual limitations in learning new skills are not a
sufficient explanation. For even if mature individuals do not relearn—as psychological evidence suggests, an organization may reconstitute its knowledge by recruiting
new workers with the requisite skills. The problem of the "inertness" of what an
organization knows is not reduceable to individuals, except for the degenerate case of
restrictions on the recruitment and retirement of human resources.

What makes the innovative search localized is that "proximate" technologies do
not require a change in an organization's recipes of organizing research. If current
knowledge is inadequate, it may well be that a firm does not know what changes are
required in the existing principles and structure of relationships. Even if identified,
they may not be feasible, because the relational structure in the organization would
be disturbed. Knowledge advances by recombinations because a firm's capabilities
cannot be separated from how it is currently organized.

Selection Environment

Up to now, we have been concerned with explaining the role of organizing
principles to facilitate the transfer of technology and ideas within the organization of
the firm. The distinction between the ability to produce a product and the capability
to generate it is fundamental to broadening our perspective to the competitive
conditions of imitation. The ability to build on current technology is instrumental in
the deterrence of the imitation of a firm's knowledge by competitors.

Imitation differs from technology transfer in a fundamental sense. Whereas technology transfer is concerned with adapting the technology to the least capable user,
the threat of imitation is posed by the most capable competitors. In abstraction from
a particular technology, it is, *a priori*, impossible to state in general what aspects of
the transformation of ideas into marketable products will deter imitation. No matter
which factor, however, is the most important, imitation is impeded by the possession
of at least one bottleneck capability, as long as this capability is rewarded in the

---

[10]The view that knowledge can be created only as combinations of what is already known has a long
lineage, from Plato's *Meno* to Polanyi's (1966) idea of tacitness.

market.[11] This bottleneck can possibly arise through the benefits of reputation among consumers, patent protection, or the exercise of monopoly restrictions.

When these entry-deterring benefits are absent, competition switches from traditional elements of market structure to the comparative capabilities of firms to replicate and generate new knowledge. The nature of this competition is frequently characterized as a race between an innovator and the ability of the imitating firm either to reverse engineer and to decode the substantive technology. The growth of the firm is determined by a combination of the speed of technology transfer and of the imitative efforts of rivals.

Reverse engineering is often not a required response by competitors to new innovations. Incumbent competitors may simply respond to new product innovations by relying on other capabilities, such as brand labeling or distribution channels. Of more interest to our concerns, some competitors can imitate the function of the technology without necessitating reverse engineering of the substantive code. (As an example, many distinctive kinds of software can provide a spreadsheet function; the function is imitated, but not the underlying technology.) Many new products are only re-designs (i.e., recombinations) of existing components (Henderson and Clark 1990). In this kind of competition, the need to decipher the elements of the innovator's knowledge that generated the product can be simply bypassed.

In this on-going competition, there is a short-term consideration, i.e., at what speed and cost can a firm replicate its current technology and imitate others. In innovative industries, competition is frequently a question of the speed and efficiency by which diverse groups within a corporation cooperate, a problem exacerbated when multifunctional coordination is required in order to increase transfer times to the market (Dougherty forthcoming). Over time and across multiple products, small differences in efficiencies can generate significant variations in profitability and (as well established in evolutionary biology) survival.

Short-term competitive pressures can, however, draw from the investments required to build new capabilities. The direct effect of selection is on the acceptance and rejection of new products, but indirectly it is operating to reward or to penalize the economic merits of the underlying stock of knowledge.[12] Knowledge, no matter how resistant to imitation, is of little value if it results in products that do not correspond competitively to consumers' wants. Selection on product types acts to develop and retard the capabilities of firms.

The ability to indulge in a forward-looking development of knowledge is strongly contingent on the selection environment. Long-term survival involves a complex tradeoff between current profitability and investing in future capability. Future capabilities are of little value if the firm does not survive. In this sense, we have returned to Papert's concerns. Basic may be a poor language by which to address new applications or changes in the market. But for the student facing a deadline, programming in Basic may have clear survival value.

An important question, then, is the critical balancing between short-term survival and the long-term development of capabilities. A too strong reliance on current profitability can deflect from the wider development of capabilities (Stiglitz 1987). By their ability to buffer internal ventures from an immediate market test, organizations have the possibility to create new capabilities by a process of trial-and-error learning.

Thus luxury is often too exorbitant for companies or, for that matter, developing countries facing strong survival pressures. Yet, because investments in new ways of

---

[11] This point is captured in empirical work using the survey results, whereby appropriability is defined as the item that indicates the maximum deterrence to imitation (Levin et al. 1987).

[12] This point, of course, lies at the heart of the genes versus phenotype controversy in biology. See, for example, Dawkins (1976).

doing things are expensive, it is possible for a firm to continue to develop capabilities in ways of doing things which it knows, in the long run, are inferior (Arthur 1989). A too rigid competitive environment, especially in the early years of a firm's development, may impede subsequent performance by retarding a firm's ability to invest in new learning.

The Make Decision and Firm Capabilities

The merits of the above argument can be better evaluated by considering an example. An interesting application is the make-buy question, that is, whether a firm should source a component from the outside or make it internally. The examination of this problem throws into relief how an approach based on the knowledge of the firm differs from a contracting perspective.

It has become standard to argue that markets for the exchange of technology fail because of an appeal to a poker-hand metaphor; once the cards are revealed, imitation rapidly ensues since draws from the deck are costless. Because of the work of Teece (1977), Mansfield, Schwartz, and Wagner (1981), and Levin et al. (1987), it is widely recognized this argument is a shibboleth. Yet, the consequences of this recognition are scarcely to be seen in the literature on technology transfer.

In fact, the costliness of its transfer has often been reconstrued as market failure (Teece 1980). Because a buyer cannot ascertain its value by observation, technology cannot be priced out. Thus, markets fail for the selling of technology since it is costly to transact.

The problem of this market failure argument is not only that markets for technology do exist, but also that it is over-determined. The public good argument turns on the opportunism of the buyer; the costs of transfer do not necessitate a similar behavioral assumption, though one can always throw it in for good measure. Opportunism is not a necessary condition to explain why technology is transferred within a firm instead of the market. Rather, the issue becomes why and when are the costs of transfer of technology lower inside the firm than alternatives in the market, independent of contractual hazards. The relevant market comparison, in this sense, are the efficiencies of other firms.

This issue extends to the more commonly studied case of contractual hazards affecting the make or buy decision, that is, whether to source from outside the firm. In the seminal empirical study of Walker and Weber (1984), evidence was found for the claim that the transaction costs of relying on outside suppliers lead to decisions to source internally. Yet, the most important variable is the indicator of differential firm capabilities, that is, whether the firm or the supplier has the lower production costs. Transaction cost considerations matter but are subsidiary to whether a firm or other suppliers are more efficient in the production of the component.

In the Monteverde and Teece (1982) paper that also supported the transaction cost argument, the most significant variable is the dummy for the firm. In other words, despite controls, the heterogeneous and unobserved firm effects were the dominant influence on the make-buy decision. Yet, both firms faced the same environment and transactional hazards.

While the boundaries of the firm are, unquestionably, influenced by transactional dilemmas, the question of capabilities points the analysis to understanding why organizations differ in their performance. The decision which capabilities to maintain and develop is influenced by the current knowledge of the firm and the expectation of the economic gain from exploring the opportunities in new technologies and organizing principles as platforms into future market developments. (See Figure 1.) We propose that firms maintain those capabilities in-house that are expected to lead to recombinations of economic value.

The evaluation of this economic gain rests critically upon a firm's ability to create and transfer technology more quickly than it is imitated in the market. Many investment decisions inside a firm do not include a make-buy calculation, for the presumption is that the new assets are extensions, or combinations, of the existing knowledge base.[13] Nor should it be surprising that there is a sense of ownership over the right to make and control the investment, for the physical assets are embedded within the replication of the existing social relationships and political structure of the firm. Because these relationships exist, an ongoing firm should have a greater capability to expand in current businesses than new entrants.

Path dependence is a rephrasing of the simple statement that firms persist in making what they have made in the past; for existing firms, knowledge advances on the basis of its current information and ways of doing things. To return to the Monteverde and Teece study, the finding that firms tended to produce internally those parts with high engineering content is a confirmation that auto companies specialize in engineering design and production. They make those parts that reflect their knowledge. (In fact, we should expect that they imitate those technologies which correspond closely to their knowledge.)

There are, of course, investment opportunities which are uncertain in terms of the applicability of a firm's current knowledge. Internal development, and imitation, are deterred because the organizing principles and information cannot be easily identified. Thus, investments in new knowledge often have a characteristic of trial-and error learning, much like buying options on future opportunities.

Joint ventures frequently serve as options on new markets distantly related to current knowledge by providing a vehicle by which firms transfer and combine their organizationally-embedded learning. A common purpose of joint ventures is to experiment with new ways by which relationships are structured. That they frequently end by acquisition is a statement of their value as an ongoing entity of enduring social relationships which serve as platforms into new markets (Kogut 1991).

The decision to make or buy is, thus, dependent upon three elements: how good a firm is currently at **doing** something, how good it is at **learning** specific capabilities, and the value of these capabilities as **platforms** into new markets. To formalize the implications of these elements in terms of propositions, we would expect the following to hold:

1. Firms make those components that require a production knowledge similar to their current organizing principles and information.

2. The purchasing of technologies is carried out by the market when suppliers have superior knowledge which is complex and difficult to codify; by licensing when the transferred knowledge is close to current practice.

3. Firms develop internally projects that build related capabilities leading to platforms into new markets or rely on joint ventures (or acquisitions) when the capabilities are distantly related.

4. Immediate survival pressures encourage firms towards a policy of buying.

Similar propositions could be made in reference to other applications, such as acquisitions, the composition of a technology portfolio, and the sequence by which a firm invests in a foreign market.

---

[13] We would like to thank Gordon Walker for emphasizing that many new investment decisions entail only whether to and not to make internally; there is often no external evaluation.

396   BRUCE KOGUT AND UDO ZANDER

Conclusions

The study of the knowledge of a firm raises issues, such as relatedness, technical core, or corporate culture, that are familiar to organizational theorists, but that have been hard to pin down. To a large extent, the theory of firm knowledge, as we have sketched it above, neglects the problem of individual motivation by focusing on organizing principles as the primary unit of analysis for understanding the variation in firm performance and growth. Because these principles are expressions of how a firm organizes its activities, they represent the procedures by which social relations are recreated and coordinated in an organizational context.

In contrast to a perspective based on the failure to align incentives in a market as an explanation for the firm, we began with the view that firms are a repository of capabilities, as determined by the social knowledge embedded in enduring individual relationships structured by organizing principles. Switching to new capabilities is difficult, as neither the knowledge embedded in the current relationships and principles is well understood, nor the social fabric required to support the new learning known. It is the stability of these relationships that generates the characteristics of inertia in a firm's capabilities.

Without question, there are issues, such as the creation of compatible incentives to induce behavior from individuals in accordance with the welfare of the organization, that can be fruitfully examined from a contracting perspective. But the transaction as the unit of analysis is an insufficient vehicle by which to examine organizational capabilities, because these capabilities are a composite of individual and social knowledge. After nearly two decades of research in organizational and market failure, it is time to investigate what organizations do.

Acknowledgements

We would like to thank Ned Bowman, Farok Contractor, Deborah Dougherty, Lars Hakanson, Gunnar Hedlund, Arie Lewin, and the anonymous referees for their comments. Partial funding for the research has been provided by AT & T under the auspices of the Reginald H. Jones Center of The Wharton School.

References

Allen, Thomas and Stephen Cohen (1969), "Information Flow in Research and Development Laboratories," *Administrative Science Quarterly*, 14, 12–20.
Argyris, Chris and Donald Schoen (1978), *Organizational Learning: A Theory of Action Perspective*, Reading, MA: Addison-Wesley.
Arrow, Kenneth (1974), *The Limits of Organization*, New York: Norton.
Arthur, Brian (1989), "Competing Technologies, Increasing Returns, and Lock-in by Historical Events," *Economic Journal*, 99, 116–131.
Barney, Jay (1986), 'Strategic Factor Markets: Expectations, Luck, and Business Strategy," *Management Science*, 32, 1231–1241.
Cyert, Richard M. and James G. March (1963), *A Behavioral Theory of the Firm*, Englewood Cliffs, NJ: Prentice-Hall.
Dawkins, Richard (1976), *The Selfish Gene*, Oxford: Oxford University Press.
_____ (1987), *The Blind Watchmaker*, New York: Basic Books.
Dierickx, Ingemar and Karel Cool (1989), "Asset Stock Accumulation and Sustainability of Competitive Advantage," *Management Science*, 33, 1504–1513.
Dougherty, Deborah (1992), "Interpretative Barriers to Successful Product Innovation in Large Firms," *Organization Science*, 3, 2, 179–202.
Dreyfus, Hubert and Stuart Dreyfus (1988), "Making a Mind versus Modeling the Brain: Artificial Intelligence Back at a Branchpoint," in *The Artificial Debate*, Stephen Graubard (Ed.), Cambridge: MIT Press.
Hannan, Michael and John Freeman (1977), "The Population Ecology of Organizations," *American Journal of Sociology*, 82, 929–964.

Hedlund, Gunnar and Ikujiro Nonaka (1991), "Models of Knowledge Management in the West and Japan," mimeo, Stockholm School of Economics.

Henderson, Rebecca and Kim Clark (1990), "Architectural Innovation: The Reconfiguration of Existing Product Technologies and the Failure of Established Firms," *Administrative Science Quarterly*, 35, 9–31.

Kogut, Bruce (1987), "Country Patterns in International Competition: Appropriability and Oligopolistic Agreement," *Strategies in Global Competition*, N. Hood and J.-E. Vahlne (Ed.), London: Croom Helm.

―――― (1991), "Joint Ventures and the Option to Expand and Acquire," *Management Science*, 37, 19–33.

―――― and Dong Jae Kim (1991), "Technological Platforms and the Sequence of Entry," Working Paper, Reginald H. Jones Center, Wharton School.

―――― and Udo Zander (1990), "The Imitation and Transfer of New Technologies," mimeo.

Leonard-Barton, Dorothy (1988), "Implementations as Mutual Adaptation of Technology and Organization," *Research Policy*, 17, 251–267.

Levin, Richard, Alvin Klevorick, Richard Nelson and Sidney Winter (1987), "Appropriating the Returns from Industrial Research and Development," *Brookings Papers on Economic Activity*, 3, 783–831.

Lippman, Stephen and Richard Rumelt (1982), "Uncertain Imitability: An Analysis of Interfirm Differences in Efficiency Under Competition," *Bell Journal of Economics*, 13, 418–438.

March, James and Herbert Simon (1958), *Organizations*, New York: John Wiley.

Monteverde, Kirk and David Teece (1982), "Supplier Switching Costs and Vertical Integration in the Automobile Industry," *Bell Journal of Economics*, 13, 206–213.

Nelson, Richard (1982), "The Role of Knowledge in R & D Efficiency," *Quarterly Journal of Economics*, 96, 453–470.

―――― and Sidney Winter (1982), *An Evolutionary Theory of Economic Change*, Cambridge: Belknap Press.

Papert, Seymour (1979), "Computers and Learning," in M. Dertouzos and J. Moses (Eds.), *The Computer Age: A Twenty-Year View*, Cambridge, MA: MIT Press.

Piore, Michael (1985), "Introduction," in P. Doeringer and M. Piore, *Internal Labor Markets and Manpower Analysis*, New York: M. E. Sharpe Inc.

Polanyi, Michael (1966), *The Tacit Dimension*, New York: Anchor Day Books.

Prahalad, C. K. and Gary Hamel (1990), "The Core Competence of the Corporation," *Harvard Business Review*, (May–June), 79–91.

Pringle, J. W. S. (1951), "On the Parallel Between Learning and Evolution," *Behavior*, 3, 175–215.

Rogers, Everett (1983), *The Diffusion of Innovations*, (Third Ed.) (First Ed., 1962), New York: Free Press.

Rosenberg, Nathan (1976), *Perspectives on Technology*, Cambridge, UK: Cambridge University Press.

Rumelt, R. P. (1984), "Towards a Strategic Theory of the Firm," In *Competitive Strategic Management*, Robert Boyden Lamb (Ed.), Englewood Cliffs, NJ: Prentice-Hall, Inc.

Schumpeter, Joseph (1934), *The Theory of Economic Development*, Cambridge, MA: Harvard University Press, (First Published in 1911; republished 1968).

Simon, Herbert (1962), "The Architecture of Complexity," *Proceedings of the American Philosophical Society*, 106, 467–482.

Teece, David (1977), "Technology Transfer by Multinational Corporations: The Resource Cost of Transferring Technological Know-how," *Economical Journal*, 87 242–261.

―――― (1980), "Economies of Scope and the Scope of an Enterprise," *Journal of Economic Behavior and Organization*, 1, 223–247.

Tushman, Michael (1977), "Special Boundary Roles in the Innovation Process," *Administrative Science Quarterly*, 22, 587–605.

von Hippel, Eric (1988), *The Sources of Innovation*, Cambridge: MIT Press.

Walker, Gordon and David Weber (1984), A Transaction Cost Approach to Make or Buy Decisions," *Administrative Science Quarterly*, 29, 373–391.

Wernerfelt, Birger (1984), "A Resource-Based View of the Firm," *Strategic Management Journal*, 5, 171–180.

Winter, Sidney (1987), "Knowledge and Competence as Strategic Assets," in *The Competitive Challenge—Strategies for Industrial Innovation and Renewal*, D. Teece (Ed.), Cambridge, MA: Ballinger.

Part III
Global Strategy

[20]

International Investment and International Trade in the Product Cycle[*]

Raymond Vernon

Anyone who has sought to understand the shifts in international trade and international investment over the past twenty years has chafed from time to time under an acute sense of the inadequacy of the available analytical tools. While the comparative cost concept and other basic concepts have rarely failed to provide some help, they have usually carried the analyst only a very little way toward adequate understanding. For the most part, it has been necessary to formulate new concepts in order to explore issues such as the strengths and limitations of import substitution in the development process, the implications of common market arrangements for trade and investment, the underlying reasons for the Leontief paradox, and other critical issues of the day.

As theorists have groped for some more efficient tools, there has been a flowering in international trade and capital theory. But the very proliferation of theory has increased the urgency of the search for unifying concepts. It is doubtful that we shall find many propositions that can match the simplicity, power, and universality of application of the theory of comparative advantage and the international equilibrating mechanism; but unless the search for better tools goes on, the usefulness of economic theory for the solution of problems in international trade and capital movements will probably decline.

The present paper deals with one promising line of generalization and synthesis which seems to me to have been somewhat neglected by the main stream of trade theory. It puts less emphasis upon comparative cost doctrine and more upon the timing of innovation, the effects of scale economies, and the roles of ignorance and uncertainty in influencing trade patterns. It is an approach with respectable sponsorship deriving bits and pieces of its inspiration from the writings of such persons as Williams, Kindleberger, MacDougall, Hoffmeyer, and Burenstam-Linder.[1]

Emphases of this sort seem first to have appeared when economists were searching for an explanation of what looked like a persistent, structural shortage of dollars in the world. When the shortage proved ephemeral in the late 1950s, many of the ideas which the shortage had stimulated were tossed overboard as prima facie wrong.[2] Nevertheless, one cannot be exposed to the main currents of international trade for very long without feeling that any theory which neglected the roles of innovation, scale, ignorance and uncertainty would be incomplete.

Location of New Products

We begin with the assumption that the enterprises in any one of the advanced countries of the world are not distinguishably different from those in any other advanced country, in terms of their access to scientific knowledge and their capacity to comprehend scientific principles.[3] All of them, we may safely assume, can secure access to the knowledge that exists in the physical, chemical and biological sciences. These sciences at times may be difficult, but they are rarely occult.

It is a mistake to assume, however, that equal access to scientific principles in all the advanced countries means equal probability of the application of these principles in the generation of new products. There is ordinarily a large gap between the knowledge of a scientific principle and the embodiment of the principle in a marketable product. An entrepreneur usually has to intervene to accept the risks involved in testing whether the gap can be bridged.

If all entrepreneurs, wherever located, could be presumed to be equally conscious of and equally responsive to all entrepreneurial opportunities, wherever they arose, the classical view of the dominant role of price in resource allocation might be highly relevant. There is good reason to believe, however, that the entrepreneur's consciousness of and responsiveness to opportunity are a function of ease of communication; and further, that ease of communication is a function of geographical proximity.[4] Accordingly, we abandon the powerful simplifying notion that knowledge is a universal free good, and introduce it as an independent variable in the decision to trade or to invest.

The fact that the search for knowledge is an inseparable part of the decision-making process and that relative ease of access to knowledge can profoundly affect the outcome are now reasonably well established through empirical research.[5] One implication of that fact is that producers in any market are more likely to be aware of the possibility of introducing new products in that market than producers located elsewhere would be.

The United States market offers certain unique kinds of opportunities to those who are in a position to be aware of them.

First, the United States market consists of consumers with an average income which is higher (except for a few anomalies like Kuwait) than that in any other national market – twice as high as that of Western Europe, for instance. Wherever there was a chance to offer a new product responsive to wants at high levels of income, this chance would presumably first be apparent to someone in a position to observe the United States market.

Second, the United States market is characterized by high unit labor costs and relatively unrationed capital compared with practically all other markets. This is a fact which conditions the demand for both consumer goods and industrial products. In the case of consumer goods, for instance, the high cost of laundresses contributes to the origins of the drip-dry shirt and the home washing machine. In the case of industrial goods, high labor cost leads to the early development and use of the conveyor belt, the fork-lift truck and the automatic control system. It seems to follow that wherever there was a chance successfully to sell a new product responsive to the need to conserve labor, this chance would be apparent first to those in a position to observe the United States market.

Assume, then, that entrepreneurs in the United States are first aware of opportunities to satisfy new wants associated with high income levels or high unit labor costs. Assume further that the evidence of an unfilled need and the hope of some kind of monopoly windfall for the early starter both are sufficiently strong to justify the initial investment that is usually involved in converting an abstract idea into a marketable product. Here we have a reason for expecting a consistently higher rate of expenditure on product development to be undertaken by United States producers than by producers in other countries, at least in lines which promise to substitute capital for labor or which promise to satisfy high-income wants. Therefore, if United States firms spend more than their foreign counterparts on new product development (often misleadingly labeled 'research'), this may be due not to some obscure sociological drive for innovation but to more effective communication between the potential market and the potential supplier of the market. This sort of explanation is consistent with the pioneer appearance in the United States (conflicting claims of the Soviet Union notwithstanding) of the sewing machine, the typewriter, the tractor, etc.

At this point in the exposition, it is important once more to emphasize that the discussion so far relates only to innovation in certain kinds of products, namely to those associated with high income and those which substitute capital for labor. Our hypothesis says nothing about industrial innovation in general; this is a larger subject than we have tackled here. There are very few countries that have failed to introduce at least a few products; and there are some, such as Germany and Japan, which have been responsible for a considerable number of such introductions. Germany's outstanding successes in the development and use of plastics may have been due, for instance, to a traditional concern with her lack of a raw materials base, and a recognition that a market might exist in Germany for synthetic substitutes.[6]

Our hypothesis asserts that United States producers are likely to be the first to spy an opportunity for high-income or labor-saving new products.[7] But it goes on to assert that the first producing facilities for such products will be located in the United States. This is not a self-evident proposition. Under the calculus of least cost, production need not automatically take place at a location close to the market, unless the product can be produced and delivered from that location at lowest cost. Besides, now that most major United States companies control facilities situated in one or more locations outside of the United States, the possibility of considering a non-United States location is even more plausible than it might once have been.

Of course, if prospective producers were to make their locational choices on the basis of least-cost considerations, the United States would not always be ruled out. The costs of international transport and United States import duties, for instance, might be so high as to argue for such a location. My guess is, however, that the early producers of a new product intended for the United States market are attracted to a United States location by forces which are far stronger than relative factor-cost and transport considerations. For the reasoning on this point, one has to take a long detour away from comparative cost analysis into areas which fall under the rubrics of communication and external economies.

By now, a considerable amount of empirical work has been done on the factors affecting the location of industry.[8] Many of these studies try to explain observed locational patterns in conventional cost-minimizing terms, by implicit or explicit reference to labor cost and transportation cost. But some explicitly introduce problems of communication and external economies as powerful locational forces. These factors were given special emphasis in the analyses which were a part of the New York Metropolitan Region Study of the 1950s. At the risk of oversimplifying, I shall try to summarize what these studies suggested.[9]

In the early stages of introduction of a new product, producers were usually confronted with a number of critical, albeit transitory, conditions. For one thing, the product itself may be quite unstandardized for a time; its inputs, its processing, and its final specifications may cover a wide range. Contrast the great variety of automobiles produced and marketed before 1910 with the thoroughly standardized product of the 1930s, or the variegated radio designs of the 1920s with the uniform models of the 1930s. The unstandardized nature of the design at this early stage carries with it a number of locational implications.

First, producers at this stage are particularly concerned with the degree of freedom they have in changing their inputs. Of course, the cost of the inputs is also relevant. But as long as the nature of these inputs cannot be fixed in advance with assurance, the calculation of cost must take into account the general need for flexibility in any locational choice.[10]

Second, the price elasticity of demand for the output of individual firms is comparatively low. This follows from the high degree of production differentiation, or the existence of monopoly in the early stages.[11] One result is, of course, that small cost differences count less in the calculations of the entrepreneur than they are likely to count later on.

Third, the need for swift and effective communication on the part of the producer with customers, suppliers, and even competitors is especially high at this stage. This is a corollary of the fact that a considerable amount of uncertainty remains regarding the ultimate dimensions of the market, the efforts of rivals to preempt that market, the specifications of the inputs needed for production, and the specifications of the products likely to be most successful in the effort.

All of these considerations tend to argue for a location in which communication between the market and the executives directly concerned with the new product is swift and easy, and in which a wide variety of potential types of input that might be needed by the production unit are easily come by. In brief, the producer who sees a market for some new product in the United States may be led to select a United States location for production on the basis of national locational considerations which extend well beyond simple factor cost analysis plus transport considerations.

The Maturing Product[12]

As the demand for a product expands, a certain degree of standardization usually takes place. This is not to say that efforts at product differentiation come to an end. On the contrary; such efforts may even intensify, as competitors try to avoid the full brunt of price competition. Moreover, variety may appear as a result of specialization. Radios, for instance, ultimately acquired such specialized forms as clock radios, automobile radios, portable radios, and so on. Nevertheless, though the subcategories may multiply and the efforts at product differentiation increase, a growing acceptance of certain general standards seems to be typical.

Once again, the change has locational implications. First of all, the need for flexibility declines. A commitment to some set of product standards opens up technical possibilities for achieving economies of scale through mass output, and encourages long-term commitments to some given process and some fixed set of facilities. Second, concern about production cost begins to take the place of concern about product characteristics. Even if increased price competition is not yet present, the reduction of the uncertainties surrounding the operation enhances the usefulness of cost projections and increases the attention devoted to cost.

The empirical studies to which I referred earlier suggest that at this stage in an industry's development, there is likely to be considerable shift in the location of production facilities at least as far as internal United States locations are concerned. The empirical materials on international locational shifts simply have not yet been analyzed sufficiently to tell us very much. A little speculation, however, indicates some hypotheses worth testing.

Picture an industry engaged in the manufacture of the high-income or labor-saving products that are the focus of our discussion. Assume that the industry has begun to settle down in the United States to some degree of large-scale production. Although the first mass market may be located in the United States, some demand for the product begins almost at once to appear elsewhere. For instance, although heavy fork-lift trucks in general may have a comparatively small market in Spain because of the relative cheapness of unskilled labor in that country, some limited demand for the product will appear there almost as soon as the existence of the product is known.

If the product has a high income elasticity of demand or if it is a satisfactory substitute for high-cost labor, the demand in time will begin to grow quite rapidly in relatively advanced countries such as those of Western Europe. Once the market expands in such an advanced country, entrepreneurs will begin to ask themselves whether the time has come to take the risk of setting up a local producing facility.[13]

How long does it take to reach this stage? An adequate answer must surely be a complex one. Producers located in the United States, weighing the wisdom of setting up a new production facility in the importing country, will feel obliged to balance a number of complex considerations. As long as the marginal production cost plus the transport cost of the goods exported from the United States is lower than the average cost of prospective production in the market of import, United States producers will presumably prefer to avoid an investment. But that calculation depends on the producer's ability to project the cost of production in a market in which factor costs and the appropriate technology differ from those at home.

Now and again, the locational force which determined some particular overseas investment is so simple and so powerful that one has little difficulty in identifying it. Otis Elevator's early proliferation of production facilities abroad was quite patently a function of the high cost of shipping assembled elevator cabins to distant locations and the limited scale advantages involved in manufacturing elevator cabins at a single location.[14] Singer's decision to invest in Scotland as early as 1867 was also based on considerations of a sort sympathetic with our hypothesis.[15] It is not unlikely that the overseas demand for its highly standardized product was already sufficiently large at that time to exhaust the obvious scale advantages of manufacturing in a single location, especially if that location was one of high labor cost.

In an area as complex and 'imperfect' as international trade and investment, however, one ought not anticipate that any hypothesis will have more than a limited explanatory power. United States airplane manufacturers surely respond to many 'noneconomic' locational forces, such as the desire to play safe in problems of military security. Producers in the United States who have a protected patent position overseas presumably take that fact into account in deciding whether or when to produce abroad. And other producers often are motivated by considerations too complex to reconstruct readily, such as the fortuitous timing of a threat of new competition in the country of import, the level of tariff protection anticipated for the future, the political situation in the country of prospective investment and so on.

We arrive, then, at the stage at which United States producers have come around to the establishment of production units in the advanced countries. Now a new group of forces are set in train. In an idealized form, Figure 1 suggests what may be anticipated next.

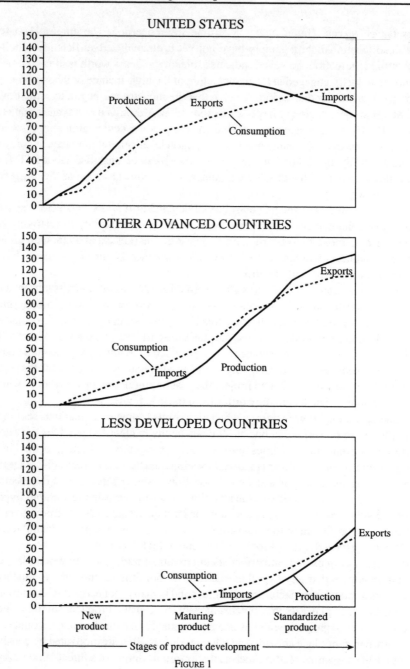

UNITED STATES

OTHER ADVANCED COUNTRIES

LESS DEVELOPED COUNTRIES

FIGURE 1

As far as individual United States producers are concerned, the local markets thenceforth will be filled from local production units set up abroad. Once these facilities are in operation, however, more ambitious possibilities for their use may be suggested. When comparing a United States producing facility and a facility in another advanced country, the obvious production-cost differences between the rival producing areas are usually differences due to scale and differences due to labor costs. If the producer is an international firm with producing locations in several countries, its costs of financing capital at the different locations may not be sufficiently different to matter very much. If economies of scale are being fully exploited, the principal differences between any two locations are likely to be labor costs.[16] Accordingly, it may prove wise for the international firm to begin servicing third-country markets from the new location. And if labor cost differences are large enough to offset transport costs, then exports back to the United States may become a possibility as well.

Any hypotheses based on the assumption that the United States entrepreneur will react rationally when offered the possibility of a lower-cost location abroad is, of course, somewhat suspect. The decision-making sequence that is used in connection with international investments, according to various empirical studies, is not a model of the rational process.[17] But there is one theme that emerges again and again in such studies. Any threat to the established position of an enterprise is a powerful galvanizing force to action; in fact, if I interpret the empirical work correctly, threat in general is a more reliable stimulus to action than opportunity is likely to be.

In the international investment field, threats appear in various forms once a large-scale export business in manufactured products has developed. Local entrepreneurs located in the countries which are the targets of these exports grow restive at the opportunities they are missing. Local governments concerned with generating employment or promoting growth or balancing their trade accounts begin thinking of ways and means to replace the imports. An international investment by the exporter, therefore, becomes a prudent means of forestalling the loss of a market. In this case, the yield on the investment is seen largely as the avoidance of a loss of income to the system.

The notion that a threat to the status quo is a powerful galvanizing force for international investment also seems to explain what happens after the initial investment. Once such an investment is made by a United States producer, other major producers in the United States sometimes see it as a threat to the status quo. They see themselves as losing position relative to the investing company, with vague intimations of further losses to come. Their 'share of the market' is imperiled, viewing 'share of the market' in global terms. At the same time, their ability to estimate the production-cost structure of their competitors, operating far away in an unfamiliar foreign area, is impaired; this is a particularly unsettling state because it conjures up the possibility of a return flow of products to the United States and a new source of price competition, based on cost differences of unknown magnitude. The uncertainty can be reduced by emulating the pathfinding investor and by investing in the same area; this may not be an optimizing investment pattern and it may be costly, but it is least disturbing to the status quo.

Pieces of this hypothetical pattern are subject to empirical tests of a sort. So far, at any rate, the empirical tests have been reassuring. The office machinery industry, for instance, has seen repeatedly the phenomenon of the introduction of a new product in the United States, followed by United States exports,[18] followed still later by United States imports. (We have still to test whether the timing of the commencement of overseas production by United States subsidiaries fits into the expected pattern.) In the electrical and electronic products industry, those elements in the pattern which can be measured show up nicely.[19] A broader effort is now under way to test the United States trade patterns of a group of products with high income elasticities; and, here too, the preliminary results are encouraging.[20] On a much more general basis, it is reassuring for our hypotheses to observe that the foreign manufacturing subsidiaries of United States firms have been increasing their exports to third countries.

It will have occurred to the reader by now that the pattern envisaged here also may shed some light on the Leontief paradox.[21] Leontief, it will be recalled, seemed to confound comparative cost theory by establishing the fact that the ratio of capital to labor in United States exports was lower, not higher, than the like ratio in the United States production which had been displaced by competitive imports. The hypothesis suggested in this paper would have the United States exporting high-income and labor-saving products in the early stages of their existence, and importing them later on.[22] In the early stages, the value-added contribution of industries engaged in producing these items probably contains an unusually high proportion of labor cost. This is not so much because the labor is particularly skilled, as is so often suggested. More likely, it is due to a quite different phenomenon. At this stage, the standardization of the manufacturing process has not gotten very far; that is to come later, when the volume of output is high enough and the degree of uncertainty low enough to justify investment in relatively inflexible, capital-intensive facilities. As a result, the production process relies relatively heavily on labor inputs at a time when the United States commands an export position; and the process relies more heavily on capital at a time when imports become important.

This, of course, is an hypothesis which has not yet been subjected to any really rigorous test. But it does open up a line of inquiry into the structure of United States trade which is well worth pursuing.

The Standardized Product

Figure 1, the reader will have observed, carries a panel which suggests that, at an advanced stage in the standardization of some products, the less-developed countries may offer competitive advantages as a production location.

This is a bold projection, which seems on first blush to be wholly at variance with the Heckscher-Ohlin theorem. According to that theorem, one presumably ought to anticipate that the exports of the less-developed countries would tend to be relatively labor-intensive products.

One of the difficulties with the theorem, however, is that it leaves marketing considerations out of account. One reason for the omission is evident. As long as knowledge is regarded as a free good, instantaneously available, and as long as individual producers are regarded as atomistic contributors to the total supply, marketing problems cannot be expected to find much of a place in economic theory. In projecting the patterns of export from less-developed areas, however, we cannot afford to disregard the fact that information comes at a cost; and that entrepreneurs are not readily disposed to pay the price of investigating overseas markets of unknown dimensions and unknown promise. Neither are they eager to venture into situations which they know will demand a constant flow of reliable marketing information from remote sources.

If we can assume that highly standardized products tend to have a well-articulated, easily accessible international market and to sell largely on the basis of price (an assumption inherent in the definition), then it follows that such products will not pose the problem of market information quite so acutely for the less-developed countries. This establishes a necessary if not a sufficient condition for investment in such industries.

Of course, foreign investors seeking an optimum location for a captive facility may not have to concern themselves too much with questions of market information; presumably, they are thoroughly familiar with the marketing end of the business and are looking for a low-cost captive source of supply. In that case, the low cost of labor may be the initial attraction drawing the investor to less-developed areas. But other limitations in such areas, according to our hypothesis, will bias such captive operations toward the production of standardized items. The reasons in this case turn on the part played in the production process by external economies. Manufacturing processes which receive significant inputs from the local economy, such as skilled labor, repairmen, reliable power, spare parts, industrial materials processed according to exacting specification, and so on, are less appropriate to the less-developed areas than those that do not have such requirements. Unhappily, most industrial processes require one or another ingredient of this difficult sort. My guess is, however, that the industries which produce a standardized product are in the best position to avoid the problem, by producing on a vertically-integrated self-sustaining basis.

In speculating about future industrial exports from the less-developed areas, therefore, we are led to think of products with a fairly clear-cut set of economic characteristics.[23] Their production function is such as to require significant inputs of labor; otherwise there is no reason to expect a lower production cost in less-developed countries. At the same time, they are products with a high price elasticity of demand for the output of individual firms; otherwise, there is no strong incentive to take the risks of pioneering with production in a new area. In addition, products whose production process did not rely heavily upon external economies would be more obvious candidates than those which required a more elaborate industrial environment. The implications of remoteness also would be critical; products which could be precisely described by standardized specifications and which could be produced for inventory without fear of obsolescence would be more relevant than those which had less precise specifications and which could not easily be ordered from remote locations. Moreover, high-value items capable of absorbing significant freight costs would be more likely to appear than bulky items low in value by weight. Standardized textile products are, of course, the illustration par excellence of the sort of product that meets the criteria. But other products come to mind such as crude steel, simple fertilizers, newsprint, and so on.

Speculation of this sort draws some support from various interregional experiences in industrial location. In the United States, for example, the 'export' industries which moved to the low-wage south in search of lower costs tended to be industries which had no great need for a sophisticated industrial environment and which produced fairly standardized products. In the textile industry, it was the grey goods, cotton sheetings and men's shirt plants that went south; producers of high-style dresses or other unstandardized items were far more reluctant to move. In the electronics industry, it was the mass producers of tubes, resistors and other standardized high-volume components that showed the greatest disposition to move south; custom-built and research-oriented production remained closer to markets and to the main industrial complexes. A similar pattern could be discerned in printing and in chemicals production.

In other countries, a like pattern is suggested by the impressionistic evidence. The under-developed south of Italy and the laggard north of Britain and Ireland both seem to be attracting industry with standardized output and self-sufficient process.[25]

Once we begin to look for relevant evidence of such investment patterns in the less-developed countries proper, however, only the barest shreds of corroboratory information can be found. One would have difficulty in thinking of many cases in which manufacturers of standardized products in the more advanced countries had made significant investments in the less-developed countries with a view of exporting such products from those countries. To be sure, other types of foreign investment are not uncommon in the less-developed countries, such as investments in import-replacing industries which were made in the face of a threat of import restriction. But there are only a few export-oriented cases similar to that of Taiwan's foreign-owned electronics plants and Argentina's new producing facility, set up to manufacture and export standard sorting equipment for computers.

If we look to foreign trade patterns, rather than foreign investment patterns, to learn something about the competitive advantage of the less-developed countries, the possibility that they are an attractive locus for the output of standardized products gains slightly more support. The Taiwanese and Japanese trade performances are perhaps the most telling ones in support of the projected pattern; both countries have managed to develop significant overseas markets for standardized manufactured products. According to one major study of the subject (a study stimulated by the Leontief paradox), Japanese exports are more capital-intensive than is the Japanese production which is displaced by imports;[26] this is what one might expect if the hypothetical patterns suggested by Figure 1 were operational. Apart from these cases, however, all that one sees are a few provocative successes such as some sporadic sales of newsprint from Pakistan, the successful export of sewing machines from India, and so on. Even in these cases, one cannot be sure that they are consistent with the hypothesis unless he has done a good deal more empirical investigation.

The reason why so few relevant cases come to mind may be that the process has not yet advanced far enough. Or it may be that such factors as extensive export constraints and overvalued exchange rates are combining to prevent the investment and exports that otherwise would occur.

If there is one respect in which this discussion may deviate from classical expectations, it is in the view that the overall scarcity of capital in the less-developed countries will not prevent investment in facilities for the production of standardized products.

There are two reasons why capital costs may not prove a barrier to such investment.

First, according to our hypotheses, the investment will occur in industries which require some significant labor inputs in the production process; but they will be concentrated in that subsector of the industry which produces highly standardized products capable of self-contained production establishments. The net of these specifications is indeterminate so far as capital-intensiveness is concerned. A standardized textile item may be more or less capital-intensive than a plant for unstandardized petro-chemicals.

Besides, even if the capital requirements for a particular plant are heavy, the cost of the capital need not prove a bar. The assumption that the capital costs come high in the less-developed countries requires a number of fundamental qualifications. The reality, to the extent that it is known, is more complex.

One reason for this complexity is the role played by the international investor. Producers of chemical fertilizers, when considering whether to invest in a given country, may be less concerned with the going rate for capital in that country than with their opportunity costs as they see such costs. For such investors the alternatives to be weighed are not the full range of possibilities calling for capital but only a very restricted range of alternatives, such as the possibilities offered by chemical fertilizer investment elsewhere. The relevant capital cost for a chemical fertilizer plant, therefore, may be fairly low if the investor is an international entrepreneur.

Moreover, the assumption that finance capital is scarce and that interest rates are high in a less-developed country may prove inapplicable to the class of investors who concern us here.[27] The capital markets of the less-developed countries typically consist of a series of water-tight, insulated, submarkets in which wholly different rates prevail and between which arbitrage opportunities are limited. In some countries, the going figures may vary from 5 to 40 per cent, on grounds which seem to have little relation to issuer risk or term of loan. (In some economies, where inflation is endemic, interest rates which in effect represent a negative real cost are not uncommon.)

These internal differences in interest rates may be due to a number of factors: the fact that funds generated inside the firm usually are exposed to a different yield test than external borrowings; the fact that government loans are often floated by mandatory levies on banks and other intermediaries; and the fact that funds borrowed by governments from international sources are often re-loaned in domestic markets at rates which are linked closely to the international borrowing rate, however irrelevant that may be. Moreover, one has to reckon with the fact that public international lenders tend to lend at near-uniform rates, irrespective of the identity of the borrower and the going interest rate in his country. Access to capital on the part of underdeveloped countries, therefore, becomes a direct function of the country's capacity to propose plausible projects to public international lenders. If a project can plausibly be shown to 'pay its own way' in balance-of-payment and output terms at 'reasonable' interest rates, the largest single obstacle to obtaining capital at such rates has usually been overcome.

Accordingly, one may say that from the entrepreneur's viewpoint certain systematic and predictable 'imperfections' of the capital markets may reduce or eliminate the capital-shortage handicap which is characteristic of the less-developed countries; and, further, that as a result of the reduction or elimination such countries may find themselves in a position to compete effectively in the export of certain standardized capital-intensive goods. This is not the statement of another paradox; it is not the same as to say that the capital-poor countries will develop capital-intensive economies. All we are concerned with here is a modest fraction of the industry of such countries, which in turn is a minor fraction of their total economic activity. It may be that the anomalies such industries represent are systematic enough to be included in our normal expectations regarding conditions in the less-developed countries.

*   *   *   *   *

Like the other observations which have preceded, these views about the likely patterns of exports by the less-developed countries are attempts to relax some of the constraints imposed by purer and simpler models. Here and there, the hypotheses take on plausibility because they jibe with the record of past events. But, for the most part, they are still speculative in nature, having been subjected to tests of a very low order of rigorousness. What is needed, obviously, is continued probing to determine whether the 'imperfections' stressed so strongly in these pages deserve to be elevated out of the footnotes into the main text of economic theory.

Notes

* The preparation of this article was financed in part by a grant from the Ford Foundation to the Harvard Business School to support a study of the implications of United States foreign direct investment. This paper is a by-product of the hypothesis-building stage of the study.

1. J.H. Williams, 'The Theory of International Trade Reconsidered', reprinted as Chap. 2 in his *Postwar Monetary Plans and Other Essays* (Oxford: Basil Blackwell, 1947); C.P. Kindleberger, *The Dollar Shortage* (New York: Wiley, 1950); Erik Hoffmeyer, *Dollar Shortage* (Amsterdam: North-Holland, 1958); Sir Donald MacDougall, *The World Dollar Problem* (London: Macmillan, 1957); Staffen Burenstam-Linder, *An Essay on Trade and Transformation* (Uppsala: Almqvist & Wicksells, 1961).

2. The best summary of the state of trade theory that has come to my attention in recent years is J. Bhagwati, 'The Pure Theory of International Trade', *Economic Journal*, LXXIV (Mar. 1964), 1–84. Bhagwati refers obliquely to some of the theories which concern us here; but they receive much less attention than I think they deserve.

3. Some of the account that follows will be found in greatly truncated form in my 'The Trade Expansion Act in Perspective', in *Emerging Concepts in Marketing*, Proceedings of the American Marketing Association, December 1962, pp. 384–89. The elaboration here owes a good deal to the perceptive work of Se'ev Hirsch, summarized in his unpublished doctoral thesis, 'Location of Industry and International Competitiveness', Harvard Business School, 1965.

4. Note C.P. Kindleberger's reference to the 'horizon' of the decision-maker, and the view that he can only be rational within that horizon; see his *Foreign Trade and The National Economy* (New Haven: Yale University Press, 1962), p. 15 *passim*.

5. See, for instance, Richard M. Cyert and James G. March, *A Behavioral Theory of the Firm* (Englewood Cliffs, N.J.: Prentice-Hall, 1963), esp. Chap. 6; and Yair Aharoni, *The Foreign Investment Decision Process*, to be published by the Division of Research of the Harvard Business School, 1966.

6. See two excellent studies: C. Freeman, 'The Plastics Industry: A Comparative Study of Research and Innovation', in *National Institute Economic Review*, no. 26 (Nov. 1963), p. 22 *et seq.*; G.C. Hufbauer, *Synthetic Materials and the Theory of International Trade* (London: Gerald Duckworth, 1965). A number of links in the Hufbauer arguments are remarkably similar to some in this paper; but he was not aware of my writings nor I of his until after both had been completed.

7. There is a kind of first-cousin relationship between this simple notion and the 'entrained want' concept defined by H.G. Barnett in *Innovation: The Basis of Cultural Change* (New York: McGraw-Hill, 1953) p. 148. Albert O. Hirschman, *The Strategy of Economic Development* (New Haven: Yale University Press, 1958), p. 68, also finds the concept helpful in his effort to explain certain aspects of economic development.

8. For a summary of such work, together with a useful bibliography, *see* John Meyer, 'Regional Economics: A Survey', in the *American Economic Review*, LIII (Mar. 1963), 19–54.

9. The points that follow are dealt with at length in the following publications: Raymond Vernon, *Metropolis, 1985* (Cambridge, MA: Harvard University Press, 1960), pp. 38–85 ; Max Hall (ed.), *Made in New York* (Cambridge, MA: Harvard University Press, 1959), pp. 3–18, 19 *passim*; Robert M. Lichtenberg, *One-Tenth of a Nation* (Cambridge, MA: Harvard University Press, 1960), pp. 31–70.

10. This is, of course, a familiar point elaborated in George F. Stigler, 'Production and Distribution in the Short Run', *Journal of Political Economy*, XLVII (June 1939), 305, *et seq.*

11. Hufbauer, *op. cit.*, suggests that the low price elasticity of demand in the first stage may be due simply to the fact that the first market may be a 'captive market' unresponsive to price changes; but

that later, in order to expand the use of the new product, other markets may be brought in which are more price responsive.

12. Both Hirsch, *op. cit.*, and Freeman, *op. cit.*, make use of a three-stage product classification of the sort used here.

13. M.V. Posner, 'International Trade and Technical Change', *Oxford Economic Papers*, Vol. 13 (Oct. 1961), p. 323, *et seq.* presents a stimulating model purporting to explain such familiar trade phenomena as the exchange of machine tools between the United Kingdom and Germany. In the process he offers some particularly helpful notions concerning the size of the 'imitation lag' in the responses of competing nations.

14. Dudley M. Phelps, *Migration of Industry to South America* (New York: McGraw-Hill, 1963), p. 4.

15. John H. Dunning, *American Investment in British Manufacturing Industry* (London: George Allen & Unwin, 1958), p. 18. The Dunning book is filled with observations that lend casual support to the main hypotheses of this paper.

16. Note the interesting finding of Mordecai Kreinin in his 'The Leontief Scarce-Factor Paradox', *The American Economic Review*, LV (Mar. 1965), 131–39. Kreinin finds that the higher cost of labor in the United States is not explained by a higher rate of labor productivity in this country.

17. Aharoni, *op. cit.*, provides an excellent summary and exhaustive bibliography of the evidence on this point.

18. Reported in U.S. Senate, Interstate and Foreign Commerce Committee, *Hearings on Foreign Commerce*, 1960, pp. 130–39.

19. See Hirsch, *op. cit.*

20. These are to appear in a forthcoming doctoral thesis at the Harvard Business School by Louis T. Wells, tentatively entitled 'International Trade and Business Policy'.

21. See Wassily Leontief, 'Domestic Production and Foreign Trade: The American Capital Position Re-examined', *Proceedings of the American Philosophical Society*, Vol. 97 (Sept. 1953), and 'Factor Proportions and the Structure of American Trade: Further Theoretical and Empirical Analysis', *Review of Economics and Statistics*, XXXVIII (Nov. 1956).

22. Of course, if there were some systematic trend in the inputs of new products – for example, if the new products which appeared in the 1960s were more capital-intensive than the new products which appeared in the 1950s – then the tendencies suggested by our hypotheses might be swamped by such a trend. As long as we do not posit offsetting systematic patterns of this sort, however, the Leontief findings and the hypotheses offered here seem consistent.

23. The concepts sketched out here are presented in more detail in my 'Problems and Prospects in the Export of Manufactured Products from the Less-developed Countries', U.N. Conference on Trade and Development, Dec. 16, 1963 (mimeo.).

24. This conclusion derives largely from the industry studies conducted in connection with the New York Metropolitan Region study. There have been some excellent more general analyses of shifts in industrial location among the regions of the United States. See e.g., Victor R. Fuchs, *Changes in the Location of Manufacturing in the United States Since 1929* (New Haven: Yale University Press, 1962). Unfortunately, however, none has been designed, so far as I know, to test hypotheses relating locational shifts to product characteristics such as price elasticity of demand and degree of standardization.

25. This statement, too, is based on only impressionistic materials. Among the more suggestive, illustrative of the best of the available evidence, see J.N. Toothill, *Inquiry into the Scottish Economy* (Edinburgh: Scottish Council, 1962).

26. M. Tatemoto and S. Ichimura, 'Factor Proportions and Foreign Trade: Case of Japan', *Review of Economics and Statistics*, XLI (Nov. 1959), 442–46.

27. See George Rosen, *Industrial Change in India* (Glencoe, Ill.: Free Press, 1958). Rosen finds that in the period studied from 1937 to 1953, 'there was no serious shortage of capital for the largest firms in India'. Gustav F. Papanek makes a similar finding for Pakistan for the period from 1950 to 1964 in a book about to be published.

[21]

THE PRODUCT CYCLE HYPOTHESIS IN A NEW INTERNATIONAL ENVIRONMENT

By RAYMOND VERNON*

The last decade has produced a flowering of hypotheses that purport to explain the international trade and direct investment activities of firms in terms of the so-called product cycle. My purpose in this paper is to suggest that the power of such hypotheses has been changing. Two reasons account for that change: one, an increase in the geographical reach of many of the enterprises that are involved in the introduction of new products, a consequence of their having established many overseas subsidiaries; the other, a change in the national markets of the advanced industrialized countries, which has reduced some of the differences that had previously existed between such markets.

A Word on Theory

The fact that new products constantly appear, then mature, and eventually die has always fitted awkwardly into the mainstream theories of international trade and international investment. Hume, Ricardo, Marshall, Ohlin, Williams, and others have observed the phenomenon in passing, without attempting any rigorous formulation of its implications for international trade and investment theory. In the past decade or two, however, numerous efforts have been made to fill the gap. Some have dealt mainly with the trade aspects of the phenomenon.[1] But some have pushed beyond the immediate trade effects, tracing out a pattern that eventually culminated in foreign direct investments on the part of the innovating firm.[2]

According to the product cycle hypothesis, firms that set up foreign producing facilities characteristically do so in reliance on some real or imagined monopolistic advantage. In the absence of such a perceived advantage, firms are loath to take

---

* David Felix, Seev Hirsch,Sanjaya Lall, L. T. Wells, Jr. and L. H. Wortzel reacted critically to various points in an earlier draft, a fact that led to some significant revisions.

[1] For instance, M. V. Posner, 'International Trade and Technical Change', *Oxford Economic Papers*, October 1961, pp. 323–341; Gary Hufbauer, *Synthetic Materials and the Theory of International Trade* (Cambridge: Harvard University Press, 1966); Seev Hirsch, 'The Product Cycle Model of International Trade—A Multi-Country Cross Section Analysis', *Oxford Bulletin of Economics and Statistics*, November 1975, vol. 37, no. 4, pp. 305–317; W. B. Walker, 'Industrial Innovation and International Trading Performance', mimeo. Science Policy Research Unit, Sussex University, October 30, 1975; and M. P. Claudon, *International Trade and Technology: Models of Dynamic Comparative Advantages* (Washington, D.C.: University Press of America, 1977).

[2] S. H. Hymer, *The International Operations of National Firms* (Cambridge: MIT Press, 1976) based on the author's 1960 Ph.D. thesis; Raymond Vernon, 'International Investment and International Trade in the Product Cycle', *Quarterly Journal of Economics*, May 1966, pp. 190–207; W. H. Gruber and others, 'The R & D Factor in International Investment of US Industries', *Journal of Political Economy*, February 1967, pp. 20–37; Thomas Horst, 'The Firm and Industry Determinants of the Decision to Invest Abroad: An Empirical Study', *Review of Economics and Statistics*, vol. 54, August 1972, pp. 258–66; S. P. Magee, 'Multinational Corporations, The Industry Technology Cycle and Development', *Journal of World Trade Law*, vol. 11, no. 4, July–August 1977, pp. 297–321; P. J. Buckley and Mark Casson, *The Future of the Multinational Enterprise* (New York: Holmes and Meier, 1976); Paul Krugman, 'A Model of Innovation, Technology Transfer, and The World Distribution of Income', *Journal of Political Economy*, April 1979, pp. 253–266.

255

256   BULLETIN

on the special costs and uncertainties of operating a subsidiary in a foreign environment.[3] One such special strength is an innovational lead.

The product cycle hypothesis begins with the assumption that the stimulus to innovation is typically provided by some threat or promise in the market.[4] But according to the hypothesis, firms are acutely myopic; their managers tend to be stimulated by the needs and opportunities of the market closest at hand, the home market.

The home market in fact plays a dual role in the hypothesis. Not only is it the source of stimulus for the innovating firm; it is also the preferred location for the actual development of the innovation. The first factor that has pushed innovating firms to do their development work in the home market has been simply the need for engineers and scientists with the requisite skills. That requirement, when gauged through the eyes of the typical innovating form, has tended to rule out sites in most developing countries and has narrowed the choice to some site in the advanced industrialized world. As between such advanced country sites, the home market has generally prevailed.[5] Locating in the home market, engineers and scientists can interact easily with the prospective customers whose needs they hope to satisfy, and can check constantly with (or be checked by) the specialists at headquarters who are concerned with financial and production planning.

The propensity to cluster in the home market is fortified by the fact that there are some well-recognized economies to be captured by an innovating team that is brought together at a common location.[6] These include the usual advantages that go with subdividing any task among a number of specialists, and the added advantages of maintaining efficiency of communication among the research specialists.[7]

The upshot is that the innovations of firms headquartered in some given market tend to reflect the characteristics of that market. Historically, therefore, US firms have developed and produced products that were labour-saving or responded to high-income wants; continental European firms, products and processes that were material-saving and capital-saving; and Japanese firms, products that conserved not only material and capital but also space.[8]

---

[3] That is a central proposition of the S. H. Hymer work, cited earlier. See also my 'The Location of Economic Activity', in J. H. Dunning, *Economic Analysis and the Multinational Enterprise* (London: George Allen and Unwin, 1970), pp. 83–114.

[4] Various empirical studies demonstrate that innovations which do not arise out of a market stimulus—innovations, for instance, that are dreamed up by the laboratory as a clever application of some new scientific capability—have a relatively low chance of industrial success. See for instance Sumner Myers and Donald Marquis, *Successful Industrial Innovations*, National Science Foundation Report No. 69–17, G.P.O., Washington, 1969, p. 31.

[5] For econometric evidence of the tie between the choice of a production location, skills and innovation, see Sanjaya Lall, 'Monopolistic Advantages and Foreign Involvement by U.S. Manufacturing Industry', *Oxford Economic Papers*, forthcoming, March 1980.

[6] For evidence of such clustering, see D. B. Creamer, *Overseas Research and Development by United States Multinationals, 1966–1975* (New York: The Conference Board, 1976); Robert Ronstadt, *Research and Development Abroad by U.S. Multinationals* (New York: Praeger Publishers, 1977); and Vernon, *Storm Over the Multinationals*, pp. 43–45.

[7] See especially T. J. Allen, *Managing the Flow of Technology* (Cambridge: MIT Press, 1978). An important exception is pharmaceuticals, a case in which US regulation has driven the innovation process abroad. See e.g. H. G. Grabowski and J. M. Vernon, 'Innovation and Invention: Consumer Protection Regulation in Ethical Drugs', *American Economic Review*, vol. 67, no. 1, 1977, pp. 359–364.

[8] For evidence, see W. H. Davidson, 'Patterns of Factor-Saving Innovation in the Industrialized World', *European Economic Review*, No. 8, 1976, pp. 207–217.

If innovating firms tend to scan their home markets with special intensity, the chances are greatly increased that their first production facilities will also be located in the home market. In many cases, the transitions from development work to pilot plant operation to first commercial production take place in imperceptible steps. But other factors also figure in the choice. One is the fact that if the firm perceives its principal market as being at home, it may prefer a home location to minimize transport costs. The second factor is that the specifications for new products and the optimal methods for manufacturing such products are typically in flux for some time; hence, fixing the optimal location of the first production site is bound to be an exercise based on guesswork. A final factor that may explain the tendency to produce at home is the characteristic inelasticity in the demand of the earliest users of many new products. That inelasticity is thought to make the innovator relatively indifferent to questions of production cost at the time of introduction of a new product.

Once the innovator has set up its first production unit in the home market, any demand that may develop in a foreign market would ordinarily be served from the existing production unit. Eventually, however, the firm may consider other alternatives, such as that of licensing a foreign producer or of setting up its own producing subsidiary abroad. For new products, the licensing alternative may prove an inferior choice because of inefficiencies in the international market for technology.[9] If licensing is not the preferred choice, then the firm makes the usual familiar comparison between the delivered cost of exports and the cost of overseas production. That is, the marginal costs of producing for export in the home unit plus international transport costs and duties are compared with the full cost of producing the required amount in a foreign subsidiary.

Although not essential to the product cycle hypothesis, it is commonly assumed that a triggering event is likely to be required before the producer will seriously make the calculations that could lead to the creation of a foreign producing facility. The triggering event ordinarily occurs when the innovator is threatened with losing its monopoly position. In the usual case, rival producers appear, prepared to manufacture the product from locations that could undersell the original innovator.

The obvious question is why the original innovator was not already aware that the costs of production might be lower abroad. Part of the answer may lie in the indeterminateness of the threat before it has actually materialized: the difficulty of deciding what is at stake in failing to find the least-cost location, what alternative sites need to be investigated, and what the costs of investigation are likely to be.

These conditions change, however, as the threat begins to crystallize. Eventually, it may be clear that the innovator is threatened with the loss of its

---

[9] See Buckley and Casson, pp. 36–45, 68–69. Their observations are strengthened by data presented in Raymond Vernon and W. H. Davidson, 'Foreign Production of Technology-Intensive Products by US-Based Multinational Enterprises', Working Paper 79–5, Harvard Business School, 1979, xeroxed, p. 66. These data show that in establishing a source of foreign production for 221 innovations, 32 large US-based multinational enterprises elected the subsidiary route far more frequently than licensing, but the degree of preference declined as the innovation aged. For similar conclusions relating to petrochemicals, see R. B. Stobaugh, 'The Product Life Cycle, U.S. Exports, and International Investment', unpublished D.B.A. thesis, Harvard Business School, 1968.

258   BULLETIN

business in a given foreign market. At that point, the areas to be investigated as possible production sites have been narrowed while the size of the risk has been more explicitly defined. Accordingly, the decision whether to invest in added information is more readily made. Once having felt compelled to focus on the issue, the innovator will decide in some cases to set up a local producing unit in order to prolong some of the advantages that were created by its original monopoly.

Two Critical Changes

The networks' spread. For the past three decades or so, the process of innovation, export, and investment has been progressing full tilt. One result has been a transformation in the industries in which innovations tend to be especially prominent, such as chemicals, electronics, machinery, and transportation equipment. In industries such as these, innovating firms that are limited to their own home markets no longer are very common. Instead, enterprises with highly developed multinational networks of producing units typically account for more than half the global output in their respective product lines.

In spreading their networks of subsidiaries around the world, multinational companies have followed some reasonably well-defined patterns. These patterns offer some strong clues regarding the changing perceptions of the enterprises and their likely lines of future behaviour.

First, a word on the extent of the spread itself. Table 1 compares the scope of

TABLE 1

Networks of Foreign Manufacturing Subsidiaries of 315 Multinational Companies 1950 and 1970s

Number of enterprises with networks including	180 US-based MNCs		135 MNCs based in UK and Europe	
	1950	1975	1950	1970
Fewer than 6 countries	138	9	116	31
6 to 20 countries	43	128	16	75
More than 20 countries	0	44	3	29

Source: Harvard Multinational Enterprise Project.

the overseas subsidiary networks of a group of the world's largest firms in 1950 with the networks of those same firms in the 1970s. The dramatic increase in the overseas networks of such firms is apparent.

Detailed data have been developed for the 180 US firms in the group, indicating more exactly how the overseas spread took place.[10] According to these data, the overseas spread of the firms in our sample was consistent and stable throughout the three decades following World War II. Firms typically set up their subsidiaries, product lines, and new products in a sequence that began with the geographical areas with which they were most familiar, such as Canada and the United Kingdom, and eventually spread to those that had originally been least familiar, such as Asia and Africa. As time went on, however, the unfamiliar became less so, and the

[10] The data on which the next few paragraphs are based are presented in detail in Raymond Vernon and W. H. Davidson, 'Foreign Production of Technology-Intensive Products by U.S.-Based Multinational Enterprises', cited earlier.

THE PRODUCT CYCLE HYPOTHESIS IN A NEW INTERNATIONAL ENVIRONMENT   259

disposition to move first into the traditional areas visibly declined. To illustrate: For product lines introduced abroad by the 180 firms before 1946, the probability that a Canadian location would come earlier than an Asian location was 79 percent; but for product lines that were introduced abroad after 1960, the probability that Canada would take precedence over Asia had dropped to only 59 percent.

The consequences of this steady shift in preferences could be seen in a corresponding shift in the geographical distribution of the foreign subsidiaries of the 180 firms. Before 1946, about 23 percent of the subsidiaries had been located in Canada; but by 1975, the proportion was about 13 percent, with the offsetting gains being recorded principally in Asia, Africa, and the Middle East.[11]

With numerous indications that US firms were feeling at ease over a wider portion of the earth's surface, it comes as no surprise that the interval of time between the introduction of any new product in the United States and its first production in a foreign location has been rapidly shrinking. Table 2 portrays the time lapse between the introduction of 954 products in the United States and their first overseas production via the manufacturing subsidiaries of the introducing firm.

The data also suggest in various ways that the trends just discussed have been strongly self-reinforcing. For instance, firms that had experienced a considerable number of prior transfers to their foreign producing subsidiaries were quite consistently quicker off the mark with any new product than were firms with fewer

TABLE 2

Spread of Production of 954 New Products by 57 US-Based MNCs to their Foreign Manufacturing Subsidiaries, Classified by Period when initially introduced in the United States

Period when introduced in US	Number of products	Percentage transferred abroad, by number of years between US introduction and initial transfer	
		within 1 year after %	within 2–3 years after %
1945	56	10.7	8.9
1946–1950	149	8.1	10.1
1951–1955	147	7.5	10.2
1956–1960	180	13.3	17.8
1961–1965	165	22.4	17.0
1966–1970	158	29.7	15.8
1971–1975	99	35.4	16.2
Total	954	18.0	14.0

Source: Vernon and Davidson, cited in text.

prior transfers. Besides, as firms introduced one product after another into a given country, the lapse of time between the introduction of successive products in that country steadily declined.

All told, therefore, the picture is one of an organic change in the overseas networks of large US-based firms. The rate of spread of these networks, whether measured by subsidiaries or by product lines, is slightly lower in the first half of the

---

[11] Some measures employed in the Vernon–Davidson study—counts based on 954 individual products rather than on subsidiaries or product lines—show Latin America also increasing its relative share. See Table 17, p. 52 of the report.

1970's than in the latter half of the 1960's; but the spread persists at rates that are rapid by historical standards. Besides, the changes in the rate of spread, according to various econometric tests, seem quite impervious to changes in exchange rates or in price-adjusted exchange rates;[12] so it seems reasonable to assume that we confront a basic change in the institutional structure of the MNCs concerned.[13]

The environmental changes. In the period after World War II, the descriptive power of the product cycle hypothesis, at least as it applied to US-based enterprises, had been enhanced by some special factors. In the early part of the post-war period, the US economy was the repository of a storehouse of innovations not yet exploited abroad, innovations that responded to the labour-scarce high-income conditions of the US market. As the years went on, other countries eventually achieved the income levels and acquired the relative labour costs that had prevailed earlier in the United States. As these countries tracked the terrain already traversed by the US economy, they developed an increasing demand for the products that had previously been generated in response to US needs. That circumstance provided the consequences characteristically associated with the product cycle sequence: exports from the United States in mounting volume, followed eventually by the establishment of foreign producing subsidiaries on the part of the erstwhile US exporters.

But many of the advanced industrialized countries that were tracking over the US terrain were doing something more: They were closing in on the United States, narrowing or obliterating the income gap that had existed in the immediate postwar period. In 1949, for instance, the per capita income of Germany and of France was less than one-third that of the United States; but by the latter 1970's, the per capita income of all three countries was practically equal. In the same interval, Japan increased its per capita income from 6 percent of the US level to nearly 70 percent of that level. That shrinkage, of course, weakened a critical assumption of the product cycle hypothesis, namely, that the entrepreneurs of large enterprises confronted markedly different conditions in their respective home markets. As European and Japanese incomes approached those of the United States, these differences were reduced. And as the United States came to rely increasingly on imported raw materials, the differences in the factor costs of the various markets declined further still.

Not only have the differences in income levels among these major markets been shrinking; the differences in their overall dimensions also have declined. This has been due partly to the convergence of such income levels, but partly also to the development of the European Economic Community. As a result, entrepreneurs with their home base in these different markets confront conditions that are much more similar than they had been in the past.

Some of the starting assumptions of the product cycle hypothesis therefore are clearly in question. It is no longer easy to assume that innovating firms are

[12] Vernon and Davidson, pp. 19–20.
[13] Although the data for testing the assumption are not at hand, I have assumed that parallel changes are occurring in European and Japanese firms.

uninformed about conditions in foreign markets, whether in other advanced countries or in the developing world. Nor can it be assumed that US firms are exposed to a very different home environment from European and Japanese firms; although the gap between most of the developing countries and the advanced industrialized countries palpably remains, the differences among the advanced industrialized countries are reduced to trivial dimensions. With some key assumptions of the product cycle hypothesis in doubt, what organizing concepts are still available by which one can observe and assess the role of innovation in the operations of the multinational enterprises of different countries?

The Global Network in Operation

To try to answer the question, I have classified multinational companies crudely into three ideal types, and have sought to explore their likely behaviour.

The first type is purely hypothetical, a result of armchair speculation. Picture an MNC with an innovating capability that has developed a powerful capacity for global scanning. Communication is virtually costless between any two points of the globe; information, once received, is digested and interpreted at little or no cost. Ignorance or uncertainty, therefore, is no longer a function of distance; markets, wherever located, have an equal opportunity to stimulate the firm to innovation and production; and factory sites, wherever located, have an equal chance to be weighed for their costs and risks. But some significant economies of scale continue to exist in the development activities as well as in the production activities of the firm.

An enterprise of this sort, we can presume, will from time to time develop an innovation in response to the promise or threat of one of the many markets to which it was exposed. The firm might launch the innovative process in the market that had produced the stimulus; or, if economies of scale were important and an appropriate facility existed elsewhere in the system, in a location well removed from the prospective market. In either case, once the innovation was developed, the global scanner would be in a position to serve any market in which it was aware that demand existed; and would be in a position to detect and serve new demands in other markets as they subsequently arose. Presumably such demands would grow in other countries as they attained the income levels or the factor cost configurations of the country whose needs had first stimulated the invention. For some products, such as consumer goods, the demand in different national markets could be expected to appear in a predictable pecking order, based largely on income levels and labour costs.

The global scanner, therefore, would be in an advantageous position as compared with those firms without such a scanning capability. Firms that were confined to a country which was down the ladder in the pecking order, including most firms headquartered in the developing countries, would be at a disadvantage in relation to the global scanner. As the incomes of their home countries grew, the nonglobal producers might well perceive the opportunity to fill a growing demand; but they would be handicapped by comparison with the enterprises that were already producing in the higher income countries, including the global scanners.

In a world composed of such firms, the product cycle hypothesis would play only a very little role. Although innovating firms might prefer locations in one of the advanced industrialized countries due to the supply of engineers and scientists, the preference for a location in the home market would be weaker. The exports generated by the innovations might come from the country in which the product had initially been introduced; but then again they might not. Whatever the original source of the exports might be, the hold of the exporting country would be tenuous, as the global scanner continuously recalculated the parameters that determined the optimal production location.

The hypothetical global scanner, of course, is not to be found in the real world. The acquisition of information is seldom altogether costless; and the digestion and interpretation of information always entails cost. The typical patterns of behaviour that one observes in the real world reflect that fact.

One typical pattern, which provides the basis for a second model, consists of firms that develop and produce a line of standardized products which they think responds to a homogeneous world demand rather than to the distinctive needs of individual markets. Some firms have been able to take this approach from the very first, because of the nature of their products; the oil, chemical, and crude metals industries, for instance, were always in a position to develop and purvey a standardized line of products to world markets. But the trend has been moving beyond such products to well-elaborated manufactures: to aircraft, computers, pharmaceuticals, and automobiles, for instance. The trends of the automobile industry in that direction are particularly striking.[14]

By standardizing their product on a world basis, firms can hope for two kinds of benefit: they can reduce or avoid the costs of processing and interpreting the information that bears on the distinctive needs of individual markets; and they can capture the scale economies of production and marketing on a global scale. Whether those advantages outweigh the disadvantages of being unresponsive to the needs of individual markets is an empirical question the answer to which may well vary by product lines and other factors; those firms that decide in the affirmative for some or all of their product lines cannot be said to be engaged in an irrational response.

Firms in this category, innovating for a global market, are obliged to play their innovational gambles for relatively heavy stakes. Accordingly, they can be expected to maintain the central core of their innovational activities close to headquarters, where complex face-to-face consultation among key personnel will be possible; in this respect, such firms are likely to perform consistently with the product cycle pattern. To be sure, with increased ease of communication and transportation, various routine aspects of the development work, not involving the most critical choices in the development process, can be spun off to more distant

[14] See A. J. Harman, 'Innovations, Technology, and the Pure Theory of International Trade', unpublished Ph.D. thesis, MIT, September 1968, pp. 131–134; J. M. Callahan, 'GM Adopting Worldwide Purchasing Coordination', *Chilton's Automotive Industries*, July 1978, pp. 47–49; 'Ford's Fiesta Makes a Big Splash', *Business Week*, August 22, 1977, pp. 38–39; and 'SKF Reintegrates Internationally', *Multinational Business*, The Economist Intelligence Unit, No. 4, 1976, pp. 1–7.

THE PRODUCT CYCLE HYPOTHESIS IN A NEW INTERNATIONAL ENVIRONMENT   263

locations. To reduce their development costs and to respond to the pressures of various governments in whose territories they hope to do business, firms in this category are commonly prepared to establish some carefully selected development activities at distant points; but integration at the centre is still needed.[15]

Firms in this category also have a strong need to integrate their global production facilities. Seeking to exploit scale economies, they are likely to establish various component plants in both advanced industrialized countries and developing countries, and to crosshaul between plants for the assembly of final products. That pattern will be at variance with product cycle expectations.

It need not be anticipated, however, that all firms with a capacity for global scanning will commit themselves unequivocally to the development of standard global products such as the IBM 370, the Boeing 757, or the GM world car. General Motors, after all, continues to respond to certain distinctive national characteristics in some of its product lines, in spite of its commitment to a world sourcing strategy. Other automobile firms, including Renault and Chrysler, seem prepared to respond to national factors for even a larger proportion of their output, foregoing the advantages of a world product and long production runs. In computers, a number of IBM's rivals survive by their willingness and ability to adapt to the requirements of local markets, including the requirements of national governments, to a degree that would be incompatible with the standardization of their products and the global rationalization of their facilities.[16] Many European and Japanese firms still find it useful to treat the US market as a distinctive entity, justifying distinctive products and strategies.[17]

Accordingly, we can picture firms that make different decisions on the benefits of global optimization, according to the characteristics of each product line. And we can picture markets in which different firms have settled on somewhat different strategies for closely competing products. If past history is any guide, such differences can persist in a given product market over extended periods of time.[18]

A third type of innovating MNC that merits some speculative consideration is the firm whose choices of innovations and production sites remain myopically oriented to the home market while leaving all analysis of foreign markets to its individual foreign producing subsidiaries. Firms in this category simply put out their home-based innovations for production by their foreign subsidiaries; or, perhaps even more commonly, such firms allow the initiative for such decisions to

[15] Compare the observations of Sanjaya Lall, 'The International Allocation of Research Activity by U.S. Multinationals', in this issue.

[16] This point is being developed in detail by Yves Doz at the Harvard Business School.

[17] For evidence on Japanese firms in this category, see Terutomo Ozawa, *Japan's Technological Challenge to the West, 1950–1974* (Cambridge: MIT Press, 1974), pp. 97–98.

[18] This proposition is of course consistent with the theory of strategic groups; see R. E. Caves and M. E. Porter, 'From Entry Barriers to Mobility Barriers: Conjectural Decisions and Contrived Deterrence to New Competition', *Quarterly Journal of Economics*, vol. XCI, no. 2, 1977, pp. 241–261. It is consistent also with the long established observation that different geographical locations offer different combinations of benefits and costs such that widely separated locations applying different production techniques may be competitive for sustained periods. See Max Hall, *Made in New York* (Cambridge: Harvard University Press, 1959).

264 BULLETIN

come from the subsidiaries themselves.[19] Drawing from a shopping list of products generated by the headquarters unit, subsidiaries choose those that seem appropriate for intensive exploitation in their local markets. As long as the proposed production in the subsidiary seems to have no considerable impact on the facilities of the firm located in other countries, the managers at headquarters are disposed to give the local managers their head.

Firms that pursue a policy of this sort can justify their approach readily enough: One possibility is that the firm perceives the cost of interpreting the information needed for pursuing a more centralized policy in production and marketing as exceeding the likely benefits. Another possibility is that the firm has found it impossible to fashion an organization that has the capability for absorbing and being influenced by signals that originate in the subsidiaries.[20]

Where this pattern of operation exists, the hypothesized behaviour of the product cycle may still be visible. But the phase of the product cycle in which the parent is responsible for serving foreign markets will be foreshortened and the oligopolistic strength of the innovating firm will be relatively weak, given the existence of firms in other markets that face similar demands and factor cost conditions.

Cases in this category will of course deviate from the pattern that a global scanner would generate. First, as long as the subsidiary is the initiator, the geographical spread of products will be affected by the risk-taking propensities and drives of individual subsidiary managers and by the resource slack of individual subsidiaries rather than by a consistent set of decision rules and allocations from the centre.[21] Second, in cases in which the initiative for transfer comes from the subsidiary rather than the parent, the possibility of producing in some third country where neither the parent nor the subsidiary is located is unlikely to be considered.

All this leads to a simple conclusion. As we search for a hypothesis that would replace the product cycle concept as an explicator of the trading and investing behaviour of the innovating multinational company, a simple variant such as that of the global scanner will not take us very far. Global scanning is not costless, even when a network of foreign subsidiaries is already in place; costs of collecting and interpreting the information, as the firm perceives those costs, may not be commensurate with its expected benefits. In assessing the benefits, flexibility may be a problem: either the flexibility that firms have lost from decisions in the past, or the flexibility they are fearful of losing in an uncertain future.

---

[19] For illustrations, see 'IBM World Trade Corporation' and 'YKK (Yoshida Kogyo KK)', both in Stanley M. Davis, *Managing and Organizing Multinational Corporations* (New York: Pergamon Press, 1979). Also, from Intercollegiate Case Clearing House, see *Corning Glass Works (A), (B), and (C)* (numbers 9–477–024, 9–477–073, and 9–477–074); *International Calculators (Australia) Pty. Limited* (9–572–641); *Veedol France* (ICH 10 M 31); *The International Harvester Company (B)* (9–512–009); *Princess Housewares Gmb H (A)* (ICH 13 M 117); *General Foods Corporation—International Division (D2)* (ICH 13 G 214); *AB Thorsten (A)* (9–414–035); and *Sanpix Industries* (9–278–673).

[20] For indications of the formidable difficulties associated with developing such an organizational capability, see Allen, *Managing the Flow of Technology, op. cit.*

[21] This, of course, is a familiar phenomenon, long observed by business historians and organizational behaviourists. More recently the concept has been elevated to the status of theory in Harvey Leibenstein's formulation of his X-inefficiency concept: see his *Beyond Economic Man: A New Foundation for Microeconomics* (Cambridge: Harvard University Press, 1976).

So the day of the global scanner as I defined it a few pages back is not yet here. Nevertheless, even if the global scanner is not yet the dominant model, nor perhaps ever will be, the power of the product cycle hypothesis is certainly weakened.

The Product Cycle Reconsidered

The evidence is fairly persuasive that the product cycle hypothesis had strong predictive power in the first two or three decades after World War II, especially in explaining the composition of US trade and in projecting the likely patterns of foreign direct investment by US firms. But certain conditions of that period are gone. For one thing, the leading MNCs have now developed global networks of subsidiaries; for another, the US market is no longer unique among national markets either in size or factor cost configuration. It seems plausible to assume that the product cycle will be less useful in explaining the relationship of the US economy to other advanced industrialized countries, and will lose some of its power in explaining the relationship of advanced industrialized countries to developing countries. But strong traces of the sequence are likely to remain.[22]

One such trace is likely to be provided by the innovating activities of smaller firms, firms that have not yet acquired a capacity for global scanning through a network of foreign manufacturing subsidiaries already in place. The assumptions of the product cycle hypothesis may still apply to such firms, as they move from home-based innovation to the possibility of exports and ultimately of overseas investment.

Moreover, even firms with a well-developed scanning capability and a willingness to use it may be found behaving according to the expectations of the product cycle hypothesis. As noted earlier, the specifications of new products are usually in such a state of flux that it is infeasible for a time to fix on a least-cost location. Some firms therefore are unlikely to make intensive use of their scanning capability when siting their first production facility. To be sure, such innovators cannot expect to retain their innovational lead for very long, in view of the fact that the innovators of many countries now confront such similar home conditions. But a shadow of the hypothesized behaviour may well remain.

Moreover, the product cycle may gain some support as a predictive device from other developments.

One such development is the improved position of European and Japanese firms as innovators. As noted earlier, the innovations of these firms, when compared with those of US firms, have tended to place greater emphasis on material-saving and capital-saving objectives, while placing lesser relative emphasis on labour-saving measures and on new mass consumer wants. The costs of materials and capital have risen rapidly over the past few years, both in relative and absolute terms. Accordingly, it may be that the long-time emphasis of the

---

[22] But see I. H. Giddy, 'The Demise of the Product Cycle Model in International Business Theory', *Columbia Journal of World Business*, vol. xiii, no. 1, Spring 1978, pp. 90–97.

266 BULLETIN

Europeans and Japanese firms will generate an increasing demand for their innovations. The world's increased use of European and Japanese small-car technology and of Japanese steel technology are cases in point, fitting nicely within the structure of the product cycle hypothesis.

However, the product cycle hypothesis would also predict that the European-Japanese advantage on this front will only be temporary. As US firms confront factor-cost conditions in their home market that are similar to those of Europe and Japan, one would expect a stream of innovations from the Americans similar to those of their overseas competitors; General Motors, for instance, is now seen as a potential threat to European and Japanese car makers for the 1980's.

A less equivocal case for the continued usefulness of the product cycle concept is found in analysing the situation of the less-developed countries. Although income, market size, and factor cost patterns have converged among the more advanced industrialized countries, a wide gap still separates such countries from many developing areas. Accordingly, despite the fact that so many MNCs have created producing networks all over the globe, the subsidiaries of such firms located in the developing countries have yet to acquire all of the products that their parents and affiliates produce in richer and larger markets. Most of the developing countries, therefore, are still in process of absorbing the innovations of other countries introduced earlier, according to patterns that remain reasonably consistent with product cycle expectations.

The performance of firms in some developing countries, moreover, follows the expectations of the product cycle in a very different sense. Firms operating in the more rapidly industrializing group—in countries such as Mexico, Brazil, India, and Korea—are demonstrating a considerable capability for producing innovations that respond to the special conditions of their own economies.[23] Once having responded to those special conditions with a new product or process or with a significant adaptation of an existing product or process, firms of that sort are in a position to initiate their own cycle of exportation and eventual direct investment; their target, according to the hypothesis, would be the markets of the other developing countries that were lagging a bit behind them in the industrialized pecking order.

Indications that some such process was going on in a limited way in the developing countries were already being reported in the 1960's in occasional illustrations and anecdotal materials; but those early cases for the most part involved the subsidiaries of multinational enterprises, which were making modest adaptations of products and processes originally received from the foreign

[23] See, for example, Julio Fidel, et al., 'The Argentine Cigarette Industry: Technological Profile and Behavior', IDB/ECLA Research Programme in Science and Technology, Buenos Aires, September 1978, pp. 92–94; C. J. Dahlman, 'From Technological Dependence to Technological Development: The Case of the USIMINAS Steel Plant in Brazil', IDB/ECLA Research Programme in Science and Technology, Buenos Aires, October 1978; and Jorge Katz *et al.*, 'Productivity, Technology and Domestic Efforts in Research and Development', IDB/ECLA Research Programme in Science and Technology, Buenos Aires, July 1978. For evidence of the increasing capacity of some developing countries to sell plants and engineering services, see Sanjaya Lall, 'Developing Countries as Exporters of Industrial Technology', *Research Policy*, forthcoming, vol. 9, no. 1, January 1980.

parents.[24] Innovations such as these sometimes gave the subsidiaries a basis for exporting more effectively to neighbouring countries that were lower on the development scale.

In the 1970's, however, the anecdotal materials began to involve firms that were headquartered in developing countries.[25] Firms were reported developing products and processes of special importance to other developing countries, to be followed eventually by the creation of producing subsidiaries in those countries.[26] Of course, the direct investments of the firms of developing countries in other developing countries have not all been of the product cycle variety. The foreign subsidiaries of firms headquartered in developing countries often maintain their position through oligopolistic strengths other than a technological lead.[27]

Accordingly, the product cycle concept continues to explain and predict a certain category of foreign direct investments. Although it no longer can be relied on to provide as powerful an explanation of the behaviour of US firms as in decades past, it is likely to continue to provide a guide to the motivations and response of some enterprises in all countries of the world.

Harvard University

[24] W. A. Yeoman, 'Selection of Production Processes for the Manufacturing Subsidiaries of U.S.-Based Multinational Corporations', D.B.A. thesis, Harvard University, April 1968, chap. 5; Jorge Katz and Eduardo Ablin, 'Technology and Industrial Exports: A Micro-Economic Analysis of Argentina's Recent Experience', IDB/ECLA Research Programme in Science and Technology, Buenos Aires, August 1978; and by the same authors, 'From Infant Industry to Technology Exports: The Argentine Experience in the International Sale of Industrial Plants and Engineering Works', IDB/ECLA Research Programme in Science and Technology, Buenos Aires, October 1978.

[25] See for instance L. T. Wells, Jr., 'The Internationalization of Firms from Developing Countries', in Tamir Agmon and C. P. Kindleberger, *Multinationals from Small Countries* (Cambridge: MIT Press, 1977), pp. 133–166; by the same author, 'Foreign Investment from the Third World: The Experience of Chinese Firms from Hong Kong', *Columbia Journal of World Business*, Spring 1978, pp. 39–49; and A. J. Prasad, 'Export of Technology from India', unpublished Ph.D. thesis, Columbia University, 1978, pp. 123–156

[26] Extensive data on this tendency are being developed by L. T. Wells, Jr., for eventual publication.

[27] Such firms also have been known, for instance, to develop special skills in the maintenance and repair of second hand machinery, and a supply of scarce spare parts for such machinery. See Wells, 'Hong Kong', and Prasad, 'India', p. 147.

[22]

TOWARD AN ECLECTIC THEORY
OF INTERNATIONAL PRODUCTION:
SOME EMPIRICAL TESTS

JOHN H. DUNNING*
University of Reading

Abstract. This paper first sets out the main features of the eclectic theory of international production and then seeks to evaluate its significance of *ownership*- and *location*-specific variables in explaining the industrial pattern and geographical distribution of the sales of U.S. affiliates in fourteen manufacturing industries in seven countries in 1970.

INTRODUCTION
The Underlying
Theory

■ There is now a consensus of opinion that the propensity of an enterprise to engage in international production—that financed by foreign direct investment—rests on three main determinants: first, the extent to which it possesses (or can acquire, on more favorable terms) assets[1] which its competitors (or potential competitors) do not possess; second, whether it is in its interest to sell or lease these assets to other firms, or make use of—internalize—them itself; and third, how far it is profitable to exploit these assets in conjunction with the indigenous resources of foreign countries rather than those of the home country. The more the *ownership*-specific advantages possessed by an enterprise, the greater the inducement to internalize them; and the wider the attractions of a foreign rather than a home country production base, the greater the likelihood that an enterprise, given the incentive to do so, will engage in international production.

This eclectic approach to the theory of international production may be summarized as follows.[2] A national firm supplying its own market has various avenues for growth: it can diversify horizontally or laterally into new product lines, or vertically into new activities, including the production of knowledge; it can acquire existing enterprises; or it can exploit foreign markets. When it makes good economic sense to choose the last route (which may also embrace one or more of the others), the enterprise becomes an international enterprise (defined as a firm which services foreign markets). However, for it to be able to produce alongside indigenous firms domiciled in these markets, it must possess additional *ownership* advantages sufficient to outweigh the costs of servicing an unfamiliar or distant environment [Hirsch 1976].

The function of an enterprise is to transform, by the process of production, valuable inputs into more valuable outputs. Inputs are of two kinds. The first are those which are available, on the same terms, to all firms, whatever their size or nationality, but which are specific in their origin to particular locations and have to be used in that location. These include not only Ricardian type endowments—natural resources, most kinds of labor, and proximity to markets,[3] but also the legal and commercial environment in which the endowments are used—market structure, and government legislation and policies. In classical and neoclassical trade theories, differences in the possession of these endowments between countries fully explain the willingness and the ability of enterprises to become international;[4] but since all firms, whatever their nationality of ownership, were assumed to have full and free access to them (including technology), there were no advantages to be gained from foreign production.

*John H. Dunning is Professor of International Investment and Business Studies at the University of Reading. He has been working in the field of international investment and the multinational enterprise since the mid 1950s and has published several books and numerous articles on the subject.

The author is much indebted to Professor Guy Landry of Brandon University, Winnipeg who was responsible for most of the computational work behind Tables 3–6 and who assisted in writing the first draft of pages 12–23.

9

The second type of input is that which an enterprise may create for itself—certain types of technology and organizational skills—or can purchase from other institutions, but over which, in so doing, it acquires some proprietary right of use. Such *ownership*-specific inputs may take the form of a legally protected right— patents, brand names, trade marks—or of a commercial monopoly—the acquisition of a particular raw material essential to the production of the product—or of exclusive control over particular market outlets; or they may arise from the size or technical characteristics of firms—economies of large-scale production and surplus entrepreneurial capacity. It should be observed that these *ownership* advantages are not exclusive either to international or multinational firms. Some are applicable to all firms producing in the same location; others are those which a branch plant of an existing enterprise may enjoy over a *de novo* enterprise of the same nationality.[5] But, because they operate in different *location*-specific environments, multinational firms may also derive additional *ownership* advantages—such as, their ability to engage in international transfer pricing, to shift liquid assets between currency areas to take advantage of (or protect against) exchange fluctuations, to reduce risks by diversifying their investment portfolios [Rugman 1979], to reduce the impact of strikes or industrial unrest in one country by operating parallel production capacity in another and by engaging international product or process specialization [Dunning 1977].

The essential feature about these second types of inputs is that, although their *origin* may be linked to *location*-specific endowments, their *use* is not so confined. The ability of enterprises to acquire *ownership* endowments is clearly not unrelated to the endowments specific to the countries in which they operate— and particularly their country of origin. Otherwise, there would be no reason why the structure of foreign production of firms of different nationalities should be different. But, in fact, it is so—and substantially so. A recently published paper [Dunning 1979] has shown that Japanese firms have a comparative advantage in the foreign production of textiles and clothing and consumer electronics; UK firms in food and tobacco products; Swedish firms in mechanical and electrical engineering; West German firms in chemicals; and U.S. firms in transport equipment. Such differences as these can be explained only by an examination of the characteristics of the endowments of the countries in which the multinational enterprises operate, and especially those of the home country, which normally give rise to the *ownership* advantages in the first place. Raymond Vernon's product cycle theory was among the first to use this approach from the viewpoint of U.S. direct investment abroad [1966]. More recently Birgitta Swedenborg [1979] has extended and applied it to a study of Swedish, U.S., and UK direct foreign investment. The paper by Dunning [1979] deals with the industrial structure of foreign direct investment of five countries: UK, Sweden, Japan, West Germany, and the U.S. asserting that the relationship between *ownership-* and *location*-specific endowments is more complex than was once thought. Moreover, often a longish time lag may be involved; many of today's *ownership* advantages of firms are a reflection of yesterday's location advantages of countries.

But, whatever the significance of the country of origin of such inputs, they are worth separating from those which are *location*-specific, because the enterprise possessing them can exploit them wherever it wishes, usually at a minimal transfer cost. Moreover, unless it chooses to sell them, or the right to their use, to other enterprises, the endowments are—for some period of time at least—its exclusive property.

Both modern trade and international production theory have embraced this kind of endowment which is often mobile between countries but not between firms. Indeed, over the last twenty years there has been a convergence in the explanation of the movement of goods and of factor inputs across national boundaries. Alongside the neotechnology theories of trade, which assert that the extent

10

to which a country possesses technology is a key determinant of patterns of trade in manufactured goods between nations [Hufbauer 1970; Hirsch 1974], there is the knowledge theory of direct investment, which explains the pattern of international production in terms of the distribution of knowledge between firms of different nationalities [Johnson 1970]. Parallel with the hypothesis that patterns of trade can best be explained by the extent to which enterprises in different countries possess monopolistic, scale, or product differentiation advantages, are the theories of direct investment which focus on product differentiation, entrepreneurial capacity and multiplant economies [Caves 1971, 1974].

In the last five or six years, it has become increasingly recognized that neither a *location* nor an *ownership* endowment approach, by itself, can satisfactorily explain all forms of trade—although particular kinds of trade may be better explained by one approach rather than by another [Hirsch 1976]. It is now also accepted that an *ownership* endowment approach (first pioneered by Kindleberger and Hymer and later refined by Caves) is a necessary but not a sufficient condition for explaining international production. Only if both of the right dispositions of resource endowments exist between countries and firms of different nationalities will international production take place.

There is one final strand to the eclectic theory of international production. The possession of *ownership* advantages determines *which* firms will supply a particular foreign market, whereas the pattern of location endowments explains whether the firm will supply that market by exports (trade) or by local production (non-trade). But why does a firm choose to use the *ownership* advantages itself to exploit a foreign market—whatever route it chooses—rather than sell or lease these advantages to a firm located in that market to exploit? Why does it *internalize* its capital, technology, management skills itself to produce goods rather than externalize their use by engaging in portfolio investment, licensing, management contracts, and so on?

The basic incentive of a firm to internalize its ownership endowments is to avoid the disadvantages, or capitalize on the imperfections, of one or the other of the two main external mechanisms of resource allocation—the *market or price system* and the *public authority fiat*. Market imperfections arise wherever negotiation or transaction costs are high, wherever the economies of interdependent activities cannot be fully captured, and wherever information about the product or service being marketed is not readily available or is costly to acquire. From a buyer's viewpoint, such imperfections include uncertainty over the availability and price of essential supplies and inability to control their timing and delivery. From a seller's viewpoint, the preference for internalizing will be most pronounced where the market does not permit price discrimination, where the costs of enforcing property rights and controlling information flows are high, or where, in the case of forward integration, the seller wishes to protect his reputation by ensuring a control over product or service quality or after-sales maintenance [Brown 1976]. For both groups of firms, and for those considering horizontal internalization, the possession of underutilized resources—particularly entrepreneurial and organizational capacity, which may be exploited at low marginal cost to produce products complementary to those currently being supplied—also fosters internalization.

Public intervention in the allocation of resources may also encourage firms to internalize their activities. This arises particularly with respect to government legislation toward the production and licensing of technology, including the patent system, and where there are differential tax and exchange rate policies, which multinational enterprises may wish either to avoid or exploit.

As described then, the propensity to internalize ownership or location advantages[6] make up the third strand in the eclectic theory. In most of the conventional literature on trade and international investment, it is this last aspect of the theory

that has been most seriously neglected. For it is not just the possession of technology per se which gives an enterprise selling goods embodying that technology
an edge over its international competitors, but also the advantages which arise
from internalizing that technology rather than selling it to a foreign producer for
the production of those goods. In other words, without the advantages of internalization much of direct foreign investment would be replaced by the international
transaction of resources on a contractual basis between independent buyers and
sellers.

To conclude this brief theoretical introduction, a matrix is presented which attempts to relate, in an encapsulated form, the main types of activities in which
multinational enterprises may be involved to the three main determinants of international involvement. (See Table 1). Such a table may be used as a starting point
for an examination of the industrial and geographical distribution of foreign
direct investment. It will be noted that as part of the explanation of *ownership* endowments, the possession of *home* country endowments has been added because these will influence the geographical origin of such investment.

AN OVERVIEW OF CURRENT APPROACHES

Broadly speaking, there have been five approaches to testing the theory of international production. The first has attempted to explain the causes of direct *foreign investment* by examining its industrial composition from the viewpoint of
individual home countries (almost exclusively the U.S.) and host countries (notably Canada, UK, and Australia). A common thread running through all these studies[7] is that they have sought to explain the pattern of foreign direct investment
in terms of *ownership* advantages of MNEs. The second approach has been to
look at the *form* of international economic involvement and to identify the determinants of whether foreign markets are exploited by trade or nontrade routes.[8]
The third has combined the two approaches by examining both the level and composition of international involvement in terms of *ownership* and *locational* characteristics.[9] The fourth approach has been to extend the first three to incorporate
the internalization thesis;[10] and the fifth has been to relate the specific endowments of firms to those of home countries, as in Vernon [1966]; Swedenborg
[1979]; and Dunning [1979]. The empirical contribution of this paper is primarily of
the third kind but with the issues of the fourth very much in mind.

From both a technical and motivational standpoint, these strands of research
have much in common.[11] Each uses, with varying degrees of sophistication, multiple regression analysis to test explanations about the relationship between
various measures of international involvement and a variety of explanatory variables. Each, too, is beset by the same kind of methodological and statistical
problems, notably the establishment of operationally testable hypotheses, data
limitations, and multicollinearity between the individual variables. From a motivational standpoint, with one exception [Knickerbocker 1973], all the studies
assume either that enterprises are profit maximizers or that their behavior is not
inconsistent with that which might be expected from a profit–maximizing firm.

In testing empirically two of the most important hypotheses implicit in the eclectic theory of international production, only two forms of international economic
involvement—exports and production—are considered; these are assumed to be
alternative to each other in servicing foreign markets.[12]

The data used cover the foreign activities of U.S. multinationals in fourteen manufacturing industries in seven countries in 1970, as published by the U.S. Tariff
Commission [1973], details of which are set out in Appendix 2.[13] The two basic
hypotheses are:

H1 The competitive advantage of a country's enterprises in servicing foreign
markets is determined both by the *ownership* advantages of these enterprises relative to those of enterprises of other nationalities, and the *location*

TABLE 1

The Determinants of International Production

Types of International Production	Ownership Advantages	Location Advantages	Internalization Advantages	Illustration of types of activity which favor MNEs
1. Resource-based	Capital, technology, access to markets	Possession of resources	To ensure stability of supply at right price. Control of markets	Oil, copper, tin, zinc, bauxite, bananas, pineapples, cocoa, tea
2. Import substituting manufacturing	Capital, technology, management and organizational skills; surplus r & d & other capacity, economies of scale; Trade marks	Material & labor costs, markets, government policy (with respect to barrier to imports, investment incentives, etc.)	Wish to exploit technology advantages, High transaction or information costs, Buyer uncertainty, etc.	Computers, pharmaceuticals, motor vehicles, cigarettes
3. Export platform manufacturing	As above, but also access to markets	Low labor costs Incentives to local production by host governments.	The economies of vertical integration	Consumer electronics, textiles & clothing, cameras, etc.
4. Trade & distribution	Products to distribute	Local markets. Need to be near customers. After-sales servicing, etc.	Need to ensure sales outlets & to protect company's name	A variety of goods—particularly those requiring close consumer contact
5. Ancillary services	Access to markets (in the case of other foreign investors)	Markets	Broadly as for 2/4	Insurance, banking & consultancy services
6. Miscellaneous	Variety—but include geographical diversification (airlines & hotels)	Markets	Various (see above)	Various kinds a) Portfolio investment—properties b) Where spatial linkages essential (airlines & hotels)

13

advantages of the countries in which they produce relative to those of other countries.

H2 The *form* of the involvement, or participation, will essentially depend on the relative attractiveness of the *location*-specific endowments of the home and host countries.[14]

That the gains to be derived from internalizing activities, which would otherwise be allocated by markets or government fiat, make up an important part of *ownership* advantages, and, in some cases, of *location* advantages as well is also contended.

Concerning H1, we shall take as our dependent variable the share of the output of a particular industry (IS) in a particular country supplied by exports (X) plus local production (AS) of U.S.-owned firms:[15] AS + X/IS. These components can, of course, be considered separately; but, in this hypothesis, we wish to exclude *location*-specific variables influencing the form of involvement. This dependent variable is notated as DV 1.[16]

The two components of international involvement may be considered separately. DV 2 signifies the share of the affiliates' sales of total output in the host country (AS/IS), and DV 3, the share of exports from the U.S. of that output (X/IS).

Concerning H2, the dependent variable—DV 4—is defined as X/IS ÷ AS/IS (or simply X/AS); in other words, it is the ratio between exploiting a particular market by exports from the U.S. relative to local production by U.S. affiliates in the country of marketing. The higher this ratio, the more the U.S. is favored as a location for production, relative to the country in which the goods are being sold (or being exported from).

THE STATISTICAL TESTING
The Dependent Variables:

We now turn to a statistical testing of the two main hypotheses.

Hypothesis 1—The international competitive hypothesis

The overall involvement index reflects both *location*- and *ownership*-specific advantages. The explanation of the foreign production ratio lies in identifying and measuring *ownership* advantages (as the location of production is assumed to be the same for all firms) and that of the export ratio in both *location* and *ownership* advantages. Looking at the export ratio, one naturally turns to trade theories for guidance; but no attempt, to our knowledge, has been made to explain shares of a particular industry's sales accounted for by foreign imports.[17] In discussing the determinants of foreign production, one should be concerned solely with *ownership* advantages; yet, the fact that trade and production are often related to each other suggests that these advantages may also be associated with *location*-specific endowments.[18] Explanations of foreign production, which ignore the latter advantages, are likely to be inadequate, thus supporting the need for an eclectic theory of production and trade.

The share of a particular industry's output supplied by foreign affiliates is determined by the competitive advantages of the affiliates and the relative attractions of the host country as a production base. It is likely to be greatest where the barriers to entry facing indigenous producers *and* exports from the home (and other countries) are highest. Trade is similarly determined except that it will flourish where barriers to exports are low and where barriers to entry to all producers in the host country are high. International involvement is determined simply by the competitive advantage of the investing and exporting firms vis-a-vis indigenous and other foreign companies.

In symbolic terms:

DV 1   AS + X/IS = f (C)

14   where C = international competitive advantage (to be defined)

DV 2   AS/IS = f (C,X/AS)

and

DV 3   X/IS = f (C,X/AS)

Hypothesis 2—The location hypothesis

This is simple and straightforward. To produce a particular good, an enterprise will choose that location which best advances its overall goals. The interface between received location theory and the MNE is a relatively unexplored territory, but a good start has been made by Vernon [1974]. In principle, there is no reason to suppose a national multiplant firm would behave very differently if its plants were located in a different country. New variables—such as exchange risks, differences in taxation rates, and policies of host governments toward inward direct investment—may need to be incorporated, but this can be done without too much difficulty.

The location hypothesis is solely concerned with *country*-specific variables affecting (1) the size and character of markets (which may be affected by competitor's behavior) and (2) production and transfer costs, though these may have a special impact on MNEs because of their ability to internalize the costs and benefits of some of the differences which exist between countries. The hypothesis may be expressed as:

DV 4   X/AS = f (L)

where L = locational advantage of the home country

(to be defined).

Hypothesis 1

To assess the competitive advantage of firms of one nationality over those of another—both in particular industries and countries—one must evaluate: (1) allocative, technical, and scale efficiency; (2) product range and quality; and (3) market power. Because we are concerned with inter-industry comparisons, allocative efficiency of resources between industries may be discounted. However, goals may differ between firms, as may the competence of firms to achieve these goals. For example, the greater the innovative ability of an enterprise, the more resourceful and the more talented its managerial and labor force, the higher its market share is likely to be. Similarly, the advantages of size, of being part of a larger organization, and of being able to internalize external economies will affect a firm's competitive situation independently of the location of its activities.

Some of these variables, of course, reflect the industry or country characteristics of firms. Governments, for example, can and do influence the extent to which there is an adequate labor force to draw upon, the promotion of new technologies, the role of advertising in fostering product differentiation, and so on. These factors are acknowledged and have been considered explicitly elsewhere [Dunning 1979].

It may be helpful to break H1 down into two sub-hypotheses.

The first is:

H1$_a$ Given the export-participation ratio (X/IS), the foreign production–participation ratio (AS/IS) will be highest in those industries where the comparative advantage of foreign (meaning U.S. here) firms is greatest vis-a-vis indigenous firms.

In principle, many of these advantages may be captured in a catchall measure, as in the comparative productivity of U.S. firms and host country firms or some proxy for integration—such as, percent of net to gross output. The comparative advan-

The Independent Variables

15

tage of U.S. firms is presumably highest where their relative productivity or value-added ratio is highest; therefore, in those cases, the affiliate penetration ratio should be highest. In practice, difficulties in measuring productivity and identifying internalizing economies make both measures of doubtful applicability.

H1$_b$ Given the production-participation ratio (AS/IS), the export penetration–participation ratio (X/IS) will be highest in those industries where the national resource endowments of the U.S. are greatest in comparison to those of other countries, and where barriers to trade are minimal.

Location theory approaches export success more in terms of difference in *absolute* production costs and the costs of traversing space. Artificial barriers to trade include those imposed by governments or imperfect markets. An incentive to export may also result from the inability of a host country's firms to compete effectively, due to the absence of a market sufficiently large to yield economies of scale in production.

Hypothesis 2

Like H1$_b$, the second hypothesis appears to be explained best by the theories of trade and location. Among the relative costs that play an important part in determining the location choice are those of labor and material inputs. The former are particularly critical in this study because it is limited to manufacturing industries where horizontal direct investment is the rule. This is in contrast to the situation in resource industries where vertical direct investment plays a much greater role. By the same token, labor productivity and its growth will be important elements in determining the real value of labor.

Production costs may be closely related also to the scale of plant which can be built. Market size will, therefore, be relevant. So, also, will rates of growth of the markets involved because they will determine the extent to which economies of scale may be exploited in the future.

The Choice of Independent Variables for this Exercise

Table 2 lists some of the variables which might be considered as proxies for *ownership*- and *location*-specific advantages. An asterisk identifies those variables which might also be used as indices of internalization advantages.[19] Some of these are very similar to each other; not all can be used for this particular exercise, partly because it is concerned with explaining patterns of involvement by *industries* rather than by *firms*, and partly because of data constraints.

It will also be noted that for some variables set out, data are required for host countries; in others, for the home country, or for both host and home countries. Where only the home country is involved, *location* advantages become irrelevant, and one cannot use the data to determine both industry and country participation ratios. The main constraint, however, has been the paucity of good data about *host* countries which seriously inhibits testing both hypotheses for the seven countries considered separately. This exercise omits the two LDCs, partly because the data are less certain for these two countries, and partly so that a tariff variable could be used—data for which were not available for Mexico and Brazil.

In the end, the independent variables were chosen and used to test both hypotheses. Data on each relate to 1970, or the nearest year, except where otherwise stated. The data for these variables were extracted mainly from the U.S. Tariff Commission Study, except for those on imports which were obtained from the OECD Commodity Trade Statistics Series C, and tariffs from a Political and Economic Planning publication [1965].

16

A schematization of variables follows.

TABLE 2
Ownership and Location Advantages
(Internalizing Advantages Marked with *)

Determinants	By Industry and/or Country
Ownership Advantages: Specific Determinants	
1. *Access to Productive Knowledge*	
(a) Skilled (professional and technical)/ unskilled labor ratio*	Home cf. host firms
(b) R and D as percent of sales*	Home cf. host firms
2. *Economics of the Firm*	
(a) Size of enterprise*	Home firms
(b) Relative size of enterprises	(Average) Home cf. host firms
(c) Number of nonproduction to all workers* *or* wage bill of nonproduction to all workers *or* nonproduction costs[1]/total costs* (gross output) *or* R and D plus advertising costs to total costs (or sales)*	Home firms
(d) Capital/Labor ratio	Home firms
3. *Opportunities for Investment*	
(a) Size of local market	(Industry) sales of host firms
(b) Size of/or local market plus exports	(Industry) sales of host firms
4. *Diversification Indices[2]*	
(a) Average number of countries MNEs operate in* *or*	Home firms
(b) % of foreign/total production of home firms*	Home firms
(c) % of intragroup exports to total exports of MNEs*	Home firms
(d) Number of product groups in which parent companies produce *or* % of output of main product group to all output*	Home firms
(e) % of shipments from multiplant enterprises to total shipments (in home country)*	Home firms
5. *Market Concentration*	
(a) Percentage of output of industry accounted for by "x" largest firms	Home firms
6. *Efficiency*	
(a) Wage costs (per man hour) of production workers	Foreign affiliates as % of home firms
7. *Resource Availability*	
(a) % of main material(s) imported*	Either import/export ratio of home firms *or* % imports to total consumption
(b) % of main material(s) used in production process	% of main material costs to gross output
8. *Product differentiation* Advertising/sales ratio	Home firms
9. *Oligopolistic Behavior* Entry Concentration Index Knickerbocker Ph.D. thesis	Home firms in host countries

[1]Nonproduction = pre- + post-direct production costs.

[2](a)–(d) specific to MNEs; (e) general to multi-plant enterprises.

continued overleaf

TABLE 2 (continued)

Ownership Advantages: Specific Determinants
(Internalizing Advantages Marked with *)

Determinants	By Industry and/or Country

Ownership Advantages: General Determinants

1. *Productivity*
   Net output or sales per man

      1. Home firms cf. host firms
      2. Foreign affiliates cf. host firms

2. *Profitability*
   Profits/assets or sales

      1. Home firms cf. host firms
      2. Foreign affiliates cf. host firms

3. *Growth*
   Increase in sales

      1. Home firms cf. host firms
      2. Foreign affiliates cf. host firms

Location Advantages: Specific Determinants

1. *Production Costs*
   (a) Wages per man hour — Home firms cf. host firms
   (b) Energy costs (e.g. electricity or oil) — Home firms cf. host firms
   (c) Materials costs (cost of major inputs; or commodity price indicies for main materials) *or* some index of resource availability — Home firms cf. host firms
   (d) Tax rates (including, where possible, tax allowances)* — Home firms cf. host firms
   (e) Average number of countries MNEs operating in — Home firms only
2. *Transfer Costs*
   (a) Transport costs — Home-host country
   (b) Tariffs — Host country
   (c) Non-tariff barriers — Host country
3. *General*
   (a) Political risks — Host country

Location Advantages: General Determinants

1. *Productivity*
   (a) Production costs per man *or* — Home firms cf. foreign affiliates
   (b) Net output or sales per man
2. *Profitability*
   Profits/assets or sales — Home firms cf. foreign affiliates
3. *Growth*
   Increase in sales — Home firms cf. foreign affiliates

(A) For the Seven Country Exercise (i) *Ownership-specific variables*

    1a SER—Skilled employment ratio: the ratio of salaried employees to production employees for all firms in the host countries.

    2a AHC—Average hourly compensation of all employees in the host countries. (1a and 2a are both measures of human capital intensity).

18

3a RSM—Relative sales per man (an efficiency index: the sales per man year of firms in the U.S. divided by sales per man year of firms (including the affiliates of U.S. firms) in the host countries.

4a GRSPM—Growth in sales per man of all firms (in the host country), 1966–1970.

The predicted sign for each of these variables for each of the hypotheses is positive, but their significance is likely to be greater for H1 than H2. U.S. firms will invest in those industries and countries in which they have the greatest technological advantage and where their productivity, vis-a-vis local firms, is the highest.

(ii) *Location-specific variables*

5a XMR—The export/import ratio, measured by the ratio of value of exports to value of imports of *host* countries (as a measure of a country's ability to produce particular products).

6a RMS—Relative market size: value of industry sales in the U.S. divided by value of industry sales in the host countries.

7a RW—Relative wages: average hourly compensation (in particular industries) in the U.S. divided by average hourly compensation in the host countries for all employees (an often quoted cost determinant of foreign production).

8a RES—Relative export shares of U.S. and host countries: another measure of country performance.

9a CMG—Comparative market growth of U.S. (domestic industry local sales plus imports) and host countries, 1966–1970.

The predicted signs of these variables vary. In the case of RES it is positive; but in the case of XMR, RMS, and CMG it is negative. It might also be expected that these variables would be most demonstrated as an explanation of H2.

(iii) *General performance indicators*

10a AVIS—The average ratio of net income to sales of all firms in different industries and countries for 1966 and 1970.

11a MG—Market growth (domestic industry local sales plus imports) in host countries, 1966–1970.

The predicted sign of AVIS is negative for H1 but positive for H2; that for MG is positive for all hypotheses.

As per 1a–11a, but with an additional *location*-specific variable.   **(B) The Five Advanced Countries**

12b TR—Average tariffs measured on a country and industry basis.

The predicted sign of this variable is negative for DV4.

Such a large number of independent variables invites problems associated with multicollinearity. These problems were compounded when the two different groups of independent variables were tested against the 'wrong' dependent variables as well, in order to determine if the general hypotheses were too restrictive. It was, therefore, decided to correlate separately each of the independent variables with the dependent variables (DV1–4) to determine which ones appeared worthy of further statistical investigation. Only those which approached significance at a 95 percent level were incorporated into multivariate form.

The large number of equations tested, given four dependent variables and twelve independent variables, also sharply increased the possibility of chance significance. Because of this, any value below the 99 percent significance should be treated with caution.

19

STATISTICAL
RESULTS
Case A: The
Seven Countries

These countries vary quite considerably in income levels, economic structure, political ideologies, culture, proximity to the U.S., and the extent to which they, themselves, spawn MNEs which compete in international markets with U.S.-based MNEs. It would not be surprising to find that different factors explain the absolute and relative success of U.S. exports and affiliate production in these countries when tested individually; here, however, we are concerned with factors which explain export and affiliate success in the seven countries *as a group,* and which can, perhaps, be regarded as "worldwide" determinants of such success.

H1 (DV1–3)

Table 3 summarizes the more significant results of our regression analyses.[20] The explanatory variables presented were extracted from the bivariate analysis and a series of multivariate equations constructed from them. For each of the variants of H1, most of the variation in the share of U.S. firms in the output of countries can be put down to two or three variables, with the best results coming from the overall international competitiveness index (DV1).

Because there are 98 observations, the explanatory power of the three variants of the hypothesis is encouraging. All of the signs (apart from that of RW) are consistent and in the right direction.

The equations reveal that the main advantages of U.S. firms are revealed in one *location*-specific variable—relative market size (RMS)—and one *ownership*-specific variable—the skilled employment ratio (SER). This latter ratio may be used as a proxy for internalizing advantages. Both are consistently significant at the two star—i.e., 99 percent—level for each of the dependent variables. The other ownership variables which are significant at this level for DV1 and DV3 are the productivity index, relative sales per man (RSM), and average hourly compensation (AHC). Two *location*-specific variables—wage differentials (RW) and net income per sales (AVNIS)—are also significant for the same two dependent variables, but only at the 95 percent level. For DV2, no variables other than RMS and SER were significant, although average hourly compensation (AHC) came closest. That this last variable appears to be collinear with SER is not unexpected because higher salaries are usually obtained by more highly skilled nonproduction employees. These same relationships were run using the 1966 data; the results obtained were much the same with the exception that the 1966 profit variable, net income to sales (AVNIS), is never quite significant.

H2 (DV4)

The results obtained from this hypothesis set out in Table 4 are quite different from those of H1. Two variables, the export/import ratio (XMR) and net income to sales (AVNIS), are consistently significant at the 99 percent level and explain nearly 60 percent of the variation in the location ratio. Growth of relative sales per man (GRSPM) comes very close but is never quite significant. The results for 1966 were virtually the same as for 1970.

Case B: The Five
Advanced
Countries

Quite early in the study, it was decided to run the data with Mexico and Brazil excluded. Although, to a certain extent, each country exercises its own unique set of influences on the involvement of foreign firms, there is something to be said for separating Mexico and Brazil from the other five countries. Historically, LDCs have produced relatively more raw materials and semi-finished manufactures and fewer finished products for world markets than the developed countries, and investment in resource-based industries is often based on very different considerations than investment in manufacturing.[1] Mexico and Brazil, in spite of recent rates of rapid industrial growth, are still sufficiently different in their stages of development to justify separate treatment.

20

TABLE 3

H1 Determinants of Participation Ratios of U.S. MNEs in Seven Countries, 1970

	Constant	AVNIS	RMS	SER	AHC	RW	RES	CMG	R (R²)
(1) DVI (AS + XI/IS)									
1.1	0.060		-0.991 (4.058)**	1.133 (4.993)**					0.546 (0.298)
1.2	-0.068		-1.137 (4.831)**	1.007 (4.613)**			0.375 (3.422)**		0.613 (0.376)
1.3	-0.051		-1.219 (4.759)**	0.910 (3.652)**	0.027 (0.815)		0.279 (1.728)		0.617 (0.380)
1.4	0.002	-0.002 (2.474)**	-1.155 (4.635)**	0.732 (2.987)**	0.161 (2.603)*	-0.777 (2.615)*	0.494 (2.880)*		0.673 (0.452)
1.5	-0.028	-0.002 (2.365)*	-1.136 (4.519)**	0.809 (2.994)**	0.131 (1.735)	-0.648 (1.840)	0.480 (2.765)**	0.0065 (0.683)	0.675 (0.455)
(2) DV2 (AS/IS)									
2.1	0.018		-0.580 (3.459)**	0.497 (3.192)**					0.430 (0.185)
2.2	0.0026		-0.693 (3.829)**	0.374 (2.164)*	0.026 (1.585)				0.454 (0.206)
2.3	0.016	-0.0009 (1.151)	-0.717 (3.942)**	0.388 (2.129)*	0.025 (1.522)				0.466 (0.217)
2.4	0.028	-0.0010 (1.260)	-0.669 (3.545)**	0.295 (1.597)	0.084 (1.801)	-0.322 (1.438)	0.072 (0.599)		0.485 (0.235)
(3) DV3 (XI/IS)									
3.1	0.078		-1.571 (4.372)**	1.631 (4.883)**					0.553 (0.306)
3.2	-0.079		-1.750 (4.957)**	1.476 (4.510)**			0.459 (2.792)**		0.599 (0.359)
3.3	0.022		-1.987 (5.254)**	1.177 (3.260)**	0.095 (2.803)**				0.599 (0.359)
3.4	0.030	-0.0038 (2.271)*	-1.824 (4.856)**	1.027 (2.780)**	0.245 (2.627)*	-1.098 (2.454)*	0.566 (2.190)*		0.657 (0.432)

*Significant at the 95 percent level
**Significant at the 99 percent level

21

TABLE 4

H2 Determinants of Export/Local Production Ratios (X/AS) of U.S. MNEs (DV4)
in Seven Countries 1970

	Constant	XMR	AVNIS	RMS	RSM	CRSPM	R (R²)
4.1	0.308	− 0.101	0.043				0.601
		(3.301)**	(7.256)**				(0.362)
4.2	0.042	− 0.101	0.043			0.0085	0.622
		(3.363)**	(7.277)**			(1.942)	(0.386)
4.3	0.103	− 0.099	0.042	− 0.561		0.0084	0.624
		(3.210)**	(7.007)**	(0.600)		(1.896)	(0.389)
4.4	0.100	− 0.100	0.042		− 0.0000048	0.0090	0.623
		(3.287)**	(7.101)**		(0.441)	(1.983)	(0.388)

H1 (DV1–DV3)

The results are presented in Table 5. In all equations, one ownership variable, the skilled employment ratio (SER), and two location variables, relative market shares (RMS) and average hourly compensation (AHC), are consistently significant at the 99 percent level. These three variables clearly have some influence on both U.S. trade and affiliate success in each of the five countries. Relative export shares (RES) and relative wages (RW) appear significant at the 95 percent (and in one case at the 99 percent) level in some of the equations of DV2 and DV3, but only where there are few independent variables regressed together. This suggests that these latter two location variables exert some influence on the competitiveness of U.S. trade but not on that of foreign production.

The tariff variable (T) appears to be a significant explanation of the overall involvement of U.S. firms in the five countries. In combination with the three universally successful variables above (RMS, SER, and AHC), T yielded an R^2 of 0.5695, which is quite satisfactory.

The data for 1966 suggest much the same results, with the exception that, in some combinations involving four or fewer independent variables, RS and RW also become significant as an explanation of DV1. This fact rather weakens the argument, based on the 1970 data, that these two have an influence on trade but not on foreign production; but probably they are only marginally significant in all three cases. For both years, 1966 and 1970, when the number of independent variables is increased, these two variables become less significant; this suggests that the added variables capture the significant influences duplicated in RES and RW. There appears, for example, to be a fair amount of collinearity between RW and AHC and between RES and RSM. For 1970, the correlation coefficients (at the seven-country level) between these variables are 0.9445 and 0.7052, respectively.

H2 (DV4)

As seen in Table 6, quite different variables explain most of the form of penetration from those which explain the first three variables. The profitability ratio (AVNIS) and the growth in sales per man (GRSPM) are consistently significant, the former at extremely high levels of significance and the latter at either 99 or 95 percent levels of significance. These two alone explain more than half the variance in the location ratio. Other variables which are occasionally significant are two ownership variables, average hourly compensation (AHC) and relative sales per man (RSM). They are only significant in small groups, however, which suggests an overlap between many of these variables. Equation 4 of DV4 is a good example where differences in wage costs (RW) are significant at 99 percent, and RS at 95 percent, and where R^2 is 0.5633.

TABLE 5

H1 Determinants of Participation Ratios of U.S. MNEs in Five Advanced Countries, 1970

	Constant	AVNIS	RMS	SER	AHC	RW	RES	RSM	T	R(R²)
(1) DV1 (AS + X/IS)										
1.1	0.058		-0.990 (3.323)**	1.162 (4.445)**						0.587 (0.343)
1.2	0.0956	-0.0028 (1.884)	1.084 (3.653)**	1.137 (4.425)**						0.614 (0.377)
1.3	-0.014	-0.0026 (1.791)	-1.015 (3.522)**	1.289 (2.373)*					0.010 (2.373)*	0.653 (0.427)
1.4	0.470	-0.0019 (1.482)	-0.9234 (3.660)**	0.872 (3.608)**	0.152 (4.609)**				0.014 (3.486)**	0.755 (0.570)
1.5	-0.436	-0.0022 (1.688)	-0.912 (3.576)**	0.891 (3.409)**	0.173 (2.844)**	-0.318 (0.942)	0.202 (0.943)		0.013 (3.330)**	0.760 (0.577)
(2) DV2 (AS/IS)										
2.1	0.0125		-0.540 (3.595)**	0.506 (3.841)**						0.566 (0.321)
2.2	-0.096		-0.522 (3.675)**	0.334 (2.438)*	0.056 (3.007)**					0.634 (0.403)
2.3	-0.055	-0.0010 (1.346)	-0.539 (3.727)**	0.339 (2.291)*	0.077 (2.254)*	-0.274 (1.426)	0.148 (1.225)			0.657 (0.432)
2.4	-0.051	-0.0012 (1.609)	-0.545 (3.845)**	0.391 (2.648)**	0.099 (2.787)**	-0.390 (1.969)	0.283 (2.059)*	-0.0000043 (1.900)		0.681 (0.464)
(3) DV3 (X/IS)										
3.1	0.070		-1.530 (3.771)**	1.669 (4.686)**						0.617 (0.381)
3.2	0.307		-1.467 (4.007)**	1.071 (3.031)**	0.194 (4.051)**					0.710 (0.504)
3.3	-0.314		-1.466 (3.830)**	1.464 (4.282)**		0.695 (3.079)*				0.677 (0.459)
3.4	-0.250	-0.0030 (1.616)	-1.570 (4.275)**	1.070 (3.064)**	0.185 (3.903)**					0.723 (0.523)
3.5	-0.206	-0.0037 (1.938)	-1.536 (4.172)**	1.137 (3.016)**	0.221 (2.532)*	-0.627 (1.280)	0.438 (1.422)			0.735 (0.540)

*Significant at the 95 percent level
**Significant at the 99 percent level

23

TABLE 6

H2 Determinants of Export/Local Production (X/AS) Ratios (DV4) of U.S. MNEs in Five Advanced Countries, 1970

	Constant	AVNIS	AHC	RW	RSM	RES	CMG	GRSPM	MG	T	R (R²)
4.1	-0.251	0.050 (7.953)**						0.012 (2.206)*			0.717 (0.515)
4.2	-0.130	0.050 (7.857)**						0.025 (2.942)**	-1.309 (1.967)		0.736 (0.542)
4.3	1.777	0.050 (8.119)**			-0.000045 (2.510)*		-3.517 (2.845)**	0.013 (2.515)**			0.755 (0.570)
4.4	0.508	0.044 (7.150)**		-2.548 (2.657)*		1.803 (2.174)*		0.024 (2.914)**	-1.240 (1.928)		0.766 (0.587)
4.5	1.492	0.046 (7.325)**		-1.509 (1.289)	-0.000043 (1.906)	1.647 (1.645)	-2.534 (1.694)	0.012 (2.316)*			0.767 (0.588)
4.6	1.277	0.045 (7.159)**		-1.760 (1.486)	-0.000030 (1.212)	1.605 (1.608)	-1.848 (1.159)	0.021 (2.361)*	-0.864 (1.210)		0.773 (0.598)
4.7	1.603	0.045 (7.086)**	0.249 (0.859)	-2.516 (1.703)	-0.000045 (1.483)	1.672 (1.666)	-2.598 (1.427)	0.022 (2.436)*	-1.004 (1.367)		0.776 (0.602)
4.8	1.521	0.045 (7.082)**	0.307 (1.008)	-2.430 (1.630)	-0.000050 (1.600)	1.483 (1.415)	-3.002 (1.555)	0.023 (2.499)*	-0.964 (1.303)	0.012 (0.656)	0.778 (0.605)

*Significant at the 95 percent level
**Significant at the 99 percent level

24

The data for 1966 yield similar results with country or industry (rather than owner-ship) differences in profitability (AVNIS) and growth in sales per man (GRSPM, an ownership variable) being rather more significant. But, in this case, MG (market share) becomes marginally significant in combination with GRSPM. None of the labor cost and productivity variables are significant.

CONCLUSION
Comparing
Case A and
Case B

Excluding Mexico and Brazil, the seven-country analysis produced some notice-able differences in the results of the statistical analysis. This section considers a few of these and speculates on the reasons for them.

First, the general level of the R^2 rises quite noticeably. This suggests that the in-dependent variables used were more relevant in explaining export and affiliate success in the more advanced industrialized countries than in Mexico and Brazil. Running the regressions excluding Canada suggests that even higher R^2s could have been obtained. (This run was not undertaken because it would have substan-tially reduced the degrees of freedom).

Second, the data for 1966 as well as for 1970 indicate that differences in wage costs (RW) and export shares (RS) tend to be more significant in explaining H1 (DV2) in the seven-country than in the five-country case. Perhaps these vari-ables are too similar over different industries in the industrialized countries; and, not until the widely different figures for Mexico and Brazil are included, is their in-fluence clearly indicated.

Third, AHC differences are significant in the compensation of the five-country but not in the seven-country case for H2 (DV4). This discrepancy is difficult to inter-pret. It may result from the less reliable figures on hourly compensation in Mexico and Brazil than in the other countries, or from the vastly different labor force structure which influences the extent to which local firms can compete success-fully against imports in different ways.

Fourth, in the case of H1 (DV1), there are virtually no differences between Cases A and B. There is one major difference between the two cases involving DV4: the export/import ratio (XMR) is significant with the larger group but not with the smaller. This may be interpreted to mean that the export potential of an industry may be more important in a less developed economy in determining the form of penetration. The negative sign implies that U.S. firms in those industries will tend to establish affiliates rather than export to the less developed countries, perhaps, to export some portion of their output. This is consistent in both the product cy-cle model's last stage and the growth of export-platform investments in some de-veloping countries, including Mexico.

25

APPENDIX 1
Note on
Methodology

The statistical analysis was restricted to common linear regression analysis and was carried out by Guy Landry at the University of Reading Computing Center. Initially, single variable regressions with each of the independent variables and for each dependent variable were run. The purpose was to choose potentially useful explanatory variables from the number available. As a result of this a few variables were dropped because they either indicated no explanatory value or appeared less useful than very similar variables which were retained.

The next step involved multiple regressions. As explained in the body of the paper, the independent variables were divided into three categories:

   a. The *ownership*-specific variables: SER, AHC, RSM, and GRSPM. These are variables suggested by industrial organization theory.

   b. The *country*-specific variables: XMR, RMS, RW, RES, and CMG. These are mostly suggested by trade and location theory.

   c. The general performance indicators: AVNIS and MG.

For each of the dependent variables, various combinations of the independent variables in each category were subjected to regression analysis. The most significant results are those shown in the tables. The purpose of this step was to determine which independent variables in each category best explained the dependent variables. Next, these same variables were analyzed, but with the categories grouped in different combinations. Once again the tables reveal the results. These particular equations should reveal the explanatory power of various combinations of the independent variables chosen from two or all three categories.

The values in brackets are the t-values: those marked by a single asterisk are significant at the 95 percent level, while those marked by two asterisks are significant at the 99 percent level.

The last column of each table gives the values of the coefficient of determination.

APPENDIX 2

U.S. Affiliate Sales, U.S. Exports, and Total Industry Sales in Seven Countries, 1970
(Billion Dollars)

	Canada			United Kingdom			France			West Germany			Belgium-Lux			Mexico			Brazil			Total		
	AS	X	IS	AS	X	IS	AS	X	IS	AS	X	IS	AS	X	IS	AS	X	IS	AS	X	IS	AS	X	IS
Food Products	2,220	98	8,532	1,054	56	10,294	473	7	17,137	634	33	15,583	121	9	2,415	487	16	5,773	107	8	3,947	5,096	227	63,681
Paper and Allied Products	1,503	118	3,840	141	118	2,763	183	61	2,161	69	103	3,474	96	27	496	121	52	525	65	9	504	2,180	488	13,763
Chemicals and Allied Products	2,124	554	2,490	1,918	226	9,356	971	107	8,190	963	215	13,888	654	220	1,357	764	171	3,888	623	146	3,325	8,017	1,639	42,494
Rubber Products	613	146	628	373	22	1,185	119	24	1,854	211	36	1,972	79	13	96	108	19	267	175	9	363	1,678	269	6,365
Primary and Fabricated Metals	1,964	631	6,877	804	237	7,905	208	167	10,750	1,821	228	25,280	252	81	3,989	749	95	1,981	262	83	2,209	6,060	1,522	58,991
Nonelectric Mach.	2,222	1,837	2,778	2,496	578	11,862	1,439	395	10,581	1,742	508	16,529	429	221	1,059	208	367	330	304	247	895	8,840	4,153	44,034
Electrical Mach.	1,822	603	2,213	1,607	221	8,961	514	136	6,059	876	237	13,888	425	52	993	478	195	919	246	49	1,014	5,968	1,493	34,047
Transp. Equipment	5,600	2,430	6,222	3,430	211	12,645	936	180	12,086	3,250	261	12,843	275	139	1,523	567	239	1,261	1,171	88	1,792	15,229	3,548	48,372
Textiles & Apparel	532	168	3,281	77	46	10,275	21	13	8,220	100	29	10,470	207	54	2,002	66	41	1,969	124	10	2,405	1,127	361	38,622
Lumber, Wood & Furniture	1,322	91	2,632	35	22	2,763	15	4	3,135	33	25	4,475	0	2	478	5	16	316	5	1	705	1,415	161	14,504
Printing & Publishing	176	153	1,516	125	29	5,003	51	4	4,320	35	6	2,589	5	2	390	6	9	396	4	4	429	401	207	14,643
Stone, Clay & Glass	406	140	1,260	242	14	3,818	252	13	2,897	239	20	6,043	45	7	727	191	19	725	76	5	821	1,451	218	16,291
Instruments	563	219	626	739	101	1,321	399	48	1,976	406	90	1,608	15	21	33	76	42	..	91	26	..	2,289	547	5,564
Other Manufacturing	567	135	1,916	3,205	53	10,541	35	36	3,122	409	63	7,282	5	44	1,093	411	38	645	128	9	630	4,760	378	25,229
Total	21,636	7,323	44,811	16,246	1,934	98,692	5,616	1,195	92,488	10,788	1,854	135,924	2,603	892	16,651	4,236	1,319	18,995	3,381	694	19,039	64,511	15,211	426,600

.. missing

APPENDIX 3

List of Industries (and Concordance)

	BEA Code	SIC Code	SITC Code		
1. Food Products	410	20	013	047	062
			023	048	092
			024	053	099
			032	055	111
			046	061	112
2. Paper and Allied Products	420	26	64		
			251		
3. Chemical and Allied Products	430	28	5		
4. Rubber	440	30	231.2		
			62		
			893		
5. Primary and Fabricated Metals	450	33	67		
			68		
			69		
			812.3		
6. Nonelectrical Machinery	460	35	71		
7. Electrical Machinery	470	36	72		
8. Transportation Equipment	480	37	73		
9. Textiles and Apparel	491	22	65		
		23	84		
			266		
10. Lumber, Wood and Furniture	492	24	63		
		25	243		
			82		
11. Printing and Publishing	493	27	892		
12. Stone, Clay, and Glass Products	495	32	66		
			− 667		
13. Instruments	496	38	86		
			− 863		
14. Ordnance, Leather, Tobacco,	494	19	122	891	
and Other Manufacturing	497	21	61	894	
	498	31	667	895	
	499	39	81	897	
			− 812.3	899	
			83	951.0	
			85		

FOOTNOTES 1. Throughout this article, assets and endowments are used interchangeably, and in the Fisherian sense, to mean "anything capable of generating a future income stream" [Johnson 1970].

2. See John H. Dunning, "Trade, Location of Economic Activity and the Multinational Enterprise," pp. 395–418.

3. In this article, distance from foreign markets is treated as a negative *location*-specific endowment.

4. Moreover, since perfect competition and identical production functions between firms were two of the assumptions underlying the theories, they were not interested in explaining the international activities of firms—only of countries.

5. For example, unused overheads of the parent company may be supplied to a branch plant at a much lower marginal cost than the average cost of supplying them by a *de novo* firm.

6. For further details and also those which especially arise from *producing* in a foreign location see Dunning [1977] and the references at the end of the Chapter. The most comprehensive theoretical treatment of the internalizing theory of international production is contained in Buckley and Casson [1976].

7. Among these one might mention particularly those of Horst [1972 (a) and (b), 1975]. (In this latter paper the author explicitly acknowledges the importancè of internalizing advantages). The study of Wolf [1973] is also particularly pertinent to explain why firms choose to engage in foreign direct investment, rather than other forms of growth. Research on host country data includes: Baumann [1975]; Caves [1974]; Buckley and Dunning [1976]; and Owen [1979].

8. See particularly the studies of Hirsch [1976], Buckley and Pearce [1979], Hawkins and Webbink [1976], Parry [1976]. The question of the extent to which trade and foreign investment substitute for each other has been very well explored by Lipsey and Weiss [1973; 1976], Cornell [1973], and Horst [1974].

9. There has been only limited empirical testing of this approach. The Hirsch contribution [1976] is again very relevant. See also Buckley and Dunning [1977].

10. Here the work of Buckley and Casson [1976] is especially relevant.

11. A summary of each of these approaches is contained in an earlier version of this paper: "Trade, Location of Economic Activity and the Multinational Enterprise: Some Empirical Evidence." University of Reading Discussion Papers in *International Investment and Business Studies No. 37*, October 1977.

12. The complications of this assumption will be dealt with later in the paper. See also Horst, 1974.

13. For a more detailed analysis of these data, see Dunning paper quoted in footnote 11.

14. Extracted is the possibility that firms might supply foreign markets from third locations.

15. Consumption figures would have been more appropriate but these figures were not available.

16. For some purposes, we may wish to normalize the ratio AS + X/IS in a particular industry (i), $AS_i + X_i/IS_i$, by dividing the ratio by that for all industry (t), $AS_i + X_t/IS_t$. The result is an index of the comparative rather than the absolute competitive advantage of U.S. firms. This allows cross-country comparisons to be made.

17. But see Dunning and Buckley, 1976.

18. I.e., that some *ownership* advantages are not independent of the *location* or production. See also Dunning, 1979.

19. For a different approach to the measurement of these advantages see Buckley and Casson, 1976.

20. See footnote 8.

REFERENCES

Brown, W. E. "Island of Consensus Power: MNCs in the Theory of the Firm MSU." *Business Topics,* Summer 1976.

Baumann, H. G. "Merger Theory, Property Rights and the Pattern of U.S. Direct Investment in Canada." *Weltwirtschaftliches Archiv* III Heft 4, 1975.

Buckley, P. J., and Casson, M. C. *The Future of the Multinational Enterprise.* London: MacMillan, 1976.

Buckley, P. J., and Dunning, J. H. "The Industrial Structure of U.S. Direct Investment in the U.K." *Journal of International Business Studies,* Summer 1976.

Buckley, P. J., and Pearce, R. D. "Overseas Production and Exporting by the World's Largest Enterprises." *Journal of International Business Studies,* Spring/Summer 1979.

Caves, R. E. "International Corporations: The Industrial Economics of Foreign Investment." *Economica,* February 1971.

Caves. R. E. "The Causes of Direct Investment: Foreign Firms' Shares in Canadian and UK Manufacturing Industries." *Review of Economics and Statistics,* August 1974.

Cornell, R. "Trade of Multinational Firms and Nation's Comparative Advantage." Paper presented to a Conference on Multinational Corporations and Governments, UCLA, November 1973.

Dunning, J. H. "The Determinants of International Production." *Oxford Economic Papers,* November 1973.

Dunning, J. H. "Trade Location of Economic Activity and the Multinational Enterprise. A Search for an Eclectic Approach" in *The International Allocation of Economic Activity,* edited by B. Ohlin, P. O. Hesselborn, and P. J. Wiskman, London: MacMillan, 1977.

Dunning, J. H., and Buckley, P. J. *International Production and Alternative Models of Trade.* Manchester School of Economic and Social Studies *45,* December 1977.

Dunning, J. H. "Explaining Changing Patterns of International Production: in Defense of the Eclectic Theory." *Oxford Bulletin of Economics and Statistics,* November 1979.

Hawkins, R., and Webbink, E. S. "Theories of Direct Foreign Investment: A Survey of Empirical Evidence." Unpublished Manuscript.

Hirsch, S. "Capital or Technology? Confronting the Neo-Factor Proportions and Neo-Technology Accounts of International Trade." *Weltwirtschaftliches Archiv 114* Heft. 2. 1974.

Hirsch, S. "An International Trade and Investment Theory of the Firm." *Oxford Economic Papers,* July 1976.

Horst, T. "Firm and Industry Determinants of the Decision to Invest Abroad: An Empirical Study." *Review of Economics and Statistics,* August 1972 (a).

Horst, T. "The Industrial Composition of U.S. Exports and Subsidiary Sales to the Canadian Market." *American Economic Review,* March 1972 (b).

Horst, T. *American Exports and Foreign Direct Investments.* Harvard Institute of Economic Research Discussion 362, May 1974.

Horst, T. "American Investments Abroad: and Domestic Market Power." Brookings Institution: Unpublished, 1975.

Hufbauer, G. C. "The Impact of National Characteristics and Technology on the Commodity Composition of Trade in Manufactured Goods," in *The Technology Factor in International Trade,* edited by R. Vernon. New York: Columbia University Press, 1970.

Hufbauer, G. C., and Adler, M. *Overseas Manufacturing Investment and the Balance of Payments.* U.S. Treasury Department, 1968.

Johnson, H. "The Efficiency and Welfare Implications of the International Corporation," in *The International Corporation,* edited by C. P. Kindleberger. Cambridge: M.I.T. Press, 1970.

Knickerbocker, F. T. *Oligopolistic Reaction and the Multinational Enterprise.* Cambridge, MA: Harvard University Press, 1973.

Kojima, K. "A Macro-Economic Approach to Foreign Direct Investment." *Hitotsubashi Journal of Economics,* June 1973.

Lipsey, P. E., and Weiss, M. Y. "Multinational Firms and the Factor Intensity of Trade." National Bureau of Economic Research, Working Paper No. 8, 1973.

Lipsey, R. E., and Weiss, M. Y. "Exports and Foreign Investment in the Pharmaceutical Industry." National Bureau of Economic Research, Working Paper No. 87 (Revised), 1976 (a).

Lipsey, R. E., and Weiss, M. Y. "Exports and Foreign Investment in Manufacturing Industries." National Bureau of Economic Research. Working Paper No. 13 (Revised), 1976 (b).

Nurkse, R. "The Problems of International Investment Today in the Light of 19th Century Experience." *Economic Journal,* December 1954.

Owen, R. F. *Interindustry Determinants of Foreign Direct Investments: A Perspective Emphasizing the Canadian Experience.* Working Paper in International Economics (G-79-03), Princeton University, 1979.

Parry, T. C. "Trade and Non Trade Performance of US Manufacturing Industry: 'Revealed' Comparative Advantage." *Manchester School of Economics and Social Studies,* June 1973.

Parry, T. C. *Methods of Servicing Overseas Markets: The UK Owned Pharmaceutical Study.* University of Reading Discussion Paper (Series 2) 27, 1976.

Political and Economic Planning "Atlantic Tariffs and Trade." A Report by PEP. Winchester, MA: Allen and Unwin, 1967.

Rugman, A. *International Diversification and the Multinational Enterprise.* Lexington, MA: Lexington Books, 1979.

Stevens, C. V. "Determinants of Investment," in *Economic Analysis and the Multinational Enterprise,* edited by J. H. Dunning: Winchester, MA: Allen and Unwin, 1974.

Swedenborg, B. *The Multinational Operations of Swedish Firms: An Analysis of Determinants and Effects.* Stockholm: Almquist & Wiksell International, 1979.

U.S. Tariff Commission. *Implications of Multinational Firms for World Trade and Investment and for US Trade and Labor.* Washington, DC: Government Printing Office, 1973.

Vaupel, J. *Characteristics and Motivations of the US Corporations which Invest Abroad.* Unpublished ms.

Vernon, R. "International Investment and International Trade in the Product Cycle." *Quarterly Journal of Economics,* May 1966.

Vernon, R. "The Location of Economic Activity," in *Economic Analysis and the Multinational Enterprise,* edited by J. H. Dunning. Winchester, MA: Allen and Unwin, 1974.

Wolf, B. "Industrial Diversification and Internationalization: Some Empirical Evidence. *Journal of Industrial Economics,* December 1977.

[23]

Sloan Management Review   Spring 1981   3

The Multinational Enterprise: Market Failure and Market Power Considerations

David J. Teece   Stanford University

The author develops a conceptual framework to examine the relative efficiency properties of multinational firms. He examines both vertical and horizontal foreign investment. The properties of multinational firms as technology transfer agents are assessed against the market alternatives. Market failure and transactions cost issues are central to the analysis. The author contrasts this approach with analyses that focus on monopoly power considerations. He contends that the obsession with these considerations and the failure to focus on the internal technology transfer properties of the international firm have significant public policy implications. These considerations have deflected attention from some important social efficiencies afforded by foreign direct investment. *Ed.*

The multinational firm continues to attract the attention of scholars and commentators of many persuasions. It has been variously interpreted as an instrument of colonial exploitation and as an efficient vehicle for the economic development of the Third World. However, emphasis on polemics typically obfuscates an understanding of the phenomenon at hand. Indeed, it is only in the last few years that a coherent and persuasive theory of multinational enterprise has begun to emerge. The purpose of this article is to pull together the various elements of a theory of multinational enterprise (MNE). Its starting point is the conceptualization of the multinational firm as an organization that internalizes various international transactions which could conceivably take place in a market. While this observation has been made by others, the implications for economic efficiency, competition, and public policy have not been fully discussed.[1] Furthermore, to the extent that the economics of internalization has been addressed, efficiency and monopoly power considerations have often been confounded, leaving the policy implications of direct foreign investment more ambiguous than is necessary.

In order to delineate a theory of multinational enterprise, it is desirable to identify some general properties of markets and of internal organization. This will be done by following the markets and hierarchies (MH) approach recently developed by Oliver Williamson.[2] A theory of multinational enterprise emerges once the nature of the transactions typically internalized by multinational firms is delineated and once related market failure considerations are explored.

Relative Efficiency Properties of Markets and Hierarchies

The MH approach developed by Williamson attempts to assess the properties of various organizational modes by comparing their relative efficiency characteristics.[3] The market is considered to be one way of organizing economic activity. The desirability of using market processes is assessed by comparing the efficiency properties of markets with those of alternative organizational modes. The concept of market failure embedded in the MH framework, therefore, is not based principally on Pareto optimality considerations. It rests instead on relative efficiency considerations. In order to assess the relative efficiency properties of various organizational modes, Williamson, following Commons, selects the transaction as the basic unit of analysis.[4] He suggests that the relative efficiency of various organizational structures can be gauged by examining the transactions cost properties of each. Transactions costs embrace all the costs associated with organizing the economic system. In a market context, for instance, transactions costs include the costs of:

— Discovering who one wishes to deal with;
— Informing market agents that one wishes to deal and on what terms;
— Conducting negotiations leading up to the bargain;
— Drawing up the contract;
— Undertaking the inspection needed to make sure that the terms of the contract are being observed.[5]

In a nonmarket context, transactions costs

David J. Teece is Asso-
ciate Professor of Busi-
ness Economics at
Stanford University,
Graduate School of
Business and Depart-
ment of Economics. Dr.
Teece holds the B.A.
degree from the Uni-
versity of Canterbury
and the M.A. and Ph.D.
degrees from the Uni-
versity of Pennsyl-
vania. He has written a
variety of articles
which have appeared
in such journals as the
*Bell Journal of Eco-
nomics, Management
Science,* and *Econo-
mica.* Dr. Teece is the
coauthor of *Technol-
ogy Transfer, Produc-
tivity and Economic
Policy.*

similarly include the costs of identifying exchange opportunities and of employing administrative processes to organize economic
activity. Whether one is assessing market or
nonmarket modes of organization, the MH
approach involves an analysis of the facility
with which contracts can be written, executed, and enforced. This is because:

Explicitly or implicitly, the institutional device by
which transactions are organized is the contract
. . . to be sure, not every problem can usefully be
posed as a contracting problem. More can be described in these terms than is generally realized.
Not only can an actual or implicit contract be
described for every market interface, but many
nonmarket relations can be expressed in contracting terms as well. For every problem that arises as
or can be transformed into a contracting relation
without emasculating its main features, transactions cost analysis is appropriately brought to
bear. Whatever the contractual context, moreover,
such an analysis ultimately reduces to an examination of the manner in which human agents
cope with complex events in the face of uncertainty.[6]

This analytic framework will now be
brought to bear upon the study of multinational enterprise.

Multinational Firms and Market Failure

The emergence of multinational enterprise
represents a response to a number of incentives.[7] These incentives can be divided into
three groups: circumventing or minimizing
taxes and controls, monopoly, and
efficiency. Whereas all three categories yield
private gain, only the latter is likely to be
associated with a net gain to economic welfare. The first category includes such distortions as adapting to or circumventing tariffs
and taxes on differential profits. For instance, vertical integration, coupled with
transfer price manipulation to minimize
tariffs, can yield private gain without necessarily enhancing the efficient allocation of
the world's resources. Monopoly power considerations may also be important, and they
have been heavily emphasized in the litera-

ture. As Coase has observed, monopoly
power is often imputed to many poorly understood business phenomena.[8] Considering
that the multinational is a complex organizational form, it is not surprising that some
scholars have missed important features of
multinational enterprise; they are obsessed
instead with market power considerations.
But, the efficiency consequences of the organization of economic activity by multinational firms are more interesting, possibly
more important, and certainly less well understood than these market power considerations. These consequences will be the
primary focus of this article, although efforts
will also be made to delineate the circumstances under which multinational firms can
be vehicles for anticompetitive behavior.

In order to proceed with the analysis of the
multinational firm, it is first necessary to
identify the markets that are internalized by
this particular institutional mode. For purposes of analysis, it is possible to identify
several different categories of international
markets, which multinational firms typically
span. These markets, are intermediate product markets, markets for proprietary and
nonproprietary know-how, and international
capital markets. A multinational firm —
which can be defined as an enterprise which
owns assets and controls activities in different countries — may internalize aspects of
one or all of the above categories of markets.
The first category will involve vertical foreign investment. The second category will
involve horizontal foreign investment. The
third category could involve either vertical,
horizontal, lateral, or conglomerate investment.[9] The efficiency properties associated
with internalizing these markets will now be
examined.

Intermediate Product Markets and Vertical Direct Foreign Investment

The emergence of multinational firms is
often traced to the sourcing of raw materials,
such as oil, copper, and alumina.[10] If intermediate product markets for these commodities were well developed on an interna-

tional scale and worked in a frictionless fashion, there would be very few circumstances where internalizing these markets would yield efficiencies. However, intermediate product markets often do not operate according to the textbook ideal. In such cases vertical integration is likely to have compelling efficiency properties. To understand the incentive for the emergence of vertical foreign investment, it is necessary to understand the incentives for vertical integration more generally, since the reasons for vertical foreign investment are basically the same as for any form of vertical integration. Thus, if the United States were to consist of fifty independent nations, a large number of vertically integrated domestic firms would probably become classified as vertically integrated multinationals.

Perhaps the critical incentive driving backward integration abroad has been the search for reliable low-cost supplies of raw materials. Throughout much of the twentieth century, vertical integration has afforded greater security of supply than has reliance on market contracts with independent nonaffiliated enterprises. Furthermore, when the know-how and capital have not been available to develop production capacity abroad, the need for vertical integration has been even more obvious. However, assuming that an independent foreign enterprise exists abroad and that it is capable of supplying the raw materials or specialized inputs needed in downstream refining, processing, or assembling facilities, it might still be efficient to vertically integrate upstream. One reason to do so would be to avoid the hazards that are sometimes associated with relying on long- or short-term supply contracts. These hazards are sufficiently important to warrant further exploration.

In attempting to explain the complicated contractual details of actual market exchange, one can begin by noting that it is impossible or prohibitively costly to write, execute, and enforce complete, fully contingent contracts. This proposition is obvious to even the casual observer of economic phenomenon. Accordingly, the relationships be-

tween transacting parties often cannot be fully described by a court-enforceable formal document that the parties have signed.[11] Sometimes the common law of contracts supplies a body of rules and principles that are read into each contract. In many cases, though, explicit terms (which include these general unwritten terms) remain somewhat vague and incomplete. They are incomplete because uncertainty implies the existence of a large number of possible contingencies. It may be very costly to know and specify in advance responses to all of these possibilities. Therefore, contractual breach may often be difficult to prove to the satisfaction of a third party enforcer — if one happens to exist.

Given the presence of incomplete contracts, opportunistic transactors often have the ability and incentive to renege on the transaction. They do so by "holding up" the other party, in the sense of taking advantage of unspecified and unenforceable elements of the contractual relationship. Such behavior is, by definition, unanticipated. It is not sustainable in the long run.

While various forms of complex contracts can sometimes be engineered to avoid the holdup problem, there are numerous cases where this is not possible. In general, the holdup problem (and hence the incentives for vertical integration on its account) is more likely the more difficult it is to write, execute, and enforce contracts for the service in question. It is also more likely the more asymmetric the relationship, the higher the appropriable quasi rents due to firm-specific investments, and the greater the costs of "contract transfer" (the costs of switching suppliers). These considerations are developed in more detail elsewhere.[12]

By way of example, consider a smelter located in the home country. Assume that there are many different types and grades of ore and that to smelt the ore at the lowest cost the smelter needs to be designed to process a particular grade of ore. If this ore is found only in one or two locations abroad, then it may be very hazardous to rely on long-term supply contracts with another enterprise. Once the investment in idiosyncratic smelting facilities has been made, the enterprise engaged in smelting will be extremely vulnerable to changes made by the ore supplier in the conditions of sale. The supplier of the ore may well behave opportunistically, raising the price above the previously contracted level. Judicial redress may be weak, so to the extent that alternative suppliers are not available, the owner of the smelter will be obliged to honor the new terms. In extreme cases of dependence, the supplier will be able to extract a pecuniary advantage from the owner, up to the value of the smelting facility. Backward vertical integration can eliminate this risk, for if supplier and purchaser are one and the same, the incentive for postcontractual recontracting is attenuated, and trading relations can proceed in a smooth and efficient fashion. The above analysis serves to delineate an important efficiency incentive for vertical integration. But, vertical integration is not itself a costless activity, since there are control costs associated with the vertical (and horizontal) expansion of the enterprise. The international expansion of the firm, assuming organizational structure is held constant, may involve additional hierarchical layers of management. In this case, management will have less contact with personnel at lower levels. Furthermore, vertical integration may itself create various distortions. According to Williamson, three types of distortion are common: an internal procurement bias, an internal expansion bias, and a program persistence bias.[13]

The internal procurement bias has its roots in the existence of an internal source of supply that tends to distort procurement decisions. Divisional or subgroup goals tend to be given too much weight in relation to objective profitability calculations. Norms of reciprocity can develop, and the opportunities for this kind of behavior may be more extensive within the firm than in the market.

The internal expansion bias is driven by the knowledge that the reward system for top management is often positively correlated with firm size, inducing management to engage in decisions to expand the size of the firm, even if it is not in the stockholders' best interest to do so. Finally, the existence of a base for cross subsidization enables the managers of large firms to maintain uneconomic divisions where the market would lead to quicker elimination.

Supporting all three biases are the distortions of strategic information, which passes horizontally and vertically within the firm. Although the intention of internalization is to harmonize the incentives of the various individuals and groups in the firm, individuals within the firm can sometimes seek to promote personal goals by distributing false or misleading information through the firm's communication channels.

Fortunately, the adoption of appropriate organizational and control structures can relieve, if not eliminate, these problems. As a result, it is reasonable to hypothesize that a large, well-managed, integrated multinational enterprise is not subject to diminishing returns as it expands. Robin Marris has summarized the matter as follows:

Large organizations have many weaknesses. . . . But in the narrowest sense — and this I believe is the basic organizational innovation of our century — they relearned something that was lost with the Roman Empire, namely how to control central loss. Large organizations know they are susceptible to loss of control, and they set up a variety of checks against it. Many of these are crude and have costly side effects. Others are more subtly effective. As a result, in my view, the best hypothesis is that there are generally constant returns to organizational expansion. In other words, I advocate a maxim, "When in doubt, assume constant returns." Some people will be content to agree with this maxim. Others instinctively assume diminishing returns, because they are absolutely convinced that bigness brings badness. Others still feel that where large-scale organization appears to flourish, the explanation must be found in conventional increasing returns. What is not in my view even today sufficiently realized is the extent of the explanatory power of the constant-returns hypothesis. It is in my view sufficient to explain much of the world we actually see.[14]

When the intermediate product in question is to be supplied from a less developed coun-

Sloan Management Review   Spring 1981   7

try (in which the infrastructure necessary to support market processes is nonexistent or poorly developed), then there are additional efficiency incentives for vertical integration. Thus, if entrepreneurship is absent or if the know-how needed to produce the item in question is missing, then price signals may not induce the necessary reallocation of resources. That is, raising the price of an intermediate product need not call forth additional output from indigenous suppliers. In this case, the relative efficiency properties of international vertical integration are especially compelling. With vertical integration, administrative processes can be called upon to transfer know-how and to establish productive capacity abroad. These processes can be used at least until development is advanced to the point where intermediate product markets can function with an acceptable degree of efficiency.

However, the transfer of know-how is a characteristic of the multinational firm that is not just associated with vertical investment decisions. Horizontal investment abroad may also involve know-how transfer. Accordingly, this property of the multinational firm must be analyzed in more detail.

Horizontal Direct Foreign Investment and the Market for Know-how

Horizontal direct foreign investment occurs when a firm with production facilities in one country establishes similar facilities in another. This phenomenon is more difficult to explain than vertical foreign investment. However, as with vertical foreign investment, market failure considerations lie at the heart of horizontal foreign investment. If markets operate in the frictionless fashion portrayed in economics textbooks, then all of the advantages from horizontal investment could be captured using contracts. But, "failures" in the market for know-how provide an important incentive for horizontal direct foreign investment. This argument can be made apparent by examining some other possible explanations for foreign investment.

If there are economies of scale in the pro-

duction of commodities, then one would expect to see production geographically focused, with foreign markets supplied by exports. Clearly, transportation costs and tariffs often dictate that production facilities be located near the markets served. However, despite the importance of tariffs and transportation costs, they do not, in a fundamental sense, explain foreign investment. If one assumes that indigenous firms have (by virture of familiarity with language, customs, regulations, and local markets) a cost advantage over foreign firms in the home market, then one would expect to see very little direct foreign investment, since indigenous firms would be able to meet indigenous market needs. Clearly foreign firms sometimes have unique assets that confer advantages over indigenous firms. Furthermore, the assets possessed may yield their highest returns when utilized within the firm rather than being sold via arm's-length contracts.

The notion that the multinational firm possesses unique assets has been developed by others, including Caves.[15] However, the argument is incomplete unless market failure issues are addressed as well. Indeed, failure to consider this dimension of the multinational firm has led to a serious misinterpretation of the distinctive properties of direct foreign investment. In particular, it has deflected attention from efficiency considerations to monopoly power considerations. Accordingly, an investigation of the efficiency properties of the multinational firm is warranted.

A distinctive attribute of the firm is that it is an organization, which possesses knowledge and skills. Perhaps the most important efficiency property of the multinational firm is that it is an organizational mode capable of transferring this knowledge and skill abroad in a relatively efficient fashion.[16] The importance of this property becomes apparent once it is acknowledged that the world's stock of knowledge is unevenly distributed.[17] Economic growth and modernization require the utilization of the world's stock of available knowledge. The differential distribution of know-how and expertise means that mutually advantageous trading opportunities exist but will be realized only if institutional modes are established to provide the appropriate linkage mechanisms and governance structures to surround and protect transactions. Unfortunately, markets are seriously faulted as institutional devices for facilitating trading in many important kinds of technological and managerial know-how. This factor helps explain why the multinational enterprise is of great significance.

Thus, consider the modern business enterprise that is characteristic of developed Western economies. The know-how possessed by the enterprise has some of the characteristics of a public good, since it can often be used in another enterprise without its value being substantially impaired. Furthermore, the marginal cost of employing know-how abroad is likely to be much less than its average cost of production and transfer. Accordingly (although know-how is not a pure public good), the international transfer of proprietary know-how is likely to be profitable, if organizational modes can be discovered to conduct and protect the transfer at low cost.[18] In this regard, the relative efficiency properties of markets and of the multinational firm need to be examined.

An examination of the properties of markets for know-how readily leads to the identification of several transactional difficulties. These difficulties can be summarized in terms of recognition, disclosure, and team organization. Consider a firm that has accumulated know-how, which can potentially find application in foreign markets. If there are firms abroad that can apply this know-how with profit, then according to traditional microeconomic theory, trading will ensue until the gains from trade are exhausted. Or, as Calabresi has put it, "if one assumes rationality, no transactions costs, and no legal impediments to bargaining, all misallocations of resources would be fully cured in the market by bargains."[19] However, one generally cannot expect this happy result in the market for proprietary know-how. Not only are there high costs associated with obtaining the requisite information, but

there are also organizational and strategic impediments associated with using the market to effectuate transfer.

Consider the information requirements associated with using markets. In order to carry out a market transaction, it is necessary to discover who one wishes to deal with and to inform people that one wishes to deal and on what terms. It is also necessary to conduct negotiations leading up to the bargain, to draw up the contract, to undertake the inspection needed to make sure that the terms of the contract are being observed, and so on.[20] Furthermore, the opportunity for trading must be identified. As Kirzner has explained:

For an exchange transaction to be completed it is not sufficient merely that the conditions for exchange which prospectively will be mutually beneficial be present; it is necessary also that each participant be *aware* of his opportunity to gain through the exchange. . . . It is usually assumed . . . that where such scope is present, exchange will in fact occur. . . . In fact, of course, exchange may fail to occur because knowledge is imperfect, in spite of the presence of the conditions for mutually profitable exchange.[21]

The transactional difficulties identified by Kirzner are especially compelling when the commodity in question is proprietary information—be it technological or managerial — and where the potential trading partner is located in a less developed country. Protecting the ownership of technological know-how often requires the suppression of information on exchange possibilities. By its very nature, industrial R&D requires that the activities and outcomes of the R&D establishment be disguised or concealed. Marquis and Allen point out that industrial laboratories, with their strong mission orientation, must:

cut themselves off from interaction beyond the organizational perimeter. This is to a large degree intentional. The competitive environment in which they operate necessitates control over the outflow of messages. The industrial technologist or scientist is therefore essentially cut off from free interaction with his colleagues outside of the organization.[22]

Sloan Management Review   Spring 1981   9

Except insofar as production or marketing specialists within the firm perceive the transfer opportunity, transfer may fail by reason of nonrecognition. Nonrecognition might also occur if there are few indigenous enterprises that have the requisite capabilities for absorbing the foreign know-how. In short, opportunities for arm's-length trading might have to await enterprise development in the recipient market.

Even where the possessor of the technology recognizes the opportunity and has the capability to absorb know-how, markets may break down. This difficulty arises because of the problems of disclosing value to buyers in a way that is convincing and that does not destroy the basis for exchange. Due to a very severe informational problem, the less informed party (in this instance, the buyer) must be wary of opportunistic representations by the seller. Moreover, if there is sufficient disclosure (including veracity checks thereon) to assure the buyer that the information possesses great value, the "fundamental paradox" of information arises: "its value for the purchaser is not known until he has the information, but then he has in effect acquired it without cost."[23]

Suppose that recognition is no problem and that buyers concede value and are prepared to pay for information in the seller's possession. Thus, a formula for a chemical compound or the blueprints for a special device may be all that is needed to effect the transfer. However, more is frequently needed. Know-how cannot always be codified, since it has an important tacit dimension: individuals often know more than they are able to articulate. When knowledge has a high tacit component, it cannot be codified. It is, therefore, extremely difficult to transfer it without intimate personal contact, demonstration, and involvement. It is well known, for instance, that the diffusion of crafts from one country to another often depended on the migration of groups of craftsmen, such as when the Huguenots were driven from France by the repeal of the Edict of Nantes under Louis XIV. Indeed, in the absence of intimate human contact, technology transfer is sometimes impossible. As Polanyi has observed, "It is pathetic to watch the endless efforts — equipped with microscopy and chemistry, with mathematics and electronics — to reproduce a single violin of the kind the half literate Stradivarius turned out as a matter of routine more than 200 years ago."[24]

In short, the transfer of knowledge may be impossible in the absence of the transfer of people. Furthermore, it will often not suffice just to transfer individuals. While a single individual may sometimes hold the key to much organizational knowledge, team support is often needed, since the organization's total capabilities must be brought to bear on the transfer problem.[25] In some instances, the transfer can be effected through a one-time contract, which would provide a consulting team to assist in the start-up. Such contracts may be highly incomplete. The failure to reach a comprehensive agreement may give rise to dissatisfaction during execution. This dissatisfaction may be an unavoidable — which is to say an irremediable — result. Plainly, foreign investment is an extreme response to the needs of a one-time exchange. In the absence of a superior organizational alternative, one-time, incomplete contracting for a consulting team is likely to prevail.

Reliance on repeated contracting is less clearly warranted, however, where a succession of exchanges is contemplated. It is also less clearly warranted when two-way communication is needed to promote the recognition and disclosure of opportunities for information transfer as well as the actual transfer itself. The parties in these circumstances are effectively joined in a bilateral monopoly trading relation. As Williamson explains, such contracting is full of hazards.[26] A more cooperative arrangement for joining the parties would enjoy a greater comparative institutional advantage. Specifically, intrafirm transfer to a foreign subsidiary (which avoids the need for repeated negotiations and attenuates the hazards of opportunism) has advantages over autonomous trading. Better disclosure, easier agreement, better governance, and more effective team organization and reconfiguration all result. Here lies an incentive for foreign direct investment.

The above arguments, while couched in the context of technological know-how, are in fact general and extend to many different kinds of proprietary information. For instance, managerial (including organizational) know-how and goodwill (including brand loyalty) represent types of assets for which markets may falter as effective exchange mechanisms. A foreign investment strategy is, therefore, suggested.

International Capital Markets and Direct Foreign Investment

Until the late 1960s, the prevailing view of direct foreign investment by multinational firms was that it represented one process by which rates of return to capital were equalized across countries. It was subsequently realized that this interpretation was inadequate, since the equalization of rates of return did not imply ownership of the means of production. A portfolio position would appear to achieve the same objectives at lower cost. Nor are pure diversification advantages involved. Following modern financial theory, a security's risk and return can be decomposed into two elements: (1) risk that is specific to each company (called "unsystematic," because it can be diversified away) and (2) risk that is common to all securities (called "systematic," because it is nondiversifiable). Since unsystematic risk can generally be eliminated through simple portfolio diversification, the investor does not need widely diversified multinational companies to eliminate this risk. Thus, it would be surprising if capital transfers were a significant feature of foreign direct investment. Indeed, the available evidence indicates that only a small percentage of the capital expenditures of foreign affiliates is financed by the parent companies. A study of 115 foreign subsidiaries for the U.K. revealed that local sources (specifically retained earnings, depreciation allowances, liquid assets, and local bank loans) accounted for 80 percent of the subsidiaries' local investment.[27] A similar pattern appears in the investment expenditures of majority-owned foreign affiliates of U.S. companies. The ratio of these expenditures to the net capital outflows from the U.S. to all foreign incorporated and unincorporated affiliates is typically about 3:1. In short, it is doubtful that the international transfer of capital is an especially significant attribute of foreign direct investment. It is mainly incidental to the other considerations identified here.

Still, there may be a number of efficiencies associated with the internalization of international capital markets. If capital markets abroad are not well developed, then an efficient internal capital market within the multinational firm may well be able to assist in the efficient worldwide allocation of resources. Funds will be allocated to high yield uses, irrespective of national boundaries. Thus, the multinational firm can perform as an effective substitute for capital markets where these markets are poorly developed.

Potential Anticompetitive Consequences of Multinational Enterprise

An alternative explanation of the overseas growth of multinational enterprises emphasizes the role of oligopoly and monopoly. According to Hymer, direct foreign investment has a dual nature:

It is an instrument which allows business firms to transfer capital, technology, and organizational skill from one country to another. It is also an instrument for restraining competition between firms of different nations . . . . The important point is to note that the general presumption of international trade economists in favor of free trade and free factor movements, on the grounds of allocative efficiency, does not apply to direct foreign investment because of the anticompetitive effect inherently associated with it . . . . A restriction on direct investment or a policy to break up a multinational corporation may be in some cases the only way of establishing a higher degree of competition in that industry . . . . Given the oligopolistic front maintained by the firms from developed

Sloan Management Review   Spring 1981   11

countries, the underdeveloped countries need to devote an important share of their scarce resources to building up national enterprises which they can control and use in bargaining with foreign oligopolists.[28]

Given the currency of these views, it is important to ascertain the degree to which MNEs can be vehicles for anticompetitive behavior. It will also prove necessary to distinguish the concept of competitive advantage from the concept of monopoly power, since it appears that Hymer and others have imputed monopoly concerns to any kind of competitive advantage the MNE may possess. In this regard, it is of interest to contrast the "market failure" view of the MNE developed above with the imperfect competition view, which originated with the work of Hymer and extends through Kindleberger and Caves.[29] According to this latter view, the existence of multinational enterprise is predicated upon some monopolistic advantage. MNEs have unique assets (e.g., innovations or differentiated products) which enable them to offset the advantages that indigenous firms have in operating in their own familiar environment. This view of the firm is consistent with the conceptualization of horizontal direct foreign investment developed earlier. Firms have know-how and other major assets, which they transfer abroad in order to capture quasi rents. But, saying that firms have unique assets does not mean that rivalry is necessarily suppressed and that public policy intervention is thereby called for. Rather, explicit consideration of costs and benefits from foreign investment is necessary, since there may be important incidental benefits to the host country.

However, it appears that the emphasis on the "special assets" that the multinational firm possesses (and on the "monopoly advantage" which those assets confer) has been interpreted by some to imply that MNEs are vehicles for anticompetitive behavior.[30] There seems to be no other way of explaining Hymer's remark that there is an anticompetitive effect inherently associated with direct foreign investment. Nor does there seem to

be any other way of explaining his statement that "a restriction on direct investment or a policy to break up a multinational corporation may in some cases be the only way of establishing a higher degree of competition in that industry." It would appear that the relationship between the "special advantage" that a firm might possess and the "anticompetitive effect" supposedly inherent in the multinational firm is a subtle one, which must be interpreted with great care. The dynamics of Schumpetarian competition in an enterprise economy involve first the creation and then the destruction of a firm's competitive advantage. While the entrance of multinational firms into foreign markets may be explained in terms of the unique assets of these firms, consumer welfare is not necessarily injured by this process. Indeed, improvement in consumer welfare is often to be expected.

In this regard, it is of interest to examine the concept of competition and how it might be interpreted for public policy purposes. In economic theory, competition is typically defined to be a state of the market in which the individual buyer or seller does not influence the price of his purchases or sales. Competitive markets will normally arise when there are large numbers of buyers and sellers, product homogeneity, perfect knowledge, and divisibility of output. However, there may not be any real world market that meets the assumptions of the competitive model. Nevertheless, it is not necessarily true that public policy intervention will secure superior results for the consumer. Bork has suggested an alternative definition of competition, which appears to have merit as a guide for public policy. Specifically, he suggests that:

"Competition" may be read as a shorthand expression, a term of art, designating any state of affairs in which consumer welfare cannot be increased by moving to an alternative state of affairs by judicial decree. Conversely, "monopoly" and "restraint of trade" would be terms of art for situations in which consumer welfare could be so improved, and to monopolize or engage in "unfair competition" would be to use practices inimical to consumer welfare.[31]

If the multinational firm possesses a distinctive competitive advantage in the form of unique assets, then the exploitation of this advantage will typically enhance consumer welfare. The principal considerations, which arise with respect to multinational rather than indigenous enterprises, relate merely to the distribution of the quasi rents associated with the employment of the firms' unique assets. Since, by assumption, these assets are transferred from abroad, it would not appear that host country welfare would be reduced by foreign direct investment unless deleterious externalities accompanied the technology transfer process. Although appropriate public policy towards multinationals can be expected to share many features of policy commonly applied to indigenous firms, the international context raises a few special considerations, which need to be identified. The following discussion is restricted to issues raised by firm structure—particularly vertical, horizontal, and conglomerate integration.

Vertically Integrated Multinationals

Firms based in one country can engage in backward or forward integration into foreign markets. The anticompetitive aspects of vertical integration have received considerable elucidation in the past decade. The circumstances under which vertical integration can have anticompetitive consequences are now fairly well understood and seem to be narrowly circumscribed. Leverage theories of vertical integration, once commonplace, explain how vertically integrated firms in one market are supposedly able to extend their monopoly power into upstream and downstream markets. However, the application of economic analysis has largely discredited these notions. Consider an industry with two stages: component manufacture and assembly. If component manufacture is monopolized and assembly is competitive, the question then is whether the monopolist can increase profits by buying out the assemblers. If the manufacturer buys out the assemblers and increases the markup on assembly operations, then the markup on

components must be decreased by the same amount if profits are to be maximized. Since the demand for components is derived from the demand for the assembled product, the component manufacturer cannot maximize his profits by charging a price above the monopoly price (which has been determined with reference to all relevant costs, including the costs of assembly). In short, vertical integration does not permit a monopolist to extend his market power. It fails to do so at least insofar as it does not create contrived barriers to entry.[32] This consideration will now be examined.

Consider the possibility that vertical integration into assembly will delay entry (or otherwise make it more costly) at the component stage by making it necessary for a new entrant to enter at both stages. Suppose a potential entrant has developed competitive components. Because the component monopolist is integrated into assembly, the new entrant must come in at both the component and the assembly stage, or else independent new entrants must occur simultaneously at the assembly stage. One view is that vertical integration by the monopolist will not impede entry. Bork, for example, contends that:

In general, if greater than competitive profits are to be made in an industry, entry should occur whether the entrant has to come in at both levels or not. I know of no theory of imperfections in the capital market which would lead suppliers of capital to avoid areas of higher return to seek areas of lower return.[33]

Clearly, integrated entry occasions an increase in financial requirements. The issue, as Williamson points out, is whether an increase in the financial requirements is accompanied by an adverse alternation of the terms under which capital becomes available.[34] If the potential entrant is not competitive in assembly (e.g., because it has no direct or related experience), then an efficient capital market will adjust the terms of finance against the new entrant. As Williamson points out: "To contend that the terms of finance are the same . . . implies that the

Sloan Management Review   Spring 1981   13

capital market has equal confidence in the new entrants' qualifications to perform [assembly] activities as it does in firms that are already experienced in the business. Except in circumstances where experienced firms are plainly inept, this is tantamount to saying that experience counts for nought."[35]

The issues raised are somewhat technical and have been clarified elsewhere.[36] Nevertheless, it is clear that entry barriers arise if capital markets are poorly developed or if entrepreneurial skills are absent. Posner has argued that if the existing component producer owns all of the existing assembly facilities, then a new entrant would not have to engage in entry at both stages. If entry at one stage is anticipated, new firms will enter at the other stage, in order to provide a market for the new product.[37] However, there seem to be two basic requirements for this situation to occur. One is that market processes must be able to coordinate the investment expectations of the potential upstream and downstream producers. Posner claims that this requirement should not be a serious concern. The other requirement, which is related to the first, is that entrepreneurs come forth to take advantage of the opportunity. While these conditions might appear appropriate in the context of developed Western economies, they are clearly inappropriate for many less developed countries. Entry at both stages may well be necessary. The additional capital just may not be available to the potential entrant due to market failure or institutional considerations. Perfect capital markets are the exception rather than the rule, once an international perspective is adopted.

Accordingly, public policy towards the vertically integrated multinational enterprise need not be neutral. Vertical integration can be used as a barrier to entry where there is horizontal market power at one stage and where capital markets experience disabilities. The appropriate policy will depend upon the objectives of the nation-states, the ownership of the multinational, and the markets in which it is selling. Nevertheless, it is important to reiterate that in the absence

of horizontal market power, the vertically integrated firm is generally without anticompetitive implications. It may, in fact, have strong efficiency and procompetitive attributes.

There is another type of antisocial consequence which may result from vertical integration: the circumvention of taxes and tariffs. Vertical integration affords opportunities for transfer price manipulation and profit sharing. This consequence may be an especially important concern in the international context, since differential tariffs and taxes characterize international commerce. Vertical integration that is completed simply to take advantage of such considerations may yield pecuniary economies to the firm without yielding equivalent efficiency gains for the host country. Competitive implications also arise if tax shifting or tax avoidance gives multinational firms a cost advantage over equally efficient indigenous firms. The auditing of transfer prices may well be necessary.

The Horizontal Expansion of Multinational Firms

A significant portion of direct foreign investment is of the horizontal kind; that is, investment abroad is directed at producing goods and services that are currently produced domestically. Whether the potential for anticompetitive behavior exists with respect to this kind of investment will depend to a large degree on the scope of the relevant markets. If the relevant markets are national or regional in scope (so that foreign production has no impact on the home market), then foreign investment will have a substantially neutral impact on competition at home. The impact on competition abroad cannot be assessed without examining the particular circumstance of the foreign market. Competition is generally enhanced: (1) if the investment represents new entry and (2) if entry is not on such a massive scale that it results in the firm's achievement of dominance or of monopoly position in an otherwise competitive market. As Caves points out:

It is seldom recognized that the multinational company is a favored entrant to industries with high barriers to entry . . . . Thus, the multinational company is a likely potential entrant into national industries that might otherwise be cloistered by . . . entry barriers . . . . Besides its ability to enter a market, there is also some possibility that the multinational may be an entrant particularly disruptive of an oligopolistic consensus, especially in the early period of its presence. Its alien status may make it initially less sensitive to signals about an oligopolistic consensus emanating from established native firms.[38]

However, the case for a general policy of openness to market entry by MNEs is not completely clear-cut. "If the multinational company is good at scaling existing industrial barriers to the entry of new firms, it is also good at building up such barriers. The resources required to contrive such barriers . . . are often found in the portfolio of multinational companies."[39]

Evaluation

It seems clear that the MNE has few distinctive characteristics that ought to be the focus of special public policy initiatives. If offensive forms of market behavior do exist, the most direct approach is to regulate or prohibit the behavior directly rather than blocking foreign investment. Since most of the monopolistic abuses typically attributed to MNEs can also characterize indigenous firms with no extraterritorial investments,[40] nondiscriminatory regulatory approaches would appear to be desirable. Conduct designed to reduce the competitiveness of host country markets is socially undesirable, regardless of the identity of the firms involved.

In short, it is not clear that the MNE should be considered a distinctive organizational form with respect to the formulation of competition policy. To the extent that social abuse is attributable to the MNE, then the same abuses are typically open to indigenous firms as well. In this regard, consider the Brazilian electrical industry. Newfarmer identifies what he considers to be seven forms of MNE conduct: interlocking directorates, mutual forbearances, control of supply channels, cross subsidization of production, formal and informal collusion, formal political ties, and MNE acquisition behavior. He concludes that MNEs "exhibit strong propensities toward organizing and preserving various forms of market power in host economies. These tactics are often based on the advantage of global financial strength or perceived international and local interdependence."[41] While Newfarmer is able to provide persuasive evidence of collusion in the Brazilian electrical industry, the identified abuses might equally well have been characteristic of Brazilian firms. His recommendation that "as one tool of national planning, serious measures to curb restrictive practices, to prevent nonsocially beneficial takeovers, and to generally counterbalance the disadvantaged position of domestic entrepreneurs" would not seem to be a well-founded proposal if it is directed at MNEs alone.[42]

Conclusion

The multinational firm appears to have both efficiency and market power properties. However, the market power properties are more narrowly circumscribed than is commonly supposed. The analysis developed here points to the distinctive capabilities of the multinational firm as an organizational mode that is capable of establishing efficient vertical supply relations and of transferring technology in an efficient fashion. While multinational firms can be used to extend market power, their distinctive capabilities in this regard do not appear to be very significant. The general presumption in favor of free trade and free factor movements is not as readily overturned as some observers have suggested. Accordingly, the prescription that Third World countries devote an important share of their scarce resources to building up national enterprises rests on extremely weak theoretical (and empirical) underpinnings.[43]

While the establishment and enforcement

The financial support of the National Science Foundation and the Center for the Study of Organizational Innovation, University of Pennsylvania is gratefully acknowledged. A considerable intellectual debt is owed to Oliver Williamson and Richard Caves, who have had a pervasive impact on my thinking on direct foreign investment.

of industrial policies favoring competition will generally have merit, it appears that there are few circumstances where efficiency considerations would support the desirability of policies discriminating between indigenous and international firms. In any event, the internal resource allocation properties of multinational firms need careful examination before momentous policy prescriptions can be derived with confidence.

References

1
See:
P.J. Buckley and M. Casson, *The Future of the Multinational Enterprise* (London: Holmes & Meier Publishers, 1976);
S. Hymer, "The Efficiency (Contradictions) of Multinational Corporations," *American Economic Review* 60 (May 1970): 441-448;
J.C. McManus, "The Theory of the International Firm," in *The Multinational Firm and the Nation State*, ed. G. Paquet (Don Mills, Ontario: Collier Macmillan, 1972).

2
See O.E. Williamson, *Markets and Hierarchies: Analysis and Antitrust Implications* (New York: Free Press, 1975).

3
This section is based on Williamson (1975).

4
See J.R. Commons, *Institutional Economics* (Madison, WI: University of Wisconsin Press, 1934).

5
See R. Coase, "The Problem of Social Cost," *Journal of Law and Economics*, October 1960, p.15.

6
See O.E. Williamson and D. Teece, "European Economic and Political Integration: The Markets and Hierarchies Approach " (University of Pennsylvania, Center for the Study of Organizational Innovation, 1979).

7
This section is based partly on Williamson and Teece (1979) and on D. Teece, "Economies of Scope and the Scope of the Enterprise," *Journal of Economic Behavior and Organization* 1 (1980): 223-247.

8
See Coase (1960).

9
Lateral integration occurs when a firm sells products which are functionally related in production and/or distribution.

10
See R. Vernon, *Sovereignty at Bay: The Multinational Spread of U.S. Enterprises* (New York: Basic Books, 1971), ch. 2.

11
See:
B. Klein, "Transaction Cost Determinants of 'Unfair' Contractual Arrangements," *American Economic Review* (May 1980);
S. Macauley, "Non-Contractual Relations in a Business: A Preliminary Study," *American Sociological Review* 28 (1963): 55-69;
D. Teece, *Vertical Integration and Vertical Divestiture in the U.S. Petroleum Industry* (Stanford, CA: Institute for Energy Studies, 1976); Williamson (1975).

12
See:
K. Monteverde and D. Teece, "Appropriable Rents and Quasi Integration" (Stanford University Graduate School of Business, Working Paper, 1980a);
K. Monteverde and D. Teece, "Supplier Switching Costs and Vertical Integration in the U.S. Automobile Industry" (Stanford University Graduate School of Business, Working Paper, 1980b).
If it is just firm-specific physical capital that is involved, the holdup problem can be avoided by quasi integration: the supplier can require the purchaser to supply the requisite physical capital (such as tools and dies) needed for efficient supply. Hence, supplier switching costs turn out to be critical. See ibid.

13
See Williamson (1975), p. 119.

14
See R. Marris, "The Future of Corporate Society" (Working Paper, Department of Economics, University of Maryland, October 1980).

15
See R.E. Caves, "International Corporations: The Industrial Economies of Foreign Investment," *Economica* 38 (1971).

16
See:
E. Mansfield, D. Teece, and A. Romeo, "Overseas

Research and Development by U.S.-Based Firms,"
Economica 46 (1979): 187-196.
D. Teece, *The Multinational Corporation and the
Resource Cost of International Technology Transfer*
(Cambridge, MA: Ballinger, 1976).

17
See S. Kuznets, *Modern Economic Growth: Rate,
Structure and Spread* (New Haven, CT: Yale University
Press, 1966).

18
This is because the value of information often declines
with its dissemination, and it cannot be transferred at
zero marginal cost.
See D. Teece, "Technology Transfer by Multinational
Firms: The Resource of International Technology
Transfer," *Economic Journal*, June 1977.

19
See G. Calabresi, "Transactions Costs, Resource
Allocation, and Liability Rules: A Comment," *Journal
of Law and Economics*, April 1968.

20
See Coase (1960), p.15.

21
See I. Kirzner, *Competition and Entrepreneurship*
(Chicago, IL: University of Chicago Press, 1962), pp.
215-216.

22
See D. Marquis and T. Allen, "Communication Matters
in Applied Technology," *American Psychologist* 21
(1966): 1055.

23
See K.J. Arrow, *Essays in the Theory of Risk Bearing*
(Chicago, IL: Markham Publishers, 1971), p. 152.

24
See M. Polanyi, *Personal Knowledge: Towards a Post
Critical Philosophy* (Chicago, IL: University of Chicago
Press, 1958).

25
See N. Rosenberg, "Economic Development and the
Transfer of Technology: Some Historical Perspectives,"
Technology and Culture 11 (1970): 550-575.

26
See Williamson (1975).

27
See M. Brooks and H. Remmers, *The Strategy of
Multinational Enterprise* (New York: American
Elsevier, 1970).

28
See Hymer (1970).

29
See:
R.E. Caves, "Industrial Organization," in *Economic
Analysis and the Multinational Enterprise*, ed. J.
Dunning (New York: Praeger, 1974);
S. Hymer, "The International Operations of National
Firms: A Study of Direct Investment" (Cambridge, MA:
Massachusetts Institute of Technology, doctoral
dissertation, 1960);
C.P. Kindleberger, *American Business Abroad* (New
Haven, CT: Yale University Press, 1969);
Caves (1971).

30
See:
R.S. Newfarmer, "Oligopolistic Tactics to Control
Markets and the Growth of MNEs in Brazil's Electrical
Community," *Journal of Development Studies* 15 (April
1979);
Hymer (1970).

31
See R. Bork, *The Antitrust Paradox* (New York: Basic
Books, 1978), p.61.

32
However, when monopsony and monopoly stages are
integrated vertically, integration facilitates arriving at
the input choice that extracts maximum profits from
whatever monopoly power exists at either stage.
Decisions regarding how much of an input to use can be
guided by the actual marginal cost of the input, rather
than by bargaining strategems or by the monopsonist's
concern for restraining the volume of its purchases in
order to avoid driving up the supply price.

33
See R. Bork, "Vertical Integration and Competitive
Processes," in *Public Policy towards Mergers*, ed. J. Fred
Weston and S. Peltzman (Pacific Palisades, CA:
Goodyear Publishing, 1969), pp. 139-146.

34
See Williamson (1975), p. 110.

35
See Williamson (1975), p. 111.
There is an issue here of whether the potential entrant
will have the terms of finance adjusted against him by
an amount greater than the monopolist would have
experienced when the monopolist integrated into
assembly. It would seem that since, by assumption, the
monopolist had no initial advantage with respect to
assembly, it would have confronted the same capital
costs. If entry barriers are defined (following Stigler) as

a condition which imposes higher long-run costs of production on a new entrant than are borne by firms already in the market, then it is not clear that the Williamson scenario ought to be considered to generate a barrier to entry.

36
See G. Saloner and D. Teece, "Vertical Integration and Capital Market Entry Barriers: A Clarifying Note" (Stanford University, Working Paper, April 1980).

37
See R. Posner, *Antitrust Law* (Chicago, IL: University of Chicago Press, 1976), p. 198.

38
See R.E. Caves, "International Cartels and Monopolies in International Trade," in *International Economic Policy*, R. Dornbusch and J. Frankel (Baltimore, MD: Johns Hopkins University Press, 1979), p. 61.

39
See Caves (1979), p. 61.

40
However, a number of forms of abuse are open to vertically integrated MNEs which are not open to vertically integrated firms which are purely domestic in the scope of their activities. Perhaps the most obvious is transfer price manipulation designed to circumvent corporate taxes or tariffs on international trade. While wealth transfer considerations are involved, there need not be any competitive implications unless the tax shifting or tax avoidance gives multinational firms a competitive advantage over equally efficient indigenous firms.

41
See Newfarmer (1979), p. 135.

42
Ibid., p. 136.

43
See Hymer (1970).

[24]

CALIFORNIA MANAGEMENT REVIEW
Volume XXVIII, Number 2, Winter 1986
© 1986, The Regents of the University of California

Changing Patterns of International Competition

Michael E. Porter

When examining the environmental changes facing firms today, it is a rare observer who will conclude that international competition is not high on the list. The growing importance of international competition is well recognized both in the business and academic communities, for reasons that are fairly obvious when one looks at just about any data set that exists on international trade or investment. Exhibit 1, for example, compares world trade and world GNP. Something interesting started happening around the mid-1950s, when the growth in world trade began to significantly exceed the growth in world GNP. Foreign direct investment by firms in developing countries began to grow rapidly a few years later, about 1963.[1] This period marked the beginning of a fundamental change in the international competitive environment that by now has come to be widely recognized. It is a trend that is causing sleepless nights for many business managers.

There is a substantial literature on international competition, because the subject is far from a new one. A large body of literature has investigated the many implications of the Heckscher-Ohlin model and other models of international trade which are rooted in the principle of comparative advantage.[2] The unit of analysis in this literature is the country. There is also considerable literature on the multinational firm, reflecting the growing importance of the multinational since the turn of the century. In examining the reasons for the multinational, I think it is fair to characterize this literature as resting heavily on the multinational's ability to exploit intangible assets.[3] The work of Hymer and Caves among others has stressed the

This article grows out of the seventh lecture in a series of lectures on Strategy and Organization for Individual Innovation and Renewal, sponsored by the Transamerica Chair, School of Business Administration, University of California at Berkeley. March 15, 1985.

9

10   MICHAEL E. PORTER

Exhibit 1. Growth of World Trade

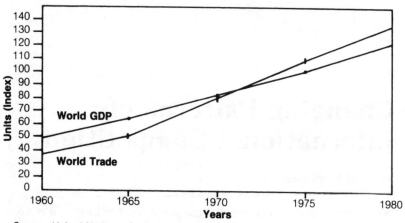

Source: United Nations, *Statistical Yearbooks*

role of the multinational in transferring know-how and expertise gained in one country market to others at low cost, and thereby offsetting the unavoidable extra costs of doing business in a foreign country. A more recent stream of literature extends this by emphasizing how the multinational firm internalizes transactions to circumvent imperfections in various intermediate markets, most importantly the market for knowledge.

There is also a related literature on the problems of entry into foreign markets and the life cycle of how a firm competes abroad, beginning with export or licensing and ultimately moving to the establishment of foreign subsidiaries. Vernon's product cycle of international trade combines a view of how products mature with the evolution in a firm's international activities to predict the patterns of trade and investment in developed and developing countries.[4] Finally, many of the functional fields in business administration research have their branch of literature about international issues—e.g., international marketing, international finance. This literature concentrates, by and large, on the problems of doing business in a foreign country.

As rich as it is, however, I think it is fair to characterize the literature on international competition as being limited when it comes to the choice of a firm's international strategy. Though the literature provides some guidance for considering incremental investment decisions to enter a new country, it provides at best a partial view of how to characterize a firm's overall international strategy and how such strategy should be selected. Put another way, the literature focuses more on the problem of becoming a multinational than on strategies for established multinationals. Although the distinction between domestic firms and multinationals is seminal in a literature focused on the problems of doing business abroad, the fact that a firm is multinational says little if anything about its international strategy except that it operates in several countries.

Broadly stated, my research has been seeking to answer the question: what does international competition mean for competitive strategy? In particular, what are the distinctive questions for competitive strategy that are raised by international as opposed to domestic competition? Many of the strategy issues for a company competing internationally are very much the same as for one competing domestically. A firm must still analyze its industry structure and competitors, understand its buyer and the sources of buyer value, diagnose its relative cost position, and seek to establish a sustainable competitive advantage within some competitive scope, whether it be across-the-board or in an industry segment. These are subjects I have written about extensively.[5] But there are some questions for strategy that are peculiar to international competition, and that add to rather than replace those listed earlier. These questions all revolve, in one way or another, around how a firm's activities in one country affect or are affected by what is going on in other countries—the connectedness among country competition. It is this connectedness that is the focus of this article and of a broader stream of research recently conducted under the auspices of the Harvard Business School.[6]

Patterns of International Competition

The appropriate unit of analysis in setting international strategy is the industry, because the industry is the arena in which competitive advantage is won or lost. The starting point for understanding international competition is the observation that its pattern differs markedly from industry to industry. At one end of the spectrum are industries that I call *multidomestic,* in which competition in each country (or small group of countries) is essentially independent of competition in other countries. A multidomestic industry is one that is present in many countries (e.g., there is a consumer banking industry in Sri Lanka, one in France, and one in the U.S.), but in which competition occurs on a country-by-country basis. In a multidomestic industry, a multinational firm may enjoy a competitive advantage from the one-time transfer of know-how from its home base to foreign countries. However, the firm modifies and adapts its intangible assets to employ them in each country and the outcome is determined by conditions in each country. The competitive advantages of the firm, then, are largely specific to each country. The international industry becomes a collection of essentially domestic industries—hence the term "multidomestic." Industries where competition has traditionally exhibited this pattern include retailing, consumer packaged goods, distribution, insurance, consumer finance, and caustic chemicals.

12   MICHAEL E. PORTER

At the other end of the spectrum are what I term *global* industries. The term global—like the word "strategy"—has become overused and perhaps under-understood. The definition of a global industry employed here is an industry in which a firm's competitive position in one country is significantly influenced by its position in other countries.[7] Therefore, the international industry is not merely a collection of domestic industries but a series of linked domestic industries in which the rivals compete against each other on a truly worldwide basis. Industries exhibiting the global pattern today include commercial aircraft, TV sets, semiconductors, copiers, automobiles, and watches.

The implications for strategy of the distinction between multidomestic and global industries are quite profound. In a multidomestic industry, a firm can and should manage its international activities like a portfolio. Its subsidiaries or other operations around the world should each control all the important activities necessary to do business in the industry and should enjoy a high degree of autonomy. The firm's strategy in a country should be determined largely by the circumstances in that country; the firm's international strategy is then what I term a "country-centered strategy."

In a multidomestic industry, competing internationally is discretionary. A firm can choose to remain domestic or can expand internationally if it has some advantage that allows it to overcome the extra costs of entering and competing in foreign markets. The important competitors in multi-domestic industries will either be domestic companies or multinationals with stand-alone operations abroad—this is the situation in each of the multidomestic industries listed earlier. In a multidomestic industry, then, international strategy collapses to a series of domestic strategies. The issues that are uniquely international revolve around how to do business abroad, how to select good countries in which to compete (or assess country risk), and mechanisms to achieve the one-time transfer of know-how. These are questions that are relatively well developed in the litera-ture.

In a global industry, however, managing international activities like a portfolio will undermine the possibility of achieving competitive advantage. In a global industry, a firm must in some way integrate its activities on a worldwide basis to capture the linkages among countries. This will require more than transferring intangible assets among countries, though it will include it. A firm may choose to compete with a country-centered strategy, focusing on specific market segments or countries when it can carve out a niche by responding to whatever local country differences are present. However, it does so at some considerable risk from competitors with global strategies. All the important competitors in the global industries listed earlier compete worldwide with coordinated strategies.

In international competition, a firm always has to perform some functions in each of the countries in which it competes. Even though a global com-petitor must view its international activities as an overall system, it has still to maintain some country perspective. It is the balancing of these two perspectives that becomes one of the essential questions in global strategy.[8]

Causes of Globalization

If we accept the distinction between multidomestic and global industries as an important taxonomy of patterns of international competition, a number of crucial questions arise. When does an industry globalize? What exactly do we mean by a global strategy, and is there more than one kind? What determines the type of international strategy to select in a particular industry?

An industry is global if there is some competitive advantage to integrating activities on a worldwide basis. To make this statement operational, however, we must be very precise about what we mean by "activities" and also what we mean by "integrating." To diagnose the sources of competitive advantage in any context, whether it be domestic or international, it is necessary to adopt a disaggregated view of the firm. In my newest book, *Competitive Advantage*. I have developed a framework for doing so, called the value chain.[9] Every firm is a collection of discrete activities performed to do business that occur within the scope of the firm—I call them value activities. The activities performed by a firm include such things as salespeople selling the product, service technicians performing repairs, scientists in the laboratory designing process techniques, and accountants keeping the books. Such activities are technologically and in most cases physically distinct. It is only at the level of discrete activities, rather than the firm as a whole, that competitive advantage can be truly understood.

A firm may possess two types of competitive advantage: low relative cost or differentiation—its ability to perform the activities in its value chain either at lower cost or in a unique way relative to its competitors. The ultimate value a firm creates is what buyers are willing to pay for what the firm provides, which includes the physical product as well as any ancillary services or benefits. Profit results if the value created through performing the required activities exceeds the collective cost of performing them. Competitive advantage is a function of either providing comparable buyer value to competitors but performing activities efficiently (low cost), or of performing activities at comparable cost but in unique ways that create greater buyer value than competitors and, hence, command a premium price (differentiation).

The value chain, shown in Figure 1, provides a systematic means of displaying and categorizing activities. The activities performed by a firm in any industry can be grouped into the nine generic categories shown. The labels may differ based on industry convention, but every firm performs these basic categories of activities in some way or another. Within each category of activities, a firm typically performs a number of discrete activities which are particular to the industry and to the firm's strategy. In

14   MICHAEL E. PORTER

Figure 1. The Value Chain

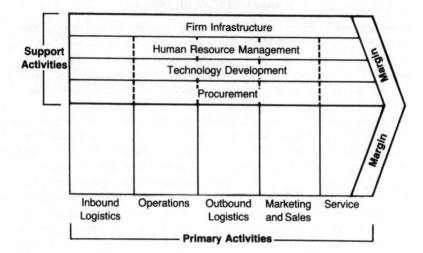

service, for example, firms typically perform such discrete activities as installation, repair, parts distribution, and upgrading.

The generic categories of activities can be grouped into two broad types. Along the bottom are what I call *primary* activities, which are those involved in the physical creation of the product or service, its delivery and marketing to the buyer, and its support after sale. Across the top are what I call *support* activities, which provide inputs or infrastructure that allow the primary activities to take place on an ongoing basis.

Procurement is the obtaining of purchased inputs, whether they be raw materials, purchased services, machinery, or so on. Procurement stretches across the entire value chain because it supports every activity—every activity uses purchased inputs of some kind. There are typically many different discrete procurement activities within a firm, often performed by different people. Technology development encompasses the activities involved in designing the product as well as in creating and improving the way the various activities in the value chain are performed. We tend to think of technology in terms of the product or manufacturing process. In fact, every activity a firm performs involves a technology or technologies which may be mundane or sophisticated, and a firm has a stock of know-how about how to perform each activity. Technology development typically involves a variety of different discrete activities, some performed outside the R&D department.

Human resource management is the recruiting, training, and development of personnel. Every activity involves human resources, and thus

CHANGING PATTERNS OF INTERNATIONAL COMPETITION   15

human resource management activities cut across the entire chain. Finally, firm infrastructure includes activities such as general management, accounting, legal, finance, strategic planning, and all the other activities decoupled from specific primary or support activities but that are essential to enable the entire chain's operation.

Activities in a firm's value chain are not independent, but are connected through what I call linkages. The way one activity is performed frequently affects the cost or effectiveness of other activities. If more is spent on the purchase of a raw material, for example, a firm may lower its cost of fabrication or assembly. There are many linkages that connect activities, not only within the firm but also with the activities of its suppliers, channels, and ultimately its buyers. The firm's value chain resides in a larger stream of activities that I term the value system. Suppliers have value chains that provide the purchased inputs to the firm's chain; channels have value chains through which the firm's product or service passes; buyers have value chains in which the firm's product or service is employed. The connections among activities in this vertical system also become essential to competitive advantage.

A final important building block in value chain theory, necessary for our purposes here, is the notion of *competitive scope*. Competitive scope is the breadth of activities the firm employs together in competing in an industry. There are four basic dimensions of competitive scope:

- *segment* scope, or the range of segments the firm serves (e.g., product varieties, customer types);
- *industry* scope, or the range of industries the firm competes in with a coordinated strategy;
- *vertical* scope, or what activities are performed by the firm versus suppliers and channels; and
- *geographic* scope, or the geographic regions the firm operates in with a coordinated strategy.

Competitive scope is vital to competitive advantage because it shapes the configuration of the value chain, how activities are performed, and whether activities are shared among units. International strategy is an issue of geographic scope, and can be analyzed quite similarly to the question of whether and how a firm should compete locally, regionally, or nationally within a country. In the international context, government tends to have a greater involvement in competition and there are more significant variations among geographic regions in buyer needs, although these differences are matters of degree.

International Configuration and Coordination of Activities—A firm that competes internationally must decide how to spread the activities in the value chain among countries. A distinction immediately arises between the activities labeled downstream on Figure 2, and those labeled

16   MICHAEL E. PORTER

Figure 2. Upstream and Downstream Activities

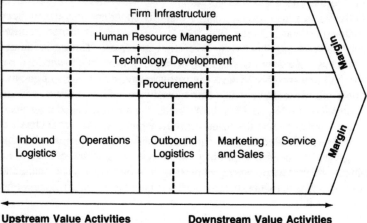

Upstream Value Activities   Downstream Value Activities

upstream activities and support activities. The location of downstream activities, those more related to the buyer, is usually tied to where the buyer is located. If a firm is going to sell in Japan, for example, it usually must provide service in Japan and it must have salespeople stationed in Japan. In some industries it is possible to have a single sales force that travels to the buyer's country and back again; some other specific downstream activities such as the production of advertising copy can also sometimes be done centrally. More typically, however, the firm must locate the capability to perform downstream activities in each of the countries in which it operates. Upstream activities and support activities, conversely, can at least conceptually be decoupled from where the buyer is located.

This distinction carries some interesting implications. The first is that downstream activities create competitive advantages that are largely country-specific: a firm's reputation, brand name, and service network in a country grow out of a firm's activities in that country and create entry/mobility barriers largely in that country alone. Competitive advantage in upstream and support activities often grows more out of the entire system of countries in which a firm competes than from its position in any one country, however.

A second implication is that in industries where downstream activities or buyer-tied activities are vital to competitive advantage, there tends to be a more multidomestic pattern of international competition. In industries where upstream and support activities (such as technology development and operations) are crucial to competitive advantage, global competition

CHANGING PATTERNS OF INTERNATIONAL COMPETITION   17

is more common. In global competition, the location and scale of these potentially footloose activities is optimized from a worldwide perspective.[10]

The distinctive issues in international, as contrasted to domestic, strategy can be summarized in two key dimensions of how a firm competes internationally. The first is what I term the *configuration* of a firm's activities worldwide, or where in the world each activity in the value chain is performed, including in how many places. The second dimension is what I term *coordination*, which refers to how like activities performed in different countries are coordinated with each other. If, for example, there are three plants—one in Germany, one in Japan, and one in the U.S.—how do the activities in those plants relate to each other?

A firm faces an array of options in both configuration and coordination for each activity. Configuration options range from concentrated (performing an activity in one location and serving the world from it—e.g., one R&D lab, one large plant) to dispersed (performing every activity in each country). In the latter case, each country would have a complete value chain. Coordination options range from none to very high. For example, if a firm produces its product in three plants, it could, at one extreme, allow each plant to operate with full autonomy—e.g., different product standards and features, different steps in the production process, different raw materials, different part numbers. At the other extreme, the plants could be tightly coordinated by employing the same information system, the same production process, the same parts, and so forth. Options for coordination in an activity are typically more numerous than the configuration options because there are many possible levels of coordination and many different facets of the way the activity is performed.

Figure 3 lists some of the configuration issues and coordination issues for several important categories of value activities. In technology development, for example, the configuration issue is where R&D is performed: one location? two locations? and in what countries? The coordination issues have to do with such things as the extent of interchange among R&D centers and the location and sequence of product introduction·around the world. There are configuration issues and coordination issues for every activity.

Figure 4 is a way of summarizing these basic choices in international strategy on a single diagram, with coordination of activities on the vertical axis and configuration of activities on the horizontal axis. The firm has to make a set of choices for each activity. If a firm employs a very dispersed configuration—placing an entire value chain in every country (or small group of contiguous countries) in which it operates, coordinating little or not at all among them—then the firm is competing with a country-centered strategy. The domestic firm that only operates in one country is the extreme case of a firm with a country-centered strategy. As we move from the lower left-hand corner of the diagram up or to the right, we have strategies that are increasingly global.

18   MICHAEL E. PORTER

Figure 3. Configuration and Coordination Issues
by Category of Activity

Value Activity	Configuration Issues	Coordination Issues
Operations	• Location of production facilities for components and end products	• Networking of international plants • Transferring process technology and production know-how among plants
Marketing and Sales	• Product line selection • Country (market) selection	• Commonality of brand name worldwide • Coordination of sales to multinational accounts • Similarity of channels and product positioning worldwide • Coordination of pricing in different countries
Service	• Location of service organization	• Similarity of service standards and procedures worldwide
Technology Development	• Number and location of R&D centers	• Interchange among dispersed R&D centers • Developing products responsive to market needs in many countries • Sequence of product introductions around the world
Procurement	• Location of the purchasing function	• Managing suppliers located in different countries • Transferring market knowledge • Coordinating purchases of common items

Figure 5 illustrates some of the possible variations in international strategy. The purest global strategy is to concentrate as many activities as
possible in one country, serve the world from this home base, and tightly
coordinate those activities that must inherently be performed near the
buyer. This is the pattern adopted by many Japanese firms in the 1960s
and 1970s, such as Toyota. However, Figures 4 and 5 make it clear that
there is no such thing as one global strategy. There are many different
kinds of global strategies, depending on a firm's choices about configuration
and coordination throughout the value chain. In copiers, for example, Xerox
has until recently concentrated R&D in the U.S. but dispersed other

Figure 4. The Dimensions of International Strategy

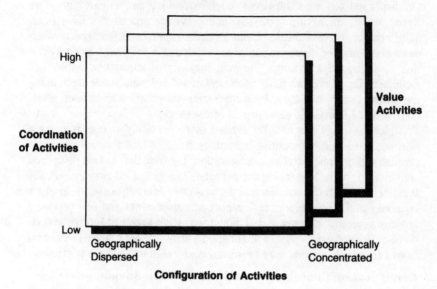

Figure 5. Types of International Strategy

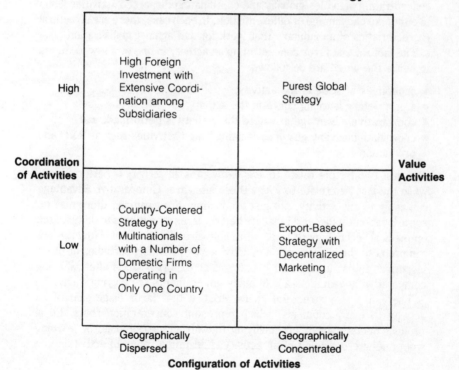

20   MICHAEL E. PORTER

activities, in some cases using joint-venture partners to perform them. On dispersed activities, however, coordination has been quite high. The Xerox brand, marketing approach, and servicing procedures have been quite standardizd worldwide. Canon, on the other hand, has had a much more concentrated configuration of activities and somewhat less coordination of dispersed activities. The vast majority of support activities and manufacturing of copiers have been performed in Japan. Aside from using the Canon brand, however, local marketing subsidiaries have been given quite a bit of latitude in each region of the world.

A global stratgy can now be defined more precisely as one in which a firm seeks to gain competitive advantage from its international presence through either concentrating configuration, coordination among dispersed activities, or both. Measuring the presence of a global industry empirically must reflect both dimensions and not just one. Market presence in many countries and some export and import of components and end products are characteristic of most global industries. High levels of foreign investment or the mere presence of multinational firms are not reliable measures, however, because firms may be managing foreign units like a portfolio.

Configuration/Coordination and Competitive Advantage—Understanding the competitive advantages of a global strategy and, in turn, the causes of industry globalization requires specifying the conditions in which concentrating activities globally and coordinating dispersed activities leads to either cost advantage or differentiation. In each case, there are structural characteristics of an industry that work for and against globalization.

The factors that favor concentrating an activity in one or a few locations to serve the world are as follows:

- economies of scale in the activity;
- a proprietary learning curve in the activity;
- comparative advantage in where the activity is performed; and
- coordination advantages of co-locating linked activities such as R&D and production.

The first two factors relate to *how many* sites an activity is performed at, while the last two relate to *where* these sites are. Comparative advantage can apply to any activity, not just production. For example, there may be some locations in the world that are better places than others to do research on medical technology or to perform software development. Government can promote the concentration of activities by providing subsidies or other incentives to use a particular country as an export base, in effect altering comparative advantage—a role many governments are playing today.

There are also structural characteristics that favor dispersion of an activity to many countries, which represent concentration costs. Local product needs may differ, nullifying the advantages of scale or learning from one-site operation of an activity. Locating a range of activities in a

CHANGING PATTERNS OF INTERNATIONAL COMPETITION 21

country may facilitate marketing in that country by signaling commitment to local buyers and/or providing greater responsiveness. Transport, communication, and storage costs may make it inefficient to concentrate the activity in one location. Government is also frequently a powerful force for dispersing activities. Governments typically want firms to locate the entire value chain in their country, because this creates benefits and spillovers to the country that often go beyond local content. Dispersion is also encouraged by the risks of performing an activity in one place: exchange-rate risks, political risks, and so on. The balance between the advantages of concentrating and dispersing an activity normally differ for each activity (and industry). The best configuration for R&D is different from that for component fabrication, and this is different from that for assembly, installation, advertising, and procurement.[11]

The desirability of coordinating like activities that are dispersed involves a similar balance of structural factors. Coordination potentially allows the sharing of know-how among dispersed activities. If a firm learns how to operate the production process better in Germany, transferring that learning may make the process run better in plants in the United States and Japan. Differing countries, with their inevitably differing conditions, provide a fertile basis for comparison as well as opportunities for arbitraging knowledge, obtained in different places about different aspects of the business. Coordination among dispersed activities also potentially improves the ability to reap economies of scale in activities if subtasks are allocated among locations to allow some specialization—e.g., each R&D center has a different area of focus. While there is a fine line between such forms of coordination and what I have termed configuration, it does illustrate how the way a network of foreign locations is managed can have a great influence on the ability to reap the benefits of any given configuration of activities. Viewed another way, close coordination is frequently a partial offset to dispersing an activity.

Coordination may also allow a firm to respond to shifting comparative advantage, where shifts in exchange rates and factor costs are hard to forecast. Incrementally increasing the production volume at the location currently enjoying favorable exchange rates, for example, can lower overall costs. Coordination can reinforce a firm's brand reputation with buyers (and hence lead to differentiation) through ensuring a consistent image and approach to doing business on a worldwide basis. This is particularly likely if buyers are mobile or information about the industry flows freely around the world. Coordination may also differentiate the firm with multinational buyers if it allows the firm to serve them anywhere and in a consistent way. Coordination (and a global approach to configuration) enhances leverage with local governments if the firm is able to grow or shrink activities in one country at the expense of others. Finally, coordination yields flexibility in responding to competitors, by allowing the firm to differentially respond across countries and to respond in one country to a challenge in another.

Coordination of dispersed activities usually involves costs that differ by form of coordination and industry. Local conditions may vary in ways that may make a common approach across countries suboptimal. If every plant in the world is required to use the same raw material, for example, the firm pays a penalty in countries where the raw material is expensive relative to satisfactory substitutes. Business practices, marketing systems, raw material sources, local infrastructures, and a variety of other factors may differ across countries as well, often in ways that may mitigate the advantages of a common approach or of the sharing of learning. Governments may restrain the flow of information required for coordination or may impose other barriers to it. The transaction costs of coordination, which have recently received increased attention in domestic competition, are vitally important in international strategy.[12] International coordination involves long distances, language problems, and cultural barriers to communication. In some industries, these factors may mean that coordination is not optimal. They also suggest that forms of coordination which involve relatively infrequent decisions will enjoy advantages over forms of coordination involving on-going interchange.

There are also substantial organizational difficulties involved in achieving cooperation among subsidiaries, which are due to the difficulty in aligning subsidiary managers' interests with those of the firm as a whole. The Germans do not necessarily want to tell the Americans about their latest breakthroughs on the production line because it may make it harder for them to outdo the Americans in the annual comparison of operating efficiency among plants. These vexing organizational problems mean that country subsidiaries often view each other more as competitors than collaborators.[13] As with configuration, a firm must make an activity-by-activity choice about where there is net competitive advantage from coordinating in various ways.

Coordination in some activities may be necessary to reap the advantages of configuration in others. The use of common raw materials in each plant, for example, allows worldwide purchasing. Moreover, tailoring some activities to countries may allow concentration and standardization of other activities. For example, tailored marketing in each country may allow the same product to be positioned differently and hence sold successfully in many countries, unlocking possibilities for reaping economies of scale in production and R&D. Thus coordination and configuration interact.

Configuration/Coordination and the Pattern of International Competition—When benefits of configuring and/or coordinating globally exceed the costs, an industry will globalize in a way that reflects the net benefits by value activity. The activities in which global competitors gain competitive advantage will differ correspondingly. Configuration/coordina-

CHANGING PATTERNS OF INTERNATIONAL COMPETITION 23

tion determines the ongoing competitive advantages of a global strategy which are additive to competitive advantages a firm derives/possesses from its domestic market positions. An initial transfer of knowledge from the home base to subsidiaries is one, but by no means the most important, advantage of a global competitor.[14]

An industry such as commercial aircraft represents an extreme case of a global industry (in the upper right-hand corner of Figure 4). The three major competitors in this industry—Boeing, McDonnell Douglas, and Airbus—all have global strategies. In activities important to cost and differentiation in the industry, there are compelling net advantages to concentrating most activities and coordinating the dispersed activities extensively.[15] In R&D, there is a large fixed cost of developing an aircraft model ($1 billion or more) which requires worldwide sales to amortize. There are significant economies of scale in production, a steep learning curve in assembly (the learning curve was born out of research in this industry), and apparently significant advantages of locating R&D and production together. Sales of commercial aircraft are infrequent (via a highly skilled sales force), so that even the sales force can be partially concentrated in the home country and travel to buyers.

The costs of a concentrated configuration are relatively low in commercial aircraft. Product needs are homogenous, and there are the low transport costs of delivering the product to the buyer. Finally, worldwide coordination of the one dispersed activity, service, is very important—obviously standardized parts and repair advice have to be available wherever the plane lands.

As in every industry, there are structural features which work against a global strategy in commercial aircraft. These are all related to government, a not atypical circumstance. Government has a particular interest in commercial aircraft because of its large trade potential, the technological sophistication of the industry, its spillover effects to other industries, and its implications for national defense. Government also has an unusual degree of leverage in the industry: in many instances, it is the buyer. Many airlines are government owned, and a government official or appointee is head of the airline.

The competitive advantages of a global strategy are so great that all the successful aircraft producers have sought to achieve and preserve them. In addition, the power of government to intervene has been mitigated by the fact the there are few viable worldwide competitors and that there are the enormous barriers to entry created in part by the advantages of a global strategy. The result has been that firms have sought to assuage government through procurement. Boeing, for example, is very careful about where it buys components. In countries that are large potential customers, Boeing seeks to develop suppliers. This requires a great deal of extra effort by Boeing both to transfer technology and to work with

24   MICHAEL E. PORTER

suppliers to assure that they meet its standards. Boeing realizes that this is preferable to compromising the competitive advantage of its strongly integrated worldwide strategy. It is willing to employ one value activity (procurement) where the advantages of concentration are modest to help preserve the benefits of concentration in other activities. Recently, commercial aircraft competitors have entered into joint ventures and other coalition arrangements with foreign suppliers to achieve the same effect, as well as to spread the risk of huge development costs.

The extent and location of advantages from a global strategy vary among industries. In some industries, the competitive advantage from a global strategy comes in technology development, although firms gain little advantage in the primary activities so that these are dispersed around the world to minimize concentration costs. In other industries such as cameras or videocassette recorders, a firm cannot succeed without concentrating production to achieve economies of scale, but instead it gives subsidiaries much local autonomy in sales and marketing. In some industries, there is no net advantage to a global strategy and country-centered strategies dominate—the industry is multidomestic.

Segments or stages of an industry frequently vary in their pattern of globalization. In aluminum, the upstream (alumina and ingot) stages of the industry are global businesses. The downstream stage, semifabrication, is a group of multidomestic businesses because product needs vary by country, transport costs are high, and intensive local customer service is required. Scale economies in the value chain are modest. In lubricants, automotive oil tends to be a country-centered business while marine motor oil is a global business. In automotive oil, countries have varying driving standards, weather conditions, and local laws. Production involves blending various kinds of crude oils and additives, and is subject to few economies of scale but high shipping costs. Country-centered competitors such as Castrol and Quaker State are leaders in most countries. In the marine segment, conversely, ships move freely around the world and require the same oil everywhere. Successful competitors are global.

The ultimate leaders in global industries are often first movers—the first firms to perceive the possibilities for a global strategy. Boeing was the first global competitor in aircraft, for example, as was Honda in motorcycles, and Becton Dickinson in disposable syringes. First movers gain scale and learning advantages which are difficult to overcome. First mover effects are particularly important in global industries because of the association between globalization and economies of scale and learning achieved through worldwide configuration/coordination. Global leadership shifts if industry structural change provides opportunities for leapfrogging to new products or new technologies that nullify past leaders' scale and learning—again, the first mover to the new generation/technology often wins.

Global leaders often begin with some advantage at home, whether it be low labor cost or a product or marketing advantage. They use this as a lever to enter foreign markets. Once there, however, the global competitor converts the initial home advantage into competitive advantages that grow out of its overall worldwide system, such as production scale or ability to amortize R&D costs. While the initial advantage may have been hard to sustain, the global strategy creates new advantages which can be much more durable.

International strategy has often been characterized as a choice between worldwide standardization and local tailoring, or as the tension between the economic imperative (large-scale efficient facilities) and the political imperative (local content, local production). It should be clear from the discussion so far that neither characterization captures the richness of a firm's international strategy choices. A firm's choice of international strategy involves a search for competitive advantage from configuration/coordination throughout the value chain. A firm may standardize (concentrate) some activities and tailor (disperse) others. It may also be able to standardize and tailor at the same time through the coordination of dispersed activities, or use local tailoring of some activities (e.g., different product positioning in each country) to allow standardization of others (e.g., production). Similarly, the economic imperative is not always for a global strategy —in some industries a country-centered strategy is the economic imperative. Conversely, the political imperative is to concentrate activities in some industries where governments provide strong export incentives and locational subsidies.

Global Strategy vs. Comparative Advantage—Given the importance of trade theory to the study of international competition, it is useful to pause and reflect on the relationship to the framework I have presented to the notion of comparative advantage. Is there a difference? The traditional concept of comparative advantage is that factor-cost or factor-quality differences among countries lead to production of products in countries with an advantage which export them elsewhere in the world. Competitive advantage in this view, then, grows out of *where* a firm performs activities. The location of activities is clearly one source of potential advantage in a global firm. The global competitor can locate activities wherever comparative advantage lies, decoupling comparative advantage from its home base or country of ownership.

Indeed, the framework presented here suggests that the comparative advantage story is richer than typically told, because it not only involves production activities (the usual focus of discussions) but also applies to other activities in the value chain such as R&D, processing orders, or designing advertisements. Comparative advantage is specific to the *activity* and not the location of the value chain as a whole.[16] One of the potent advantages of the global firm is that it can spread activities among locations to reflect different preferred locations for different activities, something a

26   MICHAEL E. PORTER

domestic or country-centered competitor does not do. Thus components can be made in Taiwan, software written in India and basic R&D performed in Silicon Valley, for example. This international specialization of activities within the firm is made possible by the growing ability to coordinate and configure globally.

At the same time as our framework suggests a richer view of comparative advantage, however, it also suggests that many forms of competitive advantage for the global competitor derive less from *where* the firm performs activities than from *how* it performs them on a worldwide basis; economies of scale, proprietary learning, and differentiation with multinational buyers are not tied to countries but to the configuration and coordination of the firm's worldwide system. Traditional sources of comparative advantage can be very elusive and slippery sources of competitive advantage for an international competitor today, because comparative advantage frequently shifts. A country with the lowest labor cost is overtaken within a few years by some other country—facilities located in the first country then face a disadvantage. Moreover, falling direct labor as a percentage of total costs, increasing global markets for raw materials and other inputs, and freer flowing technology have diminished the role of traditional sources of comparative advantage.

My research on a broad cross-section of industries suggests that the achievement of sustainable world market leadership follows a more complex pattern than the exploitation of comparative advantage per se. A competitor often starts with a comparative advantage-related edge that provides the basis for penetrating foreign markets, but this edge is rapidly translated into a broader array of advantages that arise from a global approach to configuration and coordination as described earlier. Japanese firms, for example, have done a masterful job of converting temporary labor-cost advantages into durable systemwide advantages due to scale and proprietary know-how. Ultimately, the systemwide advantages are further reinforced with country-specific advantages such as brand identity as well as distribution channel access. Many Japanese firms were fortunate enough to make their transitions from country-based comparative advantage to global competitive advantage at a time when nobody paid much attention to them and there was a buoyant world economy. European and American competitors were willing to cede market share in "less desirable" segments such as the low end of the producer line, or so they thought. The Japanese translated these beachheads into world leadership by broadening their lines and reaping advantages in scale and proprietary technology. The Koreans and Taiwanese, the latest low labor cost entrants to a number of industries, may have a hard time replicating Japan's success, given slower growth, standardized products, and now alert competitors.

Global Platforms—The interaction of the home-country conditions and competitive advantages from a global strategy that transcend the country suggest a more complex role of the country in firm success than implied

CHANGING PATTERNS OF INTERNATIONAL COMPETITION   27

by the theory of comparative advantage. To understand this more complex role of the country, I define the concept of a *global platform*. A country is a desirable global platform in an industry if it provides an environment yielding firms domiciled in that country an advantage in competing globally in that particular industry.[17] An essential element of this definition is that it hinges on success *outside* the country, and not merely country conditions which allow firms to successfully master domestic competition. In global competition, a country must be viewed as a platform and not as the place where all a firm's activities are performed.

There are two determinants of a good global platform in an industry, which I have explored in more detail elsewhere.[18] The first is comparative advantage, or the factor endowment of the country as a site to perform particular activities in the industry. Today, simple factors such as low-cost unskilled labor and natural resources are increasingly less important to global competition compared to complex factors such as skilled scientific and technical personnel and advanced infrastructure. Direct labor is a minor proportion of cost in many manufactured goods and automation of non-production activities is shrinking it further, while markets for resources are increasingly global, and technology has widened the number of sources of many resources. A country's factor endowment is partly exogenous and partly the result of attention and investment in the country.

The second determinant of the attractiveness of a country as a global platform in an industry are the characteristics of a country's demand. A country's demand conditions include the size and timing of its demand in an industry, factors recognized as important by authors such as Linder and Vernon.[19] They also conclude the sophistication and power of buyers and channels and the product features and attributes demanded. Local demand conditions provide two potentially powerful sources of competitive advantage to a global competitor based in that country. The first is *first-mover advantages* in perceiving and implementing the appropriate global strategy. Pressing local needs, particularly peculiar ones, lead firms to embark early to solve local problems and gain proprietary know-how. This is then translated into scale and learning advantages as firms move early to compete globally. The other potential benefit of local demand conditions is a baseload of demand for product varieties that will be sought after in international markets. These two roles of the country in the success of a global firm reflect the interaction between conditions of local supply, the composition and timing of country demand, and economies of scale and learning in shaping international success.

The two determinants interact in important and sometimes counterintuitive ways. Local demand and needs frequently influence private and social investment in endogenous factors of production. A nation with oceans as borders and dependence on sea trade, for example, is more prone to have universities and scientific centers dedicated to oceanographic education and research. Similarly, factor endowment seems to influence local demand.

28   MICHAEL E. PORTER

The per capita consumption of wine is highest in wine-growing regions, for example.

Comparative disadvantage in some factors of production can be an advantage in global competition when combined with pressing local demand. Poor growing conditions have led Israeli farmers to innovate in irrigation and cultivation techniques, for example. The shrinking role in competition of simple factors of production relative to complex factors such as technical personnel seem to be enhancing the frequency and importance of such circumstances. What is important today is unleashing innovation in the proper direction, instead of passive exploitation of static cost advantages in a country which can shift rapidly and be overcome. International success today is a dynamic process resulting from continued development of products and processes. The forces which guide firms to undertake such activity thus become central to international competition.

A good example of the interplay among these factors is the television set industry. In the U.S., early demand was in large screen console sets because television sets were initially luxury items kept in the living room. As buyers began to purchase second and third sets, sets became smaller and more portable. They were used increasingly in the bedroom, the kitchen, the car, and elsewhere. As the television set industry matured, table model and portable sets became the universal product variety. Japanese firms, because of the small size of Japanese homes, cut their teeth on small sets. They dedicated most of their R&D to developing small picture tubes and to making sets more compact. In the process of naturally serving the needs of their home market, then, Japanese firms gained early experience and scale in segments of the industry that came to dominate world demand. U.S. firms, conversely, cut their teeth on large-screen console sets with fine furniture cabinets. As the industry matured, the experience base of U.S. firms was in a segment that was small and isolated to a few countries, notably the U.S. Japanese firms were able to penetrate world markets in a segment that was both uninteresting to foreign firms and in which they had initial scale, learning, and labor cost advantages. Ultimately the low-cost advantage disappeared as production was automated, but global scale and learning economies took over as the Japanese advanced product and process technology at a rapid pace.

The two broad determinants of a good global platform rest on the interaction between country characteristics and firms' strategies. The literature on comparative advantage, through focusing on country factor endowments, ignoring the demand side, and suppressing the individual firm, is most appropriate in industries where there are few economies of scale, little proprietary technology or technological change, or few possibilities for product differentiation.[20] While these industry characteristics are those of many traditionally traded goods, they describe few of today's important global industries.

The Evolution of International Competition

Having established a framework for understanding the globalization of industries, we are now in a position to view the phenomenon in historical perspective. If one goes back far enough, relatively few industries were global. Around 1880, most industries were local or regional in scope.[21] The reasons are rather self-evident in the context of our framework. There were few economies of scale in production until fuel-powered machines and assembly-line techniques emerged. There were heterogeneous product needs among regions within countries, much less among countries. There were few if any national media—the *Saturday Evening Post* was the first important national magazine in the U.S. and developed in the teens and twenties. Communicating between regions was difficult before the telegraph and telephone, and transportation was slow until the railroad system became well developed.

These structural conditions created little impetus for the widespread globalization of industry. Those industries that were global reflected classic comparative advantage considerations—goods were simply unavailable in some countries (who then imported them from others) or differences in the availability of land, resources, or skilled labor made some countries desirable suppliers to others. Export of local production was the form of global strategy adapted. There was little role or need for widespread government barriers to international trade during this period, although trade barriers were quite high in some countries for some commodities.

Around the 1880s, however, were the beginnings of what today has blossomed into the globalization of many industries. The first wave of modern global competitiors grew up in the late 1800s and early 1900s. Many industries went from local (or regional) to national in scope, and some began globalizing. Firms such as Ford, Singer, Gillette, National Cash Register, Otis, and Western Electric had commanding world market shares by the teens, and operated with integrated worldwide strategies. Early global competitors were principally American and European companies.

Driving this first wave of modern globalization were rising production scale economies due to advancements in technology that outpaced the growth of the world economy. Product needs also became more homogenized in different countries as knowledge and industrialization diffused. Transport improved, first through the railroad and steamships and later in trucking. Communication became easier with the telegraph then the telephone. At the same time, trade barriers were either modest or overwhelmed by the advantages of the new large-scale firms.

The burst of globalization soon slowed, however. Most of the few industries that were global moved increasingly towards a multidomestic pattern—multinationals remained, but between the 1920s and 1950 they often evolved towards federations of autonomous subsidiaries. The principal reason was a strong wave of nationalism and resulting high tariff barriers, partly caused by the world economic crisis and world wars. Another barrier to global strategies, chronicled by Chandler,[22] was a growing web of cartels and other interfirm contractual agreements. These limited the geographic spread of firms.

The early global competitors began rapidly dispersing their value chains. The situation of Ford Motor Company was no exception. While in 1925 Ford had almost no production outside the U.S., by World War II its overseas production had risen sharply. Firms that became multinationals during the interwar period tended to adopt country-centered strategies. European multinationals, operating in a setting where there were many sovereign countries within a relatively small geographical area, were quick to establish self-contained and quite autonomous subsidiaries in many countries. A more tolerant regulatory environment also encouraged European firms to form cartels and other cooperative agreements among themselves, which limited their foreign market entry.

Between the 1950s and the late 1970s, however, there was a strong reversal of the interwar trends. As Exhibit 1 illustrated, there have been very strong underlying forces driving the globalization of industries. The important reasons can be understood using the configuration/coordination dichotomy. The competitive advantage of competing worldwide from concentrated activities rose sharply, while concentration costs fell. There was a renewed rise in scale economies in many activities due to advancing technology. The minimum efficient scale of an auto assembly plant more than tripled between 1960 and 1975, for example, while the average cost of developing a new drug more than quadrupled.[23] The pace of technological change has increased, creating more incentive to amortize R&D costs against worldwide sales.

Product needs have continued to homogenize among countries, as income differences have narrowed, information and communication has flowed more freely around the world, and travel has increased.[24] Growing similarities in business practices and marketing systems (e.g., chain stores) in different countries have also been a facilitating factor in homogenizing needs. Within countries there has been a parallel trend towards greater market segmentation, which some observers see as contradictory to the view that product needs in different countries are becoming similar. However, segments today seem based less on country differences and more on buyer differences that transcend country boundaries, such as demographic, user industry, or income groups. Many firms successfully employ global focus strategies in which they serve a narrow segment of an industry worldwide, as do Daimler-Benz and Rolex.

Another driver of post-World War II globalization has been a sharp reduction in the real costs of transportation. This has occurred through innovations in transportation technology including increasingly large bulk carriers, container ships, and larger, more efficient aircraft. At the same time, government impediments to global configuration/coordination have been falling in the postwar period. Tariff barriers have gone down, international cartels and patent-sharing agreements have disappeared, and regional economic pacts such as the European Community have emerged to facilitate trade and investment, albeit imperfectly.

The ability to coordinate globally has also risen markedly in the postwar period. Perhaps the most striking reason is falling communication costs (in voice and data) and reduced travel time for individuals. The ability to coordinate activities in different countries has also been facilitated by growing similarities among countries in marketing systems, business practices, and infrastructure—country after country has developed supermarkets and mass distributors, television advertising, and so on. Greater international mobility of buyers and information has raised the payout to coordinating how a firm does business around the world. The increasing number of firms who are multinational has created growing possibilities for differentiation by suppliers who are global.

The forces underlying globalization have been self-reinforcing. The globalization of firms' strategies has contributed to the homogenization of buyer needs and business practices. Early global competitors must frequently stimulate the demand for uniform global varieties; for example, as Becton Dickinson did in disposable syringes and Honda did in motorcycles. Similarly, globalization of industries begets globalization of supplier industries—the increasing globalization of automotive component suppliers is a good example. Pioneering global competitors also stimulate the development and growth of international telecommunication infrastructure as well as the creation of global advertising media—e.g., *The Economist* and *The Wall Street Journal*.

Strategic Implications of Globalization

When the pattern of international competition shifts from multidomestic to global, there are many implications for the strategy of international firms. While a full treatment is beyond the scope of this paper, I will sketch some of the implications here.[25]

At the broadest level, globalization casts new light on many issues that have long been of interest to students of international business. In areas such as international finance, marketing, and business-government relations, the emphasis in the literature has been on the unique problems of adapting to local conditions and ways of doing business in a foreign country in a foreign currency. In a global industry, these concerns must be supplemented with an overriding focus on the ways and means of international configuration and coordination. In government relations, for example, the focus must shift from stand-alone negotiations with host countries (appropriate in multidomestic competition) to a recognition that negotiations

32   MICHAEL E. PORTER

in one country will both affect other countries and be shaped by possibilities
for performing activities in other countries. In finance, measuring the
performance of subsidiaries must be modified to reflect the contribution
of one subsidiary to another's cost position or differentiation in a global
strategy, instead of viewing each subsidiary as a stand-alone unit. In battling
with global competitors, it may be appropriate in some countries to accept
low profits indefinitely—in multidomestic competition this would be unjusti-
fied.[26] In global industries, the overall system matters as much or more
than the country.

Of the many other implications of globalization for the firm, there are
two of such significance that they deserve some treatment here. The first
is the role of *coalitions* in global strategy. A coalition is a long-term agreement linking firms but falling short of merger. I use the term coalition to
encompass a whole variety of arrangements that include joint vertnures,
licenses, supply agreements, and many other kinds of interfirm relationships. Such interfirm agreements have been receiving more attention in
the academic literature, although each form of agreement has been looked
at separately and the focus has been largely domestic.[27] International coalitions, linking firms in the same industry based in different countries, have
become an even more important part of international strategy in the past
decade.

International coalitions are a way of configuring activities in the value
chain on a worldwide basis jointly with a partner. International coalitions
are proliferating rapidly and are present in many industries.[28] There is a
particularly high incidence in automobiles, aircraft, aircraft engines, robotics, consumer electronics, semiconductors and pharmaceuticals. While international coalitions have long been present, their character has been
changing. Historically, a firm from a developed country formed a coalition
with a firm in a lesser-developed country to perform marketing activities
in that country. Today, we observe more and more coalitions in which
two firms from developed countries are teaming up to serve the world,
as well as coalitions that extend beyond marketing activities to encompass
activities throughout the value chain.[29] Production and R&D coalitions are
very common, for example.

Coalitions are a natural consequence of globalization and the need for
an integrated worldwide strategy. The same forces that lead to globalization
will prompt the formation of coalitions as firms confront the barriers to
establishing a global strategy of their own. The difficulties of gaining access
to foreign markets and in surmounting scale and learning thresholds in
production, technology development, and other activities have led many
firms to team up with others. In many industries, coalitions can be a
transitional state in the adjustment of firms to globalization, reflecting the
need of firms to catch up in technology, cure short-term imbalances between their global production networks and exchange rates, and accelerate

CHANGING PATTERNS OF INTERNATIONAL COMPETITION   33

the process of foreign market entry. Many coalitions are likely to persist in some form, however.

There are benefits and costs of coalitions as well as difficult implementation problems in making them succeed (which I have discussed elsewhere). How to choose and manage coalitions is among the most interesting questions in international strategy today. When one speaks to managers about coalitions, almost all have tales of disaster which vividly illustrate that coalitions often do not succeed. Also, there is the added burden of coordinating global strategy with a coalition partner because the partner often wants to do things its own way. Yet, in the face of copious corporate experience that coalitions do not work and a growing economics literature on transaction costs and contractual failures, we see a proliferation of coalitions today of the most difficult kind—those between companies in different countries.[30] There is a great need for researching in both the academic community and in the corporate world about coalitions and how to manage them. They are increasingly being forced on firms today by new competitive circumstances.

A second area where globalization carries particular importance is in *organizational structure*. The need to configure and coordinate globally in complex ways creates some obvious organizational challenges.[31] Any organization structure for competing internationally has to balance two dimensions; there has to be a *country* dimension (because some activities are inherently performed in the country) and there has to be a *global* dimension (because the advantages of global configuration/coordination must be achieved). In a global industry, the ultimate authority must represent the global dimension if a global strategy is to prevail. However, within any international firm, once it disperses any activities there are tremendous pressures to disperse more. Moreover, forces are unleashed which lead subsidiaries to seek growing autonomy. Local country managers will have a natural tendency to emphasize how different their country is and the consequent need for local tailoring and control over more activities in the value chain. Country managers will be loath to give up control over activities or how they are performed to outside forces. They will also frequently paint an ominous picture of host government concerns about local content and requirements for local presence. Corporate incentive systems frequently encourage such behavior by linking incentives narrowly to subsidiary results.

In successful global competitors, an environment is created in which the local managers seek to exploit similarities across countries rather than emphasize differences. They view the firms's global presence as an advantage to be tapped for their local gain. Adept global competitors often go to great lengths to devise ways of circumventing or adapting to local differences while preserving the advantages of the similarities. A good example is Canon's personal copier. In Japan, the typical paper size is

34 MICHAEL E. PORTER

bigger than American legal size and the standard European size. Canon's personal copier will not handle this size—a Japanese company introduced a product that did not meet its home market needs in the world's largest market for small copiers! Canon gathered its marketing managers from around the world and cataloged market needs in each country. They found that capacity to copy the large Japanese paper was only needed in Japan. In consultation with design and manufacturing engineers, it was determined that building this feature into the personal copier would significantly increase its complexity and cost. The decision was made to omit the feature because the price elasticity of demand for the personal copier was judged to be high. But this was not the end of the deliberations. Canon's management then set out to find a way to make the personal copier saleable in Japan. The answer that emerged was to add another feature to the copier—the ability to copy business cards—which both added little cost and was particularly valuable in Japan. This case illustrates the principle of looking for the similarities in needs among countries and in finding ways of creating similarities, not emphasizing the differences.

Such a change in orientation is something that typically occurs only grudgingly in a multinational company, particularly if it has historically operated in a country-centered mode (as has been the case with early U.S. and European multinationals). Achieving such a reorientation requires first that managers recognize that competitive success demands exploiting the advantages of a global strategy. Regular contact and discussion among subsidiary managers seems to be a prerequisite, as are information systems that allow operations in different countries to be compared.[32] This can be followed by programs for exchanging information and sharing know-how and then by more complex forms of coordination. Ultimately, the reconfiguring of activities globally may then be accepted, even though subsidiaries may have to give up control over some activities in the process.

The Future of International Competition

Since the late 1970s, there have been some gradual but significant changes in the pattern of intenational competition which carry important implications for international strategy. Our framework provides a template with which we can examine these changes and probe their significance. The factors shaping the global configuration of activities by firms are developing in ways which contrast with the trends of the previous thirty years. Homogenization of product needs among countries appears to be continuing, though segmentation within countries is as well. As a result, consumer packaged goods are becoming increasingly prone toward globalization, though they have long been characterized by multidomestic competition. There are also signs of globalization in some service industries as the introduction of information technology creates scale economies in support activities and facilitates coordination in primary activities. Global service

Figure 6. Future Trends in International Competition

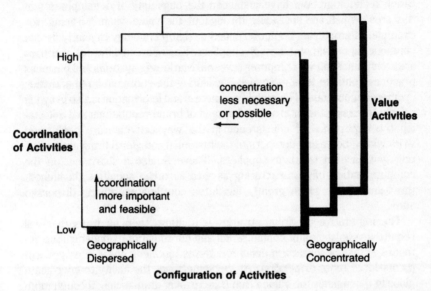

firms are reaping advantages in hardware and software development as well as procurement.

In many industries, however, limits have been reached in the scale economies that have been driving the concentration of activities. These limits grow out of classic diseconomies of scale that arise in very large facilities, as well as out of new, more flexible technology in manufacturing and other activities that is often not as scale sensitive as previous methods. At the same time, though, flexible manufacturing allows the production of multiple varieties (to serve different countries) in a single plant. This may encourage new movement towards globalization in industries in which product differences among countries have remained significant and have blocked globalization in the past.

There also appear to be some limits to further decline in transport costs, as innovations such as containerization, bulk ships, and larger aircraft have run their course. However, a parallel trend toward smaller, lighter products and components may keep some downward pressure on transport costs. The biggest change in the benefits and costs of concentrated configuration has been the sharp rise in protectionism in recent years and the resulting rise in nontariff barriers, harkening back to the 1920s. As a group, these factors point to less need and less opportunity for highly concentrated configurations of activities.

36   MICHAEL E. PORTER

When we examine the coordination dimension, the picture looks starkly different. Communication and coordination costs are dropping sharply, driven by breathtaking advances in information systems and telecommunication technology. We have just seen the beginning of developments in this area, which are spreading throughout the value chain.[33] Boeing, for example, is employing computer-aided design technology to jointly design components on-line with foreign suppliers. Engineers in different countries are communicating via computer screens. Marketing systems and business practices continue to homogenize, facilitating the coordination of activities in different countries. The mobility of buyers and information is also growing rapidly, greasing the international spread of brand reputations and enhancing the importance of consistency in the way activities are performed worldwide. Increasing numbers of multinational and global firms are begetting globalization by their suppliers. There is also a sharp rise in the computerization of manufacturing as well as other activities throughout the value chain, which greatly facilitates coordination among dispersed sites.

The imperative of global strategy is shifting, then, in ways that will require a rebalancing of configuration and coordination. Concentrating activities is less necessary in economic terms, and less possible as governments force more dispersion. At the same time, the ability to coordinate globally throughout the value chain is increasing dramatically through modern technology. The need to coordinate is also rising to offset greater dispersion and to respond to buyer needs.

Thus, today's game of global strategy seems increasingly to be a game of coordination—getting more and more dispersed production facilities, R&D laboratories, and marketing activities to truly work together. Yet, widespread coordination is the exception rather than the rule today in many multinationals, as I have noted. The imperative for coordination raises many questions for organizational structure, and is complicated even more when the firm has built its global system using coalitions with independent firms.

Japan has clearly been the winner in the postwar globalization of competition. Japan's firms not only had an initial labor cost advantage but the orientation and skills to translate this into more durable competitive advantages such as scale and proprietary technology. The Japanese context also offered an excellent platform for globalization in many industries, given postwar environmental and technological trends. With home market conditions favoring compactness, a lead in coping with high energy costs, and a national conviction to raise quality, Japan has proved a fertile incubator of global leaders. Japanese multinationals had the advantage of embarking on international strategies in the 1950s and 1960s when the imperatives for a global approach to strategy were beginning to accelerate, but without the legacy of past international investments and modes of behavior.[34]

CHANGING PATTERNS OF INTERNATIONAL COMPETITION   37

Japanese firms also had an orientation towards highly concentrated activities that fit the strategic imperative of the time. Most European and American multinationals, conversely, were well established internationally before the war. They had legacies of local subsidiary autonomy that reflected the interwar environment. As Japanese firms spread internationally, they dispersed activities only grudgingly and engaged in extensive global coordination. European and country-centered American companies struggled to rationalize overly dispersed configurations of activities and to boost the level of global coordination among foreign units. They found their decentralized organization structures—so fashionable in the 1960s and 1970s—to be a hindrance to doing so.

As today's international firms contemplate the future, Japanese firms are rapidly dispersing activities, due largely to protectionist pressures but also because of the changing economic factors I have described. They will have to learn the lessons of managing overseas activities that many European and American firms learned long ago. However, Japanese firms enjoy an organizational style that is supportive of coordination and a strong commitment to introducing new technologies such as information systems that facilitate it. European firms must still overcome their country-centered heritage. Many still do not compete with truly global strategies and lack modern technology. Moreover, the large number of coalitions formed by European firms must overcome the barriers to coordination if they are not to prove ultimately limiting. The European advantage may well be in exploiting an acute and well-developed sensitivity to local market conditions as well as a superior ability to work with host governments. By using modern flexible manufacturing technology and computerizing elsewhere in the value chain, European firms may be able to serve global segments and better differentiate products.

Many American firms tend to fall somewhere in between the European and Japanese situations. Their awareness of international competition has risen dramatically in recent years, and efforts at creating global strategies are more widespread. The American challenge is to catch the Japanese in a variety of technologies, as well as to learn how to gain the benefits of coordinating among dispersed units instead of becoming trapped by the myths of decentralization. The changing pattern of international competition is creating an environment in which no competitor can afford to allow country parochialism to impede its ability to turn a worldwide position into a competitive edge.

References

1. United Nations Center on Transnational Corporations, *Salient Features and Trends in Foreign Direct Investment* (New York, NY: United Nations, 1984).
2. For a survey, see R.E. Caves and Ronald W. Jones, *World Trade and Payments*, 4th ed. (Boston, MA: Little, Brown, 1985).

38   MICHAEL E. PORTER

3. There are many books on the theory and management of the multinational, which are too numerous to cite here. For an excellent survey of the literature, see R.E. Caves, *Multinational Enterprise and Econonomic Analysis* (Cambridge, England: Cambridge University Press, 1982).

4. Raymond Vernon, "International Investment and International Trade in the Product Cycle," *Quarterly Journal of Economics*, Vol. 80 (May 1966):190-207. Vernon himself, among others, has raised questions about how general the product cycle pattern is today.

5. Michael E. Porter, *Competitive Strategy: Techniques for Analyzing Industries and Competitors* (New York, NY: The Free Press, 1980); Michael E. Porter, "Beyond Comparative Advantage," Working Paper, Harvard Graduate School of Business Administration, August 1985.

6. For a description of this research, see Michael E. Porter, ed., *Competition in Global Industries* (Boston, MA: Harvard Business School Press, forthcoming).

7. The distinction between multidomestic and global competition and some of its strategic implications were described in T. Hout, Michael E. Porter, and E. Rudden, "How Global Companies Win Out," *Harvard Business Review* (September/October 1982), pp. 98-108.

8. Howard V. Perlmutter, "The Tortuous Evolution of the Multinational Corporation," *Columbia Journal of World Business* (January/February 1969), pp. 9-18. Perlmutter's concept of ethnocentric, polycentric, and geocentric multinationals takes the *firm* not the industry as the unit of analysis and is decoupled from industry structure. It focuses on management attitudes, the nationality of executives, and other aspects of organization. Perlmutter presents ethnocentric, polycentric, and geocentric as stages of an organization's development as a multinational, with geocentric as stages of an organization's development as a multinational, with geocentric as the goal. A later paper (Yoram Wind, Susan P. Douglas, and Howard V. Perlmutter, "Guidelines for Developing International Marketing Strategies," *Journal of Marketing*, Vol. 37 (April 1973: 14-23) tempers this conclusion based on the fact that some companies may not have the required sophistication in marketing to attempt a geocentric strategy. Products embedded in the lifestyle or culture of a country are also identified as less susceptible to geocentrism. The Perlmutter et al. view does not link management orientation to industry structure and strategy. International strategy should grow out of the net competitive advantage in a global industry of different types of worldwide coordination. In some industries, a country-centered strategy, roughly analogous to Perlmutter's polycentric idea, may be the best strategy irrespective of company size an international experience. Conversely, a global strategy may be imperative given the competitive advantage that accrues from it. Industry and strategy should define the organization approach, not vice versa.

9. Michael E. Porter, *Competitive Advantage: Creating and Sustaining Superior Performance* (New York, NY: The Free Press, 1985).

10. Buzzell (Robert D. Buzzell, "Can You Standardize Multinational Marketing," *Harvard Business Review* [November/December 1980], pp. 102-113); Pryor (Millard H. Pryor, "Planning in a World-Wide Business," *Harvard Business Review*, Vol. 23 [January/February 1965]); and Wind, Douglas, and Perlmutter (op. cit.) point out that national differences are in most cases more critical with respect to marketing than with production and finance. This generalization reflects the fact that marketing activities are often inherently country-based. However, this generalization is not reliable because in many industries, production and other activities are widely dispersed.

11. A number of authors have framed the globalization of industries in terms of the balance between imperatives for global integration and imperatives for national responsiveness, a useful distinction. See, C.K. Prahalad, "The Stategic Process in a Multinational Corporation," unpublished DBA dissertation, Harvard Graduate School of Business Administration, 1975; Yves Doz, "National Policies and Multinational Management," an unpublished DBA dissertation, Harvard Graduate School of Business Administration, 1976; and Christopher

CHANGING PATTERNS OF INTERNATIONAL COMPETITION   39

A. Bartlett, "Multinational Structural Evolution: The Changing Decision Environment in the International Division," unpublished DBA dissertation, Harvard Graduate School of Business Administration, 1979. I link the distinction here to where and how a firm performs the activities in the value chain internationally.

12. See, for example, Oliver Williamson, *Markets and Hierarchies* (New York, NY: The Free Press, 1975). For an international application, see Mark C. Casson, "Transaction Costs and the Theory of the Multinational Enterprise," in Alan Rugman, ed., *New Theories of the Multinational Enterprise* (London: Croom Helm, 1982); David J. Teece, "Transaction Cost Economics and the Multinational Enterprise: An Assessment," *Journal of Economic Behavior and Organization* (forthcoming, 1986).

13. The difficulties in coordinating are internationally parallel to those in coordinating across business units competing in different industries with the diversified firm. See Michael E. Porter, *Competitive Advantage: Creating and Sustaining Superior Performance* (New York, NY: The Free Press, 1985), Chapter 11.

14. Empirical research has found a strong correlation between R&D and advertising intensity and the extent of foreign direct investment (for a survey, see Caves, 1982, op cit.). Both these factors have a place in our model of the determinants of globalization, but for quite different reasons. R&D intensity suggests scale advantages for the global competitor in developing products or processes that are manufactured abroad either due to low production scale economies or government pressures, or which require investments in service infrastructure. Advertising intensity, however, is much closer to the classic transfer of marketing knowledge to foreign subsidiaries. High advertising industries are also frequently those where local tastes differ and manufacturing scale economies are modest, both reasons to disperse many activities.

15. For an interesting description of the industry, see the paper by Michael Yoshino in Porter, ed., op. cit., (forthcoming).

16. It has been recognized that comparative advantage in different stages in a vertically integrated industry sector such as aluminum can reside in different countries. Bauxite mining will take place in resource-rich countries, for example, while smelting will take place in countries with low electrical power cost. See R.E. Caves and Ronald W. Jones, op. cit. The argument here extends this thinking *within* the value chain of any stage and suggests that the optimal location for performing individual activities may vary as well.

17. The firm need not necessarily be owned by investors in the country, but the country is its home base for competing in a particular country.

18. See Porter, *Competitive Advantage*, op. cit.

19. See S. Linder, *An Essay on Trade and Transformation* (New York, NY: John Wiley, 1961); Vernon, op. cit., (1966); W. Gruber, D. Mehta, and R. Vernon, "R&D Factor in International Trade and International Investment of United States Industries," *Journal of Political Economics*, 76/1 (1967):20-37.

20. Where it does recognize scale economies, trade theory views them narrowly as arising from production in one country.

21. See Alfred Chandler in Porter, ed., op. cit., (forthcoming) for a penetrating history of the origins of the large industrial firm and its expansion abroad, which is consistent with the discussion here.

22. Ibid.

23. For data on auto assembly, see "Note on the World Auto Industry in Transition," Harvard Business School Case Services (#9-382-122).

24. For a supporting view, see Theodore Levitt, "The Globalization of Markets," *Harvard Business Review* (May/June 1983), pp. 92-102.

25. The implications of the shift from multidomestic to global competition were the theme of a series of papers on each functional area of the firm prepared for the Harvard Business School Colloquium on Competition in Global Industries. See Porter, ed., op. cit., (forthcoming).

40   MICHAEL E. PORTER

26. For a discussion, see Hout, Porter, and Rudden, op. cit. For a recent treatment, see Gary Hamel and C.K. Prahalad, "Do You Really Have a Global Strategy," *Harvard Business Review* (July/August 1985), pp. 139-148.

27. David J. Teece, "Firm Boundaries, Technological Innovation, and Strategic Planning," in L.G. Thomas, ed., *Economics of Strategic Planning* (Lexington, MA: Lexington Books, 1985).

28. For a treatment of coalitions from this perspective, see Porter, Fuller, and Rawlinson, in Porter, ed., op. cit., (forthcoming).

29. Hladik's recent study of international joint ventures provides supporting evidence. See K. Hladik, "International Joint Ventures: An Empirical Investigation into the Characteristics of Recent U.S.-Foreign Joint Venture Partnerships," unpublished Doctoral dissertation, Business Economics Program, Harvard University, 1984.

30. For the seminal work on contractual failures, see Williamson, op. cit.

31. For a thorough and sophisticated treatment, see Christopher A. Bartlett's paper in Porter, ed., op. cit., (forthcoming).

32. For a good discussion of the mechanisms for facilitating international coordination in operations and technology development, see M.T. Flaherty in Porter, ed., op. cit., (forthcoming). Flaherty stresses the importance of information systems and the many dimensions that valuable coordination can take.

33. For a discussion, see Michael E. Porter and Victor Millar, "How Information Gives You Competitive Advantage," *Harvard Business Review* (July/August 1985), pp. 149-160.

34. Prewar international sales enjoyed by Japanese firms were handled largely through trading companies. See Chandler, op. cit.

[25]

Global Strategy. . .
In a World of Nations?

George S. Yip

Georgetown University

THIS ARTICLE gives a detailed framework for evaluating whether—and how—to globalize an individual firm's corporate strategy. The author stresses the opportunities for gaining competitive advantage and provides examples of companies that have exploited globalization drivers and strategy levers. He also discusses the relative merits of *global* and *multidomestic* strategies in various strategic situations. *Ed.*

Sloan
Management
Review

29

Fall 1989

WHETHER TO GLOBALIZE, and how to globalize, have become two of the most burning strategy issues for managers around the world. Many forces are driving companies around the world to globalize by expanding their participation in foreign markets. Almost every product market in the major world economies—computers, fast food, nuts and bolts—has foreign competitors. Trade barriers are also falling; the recent United States/Canada trade agreement and the impending 1992 harmonization in the European Community are the two most dramatic examples. Japan is gradually opening up its long barricaded markets. Maturity in domestic markets is also driving companies to seek international expansion. This is particularly true of U.S. companies that, nourished by the huge domestic market, have typically lagged behind their European and Japanese rivals in internationalization.

Companies are also seeking to globalize by integrating their worldwide strategy. Such global integration contrasts with the multinational approach whereby companies set up country subsidiaries that design, produce, and market products or services tailored to local needs. This multinational model (also described as a "multidomestic strategy") is now in question.[1] Several changes seem to increase the likelihood that, in some industries, a global strategy will be more successful than a multidomestic one. One of these changes, as argued forcefully and controversially by Levitt, is the growing similarity of what citizens of different countries want to buy.[2] Other changes include the reduction of tariff and

nontariff barriers, technology investments that are becoming too expensive to amortize in one market only, and competitors that are globalizing the rules of the game.

Companies want to know how to globalize—in other words, expand market participation—and how to develop an integrated worldwide strategy. As depicted in Figure 1, three steps are essential in developing a total worldwide strategy:
• Developing the core strategy—the basis of sustainable competitive advantage. It is usually developed for the home country first.
• Internationalizing the core strategy through international expansion of activities and through adaptation.
• Globalizing the international strategy by integrating the strategy across countries.

Multinational companies know the first two steps well. They know the third step less well since globalization runs counter to the accepted wisdom of tailoring for national markets.[3]

This article makes a case for how a global strategy might work and directs managers toward opportunities to exploit globalization. It also presents the drawbacks and costs of globalization. Figure 2 lays out a framework for thinking through globalization issues.[4]

Industry globalization drivers (underlying market, cost, and other industry conditions) are externally determined, while global strategy levers are choices available to the worldwide business. Drivers create the potential for a multinational business to achieve the benefits of global strategy. To achieve

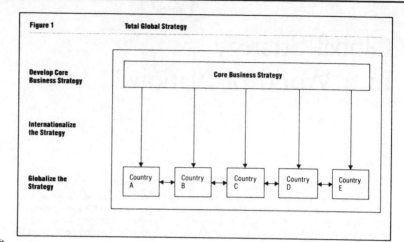

Figure 1   Total Global Strategy

Develop Core
Business Strategy

Internationalize
the Strategy

Globalize the
Strategy

Global
Strategy

30

Yip

George S. Yip is Visiting Associate Professor at the School of Business Administration, Georgetown University, and also Director of the PIMS Global Strategy Program. Dr. Yip holds the B.A. and M.A. degrees from Cambridge University, the M.B.A. degree from Cranfield Institute of Technology, and the M.B.A. and D.B.A. degrees from the Graduate School of Business Administration, Harvard University. His business experience includes marketing and advertising responsibilities with Unilever and Lintas and management consulting with Price Waterhouse and the MAC Group. He is the author of Barriers to Entry and of numerous articles.

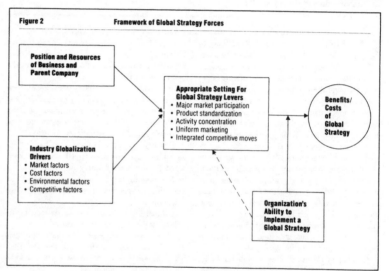

Figure 2   Framework of Global Strategy Forces

these benefits, a multinational business needs to set its *global strategy levers* (e.g., use of product standardization) appropriately to industry drivers, and to the position and resources of the business and its parent company.[5] The organization's ability to implement the strategy affects how well the benefits can be achieved.

What Is Global Strategy?

Setting strategy for a worldwide business requires making choices along a number of strategic dimensions. Table 1 lists five such dimensions or "global strategy levers" and their respective positions under a pure multidomestic strategy and a pure global strategy. Intermediate positions are, of course, feasible. For each dimension, a multidomestic strategy seeks to maximize worldwide performance by maximizing local competitive advantage, revenues, or profits; a global strategy seeks to maximize worldwide performance through sharing and integration.

Market Participation

In a multidomestic strategy, countries are selected on the basis of their stand-alone potential for revenues and profits. In a global strategy, countries need to be selected for their potential contribution to globalization benefits. This may mean entering a market that is unattractive in its own right, but has global strategic significance, such as the home market of a global competitor. Or it may mean building share in a limited number of key markets rather than undertaking more widespread coverage. A pattern of major share in major markets is advocated in Ohmae's USA-Europe-Japan "triad" concept.[6] In contrast, under a multidomestic strategy, no particular pattern of participation is required—rather, the pattern accrues from the pursuit of local advantage. The Electrolux Group, the Swedish appliance giant, is pursuing a strategy of building significant share in major world markets. The company aims to be the first global appliance maker. In 1986, Electrolux took over Zanussi Industries to become the top producer of appliances in Western Europe. Later that year, Electrolux acquired White Consolidated Industries, the third largest American appliance manufacturer.

Product Offering

In a multidomestic strategy, the products offered in each country are tailored to local needs. In a global strategy, the ideal is a standardized core product that requires minimal local adaptation. Cost reduction is usually the most important benefit of product standardization. Levitt has made the most extreme case for product standardization. Others stress the need for flexibility, or the need for a broad product portfolio, with many product varieties in order to share technologies and distribution channels.[7] In practice, some multinationals have pursued product standardization to a greater or lesser extent.[8] Differing worldwide needs can be met by adapting a standardized core product. In the early 1970s, sales of the Boeing 737 began to level off. Boeing turned to developing countries as an attractive new market, but found initially that its product did not fit the new environments. Because of the shortness of runways, their greater softness, and the lower technical expertise of their pilots, the planes tended to bounce a great deal. When the planes bounced on landing, the brakes failed. To fix this problem, Boeing modified the design by adding thrust to the engines, redesigning the wings and landing gear, and installing tires with lower pressure. These adaptations to a standardized core product enabled the 737 to become the best selling plane in history.

Location of Value-Added Activities

In a multidomestic strategy, all or most of the value chain is reproduced in every country. In another type of international strategy—exporting—most of the value chain is kept in one country. In a global strategy, costs are reduced by breaking up the value chain so each activity may be conducted in a different country. One value chain strategy is partial concentration and partial duplication. The key feature of a global position on this dimension is the strategic placement of the value chain around the globe.

Many electronics companies now locate part or all of their manufacturing operations in Southeast Asia because of that region's low-cost, skilled labor. In addition, a key component (the semiconductor chip) is very cheap there. Under the United States-Japan Semiconductor Agreement, the Japanese agreed not to sell chips in the United States below cost. But in an industry plagued by overcapacity, the chips had to go somewhere. The agreement resulted in Japanese chips being sold below cost in Southeast Asia. The lower cost of chips

Sloan
Management
Review

31

Fall 1989

Table 1	Globalization Dimensions/Global Strategy Levers	
Dimension	Setting for Pure Multidomestic Strategy	Setting for Pure Global Strategy
Market Participation	No particular pattern	Significant share in major markets
Product Offering	Fully customized in each country	Fully standardized worldwide
Location of Value-Added Activities	All activities in each country	Concentrated—one activity in each (different) country
Marketing Approach	Local	Uniform worldwide
Competitive Moves	Stand-alone by country	Integrated across countries

combined with the lower labor cost has attracted many manufacturers of computers and other electronic equipment to Southeast Asia.

Marketing Approach

In a multidomestic strategy, marketing is fully tailored for each country, being developed locally. In a global strategy, a uniform marketing approach is applied around the world, although not all elements of the marketing mix need be uniform.[9] Unilever achieved great success with a fabric softener that used a globally common positioning, advertising theme, and symbol (a teddy bear), but a brand name that varied by country. Similarly, a product that serves a common need can be geo-

graphically expanded with a uniform marketing program, despite differences in marketing environments.

Competitive Moves

In a multidomestic strategy, the managers in each country make competitive moves without regard for what happens in other countries. In a global strategy, competitive moves are integrated across countries. The same type of move is made in different countries at the same time or in a systematic sequence: a competitor is attacked in one country in order to drain its resources for another country, or a competitive attack in one country is countered in a different country. Perhaps the best ex-

Figure 3	How Global Strategy Levers Achieve Globalization Benefits				
	Benefits				**Major Drawbacks**
Global Strategy Levers	**Cost Reduction**	**Improved Quality of Products and Programs**	**Enhanced Customer Preference**	**Increased Competitive Leverage**	**All Levers Incur Coordination Costs, Plus**
Major Market Participation	Increases volume for economies of scale		Via global availability, global serviceability, and global recognition	Advantage of earlier entry Provides more sites for attack and counter-attack, hostage for good behavior	Earlier or greater commitment to a market than warranted on own merits
Product Standardization	Reduces duplication of development efforts Allows concentration of production to exploit economies of scale	Focuses development and management resources	Allows consumers to use familiar product while abroad Allows organizations to use same product across country units	Basis for low-cost invasion of markets	Less responsive to local needs
Activity Concentration	Reduces duplication of activities Helps exploit economies of scale Exploits differences in country factor costs Partial concentration allows flexibility vs. currency changes, and vs. bargaining parties	Focuses effort Allows more consistent quality control		Allows maintenance of cost advantage independent of local conditions	Distances activities from the customer Increases currency risk
Uniform Marketing	Reduces design and production costs of marketing programs	Focuses talent and resources Leverages scarce, good ideas	Reinforces marketing messages by exposing customer to same mix in different countries		Reduces adaptation to local customer behavior and marketing environment
Integrated Competitive Moves				Provides more options and leverage in attack and defense	Local competitiveness may be sacrificed

ample is the counterattack in a competitor's home market as a parry to an attack on one's own home market. Integration of competitive strategy is rarely practised, except perhaps by some Japanese companies.[10]

Bridgestone Corporation, the Japanese tire manufacturer, tried to integrate its competitive moves in response to global consolidation by its major competitors—Continental AG's acquisition of Gencorp's General Tire and Rubber Company, General Tire's joint venture with two Japanese tire makers, and Sumitomo's acquisition of an interest in Dunlop Tire. These competitive actions forced Bridgestone to establish a presence in the major U.S. market in order to maintain its position in the world tire market. To this end, Bridgestone formed a joint venture to own and manage Firestone Corporation's worldwide tire business. This joint venture also allowed Bridgestone to gain access to Firestone's European plants.

Benefits of a Global Strategy

Companies that use global strategy levers can achieve one or more of these benefits (see Figure 3):[11]

- cost reductions;
- improved quality of products and programs;
- enhanced customer preference; and
- increased competitive leverage.

Cost Reductions

An integrated global strategy can reduce worldwide costs in several ways. A company can increase the benefits from economies of scale by *pooling production or other activities* for two or more countries. Understanding the potential benefit of these economies of scale, Sony Corporation has concentrated its compact disc production in Terre Haute, Indiana, and Salzburg, Austria.

A second way to cut costs is by *exploiting lower factor costs* by moving manufacturing or other activities to low-cost countries. This approach has, of course, motivated the recent surge of offshore manufacturing, particularly by U.S. firms. For example, the Mexican side of the U.S.-Mexico border is now crowded with "maquiladoras"—manufacturing plants set up and run by U.S. companies using Mexican labor.

Global strategy can also cut costs by *exploiting flexibility*. A company with manufacturing locations

in several countries can move production from location to location on short notice to take advantage of the lowest costs at a given time. Dow Chemical takes this approach to minimize the cost of producing chemicals. Dow uses a linear programming model that takes account of international differences in exchange rates, tax rates, and transportation and labor costs. The model comes up with the best mix of production volume by location for each planning period.

An integrated global strategy can also reduce costs by *enhancing bargaining power*. A company whose strategy allows for switching production among different countries greatly increases its bargaining power with suppliers, workers, and host governments. Labor unions in European countries are very concerned that the creation of the single European market after 1992 will allow companies to switch production from country to country at will. This integrated production strategy would greatly enhance companies' bargaining power at the expense of unions.

Improved Quality of Products and Programs

Under a global strategy, companies focus on a smaller number of products and programs than under a multidomestic strategy. This concentration can improve both product and program quality. Global focus is one reason for Japanese success in automobiles. Toyota markets a far smaller number of models around the world than does General Motors, even allowing for its unit sales being half that of General Motors's. Toyota has concentrated on improving its few models while General Motors has fragmented its development funds. For example, the Toyota Camry is the U.S. version of a basic worldwide model and is the successor to a long line of development efforts. The Camry is consistently rated as the best in its class of medium-sized cars. In contrast, General Motors's Pontiac Fiero started out as one of the most successful small sports cars, but was recently withdrawn. Industry observers blamed this on a failure to invest development money to overcome minor problems.

Enhanced Customer Preference

Global availability, serviceability, and recognition can enhance customer preference through reinforcement. Soft drink and fast food companies are, of

Sloan Management Review

33

Fall 1989

course, leading exponents of this strategy. Many suppliers of financial services, such as credit cards, must have a global presence because their service is travel-related. Manufacturers of industrial products can also exploit this benefit. A supplier that can provide a multinational customer with a standard product around the world gains from worldwide familiarity. Computer manufacturers have long pursued this strategy.

Increased Competitive Leverage

A global strategy provides more points from which to attack and counterattack competitors. In an effort to prevent the Japanese from becoming a competitive nuisance in disposable syringes, Becton Dickinson, a major U.S. medical products company, decided to enter three markets in Japan's backyard. Becton entered the Hong Kong, Singapore, and Philippine markets to prevent further Japanese expansion.[12]

Drawbacks of Global Strategy

Globalization can incur significant management costs through increased coordination, reporting requirements, and even added staff. It can also reduce the firm's effectiveness in individual countries if overcentralization hurts local motivation and morale. In addition, each global strategy lever has particular drawbacks.

A global strategy approach to *market participation* can incur an earlier or greater commitment to a market than is warranted on its own merits. Many American companies, such as Motorola, are struggling to penetrate Japanese markets, more in order to enhance their global competitive position than to make money in Japan for its own sake.

Product standardization can result in a product that does not entirely satisfy *any* customers. When companies first internationalize, they often offer their standard domestic product without adapting it for other countries, and suffer the consequences. For example, Procter & Gamble stumbled recently when it introduced Cheer laundry detergent in Japan without changing the U.S. product or marketing message (that the detergent was effective in all temperatures). After experiencing serious losses, P&G discovered two instances of insufficient adaptation. First, the detergent did not suds up as it should because the Japanese use a great deal of fabric

softener. Second, the Japanese usually wash clothes in either cold tap water or bath water, so the claim of working in all temperatures was irrelevant. Cheer became successful in Japan only after the product was reformulated and the marketing message was changed.

A globally standardized product is designed for the global market but can seldom satisfy all needs in all countries. For instance, Canon, a Japanese company, sacrificed the ability to copy certain Japanese paper sizes when it first designed a photocopier for the global market.

Activity concentration distances customers and can result in lower responsiveness and flexibility. It also increases currency risk by incurring costs and revenues in different countries. Recently volatile exchange rates have required companies that concentrate their production to hedge their currency exposure.

Uniform marketing can reduce adaptation to local customer behavior. For example, the head office of British Airways mandated that every country use the "Manhattan Landing" television commercial developed by advertising agency Saatchi and Saatchi. While the commercial did win many awards, it has been criticized for using a visual image (New York City) that was not widely recognized in many countries.

Integrated competitive moves can mean sacrificing revenues, profits, or competitive position in individual countries, particularly when the subsidiary in one country is asked to attack a global competitor in order to send a signal or to divert that competitor's resources from another country.

Finding the Balance

The most successful worldwide strategies find a balance between overglobalizing and underglobalizing. The ideal strategy matches the level of strategy globalizaton to the globalization potential of the industry. In Figure 4 both Business A and Business C achieve balanced global and national strategic advantage. Business A does so with a low level of strategy globalization to match the low globalization potential of its industry (e.g., frozen food products). Business C uses a high level of strategy globalization to match the high globalization potential of its industry (e.g., computer equipment). Business B is at a global disadvantage because it uses a strategy that is less globalized than the potential offered by its industry. The business is failing to exploit potential global benefits such as cost savings via product standardization. Business D is at a national disadvantage because it is too globalized relative to the potential offered by its industry. The business is not tailoring its products and programs as much as it should. While there is no systematic evidence, executives' comments suggest that far more businesses suffer from insufficient globalization than from excessive globalization. Figure 4 is oversimplified in that it shows only one overall dimension for both strategy and industry potential. As argued earlier, a global strategy has five major dimensions and many subdimensions. Similarly, the potential of industry globalization is multidimensional.

Industry Globalization Drivers

To achieve the benefits of globalization, the managers of a worldwide business need to recognize when industry globalization drivers (industry conditions) provide the opportunity to use global strategy levers. These drivers can be grouped in four categories: market, cost, governmental, and competitive. Each industry globalization driver affects the potential use of global strategy levers (see Figure 5).

Market Drivers

Market globalization drivers depend on customer behavior and the structure of distribution channels. These drivers affect the use of all five global strategy levers.
• **Homogeneous Customer Needs.** When customers in different countries want essentially the same type of product or service (or can be so persuaded), opportunities arise to market a standardized product. Understanding which aspects of the product can be standardized and which should be customized is key. In addition, homogeneous needs make participation in a large number of markets easier because fewer different product offerings need to be developed and supported.
• **Global Customers.** Global customers buy on a centralized or coordinated basis for decentralized use. The existence of global customers both allows and requires a uniform marketing program. There are two types of global customers: national and multinational. A national global customer searches the world for suppliers but uses the purchased prod-

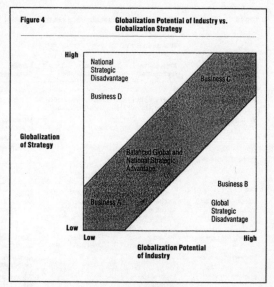

Figure 4   **Globalization Potential of Industry vs. Globalization Strategy**

uct or service in one country. National defense agencies are a good example. A multinational global customer also searches the world for suppliers, but uses the purchased product or service in many countries. The World Health Organization's purchase of medical products is an example. Multinational global customers are particularly challenging to serve and often require a global account management program. Companies that implement such programs have to beware of global customers using the unified account management to extract lower global prices. Having a single global account manager makes it easier for a global customer to negotiate a single global price. Typically, the global customer pushes for the lowest country price to become the global price. But a good global account manager should be able to justify differences in prices across countries.
• **Global Channels.** Analogous to global customers, channels of distribution may buy on a global or at least a regional basis. Global channels or middlemen are also important in exploiting differences in prices by buying at a lower price in one country and selling at a higher price in another country. Their presence makes it more necessary for a business to rationalize its worldwide pric-

Figure 5   **Effects of Industry Globalization Drivers on the Potential Use of Global Strategy Levers**

Strategy Levers

Industry Drivers	Major Market Participation	Product Standardization	Activity Concentration	Uniform Marketing	Integrated Competitive Moves
Market					
Homogeneous needs	Fewer varieties needed to serve many markets	Standardized product is more acceptable			Allows sequenced invasion of markets
Global customers			Marketing process has to be coordinated	Marketing content needs to be uniform	
Global channels			Marketing process has to be coordinated	Marketing content needs to be uniform	
Transferable marketing	Easier to expand internationally			Allows use of global brands/advertising, etc.	
Cost					
Economies of scale and scope	Multiple markets needed to reach economic scale	Standardization needed to reach economic scale	Concentration helps reach economic scale	Uniform marketing cuts program development and production costs	Country interdependence affects overall scale economies
Learning and experience	Multiple markets accelerate learning	Standardization accelerates learning	Concentration accelerates learning		
Sourcing efficiencies			Centralized purchasing exploits efficiencies		
Favorable logistics	Easier to expand internationally		Allows concentrated production		Allows export competition
Differences in country costs & skills			Exploited by activity concentration		Increase vulnerability of high-cost countries
Product development costs	Multiple markets needed to payback investment	Standardization reduces development needs	Concentration cuts cost of development		
Government					
Favorable trade policies	Affects nature/extent of participation	May require or prevent product features	Local content rules affect extent of concentration possible		Integration needed to deal with competitive effects of tariffs/subsidies
Compatible technical standards	Affects markets that can be entered	Affects standardization possible			
Common marketing regulations				Affects approaches possible	
Competitive					
Interdependence of countries	More participation leverages benefits	Accept tradeoffs to get best global product	Locate key activities in lead countries	Use lead country to develop programs	Integration needed to exploit benefits
Competitors globalized or might globalize	Expand to match or preempt	Match or preempt	Match or preempt	Match or preempt	Integration needed to exploit benefits

ing. Global channels are rare, but regionwide channels are increasing in number, particularly in European grocery distribution and retailing.
• **Transferable Marketing**. The buying decision may be such that marketing elements, such as brand names and advertising, require little local adapta-

tion. Such transferability enables firms to use uniform marketing strategies and facilitates expanded participation in markets. A worldwide business can also adapt its brand names and advertising campaigns to make them more transferable, or, even better, design global ones to start with. Offsetting risks include the blandness of uniformly acceptable brand names or advertising, and the vulnerability of relying on a single brand franchise.

Cost Drivers

Cost drivers depend on the economics of the business; they particularly affect activity concentration.
• **Economies of Scale and Scope.** A single-country market may not be large enough for the local business to achieve all possible economies of scale or scope. Scale at a given location can be increased through participation in multiple markets combined with product standardization or concentration of selected value activities. Corresponding risks include rigidity and vulnerability to disruption.

In the past few years, the economics of the electronics industry have shifted. As the cost of circuits has decreased, the economic advantage has gone to companies that can produce the lowest-cost components. Size has become a major asset. Thomson, the French electronics firm, understands the need to have a worldwide presence in an industry characterized by economies of scale. In 1987, Thomson greatly increased both its operating scale and its global coverage by acquiring the RCA television business from General Electric.
• **Learning and Experience.** Even if economies of scope and scale are exhausted, expanded market participation and activity concentration can accelerate the accumulation of learning and experience. The steeper the learning and experience curves, the greater the potential benefit will be. Managers should beware, though, of the usual danger in pursuing experience curve strategies—overaggressive pricing that destroys not just the competition but the market as well. Prices get so low that profit is insufficient to sustain any competitor.
• **Sourcing Efficiencies.** Centralized purchasing of new materials can significantly lower costs. Himont began as a joint venture between Hercules Inc. of the United States and Montedison Petrolchimica SpA of Italy, and is the leader in the global polypropylene market. Central to Himont's strategy is global coordination among manufacturing facilities in the purchase of raw materials, particularly monomer, the key ingredient in polypropylene production. Rationalization of raw material orders significantly strengthens the venture's low-cost production advantage.
• **Favorable Logistics.** A favorable ratio of sales value to transportation cost enhances the company's ability to concentrate production. Other logistical factors include nonperishability, the absence of time urgency, and little need for location close to customer facilities. Even the shape of the product can make a crucial difference. Cardboard tubes, such as those used as cores for textiles, cannot be shipped economically because they are mostly air. In contrast, cardboard cones are transportable because many units can be stacked in the same space.
• **Differences in Country Costs and Skills.** Factor costs generally vary across countries; this is particularly true in certain industries. The availability of particular skills also varies. Concentration of activities in low-cost or high-skill countries can increase productivity and reduce costs, but managers need to anticipate the danger of training future offshore competitors.[13]

Under attack from lower-priced cars, Volkswagen has needed to reduce its costs. It is doing so by concentrating its production to take advantage of the differences in various country costs. In Spain, hourly labor costs are below DM 20 per hour, while those in West Germany are over DM 40 per hour. To take advantage of this cost differential, the company moved production of Polos from Wolfsburg to Spain, freeing up the high-wage German labor to produce the higher-priced Golf cars. Another example of this concentration occurred when Volkswagen shut down its New Stanton, Pennsylvania, plant that manufactured Golfs and Jettas. The lower end of the U.S. market would be served by its low-wage Brazilian facility that produced the Fox. The higher end of the product line (Jetta and Golf) would be exported from Europe. This concentration and coordination of production has enabled the company to lower costs substantially.
• **Product Development Costs.** Product development costs can be reduced by developing a few global or regional products rather than many national products. The automobile industry is characterized by long product development periods and high product development costs. One reason for the high costs is duplication of effort across countries. The Ford Motor Company's "Centers of Excellence" program aims to reduce these duplicating efforts and to exploit the differing expertise of Ford specialists worldwide. As part of the concentrated effort, Ford of Europe is designing a common platform for all compacts, while Ford of North America is developing platforms for the replace-

Sloan
Management
Review

37

Fall 1989

ment of the midsized Taurus and Sable. This concentration of design is estimated to save "hundreds of millions of dollars per model by eliminating duplicative efforts and saving on retooling factories."[14]

Governmental Drivers

Government globalization drivers depend on the rules set by national governments and affect the use of all global strategy levers.

• **Favorable Trade Policies.** Host governments affect globalization potential through import tariffs and quotas, nontariff barriers, export subsidies, local content requirements, currency and capital flow restrictions, and requirements on technology transfer.[15] Host government policies can make it difficult to use the global levers of major market participation, product standardization, activity concentration, and uniform marketing; they also affect the integrated-competitive-moves lever.

National trade policies constrain companies' concentration of manufacturing activities. Aggressive U.S. government actions including threats on tariffs, quotas, and protectionist measures have helped convince Japanese automakers and other manufacturers to give up their concentration of manufacturing in Japan. Reluctantly, Japanese companies are opening plants in the United States. Honda has even made a public relations virtue out of necessity. It recently gave great publicity to the first shipment of a U.S.-made Honda car to Japan.

The easing of government restrictions can set off a rush for expanded market participation. European Community regulations for banking and financial services will be among those harmonized in 1992. The European Community decision to permit the free flow of capital among member countries has led European financial institutions to jockey for position. Until recently, the Deutsche Bank had only fifteen offices outside of Germany, but it has recently established a major presence in the French market. In 1987, Deutsche Bank also moved into the Italian market by acquiring Bank of America's one hundred branches there. Other financial organizations, such as J.P. Morgan of the United States, Swiss Bank Corporation, and the S.P. Warburg Group in Britain have increased their participation in major European markets through acquisitions.

• **Compatible Technical Standards.** Differences in technical standards, especially government-imposed standards, limit the extent to which products can be standardized. Often, standards are set with protectionism in mind. Motorola found that many of their electronics products were excluded from the Japanese market because these products operated at a higher frequency than was permitted in Japan.

• **Common Marketing Regulations.** The marketing environment of individual countries affects the extent to which uniform global marketing approaches can be used. Certain types of media may be prohibited or restricted. For example, the United States is far more liberal than Europe about the kinds of advertising claims that can be made on television. The British authorities even veto the depiction of socially undesirable behavior. For example, British television authorities do not allow scenes of children pestering their parents to buy a product. And, of course, the use of sex is different. As one extreme, France is far more liberal than the United States about sex in advertising. Various promotional devices, such as lotteries, may also be restricted.

Competitive Drivers

Market, cost, and governmental globalization drivers are essentially fixed for an industry at any given time. Competitors can play only a limited role in affecting these factors (although a sustained effort can bring about change, particularly in the case of consumer preferences). In contrast, competitive drivers are entirely in the realm of competitor choice. Competitors can raise the globalization potential of their industry and spur the need for a response on the global strategy levers.

• **Interdependence of Countries.** A competitor may create competitive interdependence among countries by pursuing a global strategy. The basic mechanism is through sharing of activities. When activities such as production are shared among countries, a competitor's market share in one country affects its scale and overall cost position in the shared activities. Changes in that scale and cost will affect its competitive position in all countries dependent on the shared activities. Less directly, customers may view market position in a lead country as an indicator of overall quality. Companies frequently promote a product as, for example, "the leading brand in the United States." Other competitors then need to respond via increased market participation, uniform marketing, or integrated competitive strategy to avoid a downward spiral of sequentially weakened positions in individual countries.

In the automobile industry, where economies of scale are significant and where sharing activities can lower costs, markets have significant competitive interdependence. As companies like Ford and Volkswagen concentrate production and become more cost competitive with the Japanese manufacturers, the Japanese are pressured to enter more markets so that increased production volume will lower costs. Whether conscious of this or not, Toyota has begun a concerted effort to penetrate the German market: between 1984 and 1987, Toyota doubled the number of cars produced for the German market.

• **Globalized Competitors.** More specifically, matching or preempting individual competitor moves may be necessary. These moves include expanding into or within major markets, being the first to introduce a standardized product, or being the first to use a uniform marketing program.

The need to preempt a global competitor can spur increased market participation. In 1986, Unilever, the European consumer products company, sought to increase its participation in the U.S. market by launching a hostile takeover bid for Richardson-Vicks Inc. Unilever's global archrival, Procter & Gamble, saw the threat to its home turf and outbid Unilever to capture Richardson-Vicks. With Richardson-Vicks's European system, P&G was able to greatly strengthen its European positioning. So Unilever's attempt to expand participation in a rival's home market backfired to allow the rival to expand participation in Unilever's home markets.

In summary, industry globalization drivers provide opportunities to use global strategy levers in many ways. Some industries, such as civil aircraft, can score high on most dimensions of globalization.[16] Others, such as the cement industry, seem to be inherently local. But more and more industries are developing globalization potential. Even the food industry in Europe, renowned for its diversity of taste, is now a globalization target for major food multinationals.

Changes over Time

Finally, industry evolution plays a role. As each of the industry globalization drivers changes over time, so too will the appropriate global strategy

change. For example, in the European major appliance industry, globalization forces seem to have reversed. In the late 1960s and early 1970s, a regional standardization strategy was successful for some key competitors.[17] But in the 1980s the situation appears to have turned around, and the most successful strategies seem to be national.[18]

In some cases, the actions of individual competitors can affect the direction and pace of change; competitors positioned to take advantage of globalization forces will want to hasten them. For example, a competitor with strong central manufacturing capabilities may want to accelerate the worldwide acceptance of a standardized product.

More Than One Strategy Is Viable

Although they are powerful, industry globalization drivers do not dictate one formula for success. More than one type of international strategy can be viable in a given industry.

Industries vary across drivers. No industry is high on every one of the many globalization drivers. A particular competitor may be in a strong position to exploit a driver that scores low on globalization. For example, the dominance of national government customers offsets the globalization potential from other industry drivers, because government customers typically prefer to do business with their own nationals. In such an industry a competitor with a global strategy can use its other advantages, such as low cost from centralization of global production, to offset this drawback. At the same time, another multinational competitor with good government contacts can pursue a multidomestic strategy and succeed without globalization advantages, and single-country local competitors can succeed on the basis of their very particular local assets. The hotel industry provides examples both of successful global and of successful local competitors.

Global effects are incremental. Globalization drivers are not deterministic for a second reason: the appropriate use of strategy levers adds competitive advantage to existing sources. These other sources may allow individual competitors to thrive with international strategies that are mismatched with industry globalization drivers. For example, superior technology is a major source of competitive advantage in most industries, but can be quite independent of globalization drivers. A competitor with sufficiently superior technology can use it to

Sloan
Management
Review

39

Fall 1989

Global
Strategy

40

Yip

offset globalization disadvantages.

Business and parent company position and resources are crucial. The third reason that drivers are not deterministic is related to resources. A worldwide business may face industry drivers that strongly favor a global strategy. But global strategies are typically expensive to implement initially even though great cost savings and revenue gains should follow. High initial investments may be needed to expand within or into major markets, to develop standardized products, to relocate value activities, to create global brands, to create new organization units or coordination processes, and to implement other aspects of a global strategy. The strategic position of the business is also relevant. Even though a global strategy may improve the business's long-term strategic position, its immediate position may be so weak that resources should be devoted to short-term, country-by-country improvements. Despite the automobile industry's very strong globalization drivers, Chrysler Corporation had to deglobalize by selling off most of its international automotive businesses to avoid bankruptcy. Lastly, investing in nonglobal sources of competitive advantage, such as superior technology, may yield greater returns than global ones, such as centralized manufacturing.

Organizations have limitations. Finally, factors such as organization structure, management processes, people, and culture affect how well a desired global strategy can be implemented. Organizational differences among companies in the same industry can, or should, constrain the companies' pursuit of the same global strategy. Organization issues in globalization are a major topic, and cannot be covered in the space here.[19] ∎

References

1
See:
T. Hout, M.E. Porter, and E. Rudden, "How Global Companies Win Out," *Harvard Business Review*, September-October 1982, pp. 98-108.
My framework, developed in this article, is based in part on M.E. Porter's pioneering work on global strategy. His ideas are further developed in:
M.E. Porter, "Competition in Global Industries: A Conceptual Framework," in *Competition in Global Industries*, ed. M.E. Porter (Boston: Harvard Business School Press, 1986).
Bartlett and Ghoshal define a "transnational industry" that is somewhat similar to Porter's "global industry." See:

C.A. Bartlett and S. Ghoshal, "Managing across Borders: New Strategic Requirements," *Sloan Management Review*, Summer 1987, pp. 7-17.

2
T. Levitt, "The Globalization of Markets," *Harvard Business Review*, May-June 1983, pp. 92-102.

3
These obstacles are laid out in one of the rejoinders provoked by Levitt's article. See:
S.P. Douglas and Y. Wind, "The Myth of Globalization," *Columbia Journal of World Business*, Winter 1987, pp. 19-29.

4
For a more theoretical exposition of this framework see:
G.S. Yip, "An Integrated Approach to Global Competitive Strategy," in *Frontiers of Management*, ed. R. Mansfield (London: Routledge, forthcoming).

5
The concept of the global strategy lever was first presented in:
G.S. Yip, P.M. Loewe, and M.Y. Yoshino, "How to Take Your Company to the Global Market," *Columbia Journal of World Business*, Winter 1988, pp. 37-48.

6
K. Ohmae, *Triad Power: The Coming Shape of Global Competition* (New York: The Free Press, 1985).

7
G. Hamel and C.K. Prahalad, "Do You Really Have a Global Strategy?" *Harvard Business Review*, July-August 1985, pp. 139-148;
B. Kogut, "Designing Global Strategies: Profiting from Operational Flexibility," *Sloan Management Review*, Fall 1985, pp. 27-38.

8
P.G.P. Walters, "International Marketing Policy: A Discussion of the Standardization Construct and Its Relevance for Corporate Policy," *Journal of International Business Studies*, Summer 1986, pp. 55-69.

9
For a discussion of the possibilities and merits of uniform marketing see:
R.D. Buzzell, "Can You Standardize Multinational Marketing?" *Harvard Business Review*, November-December 1968, pp. 102-113; and
J.A. Quelch and E.J. Hoff, "Customizing Global Marketing," *Harvard Business Review*, May-June 1986, pp. 59-68.

10
P. Kotler et al., *The New Competition* (Englewood Cliffs, NJ: Prentice-Hall, 1985), p. 174.

11
Figure 3 is also presented in Yip (forthcoming).

12
M.R. Cvar, "Case Studies in Global Competition," in Porter (1986).

13
See:
C.C. Markides and N. Berg, "Manufacturing Offshore Is Bad Business," *Harvard Business Review*, September-October 1988, pp. 113-120.

14
"Can Ford Stay on Top?" *Business Week*, 28 September 1987, pp. 78–86.

15
Three public sector activities that can protect domestic competitors are blocking access to the domestic market, providing subsidies, and creating spillovers in research and development. See:
M.A. Spence, "Industrial Organization and Competitive Advantage in Multinational Industries," *American Economic Review* 74 (May 1984): 356–360.

16
M.Y. Yoshino, "Global Competition in a Salient Industry: The Case of Civil Aircraft," in Porter (1986).

17
Levitt (May-June 1983).

18
C. Baden Fuller et al., "National or Global? The Study of Company Strategies and the European Market for Major Appliances" (London: London Business School Centre for Business Strategy, working paper series, No. 28, June 1987).

19
See:
Yip et al. (1988); and
C.K. Prahalad and Y.L. Doz, *The Multinational Mission: Balancing Local Demands and Global Vision* (New York: The Free Press, 1987).

Sloan
Management
Review

41

Fall 1989

[26]

Managing across Borders: New Strategic Requirements

Christopher A. Bartlett
Sumantra Ghoshal

Harvard Business School
INSEAD

INTERNATIONAL BUSINESSES FACED NEW STRATEGIC challenges in the 1980s. Corporations that had once succeeded with relatively one-dimensional strategies—efficiency, responsiveness, or ability to exploit learning—were forced to broaden their outlook. Successful "transnational" corporations integrated all three of those characteristics. They did so by building on the strengths— but accepting the limitations—of their administrative heritages. This is the first of two articles; the second will describe how actual companies made that transition. *Ed.*

Sloan
Management
Review

7

Summer 1987

THE DEMANDS OF MANAGING in an international operating environment changed considerably over the past decade. In an increasing number of industries, the benefits of exploiting global economies of scale and scope enhanced the need for integration and coordination of activities. At the same time, volatile exchange rates, industrial policies of host governments, resistance of consumers to standardized global products, and the changing economies of flexible manufacturing technologies increased the value of more nationally responsive differentiated approaches.[1] And with the emergence of competitive battles among a few large firms with comparable resources and skills in global-scale efficiency *and* nationally responsive strategies, the ability to learn— to transfer knowledge and expertise from one part of the organization to others worldwide—became more important in building durable competitive advantage. Managers of multinational companies (MNCs) are now faced with the task of optimizing efficiency, responsiveness, and learning *simultaneously* in their worldwide operations—which suggests new strategic and organizational challenges.

This is the first of two articles that explore this new situation; they are based on a research project that involved extensive discussions with more than 250 managers in nine of the world's largest multinational companies.[2] In this article we will describe the strategic challenges these companies faced because of increasing complexity of environmental demands, and the ways in which they tried to respond to those challenges. Our analysis suggests that, for most MNCs, limited organizational capability (rather than lack of analysis or insight) represents the most critical constraint in responding to new strategic demands. In the follow-up article, we will describe how companies are trying to overcome this constraint by building a very different kind of multinational organization, one that can cope with the increasing complexity of the international environment.

New Challenges: Mixed Responses

The international operations of all the companies we studied were in a state of transition. The 1980s brought new demands and pressures that forced them to question their worldwide strategic approach and to adapt their organizational capabilities. Some seemed to be managing the transitions successfully, others were simply surviving, and a few were encountering major difficulties.

• In the branded packaged goods industry, both Unilever and Procter & Gamble responded to the need for greater scale efficiency and more globally integrated marketing strategies and technology development by providing better coordination and control over their worldwide operations. Kao, the leading Japanese consumer chemicals company, was able to use its formidable technological capabilities, scale-efficient plants, and marketing creativity to score major victories against both these competitors in its home market, yet it was unable to leverage those skills worldwide. Despite significant investments and substantial management effort, the

International
Strategy

8

Bartlett
& Ghoshal

*Christopher A. Bartlett
is Associate Professor of
Business Administra-
tion at the Graduate
School of Business Ad-
ministration, Harvard
University. Dr. Bart-
lett holds the B. Econ.
degree from the
University of Queens-
land, Australia, and
the M.B.A. and
D.B.A. degrees from
Harvard University.
Prior to his academic
career, Dr. Bartlett
had extensive manage-
ment experience in Al-
coa, McKinsey and
Co., and Baxter
Travenol, where he
was general manager
of the French subsidi-
ary. His research has
focused on the strategic
and organizational
problems facing mul-
tinationals.*

company's internationalization thrust stalled out
in the small developing markets of neighboring East
Asia.
• Turbulence in the consumer electronics industry led both Philips and Matsushita to make major readjustments over the past decade. Philips made
heroic changes to its historically decentralized organization to achieve greater global-scale efficiency.
More recently, Matsushita has begun to reconfigure
its operations to make them more localized and
responsive to host country pressures. But for
General Electric, the once-cherished dream of becoming a leading player in the global consumer
electronics industry was abandoned in favor of the
more modest goal of defending its home-market
position in televisions, radios, and other such products, based on an outsourcing strategy.
• Over the past decade, Japan's NEC used the
technological changes and political upheaval in the
telecommunications switching business to build a
strong presence in the global marketplace. In the
same period, the Swedish electronics company
L.M. Ericsson successfully adapted its strategic approach and realigned its worldwide organization
to protect, then build, its global-market position
in telecommunications. ITT, meanwhile, floundered in this business. Despite being the second
largest supplier of telecommunications equipment
in the world in the late 1970s, and the leading company outside the U.S., and despite a staggering investment of over $1 billion in new switching tech-
nology, ITT was forced to abandon its attempt to
enter the U.S. switching market. And it finally had
to sell the crown jewel, its formidable European
telecommunications business.
    Why was it that some companies fell behind,
while others adapted to the changing demands of
international industry's competitive environment
in the 1980s? The inability of certain businesses
within Kao, GE, and ITT to adjust to important
new demands is not presented as an example of
strategic incompetence or managerial ineptitude.
Indeed, all three companies are frequently cited
as examples of corporate excellence. To understand
the source of their problems, one must first analyze the changes occurring in the international environment, and how they affect each of these companies differently. Then it is important to study
how each organization adjusted in order to understand why results have been so different from one
company to the next.

Traditional Strategic Demands

Trying to distill the key strategic tasks in large and
complex industries is a hazardous venture but, at
the risk of oversimplification, one can make the
case that until recently most worldwide industries
presented relatively unidimensional strategic requirements. In each industry, a particular set of
forces dominated the environment and led to the
success of firms that possessed a particular set of
corresponding competencies.

Rewarding Efficiency in Global Industries

Bell Laboratories' development of the transistor in
1947 paved the way for global efficiency in the
consumer electronics industry. Transistors led to
printed circuit boards, and then to integrated circuits, which made mass production feasible by
reducing both the amount and skill level of labor
required for assembly. The automation of component insertion, in-line testing, materials handling,
final assembly, and packaging further reduced
manufacturing costs and increased product quality. As a result of all these developments, the
efficient scale for production of color televisions
went from 50,000 sets per annum in the early
1960s to 500,000 sets by the late 1970s.
    Meanwhile, scale economies in R&D and mar-
keting were also increasing. State-of-the-art skills
in micromechanics, micro-optics, and electronics
could not be supported by revenues from a single
market. Funding from global volume was essential to support the breadth and depth of expertise
required by the three diverse technologies.
    Furthermore, the emergence of giant chain stores
caused increasing concentration in distribution
channels worldwide and raised the need for marketing economies. The resulting shift in bargaining power from manufacturers to resellers changed
the rules of the distribution game. Instead of delivering small lot sizes to single-store operators and
recovering fairly large marketing overheads,
manufacturers could ship large lot-size deliveries
to giant chain outlets, but also had to operate within
very low margins. Because these outlets sold on
price, manufacturers could no longer rely on
knowledgeable store personnel to move their mer-
chandise. To educate the consumer and communicate product benefits, they had to invest heavily

in advertising, and this too raised break-even volumes. Finally, local service capability, once an entry barrier to global firms, also became less important as increased product reliability reduced the need for service, and as the development of replaceable service boards practically eliminated the need for skilled service technicians.

According to some industry members, by the late 1970s the new manufacturing, research, and marketing economies meant that a global player in the color TV business needed to produce at least 2.0 or 2.5 million sets annually—forty to fifty times the minimum efficient scale in the early 1960s.

In an environment characterized by incrementally changing technologies, falling transportation and communication costs, relatively low tariffs and other protectionist barriers, and increasing homogenization of national markets, these huge scale economies progressively increased the benefits of global efficiency in the consumer electronics business. The industry gradually assumed the attributes of a classic *global industry*—one in which important characteristics like consumer needs, minimum efficient scale, and context of competitive strategy were defined not by individual national environments, but by the global economy.

Firms like Matsushita were ideally placed to exploit the emerging global-industry demands. Having expanded internationally much later than their American and European counterparts, they were able to capitalize on highly centralized scale-intensive manufacturing and R&D operations, and leverage them through worldwide exports of standardized global products. Such *global strategies* fit the emerging industry characteristics far better than the more tailored country-by-country approach that companies like Philips and GE had been forced to adopt in an earlier era of high trade barriers, differences in consumer preferences, and pretransistor technological and economic characteristics.[3]

Building Responsiveness in Multinational Industries

If global efficiency was the dominant strategic demand in the consumer electronics industry, the consumer packaged goods business represented an interesting contrast. Traditionally, global integration of activities offered this industry few benefits. Instead, national responsiveness appeared to be the key strategic requirement.

In laundry detergents, for example, there was very little scope for standardizing products within Europe, let alone worldwide. As late as 1980, washing machine penetration varied from less than 30 percent of all households in the U.K. to over 85 percent in Germany. Washing practices varied from northern European countries, where "boil washing" had long been standard, to Mediterranean countries, where hand washing in cold water represented an important demand segment. Differences in water hardness, perfume preference, fabric mix, and phosphate legislation made product differentiation from country to country a strategic requirement.

Not only product attributes, but even marketing strategies, had to be responsive to the different conditions in different national markets. Concentration in distribution channels varied greatly— five chains controlled 65 percent of the market in Germany, but no chain controlled even 2 percent of the retail market in neighboring Italy. The possibility of using advertising and promotional tools also varied by market. In Holland, for example, each brand was allowed a maximum number of minutes of commercial television air time per annum, while in Germany the use of coupons, refunds, and similar forms of promotion was virtually blocked by national laws.

Against this strong need for differentiated approaches to each national market, global scale offered few benefits. In R&D, most of the consumer chemicals companies were involved only in formulating the final products; basic research for developing the ingredients was carried out by the chemical manufacturers. Similarly, the relatively simple operations of soap making could be carried out efficiently at a scale that could support a separate plant for all but the smallest markets. In any case, with raw material purchases accounting for 40 to 50 percent of costs, and advertising and marketing accounting for another 20 percent, development and production represented only a modest part of total costs.

This and many other industries with similar characteristics were what we call *multinational industries*—worldwide businesses in which the need for local differentiation made multiple national industry structures flourish. In such an environment, Unilever's *multinational strategy* was a natural fit— the company had a long history of building strong national companies that were sensitive to local needs

Sloan
Management
Review

9

Summer 1987

and opportunities, then allowing them the freedom to manage their local businesses entrepreneurially, with minimal direction from headquarters. It took Procter & Gamble time to learn that transferring the parent company's products and marketing approaches abroad would not guarantee success, but the company was able to adapt. At Kao, subsidiaries were almost totally dependent on efficient, but highly centralized, operations. This proved to be an even less appropriate fit, and prevented the company from responding to the dominant industry requirements.

International Strategy

10

Bartlett & Ghoshal

Sumantra Ghoshal is Assistant Professor of Business Policy at the European Institute of Business Administration (INSEAD) in Fontainebleau, France. Dr. Ghoshal holds the undergraduate degree from the University of Delhi, India. He also holds the S.M. and Ph.D. degrees from the Sloan School of Management, M.I.T., and the D.B.A. degree from the graduate School of Business Administration, Harvard University. He is coauthor of Strategic Control and has written ten articles for Sloan Management Review and Harvard Business Review. He has teaching or consulting relationships with a number of U.S. and European companies.

Exploiting Learning in International Industries

Unlike the consumer electronics industry, which was dominated by the need for efficiency, or the branded packaged goods industry, where responsiveness was the key strategic task, the telecommunications switching industry traditionally required a more multidimensional strategic capability. Monopoly purchasing in most countries by a government-owned post, telegraph, and telephone authority created a demand for responsiveness—a demand enhanced by the strategic importance almost all governments accord to developing local manufacturers of telecom equipment. Significant scale economies in production, and the need to arrange complex credit facilities for buyers through multinational lending agencies, required global integration and activity coordination. However, the most critical task for the manufacturers of telecom switching equipment was the ability to develop and harness new technologies and to exploit them worldwide. The ability to learn and to appropriate the benefits of learning in multiple national markets differentiated the winners from the losers in this highly complex business.

The historical diffusion of telecommunications switching technologies followed the classic international product cycle described by Vernon.[4] In most cases, new products were developed in one of the advanced Western economies, often because of the powerful research capabilities of AT&T's Bell Labs in North America. Next, they were adopted in other developed countries, typically in European countries first, then in Japan. Once the new technology was understood, and the product design was standardized, companies in the developed nations began to export to countries using earlier

generation products. Exports were usually replaced quickly by local manufacturing in response to host government demands. After the local subsidiary developed adequate understanding of the technology, it was allowed to develop and adapt the product locally, to suit unique attributes of the local markets or to help local vendors. By this time, the next new product—an augmented version based on the same technology, or built on an altogether new technology—would be ready for transfer, and the same cycle would be repeated.

We call industries such as this one, where the key to success lies in one's ability to transfer knowledge (particularly technology) to overseas units and to manage the product life-cycle efficiently and flexibly, *international industries*. This name reflects the importance of the international product cycle that lies at the core of the industry's strategic demands.

Recognizing that its small home market could not support the R&D efforts required to survive, L.M. Ericsson built its strategy around an ability to transfer and adapt its innovative product and process technologies to international markets. Its *international strategy*—sequential diffusion of innovation developed in the home market—fit the industry's requirements much better than ITT's multinational approach or NEC's global posture.

Strategic Challenge of the 1980s: Transition to Transnationality

Our portrayal of these industries' strategic demands in the late 1970s is clearly oversimplified. Different tasks in the value-added chains of the different businesses required different levels of efficiency, responsiveness, and learning capabilities. We have charted what appeared to us to be the "center of gravity" of these activities—the environmental forces that had the most significant impact on the industry's strategic demands.

In the 1980s, each of these industries underwent some major transitions. In all three, the earlier dominance of a single set of environmental forces was replaced by a much more complex set of environmental forces. Increasingly, firms must respond simultaneously to diverse and often conflicting strategic needs. Today, it is more difficult for a firm to succeed with a relatively unidimensional strategic capability that emphasizes only efficiency, or responsiveness, or learning. To win, it must now achieve all three goals at one time.

Need for Multidimensional Strategic Capabilities

In the consumer electronics industry, the trends of increasing scale economies in manufacturing, R&D, and marketing persisted, and the need for global efficiency, if anything, increased. But the very success of efficient competitors contributed to a counterbalancing set of strategic influences that heightened the need for national differentiation and responsiveness. Most noticeably, host governments reacted strongly when the trickle of imported consumer electronics became a flood that upset their trade balances and threatened local industries. In the United States and Europe, antidumping suits, orderly marketing agreements, and political pressures fragmented the manufacturing operations of global companies by forcing almost all companies to set up local plants.

Consumers also reacted to an overdose of standardized global products by showing a renewed preference for differentiated products; the advent of flexible manufacturing processes fed the trend. Amstrad, the fast-growing British computer and electronics company, got its start by recognizing and responding to this local consumer need. It captured a major share of the high-end audio market in the U.K. by moving away from the standardized, inexpensive "music centers" marketed by the global firms, and offering customers a product more reminiscent of the old "hi-fi" systems. Their product was encased in teak rather than metal cabinets, with a control panel tailor-made to appeal to the British consumers' preferences. Largely because of localized challenges such as Amstrad's, Matsushita has had to reverse its earlier bias toward standardized global designs and place more emphasis on differentiation of products. From fifteen models in its portable audio product range in 1980, the company increased the line to thirty in 1985; it also doubled the number of tape recorder models it produces, while sales per model have declined 60 percent.

The major industry shakeout of the past twenty years has left only a handful of viable competitors, all roughly equivalent in their potential to capture scale economies and develop responsive strategies. In the emerging environment, it is increasingly important for these companies to capture and interpret information, and to use the resulting knowledge and skills on a global basis. The growing sophistication of global competitive strategies means that knowledge gained about a competitor, and skills developed in response to its activities in one market, may be of vital importance for company units elsewhere in the world. Furthermore, with more sophisticated markets worldwide, rapidly changing technology, and shorter product life cycles, rich rewards are accruing to companies that can develop and diffuse successful innovations. In brief, a company's worldwide organizational learning capability is fast becoming an essential strategic asset.

In the branded packaged goods industry, similarly, responsiveness continues to be a critical task, but both efficiency and worldwide learning have become more important. In the detergent business, for example, product standardization has become more and more feasible because of standardization in the washing machine industry. Growing penetration of washing machines has also contributed, as has the increasing share of synthetic textiles, which narrows the differences in washing practices across countries. But the biggest impetus toward globalization has come from the firms themselves. Managers at P&G, Unilever, Henkel, and Colgate faced sharply rising input prices caused by the oil crisis of the mid-1970s, and the simultaneous recession in demand that made passing increased costs on to customers impossible. They found that developing standard brands, formulas, and packages created some economies in the production process. Further savings were made possible by developing common advertising and promotion approaches.

Innovations made jointly by a company's headquarters and a number of national organizations have been the most important instrument for creating standardized products that satisfied the diverse demands of customers at acceptable cost levels. For example, P&G sells a heavy-duty liquid detergent called Tide in the United States, Ariel in Europe, and Cheer in Japan. The product was truly global in its development: It incorporated surfactant technology, developed in the company's international technical coordination group to respond to cold water washing in Japan; water softening technology, developed at the European Technical Center to respond to the hardness of washing water in most European countries; and builder technology, developed in the United States to combat the higher soil content in dirty clothes. At the same time, however, the existence of regional development groups

Sloan
Management
Review

11

Summer 1987

ensured that the detergent satisfied primary requirements of customers in each country. Such successes have stimulated other global competitors, and have broadened the competitive game from one based primarily on national marketing capability to a much more complex one where local responsiveness, global efficiency, and worldwide innovation and learning are all part of the rules.

Similarly, the new digital technology, at one stroke, enhanced the need for efficiency, responsiveness, and learning in the telecommunications switching business. The increasing need for efficiency and integration is driven by soaring R&D costs that can only be supported through global volume and higher scale economies in component production. The magnitude of skills and resources required to create a new digital switch is difficult for most companies to assemble in one organizational unit, and this has made global innovations essential. At the same time, the growing strategic importance of the switch—it is now the core of a country's information infrastructure—has enhanced its importance to national governments, thereby enhancing the need for companies to be responsive to local demands.

These transitions were not unique to the three industries we have described. Many other industries, from heavy earth-moving equipment and automobiles to photocopiers and power tools, have confronted similar environmental changes. In the emerging international environment, therefore, there are fewer and fewer examples of industries that are pure global, textbook multinational, or classic international. Instead, more and more businesses are being driven by *simultaneous* demands for global efficiency, national responsiveness, and worldwide learning. These are the characteristics of what we call a *transnational industry*.

This is not to suggest that the strategic challenges facing companies in the branded packaged goods business are the same as those confronting global competitors in the consumer electronics industry. The nature, the strength, and the mix of the three broad demands obviously vary widely. But it is true that companies in both these businesses—and many others besides—will find it increasingly difficult to defend a competitive position based on only one dominant capability. They will need to develop their strategy to a point where they can manage efficiency, responsiveness, and learning on a worldwide basis.

Responding to the Challenge: Toward Transnational Capabilities

These new demands had a profound impact on all the companies we studied. Firms whose key competencies had previously fit the dominant industry requirement found they needed to develop entirely new capabilities. Those whose strategic posture was an industry mismatch in the era of unidimensional strategic demands also faced the challenge of developing multidimensional capabilities. For many, however, there was the incentive of being able to leverage previously inappropriate organizational capabilities.

Companies like Philips, Unilever, and ITT, which had traditionally operated in a multinational strategic mode (with responsiveness as their dominant posture), faced the challenge of developing global efficiency and improving their ability to develop knowledge and skills worldwide and diffuse it throughout the organization. Firms such as Kao, NEC, and Matsushita, on the other hand, had traditionally adopted a global strategic posture with efficiency as their trump card, and confronted the need for more national responsiveness and improved access to worldwide innovative resources and stimuli. GE, Procter & Gamble, and L.M. Ericsson had been exponents of the international product cycle model, efficiently transferring domestic innovations and expertise to worldwide operations. They faced the challenge of expanding their capability to create more global innovations while ensuring that their international operations retained the appropriate balance of responsiveness and efficiency.

The Organizational Constraint

One thing was clear. In all the companies we studied, there was either an explicit or an implicit recognition of the changing strategic task demands we have described. Even in those organizations that were lagging in their adaptation to the new demands, or that had abandoned their attempts to adjust, the issue was not a poor understanding of environmental forces or inappropriate strategic intent. Without exception, they knew *what* they had to do; their difficulties lay in *how* to achieve the necessary changes.

• Kao had been trying unsuccessfully since the late 1960s to establish a foothold in the European and

North American markets. Management recognized that a lack of responsiveness to the very different customer preferences and market structures was limiting the company's potential outside Japan. Emulating the practices of Unilever and P&G, the company created regional headquarters in Asia, America, and Europe. It also undertook a personnel development program to upgrade the skills and organizational status of its overseas groups, and to internationalize the perspectives of managers at headquarters.

However, functional managers at headquarters—the dominant group in this traditionally centralized company—saw the localization thrust as a signal to become more directly involved in overseas operations. The company failed to develop the national responsiveness it was seeking, since its established processes reinforced the strong direct control of headquarters functional staff and prevented regional and country managers from significantly influencing product development or even local product-market strategies.

• Many GE managers foresaw that superior global efficiency of its Japanese competitors would erode the company's competitive position in the consumer electronics business. It was manifest to them that GE's philosophy of building autonomous mini-GEs in each country had become inappropriate; greater integration and coordination of activities were necessary. Plans were made to develop more globally efficient operations by shifting production to Southeast Asia and developing specialized internal sourcing plants.

But, in an organization that had historically considered foreign subsidiaries appendages to a dominant home country operation, the importance and urgency of these plans were lost. It was a case of too little too late, and the company could not reverse the traditional role of international operations as sales outlets dependent on the parent. By this stage, the Japanese competitors had developed insurmountable leads in the battle for low-cost position, and GE had lost the opportunity to develop a global presence.

• Soon after Rand Araskog took over as ITT's chief executive, he committed himself to selling off many of its diverse businesses to provide the resources and management focus that would be necessary to make the company a leader in the emerging battle for domination of global telecommunications. He also recognized that ITT would

have to change the way it managed this business. In particular, there was an urgent need to change the company's product development process in response to the emerging digital technology. All but the smallest national subsidiaries of the company had traditionally developed their own products in cooperation with their local post, telegraph, and telephone authorities. While this had generated multiple standards and a plethora of product varieties, the company had reaped considerable political rewards from being able to present a locally designed product to each government.

But the resources and technological capabilities required to develop a digital switch were clearly beyond the ability of any single country unit. At the same time, the trend toward deregulation had reduced the rewards of local differentiation. As a result, integrating the technological capabilities and financial resources of different national entities to design a standard global product had become a strategic imperative.

However, despite its best efforts, ITT management failed to persuade the different national units to cooperate with each other in building a standard switch. Conditioned by a long history of local autonomy, and driven by systems that measured performance on a local basis, national units strongly resisted joint efforts and common standards. Fierce turf protection led to constant duplication of efforts and divergence of specifications; total development costs ballooned to over $1 billion. The biggest problem appeared when the company decided to take the System 12 switch to the U.S. market. In true ITT tradition, the U.S. group asserted its right to develop its own product and launched a major new R&D effort, despite concerns from the company's chief technological officer that they risked developing what he called System 13. After years of effort and hundreds of millions of dollars in additional development costs, the product was still not ready for the market. Ultimately, it was this failure to create an integrated process for global product development that led to ITT's withdrawal from the telecommunications switching business.

The problems these companies faced were not caused by a lack of strategic analysis or insight, but instead by the limitations and biases in their own organizations that prevented the development of required strategic competencies. While the consequences were somewhat extreme in their cases, all the other companies we surveyed faced basically

Sloan
Management
Review

13

Summer 1987

the same kind of organizational constraints in developing the multidimensional strategic capability that the environment of the 1980s required.

The Critical Role of Administrative Heritage

International
Strategy

14

Bartlett
& Ghoshal

Managers of all these companies have since learned that while strategic plans can be scrapped and redrawn overnight, a company's organizational capability is much more durable and difficult to restructure. There is no such thing as a zero-based organization. A company's organizational capability develops over many years and is tied to a number of attributes: a configuration of organizational assets and capabilities that are built up over decades; a distribution of managerial responsibilities and influence that cannot be shifted quickly; and an ongoing set of relationships that endure long after any structural change has been made. Collectively, these factors constitute a company's *administrative heritage*. It can be, at the same time, one of the company's greatest assets – the underlying source of its key competencies – and also one of its most significant liabilities, since it resists change and thereby prevents realignment or broadening of strategic capabilities.

A company's administrative heritage is shaped by many factors. Strong leaders often leave indelible impressions on their organizations, as Kenosuke Matsushita has in the company that bears his name, and as Harold Geneen has in a company that still reflects his philosophies.

• Geneen is best known for strengthening the corporate controller's function in ITT, but he also built up a strong tradition that headquarters managers could not interfere with either the strategic autonomy or the day-to-day operating decisions of national management in subsidiaries. He resisted the development of a central research function in the telecommunications business, and instead ensured that the national units controlled almost all the key resources and technological expertise of the company. He also placed the strongest managers in different national units, and held them fully accountable for their performance. This led to a distribution of resources and power that was strongly biased in favor of the area organization at the cost of central functional and business management. It was this administrative heritage that resisted subsequent efforts to achieve global integration.

Home country culture and social systems also have significant influences on a company's administrative heritage. For example, the more important roles that owners and bankers play in corporate-level decision making in many European companies led to an internal culture quite different from that of their American counterparts. These companies tended to emphasize personal relationships rather than formal structures, and financial controls rather than coordination of technical or operational detail.[5] This management style led companies like Unilever to develop highly autonomous national subsidiaries that were managed like a portfolio of offshore investments, rather than like a single worldwide business. In contrast, Japanese cultural norms that emphasized group decision making and commitment to long-term welfare of employees led to highly centralized management processes that resisted the growth in the resources and influence of foreign units.[6]

• Decision-making processes based on *nemawashi* and *ringi* require close face-to-face contact among participating managers. These processes lay at the core of Kao's management systems and obstructed management's efforts to give foreign subsidiaries greater access, legitimacy, and influence. Further, a commitment to maintain and increase domestic employment impeded the company's ability to expand the activities and resources of the offshore units.

Finally, the internationalization history of a firm also influences its administrative heritage.[7] Expanding in the pre–Second World War period of rising tariffs and discriminatory legislation, many European companies were forced to transfer most value-adding activities to their foreign subsidiaries. High tariff barriers in the 1920s and 1930s forced Philips to decentralize not only assembly but even component production; the dangers of German occupation of Holland led to decentralization of R&D; and, finally, the postwar boom further strengthened the roots of decentralization, since the war-ravished headquarters did not have the capability to coordinate the company's rapidly growing international operations. Japanese companies faced quite the opposite situation. Making their main international thrust in the 1970s – the era of falling tariffs and transport costs, and increasing homogenization of national markets – their centrally controlled, export-based internationalization strategy represented a perfect fit with the external environment, besides being consistent with their own cultural norms and internal management processes. American companies, many of which enjoyed their fastest international expansion in the 1950s and 1960s, grew primarily on the strength of new technologies and management processes that they had developed during the war.[8] The creation of new products and technologies at home, and their exploitation abroad, became the core of internationalization strategies.

• While delegating most application engineering, manufacturing, sourcing, and marketing responsibilities to its foreign subsidiaries, GE kept basic research tightly centralized at home. The assumption was that a domestic operation could create new products that would then be available to foreign units for adoption and adaptation. This parent-company-as-leader mentality proved a major impediment to building a worldwide manufacturing function. It compromised the willingness of the U.S. company to rely on offshore sources, and kept it from recognizing the need to tap into the multiple centers of technological excellence that had emerged in different parts of the world.

In developing the capabilities required to cope with the complex demands of transnational industries, each of the companies we studied was confronted with the limiting constraints of its administrative heritage. Yet such limitations were not always immediately recognized. The more normal approach was to respond to new demands by emulating those competitors that were most successful in dealing with the situation. Philips's initial reaction to the growing competitive challenge from Japan was to pull product decisions and sourcing control to headquarters. This step was intended to replicate (and therefore, enable Philips to compete with) companies like Matsushita, whose global efficiency was dependent on standardized products and centralized production. Meanwhile, managers at Matsushita were extremely aware of the growing need for responsiveness, and launched a localization program aimed at enhancing the self-sufficiency and entrepreneurship of the worldwide subsidiary companies—attributes of Philips's national organizations that were greatly admired and envied in Osaka.

Initially, both approaches not only failed, but also had unfortunate consequences, primarily because they did not take into account the powerful administrative heritage of the organization that had to implement the changes. At Philips, the national subsidiaries were not only the main sources of international knowledge and skill, but also the entrepreneurial spark plugs that fired many strategic initiatives. Denying their traditional roles and diminishing their influence damaged their motivation and deprived corporate management of the benefits of their considerable resources. Instead of improving global efficiency, the action jeopardized the company's key organizational asset. Philips has since recognized that, while global efficiency has to be achieved, it must be done in a way that is consistent with its administrative heritage and that protects and indeed builds on the formidable strengths of its national organizations. Facing limited success in its localization program, Matsushita has also learned that the way to build national responsiveness is not to weaken central management, but to leverage the strengths of its centralized and culture-bound systems.

Philips and Matsushita (and many of the other companies we studied) eventually recognized the importance of both harnessing and offsetting the powerful influence of their administrative heritage as they adapted to new strategic demands. (In the companion article, we will describe some of the ways in which these companies were able to do so.) In constrast, as the earlier examples showed, the companies that were slow to adapt to the new environment never seemed to recognize the importance of their administrative heritage, and were therefore unable to leverage its strengths while counterbalancing its limitations.

Organizational Capability as Key Competence

The ability of a company to survive and succeed in today's turbulent international environment depends on two factors: The fit between its strategic posture and the dominant industry characteristics, and its ability to adapt that posture to the multidimensional task demands shaping the current competitive environment. Kao's inability to succeed internationally stemmed from a poor fit between its centralized scale and technology-driven strategy in an industry that demanded a more differentiated and market-responsive approach. ITT's problems, on the other hand, were due more to an inability to adapt strongly focused organizational norms and behaviors, shaped by its unique administrative heritage, to the fast-changing, multidimensional demands of today's telecommunications industry. And GE experienced both fit and adaptation problems.

Sloan
Management
Review

15

Summer 1987

International
Strategy

16

Bartlett
& Ghoshal

Despite the very different tasks facing the other companies in our study, in broad terms they are all moving toward a common goal, though from diverse directions. In the terminology we have adopted, they are making the transition from being multinational, international, or global companies to being transnational corporations. Obviously, these companies are not adopting a common strategy—the differences in their industry characteristics and administrative heritages prevent that. Indeed, neither a particular competitive posture nor a specific organizational form characterizes these companies. What *is* emerging as common to all of them is a new set of beliefs about managing across borders.[9] Fundamental to this new mentality is the awareness of the importance of administrative heritage both as an asset to protect and as a constraint to overcome. To respond to the complexity, diversity, and dynamism of the external environment, and to build the multidimensional strategic postures that are required, each of these companies has to overcome the unidimensional bias shaped by its administrative heritage. To become a transnational, each must build a multidimensional organization capable of developing new strategic competences while protecting the existing strengths. What are the key attributes of such an organization? How can managers develop those attributes? How should such an organization be managed once it is built? These are some of the questions that we will address in the following article. ∎

References

1
The tension between the strategic requirement for integration and differentiation has a long intellectual history, but is perhaps best captured in the classic Lawrence and Lorsch study [P. Lawrence and J. Lorsch, *Organization and Environment* (Boston: Harvard Business School Press, 1967)]. Their differentiation-integration framework was first applied to the international organization task by Prahalad [C.K. Prahalad, "The Strategic Process in a Multinational Corporation," (Boston: unpublished doctoral dissertation, Harvard Graduate School of Business Administration, 1976)], and subsequently adapted by others, including Doz and Bartlett [see Y. Doz, *National Policies and Multinational Strategic Management* (New York: Praeger, 1979)]; and [C.A. Bartlett, "Multinational Structural Evolution: The Changing Decision Environment" (Boston: unpublished doctoral dissertation, Harvard Graduate School of Business Administration, 1979)].

2
This research project consisted of three phases. The first aimed at identifying and describing the key challenges faced by managers of worldwide companies and documenting "leading practice" in coping with these challenges. That was also the hypothesis-generating phase, and the sample was selected to represent the greatest variety of strategic and organizational situations. In the consumer electronics industry, globalization offered the greatest benefits; in the consumer packaged products business, the forces of national responsiveness were especially strong; and in the telecommunications switching industry, both global and local forces were very important. Within each industry, we selected a group of firms that represented the greatest variety of administrative heritages, including differences in nationality, internationalization history, and corporate culture. The research sites we chose were Philips, Matsushita, and GE in consumer electronics, Kao, Procter & Gamble, and Unilever in consumer chemicals, and ITT, NEC, and L.M. Ericsson in telecommunications switching.

In each of these companies, we interviewed a great many managers in the corporate headquarters and also in a number of national organizations in the U.S., Brazil, U.K., Germany, France, Italy, Taiwan, Singapore, Japan, and Australia. In addition, we studied company documents, and also collected information about the industries and the companies from a range of external sources. This two-article series is written primarily on the basis of data collected in this first phase of the project.

In the next stage, we conducted detailed questionnaire surveys in three of these nine companies. The principal objective of the survey was to carry out a preliminary test of some hypotheses generated during the first phase of clinical research, to define the hypotheses more precisely, and to develop suitable instruments for testing them more rigorously. Approximately 100 managers each from NEC, Matsushita, and Philips participated in the survey.

Finally, in the third phase of the study, the hypotheses were tested through a large-sample mailed questionnaire survey that yielded data on 720 cases of headquarters-subsidiary relations in sixty-six of the largest U.S. and European multinational corporations.

The overall findings of the project are being reported in our forthcoming book, tentatively entitled *Managing across Borders: The Transnational Solution*, to be published by the Harvard Business School Press.

3
The term "global," applied to industries, companies, and strategies, has been subject to widely differing definition and usage. For further discussion, see M.E. Porter, "Competition in Global Industries: A Conceptual Framework," in M.E. Porter, ed., *Competition in Global Industries* (Boston: Harvard Business School Press, 1986). We will use the term *global strategy* in its purest sense—one that defines product, manufacturing scale, technology, sourcing patterns, and competitive strategy on the assumption of a unified world market. It is the classic standardized product exported from a centralized global-scale plant and distributed according to a centrally managed global strategy.

4
See R. Vernon, "International Investment and International

Trade in the Product Cycle," *Quarterly Journal of Economics*, May 1966, pp. 190–207.

5
The internationalization processes and accompanying organizational attributes of many European multinationals have been described by L.G. Franko, *The European Multinationals* (Stanford, CA: Graylock, 1976).

6
For a detailed discussion of the management process in Japanese firms and their impact on strategy, see M.Y. Yoshino, *Japan's Managerial System: Tradition and Innovation* (Cambridge: MIT Press, 1968).

7
Readers with a particular interest in the history of international business will find a far richer historical analysis in A.D.

Chandler, "The Evolution of Modern Global Enterprise," in *Competition in Global Industries*, ed. M.E. Porter (Boston: Harvard Business School Press, 1986).

8
Documenting the postwar expansion of U.S.-based companies, Jean Jacques Servan-Schreiber attributed the Americans' success to their technological and managerial abilities. See J.J. Servan-Schreiber, *The American Challenge* (New York: Atheneum, 1968).

9
The issue of a management mind-set being critical to the task of managing MNCs was highlighted almost two decades ago by Perlmutter. See H.V. Perlmutter, "The Tortuous Evolution of the Multinational Corporation," *Columbia Journal of World Business*, January-February 1969, pp. 9–18.

Sloan
Management
Review

17

Summer 1987

Strategic Management Journal, Vol. 8, 425–440 (1987)

GLOBAL STRATEGY: AN ORGANIZING FRAMEWORK

SUMANTRA GHOSHAL
INSEAD, Fontainebleau, France

Global strategy has recently emerged as a popular concept among managers of multinational corporations as well as among researchers and students in the field of international management. This paper presents a conceptual framework encompassing a range of different issues relevant to global strategies. The framework provides a basis for organizing existing literature on the topic and for creating a map of the field. Such a map can be useful for teaching and also for guiding future research in this area. The article, however, is primarily directed at managers of multinational corporations, and is aimed at providing them with a basis for relating and synthesizing the different perspectives and prescriptions that are currently available for global strategic management.

Over the past few years the concept of global strategy has taken the world of multinational corporations (MNCs) by storm. Scores of articles in the *Harvard Business Review, Fortune, The Economist* and other popular journals have urged multinationals to 'go global' in their strategies. The topic has clearly captured the attention of MNC managers. Conferences on global strategy, whether organized by the Conference Board in New York, *The Financial Times* in London, or Nomura Securities in Tokoyo, have invariably attracted enthusiastic corporate support and sizeable audiences. Even in the relatively slow-moving world of academe the issue of globalization of industries and companies has emerged as a new bandwagon, as manifest in the large number of papers on the topic presented at recent meetings of the Academy of Management, the Academy of International Business and the Strategic Management Society. 'Manage globally' appears to be the latest battlecry in the world of international business.

MULTIPLE PERSPECTIVES, MANY PRESCRIPTIONS

This enthusiasm notwithstanding, there is a great deal of conceptual ambiguity about what a 'global' strategy really means. As pointed out by Hamel and Prahalad (1985), the distinction among a global industry, a global firm, and a global strategy is somewhat blurred in the literature. According to Hout, Porter and Rudden (1982), a global strategy is appropriate for global industries which are defined as those in which a firm's competitive position in one national market is significantly affected by its competitive position in other national markets. Such interactions between a firm's positions in different markets may arise from scale benefits or from the potential of synergies or sharing of costs and resoures across markets. However, as argued by Bartlett (1985), Kogut (1984) and many others, those scale and synergy benefits may often be created by strategic actions of individual firms and may

0143-2095/87/050425–16$08.00

Received 6 January 1986
Revised 3 October 1986

not be 'given' in any *a priori* sense. For some industries, such as aeroframes or aeroengines, the economies of scale may be large enough to make the need for global integration of activities obvious. However, in a large number of cases industries may not be born global but may have globalness thrust upon them by the entrepreneurship of a company such as Yoshida Kagyo KK (YKK) or Procter and Gamble. In such cases the global industry–global strategy link may be more useful for ex-post explanation of outcomes than for ex-ante predictions or strategizing.

Further, the concept of a global strategy is not as new as some of the recent authors on the topic have assumed it to be. It was stated quite explicitly about 20 years ago by Perlmutter (1969) when he distinguished between the geocentric, polycentric, and ethnocentric approaches to multinational management. The starting point for Perlmutter's categorization scheme was the worldview of a firm, which was seen as the driving force behind its management processes and the way it structured its world-wide activities (see Robinson, 1978 and Rutenberg, 1982 for detailed reviews and expositions). In much of the current literature, in contrast, the focus has been narrowed and the concept of global strategy has been linked almost exclusively with how the firm structures the flow of tasks within its world-wide value-adding system. The more integrated and rationalized the flow of tasks appears to be, the more global the firm's strategy is assumed to be (e.g. Leontiades, 1984). On the one hand, this focus has led to improved understanding of the fact that different tasks offer different degrees of advantages from global integration and national differentiation and that, optimally, a firm must configure its value chain to obtain the best possible advantages from both (Porter, 1984). But, on the other hand, it has also led to certain dysfunctional simplifications. The complexities of managing large, world-wide organizations have been obscured by creating polar alternatives between centralization and decentralization, or between global and multidomestic strategies (e.g. Hout *et al.*, 1982). Complex management tasks have been seen as composites of simple global and local components. By emphasizing the importance of rationalizing the flow of components and final products within a multinational system, the importance of internal flows of

people, technology, information, and values has been de-emphasized.

Differences among authors writing on the topic of global strategy are not limited to concepts and perspectives. Their prescriptions on how to manage globally have also been very different, and often contradictory.

1. Levitt (1983) has argued that effective global strategy is not a bag of many tricks but the successful practice of just one: product standardization. According to him, the core of a global strategy lies in developing a standardized product to be produced and sold the same way throughout the world.

2. According to Hout, *et al.* (1982), on the other hand, effective global strategy requires the approach not of a hedgehog, who knows only one trick, but that of a fox, who knows many. Exploiting economies of scale through global volume, taking pre-emptive positions through quick and large investments, and managing interdependently to achieve synergies across different activities are, according to these authors, some of the more important moves that a winning global strategist must muster.

3. Hamel and Prahalad's (1985) prescription for a global strategy contradicts that of Levitt (1983) even more sharply. Instead of a single standardized product, they recommend a broad product portfolio, with many product varieties, so that investments on technologies and distribution channels can be shared. Cross-subsidization across products and markets, and the development of a strong world-wide distribution system, are the two moves that find the pride of place in these authors' views on how to succeed in the game of global chess.

4. If Hout, *et al.*'s (1982) global strategist is the heavyweight champion who knocks out opponents with scale and pre-emptive investments, Kogut's (1985b) global strategist is the nimble-footed athelete who wins through flexibility and arbitrage. He creates options so as to turn the uncertainties of an increasingly volatile global economy to his own advantage. Multiple sourcing, production shifting to benefit from changing factor costs and exchange rates, and arbitrage to exploit imperfections in financial and information markets are,

according to Kogut, some of the hallmarks of a superior global strategy.

These are only a few of the many prescriptions available to MNC managers about how to build a global strategy for their firms. All these suggestions have been derived from rich and insightful analyses of real-life situations. They are all reasonable and intuitively appealing, but their managerial implications are not easy to reconcile.

THE NEED FOR AN ORGANIZING FRAMEWORK

The difficulty for both practitioners and researchers in dealing with the small but rich literature on global strategies is that there is no organizing framework within which the different perspectives and prescriptions can be assimilated. An unfortunate fact of corporate life is that any particular strategic action is rarely an unmixed blessing. Corporate objectives are multidimensional, and often mutually contradictory. Contrary to received wisdom, it is also usually difficult to prioritize them. Actions to achieve a particular objective often impede another equally important objective. Each of these prescriptions is aimed at achieving certain objectives of a global strategy. An overall framework can be particularly useful in identifying the trade-offs between those objectives and therefore in understanding not only the benefits but also the potential costs associated with the different strategic alternatives.

The objective of this paper is to suggest such an organizing framework which may help managers and academics in formulating the various issues that arise in global strategic management. The underlying premise is that simple categorization schemes such as the distinction between global and multidomestic strategies are not very helpful in understanding the complexities of corporate-level strategy in large multinational corporations. Instead, what may be more useful is to understand what the key strategic objectives of an MNC are, and the tools that it possesses for achieving them. An integrated analysis of the different means and the different ends can help both managers and researchers in formulating, describing, classifying and analyzing

the content of global strategies. Besides, such a framework can relate academic research, that is often partial, to the totality of real life that managers must deal with.

THE FRAMEWORK: MAPPING MEANS AND ENDS

The proposed framework is shown in Table 1. While the specific construct may be new, the conceptual foundation on which it is built is derived from a synthesis of existing literature.

The basic argument is simple. The goals of a multinational—as indeed of any organization—can be classified into three broad categories. The firm must achieve efficiency in its current activities; it must manage the risks that it assumes in carrying out those activities; and it must develop internal learning capabilities so as to be able to innovate and adapt to future changes. Competitive advantage is developed by taking strategic actions that optimize the firm's achievement of these different and, at times, conflicting goals.

A multinational has three sets of tools for developing such competitive advantage. It can exploit the differences in input and output markets among the many countries in which it operates. It can benefit from scale economies in its different activities. It can also exploit synergies or economies of scope that may be available because of the diversity of its activities and organization.

The strategic task of managing globally is to use all three sources of competitive advantage to optimize efficiency, risk and learning simultaneously in a world-wide business. The key to a successful global strategy is to manage the interactions between these different goals and means. That, in essence, is the organizing framework. Viewing the tasks of global strategy this way can be helpful to both managers and academics in a number of ways. For example, it can help managers in generating a comprehensive checklist of factors and issues that must be considered in reviewing different strategic alternatives. Such a checklist can serve as a basis for mapping the overall strategies of their own companies and those of their competitors so as to understand the comparative strengths and

428   S. Ghoshal

Table 1. Global strategy: an organizing framework

Strategic objectives	Sources of competitive advantage		
	National differences	Scale economies	Scope economies
Achieving efficiency in current operations	Benefiting from differences in factor costs—wages and cost of capital	Expanding and exploiting potential scale economies in each activity	Sharing of investments and costs across products, markets and businesses
Managing risks	Managing different kinds of risks arising from market or policy-induced changes in comparative advantages of different countries	Balancing scale with strategic and operational flexibility	Portfolio diversification of risks and creation of options and side-bets
Innovation learning and adaptation	Learning from societal differences in organizational and managerial processes and systems	Benefiting from experience—cost reduction and innovation	Shared learning across organizational components in different products, markets or businesses

vulnerabilities of both. Table 1 shows some illustrative examples of factors that must be considered while carrying out such comprehensive strategic audits. Another practical utility of the framework is that it can highlight the contradictions between the different goals and between the different means, and thereby make salient the strategic dilemmas that may otherwise get resolved through omission.

In the next two sections the framework is explained more fully by describing the two dimensions of its construct, viz. the strategic objectives of the firm and the sources of competitive advantage available to a multinational corporation. Subsequent sections show how selected articles contribute to the literature and fit within the overall framework. The paper concludes with a brief discussion of the trade-offs that are implicit in some of the more recent prescriptions on global strategic management.

THE GOALS: STRATEGIC OBJECTIVES

Achieving efficiency

A general premise in the literature on strategic management is that the concept of strategy is relevant only when the actions of one firm can affect the actions or performance of another. Firms competing in imperfect markets earn different 'efficiency rents' from the use of their resources (Caves, 1980). The objective of strategy, given this perspective, is to enhance such efficiency rents.

Viewing a firm broadly as an input–output system, the overall efficiency of the firm can be defined as the ratio of the value of its outputs to the costs of all its inputs. It is by maximizing this ratio that the firm obtains the surplus resources required to secure its own future. Thus it differentiates its products to enhance the exchange value of its outputs, and seeks low cost factors to minimize the costs of its inputs. It also tries to enhance the efficiency of its throughput processes by achieving higher scale economies or by finding more efficient production processes.

The field of strategic management is currently dominated by this efficiency perspective. The generic strategies of Porter (1980), different versions of the portfolio model, as well as overall strategic management frameworks such as those proposed by Hofer and Schendel (1978) and Hax and Majluf (1984) are all based on the underlying notion of maximizing efficiency rents of the different resources available to the firm.

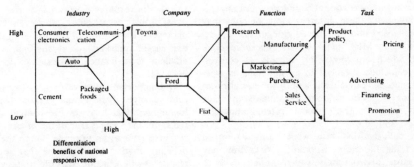

Figure 1.   The integration–responsiveness framework (reproduced from Bartlett, 1985)

In the field of global strategy this efficiency perspective has been reflected in the widespread use of the integration–responsiveness framework originally proposed by Prahalad (1975) and subsequently developed and applied by a number of authors including Doz, Bartlett and Prahalad (1981) and Porter (1984). In essence, the framework is a conceptual lens for visualizing the cost advantages of global integration of certain tasks *vis-à-vis* the differentiation benefits of responding to national differences in tastes, industry structures, distribution systems, and government regulations. As suggested by Bartlett (1985), the same framework can be used to understand differences in the benefits of integration and responsiveness at the aggregate level of industries, at the level of individual companies within an industry, or even at the level of different functions within a company (see Figure 1, reproduced from Bartlett, 1985). Thus the consumer electronics industry may be characterized by low differentiation benefits and high integration advantages, while the position of the packaged foods industry may be quite the opposite. In the telecommunications switching industry, in contrast, both local and global forces may be strong, while in the automobile industry both may be of moderate and comparable importance.

Within an industry (say, automobile), the strategy of one firm (such as Toyota) may be based on exploiting the advantages of global integration through centralized production and decision-making, while that of another (such as Fiat) may aim at exploiting the benefits of national differentiation by creating integrated and autonomous subsidiaries which can exploit strong links with local stakeholders to defend themselves against more efficient global competitors. Within a firm, research may offer greater efficiency benefits of integration, while sales and service may provide greater differentiation advantages. One can, as illustrated in Figure 1, apply the framework to even lower levels of analysis, right down to the level of individual tasks. Based on such analysis, a multinational firm can determine the optimum way to configure its value chain so as to achieve the highest overall efficiency in the use of its resources (Porter, 1984).

However, while efficiency is clearly an important strategic objective, it is not the only one. As argued recently by a number of authors, the broader objective of strategic management is to create value which is determined not only by the returns that specific assets are expected to generate, but also by the risks that are assumed in the process (see Woo and Cool (1985) for a review). This leads to the second strategic objective of firms—that of managing risks.[1]

Managing risks

A multinational corporation faces many different kinds of risks, some of which are endemic to all firms and some others are unique to organizations

---

[1] In the interest of simplicity the distinction between risk and uncertainty is ignored, as is the distinction between systematic and unsystematic risks.

operating across national boundaries. For analytical simplicity these different kinds of risks may be collapsed into four broad categories.

First, an MNC faces certain *macroeconomic risks* which are completely outside its control. These include cataclysmic events such as wars and natural calamities, and also equilibrium-seeking or even random movements in wage rates, interest rates, exchange rates, commodity prices, and so on.

Second, the MNC faces what is usually referred to in the literature as political risks but may be more appropriately called *policy risks* to emphasize that they arise from policy actions of national governments and not from either long-term equilibrium-seeking forces of global markets, nor from short-term random fluctuations in economic variables arising out of stickiness and unpredictability of market mechanisms. The net effect of such policy actions may often be indistinguishable from the effect of macroeconomic forces; for example, both may lead to changes in the exchange rate of a particular currency. But from a management perspective the two must be distinguished, since the former is uncontrollable but the latter is at least partially controllable.

Third, a firm also faces certain *competitive risks* arising from the uncertainties of competitors' responses to its own strategies (including the strategy of doing nothing and trying to maintain the status quo). While all companies face such risks to varying extents (since both monopolies and perfect competition are rare), their implications are particularly complex in the context of global strategies since the responses of competitors may take place in many different forms and in many different markets. Further, technological risk can also be considered as a part of competitive risk since a new technology can adversely affect a firm only when it is adopted by a competitor, and not otherwise.[2]

Finally, a firm also faces what may be called *resource risks*. This is the risk that the adopted strategy will require resources that the firm does not have, cannot acquire, or cannot spare. A key scarce resource for most firms is managerial

talent. But resource risks can also arise from lack of appropriate technology, or even capital (if managers, for reasons of control, do not want to use capital markets, or if the market is less efficient than finance theorists would have us believe).

One important issue with regard to risks is that they change over time. Vernon (1977) has highlighted this issue in the context of policy risks, but the same is true of the others. Consider resource risks as an example. Often the strategy of a multinational will assume that appropriate resources will be acquired as the strategy unfolds. Yet the initial conditions on which the plans for on-going resource acquisition and development have been based may change over time. Nissan, for instance, based its aggressive internationalization strategy on the expectation of developing technological, financial, and managerial resources out of its home base. Changing competitive positions among local car manufacturers in Japan have affected these resource development plans of the company, and its internationalizing strategy has been threatened significantly. A more careful analysis of alternative competitive scenarios, and of their effects on the resource allocation plans of the company, may have led Nissan to either a slower pace of internationalization, or to a more aggressive process of resource acquisition at an earlier stage of implementing its strategy.

The strategic task, with regard to management of risks, is to consider these different kinds of risks *jointly* in the context of particular strategic decisions. However, not all forms of risk are strategic since some risks can be easily diversified, shifted, or shared through routine market transactions. It is only those risks which cannot be diversified through a readily available external market that are of concern at the strategic level.

As an example, consider the case of currency risks. These can be classified as contractual, semi-contractual and operating risks (Lessard and Lightstone, 1983). Contractual risks arise when a firm enters into a contract for which costs and revenues are expected to be generated in different currencies: for example a Japanese firm entering into a contract for supplying an item to be made in Japan to an American customer at a price fixed in dollars. Semi-contractual risks are assumed when a firm offers an option denominated in foreign currencies, such as a British

---

[2] This assumes that the firm has defined its business correctly and has identified as competitors all the firms whose offerings are aimed at meeting the same set of market needs that the firm meets.

company quoting a firm rate in guilders. Operating risks, on the other hand, refer to exchange rate-related changes in the firm's competitiveness arising out of long-term commitments of revenues or costs in different currencies. For example, to compete with a Korean firm, an American firm may set up production facilities in Singapore for supplying its customers in the United States and Europe. A gradual strengthening of the Singapore dollar, in comparison with the Korean won, can erode the overall competitiveness of the Singapore plant.

Both contractual and semi-contractual currency risks can be easily shifted or diversified, at relatively low cost, through various hedging mechanisms. If a firm does not so hedge these risks, it is essentially operating as a currency speculator and the risks must be associated with the speculation business and not to its product-market operations. Operating risks, on the other hand, cannot be hedged so easily, [3] and must be considered at the strategic rather than the operational level.

Analysis of strategic risks will have significant implications for a firm's decisions regarding the structures and locations of its cost and revenue streams. It will lead to more explicit analysis of the effects of environmental uncertainties on the configuration of its value chain. There may be a shift from ownership to rental of resources; from fixed to variable costs. Output and activity distributions may be broadened to achieve the benefits of diversification. Incrementalism and opportunism may be given greater emphasis in its strategy in comparison to pre-emptive resource commitments and long-term planning. Overall strategies may be formulated in more general and flexible terms, so as to be robust to different environmental scenarios. In addition, side-bets may be laid to cover contingencies and to create strategic options which may or may not be exercised in the future (see Kogut, 1985b; Aaker and Mascarenhas, 1984; and Mascarenhas, 1982).

Innovation, learning and adaptation

Most existing theories of the multinational corpor-

ation view it as an instrument to extract additional rents from capabilities internalized by the firm (see Calvet, 1981, for a review). A firm goes abroad to make more profits by exploiting its technology, or brand name, or management capabilities in different countries around the world. It is assumed that the key competencies of the multinational always reside at the center.

While the search for additional profits or the desire to protect existing revenues may explain why multinationals come to exist, they may not provide an equally complete explanation of why some of them continue to grow and flourish. An alternative view may well be that a key asset of the multinational is the diversity of environments in which it operates. This diversity exposes it to multiple stimuli, allows it to develop diverse capabilities, and provides it with a broader learning opportunity than is available to a purely domestic firm. The enhanced organizational learning that results from the diversity internalized by the multinational may be a key explanator of its ongoing success, while its initial stock of knowledge may well be the strength that allows it to create such organizational diversity in the first place (Bartlett and Ghoshal, 1985).

Internal diversity may lead to strategic advantages for a firm in many different ways. In an unpredictable environment it may not be possible, ex ante, to predict the competencies that will be required in the future. Diversity of internal capabilities, following the logic of population ecologists (e.g. Hannan and Freeman, 1977; Aldrich, 1979), will enhance the probability of the firm's survival by enhancing the chances that it will be in possession of the capabilities required to cope with an uncertain future state. Similarly, diversity of resources and competencies may also enhance the firm's ability to create joint innovations, and to exploit them in multiple locations. One example of such benefits of diversity was recently described in the *Wall Street Journal* (April 29, 1985):

> P&G [Procter and Gamble Co.] recently introduced its new Liquid Tide, but the product has a distinctly international heritage. A new ingredient that helps suspend dirt in wash water came from the company's research center near P&G's Cincinnati headquarters. But the formula for Liquid Tide's surfactants, or cleaning agents, was developed by P&G technicians in Japan.

---

[3] Some market mechanisms such as long-term currency swaps are now available which can allow at least partial hedging of operating risks.

The ingredients that fight mineral salts present in hard water came from P&G's scientists in Brussels.

As discussed in the same *WSJ* article, P&G's research center in Brussels has developed a special capability in water softening technology due, in part, to the fact that water in Europe contains more than twice the level of mineral content compared to wash water available in the United States. Similarly, surfactant technology is particularly advanced in Japan because Japanese consumers wash their clothes in colder waters compared to consumers in the US or Europe, and this makes greater demands on the cleaning ability of the surfactants. The advantage of P&G as a multinational is that it is exposed to these different operating environments and has learned, in each environment, the skills and knowledge that coping with that environment specially requires. Liquid Tide is an example of the strategic advantages that accrue from such diverse learning.

The mere existence of diversity, however, does not enhance learning. It only creates the potential for learning. To exploit this potential, the organization must consider learning as an explicit objective, and must create mechanisms and systems for such learning to take place. In the absence of explicit intention and appropriate mechanisms, the learning potential may be lost. In some companies, where all organizational resources are centralized and where the national subsidiaries are seen as mere delivery pipelines to supply the organization's value-added to different countries, diverse learning may not take place either because the subsidiaries may not possess appropriate sensing, analyzing, and responding capabilities to learn from their local environments, or because the centralized decision processes may be insensitive to knowledge accumulated outside the corporate headquarters. Other companies, in which the subsidiaries may enjoy very high levels of local resources and autonomy, may similarly fail to exploit global learning benefits because of their inability to transfer and synthesize knowledge and expertise developed in different organizational components. Local loyalties, turf protection, and the 'not invented here' (NIH) syndrome—the three handmaidens of decentralization—may restrict internal flow of information across national boundaries which is essential for global learning to occur. In other words, both centralization and decentralization may impede learning.

THE MEANS: SOURCES OF COMPETITIVE ADVANTAGE

Most recent articles on global strategy have been aimed at identifying generic strategies (such as global cost leadership, focus or niche) and advocating particular strategic moves (such as cross-subsidy or pre-emptive investments). Underlying these concepts, however, are three fundamental tools for building global competitive advantage: exploiting differences in input and output markets in different countries, exploiting economies of scale, and exploiting economies of scope (Porter, 1985).

National differences

The comparative advantage of locations in terms of differences in factor costs is perhaps the most discussed, and also the best understood, source of competitive advantage in international business.

Different nations have different factor endowments, and in the absence of efficient markets this leads to inter-country differences in factor costs. Different activities of the firm, such as R&D, production, marketing, etc., have different factor intensities. A firm can therefore gain cost advantages by configuring its value-chain so that each activity is located in the country which has the least cost for the factor that the activity uses most intensely. This is the core concept of comparative advantage-based competitive advantage—a concept for which highly developed analytical tools are available from the discipline of international economics. Kogut (1985a) provides an excellent managerial overview of this concept.

National differences may also exist in output markets. Customer tastes and preferences may be different in different countries, as may be distribution systems, government regulations applicable to the concerned product-markets, or the effectiveness of different promotion strategies and other marketing techniques. A firm can augment the exchange value of its ouput by tailoring its offerings to fit the unique requirements in each national market. This, in essence, is the strategy of national differentiation, and it lies at the core of what has come to be referred to as the multidomestic approach in multinational management (Hout *et al.*, 1982).

From a strategic perspective, however, this static and purely economic view of national differences may not be adequate. What may be more useful is to take a dynamic view of comparative advantage and to broaden the concept to include both societal and economic factors.

In the traditional economics view, comparative advantages of countries are determined by their relative factor endowments and they do not change. However, in reality one lesson of the past four decades is that comparative advantages change and a prime objective of the industrial policies of many nations is to effect such changes. Thus, for any nation, the availability and cost of capital change, as do the availability of technical manpower and the wages of skilled and unskilled labor. Such changes take place, in the long run, to accommodate different levels of economic and social performance of nations, and in the short run they occur in response to specific policies and regulations of governments.

This dynamic aspect of comparative advantages adds considerable complexity to the strategic considerations of the firm. There is a first-order effect of such changes—such as possible increases in wage rates, interest rates or currency exchange rates for particular countries that can affect future viability of a strategy that has been based on the current levels of these economic variables. There can also be a more intriguing second-order effect. If an activity is located in an economically inefficient environment, and if the firm is able to achieve a higher level of efficiency in its own operations compared to the rest of the local economy, its competitive advantage may actually increase as the local economy slips lower and lower. This is because the macroeconomic variables such as wage or exchange rates may change to reflect the overall performance of the economy relative to the rest of the world and, to the extent that the firm's performance is better than this national aggregate, it may benefit from these macro-level changes (Kiechel, 1981).

Consistent with the discipline that gave birth to the concept, the usual view of comparative advantage is limited to factors that an economist

admits into the production function, such as the costs of labor and capital. However, from a managerial perspective it may be more appropriate to take a broader view of societal comparative advantages to include 'all the relative advantages conferred on a society by the quality, quantity and configuration of its material, human and institutional resources, including "soft" resources such as inter-organizational linkages, the nature of its educational system, and organizational and managerial know-how' (Westney, 1985: 4). As argued by Westney, these 'soft' societal factors, if absorbed in the overall organizational system, can provide benefits as real to a multinational as those provided by such economic factors as cheap labor or low-cost capital.

While the concept of comparative advantage is quite clear, available evidence on its actual effect on the overall competitiveness of firms is weak and conflicting. For example, it has often been claimed that one source of competitive advantage for Japanese firms is the lower cost of capital in Japan (Hatsopoulos, 1983). However, more systematic studies have shown that there is practically no difference in the risk-adjusted cost of capital in the United States and Japan, and that capital cost advantages of Japanese firms, if any, arise from complex interactions between government subsidies and corporate ownership structures (Flaherty and Itami, 1984). Similarly, relatively low wage rates in Japan have been suggested by some authors as the primary reason for the success of Japanese companies in the US market (Itami, 1978). However, recently, companies such as Honda and Nissan have commissioned plants in the USA and have been able to retain practically the same levels of cost advantages over US manufacturers as they had for their production in Japan (Allen, 1985). Overall, there is increasing evidence that while comparative advantages of countries can provide competitive advantages to firms, the realization of such benefits is not automatic but depends on complex organizational factors and processes.

Scale economies

Scale economies, again, is a fairly well established concept, and its implications for competitive advantage are quite well understood. Microeconomic theory provides a strong theoretical and empirical basis for evaluating the effect of scale on cost reduction, and the use of scale as a competitive tool is common in practice. Its primary implication for strategy is that a firm must expand the volume of its output so as to achieve available scale benefits. Otherwise a competitor who can achieve such volume can build cost advantages, and this can lead to a vicious cycle in which the low-volume firm can progressively lose its competitive viability.

While scale, by itself, is a static concept, there may be dynamic benefits of scale through what has been variously described as the experience or learning effect. The higher volume that helps a firm to exploit scale benefits also allows it to accumulate learning, and this leads to progressive cost reduction as the firm moves down its learning curve.

The concept of the value-added chain recently popularized by Porter (1985) adds considerable richness to the analysis of scale as a source of competitive advantage. This conceptual apparatus allows a disaggregated analysis of scale benefits in different value-creating activities of the firm. The efficient scale may vary widely by activity— being higher for component production, say, than for assembly. In contrast to a unitary view of scale, this disaggregated view permits the firm to configure different elements of its value chain to attain optimum scale economies in each.

Traditionally, scale has been seen as an unmixed blessing—something that always helps and never hurts. Recently, however, many researchers have argued otherwise (e.g. Evans, 1982). It has been suggested that scale efficiencies are obtained through increased specialization and through creation of dedicated assets and systems. The same processes cause inflexibilities and limit the firm's ability to cope with change. As environmental turbulence has increased, so has the need for strategic and operational flexibility (Mascarenhas, 1982). At the extreme, this line of argument has led to predictions of a re-emergence of the craft form of production to replace the scale-dominated assembly form (Piore and Sabel, 1984). A more typical argument has been to emphasize the need to balance scale and flexibility, through the use of modern technologies such as CAD/CAM and flexible manufacturing systems (Gold, 1982).

Scope economies

Relatively speaking, the concept of scope economies is both new and not very well understood. It is based on the notion that certain economies arise from the fact that the cost of the joint production of two or more products can be less than the cost of producing them separately. Such cost reductions can take place due to many reasons—for example resources such as information or technologies, once acquired for use in producing one item, may be available costlessly for production of other items (Baumol, Panzer and Willig, 1982).

The strategic importance of scope economies arise from a diversified firm's ability to share investments and costs across the same or different value chains that competitors, not possessing such internal and external diversity, cannot. Such sharing can take place across segments, products, or markets (Porter, 1985) and may involve joint use of different kinds of assets (see Table 2).

A diversified firm may share physical assets such as production equipment, cash, or brand names across different businesses and markets. Flexible manufacturing systems using robots, which can be used for production of different items, is one example of how a firm can exploit such scope benefits. Cross-subsidization of markets and exploitation of a global brand name are other examples of sharing a tangible asset across different components of a firm's product and market portfolios.

A second important source of scope economies is shared external relations: with customers, suppliers, distributors, governments, and other institutions. A multinational bank like Citibank can provide relatively more effective service to a multinational customer than can a bank that operates in a single country (see Terpstra, 1982). Similarly, as argued by Hamel and Prahalad (1985), companies such as Matsushita have benefited considerably from their ability to market a diverse range of products through the same distribution channel. In another variation, Japanese trading companies have expanded into new businesses to meet different requirements of their existing customers.

Finally, shared knowledge is the third important component of scope economies. The fundamental thrust of NEC's global strategy is 'C&C'—

Table 2. Scope economies in product and market diversification

	Sources of scope economies	
	Product diversification	Market diversification
Shared physical assets	Factory automation with flexibility to produce multiple products (Ford)	Global brand name (Coca-Cola)
Shared external relations	Using common distribution channel for multiple products (Matsushita)	Servicing multi-national customers world-wide (Citibank)
Shared learning	Sharing R&D in computer and communications businesses (NEC)	Pooling knowledge developed in different markets (Procter and Gamble)

computers and communication. The company firmly believes that its even strengths in the two technologies and resulting capabilities of merging them in-house to create new products gives it a competitive edge over global giants such as IBM and AT&T, who have technological strength in only one of these two areas. Another example of the scope advantages of shared learning is the case of Liquid Tide described earlier in this paper.

Even scope economies, however, may not be costless. Different segments, products or markets of a diversified company face different environmental demands. To succeed, a firm needs to differentiate its management systems and processes so that each of its activities can develop *external consistency* with the requirments of its own environment. The search for scope economies, on the other hand, is a search for *internal consistencies* within the firm and across its different activities. The effort to create such synergies may invariably result in some compromise with the objective of external consistency in each activity.

Further, the search for internal synergies also enhances the complexities in a firm's management processes. In the extreme, such complexities can overwhelm the organization, as it did in the case of EMI, the UK-based music, electronics, and leisure products company which attempted to manage its new CT scanner business within the framework of its existing organizational structure and processes (see EMI and the CT scanner,

ICCH case 9–383–194). Certain parts of a company's portfolio of businesses or markets may be inherently very different from some others, and it may be best not to look for economies of scope across them. For example, in the soft drinks industry, bottling and distribution are intensely local in scope, while the tasks of creating and maintaining a brand image, or that of designing efficient bottling plants, may offer significant benefits from global integration. Carrying out both these sets of functions in-house would clearly lead to internalizing enormous differences within the company with regard to the organizing, coordinating, and controlling tasks. Instead of trying to cope with these complexities, Coca-Cola has externalized those functions which are purely local in scope (in all but some key strategic markets). In a variation of the same theme, IBM has 'externalized' the PC business by setting up an almost stand-alone organization, instead of trying to exploit scope benefits by integrating this business within the structure of its existing organization (for a more detailed discussion on multinational scope economies and on the conflicts between internal and external consistencies, see Lorange, Scott Morton and Ghoshal, 1986).

PRESCRIPTIONS IN PERSPECTIVE

Existing literature on global strategy offers analytical insights and helpful prescriptions for

436   *S. Ghoshal*

Table 3. Selected references for further reading

Strategic objectives	Sources of competitive advantage		
	National differences	Scale economies	Scope economies
Achieving efficiency in current operations	Kogut (1985a); Itami (1978); Okimoto, Sugano and Weinstein (1984)	Hout, Porter and Rudden (1982); Levitt (1983); Doz (1978); Leontiades (1984); Gluck (1983)	Hamel and Prahalad (1985); Hout, Porter and Rudden (1982); Porter (1985); Ohmae (1985)
Managing risks	Kiechel (1981); Kobrin (1982); Poynter (1985); Lessard and Lightstone (1983); Srinivasulu (1981); Herring (1983)	Evans (1982); Piore and Sabel (1984); Gold (1982); Aaker and Mascarenhas (1984)	Kogut (1985b); Lorange, Scott Morton and Ghoshal (1986)
Innovation, learning and adaptation	Westney (1985); Terpstra (1977); Ronstadt and Krammer (1982)	BCG (1982); Rapp (1973)	Bartlett and Ghoshal (1985)

almost all the different issues indicated in Table 1. Table 3 shows a selective list of relevant publications, categorized on the basis of issues that, according to this author's interpretations, the pieces primarily focus on.[4]

Pigeon-holing academic contributions into different parts of a conceptual framework tends to be unfair to their authors. In highlighting what the authors focus on, such categorization often amounts to an implicit criticism for what they did not write. Besides, most publications cover a broader range of issues and ideas than can be reflected in any such categorization scheme. Table 3 suffers from all these deficiencies. At the same time, however, it suggests how the proposed framework can be helpful in integrating the literature and in relating the individual pieces to each other.

[4] From an academic point of view, strategy of the multinational corporation is a specialized and highly applied field of study. It is built on the broader field of business policy and strategy which, in turn, rests on the foundation of a number of academic disciplines such as economics, organization theory, finance theory, operations research, etc. A number of publications in those underlying disciplines, and a significant body of research carried out in the field of strategy, in general, provide interesting insights on the different issues highlighted in Table 1. However, given the objective of suggesting a limited list of further readings that *managers* may find useful, such publications have not been included in Table 3. Further, even for the more applied and prescriptive literature on global strategy, the list is only illustrative and not exhaustive.

From parts to the whole

For managers, the advantage of such synthesis is that it allows them to combine a set of insightful but often partial analyses to address the totality of a multidimensional and complex phenomenon. Consider, for example, a topic that has been the staple for academics interested in international management: explaining and drawing normative conclusions from the global successes of many Japanese companies. Based on detailed comparisons across a set of matched pairs of US and Japanese firms, Itami concludes that the relative successes of the Japanese firms can be wholly explained as due to the advantages of lower wage rates and higher labor productivity. In the context of a specific industry, on the other hand, Toder (1978) shows that manufacturing scale is the single most important source of the Japanese competitive advantage. In the small car business, for example, the minimum efficient scale requires an annual production level of about 400,000 units. In the late 1970s no US auto manufacturer produced even 200,000 units of any subcompact configuration vehicle, while Toyota produced around 500,000 Corollas and Nissan produced between 300,000 and 400,000 B210s per year. Toder estimates that US manufacturers suffered a cost disadvantage of between 9 and 17 percent on account of inefficient scale alone. Add to it the effects of wage rate differentials and exchange rate movements, and Japanese success in the

US auto market may not require any further explanation. Yet process-orientated scholars such as Hamel and Prahalad suggest a much more complex explanation of the Japanese tidal wave. They see it as arising out of a dynamic process of strategic evolution that exploits scope economies as a crucial weapon in the final stages. All these authors provide compelling arguments to support their own explanations, but do not consider or refute each other's hypotheses.

This multiplicity of explanations only shows the complexity of global strategic management. However, though different, these explanations and prescriptions are not always mutually exclusive. The manager's task is to find how these insights can be combined to build a multidimensional and flexible strategy that is robust to the different assumptions and explanations.

The strategic trade-offs

This, however, is not always possible because there are certain inherent contradictions between the different strategic objectives and between the different sources of competitive advantage. Consider, for instance, the popular distinction between a global and a multidomestic strategy described by Hout *et al.* (1982). A global strategy requires that the firm should carefully separate different value elements, and should locate each activity at the most efficient level of scale in the location where the activity can be carried out at the cheapest cost. Each activity should then be integrated and managed interdependently so as to exploit available scope economies. In essence, it is a strategy to maximize efficiency of current operations.

Such a strategy may, however, increase both endogenous and exogenous risks for the firm. Global scale of certain activities such as R&D ana manufacturing may result in the firm's costs being concentrated in a few countries, while its revenues accrue globally, from sales in many different countries. This increases the operating exposure of the firm to the vicissitudes of exchange rate movements because of the mismatch between the currencies in which revenues are obtained and those in which costs are incurred. Similarly, the search for efficiency in a global business may lead to greater amounts of intra-company, but inter-country, flows of goods, capital, information and other resources. These

flows are visible, salient and tend to attract policy interventions from different host governments. Organizationally, such an integrated system requires a high degree of coordination, which enhances the risks of management failures. These are lessons that many Japanese companies have learned well recently.

Similarly, consideration of the learning objective will again contradict some of the proclaimed benefits of a global strategy. The implementation of a global strategy tends to enhance the forces of centralization and to shift organizational power from the subsidiaries to the headquarters. This may result in demotivation of subsidiary managers and may erode one key asset of the MNC—the potential for learning from its many environments. The experiences of Caterpillar is a case in point. An exemplary practioner of global strategy, Cat has recently spilled a lot of red ink on its balance sheet and has lost ground steadily to its archrival, Komatsu. Many factors contributed to Caterpillar's woes, not the least of which was the inability of its centralized management processes to benefit from the experiences of its foreign subsidiaries.

On the flipside of the coin, strategies aimed at optimizing risk or learning may compromise current efficiency. Poynter (1985) has recommended 'upgrade', i.e. increasing commitment of technology and resources in subsidiaries, as a way to overcome risk of policy interventions by host governments. Kogut (1985b), Mascarenhas (1982) and many others have suggested creating strategic and operational flexibility as a mechanism for coping with macroenvironmental risks. Bartlett and Ghoshal (1985) have proposed the differentiated network model of multinational organizations as a way to operationalize the benefits of global learning. All these recommendations carry certain efficiency penalties, which the authors have ignored.

Similar trade-offs exist between the different sources of competitive advantages. Trying to make the most of factor cost economies may prevent scale efficiency, and may impede benefiting from synergies across products or functions. Trying to benefit from scope through product diversification may affect scale, and so on. In effect these contradictions between the different strategic objectives, and between the different means for achieving them, lead to trade-offs between each cell in the framework and practically all others.

These trade-offs imply that to formulate and implement a global strategy, MNC managers must consider all the issues suggested in Table 1, and must evaluate the implications of different strategic alternatives on each of these issues. Under a particular set of circumstances a particular strategic objective may dominate and a particular source of competitive advantage may play a more important role than the others (Fayerweather, 1981). The complexity of global strategic management arises from the need to understand those situational contingencies, and to adopt a strategy after evaluating the trade-offs it implies. Existing prescriptions can sensitize MNC managers to the different factors they must consider, but cannot provide ready-made and standardized solutions for them to adopt.

CONCLUSION

This paper has proposed a framework that can help MNC managers in reviewing and analyzing the strategies of their firms. It is not a blueprint for formulating strategies; it is a road map for reviewing them. Irrespective of whether strategies are analytically formulated or organizationally formed (Mintzberg, 1978), every firm has a realized strategy. To the extent that the realized strategy may differ from the intended one, managers need to review what the strategies of their firms really are. The paper suggests a scheme for such a review which can be an effective instrument for exercising strategic control.

Three arguments underlie the construct of the framework. First, in the global strategy literature, a kind of industry determinism has come to prevail not unlike the technological determinism that dominated management literature in the 1960s. The structures of industries may often have important influences on the appropriateness of corporate strategy, but they are only one of many such influences. Besides, corporate strategy may influence industry structure just as much as be influenced by it.

Second, simple schemes for categorizing strategies of firms under different labels tend to hide more than they reveal. A map for more detailed comparison of the content of strategies can be more helpful to managers in understanding and improving the competitive positions of their companies.

Third, the issues of risk and learning have not been given adequate importance in the strategy literature in general, and in the area of global strategies in particular. Both these are important strategic objectives and must be explicitly considered while evaluating or reviewing the strategic positions of companies.

The proposed framework is not a replacement of existing analytical tools but an enhancement that incorporates these beliefs. It does not present any new concepts or solutions, but only a synthesis of existing ideas and techniques. The benefit of such synthesis is that it can help managers in integrating an array of strategic moves into an overall strategic thrust by revealing the consistencies and contradictions among those moves.

For academics this brief view of the existing literature on global strategy will clearly reveal the need for more empirically grounded and systematic research to test and validate the hypotheses which currently appear in the literature as prescriptions and research conclusions. For partial analyses to lead to valid conclusions, excluded variables must be controlled for, and rival hypotheses must be considered and eliminated. The existing body of descriptive and normative research is rich enough to allow future researchers to adopt a more rigorous and systematic approach to enhance the reliability and validity of their findings and suggestions. The proposed framework, it is hoped, may be of value to some researchers in thinking about appropriate research issues and designs for furthering the field of global strategic management.

ACKNOWLEDGEMENTS

The ideas presented in this paper emerged in the course of discussions with many friends and colleagues. Don Lessard, Eleanor Westney, Bruce Kogut, Chris Bartlett and Nitin Nohria were particularly helpful. I also benefited greatly from the comments and suggestions of the two anonymous referees from the *Strategic Management Journal*.

REFERENCES

Aaker, D. A. and B. Mascarenhas. 'The need for strategic flexibility', *Journal of Business Strategy*, **5**(2), Fall 1984, pp. 74–82.

Aldrich, H. E. *Organizations and Environments*, Prentice-Hall, Englewood Cliffs, NJ, 1979.

Allen, M. K. 'Japanese companies in the United States: the success of Nissan and Honda'. Unpublished manuscript, Sloan School of Management, MIT, November 1985.

Bartlett, C. A. 'Global competition and MNC managers', ICCH Note No. 0–385–287, Harvard Business School, Boston. 1985.

Bartlett, C. A. and S. Ghoshal. 'The new global organization: differentiated roles and dispersed responsibilities', Working Paper No. 9–786–013, Harvard Business School, Boston, October 1985.

Baumol, W. J., J. C. Panzer and R. D. Willig. *Contestable Markets and the Theory of Industry Structure*, Harcourt, Brace, Jovanovich, New York, 1982.

Boston Consulting Group, *Perspectives on Experience*, BCG, Boston, MA, 1982.

Calvet, A. L. 'A synthesis of foreign direct investment theories and theories of the multinational firm', *Journal of International Business Studies*, Spring–Summer 1981, pp. 43–60.

Caves, R. E. 'Industrial organization, corporate strategy and structure', *Journal of Economic Literature*, **XVIII**, March 1980, pp. 64–92.

Doz, Y. L. 'Managing manufacturing rationalization within multinational companies', *Columbia Journal of World Business*, Fall 1978, pp. 82–94.

Doz, Y. L., C. A. Bartlett and C. K. Prahalad. 'Global competitive pressures and host country demands: managing tensions in MNC's', *California Management Review*, Spring 1981, pp. 63–74.

Evans, J. S. *Strategic Flexibility in Business*, Report No. 678, SRI International, December 1982.

Fayerweather, J. 'Four winning strategies for the international corporation', *Journal of Business Strategy*, Fall 1981, pp. 25–36.

Flaherty, M. T. and H. Itami. 'Finance', in Okimoto, D.I., T. Sugano and F. B. Weinstein (Eds), *Competitive Edge*, Stanford University Press, Stanford, CA, 1984.

Gluck, F. 'Global competition in the 1980's', *Journal of Business Strategy*, Spring 1983, pp. 22–27.

Gold, B. 'Robotics, programmable automation, and international competitiveness', *IEEE Transactions on Engineering Management*, November 1982.

Hamel, G. and C. K. Prahalad. 'Do you really have a global strategy?', *Harvard Business Review*, July–August 1985, pp. 139–148.

Hannan, M. T. and J. Freeman. 'The population ecology of organizations', *American Journal of Sociology*, **82**, 1977, pp. 929–964.

Hatsopoulos, G. N. 'High cost of capital: handicap of American industry', Report Sponsored by the American Business Conference and Thermo-Electron Corporation, April 1983.

Hax, A. C. and N. S. Majluf. *Strategic Management: An Integrative Perspective*, Prentice-Hall, Englewood Cliffs, NJ, 1984.

Herring, R. J. (ed.), *Managing International Risk*, Cambridge University Press, Cambridge, 1983.

Hofer, C. W. and D. Schendel. *Strategy Formulation: Analytical Concepts*, West Publishing Co., St Paul, MN, 1978.

Hout, T., M. E. Porter and E. Rudden. 'How global companies win out', *Harvard Business Review*, September–October 1982, pp. 98–108.

Itami, H. 'Japanese–U.S. comparison of managerial productivity', *Japanese Economic Studies*, Fall 1978.

Kiechel, W. 'Playing the global game', *Fortune*, November 16, 1981, pp. 111–126.

Kobrin, S. J. *Managing Political Risk Assessment*, University of California Press, Los Angeles, CA, 1982.

Kogut, B. 'Normative observations on the international value-added chain and strategic groups', *Journal of International Business Studies*, Fall 1984, pp. 151–167.

Kogut, B. 'Designing global strategies: comparative and competitive value added chains', *Sloan Management Review*, **26**(4), Summer 1985a, pp. 15–28.

Kogut, B. 'Designing global strategies: profiting from operational flexibility', *Sloan Management Review*, Fall 1985b, pp. 27–38.

Leontiades, J. 'Market share and corporate strategy in international industries', *Journal of Business Strategy*, **5**(1), Summer 1984, pp. 30–37.

Lessard, D. and J. Lightstone. 'The impact of exchange rates on operating profits: new business and financial responses', mimeo, Lightstone-Lessard Associates, 1983.

Levitt, T. 'The globalization of markets', *Harvard Business Review*, May–June 1983, pp. 92–102.

Lorange, P., M. S. Scott Morton and S. Ghoshal. *Strategic Control*, West Publishing Co., St Paul, MN, 1986.

Mascarenhas, B. 'Coping with uncertainty in international business', *Journal of International Business Studies*, Fall 1982, pp. 87–98.

Mintzberg, H. 'Patterns in strategic formation', *Management Science*, **24**, 1978, pp. 934–948.

Ohmae, K. *Triad Power: The Coming Shape of Global Competition*, Free Press, New York, 1985.

Okimoto, D. I., T. Sugano and F. B. Weinstein (eds). *Competitive Edge*, Stanford University Press, Stanford, CA, 1984.

Perlmutter, H. V. 'The tortuous evolution of the multinational corporation', *Columbia Journal of World Business*, January–February 1969, pp. 9–18.

Piore, M. J. and C. Sabel. *The Second Industrial Divide: Possibilities and Prospects*, Basic Books, New York, 1984.

Porter, M. E. *Competitive Strategy*, Basic Books, New York, 1980.

Porter, M. E. 'Competition in global industries: a conceptual framework', paper presented to the Colloquium on Competition in Global Industries, Harvard Business School, 1984.

440   S. Ghoshal

Porter, M. E. *Competitive Advantage*, Free Press, New York, 1985.

Poynter, T. A. *International Enterprises and Government Intervention*, Croom Helm, London, 1985.

Prahalad, C. K. 'The strategic process in a multinational corporation'. Unpublished doctoral dissertation, Graduate School of Business Administration, Harvard University, 1975.

Rapp, W. V. 'Strategy formulation and international competition', *Columbia Journal of World Business*, Summer 1983, pp. 98–112.

Robinson, R. D. *International Business Management: A Guide to Decision Making*, Dryden Press, Illinois, 1978.

Ronstadt, R. and R. J. Krammer. 'Getting the most out of innovations abroad', *Harvard Business Review*, March–April 1982, pp. 94–99.

Rutenberg, D. P. *Multinational Management*, Little, Brown, Boston, MA, 1982.

Srinivasula, S. 'Strategic response to foreign exchange risks', *Columbia Journal of World Business*, Spring 1981, pp. 13–23.

Terpstra, V. 'International product policy: the role of foreign R&D', *Columbia Journal of World Business*, Winter 1977, pp. 24–32.

Terpstra, V. *International Dimensions of Marketing*, Kent, Boston, MA, 1982.

Toder, E. J. *Trade Policy and the U.S. Automobile Industry*, Praeger Special Studies, New York, 1978.

Vernon, R. *Storm Over the Multinationals*, Harvard University Press, Cambridge, MA, 1977.

The Wall Street Journal, April 29, 1985, p. 1.

Westney, D. E. 'International dimensions of information and communications technology'. Unpublished manuscript, Sloan School of Management, MIT, 1985.

Woo, C. Y. and K. O. Cool. 'The impact of strategic management of systematic risk', Mimeo, Krannert Graduate School of Management, Purdue University, 1985.

[28]

Strategic Management Journal, Vol. 16, 637–655 (1995)

STRUCTURAL AND COMPETITIVE DETERMINANTS OF A GLOBAL INTEGRATION STRATEGY

JULIAN BIRKINSHAW
Western Business School, University of Western Ontario, London, Ontario, Canada

ALLEN MORRISON
American Graduate School of International Management–Thunderbird, Glendale, Arizona, U.S.A.

JOHN HULLAND
Western Business School, University of Western Ontario, London, Ontario, Canada

Both structural determinants and competitive factors can work to define the relevant environment for strategy formulation within an industry. This study examines the effects of each of these two sets of factors on global integration strategies, and finds that their impacts vary considerably from one industry to another. The study also investigates the relationship between a business's global integration strategy and its performance, using an industry-specific perspective. In the aggregate, the businesses studied appear to be under-globalized. However, this relationship varied significantly by industry; four of the industries studied appeared to be under-globalized, while the remaining three industries were at or near an optimal level of globalization.

Recent literature on international business has proclaimed a 'new era of globalization' (Bartlett and Ghoshal, 1989) and the 'new reality of global competition' (Prahalad and Doz, 1987). Some have suggested that globalization has become so pervasive that businesses that do not think and act globally will be at a competitive disadvantage in the 1990s (Levitt, 1983; Ohmae, 1989; Holstein, 1990; UNCTAD, 1993). Much of this writing has captured the attention of practitioners who are increasingly searching for new ways to compete in an ever-changing world. For managers, the message seems clear: markets are fast becoming 'borderless,' and strategies that fail to

recognize the integration of markets are both shortsighted and misguided.

While few have taken issue with generalized claims of the increasing globalization of competition, a growing number of researchers have raised questions about the appropriateness of blindly adopting global strategies. Morrison, Ricks, and Roth (1991), for example, highlighted the success of regional strategies in health care products and pharmaceuticals. In other studies, Baden-Fuller and Stopford (1991) and *The Economist* (1991) showed that in white goods and tires, respectively, businesses pursuing global strategies were losing out to smaller, regional competitors. Other studies have shown that pressures for global integration are often misinterpreted and that competitors frequently adopt strategies that are either too global or not global

Key words: global strategy; globalization; global industries; performance

CCC 0143–2095/95/090637–19
© 1995 by John Wiley & Sons, Ltd.

Received 7 January 1993
Final revision received 2 March 1995

638   *J. Birkinshaw, A. Morrison and J. Hulland*

enough (Douglas and Wind, 1987; Morrison, 1990; Yip, 1992; Stopford, 1993).

The degree to which strategies have or should become globalized is clearly a matter of debate. This paper examines this issue by studying the relationship between industry globalization, business strategy, and business performance. The paper begins by distinguishing an industry's structural characteristics from the competitive actions of businesses. Under a systems-structural view, competitive actions should coincide with structural imperatives (Astley and Van de Ven, 1983). However, evidence in global industries suggests that collective competitive actions are often inconsistent with structural characteristics (Morrison, 1990; Yip, 1992; Stopford, 1993). In industries where collective competitive actions coincide with structural characteristics, the imperatives for an individual business are clear and unequivocal. However, in industries where collective strategy is mismatched with structural imperatives, the determination of an appropriate business strategy is much more difficult. For an individual business, the question is: when structural characteristics conflict with the competitive norms, which should drive strategy? Based on a sample of 124 businesses competing in 10 different industries, we address this question by examining the relationship between structural determinants and competitive action. Issues of fit between these two imperatives are then studied in the context of individual business strategy and performance on an industry-specific basis.

The paper is organized in six sections. In the first section the relevant literature on structural forces and global competition is reviewed. In the next section, a conceptual framework is developed that integrates both the structural and competitive perspectives of globalization. Propositions are developed in the third section of the paper. In the fourth section, the research methodology and data are discussed. The empirical analysis and results are presented in the fifth section. In the final section of the paper, a discussion of the results including the implications of our findings is presented.

GLOBAL COMPETITION: STRUCTURAL AND COMPETITIVE FORCES

Despite the growing body of literature on the globalization of competition, confusion remains over a variety of globalization-related issues. Many managers, for example, continue to associate global with anything international. 'International' and 'global' are frequently used interchangeably to describe a variety of strategies that mean different things to different people. In reality, however, the term 'global' has unique connotations. 'Global' refers to a particular type of industry (Porter, 1980, 1986) as well as a specific type of international strategy (Doz, 1980; Porter, 1986; Morrison, 1990; Yip, 1992). Examples of other international industry and strategy types include multidomestic, regional, and transnational (Bartlett and Ghoshal, 1989; Prahalad and Doz, 1987; Morrison *et al.*, 1991). All three alternate industry and strategy types have 'aspects that are global or potentially global' (Yip, 1992: 1).

At the industry level, globalization can be meaningfully defined through references to either structural forces or the collective actions of businesses. For an *individual* business, structural forces and competitive actions are both relevant aspects of the environment and form the basis of a comprehensive industry analysis. At the macro level, however, the two are distinct in that the structural imperatives of the industry may well be different than the collective competitive actions in the industry (Porter, 1980; Cvar, 1984).

Structural forces perspective

The structural forces perspective has its roots in industry organization economics and contingency theory. The synthesis of contingency theory and industry organization economics has enabled researchers to identify alternative strategies for distinct industry contexts. A key assumption of this approach is that pressures to globally integrate or respond to local markets vary along a broad spectrum with endpoints that can be labeled 'global' and 'national' (Bartlett, 1987; Morrison and Roth, 1992). By examining relevant structural forces, researchers and managers can classify industries with resulting normative implications for business strategy content (Hunt, 1972; Hatten, 1974). For example, Kobrin (1991) developed an empirical measure of 'transnational integration' in 56 industries based on intrafirm trade. Structural forces have also been used to effectively identify other contexts, including fragmented industries (Dess, 1987; Keels *et al.*, 1987), mature industries (Harrigan, 1982; Hambrick and Scheter, 1983; Zeithaml and Fry, 1984), and emerging industries (Aaker and Day, 1986).

The importance of individual structural forces varies from industry to industry (Vernon, 1966; Caves, 1977; Porter, 1980; Fiegenbaum, McGee, and Thomas, 1987). In the case of global industries, three broad factors have been cited as structural determinants or 'drivers:' (1) the potential for economies of scale in value adding activities; (2) differences in comparative advantages across countries; and (3) standardized market demand across countries (Porter, 1980; Hout, Porter, and Rudden, 1982; Kogut, 1991). While all industries share in these drivers to varying degrees, all three determinants function at high levels in global industries. In contrast, all three drivers would have little functionality in national or multidomestic industries.

All things being equal, global business strategies are encouraged in an industry dominated by global industry drivers (Hout *et al.*, 1982; Yip, 1992). A global strategy consists of globally integrated operations and the cross-subsidization of international market share battles (Doz, 1986; Graham, 1978; Hamel and Prahalad, 1985; Jolly, 1988). In theory, a business which adopts a global strategy maximizes its 'fit' with structural imperatives.

Competitive action perspective

The second stream of literature relating to competition in global industries focuses on the 'collective' strategies of businesses. Rooted in social ecology, and with other linkages to population ecology (Aldrich, McKelvey, and Ulrich, 1984), the competitive action perspective makes a clear distinction between individual business strategy and group responses to the industry pressures. As argued by Astley and Fombrun (1983), the collective activities of organizations overwhelm individual strategies, and while businesses act collectively, they do not independently maintain control over the environment. As a result, the common or shared strategy of group members overwhelms the strategy of an individual business (Astley and Fombrun, 1983), thus putting intense pressure on individual businesses to develop strategies consistent with group norms. Under this perspec-

tive, the collective group represents shared industry membership, with strategic norms superseding exogenous structural forces as the relevant contingency for individual businesses (Thomas and Venkatraman, 1988; Fiegenbaum, McGee, and Thomas, 1987).

A related body of work that sheds additional light on the collective action phenomenon is institutionalization theory (Meyer and Rowan, 1977; DiMaggio and Powell, 1983). Institutionalization theory views organizations as social (as well as technical) phenomena that adopt patterns of behavior and activity that are appropriate to their environments. Thus, within an organizational field—the broad analogue of industry in IO Economics—member organizations move towards common structures and processes (termed 'isomorphism') through a combination of coercion, imitation, and normative expectation (DiMaggio and Powell, 1983). What this means for collective strategy is that there are typically strong social forces at work within an industry that push members to act in like fashion, even when such actions are in conflict with 'technical' imperatives. As stated by Meyer and Rowan (1977: 340), 'conformity to institutionalized rules often conflicts sharply with efficiency criteria.' One of the best examples of imitative behavior driving strategy in an international context is the movement of Japanese financial institutions and developers into North American real estate in the late 1980s (Carlton and Barsky, 1992). In this example, competitive actions and imitative behavior dominated decision making for all but the first movers in the industry. Structural imperatives appeared to have only a limited impact on Japanese decision making.

In the international domain, the roots of the competitive action perspective can be traced to Vernon (1966) and Wells (1968), who applied oligopoly theory developed by Hymer (1960) and later Kindleberger (1969) to show that the internationalization of businesses can be explained by the competitive dynamics of the industry. Vernon (1966) best articulated the role of collective action by arguing that the internationalization of competition is tied to three distinct factors: first, to the individual actions of an innovative business; second, the presence of favorable international structural conditions; and third—and most important at the industry level—the timely, collective reaction of

640   *J. Birkinshaw, A. Morrison and J. Hulland*

numerous other businesses to the threat of
market loss in emerging international markets.
Knickerbocker (1973) also argued that competitive actions rather than structural imperatives
dominate decisions to go international. In an
examination of U.S. manufacturers, Knickerbocker (1973) asserted that oligopolists had a
tendency to follow each other into international
markets to protect their competitive interests.

Thus, under a competitive action perspective,
a global industry is one which 'pits one multinational's entire worldwide system of product and
market positions against another's' (Hout *et al.*,
1982: 103). Using this approach, a great deal of
research has relied on high-profile competitors
to identify global industries (see, for example,
Cvar, 1984; Flaherty, 1986; Yoshino, 1986; Jolly,
1988). In these studies, industries are frequently
classified as 'global' because researchers identified
either individual businesses or two or three
businesses competing with global strategies.
These global businesses are then cited as representative of collective action or the competitive
norms in the industry.[1] Aircraft parts, tires,
construction equipment, and pet food are
examples of industries that have been classified
as global through the extrapolation of case studies
of high-profile businesses to all businesses in
the industry. In the construction industry, for
example, the strategies of Caterpillar and Komatsu discussed by Hout *et al.* (1982) were used
by Doz (1987) to illustrate the global nature of
the entire industry. Looking at the same industry
a few years later, Johnson (1991) characterized the
entire 1800-member U.S. construction equipment
industry as global after examining seven key
competitors in the industry.

BRINGING THE TWO SIDES TOGETHER: A CONCEPTUAL FRAMEWORK

The competitive action and structural forces
perspectives represent divergent yet ultimately

reconcilable views of global industries and global
strategy. On the one hand, global competition is
shaped through structural drivers (Yip, 1992),
while on the other hand, global competition
occurs through imitative behavior based on
competitive norms that may or may not be
structurally justified. The distinction between
these two perspectives has become increasingly
recognized in the literature. Bartlett (1987),
Ghoshal (1987), Kogut (1989), and Stopford
(1993) have all highlighted the need to distinguish
between global industry structure and the competitive actions of businesses. To this end, Kobrin
(1991: 18) has argued that a distinction must be
made 'between the inherent structure or economic
organization of a business or industry and the
characteristics of competition or the strategy of
companies in that industry.'

Global industry is defined here in terms of
'the significance of the competitive advantages
of international operations' (Kobrin, 1991: 18).
This definition is consistent with both the
structural forces and competitive action perspectives, in that competitive advantage is obtained
only by achieving a low-cost or differentiated
position (e.g. through international operations)
relative to competing businesses in the industry
(Porter, 1985). In other words, neither the
structural forces nor competitive action perspectives is sufficient on its own to completely
explain international industry imperatives for
an individual business. However, both converge
in that they represent the 'broad operating
environment' for the business, and thus define
the relevant context of business decision making
(Bartlett, 1987). A two-dimensional space with
axes representing structural determinants or
the 'degree to which industry structure favors
globalization' and competitive determinants or
the 'level of collective global competition in
the industry' can be constructed to represent
the interaction of these two approaches (see
Figure 1).

Figure 1 identifies the mismatches that often
occur between structural pressures and the
competitive actions of industry members. Three
domains can be identified in the figure. First, a
broad diagonal in which the level of competition
matches the industry context. The funeral
parlor industry, for example, exhibits a low
need for integration and few economies of
scale, indicating that competition should corre-

[1] An important implicit assumption in this work is that global
industry structure is oligopolistic, and hence that individual
firm behavior matters. In the case of an atomistic industry
where all participants are price takers, competitive actions
by individual firms would not be expected to have any impact
on business integration.

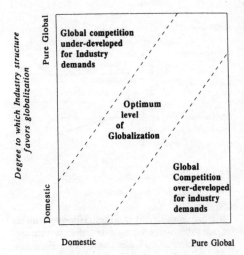

Figure 1. Industry responses to pressures for global integration

spondingly occur at a local level. The shipbuilding industry, in contrast, has the potential for global economies of scale as well as a high degree of integration, suggesting that competition should respond accordingly. Note that the diagonal band in Figure 1 represents an ideal 'fit' between industry structure and competitive state, and as such it is time specific; as structural drivers evolve so will the optimum level of global competition.

The second domain in Figure 1, the top left triangle, indicates the condition in which global competition is underdeveloped given the structural pressures of the industry. This area could include a number of 'undiscovered' global industries in which the structure favors globalization but the majority of businesses are still competing with less than global strategies. Over-the-counter pharmaceuticals and credit cards are industries that have been cited as having a much higher latent global potential than currently demonstrated by competitor strategy (Cvar, 1986; Yip, 1992). These industries offer potential first mover advantages for businesses which can rapidly adopt global strategies.

The third domain in Figure 1, the bottom

right triangle, indicates the condition in which competition has overglobalized *vis-à-vis* existing industry pressures. As mentioned above, the tire and white goods industries have been cited as examples of industries that have overglobalized. Two possible reasons help explain why overly global competition has occurred in these industries: first, management may have misread the signs and pushed globalization when the industry could not support it; or second, competition may have become global because of oligopolistic games that, while often suboptimizing for the business, may meet ulterior corporate objectives (Kim, Hwang, and Burgers, 1989).

Matching business and industry responses

Inherent in the structural forces and competitive action perspectives is the recognition that businesses may not always realize the global opportunities and threats in their industry. Because an industry's structure is defined independent of business strategy, a large number of international industries may consequentially have 'global potential, even though they may not know it' (Hout, *et al.*, 1982: 99). This suggests that a business can gain a competitive advantage through accurately assessing the underlying structural potential for globalization rather than through examining the dominant competitive patterns in the industry (Bartlett, 1987; Stopford, 1993). As a result, performance can be maximized when businesses develop strategies that accurately reflect industry structure (Ginsberg and Venkatraman, 1985; Hofer, 1975).

The appropriate dimension of strategy here is the business unit's global integration strategy, which can be defined as 'rationalization that may entail standardization of product, centralization of technological development, or the vertical or horizontal integration of manufacturing' (Kobrin, 1991: 18). A similar definition was proposed by Prahalad and Doz (1987: 14): 'The centralized management of geographically dispersed activities on an ongoing basis.' However, Kobrin's definition is preferred because 'centralization' implies a concentration of activities at head office. In reality, many multinational corporations assign world product mandates to their affiliates that offer a form of 'decentralized centralization' (Roth and

642   *J. Birkinshaw, A. Morrison and J. Hulland*

Morrison, 1992), which is entirely consistent with the notion of a global integration strategy.[2]

While structural conditions can be conceptually disentangled from the combined actions of competitors at the industry level of analysis, such a distinction cannot be made from the perspective of an individual business which views both sets of factors as part of its relevant operating environment. In broad terms, three possible industry configurations may develop in response to globalization pressures: an appropriate level of collective global competition; too much global competition; or too little. In turn, there are three possible positions that each business can take with respect to the industry's position, namely more globally integrated, integrated to an equivalent extent, and less globally integrated. All else being equal, one would expect that a business whose relative global integration is more closely matched with environmental pressures would perform better. In graphical terms, it would be expected that the performance–integration plot in suitably global industries would be horizontal, whereas the under-integrated and over-integrated industries would have upward sloping and downward sloping plots respectively (see Figure 2).

It should be stressed here that the proposed relationships between business unit integration and performance assume a homogeneous set of industry participants that differ primarily in terms of their level of integration. Strategic group theory (Hatten and Schendel, 1977; McGee and Thomas, 1986; Porter, 1980) challenges this notion, by showing that within a given industry distinct groups can be identified which may be asymmetrically exposed to both structural forces and competitive actions, on account of mobility barriers which exist between the groups. There are industries where the appropriate dimension on which to identify strategic groups is the level of global integration. For example, Baden-Fuller and Stopford (1991) identified national (exporting), regional, and global players in the

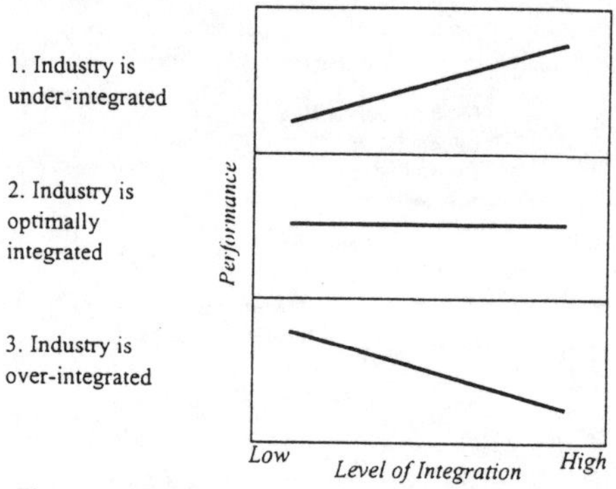

Figure 2.   Expected performance–integration plots

European white goods market. However, there are also industries where other dimensions are more appropriate. Determination of the critical dimensions for strategic group identification requires careful industry analysis. For the purposes of our study, the decision to focus on the business-unit level precluded such analysis, but the possible impact of intraindustry groups on the results should be kept in mind.

RESEARCH PROPOSITIONS

Structural forces

A number of testable propositions emerge from the preceding discussion. Following the structural forces perspective, structurally determined drivers can be expected to influence the global integration strategies of businesses. As discussed earlier, one such structural driver involves economies of scale that can be gained from integrating operations across countries (Porter, 1986; Ghoshal, 1987). Scale economies are associated with such activities as research and development, raw material procurement, manufacturing operations, marketing, and sales. Strictly speaking, the minimum efficient scale (MES) for the activity is the critical variable, since there can be no further reductions in product unit cost above this level. However as Scherer *et al.* (1975) point out, measurement of the MES is fraught with difficulties. Furthermore, the concept has been applied primarily to manufacturing plants, where unit costs and size can be measured with some degree of accuracy.

---

[2] Note that high global integration embraces two somewhat different scenarios: one in which all activity is centralized, and the other in which it is dispersed, but centrally coordinated (Porter, 1986). While this distinction is important, it cannot be captured in a single index, as used in this paper and by Kobrin (1991). Instead, industry-specific analyses are conducted later in the paper to control for the different levels of configuration and coordination that are found from industry to industry.

Because the current study is concerned with the broader integration of all value-adding activities, and not just manufacturing, MES could not be measured adequately. Instead, the broader notion of economies of scale is used here.

Proposition 1: Economies of scale are positively associated with the global integration of business activities.

A second structural driver is the differential comparative advantage that may exist between countries. The decision to locate certain value-added activities in a single global location is a function of both the availability of scale economies and also the existence of differential comparative advantage between countries (Kogut, 1985; Porter, 1986). While there are costs associated with globalizing activities—including transportation costs and government-induced tariffs or standards—evidence suggests that in global industries they are relatively insignificant (Porter, 1986). Differences in comparative advantage can be exploited only in an international context, and are maximized when comparative advantages for multiple activities can be linked across the value chain (Dunning, 1981; Porter, 1986). Because of this, businesses competing in global industries should, all things being equal, limit foreign direct investment to those countries with either low cost resource endowments or comparatively high national investment incentive levels (Buckley and Casson, 1981; Casson, 1986; Dunning, 1981). By contrast, in multidomestic industries, business strategy is based on market access with little global sourcing. Note that the issue of relevance here is *whether* or not value activities are cited according to country advantages in general, rather than *where* specific value elements are located.

Proposition 2: Differential comparative advantages between countries is positively associated with the global integration of business activities.

The third structural driver is the permeability of borders to the flow of information and technology. This has led to a gradual homogenization in demand patterns among consumers worldwide, and a corresponding increase in standardization for product offerings and distribution systems

(Levitt, 1983; Ohmae, 1989). While a number of writers (e.g. Douglas and Wind, 1987; Morrison *et al.*, 1991) have argued that national differences are converging much more slowly than has been suggested, linkages between the standardization of demand and the global integration of business activities have considerable support in the literature (Quelch and Hoff, 1986; Doz, 1987).

Proposition 3: Standardization of market demand is positively associated with the global integration of business activities.

Competitive action

Research has shown that a business's global integration strategy is frequently determined in response to the actions of competitors independent of structural forces (Knickerbocker, 1973; Hamel and Prahalad, 1985). In the context of this study, businesses would be expected to adopt global integration strategies that matched or improved upon those of competitors. In particular, as competitors make decisions to globalize, businesses are likely to perceive increasing pressures to integrate operations.

Proposition 4: Global competitive actions within the industry are positively associated with the global integration of business activities.

Performance

The industrial organization paradigm suggests that business performance is contingent on the fit between environment and conduct (strategy) (Porter, 1981). We would therefore expect to see superior performance in those businesses that have effectively matched their global integration strategy with the structural drivers in the industry. Using Figure 2, this establishes three rival propositions relating to global integration and performance.

Proposition 5a: The global integration of business activities is positively associated with performance in industries that have underglobalized.

Proposition 5b: The global integration of business activities is negatively associated with

performance in industries that have overglobalized.

Proposition 5c: In industries that are neither overglobalized nor underglobalized, no relationship exists between global integration of business activities and performance.

Environment–performance relationships

The relationship between industry structure and business performance has been the focus of considerable discussion in the management literature (Porter, 1980; Caves, 1982; Hitt, Ireland, and Stadter, 1982; Ginsberg and Venkatraman, 1985). Industry structure helps explain why some industries are consistently more profitable than others (Porter, 1980). However, according to contingency theory, industry structure has only an indirect effect (via business strategy) on business performance. It is only by achieving an appropriate fit between industry demands and strategy that the business can realize superior performance (Drazin and Van de Ven, 1985; Galbraith and Kazanjian, 1986; Miller, 1988). Thus, it is proposed that industry structure will have a strong effect on business strategy, but no direct effect on business performance.

Proposition 6: Economies of scale will have no direct effect on business peformance.

Proposition 7: Differential comparative advantage between countries will have no direct effect on business performance.

Proposition 8: Standardization of market demand will have no direct effect on business performance.

In contrast, the direct relationship between global competitive actions and performance is expected to be positive. While a traditional microeconomic perspective would suggest that high levels of competition are associated with average returns, there are some factors specific to globalization that may challenge this relationship. Specifically, global competition opens up a number of new markets to businesses, allowing them to amortize fixed costs over larger sales volumes, realize greater economies of scale, and sell into national

markets that are often less price discerning. Geringer, Beamish, and DaCosta (1989) showed, for example, that for a sample of 200 large multinational enterprises the level of internationalization was positively related to performance, without regard to the level of integration. Thus:

Proposition 9: Global competitive actions are positively associated with business performance.

The nine preceding propositions are summarized in Figure 3. Propositions 6 through 9 are included in order to assess the validity of the contingency framework, and to investigate conditions under which this perspective may be too limiting.

RESEARCH METHODOLOGY AND DATA

Sample

Given that a variety of researchers have identified rising trade levels as a key indicator of industry globalization (Cvar, 1984; Morrison, 1990; Kobrin, 1991; Yip, 1992), industries were selected from the *U.S. International Trade Commission* and industry sources that exhibited high levels (greater than 50%) of international, intraindustry trade. In all, 12 industries (four-digit SIC code) were selected. Questionnaires were subsequently sent to the CEO or president of medium and large-sized U.S.-based businesses in each of these industries (322 in total), as identified in *America's Corporate Families* and *The Directory of Corporate Affiliations*. Responses were received from 147 businesses, but for the purposes of this study two industries were dropped due to the low response rate of member businesses; a further 20 businesses were dropped due to incomplete survey responses. As a result, the final sample contained 124 businesses from 10 industries, with between 4 and 26 businesses responding per industry.

Measures

Structural forces and global competitive action

Despite the conceptual distinction between structural drivers and competitive forces, an empirical distinction between the two can be difficult to

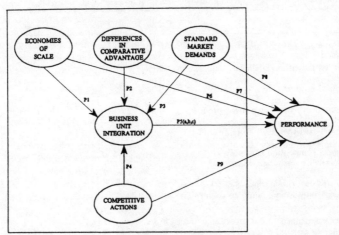

Figure 3.   Summary of proposed relationships

achieve. In part this is due to the fact that several potentially relevant measures are related to both constructs. As a result, a principal components factor analysis was performed on an eight-item scale which included measures of both the structural drivers and the competitive forces in the industry.[3] This analysis yielded four factors: (1) standardization of market demands; (2) evidence of competitive action within the industry; (3) economies of scale; and (4) differences in comparative advantage across countries.[4] Table 1 indicates the individual items associated with these four factors, along with key statistical information. As a result of this analysis, conceptual separation between the four independent variables was confirmed. Evidence of three distinct structural driver variables was also consistent with Hout *et al.* (1982). Subsequent analysis was undertaken using these four factors.

Global integration of business activities

This construct was measured using an eight-item scale. A principal components factor analysis conducted on this scale indicated a single construct representing the global integration of business activities.[5] Two of these items (3 and 7) were subsequently dropped in order to improve the scale reliability.

Given the focus on industry-specific relationships in this paper, it was important to measure managers' assessments of the global integration of business activities relative to their specific industries. This was necessary to control for the variation in overall global integration levels between industries. A

[3] A preliminary factor analysis was performed for a 12-item scale. However, four of these items were subsequently dropped due to either high cross-loadings or a high loading on a conceptually inconsistent factor.

[4] Although the eigenvalue for the fourth factor is less than one, we retained all four factors as suggested by both prior theory and a factor scree plot.

[5] This factor (eigenvalue = 4.19; explained variance = 52%) consists of items assessing the importance of methods potentially used to compete internationally. These items (and their factor loadings): (1) 'international control of the manufacturing cycle from raw materials to distribution of finished product' (0.67); (2) 'control within the organization of the international transfer of intangible assets (e.g., skills/technology)' (0.73); (3) 'sourcing capital funds internationally' (0.60); (4) 'investing in countries which offer investment incentives (e.g., tax holidays)' (0.66); (5) 'vertically integrate operations worldwide' (0.70); (6) 'minimizing tax liabilities through transfer pricing and method of cash remittance' (0.79); (7) 'safeguarding operations from foreign intervention' (0.58); and (8) 'horizontally integrating operations world wide' (0.62).

646   *J. Birkinshaw, A. Morrison and J. Hulland*

Table 1. Factor analysis results confirming distinct structural and competitive drivers

	Item	Factor 1	Factor 2	Factor 3	Factor 4
1.	Buyer/customer needs are standardized worldwide	0.78			
2.	Standardized purchasing practices exist worldwide	0.60			
3.	Standardized product technology exists worldwide	0.74			
4.	Competitors market a standardized product worldwide	0.81			
5.	Competitors exist that have a presence in all key markets		0.86		
6.	International competition is intense		0.82		
7.	Business activities are susceptible to scale economies			0.86	
8.	Factor costs (wages, materials, capital) differ significantly from country to country				0.86
	Eigenvalue	2.47	1.54	1.13	0.71
	% Variance explained	30.8%	19.3%	14.1%	8.8%
	% Cumulative variance	30.8%	50.1%	64.2%	73.1%
	Factor name	Standardized market demands	Competitive actions	Economics of scale	Differences in comparative advantage

Note: Only factor loadings greater than or equal to 0.50 are included in the table.

correlation analysis of individual responses with the average of all businesses in the relevant industry was conducted. Correlations ranged from 0.92 to 0.97, confirming that the responses were industry specific and relative rather than absolute.

Performance

Performance was measured using subjective assessments of a business's performance relative to other businesses in the same industry. While there are potential reporting biases in such measures, research has shown that self-reported performance data are generally reliable (e.g. Dess and Robinson, 1984). In addition, objective data are frequently not available at the business-unit level. Conceptually, it is the ability of the business to generate a superior performance relative to its industry that was viewed as most relevant, rather than absolute measures of performance. Three aspects of performance were assessed: return on assets, return on total investment, and sales growth. By combining financial and competitive performance character-

istics in this way, greater construct validity was achieved.[6]

RESULTS

Partial least squares

To estimate the paths between the constructs shown in Figure 3, and thereby test the propositions advanced previously, a relatively new and powerful multivariate analysis technique known as partial least squares (PLS) was used (see Fornell and Bookstein, 1982, for a complete description). Partial least squares belongs to a family of techniques which also includes the better-known LISREL (Lohmoller, 1988).

PLS is most appropriate when sample sizes are small, when assumptions of multivariate normality and interval scaled data cannot be made, and when the researcher is primarily concerned with prediction of the dependent

---

[6] A confirmatory factor analysis conducted on these three measures indicated a single construct (eigenvalue 2.28) which explained 76 percent of the variance in the original measures.

variable (Fornell and Bookstein, 1982). PLS is ideally suited to the early stages of theory building and testing, and it has been used by a growing number of researchers from a variety of disciplines (e.g., Barclay, 1991; Fornell and Robinson, 1983; Higgins, Duxbury, and Irving, 1992).

While it is possible to test the nine preceding propositions using univariate analysis, this was viewed as not totally appropriate given that the model proposed in Figure 3 involves independent equations that need to be estimated simultaneously. That is, the structural and competitive drivers are expected to influence business strategy at the same time that business strategy (and potentially the structural and competitive drivers) influence business performance. To avoid obtaining biased and inconsistent parameter estimates for these equations, the Figure 3 model must be analyzed using a multivariate estimation technique such as two-stage least squares (Pindyck and Rubinfeld, 1981) or PLS. While both techniques will provide acceptable parameter estimates, two-stage least squares requires the use of single measures for all dependent variables. In contrast, PLS permits multiple measures of both dependent and independent variables. Because global integration and performance were both assessed using multiple measures, use of PLS appeared to be more appropriate for the current study.

The path coefficients obtained from a PLS analysis are standardized regression coefficients, while the loadings of items on individual constructs are factor loadings. Factor scores created using these loadings are equivalent to weighted composite indices. Thus, PLS results can be easily interpreted by considering them in the context of regression and factor analysis. PLS provides a clear advantage over regression for two reasons: (1) it considers all path coefficients simultaneously to allow the analysis of direct, indirect, and spurious relationships; and (2) it estimates the individual item weightings in the context of the theoretical model rather than in isolation.

Generally, PLS results are presented in two stages. In the first stage, the researcher ensures that the measures used as operationalizations of the underlying constructs are both reliable and valid. Once convinced of the adequacy of the measurement model, the researcher can then proceed to interpret the resulting model coefficients.

Validity and reliability of measures

The acceptability of the measurement model used here was assessed by looking at the reliability of individual items, the internal consistency between items expected to measure the same construct, and the discriminant validity between constructs. Individual item reliability was determined by examining the loadings of measures on their corresponding constructs. In all cases, only individual factor loadings greater than 0.6 were retained, with most greater than 0.7, indicating a high degree of individual item reliability.

Internal consistency was assessed using a measure suggested by Fornell and Larcker (1981). This measure is similar to Cronbach's alpha as a measure of internal consistency, and interpretation of the values obtained is similar. Following the guideline proposed by Nunnally (1978), an internal consistency value of 0.7 or greater is reasonable for exploratory research. In the current study, the internal consistency values for all six contructs exceeded the 0.7 guideline (see Table 2), indicating good internal consistency.

The discriminant validity of constructs used in the model also needs to be assessed (Fornell and Larcker, 1981). This can be done in two ways. Table 3 shows the correlation matrix of the constructs. The diagonal elements in this matrix show the square root of the average variance extracted. For adequate discriminant validity, the diagonal elements should be greater than all other entries in the corresponding rows and columns, as is the case here. Second, no item loaded more highly on another construct than it did on its associated construct. Both of these criteria indicate that the discriminant validity of the constructs used in the current model is more than adequate.

Tests of propositions

Results for tests of the propositions are shown in Figure 4. All nine of the relationships examined were significant. The model explained 36 percent of the variance in global integration, and 12 percent of the variance in business performance.

As predicted, the impacts of economies of scale (P1), differential comparative advantage

648   J. Birkinshaw, A. Morrison and J. Hulland

Table 2. Measurement model

Construct	Number of items	Internal consistency
Economies of scale	1	1.000
Differences in comparative advantage	1	1.000
Standard market demands	4	0.824
Competitive actions	2	0.809
Business unit integration	6	0.878
Business unit performance	3	0.857

Table 3. Discriminant validity

	Correlations between constructs					
Economies of scale	1.000					
Differences in comparative advantage	0.201	1.000				
Standard market demands	−0.048	−0.197	0.736			
Competitive actions	0.092	0.013	0.088	0.824		
Business unit integration	0.459	0.234	−0.230	0.098	0.740	
Business unit performance	0.219	0.003	−0.096	0.174	0.271	0.817

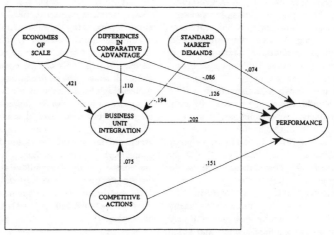

Figure 4.   Summary of results. Note: all path coefficients are significant at *p* < 0.001

(P2), and competitive actions (P4) on global integration were all statistically significant and positive. In contrast, the relationship between standardized market demand and global integration was statistically significant and negative, contrary to prediction (P3).

The relationship between the global integration of business unit activities and performance was positive and significant. At an aggregate level of analysis, this finding supports P5a, while refuting P5b and P5c. On average, then, the businesses included in this study tended to be underglobalized.

Significant direct effects on performance were obtained for economies of scale (P6), comparative advantage (P7), and standardized market demands (P8), contrary to expectations. Competitive actions also had a significant positive impact on performance, as predicted (P9). The direct effects of these constructs on performance are in addition to their indirect effects through integration.

Although all four drivers have a significant impact on integration, the economies of scale factor is more than twice as important as the next closest driver, standard market demands (i.e., $0.421/0.194 = 2.2$). Furthermore, when the direct and indirect effects of the structural and competitive factors on performance are combined, the economies of scale factor emerges as the single most important. That is, the total effect of economies of scale on performance $(0.126 + (0.421)(0.202) = 0.211)$ is greater than each of the individual total effects of comparative advantage (-0.064), market demands (-0.113), and competitive actions (0.166). These results also suggest that use of the contingency framework may ignore strong direct effects of structural and competitive factors on business performance. In part, this may be a reflection of a time lag between the strategic and structural responses of businesses relative to industry changes. Although the implicit assumption of contingency theory is that such time lags do not occur, the removal of this assumption would help explain the direct relationship that was observed between performance and structural and competitive factors.

Additional analysis

The preceding analysis provides significant insights into the relationships between key structural determinants, global integration, and business performance, and offers a complete test of the nine propositions advanced earlier. However, as indicated in the introductory sections of this paper, distinct differences may exist between individual industries in the relative importance of structural and competitive drivers. Furthermore, the nature of the relationship between global integration and performance may vary substantially from one industry to another. As argued previously, businesses in one industry may tend to be underglobalized, while businesses in a second may tend to be overglobalized.

In this section, the relationships between the key structural determinants, global integration, and performance are examined at an industry-specific level of analysis. This was done in two stages. First, industry-specific multivariate regression analyses were completed, using a global integration index based on the six measurement items used previously as the dependent variable, and indices for the structural and competitive factors (formed by averaging the relevant items identified earlier in Table 1) as the independent variables.

In the second stage, a second set of regression analyses examined the relationship between global integration and performance at the industry-specific level, using a performance index as the dependent variable and the global integration index as the independent variable. Only 7 of the 10 industries surveyed were included in these analyses due to sample size problems. The three excluded industries had six or fewer observations, precluding meaningful analysis. Given the relatively small sample sizes for many of the retained industries, the following results should be interpreted with some degree of caution.

Results for the seven remaining industries are shown in Table 4. Each industry is identified by its four-digit SIC code and by its SIC descriptor. Three industries were found to have a significant relationship ($p < 0.10$) between at least one of the structural and competitive determinants and global integration. Furthermore, for four industries, the relationship between global integration and performance was significant ($p < 0.10$) and positive, while for the remaining three industries no significant relationship was found. There were no industries for which the global integration–performance relationship was found to be negative. Thus, four of the industries surveyed here appear to be underglobalized (P5a), while the other three are apparently already at an appropriate level of globalization (P5c).

No significant relationships between the structural and competitive determinants and global integration were found for the pesticides and agricultural chemicals industry ($F_{4,11} = 1.47$), the mining machinery and equipment industry ($F_{4,11} = 0.08$), the oil and gas field machinery and equipment industry ($F_{4,14} = 0.20$), or the aircraft engines and parts industry ($F_{4,3} = 5.40$). Both economies of scale and competitive actions were found to have a significant positive impact

Table 4. Industry-specific results

Industry Name			Significant determinants of integration	Integration–performance slope
SIC		N		
2879	Pesticides and agricultural chemicals	16	None	+
3532	Mining machinery and equipment, except oil and gas	16	None	+
3533	Oil and gas field machinery and equipment	19	None	+
3651	Household audio and video equipment	12	Economies of scale, Competitive actions	0
3674	Semiconductors and related devices	26	Competitive actions	0
3724	Aircraft engines and parts	8	None	0
3728	Aircraft parts and auxiliary equipment	14	Differential comparative advantage	+

on global integration in the household audio and video equipment industry ($F_{4,7} = 24.50$, $p < 0.001$), while competitive actions alone had a significant positive impact on integration in the semiconductors and related devices industry $F_{4,21} = 6.00$, $p < 0.01$). Finally, differential comparative advantage had a significant and positive influence on global integration for the aircraft parts and auxiliary equipment industry ($F_{4,9} = 5.20$, $p < 0.05$).

The relationship between the extent of global integration and performance was significant and positive for pesticides and agricultural chemicals ($F_{1,14} = 3.98$, $p < 0.10$), mining machinery and equipment ($F_{1,14} = 5.35$, $p < 0.05$), oil and gas field machinery and equipment ($F_{1,17} = 3.44$, $p < 0.10$), and aircraft parts and auxiliary equipment ($F_{1,12} = 7.11$, $p < 0.025$). In all four cases, more globally integrated businesses exhibited superior performance, suggesting that these industries tended to be underglobalized on average. In contrast, the relationship between global integration and performance was not significant for businesses in the household audio and video industry ($F_{1,10} = 0.19$), the semiconductor and related devices industry ($F_{1,14} = 2.05$), and the aircraft engines and parts industry ($F_{1,6} = 0.71$), indicating an acceptable level of globalization in these three cases.

DISCUSSION

Three broad findings emerge from the preceding examination of the relationships between indus-

try, business strategy and performance. First, business strategy (in the form of decisions relating to the appropriate level of global integration for a business) is responsive to all of the underlying structural pressures for global integration, although the direction of the relationship was opposite to what was predicted in the case of standardized market demands. Second, competitive action pressures play a somewhat limited, though significant, role in shaping global integration strategies. Third, there is evidence that, in the aggregate, the industries studied here were 'underglobalized,' while at the industry-specific level there were examples of both 'underglobalized' and 'optimally globalized' industries.

Structural pressures

The global integration of business activities was shown to be heavily influenced by economies of scale and differences in comparative advantage, as predicted. The surprising result was a significant negative relationship between standardized market demands and global integration. This suggests that the businesses surveyed believed that differences between national markets remain important despite the trends towards global integration. A number of researchers have put forward arguments supporting this position. For example, Douglas and Wind (1987) noted that homogenization of demand is not pervasive, and that discerning customers continue to pay a premium for nonstandard products. Similarly, Takeuchi and Porter (1986) proposed that certain value activities *not* be integrated to achieve competitive advantage. Finally, Morrison *et al.* (1991) have documented the increasing use of regional, rather than global, strategies.

With regard to direct influences on performance, there was evidence of significant associations from all three structural drivers: positive in the case of economies of scale, and negative for the other two. While the magnitudes of these paths were relatively small, this finding suggests that the contingency framework is only partially supported here. The implication is that business unit performance is impacted directly by these structural drivers, regardless of the level of global integration. 'Fit' between environmental demands and business strategy is still important, but not to such a degree that direct relationships between industry factors and performance can be overlooked.

In broader terms, it is interesting to note the predominance of economies of scale as a structural driver in this study. In a similar study, Johansson and Yip (1994) found economies of scale, as part of a larger construct called 'structural drivers,' to be significant, but less so than 'market drivers' such as standardization of demand. Kobrin (1991), however, using an objective measure of the minimum efficient scale (MES), found no significant relationship between MES and global integration ($r = 0.178$). This discrepancy bears discussion.

Kobrin's discussion (1991: 25) of the lack of relationship between MES and transnational integration made three main points: (1) the MES measure was a crude proxy based on a 'top 50' estimate and aggregated at the three-digit SIC code level; (2) the use of CAD–CAM technology had gone some way towards reducing the superiority of large manufacturing plants; and (3) clear anecdotal evidence, on an industry-by-industry basis, existed both to support and deny the existence of a relationship between MES and integration. He concluded that the importance of MES 'across all global industries may have been overstated' (1991: 28).

This study actually complements Kobrin's analysis quite effectively. The industry-specific analysis suggested that economies of scale were a significant driver of global integration in only three cases, namely mining machinery and equipment, semiconductors and related devices, and aircraft engines and parts. Building on Kobrin's anecdotal evidence, and his observation that the three-digit SIC code represents a very broad level of aggregation, the implication is that detailed industry analysis may be the only effective way of truly understanding the nature of economies of scale. Furthermore, the current study did not distinguish between manufacturing economies of scale and other capital-intensive business activities such as research and development. Kobrin actually found a very strong positive relationship between technological intensity and transnational integration, which is wholly consistent with the findings of the current study. In sum, while the relationship between economies of scale and integration was strong, it was not supported in every industry. Kobrin's assessment of the declining importance of MES as a driver of transnational integration cannot, therefore, be refuted.

Competitive action

The observed relationship between the competitive actions of industry players and the global integration strategies of businesses was significant. This is consistent with much of the literature on global strategy (Knickerbocker, 1973; Hamel and Prahalad, 1985) and with institutionalization theory (DiMaggio and Powell, 1983; Scott, 1987), although the magnitude of the relationship was relatively small. The issue here may, in fact, be less the phenomenon itself, but more the ability and/or willingness of managers to recognize it. The motives for competitive actions are often ambiguous; cross-subsidization, for example, can be undertaken for a variety of reasons including the benign (market entry), the devious (a threat of further action), or the illegal (dumping). Management's acknowledgement of the action is likely to depend more on the motive for, than the preponderance of, the action. Furthermore, management's rationalization of their actions on a post hoc basis will frequently obscure their genuine motives. Thus, while Knickerbocker's (1973) research, based on objective, industry-level data, yielded strong evidence for the phenomenon of competitive actions, Baden-Fuller and Stopford (1991: 504) effectively found no such evidence. Results from the current study fall between these two extremes. It is certainly possible that imitative behavior is less common now than it was in the late 1960s, but it would take an objective study akin to Knickerbocker's

652   *J. Birkinshaw, A. Morrison and J. Hulland*

study to verify this assertion. A separate, intriguing possibility is that imitative behavior is still a powerful force, but that U.S. businesses are fixating on overseas competitors not included in this study.

The existence of a positive relationship between competitive actions and performance was as predicted. The finding suggests that high levels of global competition—with or without business integration—are sufficient to induce superior performance. As discussed earlier, this is probably a facet of the broader relationship previously found between level of internationalization and performance (e.g., Geringer *et al.*, 1989). Furthermore, because the current study's findings are based on management perceptions, it is possible to speculate that those businesses that have recognized the intensity and importance of global competitors are also the ones exhibiting superior performance, while the poorer performers are those that have failed to acknowledge the new realities of global competition.

Global integration–performance

The positive relationship between the global integration of business activities and performance supported the proposition that the majority of industries are 'underglobalized' through the observation that the stronger performers are also those with more globally integrated strategies. At the industry level the proposition was confirmed, with the additional finding that four industries are 'underglobalized' and three are at an optimal level of global integration. While this interpretation was supported by the data, additional information is required to more fully understand the details of this relationship. It may be, for example, that groupings exist, such that the 'global' players outperform the 'regional' players, who outperform the 'national' players. This is a fruitful line of inquiry, building on a long tradition of research into strategic groups, but it would be unwise to attempt to infer such groupings from the data collected in this study. As noted earlier, meaningful strategic groups research relies on careful industry analysis to ensure that groups are constructed along the relevant dimensions, and this was precluded by the current data.

The broad conclusion that industries are either underglobalized or optimally globalized is consistent with the anecdotal evidence of several researchers including Hout *et al.* (1982), Porter (1986), and Yip (1992). However, the finding that underglobalized industries exist, and even appear to persist, raises an important question: why do managers in such industries fail to recognize the latent profit potential of integration and therefore adopt a more globally integrated strategy? The answer, in part, has to do with the norms and rules of competitive behavior that make managers myopic to paradigm-breaking strategic moves (Astley and Fombrun, 1983; DiMaggio and Powell 1983; Meyer and Rowan, 1977). The presence of groups within the industry could also be a factor. For example, the capital investment required to move from being a regional to a global player in an underglobalized industry may be prohibitively high, and thus constitute a mobility barrier. In such cases, the high-performing global players as well as the lower-performing regional players would be aware of the discrepancy in performance, but the performance gap would likely persist.

The present study has a number of limitations. The sampling frame included manufacturing businesses in industries with high levels of international intraindustry trade. Further research should be undertaken to extend this frame to businesses from multiple countries, nonmanufacturing industries, and industries with diverse levels of intraindustry trade. Another concern is that the 'competitive action' construct is inherently difficult to measure. One possibility would be to revert to Knickerbocker's measures but this would require detailed time-series data at the business-unit level. Another possibility would be a more focused questionnaire which hones in on issues such as cross-subsidization. A third limitation relates to the global integration construct. Bartlett and Ghoshal (1989), among others, have suggested that integration is a fine-grained construct that varies according to the nature of the resource flow (product, capital, technology, people). This proposition was recently assessed by Rosenzweig (1993), who demonstrated significant but weak correlations between integration of different types of resource flows. He concluded that there were limitations associated with the use of a single measure (typically physical product flows) of integration. The current study used a reliable six-item scale reflecting a broader conceptualization of integration than simply physical product flows. However, our view here of integration as a unidimensional construct is probably constraining, and future research should address this limitation.

Despite these concerns, the study adds considerably to our understanding of global competition. The study uses multiple respondents from 10 industries to investigate the impact which structural imperatives and competitive actions have on global integration strategies and performance. While some concerns need to be expressed over the use of a U.S. sample to draw global conclusions, the results offer tentative findings regarding the level of globalization in each of seven industries. It is interesting that no 'overglobalized' industries were found: this broadly concurs with Yip's findings (1992), but runs counter to one of the original assertions of the paper, namely that certain industries (e.g., tires and white goods) may have become 'overglobalized'.

ACKNOWLEDGEMENTS

The authors would like to thank Kendall Roth, George Yip, and three anonymous reviewers for this journal for their helpful comments on earlier versions of this article.

REFERENCES

Aaker, D. and G. Day (1986). 'The perils of high growth markets', Strategic Management Journal, 7(5), pp. 409–421.

Aldrich, H., B. McKelvey and D. Ulrich (1984). 'Design strategy from a population perspective', Journal of Management, 10, pp. 67–86.

Astley, G. and C. Fombrun (1983). 'Collective strategy: Social ecology of organizational environments', Academy of Management Review, 8(4), pp. 576–587.

Astley, G. and A. Van de Ven (1983). 'Central perspectives and debates in organizational theory', Administrative Science Quarterly, 28, pp. 245–273.

Baden-Fuller, C. and J. Stopford (1991). 'Globalization frustrated: The case of white goods', Strategic Management Journal, 12(7), pp. 493–507.

Barclay, D. (1991). 'Interdepartmental conflict in organizational buying: The impact of the organizational context', Journal of Marketing Research, 28, pp. 145–159.

Bartlett, C. (1987). 'Global competition and MNC managers', ICCH Note 9-385-287. Harvard Business School, Boston, MA.

Bartlett, C. and S. Ghoshal (1989). Managing across Borders: The Transnational Solution. Harvard University Press, Boston, MA.

Buckley, P. and M. Casson (March 1981). 'The optimal timing of a foreign direct investment', Economic Journal, pp. 75–87.

Carlton, J. and N. Barsky (21 February 1992). 'Japanese purchases of U.S. real estate fall on hard times', Wall Street Journal, A1.

Casson, M. (1986). Multinationals and World Trade: Vertical Integration and the Division of Labour in World Industries. Allen & Unwin, Boston, MA.

Caves, R. (1977). American Industry: Structure, Conduct, Performance (4th ed.). Prentice-Hall, Englewood Cliffs, NJ.

Caves, R. (1982). Multinational Enterprise and Economic Analysis. Cambridge University Press, Cambridge, MA.

Cvar, M. (1984). 'Competitive strategies in global industries', unpublished PhD dissertation, Harvard Business School.

Cvar, M. (1986). 'Case studies in global competition: Patterns of success and failure'. In M. Porter (ed.), Competition in Global Industries. Harvard Business School Press, Boston, MA, pp. 483–516.

Dess, G. (1987). 'Consensus on strategy formulation and organizational performance: Competitors in a fragmented industry', Strategic Management Journal, 8(3), pp. 259–277.

Dess. G. and R. Robinson (1984). 'Measuring organizational performance in the absence of objective measures: The case of the privately-held firms and conglomerate business unit', Strategic Management Journal, 5(3), pp. 265–273.

DiMaggio, P. J. and W. W. Powell (1983). 'The iron cage revisited: Institutional isomorphism and collective rationality in organizational fields', American Sociological Review, 48, pp. 147–160.

Douglas, S. and Y. Wind (Winter 1987). 'The myth of globalization', Columbia Journal of World Business, pp. 19–29.

Doz, Y. (Winter 1980). 'Strategic management in multinational companies', Sloan Management Review, pp. 27–46.

Doz, Y. (1986). Strategic Management in Multinational Companies. Pergamon Press, Oxford.

Doz, Y. (1987). 'International industries: Fragmentation versus globalization'. In B. Guile and H. Brooks (eds.), Technology and Global Industry: Companies and Nations in the World Economy. National Academy Press, Washington, DC, pp. 96–118.

Drazin, R. and A. H. Van de Ven (1985). 'Alternative forms of fit in contingency theory', Administrative Science Quarterly, 30, pp. 514–539.

Dunning, J. (1981). International Production and the Multinational Enterprise. George Allen & Unwin, London.

The Economist (8 June 1991). 'The tire industry's costly obsession with size', pp. 65–66.

Fiegenbaum, A., J. McGee and H. Thomas (1987). 'Exploring the linkage between strategic groups

654   *J. Birkinshaw, A. Morrison and J. Hulland*

and competitive strategy', *International Studies of Management and Organization*, **18**(1), pp. 6–25.

Flaherty, M. (1986). 'Coordinating international manufacturing and technology'. In M. Porter (ed.), *Competition in Global Industries*, Harvard Business School, Boston, MA, pp. 83–110.

Fornell, C. and F. Bookstein (1982). 'Two structural equations models: LISREL and PLS applied to consumer exit-voice theory', *Journal of Marketing Research*, **19**, pp. 440–452.

Fornell, C. and D. Larcker (1981). 'Evaluating structural equation models with unobservable variables and measurement error', *Journal of Marketing Research*, **18**, pp. 39–50.

Fornell, C. and W. Robinson (1983). 'Individual organization and consumer satisfaction/dissatisfaction', *Journal of Consumer Behavior*, **9**, pp. 403–412.

Galbraith, J. R. and R. K. Kazanjian (1986). *Strategy Implementation: Structure, Systems, and Process*, (2nd ed.). West, St. Paul, MN.

Geringer, J. M., P. W. Beamish and R. C. DaCosta (1989). 'Diversification strategy and internationalization: Implications for MNE performance', *Strategic Management Journal*, **10**(2), pp. 109–119.

Ghoshal, S. (1987). 'Global strategy: An organizing framework', *Strategic Management Journal*, **8**(5), pp. 425–440.

Ginsberg, A. and N. Venkatraman (1985). 'Contingency perspectives of organizational strategy: A critical review of the empirical research', *Academy of Management Review*, **10**, pp. 421–434.

Graham, E. M. (1978)). 'Transnational investment by multinational firms: A rivalistic phenomenon', *Journal of Post-Keynesian Economics*, **1**, pp. 82–99.

Hambrick, D. and S. Scheter (1983). 'Turnaround strategies for mature industrial-product business units', *Academy of Management Journal*, **26**, pp. 231–248.

Hamel, G. and C. K. Prahalad (July–August 1985). 'Do you really have a global strategy?', *Harvard Business Review*, pp. 139–148.

Harrigan, K. (1982). 'Exit decisions in mature industries', *Academy of Management Journal*, **25**, pp. 707–732.

Hatten, K. J. (1974). 'Strategic models in the brewing industry', unpublished PhD dissertation, Purdue University.

Hatten, K. J. and D. E. Schendel (1977). 'Heterogeneity within an industry: Firm conduct in the US brewing industry 1952–1971', *Journal of Industrial Economics*, **26**, pp. 97–113.

Higgins, C., L. Duxbury and R. Irving (1992). 'Work–family conflict in the dual-career family', *Organizational Behavior and Human Decision Processes*, **51**, pp. 51–75.

Hitt, M., D. Ireland and G. Stadter (1982). 'Functional importance and company performance: Moderating effects of grand strategy and industry type', *Strategic Management Journal*, **3**(4), pp. 315–330.

Hofer, C. (1975). 'Toward a contingency theory of business strategy', *Academy of Management Journal*, **18**, pp. 784–810.

Holstein, W. (14 May 1990). 'The stateless corporation', *Business Week*, pp. 98–105.

Hout, T., M. Porter and E. Rudden (September 1982). 'How global companies win out', *Harvard Business Review*, pp. 98–108.

Hunt, M. (1972). 'Competition in the major home appliance industry, 1960–1970', unpublished PhD dissertation, Harvard Business School.

Hymer, S. (1960). *The International Operations of National Firms: A Study of Direct Investment*. MIT Press, Cambridge, MA. Publication of PhD thesis of same title, Massachusetts Institute of Technology, 1976.

Johansson, J. and G. Yip (1994). 'Exploiting globalization potential: US and Japanese strategies', *Strategic Management Journal*, **15**(8), pp. 579–601.

Johnson, J. (1991). 'Strategy formulation in a global industry: The case of the U.S. construction equipment industry', unpublished doctoral dissertation, George Washington School of Public Management.

Jolly, V. (1988). 'Global competitive strategies'. In C. Snow (ed.), *Strategy, Organization Design, and Human Resource Management*. JAI Press, Greenwich, CT, pp. 55–109.

Keels, K., J. Chrisman, W. Sandberg and D. Schweiger (1987). 'A causal model of industry fragmentation', unpublished manuscript, University of South Carolina.

Kim, C., P. Hwang and W. Burgers (1989). 'Global diversification strategy and corporate profit performance', *Strategic Management Journal*, **10**(1), pp. 45–57.

Kindleberger, C. (1969). *American Business Abroad*. Yale University Press, New Haven, CT.

Knickerbocker, F. (1973). *Oligopolistic Reaction and the Multinational Enterprise*. Harvard University Press, Cambridge, MA.

Kobrin, S. (1991). 'An empirical analysis of the determinants of global integration', *Strategic Management Journal*, Summer Special Issue, **12**, pp. 17–31.

Kogut, B. (Summer 1985). 'Designing global strategies: Comparative and competitive value-added chains', *Sloan Management Review*, pp. 15–27.

Kogut, B. (1989). 'A note on global strategies', *Strategic Management Journal*, **10**(4), pp. 383–389.

Kogut, B. (1991). 'Country capabilities and the permeability of borders', *Strategic Management Journal*, Summer Special Issue, **12**, pp. 33–47.

Levitt, T. (May–June 1983). 'The globalization of markets', *Harvard Business Review*, pp. 92–102.

Lohmoller, J. (1988). 'The PLS program system: Latent variables path analysis with partial least squares estimation', *Multivariate Behavioral Research*, **23**, pp. 125–127.

McGee, J. and H. Thomas (1986). 'Strategic groups: Theory, research, and taxonomy', *Strategic Management Journal*, **7**(2), pp. 141–160.

Meyer, J. W. and B. Rowan (1977). 'Institutionalized organizations: Formal structures as myth and ceremony, *American Journal of Sociology*, **83**, pp. 340–363.

Miller, D. (1988). 'Relating Porter's business strategies

to environment and structure: Analysis and performance implications', *Academy of Management Journal*, **31**, pp. 280–308.

Morrison, A. (1990). *Strategies in Global Industries*. Quorum Books, New York.

Morrison, A., D. Ricks and K. Roth (1991). 'Globalization versus regionalization: Which way for the multinational?', *Organizational Dynamics*, **19**, pp. 17–29.

Morrison, A. J. and K. Roth (1992). 'A taxonomy of business-level strategies in global industries', *Strategic Management Journal*, **13**(6), pp. 399–417.

Nunnally, J. (1978). *Psychometric Theory* (2nd ed.). McGraw Hill, New York.

Ohmae, K. (May–June 1989). 'Managing in a borderless world', *Harvard Business Review*, pp. 152–161.

Pindyck, R. and D. Rubinfeld (1981). *Econometric Models and Econometric Forecasts* (2nd ed.). McGraw Hill, New York.

Porter, M. (1980). *Competitive Strategy*. Free Press, New York.

Porter, M. (1981). 'The contributions of industrial organization to strategic management', *Academy of Management Review*, **6**, pp. 609–620.

Porter, M. E. (1985). *Competitive Advantage*. Free Press, New York.

Porter, M. (1986). 'Changing patterns of international competition', *California Management Review*, **28**, pp. 9–40.

Takeuchi, H. and M. Porter (1986). 'Three roles of international marketing in a global strategy'. In M. E. Porter (ed.), *Competition in Global Industries*. Harvard Business School Press, Boston, MA, pp. 111–146.

Prahalad, C. K. and Y. Doz (1987). *The Multinational Mission: Balancing Local Demands and Global Vision*. Free Press, New York.

Quelch, J. and E. Hoff (1986). 'Customizing global marketing', *Harvard Business Review*, **64**, pp. 59–68.

Roth, K. and A. J. Morrison (1992). 'Implementing global strategy: Characteristics of global subsidiary mandates', *Journal of International Business Studies*, **23**, pp. 715–736.

Rosenzweig, P. M. (1993). 'The integration of MNC affiliates: An exploration of patterns and determinants'. Proceedings of the Academy of Management Conference, Atlanta, pp. 147–151.

Scherer, F. M., A. Beckenstein, E. Kaufer and R. D. Murphy (1975). *The Economics of Multi-plant Operation*. Harvard University Press, Cambridge, MA.

Scott, W. R. (1987). 'The adolescence of institutional theory', *Administrative Science Quarterly*, **32**, pp. 493–511.

Stopford, J. (Summer 1993). 'Inside the opposing general's mind', *Crossborder*, pp. 26–29.

Thomas, H. and N. Venkatraman (1988). 'Research on strategic groups: Progress and prognosis', *Journal of Management Studies*, **25**(6), pp. 537–555.

UNCTAD (1993). *World Investment Report 1993: Transational Corporations and Integrated International Production*. United National Publications, New York.

Vernon, R. (1966). 'International investment and international trade in the product cycle', *Quarterly Journal of Economics*, **80**, pp. 190–207.

Wells, L. (1968). A product cycle and international trade?', *Journal of Marketing*, **32**, pp. 1–6.

Yip, G. (1992). *Total Global Strategy: Managing for Worldwide Competitive Advantage*. Prentice-Hall, Englewood Cliffs, NJ.

Yoshino, M. (1986). 'Global competition in a salient industry: The case of civil aircraft'. In M. E. Porter (ed.), *Competition in Global Industries*. Harvard Business School Press, Boston, MA, pp. 517–538.

Zeithaml, C. and L. Fry (1984). 'Contextual and strategic differences among mature businesses in four dynamic performance situations', *Academy of Management Journal*, **27**, pp. 841–860.

Name Index